MAKING FINANCE WORK
FOR AFRICA

MAKING FINANCE WORK
FOR AFRICA

Patrick Honohan
Thorsten Beck

 THE WORLD BANK

©2007 The International Bank for Reconstruction and Development / The World Bank
1818 H Street NW
Washington DC 20433
Telephone: 202-473-1000
Internet: www.worldbank.org
E-mail: feedback@worldbank.org

All rights reserved

1 2 3 4 5 11 10 09 08 07

This volume is a product of the staff of the International Bank for Reconstruction and Development / The World Bank. The findings, interpretations, and conclusions expressed in this volume do not necessarily reflect the views of the Executive Directors of The World Bank or the governments they represent.

The World Bank does not guarantee the accuracy of the data included in this work. The boundaries, colors, denominations, and other information shown on any map in this work do not imply any judgement on the part of The World Bank concerning the legal status of any territory or the endorsement or acceptance of such boundaries.

Rights and Permissions
The material in this publication is copyrighted. Copying and/or transmitting portions or all of this work without permission may be a violation of applicable law. The International Bank for Reconstruction and Development / The World Bank encourages dissemination of its work and will normally grant permission to reproduce portions of the work promptly.

For permission to photocopy or reprint any part of this work, please send a request with complete information to the Copyright Clearance Center Inc., 222 Rosewood Drive, Danvers, MA 01923, USA; telephone: 978-750-8400; fax: 978-750-4470; Internet: www.copyright.com.

All other queries on rights and licenses, including subsidiary rights, should be addressed to the Office of the Publisher, The World Bank, 1818 H Street NW, Washington, DC 20433, USA; fax: 202-522-2422; e-mail: pubrights@worldbank.org.

ISBN-10: 0-8213-6909-1
ISBN-13: 978-0-8213-6909-8
eISBN-10: 0-8213-6910-5
eISBN-13: 978-0-8213-6910-4
DOI: 10.1596/978-0-8213-6909-8

Cover painting by Mwamba Mulangala, "Soweto Market," 2006. A visual expression of the vibrant Soweto market in Zambia, a trade engine for the Zambian economy, forging bonds between people engaged in the frantic activity of survival.
Cover design: Naylor Design.

Library of Congress Cataloging-in-Publication Data
Honohan, Patrick.
  Making finance work for Africa.
    p. cm.
  Principal authors, Patrick Honohan and Thorsten Beck.
  Includes bibliographical references and index.
   ISBN-13: 978-0-8213-6909-8
   ISBN-10: 0-8213-6909-1
   ISBN-10: 0-8213-6910-5 (electronic)
  1. Finance—Africa. 2. Banks and banking—Africa.   I. Beck, Thorsten. II. Title.
 HG187.5.A2H66 2007
 332.096—dc22

2006038456

Contents

Foreword	*xi*
Acknowledgments	*xiii*
Abbreviations	*xv*

1 Setting the Scene — 1
  Introduction: The Role of the Financial Sector — 1
  Key Policy Issues — 4
  Modernism and Activism: Two Perspectives for Reform — 7
  Ultimate Goals: Financial Sector Development for
    Growth and Poverty Reduction — 12
  Policy Perspectives for the Major Elements of the
    Formal Financial Sector — 14
  Reaching Difficult Markets — 17
  Organization of the Report — 20

2 African Financial Systems: Depth, Breadth, and Efficiency — 25
  Introduction: International Comparisons — 25
  Financial Depth and Efficiency:
    What Explains Africa's Low Score? — 26
  Nonbank Finance — 46
  Inclusive Household Finance — 57
  Enterprises Place High Value on Better Financial Services — 61

3	**Finance for Long-Term Growth: Enriching the Flow of Finance to Transform the Economy**	**71**
	Introduction: Mainstream Financial Institutions	71
	Improving the Banking System's Ability to Intermediate Funds	73
	Ownership and Industrial Structure of the Banking System	87
	Term Finance and Risk Finance: Beyond Commercial Banking	107
	Macroeconomic Aspects: Building Confidence and Absorptive Capacity	120
4	**Finance for All**	**139**
	Introduction: Access to Formal Financial Services	139
	Technology and Financial Engineering	143
	Organization: Who Needs to Do What?	162
5	**Policy Choices in Current Conditions**	**191**
	Introduction: The Vision	191
	From Vision to Policy	193
	Where Should Government Begin? Two Attainable Goals	196
	Contrasting Initial Conditions	199

Appendix: African Relationship Lending	**207**
Credit Appraisal	207
Enforcement	208

Bibliography	*211*
Index	*229*

Boxes

1.1	Stability, Certainty, and Transparency: Foundations of Financial Sector Efficiency	8
1.2	Microfinance: Sustainability and Outreach	21
2.1	Historic Explanations of Cross-Country Variation in Financial Development	45

3.1	Dollarization	76
3.2	Points to Look For in an Effective Legal System	79
3.3	Bank Regulation: Avoid Reliance on Extensive Discretionary Powers	85
3.4	Basel II in Africa	88
3.5	Foreign Banks and SME Lending: Evidence from Cross-Country Studies	96
3.6	One Country's Experience with State-Owned DFIs	101
3.7	Governance Arrangements for DFIs	105
3.8	Surges in External Inflows and Implications for Financial Stability	125
4.1	Ignoring Informal Finance?	140
4.2	Pilot Weather-Based Insurance in Malawi	152
4.3	Price Risk Insurance in Tanzania	154
4.4	Improving the Remittances Situation	160
A.1	Reputation	208

Figures

1.1	Gross Domestic Product (GDP) Growth Rates and Financial Depth, 1980–2003	3
2.1	Liquid Liabilities across Countries	28
2.2	Private Credit across Countries	29
2.3	Private Credit and GDP per Capita	30
2.4	Liquid Liabilities to GDP and GDP per Capita	31
2.5	Private Credit to GDP and GDP per Capita	32
2.6	Offshore to Domestic Bank Deposits: Regional Distributions	33
2.7	Asset Composition of Banks across Regions	34
2.8	Financial Depth in Africa, 1990–2005	34
2.9	Real Interest Rates in Africa, 1990–2005	35
2.10	Net Interest Margins across Regions	37
2.11	Governance across Countries	39
2.12	Size of Banking Systems across Countries	40
2.13	Private Credit: French and English Legal Origin	49
2.14	Financial Development and Initial Colonial Conditions	50
2.15	African Stock Exchanges: Capitalization and Value Traded as a Percentage of GDP	51

2.16	International Comparison of Stock Exchange Development: Main African Exchanges Relative to Other Developing Countries	53
2.17	Access to Finance, Regional Extremes, Medians, and Means	58
2.18	Access to Finance across Countries	59
2.19	Financing Obstacles across Regions	62
2.20	Sources of Financing for Investment across Regions	63
2.21	Share of Agriculture across Countries	66
2.22	Share of Informal Economic Activities across Countries	67
3.1	Liquidity of the Banking System in African Economies	74
3.2	African Banks: Financial Depth and Liquidity, 2004	75
3.3	Business Opinion on Courts and on the Recoverability of Overdue Amounts	78
3.4	Patterns of Bank Ownership: Africa and the Rest of the World	94
3.5	African Countries: Saving and Investment as a Percentage of GDP	121
4.1	Share of Cooperatives, NGOs, Savings, and Other Banks in Providing Access	166

Maps

2.1	Financial Depth: Average Ratio of Private Credit to GDP, 2000–04	35
2.2	Predominant Form of Bank Ownership	44
2.3	Common Law and Civil Code Countries	48
2.4	Access to Finance by Households	60

Tables

2.1	Bank Profit Comparisons, 2000–04	37
2.2	Net Interest Margins and Overhead Costs in International Comparison	38
2.3	Distribution of African Countries by Predominant Form of Bank Ownership	43
2.4	Stock Exchanges in Africa	52

2.5	Portfolio Composition of Selected Life Insurance and Pension Funds	55
2.6	Credit Demand and Constraints across African Enterprises	64
3.1	Cross-Border Banking in Africa: Locations of Branches or Subsidiaries of 26 International Banking Groups	90
4.1	Remittances: Top Sub-Saharan Recipients	159
4.2	Large Financial Intermediaries and Networks in Africa Ranked by Outreach	164

Foreword

All across Africa, access to finance is rightly seen as the key to unlocking growth for poor farm families as much as for expanding export firms. This book explains that Africa needs not only funds, but also a more effective and inclusive means of channeling funds and other financial services to where they can be most effective.

Making financial systems work better is already a widely shared goal among policy makers in Africa. Strong financial systems have helped deliver rapid overall growth, as well as direct and indirect benefits, across the income distribution. Reflecting this understanding, policy reforms that have halted and reversed earlier deterioration have been adopted over the past decade. Governments have been building needed legal, information, and regulatory infrastructures. They have facilitated entry of—and competition among—solid financial intermediaries, national, regional, and international.

Important foundations have been laid, but it is clear that the performance of national financial sectors still falls short of its potential. Policy makers in many African countries are confronting similar issues and choices: how to get credit flowing more readily to where it can boost growth, how to get more finance for long-term and riskier projects, whether small national equity markets should collaborate across national borders, how best to design the regulation of banks and microfinance institutions in the African context, and where governments should concentrate their efforts.

The fact that such a wide range of fundamental questions is being asked in so many parts of Africa motivates the present regional study. Drawing on recent experience across the region and in international comparisons, *Making Finance Work for Africa* seeks to present a coherent and consistent policy approach that addresses African priorities and can work in African conditions.

This is a wide-ranging study that defies brief summary. But I am struck by three ideas, which recur in different forms throughout the book.

First, there is a clear institution-building agenda whose building blocks will yield clear benefits over time. At the same time, scope also exists for energy and imagination in adapting and applying universally sound principles to local conditions.

Second, despite the sometimes problematic political overtones, there is much to be said for being open to regional or international solutions. The reentry of foreign banks and the renewed interest in multicountry regulatory agencies show that this thought already has its adherents. International partnerships and outsourcing are also key to making the most of new technologies that are providing innovative solutions to the challenges of access to finance.

Third, countries have benefited from adopting an inclusive approach. By an inclusive approach I mean ensuring not only that reforms are targeted at embracing all income groups and sectors, but also that regulators facilitate the emergence and growth of a range of different types of intermediaries and ownership structures, and of different types of financial products.

The low level of private sector investment is both a cause of Africa's growth shortfall and a consequence of low confidence engendered by the repeated setbacks in most countries in the region. Escape from these conditions can hardly be imagined without a central role for finance. Policies that strengthen finance will also address these core development gaps. By providing an alternative to government patronage as the basis for entry into business activities, a strong, independent financial system can transform the business environment. Financial development can also generate a lock-in effect that raises the commitment of national elites to growth-oriented policies.

Making finance work for Africa is thus one of the most central and far-reaching of development goals for the continent.

Gobind T. Nankani
Regional Vice President for Africa
The World Bank

Acknowledgments

The principal authors of this report are Patrick Honohan and Thorsten Beck, and it also draws on draft material specially provided by Erin Bryla, Juan Costain, Julie Dana, Michael Fuchs, Ufuk Guven, Olivier Mahul, Samuel Munzele Maimbo, Astrid Manroth, Thomas Muller, Marguerite Robinson, and David Scott. The final text benefited from Mark Feige's editorial advice. Exceptional research assistance on quantitative issues has been provided by Edward Al-Hussainy, as well as by Baybars Karacaovali and Heiko Hesse.

Peer reviewers for the study were Alan Gelb and Benno Ndulu, who provided valuable advice.

Thanks also for the helpful comments received on a previous draft from members of an external advisory group: Ernest Aryeetey, Chicot Eboue, Machiko Nissanke, Steve O'Connell, and Lemma Senbet.

Suggestions and comments are acknowledged from Abayomi Alawode, Sherri Archondo, Henry Bagazonzya, Bernd Balkenhol, Chris Barltrop, Priya Basu, François Boutin-Dufresne, Gabriella Braun, Colin Bruce, John Byamakuma, Jerry Caprio, Anne-Marie Chidzero, Stijn Claessens, Tiphaine Crenn, Ross Croulet, Carlos Cuevas, Bob Cull, Julie Dana, David de Groot, Aslı Demirgüç-Kunt, Ishac Diwan, Stephanie Emond, Tadashi Endo, Louise Fox, Martin Gisiger, Olivier Hassler, Brigit Helms, Jennifer Isern, Andres Jaime, William Kingsmill, Renate Kloeppinger-Todd, Lolette Kritzinger–van Niekerk, Kathie Krumm, Anjali Kumar, Luc Laeven, Zahia

Lolila-Ramin, Millard Long, Susan Marcus, John McIntire, Latifah Merican, Margaret Miller, Paul Murgatroyd, Mark Napier, Korotoumou Ouattara, John Page, Doug Pearce, Jeeva A. Perumalpillai-Essex, Michael Pomerleano, Ann Rennie, Ann Ritchie, Alan Roe, Ravi Ruparel, Andre Ryba, Rick Scobey, Sudhir Shetty, Ahmet Soylemezoglu, Martha Stein-Sochas, Robert Stone, Menbere Taye Tesfa, Mohamed Toure, Craig Thorburn, John Tucker, Marilou Uy, Jos Verbeek, Stuart Yikona, and JaeHoon Yoo. Also appreciated were the insights of officials and market participants visited for the study in Equatorial Guinea, Ethiopia, Kenya, Liberia, Mali, Mozambique, Rwanda, South Africa, and Zambia, as well as in London and Paris.

The study was carried out under the overall guidance of John Page, chief economist for the Africa Region. The task was comanaged by Patrick Honohan and Tony Thompson.

Abbreviations

AERC	African Economic Research Consortium
AGO	Angola
AIDS	Acquired immunodeficiency syndrome
AIM	Alternative Investment Market
AML–CFT	Anti-money-laundering and combating the financing of terrorism
ASSOPIL	Association pour la Promotion des Initiatives Locales (Benin)
ATM	Automated teller machine
BAO	Banque de l'Afrique Occidentale
BCCI	Bank of Credit and Commerce International
BDI	Burundi
BEN	Benin
BFA	Burkina Faso
BIMAO	Banque des Institutions Mutualistes d'Afrique de l'Ouest
BNDA	Banque Nationale de Développement Agricole (Mali)
BOAD	Banque Ouest Africaine de Développement
BRVM	Bourse Régionale des Valeurs Mobilières
BWA	Botswana
CAF	Central African Republic
CAMCCUL	Cameroon Cooperative Credit Union League
CCP	Compte chèque postal

CECP	Caisse d'Epargne et des Chèques Postaux (Côte d'Ivoire)
CEMAC	Communauté Economique et Monétaire de l'Afrique Centrale
CERUDEB	Centenary Rural Development Bank (Uganda)
CFA	Communauté Financière d'Afrique (West Africa)
CFA	Coopération Financière en Afrique Centrale (Central Africa)
CGAP	Consultative Group to Assist the Poor
CIV	Côte d'Ivoire
CMA	Common Monetary Area
CMR	Cameroon
CNE	Caisse nationale d'épargne
COG	Republic of Congo
COM	Comoros
COMESA	Common Market for Eastern and Southern Africa
COWAN	Countrywomen's Association (Nigeria)
CPV	Cape Verde
DBSA	Development Bank of Southern Africa
DFI	Development finance institution
EAC	East African Community
EADB	East African Development Bank
ECOWAS	Economic Community of West African States
EMU	European Economic and Monetary Union
ERI	Eritrea
ESAAMLG	Eastern and Southern Africa Anti-Money Laundering Group
ETH	Ethiopia
EU	European Union
FADU	Farmers' Development Union (Nigeria)
FDI	Foreign direct investment
FECECAM	Fédération des Caisses d'Epargne et de Crédit Agricole Mutuel (Benin)
FENACOOPEC-CI	Fédération Nationale des Coopératives d'Epargne et de Crédit de Côte d'Ivoire
FGHM	Fonds de Garantie Hypothecaire du Mali
FSA	Financial Services Authority (United Kingdom)
FSAP	Financial Sector Assessment Program

FUCEC	Faîtière des Unités Coop
GAB	Gabon
GDP	Gross domestic product
GHA	Ghana
GHAMFIN	Ghana Microfinance Institutions Network
GIN	Guinea
GMB	Gambia
GNB	Guinea-Bissau
GNI	Gross national income
GNQ	Equatorial Guinea
HIV	Human immunodeficiency virus
ICA	Investment Climate Assessment
ICT	Information and communications technology
IFC	International Finance Corporation
IFRS	International Financial Reporting Standards
IMF	International Monetary Fund
IPO	Initial public offering
KEN	Kenya
KenGen	Kenya Electricity Generating Company
KPOSB	Kenya Post Office Savings Bank
KUSCCO	Kenya Union of Savings & Credit Co-operatives
LBR	Liberia
LSO	Lesotho
MDG	Madagascar
MDV	Maldives
MFI	Microfinance institution
MGA	Mutual guarantee association
MLI	Mali
MOZ	Mozambique
MRFC	Malawi Rural Finance Corporation
MRT	Mauritania
MSME	Micro, small, and medium-scale enterprises
MTN	Mobile Telephone Networks (South Africa)
MTO	Money transfer operator
MUS	Mauritius
MWI	Malawi
NAM	Namibia
NASFAM	National Association of Small Farmers (Malawi)

NER	Niger
NGA	Nigeria
NGO	Nongovernmental organization
NMB	National Microfinance Bank (Tanzania)
OIBM	Opportunity International Bank of Malawi
PAMECAS	Projet d'Appui aux Mutuelles d'Epargne et de Crédit au Sénégal
PIN	Personal identification number
PoS	Point of sale
PPP	Public-private partnership
ROSCA	Rotating savings and credit association
RTS	Remote Transaction System
RWA	Rwanda
SACCO	Savings and credit cooperative
SADC	Southern African Development Community
SAFEX	South African Futures Exchange
SDN	Sudan
SEN	Senegal
SLE	Sierra Leone
SME	Small and medium-scale enterprise
SMS	Short message service
SOM	Somalia
Stanbic	Standard Bank of South Africa
STP	São Tomé and Principe
SWZ	Swaziland
SYC	Seychelles
TCD	Chad
TGO	Togo
TZA	Tanzania
UCB	Uganda Commercial Bank
UEMOA	Union Economique et Monétaire Ouest Africaine
UGA	Uganda
WAMZ	West African Monetary Zone
ZAF	South Africa
ZAR	Democratic Republic of Congo
ZMB	Zambia
ZNCB	Zambia National Commercial Bank
ZWE	Zimbabwe

CHAPTER 1

Setting the Scene

Introduction: The Role of the Financial Sector

A decade of reforms—
There are stirrings of change in African finance, some of them vigorous. Strengthened by an extended wave of reforms over the past decade, financial systems in many African countries have begun to diversify their activities, deepen their lending, and increase their reach with new products and new technologies. Financial repression and the practice of directed credit are both much diminished, and there has been extensive privatization of state-owned banks—often to foreign-owned banks, the reentry of which represents only one aspect of a growing potential in internationalization and regionalization. A microfinance movement with deep roots on the continent has strengthened with organic growth and new entrants. Growing links between microfinance institutions (MFIs) and mainstream banks illustrate the adaptation of organizational structures to local conditions.

The persistent failure—until a decade ago—of formal and semiformal finance to advance, thereby leaving a fragmented and dualistic financial system stubbornly in place, thus seems to have been overcome. A new wave of intermediaries, many of them market based, has begun to adopt new approaches that promise to address the special challenges that confront financial development in the region. Cell-phone technology is being used for retail payments and for price transparency. Modern technology also underlies the surge of retail lending in several African countries.

—But there is still much left to do
Of course, these countries still have a long way to go. The continued shallowness of finance and the limited access by small firms and households to any formal financial services, especially in rural areas, mean that this financial awakening is just a turning of the corner. The environment for financial firms remains difficult, and progress has not been as fast as had been hoped. The combination of improvements and unfulfilled potential warrants a new look at African finance.

To some extent, the condition of national financial systems reflects general economic conditions in each economy. But a two-way process is at work: a strong financial system is a powerful engine of growth—and equality.

Finance can expand opportunities and reduce risks—
The economies of East Asia have shown how putting national savings to work in productivity-increasing investment can sustain rapid growth over a generation. Microfinance innovations in Asia and Latin America have helped low-income households manage risks through savings. Such innovations have empowered energetic microentrepreneurs, giving them the first step up the ladder of prosperity and lifting living standards in the areas where they operate. Innovations in the technology for remittances and novel techniques in insurance have also played an important role in improving welfare.

By bridging the gap between savers and entrepreneurs, financial systems not only reduce the risks on both sides but also open up opportunities to both sides. They can reduce the barriers to entry for entrepreneurs, thereby allowing the economy at large to benefit in terms of increasing employment, improving the price and quality of services, and reducing the stifling influence of established monopolies. Given access to the necessary finance, farmers can move to a higher level of productivity and output. Savers, too, can share in the returns on an expanded flow of investment. Housing, insurance, and pension arrangements can be lifted onto a new plane.

—But governments must provide a supporting policy environment
Increasingly, scholars acknowledge that supportive policy for financial sector development is a key component of national development policy.

Indeed, careful comparative analysis of the growth rates of different countries over a 30-year period has produced convincing evidence that having a deeper financial system contributes to growth—and is not merely a reflection of prosperity (figure 1.1).[1] Countries with deep financial systems also seem to have a lower incidence of poverty than others at the same level of national income. At the firm level, growth also responds to access to credit and to the conditions that favor such access.

Finance and social change

Strong financial systems are built on good governance, certainly both of the intermediaries and their regulators. In addition, because all sizable enterprises and all government agencies do business with the financial sector, improvements in this dimension of the financial sector have a pervasive leavening effect on the quality of governance in the business and government sectors as a whole.

FIGURE 1.1
Gross Domestic Product (GDP) Growth Rates and Financial Depth, 1980–2003

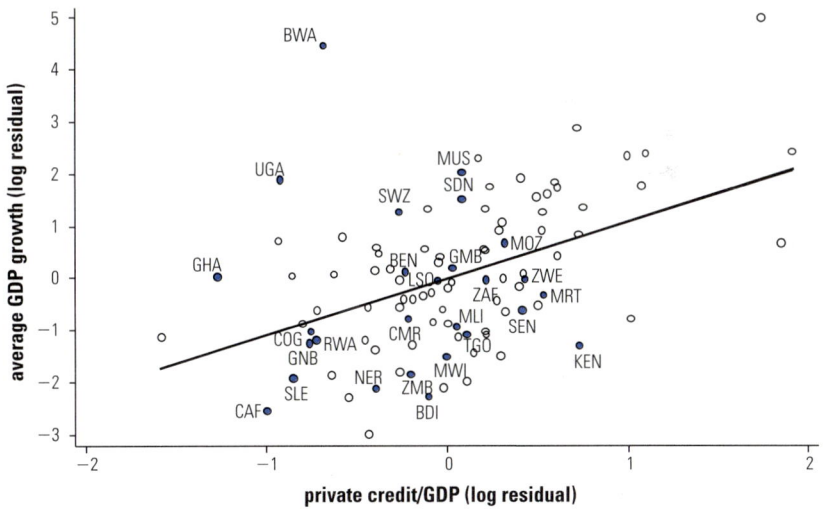

Source: Based on data in Beck 2006.

Note: Country abbreviations are included in the abbreviations list at the front of the book. This figure plots for 99 countries the relationship between private credit from the banking system, expressed as a percentage of GDP, and average annual growth in GDP per capita, controlling for the effect of initial (1980) GDP per capita, inflation, trade openness, government consumption, average years of schooling, and black-market premium.

Without a well-functioning financial sector to allocate and reallocate resources available for investment, African societies in which a closed group of incumbents (public or private) makes most of the investment and strategic decisions, because only they have the resources to implement large-scale plans, risk stagnating (see Eifert, Gelb, and Ramachandran 2006; Rajan and Zingales 2003). By allocating and reallocating resources on a more objective basis of creditworthiness and prospective returns, a finance-rich economy is more conducive to a wider distribution of economic power and influence, which in turn should feed back into improved national economic performance on many dimensions.

Financial development can help broaden the elite class because wealthy and middle-class people can acquire a share in the success of local economic ventures and begin to define their own prosperity in terms of national prosperity without reference to ethnic or local advantage. One concrete example is the way in which national elites have become interested in the fortunes of recently privatized firms, which though often majority owned by foreigners have a fraction of their ownership listed on local exchanges. If elites are invested in national economic prosperity (rather than defensively attempting to secure—for a time—their share of a static or declining pie that may at any time be swept away by social or economic crisis), they may work harder to introduce policies that underpin economic growth.[2]

Key Policy Issues

What policy responses are now needed to foster the new energy; to help ensure that modern technology, organizational innovation, and internationalization are exploited to the maximum; and to help ensure that investable funds are well allocated to underpin growth and to protect against any future risks?

The agenda for financial sector policy reform and strengthening is a long one. A practical strategy needs to take into account implementation constraints. Furthermore, some reforms require preconditions in the wider economic and political environment, without which they will be ineffective or even counterproductive.

What should guide African decision makers in prioritizing policies to strengthening financial sectors? This report suggests a two-pronged approach:

- Economic growth is the surest way to a substantial and sustained reduction in poverty in Africa; policy for long-term growth requires focusing on the larger and more formal parts of the financial system.
- But even while growth-enhancing policies are beginning to have their effect, improving the access of low-income households and microentrepreneurs to financial services should become an additional central focus of financial sector policy.

Thus, consistent with the two policy prongs of growth and access, the most pressing needs in African finance are (a) to increase the availability and lower the cost of credit to productive enterprises and (b) to extend the reach of basic savings, payments, credit, and insurance services for low-income people and for the smallholder farms and microenterprises that provide their livelihood. Africa also needs a wider range of longer-term facilities (including mortgage finance); greater possibilities for risk management and diversification, including more transparent price discovery; and improved marketability of tradable securities, such as debt and corporate equity. Each of these areas makes demands on scarce technical and managerial skills, including prudent management, regulation, and supervision.

The two prongs will have overlaps; indeed, in time these overlaps will tend to grow as the larger intermediaries find ways of applying technology to reach a wider clientele. The challenges of agricultural finance will remain central for both prongs. Scaling up high-productivity agriculture and agribusiness will remain an important part of the growth process in most African countries; large-scale agricultural enterprises will remain important customers of the main banks. For most farmers and rural workers, their main point of contact with the financial sector will be at the micro level.

For the most part, the growth and access prongs do not interfere: conflicts or tradeoffs between the two goals are encountered only rarely. It is possible to move forward on both fronts.

African financial systems are not all the same;[3] they are spread across a spectrum of financial sector performance. Nevertheless, sufficient similarities exist between the underlying economic conditions that face financial firms in most of the countries to allow several generalizations. In addition to low savings rates, finance in most African countries works within an environment that is extreme in four key dimensions: scale, informality, governance, and shocks. Although similar difficulties are found elsewhere, the frequency with which this quartet of environmental obstacles meets up together in Africa means that policy analysis in the region has a distinctive flavor.

- *Scale* refers to the small size of the economies and even more of the national financial systems and firms and their customers. Sparse population, resulting in isolation and great distances (at least in terms of travel time) to points of services, is another aspect of what is included under the heading of scale. Because most financial services involve fixed costs and increasing returns of scale (at least up to a certain point), the problem of scale translates into a problem of high unit costs and even unaffordability of certain services. Possible solutions include rigorous attention to cost control, reliance on internationalization to benefit from a sharing of some of the fixed costs, and reliance on information and communications technology that can result in lower unit costs.

- *Informality* refers to the status not just of client enterprises of financial intermediaries but also of the markets within which they work; informality reduces the degree to which reliance can be placed on systematic documentation, adherence to a predictable schedule, or even a fixed place of business.

- *Governance* problems arise at the level of private and public institutions but are probably relatively more severe in the public sector. This problem reduces the credibility and stability of government policy and increases the danger that policy goals will be subverted in implementation.

- Not all types of *shocks* are more severe or more frequent in Africa than elsewhere, but the continent's history over the past half-century has been marked by a high incidence of occasional economic or political meltdowns (associated with conflict, famine, and politico-societal collapse as well as with external factors) at a frequency of up to one per decade per country (Arnold 2005; Meredith 2005). At the micro or "idiosyncratic" level, risk is also very high for individual households near or below the poverty line and for small farms and firms.

So that financial services can be delivered safely and at reasonable cost despite these difficult conditions, stakeholders need to find solutions drawing on innovations in financial, information, and communications technology; internationalization; and well-adapted organizational structures.

Bearing in mind this quartet of environmental challenges, we now turn to the two major approaches that are conventionally adopted to pursue financial sector reform in Africa.

Modernism and Activism: Two Perspectives for Reform

Building and preserving an enabling environment for domestic finance to flourish is a goal on which all will agree. African policy reforms to date have gone some distance toward stabilizing the macroeconomy and removing incoherent administrative controls on wholesale interest rates. Regulatory authorities have rightly intervened in insolvent banks; many of them have been recapitalized and placed under better management and ownership. Among many other reforms, a lot has been done to improve the regulatory framework for banking (Aryeetey and Senbet 2004).

Clearly more is needed, but what? There can be no dispute about the importance of macroeconomic stability, contractual certainty, and policy and commercial transparency as the foundations of an effective financial system (see box 1.1). That is not to say that these foundations are securely in place throughout the continent—far from it. Macroeconomic instability, though much less evident than a decade ago, is still a threat in certain parts; crowding out by government borrowing has been evident in several countries; and the risk of major policy reversals is routinely factored into investor decisions. Reforming the legal and judicial system and improving financial information and transparency are tasks that are far from complete.

Certain building blocks, including rationalization and clarification of laws, streamlining of court procedures, establishment of credit registries, and training of financial professionals, are well accepted as key components in moving toward more effective financial systems. This book does not dwell on these widely agreed goals and building blocks—which are not Africa-specific.[4] Instead, the focus is on matters that are not so clear but speak more specifically to Africa's distinctive needs.

Two distinct but complementary perspectives to the strengthening of African financial systems prevail in current policy discussion. They can be summarized as the modernist and the activist perspectives. Both accept the

> **BOX 1.1**
>
> **Stability, Certainty, and Transparency:**
> **Foundations of Financial Sector Efficiency**
>
> Three of the most important background aspects of the economic and institutional environmental contributing to efficient financial sector functioning are macroeconomic stability, certainty of contract enforcement, and availability of information.
>
> Macroeconomic stability is particularly helpful for encouraging banking development. Low and stable inflation encourages monetary savings by making the real value of savings more predictable. Fiscal discipline allows mobilized savings to be channeled to the private sector and prevents the crowding out of private investment by government borrowing demands.
>
> Lenders and investors are more willing to enter into financial contracts where more certainty exists about the relative legal rights of borrowers, creditors, and outside (minority) investors and if fair, speedy, and impartial enforcement can be confidently expected. Legal systems giving greater relative weight to the rights of creditors compared with borrowers and to the rights of minority shareholders compared with majority shareholders and management, for example, promote deeper debt and equity markets, respectively. Ideally, creditors should have effective ways of enforcing contracts outside bankruptcy as well as maintaining creditor rights within the

importance of the overall enabling environment but seek to look beyond those basics. Both perspectives have validity and an appropriate range of application. Misunderstandings and policy debates can often be interpreted in terms of a clash over which perspective is more relevant and more likely to be effective in meeting different dimensions of African needs.

Putting in place the infrastructures necessary for effective functioning of the financial sector will require a protracted period of modernization. There is no doubt that modernization represents the bedrock of any credible vision for national financial sectors, whether in Africa or elsewhere.

The modernist perspective sees finance as an anonymous, atomistic, market-oriented mechanism that disregards the pedigree or power of its users except to the extent that such power influences the remuneration of bankruptcy procedure. Effective functioning of property registries and courts is critical to the creation, perfection, and enforcement of security interests. Shareholders need not only sufficient information but also the possibility to influence company decisions directly through votes on critical corporate decisions and indirectly by their voice in the selection of directors. More important than the laws on the books, however, is the actual enforcement in practice. In this context, fighting corruption and fortifying corporate governance are both key.

Finally, effective financial intermediation depends on tools to reduce the information asymmetries between provider and borrower that can restrict intermediation because of the associated adverse selection and moral hazard. Transparent financial statements are crucial for reducing screening and monitoring costs for lenders and thereby increasing the efficiency of resource allocation. Credit registries that give easy and reliable access to clients' credit history and both negative and positive information make borrower quality much more transparent, making it safe for lenders to lend to a wider range of customers with a satisfactory credit history (see Beck 2006).

At the same time, it is worth remembering that the link between risks and the importance of the financial sector is a two-way one. When risks are high, financial contracts can help market participants hedge or pool these risks. In this way, the financial system can be a valuable buffer for the rest of the economy, though in practice it is more effective in insulating short-term risks than long-term risks.

each financial contract. This perspective casts a suspicious eye on the integration of industrial and financial power, because the emergence of concentrated industrial-financial groups can have the effect of blocking entrepreneurship by those outside the main power groups. Integration of finance and government is also questioned for similar reasons (hence the low standing, from the modernist perspective, of state-owned banks).

The modernist perspective concerns itself mainly with large-scale finance—deepening the resource mobilization of the banking system, ensuring that banks want to and can safely lend on these resources, and enabling productive formal sector firms to find the mix of equity and debt finance they need to grow, as well as sophisticated tools for risk management.

Governments have a central role here, not least in creating the enabling environment. The policy agenda associated with the modernist perspective focuses on the macroeconomic, contractual, and information frameworks, with the objective of reducing information asymmetries, improving legal certainty, and lengthening investors' planning horizon. This agenda includes updating laws governing financial contracts and ensuring their proper and reliable enforcement through judicial reforms to make certain that property rights are clearly defined and enforceable, both in general terms and as they apply to specific modern financial instruments. It also focuses on defining and updating accounting rules and procedures to ensure that enterprise accounts are a reliable basis for investment and other financial relationships, as well as on improving systems of credit information sharing to allow borrowers to use their reputation as collateral. Increasing the predictability and stability of government policies as they affect the overall macroeconomic environment is also an important desideratum for the modernist, as systemic risk impedes the functioning of finance—even if integration with global finance can mitigate this problem.

The touchstone for the modernist is "best practice" of the advanced market economies. Transplanting best practice is acknowledged as likely to take time, but the modernist is inclined to see any move in that direction as progress. As we will argue, this view is where the modernist may overreach in Africa. Modernists sometimes neglect real-world constraints. Disappointing results can be expected from a mindless transplantation of overambitious structures from the advanced economies. Indeed, although modernization may seem low risk, it can cause problems if introduced in an unfavorable environment. For example, the design of African stock markets—influenced by what was seen as best practice in advanced economies—may (as discussed in chapter 3), through costs and prerequisites, have created barriers to listed equity finance for many African firms that could have obtained it if a more context-sensitive regulatory design had been chosen.

Applied with a realistic attention to national context, however, the modernist agenda does help to build the foundations of an effective financial system for the long run. As implied by the term we have used for it, what the modernist perspective offers directly is modernization more than economic growth, but growth comes with and as a result of successful modernization. And although modernization is maturing, policy makers need to be actively engaged in encouraging the numerous initiatives that financial market participants are already taking to reach a wider market.

The *activist* perspective to finance is concerned with achieving results in areas where the anonymous private financial sector is not conspicuously successful: finance for agriculture and the rural economy, for micro- and small enterprises, and for low-income households, as well as long-term finance in general. Inherent difficulties, risks, and costs impede the effectiveness of finance in each of these areas. The occasional collapse of financial intermediaries and the economic dislocation that often accompanies such crises are also the target of the activist perspective.

The activist sees the need for special interventions to help correct the market failures here. These interventions include enacting restrictive legislation and establishing competent and politically independent prudential regulators to guard against weak, reckless, or corrupt management of financial intermediaries that could cause their collapse. Protecting the consumer from predatory practices is also high on the activist agenda.

The activist sometimes advocates a variety of special public, charitable, or otherwise privileged intermediaries. Because of the disappointing performance of many publicly owned financial firms (all too often subverted through a politicized management or through corruption), the risk of overreaching in this regard is well known. Even though the deficiencies that gave rise to state ownership persist today, few close observers of financial systems around the world now recommend the establishment of government-owned development banks in African countries. Effective governments will have learned the lessons of the past and, to avoid counterproductive interventions resulting from weak governance, will support—but will not themselves take the lead in—implementing the activist agenda by increasing their direct engagement in providing financial services. The potential for regional entities and for partnerships with local and international nongovernmental organizations (NGOs) and with the private sector to fill this gap needs to be explored; donors, too, can have a potentially valuable role as disinterested activists in bolstering specific initiatives.

Imposing impracticably low interest rate ceilings in a misconceived attempt to protect borrowers is another familiar activist error, which chiefly results in reduced flow of formal sector credit to those who could most benefit from it.

But it would be a major mistake to think that these instances can be extrapolated to discredit the activist perspective on a broad front. In particular, the rapid growth and many success stories have encouraged individual social entrepreneurs as well as international donors and others to promote the creation and expansion of microfinance firms in Africa as in other developing countries. This result can be seen as consistent with the activist perspective.

Activism is most effective when it achieves its effects by realigning the incentives of the relevant market participants. It should be attempted only by entities that have adequate governance. This requirement poses a problem for many governments in Africa, as cross-country surveys confirm.

Sometimes it is not immediately clear whether certain policies should best be considered modernist or activist. The widespread, but relatively recent, adoption in almost all countries of a greatly intensified regime of bank regulation is sometimes presented as a modernist agenda, even though it responds to a series of market failure events. Restrictive legislation on bank behavior and the establishment of competent and politically independent prudential regulators to guard against weak, reckless, or corrupt management of financial intermediaries that could cause their collapse is part of the standard policy package in both advanced and developing economies these days, but it can easily be seen as part of the activist agenda. Indeed, as markets become more integrated and sophisticated, the modernist view among scholars has begun to emphasize market discipline in preference to regulatory discretion in bank regulation.

The conclusion of the present study is that only through a pragmatic and context-sensitive combination of *both* modernism and activism can good results be expected. Pursuing only one or the other would leave Africa without many of the financial services it so badly needs. The relevant aspects of the context that need to be taken into account in African countries include the cost and complexity of each type of intervention, the ease with which abuses and subversion of the policies can be limited (especially in the context of weak governance), and enforcement capacity.

Ultimate Goals: Financial Sector Development for Growth and Poverty Reduction

As Sachs (2005) has pointed out, well-targeted direct assistance to improve the productivity of subsistence farming productivity and to reduce disease can have a sizable effect on extreme poverty. This assistance, however, just gets the poor to the bottom rung of the ladder. Helping them to the next rungs is the task of microfinance; building the ladder requires mainstream finance.

Reducing absolute poverty in conditions of anemic growth is all but impossible for a market economy.[5] From a long-term growth perspective, the major channel for a sustained reduction in African poverty is a transformational increase in the share of the population that is working in the modern sector and with advanced economy productive techniques.

A more effective formal financial system would not only intermediate on a much larger scale, but in doing so it would help improve enterprise productivity and growth, not least in sectors that have the potential to contribute directly or indirectly to exports, especially exports of nontraditional goods and services. Faster national economic growth is the only sure way to a sizable and sustained reduction and eventual elimination of absolute poverty (as we know it today). In addition, improved access to financial services for poor people and people in rural areas would directly help improve their circumstances and help reverse what has, at least until recently, been a trend in the continent toward widening inequality and increasing poverty rates.

In terms of agriculture—which accounts for such a high proportion of output and especially of employment at present and will continue to form the backbone of the African economy for the foreseeable future—the required transition will be toward a situation in which, although farms may be largely family controlled, they will be less labor intensive and on a much larger scale than at present.

It follows that accomplishing this long-term growth agenda needs the machinery of efficient mainstream finance. Only in this way will there be a ladder for the poor to climb. Of course, in addition to having access to effective financial services, the international and domestic private sector will be able and prepared to invest in modern productive structures only to the extent that complementary factors, including human capital and physical infrastructure, as well as other necessary conditions of the business environment, are present.

Effective finance has a role to play in contributing to these complementary factors also. The right financial arrangements can speed and improve the provision of physical infrastructure. And the legal and information infrastructures needed for effective finance also help improve the overall governance and business environment.

At the small scale, finance is relevant to helping ensure that human capital gets created. Investment by households and individuals in health and education requires insurance, savings, and sometimes borrowing services, without which families are often unable to acquire the needed skills. So finance at the small scale helps support the creation of the skilled and healthy labor force, which is among the most important prerequisites for the willingness of entrepreneurs to embark on the needed investments. Returning to the analogy of climbing a ladder, these are the second and third rungs up the ladder—the part of the climb that small-scale finance can help, once the bottom rung has been reached.

Although this vision provides the long-run goal toward which policy should be aimed, much of Africa will not have completed this transition for many years to come. The bulk of the population will still depend on a more unstructured and unsystematic, low-productivity economic structure. Even if amelioration of their condition in such structures is not directly conducive to achieving the growth-delivering economic transformation spoken of above, it should not be neglected. Financial services for microenterprises, even of low productivity, and for low-income households directly speak to a reduction of poverty.

Policy Perspectives for the Major Elements of the Formal Financial Sector

Finance at the large scale is provided in general by large and influential financial firms—banks, insurance companies, pension funds, securities market specialists, and so forth. As a general observation, if the provision of mainstream financial services in African countries is to improve as to quantity and quality, more competition and a greater presence of strong, profitable financial firms are needed. That requirement certainly means policy should create a favorable environment for doing financial business, but it does not mean that what is good for existing financial firms is necessarily good for the economy as a whole.

Clearly, the managers and owners of these firms are experts, and their opinions must be taken seriously in policy design. Their recommendations often seem to represent the modern solution. But this is not necessarily always the case. After all, in a typical well-balanced economy, the financial sector serves the rest of the economy and not the other way around. This observation is crucial for policy design, because the political and economic power of major financial sector players may tend to tip the balance into policies that make financiers wealthy (regardless of their effectiveness) as distinct from policies that favor financial sector efficiency. A vivid recent example of a major policy initiative designed to improve sector performance—rather than please incumbent suppliers—is the consolidation of the Nigerian banking system resulting from the increase in minimum capital. This ownership shake-up may not have been welcomed by many incumbents, and there is the risk that the high entry barrier represented by the new minimum capital could reduce competition. It is too early to pass judgment, but if the end result is reduced rent seeking and greater professionalism by the elimination of numerous small banks, it will have been a good idea.

Banks are and will remain at the heart of African financial systems. Their effectiveness could be greatly improved if stronger underlying infrastructures existed, including in the information and, especially, legal dimensions. Banks can function without, for example, a robust regime of land-ownership rights[6] and without a predictable judiciary, but they do so in a manner that is greatly constrained. Absence of these infrastructures reduces bank lending (as is reflected in the high liquidity prevailing in many African banking systems) and increases the necessary spread for those who do get to borrow (both for covering administrative costs—because neither large depositors nor liquid asset markets will cover those—and because of heightened loan loss risks). A full resolution of these legal issues is not something for which a quick technical fix is readily available—although some easy steps can help. The long-term solutions may be country specific and will certainly require political follow-through.

Extensive ownership changes have occurred in African banking following the bankruptcy of many banks, including state-owned banks. International banks have returned in force: new entrants from South Africa, returning ex-colonial banks from Britain and France, as well as a handful of intercontinental South-South links, especially from the Gulf and South Asia. A new wave of regional banks within Africa is also flourishing. Yet state presence lingers more than is immediately evident. For one thing, numerous state-owned near-banks still exist, including development finance institutions. Furthermore, several large, formerly state-owned commercial banks remain state controlled, with direct government ownership being supplemented by parastatal shareholdings. Lip service to the concept of privatization can leave a bank even more vulnerable to the weaknesses that are often associated with state ownership. And political pressures on lending decisions of banks—both state owned and private—continue to be a problem in some countries.

The lack of long-term finance is partly a reflection of the long-term risks already mentioned and partly an endogenous response to the need for monitoring and recontracting. In some countries, it is caused by a regulatory-induced bias restricting maturity transformation. Finally, across Africa, there is a paucity of long-term resources available for investment. Although pension funds, social security, and life insurance are natural providers of such funds, more could be done to encourage those entities to actively seek out long-term uses for their funds. However, good governance of these funds needs to be ensured, and that will be facilitated if active securities exchanges exist on which their investments can be priced.[7]

For the present, most organized African securities markets are largely primary markets with relatively little secondary activity. Perhaps an over-elaborate model of regulation has been adopted for these markets (the modernist model overreaching itself), effectively precluding small issuers, yet failing to achieve substantial liquidity for larger issuers.

With the failure of several state-owned insurance companies and the entry of regional or international firms to provide the basic insurance products, general insurance is gradually making a comeback in Africa. But the potential complexity of insurance business makes it essentially a business in which the buyer must beware. Most national regulators are ill equipped to assess and discipline fraudulent or reckless insurers. Insurance is a good candidate for regional cooperation in supervision—potentially as an annex to banking supervision.

Regional cooperation and integration have long seemed to offer possible solutions to problems of small scale. Regional integration could be further pursued in numerous dimensions. Currency unions are firmly on the political agenda. At present, just three working examples survive of a more numerous set of colonial relationships. Despite political commitment to single-currency programs (undoubtedly inspired by the European Economic and Monetary Union, or EMU, project), most practitioners do not expect further single currencies to become a reality in any short time-scale, especially given the diversity of national macroeconomic policy conditions and the inability of most African governments to provide a fully credible commitment to a single currency. A more plausible candidate area for further integration is supervision of banks and other intermediaries (with the two international agencies of the CFA zones now well established and offering one potential model) and securities markets (one already, others in the planning or development stage). It might be more fruitful to redirect political will in the short run to cooperation on bank and other intermediary supervision and to exploitation of regional gains from stock market integration.

Aggregate national resource mobilization is primarily a matter of convincing the wealthy that they can safely leave their deposits in the local banks. That means macroeconomic and political stability, sound banks, adequate competition, and a quasi-tax regime that allows reasonable rates of interest to be paid. Absence of these conditions helps explain why African savings rates have been low. A new technical challenge to achieving sustained macro balance without choking off growth is emerging from increasing aid flows (as well as from the effects of the oil price boom in oil-producing countries). The willingness of the private sector to hold money onshore is likely to grow in line with the improved prospects created by these inflows, thereby allowing greater financial deepening without triggering unduly restrictive credit policies.

Helping more people to access deposit services is also important and commercially possible, but its social value lies in a different dimension entirely from that of aggregate resource mobilization—namely from affording the depositors an important liquidity, precautionary saving, and accumulation function. Offering deposit services can also be a key to the healthy growth of the MFIs that serve low-income clients.

Reaching Difficult Markets

At most, 20 percent of African households have any access to formal finance.[8] Even medium-scale enterprises have difficulty accessing credit and the other financial services they need to grow.

The major problems are twofold. First, intermediaries have difficulty delivering their products to poor or remote customers—let alone adapting product design to these customers' needs—at an affordable cost. Cost penalties particularly relevant in Africa (though also observed in other parts of the world) include the small size of the market at both national and local levels, which is partly attributable to low geographic density of population and pronounced economic isolation (especially in rural areas). This factor is compounded by the deficiencies of transport and communications, as well as extremely low transaction sizes and the inappropriateness of some standard products to the needs of small clients. Lack of competition adds to the cost penalties experienced by clients.

Second is the difficulty of assessing creditworthiness and enforcing contracts. Low levels of perceived creditworthiness in Africa relate to the poor quality and scarcity of information about individual risks as well as to high incidence of shocks (weather, health, social disruption) exogenous to the agents and often systemic or at least covariant. Weak legal and judicial and other information and contract enforcement infrastructures are also a pervasive underlying factor here.

Despite a newfound interest on the part of some of the big banks in reaching parts of the market in which they have not been active before—the small farmer, the rural or urban poor, the middle-class would-be homeowner—it would be unwise to assume that their unaided efforts are guaranteed to overcome the formidable challenges that face such an effort. Although the banks may have the resources to meet the overhead costs of setting up new systems that can help reach rural households and meet the financial service needs of small farmers, they will have to work hard to make sure that the unit costs of operating these systems are sufficiently low.

Governments can assist banks and other private financial intermediaries in this regard through efforts to build and repair various hard and soft infrastructures that are essential ingredients in rolling out financial services widely. Improving the functioning of courts as enforcers of contracts and property rights—whether through legislative changes to reduce the complexity and cost of unnecessary court procedures, through training and selection of judges and an effective system of sanctions for judicial corruption, or through efficient mechanisms for enforcing judgments—is one area in which the need for reforms is clear and on which some of the initial steps in that direction can be taken without too much difficulty, technical or political. Likewise, it is not too difficult to clarify laws and tax rules in order to smooth the way to a wider use of leasing and factoring—credit techniques that have long proved effective in reaching borrowers with limited scale and weaker creditworthiness. Building the credit information infrastructure—from registries of secured claims and credit bureaus to accounting rules and the performance of the audit profession—is a longer process but also eminently feasible. Recasting land-ownership claims in such a way as to make land usable as collateral may be a tougher challenge. It may require a political campaign to refocus public awareness of the relative benefits of modern market-based land-ownership structures in comparison with tribal or other conventional land-tenure systems or with socialism; even more important, the opposition of those who have a vested interest in the current arrangements for the control of land will need to be overcome.

Even if these modernist "meso-level" initiatives are accomplished, lending—and borrowing—in Africa will remain a challenge. The necessarily unsystematic and unstructured nature of African business transactions, especially in the informal sector, is one major reason simple solutions are not available. In these conditions, lenders must reach deeper into classic loan appraisal techniques. Micro-, small-, and medium-scale enterprises' access to credit from the formal financial sector will depend in large part on the degree to which banks and other formal intermediaries are motivated by profit or social concern to make this more elaborate and necessarily more costly effort. If the effort is to be worth making, it is crucial that neither governments nor donors spoil the market (as they have in the past) with simplistic and heavily subsidized credit interventions that will be captured by those who would have received credit anyway, do not need the subsidy, and could have provided profitable business to share the costs of market-dependent intermediaries.

Experience shows that successful lenders in Africa go beyond the mechanical rules and procedures that work well in more settled environments. *Relationship lending* is probably the best umbrella term[9] to describe the tailored investment in credit appraisal, the flexibility of response to excusable delinquency, and the imaginative approaches to renegotiation and recovery that are needed to be a successful lender to the middle market in Africa. This strategy requires experience and skills and may at first not always yield financial rewards commensurate with the skills employed. That is why charitable NGOs and donor agencies are active in these areas. Commercial concerns are also engaged, and provided that they have a long time horizon and deep pockets, they should also be able to make a success of this method if they are not undercut by subsidy or blocked by overelaborate or poorly designed prudential regulations. Facilitating their activities and helping them reach scale while controlling costs must be a top priority of financial policy authorities in African countries.

Credit and noncredit financial services—such as deposits, payments (including domestic and international remittances), and insurance—have a tough time reaching rural areas, farmers, and low-income households. Different main sources of difficulty can easily be seen for each of these three categories. Rural areas are by definition more remote than urban areas, and in most African countries the population is very dispersed indeed. Farm enterprises are rarely able to benefit as immediately and deeply from the most common techniques of sustainable microfinance as are small urban traders. This difficulty arises not only because of the short-term and progressive nature of the lending relationship but also because the relatively high break-even interest rates (see box 1.2) that have to be charged for sustainable microfinance are often out of line with the rates of return that can be achieved in most of African farming today—even if such returns are reliably in double digits. Finally, low-income households are hard to reach because they can rarely afford to pay the unavoidable fixed costs involved in any banking-type relationship, but it is not impossible.

It seems natural to look to financial engineering and technological advance to help overcome these difficulties. Already, innovators throughout Africa have been piloting a range of initiatives that can help. Several of these are described in chapter 4. Even if some have not yet reached commercial scale, they all show the general outlines of the way forward. Extending these experiments and conducting others is something in which all concerned—specialized MFIs, whether or not cooperative in structure; mainstream banks; governments; and donors—have their part to play.

Organization of the Report

Chapter 2 provides a quantitative stock-taking of Africa's financial systems. Financial depth is found to be somewhat lower than the worldwide average even after taking account of inflation and mean per capita income, especially for credit. Africans also have disproportionately high offshore deposits. Interest margins are high; international comparison pinpoints small scale, property rights institutions, and lack of competition as among the important causal factors. Apart from a few of the longest established, organized securities markets are small and inactive; institutional investors often concentrate on bank deposits and real estate instead. Microfinance has improved its outreach, though access rates in African countries remain behind those in other regions.

> **BOX 1.2**
>
> **Microfinance: Sustainability and Outreach**
>
> The goal of achieving a large outreach and sustainability drives certain microfinance principles that also mesh well with the modernist perspective to mainstream finance. The *financial systems approach* to microfinance envisages microfinance institutions converging to financial self-sustainability. According to this approach, subsidies that are provided focus on setup and head-office issues, including product development, and are not directly used to subsidize lending interest rates at the margin (even when the subsidy is received in the form of a low-interest long-term loan that the MFI invests in treasury bills, using the net revenue to cover operating costs). As scale is achieved, such subsidies will tend to assume a relatively smaller part of the microfinance business (in a way that, for example, systematically distorting marginal pricing of interest rates would not). Even though the intention is usually to eliminate them, such foundation subsidies do tend to persist for a very long time.
>
> The high interest rates (spread over wholesale rates) seen in unsubsidized microcredit—although much lower than those typically charged by moneylenders—result from the costs associated with intermediation of this sort and, in particular, costs that result from small scale. Microfinance can be successful in rural areas but is more widespread in urban and peri-urban settings, which points to the costs associated with remoteness and low density. By the same token, such high interest rates (and a fortiori such absences) mean that much potentially socially beneficial microlending simply does not take place. The same applies mutatis mutandis with respect to the pricing of deposits and insurance type products (see Helms and Reille 2004; Porteous 2006a).

Chapter 3 examines finance at the large scale and its contribution to national economic growth. The chapter considers the measures needed to boost financial depth and, in particular, to encourage banks to lend a higher fraction of the resources they mobilize. The role of different ownership structures in African banking—in particular the return of the foreign banks and the decline of development banking—is documented and interpreted. The best solution to long-term finance is not development banking. Instead, the long-term resources of pension funds and other institutional investors offer a more promising alternative source of term finance, though governance improvements are needed to underpin this source. The pricing transparency offered by active organized securities markets could help. The lack of volume and activity on existing exchanges is seen as partly attributable to an overambitious model of securities regulation: less onerous requirements could increase the scale and activity of the exchanges and their usefulness to smaller firms, without undue loss of investor protection.

Regional cooperation can help improve policy solutions in the areas considered in chapter 3, but there is a need to select the most promising among the numerous extant projects here, with intermediary supervision more immediately promising than currency union. If the external environment improves, careful policy design in other macro areas will be needed to ensure that resource mobilization increases in response and to guard against the danger that the growth dividend from incipient financial deepening is not choked off by unduly restrictive measures.

Chapter 4 turns to finance at the bottom of the pyramid, considering in turn the challenges faced in reaching a wider market for credit, insurance, deposits, and payments. Evidence and practical experience about what can work in an African environment are reviewed under each heading, with an emphasis on financial engineering and technology as key elements of the solution. Although activism is clearly needed here, different types of agents have different roles to play. The direct provision of financial services will remain largely in the hands of private financiers, albeit including cooperatives and donor-aided NGOs. Government needs to attach priority to creating policy structures that actively help these intermediaries reach cost-effective scale and that are not blocked by dysfunctional or excessive regulation. Donors can help fill gaps by acting as independent "agents of restraint" to prevent abuse where national governments so far lack the market credibility or governance institutions to intervene effectively.

Financial sector reform is a long haul, but in tackling it policy makers should be on the lookout for available shortcuts that can help without compromising stability and efficiency: they should be especially open to leveraging on what external agents can offer, and they need to ensure that policy is geared toward inclusiveness. The report ends (chapter 5) by addressing these issues of policy prioritization. It suggests two particular practical areas that may offer a high payback in most African countries today—namely (a) boosting credit flows by strengthening registries and streamlining court procedures and (b) working on enhancing the independence of regulatory authorities. More generally, priorities will vary depending on the contrasting conditions that face African countries, and this point is illustrated for some specific extreme cases—postconflict countries, oil-rich countries, small countries, sparsely populated countries, and finally the few large countries able to avail themselves of critical mass.

Notes

1. The evidence pointing to a positive causal association between better-developed financial systems and faster economic development is based on analysis of a wide range of country-level, industry-level, firm-level, and internal country data. If we consider worldwide experience as a whole, financial development's positive effect on gross domestic product per capita growth comes through improving the efficiency of resource allocation and thereby productivity, rather than through financial development's effect on investment volumes (Levine 2005). The evidence for subgroups of countries is harder to interpret. Thus, the investment-volume channel may be relatively stronger in low-income countries, for which indeed the evidence for a causal effect of finance on long-term growth is less clear (Rioja and Valev 2004a, 2004b). However, Aghion, Howitt, and Mayer-Foulkes (2005) provide evidence suggesting a complex causal pattern for variations in the effect of finance at different levels of development. They find that once a country has achieved a certain level of financial development, more finance does not contribute further to growth, but growth in countries with low financial development does benefit from further financial deepening. Studies confined to African data also find a causal link between finance and growth (see Ghirmay 2004), but some suggest that the effectiveness of finance might be lower in Africa (Kpodar 2005).
2. A major Harvard-Oxford-African Economic Research Consortium (AERC) project, building on earlier work that was surveyed in Collier and Gunning (1999a, 1999b), has combined historical case studies and cross-country econometrics to try to understand the causes of Africa's low growth performance. While noting the role of exogenous factors ("opportunities") in holding back many African countries, the study points to a set of antigrowth policy ("choice") syndromes-control regimes, adverse redistribution, unsustainable spending booms, and state failure-that have accounted for the loss of between 1 and 2.5 percent per annum in median growth rates. According to the project's conclusions, avoiding these syndromes was virtually a necessary condition for rapid growth and virtually sufficient for avoiding the growth collapses that so often undermined sustained progress in Africa (Fosu and O'Connell 2006; see also Azam, Bates, and Biais 2005; Azam, Fosu, and Ndung'u 2002).

3. For example, the AERC-Harvard-Oxford Africa growth project emphasizes contrasting physical and political geographic preconditions for growth between African countries (see Fosu and O'Connell 2006); contrasting monetary regimes in Africa are highlighted by Honohan and O'Connell (1997).
4. A useful background resource for anyone wishing to assess the quality of a country's financial sector in terms of these standard building blocks is International Monetary Fund (IMF) and World Bank (2005).
5. But note also that, up until recently, in contrast to most other developing countries where both the numbers and percentage share of the population in absolute poverty have been falling, African countries have been characterized by a widening inequality gap, with more absolutely poor people alongside a middle class whose prosperity is—on average—gradually increasing (see Artadi and Sala-i-Martin 2003; Sala-i-Martin 2006). At the same time, however, certain nonincome social indicators have improved (Silva Lopes 2005).
6. Insecurity of individual land tenure in Africa has had implications well beyond those for access to credit, notably in its chilling effect on rural investment, as documented in microstudies such as Dercon, Ayalew, and Gautam (2005).
7. Another important and underrated benefit of equity markets is the way in which they can help to give elite groups and the upper-middle class a stake in economic systemic stability and growth through diversified and interlinked claims on the system achieved by portfolio (arm's-length) equity claims on firms operating in and reliant on the local economy (including banks).
8. To be sure, many more have recourse to informal finance for both household and enterprise needs. Indeed, the richness and persistent centrality of African informal financial networks for most Africans is a phenomenon that has fascinated observers. It is not to diminish the current importance of these networks to confine the present discussion to the formal financial sector. The formal sector is the main target of policy, and it will undoubtedly become increasingly important in serving the majority of African households and firms.
9. Relationship lending is to be distinguished from related party lending, where the lender has family, social, or nonlending business relationships with the borrower.

CHAPTER 2

African Financial Systems: Depth, Breadth, and Efficiency

Introduction: International Comparisons

An underdeveloped financial system—
Given the proposition underlying the discussion of the previous chapter—namely that financial development is important for economic development and poverty alleviation—how do Africa's[1] financial systems stand in international comparison? Is a low degree of financial depth, efficiency, and access simply a question of economic development, or can other factors explain Africa's low score? This chapter assembles the key statistics allowing such a comparison as an essential starting point for policy discussion. The objective is not to belabor the shortcomings of Africa's formal financial systems. Although there are sizable differences between countries within the region, it is well known that, on average, African finance performs well below that of other regions. Instead, the goal is to pinpoint especially weak areas and to identify dimensions in which improvements might realistically be hoped for.

—in both absolute and relative terms
As measured by aggregate banking depth, African financial systems are shallow. Most of this shallowness can be related to low income, given the worldwide tendency for higher-income countries to have deeper financial systems. However, a disproportionate number of African countries are

below this average relationship, especially in terms of credit. Offshore deposit accounts explain some of the missing deposits, and an apparent inability of banks to find enough safe lending opportunities shows up in the low credit numbers. Banking spreads are high too, as are bank profits and overhead costs. Lack of competition in banking is one aspect of this problem, and it can also be traced to other structural factors that have been shown to contribute to spreads in other countries.

Only one in three African countries has an organized securities market, and though South Africa has one of the largest emerging stock markets in the world, only a handful of the rest of the stock markets have achieved significant capitalization or liquidity. Insurance is also highly variable across African countries, especially in the life sector, with considerable potential both for development and, as with pension and social security funds, for more effective portfolio allocation.

Much of the financial sector is informal
Reflecting the prevalence of poverty in the region, new data suggest that not more than 20 percent of African adults have an account at a formal or semiformal financial institution. Across countries, however, the data vary widely, and the roles of different classes of institutions—savings banks, cooperatives, microfinance institutions (MFIs) sponsored by nongovernmental organizations (NGOs)—also vary widely. Enterprises complain more about lack of finance in Africa than in other regions, and they are less likely to use formal external finance, which impedes investment and growth.

Financial Depth and Efficiency: What Explains Africa's Low Score?

As for the developing world as a whole, banking is at the heart of Africa's formal financial systems, so measures of banking depth and efficiency are the natural place to begin.

Banking Depth

Banking depth is generally measured by reference either to deposit resources mobilized by the system or by credit extended. Although these two measures of depth are closely correlated, there are differences, both in terms of their influence and in terms of measurement. The deposit side is central to analysis of monetary policy, inasmuch as it measures an important component of liquid spending power in the economy, and fluctuations in money and bank deposits may help predict inflation. But it is the level of bank credit to the private sector that is most closely correlated with medium-term growth and poverty reduction (Beck, Demirgüç-Kunt, and Levine 2004; Beck, Levine, and Loayza 2000; Honohan 2004), essentially because that measure captures the degree to which banks are channeling society's savings to productive uses.[2]

Deposit and credit measures differ for several reasons. In addition to mobilizing domestic deposits, banks can source loanable funds from the wholesale market—for example, from their affiliates or from other banks abroad. Furthermore, capital liabilities—owners' resources, for example—are also important contributors to a bank's capacity to lend. Conversely, not all the resources mobilized may be onlent to the domestic private sector. For one thing, the government and other public authorities and public enterprises will also be drawing on bank finance; furthermore, many banks invest some of their resources abroad.

We therefore focus on two standard indicators of financial depth and development: the ratio of liquid liabilities to gross domestic product (GDP) is a broad measure of monetary resources (currency plus demand and interest-bearing liabilities) mobilized by banks and near-bank intermediaries relative to economic activity. The ratio of private credit to GDP gets us closer to the growth potential of financial intermediation by measuring the claims of financial institutions in the private sector relative to economic activity.[3]

In interpreting the data, one must bear in mind that the link between financial depth and growth is a two-way one: although deeper financial systems tend to boost subsequent growth, the level of per capita income is also a major determinant of current financial depth, with lower monetary holdings in poor countries. Consistent with this relationship, we find that intermediary development in most African countries is lower than in other regions of the world (figures 2.1 and 2.2). The ratio of liquid liabilities to GDP averages 32 percent in Africa, compared with 49 percent in East Asia and Pacific and 100 percent in high-income countries. Similarly, the ratio of private credit to GDP averages 18 percent in Africa, compared with 30 percent in South Asia and 107 percent in high-income countries. The ratio of private credit to GDP averages 11 percent in low-income countries in Africa but 21 percent in low-income countries outside Africa.

FIGURE 2.1
Liquid Liabilities across Countries

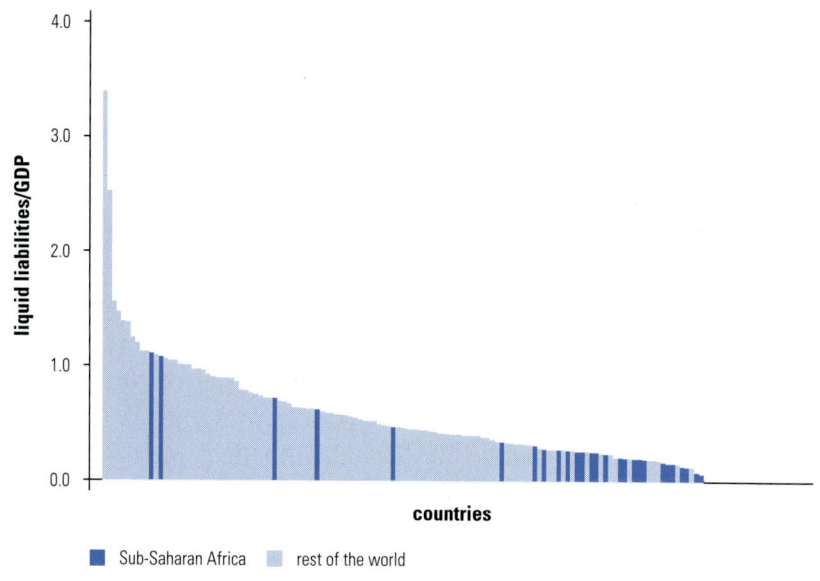

[Bar chart showing liquid liabilities/GDP ratios across 127 countries, sorted from highest to lowest. Sub-Saharan African countries shown in darker color, rest of the world in lighter color. Y-axis ranges from 0.0 to 4.0.]

Source: World Bank's Financial Structure database.

Note: This figure shows the liquid liabilities of the monetary system (M3) relative to GDP for the 127 countries available. African countries are shown in darker color. The highest African values are for the offshore financial centers of Seychelles, Mauritius, and Cape Verde, followed by those of South Africa and Ethiopia. All data are for the latest available year, 2004–05.

Within Africa, the tendency for higher-income countries to have deeper financial systems is also observed (figure 2.3). Consistent with its much higher mean income (and special economic structure), South Africa is a large outlier in all these indicators and need not be discussed further in this context. Two other outliers in the deposit data, Mauritius and the Seychelles, are offshore financial centers. An additional factor is inflation expectations; countries with long experience of inflationary surges tend to have lower monetary depth (Boyd, Levine, and Smith 2001).

Figures 2.4 and 2.5 show that much of the low level—and of the cross-country variation—in African monetary depth can be explained by national per capita income, controlling for inflation. Still, more African countries fall below the line than above it.[4] Among the low-depth countries are all but one of the members of the CFA franc zone.[5]

Monetary depth is lowered by the tendency of wealth holders to hold their liquid assets outside Africa: the ratio of offshore deposits to domestic bank deposits is significantly higher in Africa than in other regions of the

FIGURE 2.2
Private Credit across Countries

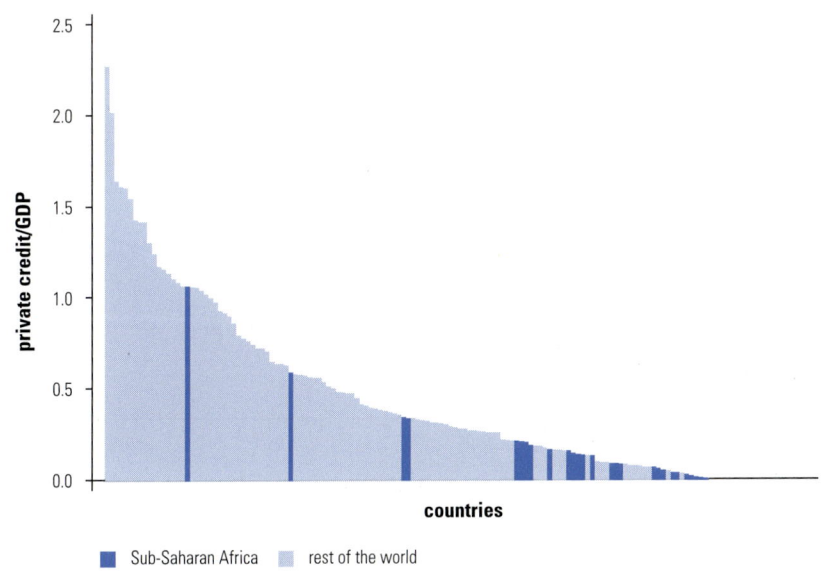

Source: World Bank's Financial Structure database.

Note: This figure shows private credit granted by deposit money banks and other financial institutions relative to GDP for the 128 countries available. African countries are shown in darker color. The highest African values are for South Africa, Mauritius, Seychelles, and Cape Verde. All data are for the latest available year, 2004–05.

world (figure 2.6). This tendency points to capital flight as one factor exacerbating the low rate of domestic savings (though additional factors are at work, including the requirement imposed by some foreign financiers for African importers to post cash collateral abroad).[6] Aggregate data point to Africa as the continent with the largest capital flight relative to private wealth, for which a variety of risk factors are likely causes (Collier and Gunning 1999a, 1999b; Collier, Hoeffler, and Pattillo 2004; Ndikumana and Boyce 2002). Unlike in other regions, capital flight in Africa is not compensated by private capital inflows; Africa is the only region where donor funding still exceeds private portfolio funding (Senbet and Otchere 2006).

Also, in terms of credit depth, more African countries fall below what would be expected from the cross-country pattern—and in several cases the gap is quite large (figure 2.5). This feature is consistent with another striking characteristic of African financial systems: the low intermediation ratio (that is, the low share of deposits intermediated into private sector credit). Figure 2.7 shows what is happening: in Africa, the median bank-

FIGURE 2.3
Private Credit and GDP per Capita

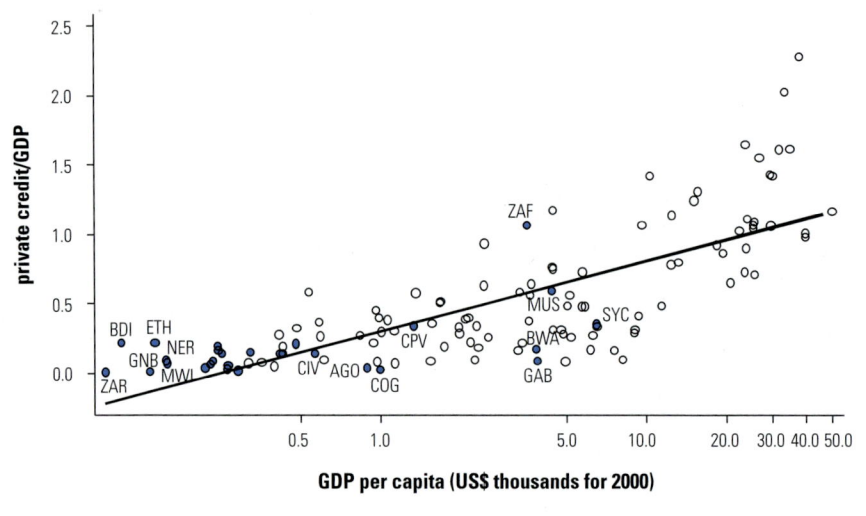

Sources: World Bank's Financial Structure database; World Bank's World Development Indicators database.

Note: Country abbreviations are included in the abbreviations list at the front of the book. This figure plots the ratio of private credit to GDP against GDP per capita (in log scale) for 122 countries. African countries are shown in darker color. All data are for the latest available year, 2004–05.

ing system allocates more of its resources to liquid assets and lending to government than do systems in other regions, thus implying a lower share of credit allocated to the private sector. Given the importance of private sector credit for economic growth, finding effective ways of ensuring that the banks channel more of their resources to the domestic private sector is crucial for financial sector development.

Though financial depth remains low, signs of recovery are unmistakable and encouraging. As figure 2.8 shows, indicators of financial development for the median African country have steadily increased over the past 10 years after hitting a low point in 1995–96. The earlier decline was partly a legacy of bank closures and rationalizations following the waves of banking failures experienced in earlier years. A cleanup of the books left private credit and deposits lower than they had been (and often saw a jump in the share of government credit when failing banks were recapitalized with government bonds). There was thus room for growth, which is now being realized.

FIGURE 2.4
Liquid Liabilities to GDP and GDP per Capita

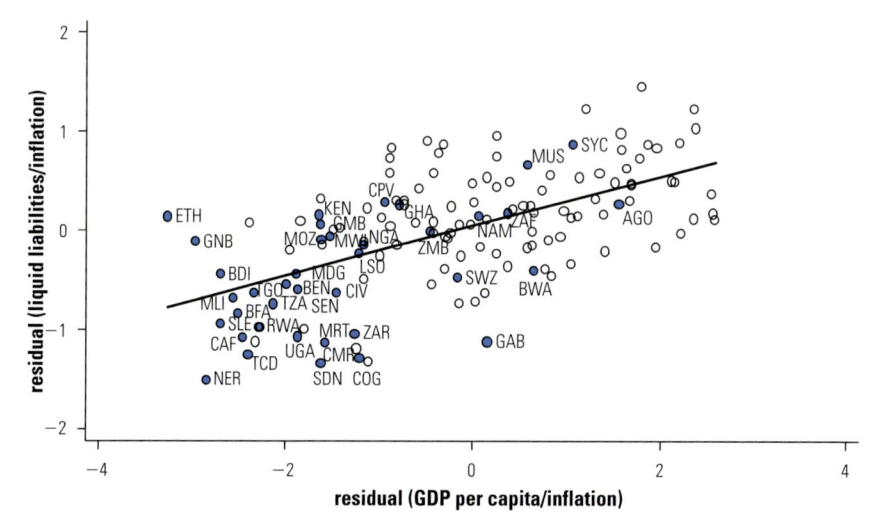

Sources: World Bank's Financial Structure database; World Bank's World Development Indicators database.

Note: Country abbreviations are included in the abbreviations list at the front of the book. This figure plots the residual from a linear regression of the ratio of liquid liabilities to GDP on inflation against the residual from a linear regression of GDP per capita on inflation for 139 countries. Liquid liabilities and GDP per capita are in log scales. African countries are shown in darker color. All data are for the latest available year, 2004–05.

Real private sector credit has, in particular, been growing at an accelerating rate, and its median value has doubled in the past decade. Even as a share of GDP, it has turned the corner, with the median share reaching almost 14 percent in 2005, about a third higher than at its anemic trough in 1996. (A regression estimate of the time trend is shown in figure 2.8.) And although some countries have not shared in the general upward movement, four of every five African countries for which data are available have seen financial depth increasing since 2000.

The continued wide variation in financial depth among African countries (map 2.1) shows considerable further upside potential, especially in countries such as the Democratic Republic of Congo and Mozambique, where private sector lending remains minuscule. A case in point is Tanzania, where the loan-to-deposit ratio of the banking system as a whole dipped to less than 18 percent after the financial restructuring of the largest banks. After a cautious resumption of lending, the ratio of private credit to

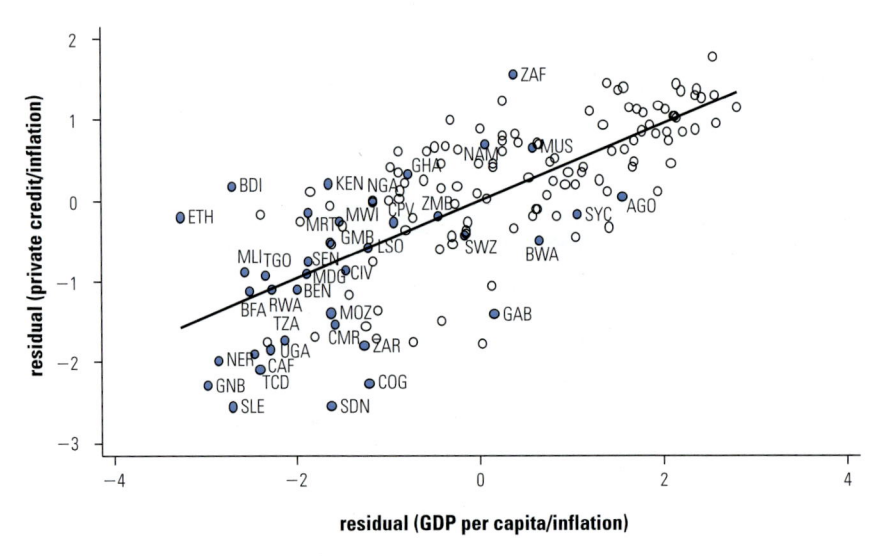

FIGURE 2.5
Private Credit to GDP and GDP per Capita

[Scatter plot showing residual (private credit/inflation) on y-axis from -3 to 2, and residual (GDP per capita/inflation) on x-axis from -4 to 4. Sub-Saharan Africa countries shown in darker color, all other countries as open circles. Countries labeled include ZAF, MUS, GHA, NAM, KEN, NGA, BDI, ETH, MRT, MWI, CPV, ZMB, AGO, SYC, MLI, TGO, GMB, SEN, LSO, SWZ, BWA, MDG, CIV, BEN, BFA, RWA, TZA, MOZ, GAB, CMR, ZAR, UGA, NER, CAF, GNB, TCD, COG, SLE, SDN.]

● Sub-Saharan Africa ○ all other countries

Sources: World Bank's Financial Structure database; World Bank's World Development Indicators database.

Note: Country abbreviations are included in the abbreviations list at the front of the book. This figure plots the residual from a linear regression of the ratio of private credit to GDP on inflation against the residual from a regression of GDP per capita on inflation for 151 countries. The ratio of private credit to GDP and GDP per capita is in log scales. African countries are shown in darker color. All data are for the latest available year, 2004–05.

GDP has increased steadily since 1996, growing from 2.8 percent in that year to about 10 percent by 2005. Tanzanian bank deposits have also been growing rapidly and these resources are still underlent: there is considerable growth potential left, even before considering the possibility of mobilizing more domestic resources. For Tanzania, as for other countries, the question remains how to unlock this growth potential.

Banking Competition and Efficiency: Interest Margins, Costs, and Profitability

Africa's banking systems are characterized not only by low levels of intermediation but also by high interest rates, wide intermediation spreads, and substantial bank profitability. High lending interest rates, whether caused by inefficiency or lack of competition, do more than add to borrowers' costs. By pricing the safer borrowers out of the market, high interest rates

FIGURE 2.6
Offshore to Domestic Bank Deposits: Regional Distributions

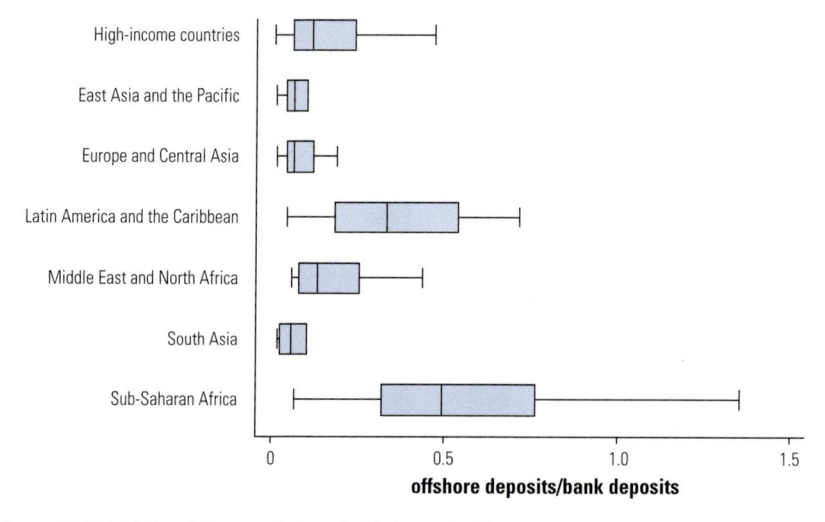

Sources: World Bank's Financial Structure database; Bank for International Settlements online database.

Note: For each region, the figure plots the minimum, maximum, and median of the ratio of offshore to domestic bank deposits for 132 countries. The shaded boxes show the interquartile range. Outliers have been omitted. All data are for the latest available year, 2004–05.

can increase the risk of lending, making banks less willing to lend and—as has been recognized since the pioneering work of Stiglitz and Weiss (1981)—potentially resulting in credit rationing combined with high bank liquidity. One source of high lending rates is high wholesale interest rates, which reflect currency and other macroeconomic uncertainties as well as the demand by governments for domestic loanable funds. The degree of efficiency and competition in the banking system is another factor that explains variation in lending rates.

Wholesale real interest rates in Africa increased significantly in the median African country in the early 1990s. This was a direct and intended consequence of interest rate and macroeconomic liberalization; it was also influenced by fiscal and macroeconomic expectation effects. Since 1993, realized wholesale interest rates have fluctuated without any discernible trend (figure 2.9).

Interest rate margins
The intermediation spread (the gap between average deposit and average lending rates) or the intermediation margin (net interest income as a per-

FIGURE 2.7
Asset Composition of Banks across Regions

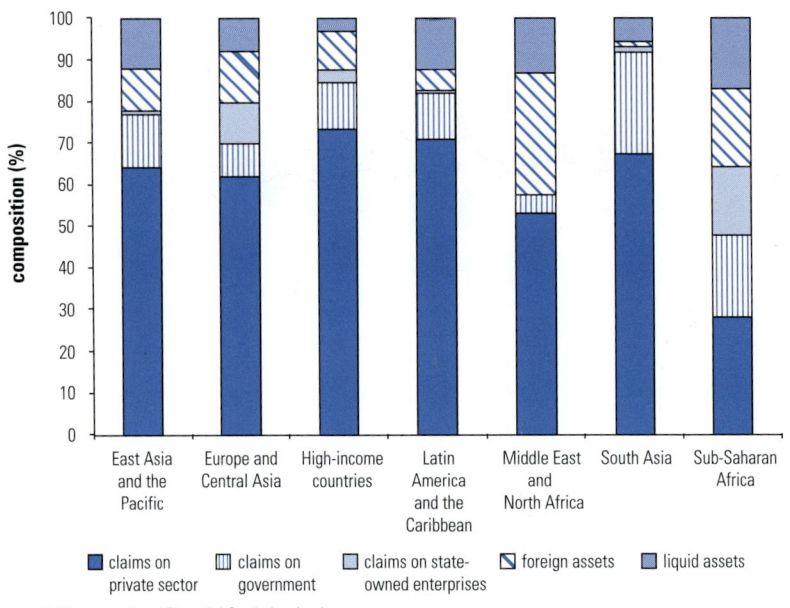

Source: IMF's International Financial Statistics database.

Note: For each region, the figure shows the composition of the asset portfolio of banks between liquid assets, foreign assets, claims on state-owned enterprises, claims on government, and claims on the private sector. All data are for 2005.

FIGURE 2.8
Financial Depth in Africa, 1990–2005

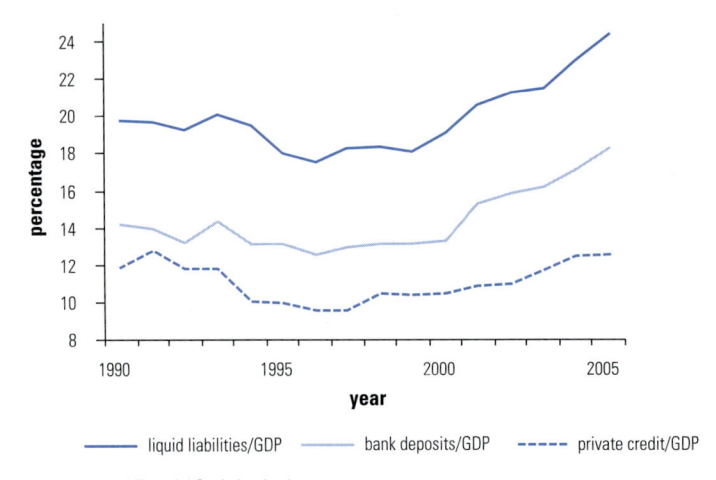

Source: IMF's International Financial Statistics database.

Note: Figure shows estimated date coefficients from pooled time-series cross-section median regressions.

MAP 2.1
Financial Depth: Average Ratio of Private Credit to GDP, 2000–04

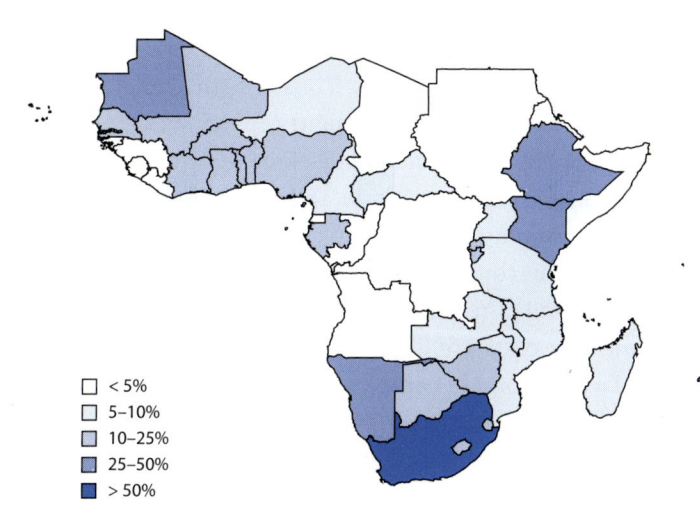

- ☐ < 5%
- ☐ 5–10%
- ☐ 10–25%
- ☐ 25–50%
- ■ > 50%

Source: World Bank Financial Structure database.

FIGURE 2.9
Real Interest Rates in Africa, 1990–2005

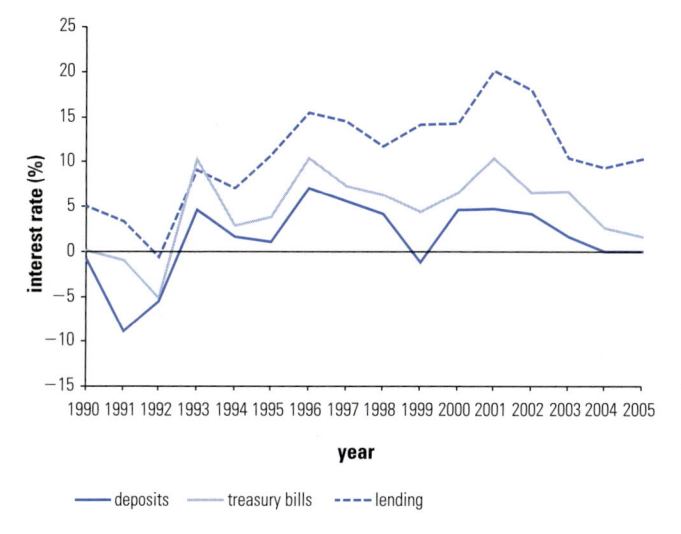

— deposits   — treasury bills   --- lending

Source: IMF's International Financial Statistics database.

Note: The figure shows estimated date coefficients from pooled time-series cross-section median regressions. Real interest rates are computed using the consumer price index as the deflator.

centage of total earning assets) are often taken as measures of banking (in)efficiency. In interpreting these numbers, one must recall that the difference between interest received and interest paid by the banks goes to pay for staff and other noninterest costs and to make provisions for loan losses, as well as to contribute to profits. Thus, a high spread could result from an uncompetitive banking environment (implying higher profits) or from factors such as a higher risk of default. Some elements of default risk may in turn be considered systemwide and outside the control of the banks, but some banks may deliberately choose a high-yield, high-risk portfolio. Banks in some countries may also face different unit prices for skilled staff members and other inputs—though within a particular market variations in unit staff costs are likely to reflect skill differentials rather than exogenous factors. Foreign banks, however, often draw on expatriate staff members, which can increase intermediation costs considerably. Given all these considerations, it is clear that the variation across countries and across banks in intermediation spreads and margins needs to be interpreted with care.

Figure 2.10 shows that African banking systems tend to have higher net interest margins than banks in many other parts of the world. On average, the net interest margin in African banks between 2000 and 2004 was 800 basis points, compared with 480 basis points in the rest of the world. However, banks in many Latin American and Eastern European countries have margins at least as high as African banks do, which raises the question of what drives high interest margins across banks and countries.[7]

One factor is bank profitability. The overall profitability of African banks in recent years has been high: in our sample, the average return on total assets was 2.1 percent, more than three times the profitability of non-African banks (0.6 percent). Similarly, the average return to equity for African banks in our sample was 20.1 percent over the period 2000 to 2004, compared with 8.5 percent for non-African banks (table 2.1). High profitability might be due to high risk premiums demanded by bankers, lack of competition, or—most likely—a combination and interaction of both.

Bank operating costs are another component of the interest margin.[8] Mean operating costs—that is, administrative (overhead) costs—in African banks averaged 650 basis points during 2000 to 2004, compared with 480 basis points on average in the rest of the world.

Breaking down the interest margins into profit and cost components is informative but also raises a deeper question: what underlying structural

FIGURE 2.10
Net Interest Margins across Regions

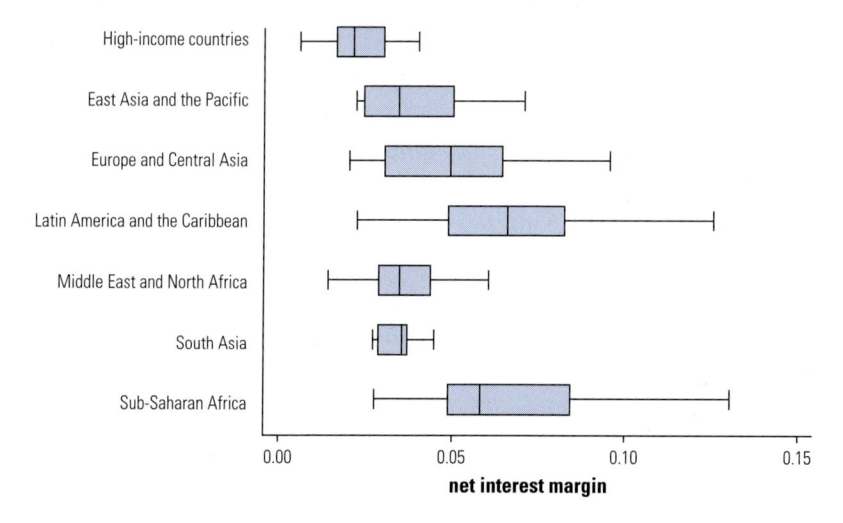

[Box plot showing net interest margins from 0.00 to 0.15 for the following regions: High-income countries, East Asia and the Pacific, Europe and Central Asia, Latin America and the Caribbean, Middle East and North Africa, South Asia, Sub-Saharan Africa]

Sources: World Bank's Financial Structure database; World Bank's World Development Indicators database.

Note: The figure shows the minimum, maximum, and median of the national mean net interest margins for banks in 146 countries, as reported in the BankScope database for the latest available year, 2004 or 2005. The shaded boxes show the interquartile range.

factors in the different economies are driving these differences? A recent study (Demirgüç-Kunt, Laeven, and Levine 2004), using bank-level data for 76 countries (including 7 from Africa) for the period 1995 to 1999 suggested that the most important drivers include the quality of property rights protection (weaker property rights lead banks to charge higher lend-

TABLE 2.1
Bank Profit Comparisons, 2000–04

	Return on assets (%)	Return on equity (%)
Africa	2.1	20.1
Foreign banks in Africa	2.8	26.7
Subsample of foreign banks in Africa	4.7	43.2
Rest of world	0.6	8.5
Foreign banks in rest of world	0.9	8.6
Subsample of foreign banks in rest of world	0.7	9.7

Source: Authors' calculations using data from BankScope.

Note: The table shows mean return on assets and return on equity for the classes of banks shown in Africa and in the rest of the world. The subsample of foreign banks consists of those banks for which data were available and that have operations both in Africa and in the rest of the world.

ing rates and also to spend more administrative resources on credit appraisal and monitoring); inflation; and bank size (smaller banks incur more overhead costs, which may also add to their interest margins).

Reestimating the same regression equation as in the 2004 study just mentioned with a larger and more recent data set allows us to obtain both confirmation and updated estimates of the importance of these underlying factors in contributing to higher operating costs and the other components of high interest margins. Table 2.2 shows the breakdown. Of the 320 basis points difference in average interest margin between Africa and the rest of the world, only 60 basis points are left unexplained by the model; of the 180 basis points difference in overhead costs, only 10 basis points remain unaccounted for. After we account for these different country and bank-level characteristics, a dummy variable for Sub-Saharan Africa does not enter either regression significantly. There seems to be no significant difference between margins and overhead costs across banks with different ownership structures, after controlling for other bank- and country-level characteristics.

By this analysis, much of the gap, especially for the interest margin, is fundamentally explained by the weaker protection in Africa of property rights, as measured by the composite governance indicator for which recent values are plotted in figure 2.11. On a scale that has been normalized to give a worldwide average of zero and a standard deviation of one, the African countries in the sample have an average governance score of –0.5. This lower governance score for Africa translates into a predicted dif-

TABLE 2.2
Net Interest Margins and Overhead Costs in International Comparison

	Interest margin (basis points)	Administrative costs (basis points)
African banks	800	650
Rest of world banks	480	480
Difference	320	180
Of which:		
Property rights protection	130	40
Bank size	70	50
Other bank characteristics	−40	70
Inflation	100	30
Africa residual	60	−10

Source: Authors' calculations using data from BankScope.

FIGURE 2.11
Governance across Countries

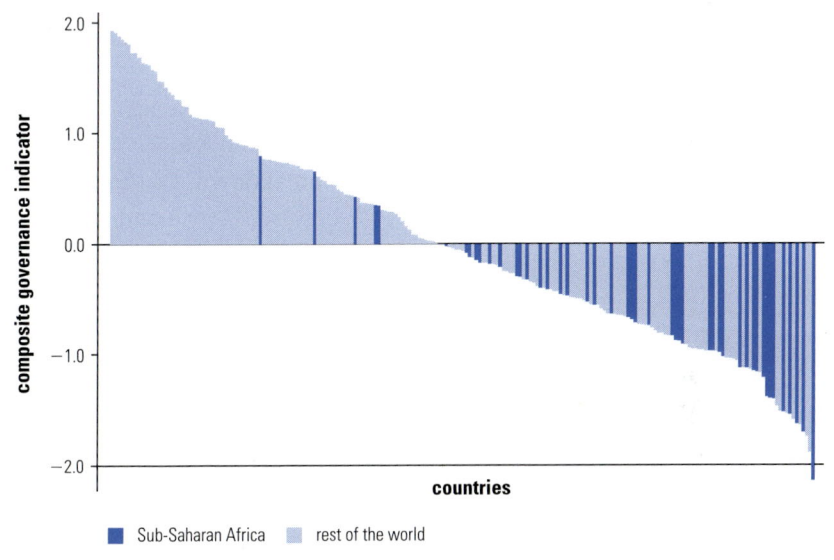

Sources: Kaufmann, Kraay, and Mastruzzi 2004; World Bank's Governance Matters IV database.

Note: The figure shows the composite governance indicator for 209 countries. African countries are shown in color. All data are for 2004.

ference of 130 basis points in the net interest margin differential and 40 basis points in the higher overhead costs. Although this indicator of governance is a very general one, the low score for Africa captures many aspects of an unsatisfactory contractual framework: weak creditor rights, seldom enforced by compromised courts; a deficient and rarely applied insolvency framework; and a general disrespect for contracts.

The small size of banks and financial systems in Africa can explain a large part of the large margins and overhead costs. The average African bank in our sample has total assets of US$81 million, compared with US$334 million for the average bank outside Africa. This difference can explain 70 basis points of the higher net interest margins and 50 basis points of the higher overhead costs in African banks, or about a quarter of the difference from the worldwide average. Small size is also reflected in the data on aggregate banking system size: African banking systems are among the smallest in the world (figure 2.12).

A number of bank-level characteristics are also important. Banks with higher fee income (as opposed to interest income) earn lower interest mar-

FIGURE 2.12
Size of Banking Systems across Countries

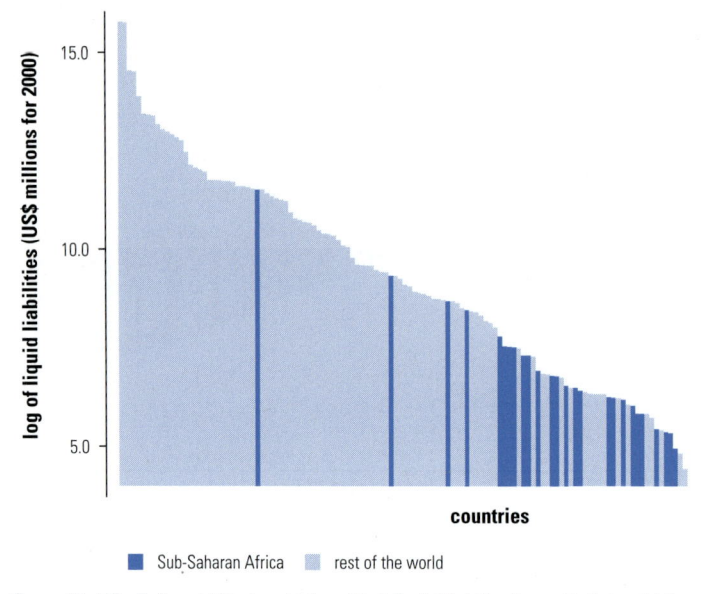

Sources: World Bank's Financial Structure database; World Bank's World Development Indicators database.

Note: The figure plots the overall size of the monetary system in 121 countries, as measured by liquid liabilities (M3) in U.S. dollars for all available countries, on a logarithmic scale. African countries are shown in color. The African country with the largest banking system is South Africa with US$98 billion, followed by Nigeria with US$11 billion, Mauritius with US$6 billion, and Ethiopia with US$5 billion. All data are for the latest available year, 2004–05.

gins but incur higher costs. Less liquid, better capitalized banks with more volatile earnings earn higher margins and incur high costs. On average, African banks' individual characteristics, other than size, tend to reduce interest margins but increase administrative costs.

Finally, monetary instability can explain a sizable part of the higher average net interest margins and overhead costs in Africa. Here differences between countries are especially substantial. Only 16 African countries have had annual average inflation in the double digits over the past decade, but the outliers—Angola and the Democratic Republic of Congo—have seen annual inflation running into the hundreds of percent, with Zimbabwe soaring above 1,000 percent per annum in 2005–06.[10] As a result, cumulative inflation over the five years from 2000 to 2004 averaged 36 percent for African countries and 20 percent for the rest of the world. The high inflation boosted interest margins in the affected countries, explaining almost 100 of the 320 basis point average difference in net interest margins and about 30 basis points of the administrative cost differences.

Some of the causal factors included in the regression estimates may have contributed to a lack of competition in African banking. Furthermore, the 60 basis points (on average) that remain unexplained may also be attributable in part to lack of competition. The same contractual and informational deficiencies that explain high overhead costs and high risk premiums in lending also reduce competitiveness by binding borrowers to specific lenders and by deterring new entrants.[11] These deficiencies also reduce the contestability of African banking by increasing entry costs for new institutions.

Most of Africa's banking systems are highly concentrated. This is not surprising, given the small size of the national markets. The market share of the top three banks (concentration ratio) in each country averages 73 percent across 22 African countries, based on total assets in the latest year for which data are available; for the median country, the figure is 74 percent. This figure compares with 60 percent for the world as a whole. No other region has a mean higher than 66 percent. The lowest ratios in Africa are for the largest economies—South Africa (41 percent) and Nigeria (48 percent).[12] All other African countries have ratios of at least 59 percent. The general picture is one of market dominance by a small number of banks. In Mozambique, the largest bank (a foreign-owned one) holds a 48 percent share in the lending market. In Mauritius, the largest two banks account for 77 percent of the lending market.

Concentrated banking systems are not necessarily uncompetitive—for example, in open systems, the threat of entry can restrain incumbents from overcharging (Claessens and Laeven 2004; Demirgüç-Kunt, Laeven, and Levine 2004). But concentration does often go hand in hand with market power, especially when contestability is weak.

This attempt at quantification of the obstacles to banking efficiency thus points to at least three major background dimensions: the contractual and informational environment, the broader issues of systemic risk, and the lack of scale. Together these dimensions can explain the high risk premiums demanded by bankers, the high profitability, and the lack of competition. The specific indicators used in the regression analysis only scratch the surface of these issues.

As can be seen in figure 2.9, the median quoted intermediation spreads (the gap between representative lending and deposit rates reported in the

International Monetary Fund [IMF] International Financial Statistics database) widened in the early 1990s—a trend that is likely attributable in part to liberalization. Since the late 1990s, the upward trend has been stabilized and even reversed, with the median for 2005 at about 1,000 basis points—compared with more than 1,500 basis points in 2001. The data are too noisy to point unambiguously to the explanation for this improvement, but one plausible explanation is that, as in other parts of the world, postliberalization competitive pressures have begun to kick in. Improvements in the underlying environmental factors discussed above will also have played their part, in countries such as Nigeria and Tanzania, for example.

Ownership issues

Following a wave of privatization and restructuring of banks—including state-owned ones—in numerous African countries, the balance of ownership has shifted dramatically in recent years. Now the foreign banks are back in force. Although somewhat similar trends have occurred in other parts of the world, the process has gone further in Africa than in other regions. Table 2.3 classifies countries according to whether their banking systems are mainly foreign owned (more than 60 percent of banking assets in foreign-controlled banks), mainly government owned (or owned by government agencies), mainly owned by the local private sector (with the same 60 percent dividing line), or foreign plus government owned (the two types accounting for at least 70 percent) or whether they fall in a residual category called "equally shared." Two of every five African banking systems are mainly foreign owned, and only three countries (7 percent) are still dominated by state-owned banks. Map 2.2 shows the variation in ownership structure across African countries.

Interestingly, although a worldwide sample of banks shows no significant difference in profitability across banks with different ownership structures, foreign-owned banks in Africa are more profitable than foreign-owned banks elsewhere (even controlling for the higher profitability of banking in Africa). They are also more profitable than locally owned banks (see table 2.1). Table 2.1 also shows data for a subsample of banks with operations both in Africa and elsewhere. For this subsample, the difference between profit performance in Africa and elsewhere is even more pronounced: a mean of 9.6 percent in Africa as against 6.2 percent elsewhere.

TABLE 2.3
Distribution of African Countries by Predominant Form of Bank Ownership

Mainly government	Mainly foreign	Mainly local private sector	Foreign plus government	Equally shared
Eritrea	Botswana	Benin	Burkina Faso	Angola
Ethiopia	Cape Verde	Mali	Congo, Dem. Rep. of	Burundi
Togo	Central African Republic	Mauritania	Sierra Leone	Cameroon
	Chad	Mauritius		Congo, Rep. of
	Côte d'Ivoire	Nigeria		Gabon
	Equatorial Guinea	Rwanda		Ghana
	Gambia	Somalia		Kenya
	Guinea-Bissau	South Africa		Rwanda
	Guinea	Sudan		Senegal
	Lesotho	Zimbabwe		
	Liberia			
	Madagascar			
	Malawi			
	Mozambique			
	Namibia			
	Niger			
	Seychelles			
	Swaziland			
	Tanzania			
	Uganda			
	Zambia			

Source: World Bank staff estimates.

Note: Mainly government, mainly foreign, and *mainly local private sector* mean more than 60 percent of total assets are held by banks majority owned by government, majority owned by foreign shareholders, or majority owned by the local private sector, respectively; *foreign plus government* means these two categories together hold more than 70 percent. *Equally shared* is a residual category. (In Senegal foreign plus private local adds to more than 70 percent.)

Volatility

Monetary volatility is only one dimension of a generally volatile political and economic environment that has hampered monetary deepening and efficiency improvements. Africa is a continent of civil strife and political violence; only nine countries have suffered no internal or external conflict during the past 50 years (Strand and others 2004). On average, an African country survives little more than a decade without a major economic, social, or political disturbance (Arnold 2005; Meredith 2005). This duration is similar to 19th-century business cycles in what are now advanced economies—though the African crises tend to be deeper and more protracted and extend to all parts of the economy and society. Such volatility does not affect only financial depth and interest rate spreads. Just as the

MAP 2.2
Predominant Form of Bank Ownership

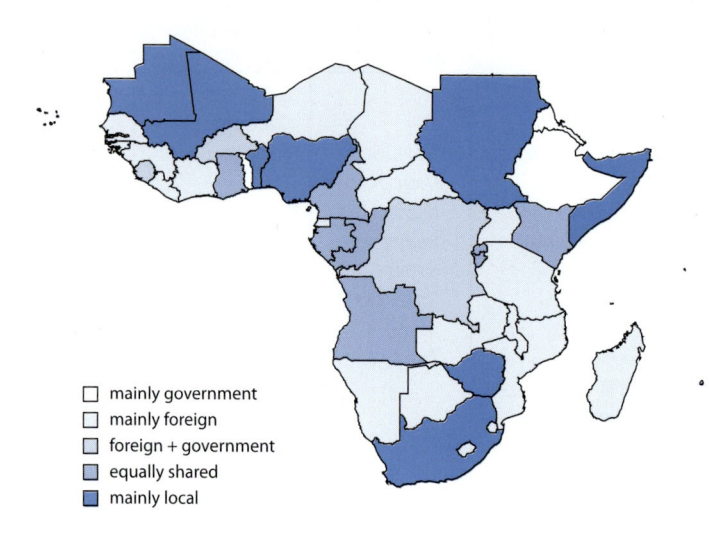

- ☐ mainly government
- ☐ mainly foreign
- ☐ foreign + government
- ☐ equally shared
- ■ mainly local

Source: World Bank Staff estimates.

business cycle impeded investment and growth in economies in the 19th century, so the likelihood that an investment in recent decades would be destroyed or made valueless by a major downturn must have impeded investment in Africa—chaining African business leaders to a short-term perspective.

The causes of these recurrent crises have been many. Part of the problem has been Africa's economic dependence on exports of primary products. The high share of natural resources and agricultural commodities in Africa's exports, combined with the high price volatility for these commodities, exposes African economies to high terms-of-trade volatility. Drought, floods, and other supply shocks add to the problems: natural disasters causing death occur frequently in Africa, as they do in much of mainland Asia. HIV/AIDS has often been mentioned as a cause in recent years. But it is the relatively high frequency of political disruption and civil strife that has most marked Africa for a seemingly endemic pattern of systemic economic instability.

Market perceptions of instability dampen financial sector development. Lack of financial development could also be contributing to the sources of instability in a variety of ways. For example, African countries lack diversified financial instruments that could broaden claims on the prosperity that could be generated by a growing and profitable business sector. This in turn represents a missed opportunity to give a wider group of influential Africans a stake in sustained economic growth. Such participation in sustained economic growth, in turn, would help shift the focus of the elites' personal and political activities away from short-term thinking.

BOX 2.1

Historic Explanations of Cross-Country Variation in Financial Development

Although current policy and institutional conditions explain much cross-country variation in financial development and efficiency, scholars have sought to uncover past causal factors, notably in terms of the origins of legal structures, of geographic endowments, and of ethnic mix. Variations across African countries provide much of the evidence and, as such, are at the center of the debates on the relative importance of each factor.

The law and finance literature points to legal tradition as a decisive factor forming contractual frameworks, which are fundamental to financial sector development. The main divide is between the English Common Law and the French Civil Code traditions, and in particular the degree of protection each provides to private property rights and their adaptability to change. At the risk of caricature, it may be said that the evolution of Common Law was strongly influenced by the attempt to protect private property rights against the state, which facilitated the ability of private parties to transact confidently with each other and the state. The Civil Code tradition reflected the reaction to a corrupt and secretive prerevolutionary judiciary that had sided with rich property holders against reformist politicians; it thus has its origin in the state's attempt to solidify state power over private citizens. Where the Civil Code tradition distrusts judges and jurisprudence and thus relies on rigid bright-line rules, the Common Law tradition allows more dynamism as judges react to changing circumstances on a case-by-case basis, enabling the law to adapt quickly to the needs of the economy and especially

(Box continues on the following page.)

BOX 2.1 (*continued*)

the financial system. The Common Law tradition spread throughout the world with British colonizers; the Napoleonic Code influenced subsequent codifications in other colonizing nations, such as Belgium, Portugal, and Spain.

Map 2.3 shows the variation in legal origin across Africa. Consistent with the stronger protection of property rights and the prediction of dynamism, Common Law countries have higher levels of financial development than do Civil Code countries. This holds true not only for a broad sample of former colonies, but also within Africa—though here the difference is less pronounced and the variation across countries much larger within legal families (figure 2.13).

The law and finance view focuses on the identity of the colonizer. The endowment view has focused on the conditions that colonizers found when they arrived and the influence those conditions had on the behavior of the colonial powers (Acemoglu, Johnson, and Robinson 2001). Specifically, European settlers adopted different colonization strategies depending on whether the disease conditions were friendly to European settlement. Where conditions were conducive to settlement, settlers chose to re-create governance structures to support their private property rights and local market exchange. Where conditions were less friendly for settlement, the European colonizers created "extractive colonies," establishing institutions that empowered colonizers to extract natural resources without protecting local business interests (Austen 1987). Congo, which was—in effect—the personal property of King Leopold I of the Belgians for a quarter-century, is often quoted as prime example of such an approach. Critically, these contrasting institutional structures survived the move to independence (Arnold 2005; Meredith 2005).

Nonbank Finance

The remainder of the formal financial system controls far smaller resources. This characteristic again is typical of low-income countries in general and not specific to Africa. But there is quite a lot of variation among African countries, revealing the potential for improvement in those that lag.

> To capture a quantitative indication of the initial colonial conditions, scholars have used historical records on the death rates of early colonial settlers. Interestingly, as shown in figure 2.14, financial depth today is negatively associated with those early death rates. Within Africa, there is considerable variation in the early mortality rates: western African countries such as Ghana and Congo had very high mortality rates, whereas Kenya and Zimbabwe, for example, had low mortality rates—which were conducive to European settlement. This variation is also reflected in the levels of financial development. The choice of institutional structure is not solely caused by climatic conditions, though: Nunn (2005) notes that the incidence of slavery is also highly correlated with subsequent institutional development.
>
> Under some conditions, ethnic diversity may produce a governing ethnic group that uses the state's powers to strengthen its dominance by restricting the rights of other groups and expropriating their resources, as well as impeding the growth of industries and sectors that will threaten the governing ethnic group. Such behavior could lead to rent seeking, inefficient and reduced allocation of public goods and services, and growth-reducing policies such as financial repression. In studies of this conjecture, diversity is measured by the so-called ethnic fractionalization index, which is the probability that two randomly selected people will not be members of the same ethnic group. African countries tend to have the highest scores on this index. However, though there is some econometric evidence that ethnic diversity could contribute to low growth in Africa (Easterly and Levine 1997), there is little evidence that it affects financial development in particular. The same is true of an alternative indicator of precolonial conditions, namely political centralization, which has been shown to be positively correlated with the provision of public goods in Africa (Gennaioli and Rainer 2005). For more detail and references to the literature, see also Beck and Levine (2005) and Levine (2005).

Nonbank financing can offer a range and variety of services that are not part of the standard product range of banks. Furthermore, a strong nonbank sector can also provide competition for banks. Financial systems in the advanced market economies are characterized by a very diverse array of institutions and markets offering a variety of products. Apart from banks, this array includes capital markets, with both equity and debt securities and contractual savings institutions, such as insurance companies,

MAP 2.3
Common Law and Civil Code Countries

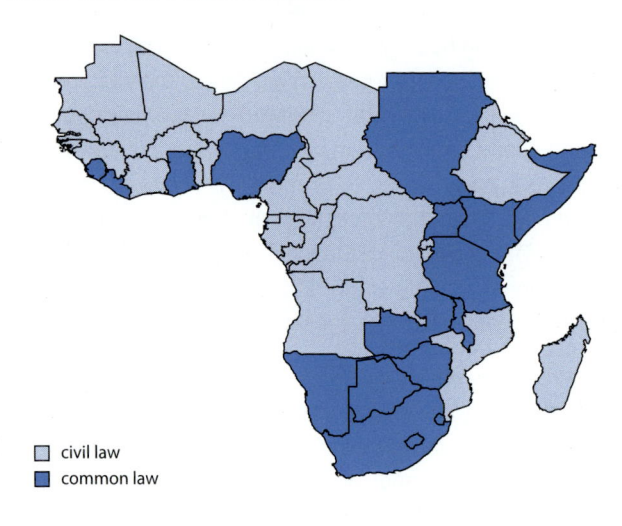

☐ civil law
■ common law

Source: World Bank staff judgment.

pension funds, and mutual funds. This wider range of institutional specializations has the potential to offer a wider range of financial services and better risk pooling, at better prices, in a more competitive environment than is characteristic of the bank-dominated systems observed in most of Africa and in most low- and lower-middle-income countries around the globe. In particular, contractual savings institutions can be major forces in providing patient capital, in equity or loans, for long-term projects. Organized securities markets help to improve the transparency of funding arrangements by determining the market-clearing price of equities, as well as market-clearing interest rates for bonds. Equity markets are particularly valuable for providing financing to risky ventures, about which there may be wide differences of opinion: banks are often reluctant to finance such ventures because the downside risk is insufficiently compensated by the contractual interest rate; well-resourced investors can build a portfolio of equity claims on such ventures for which the securities market will provide an exit mechanism, in due course, for those that are successful.

Securities Markets

With a market capitalization of US$600 billion, the South African (Johannesburg) market is the fourth-largest emerging market in the world (after

FIGURE 2.13
Private Credit: French and English Legal Origin

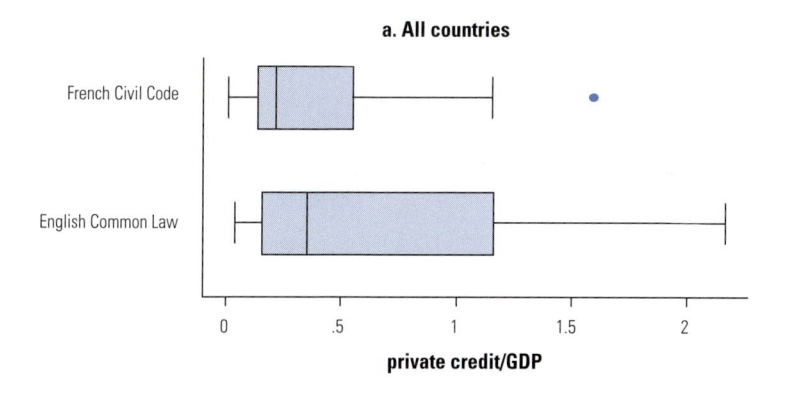

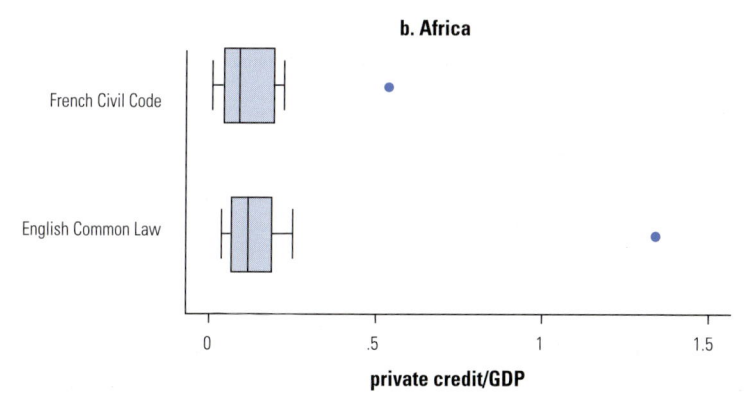

a. All countries

b. Africa

Source: World Bank's Financial Structure database.

Note: The figure shows the minimum, maximum, and median of the ratio of private credit to GDP for 84 countries of the world (panel a) and for 26 countries in Africa (panel b). The shaded boxes show the interquartile range. All data are for 2005.

those in the Republic of Korea, the Russian Federation, and India and before those in Brazil, China, and Hong Kong, China). Yet even Johannesburg is not a big enough market to retain the primary listings of several of South Africa's largest companies. Twenty-one companies listed in Johannesburg have their primary listings elsewhere—including the mining conglomerate Anglo American, the banking group Investec, the brewing company SAB-Miller, the insurance giant Old Mutual, and the technology company Dimension Data, all of which have their primary listings in London. This list shows that the context in which African securities markets operate is one in which the larger companies look abroad as well as to the home market.[13]

FIGURE 2.14
Financial Development and Initial Colonial Conditions

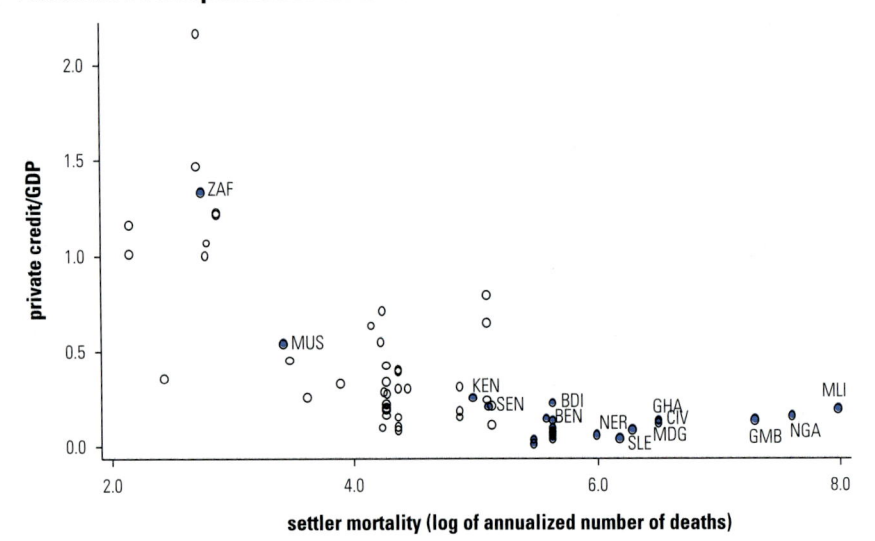

[Scatter plot: x-axis "settler mortality (log of annualized number of deaths)" from 2.0 to 8.0; y-axis "private credit/GDP" from 0.0 to 2.0. Labeled points include ZAF, MUS, KEN, SEN, BDI, BEN, NER, GHA, CIV, SLE, MDG, GMB, NGA, MLI. Legend: ● Sub-Saharan Africa ○ all other countries]

Sources: Acemoglu, Johnson, and Robinson 2001.

Note: Country abbreviations are included in the abbreviations list at the front of the book. The figure plots financial depth in 63 countries, as measured by the ratio of private credit to GDP against an index of colonial settler mortality (log of the annualized number of deaths per thousand). African countries are shown in darker color. All data are for 2004.

Africa has 15 organized securities markets. Several other projects are under discussion or partly implemented, but not yet active. (This number does not include Cameroon and Gabon, both of which recently established stock exchanges but have not yet attracted any listings.) One exchange, the Bourse Régionale des Valeurs Mobilières (BRVM) headquartered in Abidjan, caters to the eight-country Union Economique et Monétaire Ouest Africaine (UEMOA). The BRVM was expanded from the Abidjan stock exchange created in 1976. Four other exchanges started operations in the days of the British Empire: those with headquarters at Nairobi, Lagos, Harare, and Johannesburg, the last two having histories going back into the 19th century. The older exchanges also have the largest number of equities listed. These five, along with those established in 1988 and 1989 in Botswana, Ghana, and Mauritius, were the only exchanges with market capitalization at the end of 2004 in excess of 10 percent of GDP, even though market capitalization has been increasing in recent years (figure 2.15).

FIGURE 2.15
African Stock Exchanges: Capitalization and Value Traded as a Percentage of GDP

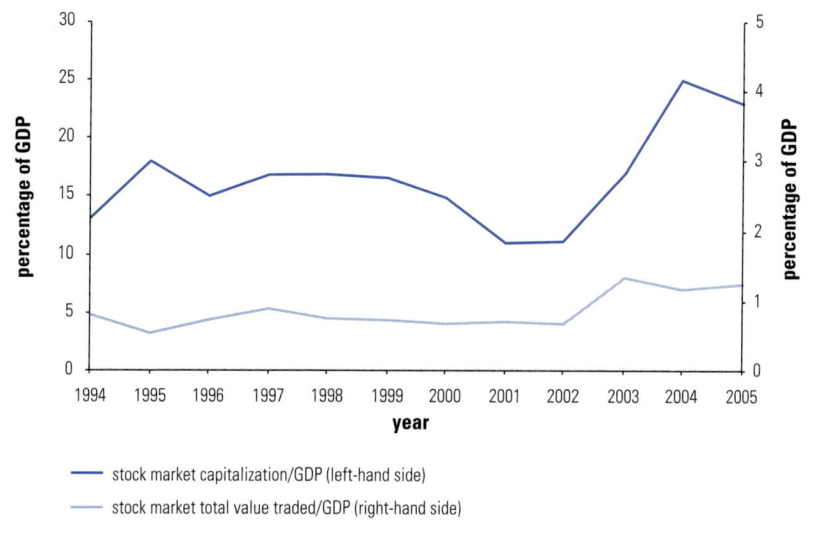

[Line chart showing stock market capitalization/GDP (left-hand side, ranging roughly 11–25%) and stock market total value traded/GDP (right-hand side, ranging roughly 0.5–1.5%) from 1994 to 2005]

— stock market capitalization/GDP (left-hand side)
— stock market total value traded/GDP (right-hand side)

Source: Compiled from published stock exchange reports.

Note: The figure shows the medians of the eight most active exchanges by value traded other than Johannesburg (that is, for Botswana, Côte d'Ivoire, Ghana, Mauritius, Mozambique, Namibia, Nigeria, and Zimbabwe).

Trading data show a different aspect of the contribution of stock exchanges in developing countries. That contribution is influenced by secondary market liquidity and also by the degree to which a large fraction of the shares in developing markets is effectively locked up in the strategic stakes of controlling shareholders and not normally available for trading. It should be noted in this context that funds actually raised on these markets—as on most capital markets14—are but a tiny fraction of market capitalization. The eight oldest exchanges also have the most active trading, with the value traded fluctuating around 2 percent of GDP for the past several years (table 2.4; see also figure 2.15). Yet even these more active African exchanges (Johannesburg aside) cannot be considered to have much trading. Except for Johannesburg, turnover on all markets is less than 15 percent of market capitalization. There was no trading on the Maputo exchange in 2004.

Low turnover is reflected in and feeds back onto a lack of liquidity, as illustrated by large gaps between buy and sell orders and high price volatil-

TABLE 2.4
Stock Exchanges in Africa

Country	Number of listed firms	Market cap (% of GDP)	Value traded (% of GDP)	Turnover (%)	Zero-return weeks (% of total)	Concentration of firms	Number of listed corporate bonds	Year established
Botswana	25	27.2	0.6	2.1	—	0.21	17	1989
Côte d'Ivoire (BRVM)	39	12.3	0.3	2.5	—	0.21	—	1976
Ghana	30	23.7	0.8	3.2	70	0.12	3	1989
Kenya	47	26.1	2.1	7.9	41	0.20	—	1954
Malawi	8	9.2	1.3	14.1	—	—	0	1996
Mauritius	41	36.0	1.6	4.4	48	0.12	1	1988
Mozambique	1	3.0	0.0	0.0	—	—	—	1999
Namibia	13	6.9	0.3	4.7	57	0.39	4	1992
Nigeria	207	16.7	2.3	13.9	67	0.08		1960
South Africa	403	170.5	76.5	44.9	13	0.06		1887
Swaziland	6	8.3	0.0	0.0	—	—	2	1990
Tanzania	6	6.2	0.2	2.5	—	—	6	1998
Uganda	5	1.4	0.0	0.2	—	—	—	1998
Zambia	13	8.0	0.1	1.5	—	—	0	1994
Zimbabwe	79	41.3	2.9	7.0	37	0.08	—	1896

Sources: World Bank's Financial Structure database; World Bank's Financial Sector Development Indicators database.

Note: — = not available. All data are for 2005, except for Malawi, for which data are from 2002, and zero-return weeks, for which data are for 2000–04. Zero-return weeks measure the average over all companies of the percentage of weeks for which there was no price change; this measure indicates illiquidity. Concentration of firms is measured using the Herfindahl index of the market capitalization of listed firms. Secondary listings are not included; for example, data for Malawi exclude the Old Mutual cross-listing.

ity. This lack of transactions is also somewhat self-reinforcing, as the transaction volume does not justify investment in technology either by the exchange itself or by member brokers. Limited trading discourages listing and raising money on the exchanges. Even linking different centers electronically (as in the BRVM or in Namibia, whose exchange is now electronically linked to the Johannesburg exchange) cannot guarantee much more trading and liquidity.

In international comparisons of composite indicators of equity market development (data are available typically only for seven or eight of the African exchanges), it appears that the main African exchanges fall behind the average in developing countries, mainly in regard to efficiency, as distinct from size, stability, and access of issuers (figure 2.16).[15] The other seven markets, all established since 1989, are small by all measures. The smaller African countries tend to have neither organized exchanges nor any prospect of one.

FIGURE 2.16
International Comparison of Stock Exchange Development: Main African Exchanges Relative to Other Developing Countries

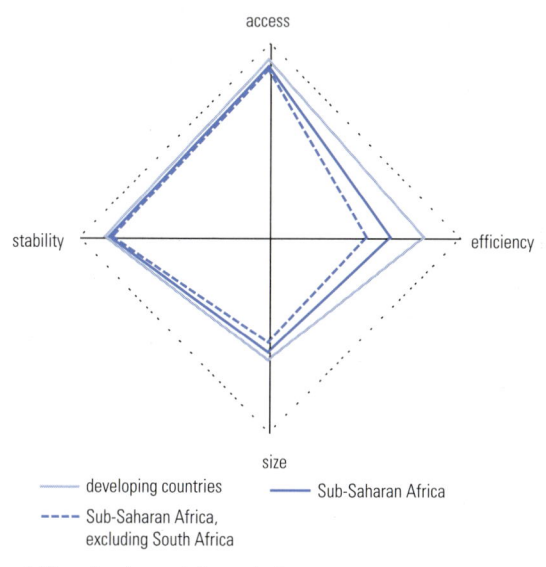

Source: World Bank's Financial Sector Development Indicators database.

Note: The figure shows the mean performance of different groups of exchanges relative to exchanges in high-income countries. Developing countries as a whole have much smaller exchanges than do high-income countries, but it is mainly in their efficiency that African exchanges fall short of the performance of other developing market exchanges. The composite indicators are defined in World Bank (2006).

The small size and illiquidity of Africa's stock exchanges partly reflect low levels of economic activity, which make it hard to reach a minimum efficient size or critical mass, and partly reflect the state of company accounts and their reliability. Several of the exchanges established in the late 1980s and 1990s were set up mainly to facilitate privatization, in the hope of attracting inward investment with the modernization and technology transfer that such investment could convey (Moss 2003). For example, the stock exchange in Maputo was established in the process of privatizing Mozambique's national brewery, which is still the only listed company and which must bear the operating costs of the stock exchange. To the extent that the establishment of stock exchanges was driven by outside influences—rather than emerging from a realistic need felt in the market, whether by investors or by issuers—it is perhaps unsurprising that many have so far struggled to reach an effective scale and activity level.

Pricing on all the markets appears to build in a sizable risk premium, to judge, for example, from the low price-earnings ratios that have been prevalent (Moss 2003; Senbet and Otchere 2006). The widespread limitations on foreign holdings of listed shares, although diminishing in recent years, have also contributed to low prices.[16] High risk perceptions affect all countries, even those with stable macroeconomic environments; indeed, most countries lack sovereign credit ratings. The perceived risk is reflected also in the very small amount of funds raised through new issues, including initial public offerings (IPOs) and other public sales of equities.[17]

Nevertheless, issuing activity has picked up. Ghana had five new equity issues in 2004, accounting for US$60 million. The Kenya Electricity Generating Company (KenGen) IPO of 2006—the country's first in five years—attracted strong demand and enormous public interest, raising more than US$100 million.[18] In Nigeria, the equivalent of almost US$3 billion in new capital was raised on the exchange in 2003 to 2005 in connection with the new capital requirements for banks.

Scale issues in equities have been mirrored in the bond market; only a limited number of private bonds have been listed, and there is little secondary market trading. In Tanzania capitalization of corporate bonds amounts to T Sh 89 billion (about US$90 million); compare that with equity market capitalization of T Sh 2.3 trillion. Ghana has three corporate bonds, but 30 listed companies. The bond market capitalization of the BRVM is relatively higher—about one-fifth of equity market capitalization. Most of the larger issues are governmental or from government-owned enterprises, and trading is very light.

African governments[19] have relied more on foreign debt than on domestic debt, though about half have issued significant domestic debt instruments (not all of them traded on an organized market), eight with domestic debt-to-GDP ratios in excess of 20 percent. Banks tend to be the biggest holders, with about two-thirds of the stock outside the central bank. With an estimated 87 percent of the debt having initial maturities of 12 months or less, there is little secondary trading (Christensen 2004). Longer-term issues have only recently appeared (or reappeared) on some of the exchanges. The 7- and 10-year issues of the regional development banks Banque Ouest Africaine de Développement (BOAD) and East African Development Bank (EADB) are noteworthy, together with a handful of government and corporate bonds. The absence of such issues in most currencies means a lack of good reference rates for long-term finance (Irving 2005).

Insurance, Pension, and Collective Savings Institutions

Insurance penetration is low across Africa with the notable exception of a few countries in southern Africa, presumably reflecting the persistence in that subregion of factors that account for the traditional success of this subsector in the United Kingdom in colonial times (that is, factors that are partly tax driven). Most countries have insurance penetration ratios (premium volume relative to GDP) of less than 1 percent. Low income explains much of the low insurance penetration, with monetary instability and weak contractual frameworks also contributing. In most countries, insurance is characterized by many small and weak institutions and inadequate supervision.

Some countries have introduced a funded national social security system and funded pensions for public servants; where these funds exist, they are in an accumulation phase. Although actuarial valuations of several of these schemes raise questions about their long-run sustainability in the absence of a change in parameters, for the medium term they will be increasingly important suppliers of investable funds. To date, however, most insurance companies and pension funds have invested mainly in real estate, government securities, and bank deposits and comparatively little in equities and corporate bonds (table 2.5).

TABLE 2.5
Portfolio Composition of Selected Life Insurance and Pension Funds

Country	Fund	Cash, deposits, and so forth (%)	Government paper (%)	Equities (%)	Real estate (%)	Other (%)	Date
Ghana	Social Security and National Insurance Trust	8.0	7.2	19.4	35.0	30.4	1999
Ghana	Insurance	21.0	14.2	5.0	14.8	45.0	1999
Kenya	Insurance	8.2	30.5	7.0	29.0	25.3	2001
Kenya	National Social Security Fund	7.3	2.0	10.9	68.8	11.0	2002
Nigeria	Life insurance	12.2	3.9	31.3	11.1	41.5	1999
Senegal	Life insurance	30.9	12.7	25.0	8.5	22.9	1999
Senegal	IPRES (public pension fund)	81.8	8.6	9.6	0.0	0.0	2000
Tanzania	National Social Security Fund	26.0	25.0	6.0	24.0	19.0	2002
Tanzania	Parastatal Pension Fund	34.0	7.0	7.0	37.0	15.0	2002
Uganda	National Social Security Fund	41.9	11.3	8.2	34.8	3.8	2000

Source: World Bank files. Data are for different years over the period 1999 to 2003.

Term Finance

Another striking characteristic of financial systems in Africa is the concentration on short-term claims across all financial institutions and financial markets. This characteristic is exemplified by the dominance of short-term rather than long-term government paper. Christensen (2004) found that the average maturity of government paper in 15 African countries was just 231 days. Four of those countries had average maturities of less than four months, compared with five and one-half years for developed countries. This lack of long-term government financing can be explained by reluctance on both sides of trading. Undoubtedly, given the systemic volatility already discussed, providers of funds are more comfortable with an arrangement in which they can decide whether to renew short-term advances on the basis of evolving conditions. Even if borrowers could secure long-term funding, it would be at unfavorable terms. This concentration on the short-term end is matched in private sector lending and on the deposit side. In Mozambique, only 35 percent of the local-currency loan portfolio and 28 percent of the foreign-currency loan portfolio have an original maturity of more than one year. In Uganda, 35 percent of the loan volume has an original maturity of more than one year, which is concentrated in 12 percent of all loans and mostly financed through donor lines of credit. A similar picture can be observed on the deposit side. In Uganda, only 0.4 percent of time deposits have an original maturity of more than a year.

Limited evidence from users, however, does not paint as bleak a picture. Firm-level surveys suggest that firms' bank loans have the same, if not longer, terms as bank loans in other regions. The average firm in the median African economy reports bank loans with maturities of 45 months, compared with 36 months in South Asia, 40 months in Latin America, and 52 months in high-income countries.

Illustrative of the limited availability of term finance is the lack of housing finance in most African economies. Although the stock of housing finance in Namibia and South Africa comes to 18 to 20 percent of GDP, the figures for other countries for which data are available are no more than 2 percent (Mali, Rwanda, Senegal) or even 1 percent (Ghana, Tanzania, and Uganda).[20] This figure is not only small in relation to GDP but also as a percentage of total private credit. In addition to the general confidence factors that have worked against the growth of term finance, many specific factors impede expansion of mortgage credit, including lack of effective title and collateral registration systems. Attempts by many African governments to address the dearth of housing finance over the years with government-owned housing finance intermediaries resulted in skewed allocations of subsidies to a small number of well-connected borrowers. As with other state-owned development finance institutions (DFIs), many of these institutions eventually became insolvent and had to be bailed out—as in Côte d'Ivoire, Niger, Rwanda, Tanzania, and elsewhere.

Inclusive Household Finance

The financial service needs of lower-income households in Africa—which have long been excluded from the formal financial system—have begun to receive more attention from governments, NGOs, and even banks. The accelerating expansion of formal and semiformal microfinance and the political changes in South Africa have been major factors in this change.

Although the closure of some state-owned banks with broad outreach may have reduced households' financial access in some countries, microfinance has grown. Taking account also of the continued effectiveness of some post offices as suppliers of banking services and piecing together available information make it possible to generate rough estimates of the percentage of the adult population with a bank or banklike account. In the median African country, the figure is less than 20 percent. This percentage is lower than in other regions, but the gap is, perhaps, smaller for this dimension than for other aspects of finance (figures 2.17 and 2.18).[21] To a significant extent, the low access percentages reflect general economic conditions (per capita income can explain a high fraction of the variation in access across countries).However, African access figures remain about 2 percentage points lower on average, a figure that is not statistically significant.

Mapping the estimated access percentages shows how widely access varies (map 2.4). In addition to relatively high percentages in Botswana, Mauritius, and South Africa, the estimated access percentages are relatively high in Angola, Benin, Gabon, and Niger, as well as in Zimbabwe. Several of the largest financial intermediaries in terms of numbers of clients are post office savings banks (even allowing for the fact that some accounts may be dormant). Although not all have been continuously effective over their lengthy histories, there have been successful turnarounds, and they remain very important in the market for small deposits and payments services.

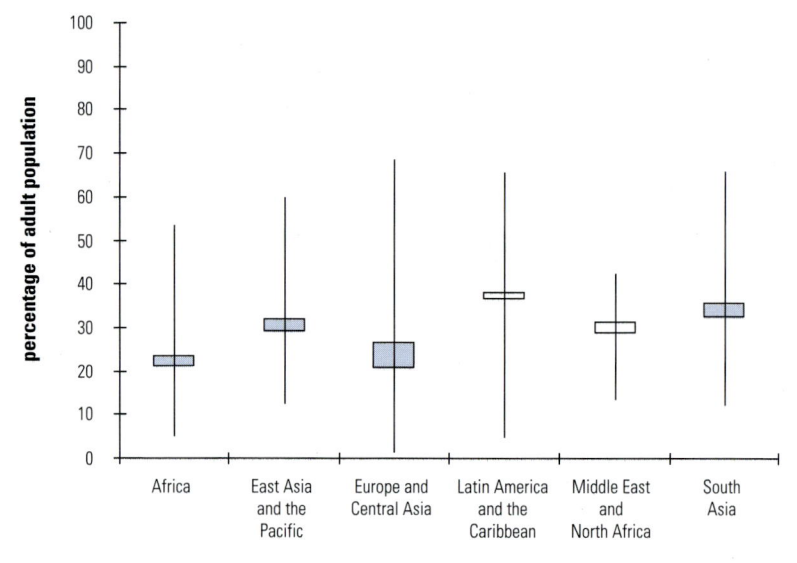

FIGURE 2.17
Access to Finance, Regional Extremes, Medians, and Means

Source: Honohan 2006.

Note: The figure shows the percentage of the adult population with access to an account. It shows mean, median, maximum and minimum values for countries in each region. The median is higher than the mean in Latin America and the Caribbean and in the Middle East and North Africa; the mean is higher than the median elsewhere.

It is worth stressing that these estimates do not purport to include traditional informal finance. In addition, of course, most Africans—perhaps as many as 80 percent—are involved in informal finance groups. Important though these informal financial services are, they are not the focus of this book. A more in-depth picture of household financial access can be obtained by survey methods, and a new wave of surveys focusing on finance is under way. So far, these kinds of data are available for only a handful of African countries, all south of the Limpopo River.

Numerous factors contribute to low access percentages. The low population densities and communications and transportation deficiencies that characterize most, although not all, African economies likely increase the cost of market exchange between different agents in the economy, as people, goods, and services must travel longer distances. Further, most Sub-Saharan African countries have lower branch and ATM penetration, both demographically and geographically, than developing countries in other regions. In addition, the difficulties of establishing and maintaining com-

FIGURE 2.18
Access to Finance across Countries

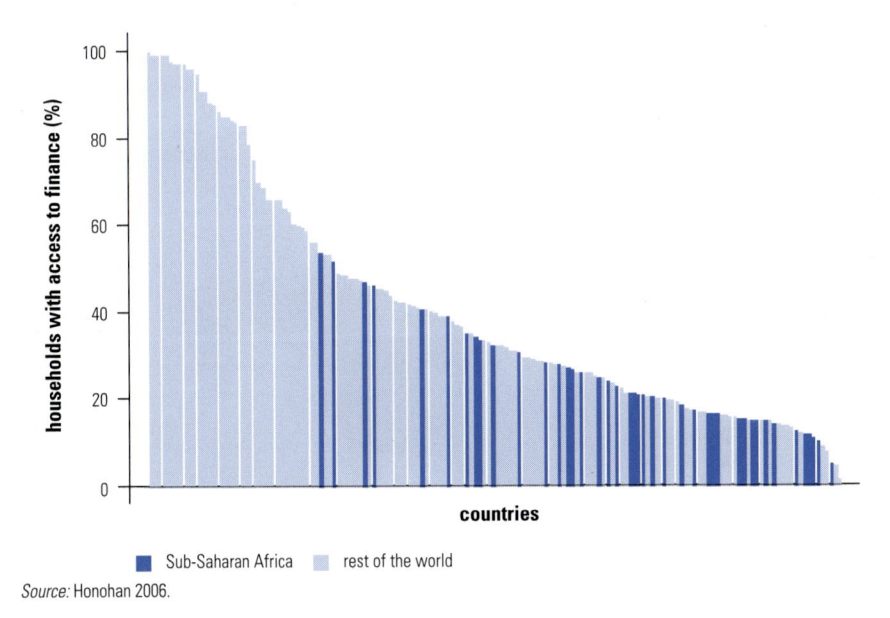

Source: Honohan 2006.

Note: The figure shows the estimated percentage of households in 158 countries with access to formal financial services. African countries are shown in color.

munication and transportation networks exacerbate the negative effect of scarcely populated economies by further increasing the cost of market exchange. Africa has the lowest road density in the world, with the notable exception of South Asia (which, in contrast, has a much higher population density). Recent technological advances and innovations, such as mobile branches or mobile banking (by mobile phones[22]) have helped reduce this barrier, as we discuss in more detail in chapter 4.

Affordability is another important barrier. Low levels of income and the lack of steady income flows make large parts of the population "unbankable" in the eyes of traditional financial service providers such as banks. Seen from the demand side, high minimum balances and monthly fees can prevent large parts of the population from accessing formal financial services.[23] In Ethiopia, Sierra Leone, and Uganda, a sum equivalent to more than 50 percent of per capita GDP is needed to open a checking account. In Malawi, Sierra Leone, Uganda, and Zimbabwe, annual fees associated with a checking account amount to more than 20 percent of per capita GDP.[24]

MAP 2.4
Access to Finance by Households

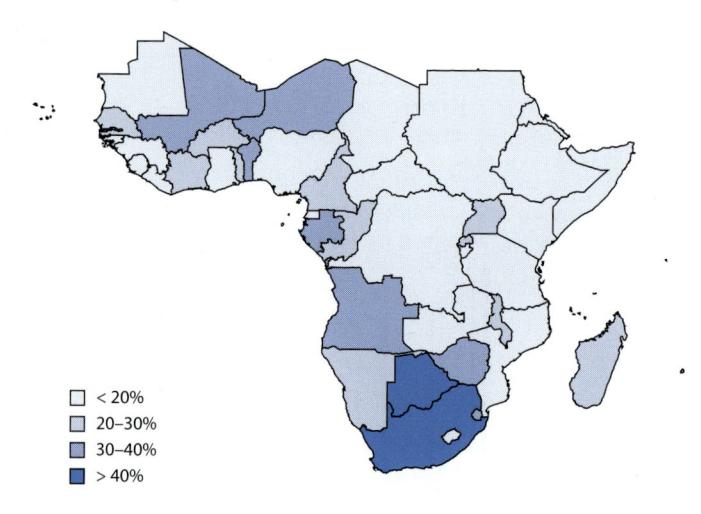

- < 20%
- 20–30%
- 30–40%
- > 40%

Sources: Honohan 2006, with additional data obtained for Guinea Bissau from Banque Centrale des Etats de l'Afrique de l'Ouest and World Bank staff estimates for Chad, Equatorial Guinea, and Somalia.

Compare this system with many developing and advanced financial systems that have no minimum balance requirements and no fees associated with routine checking account use (Beck, Demirgüç-Kunt, and 2006).[25]

Eligibility is another hurdle for accessing financial services. In Swaziland, legislation mandates that a woman can be party to a contract (such as opening an account or taking out a loan) only with the consent of her father, her husband, or another male family member. This requirement might explain the large gender gap in bank accounts—52 percent of men have accounts, but only 30 percent of women. Documentation requirements for opening a bank account can be another important hurdle. Such requirements seem to be more onerous in African countries than elsewhere. In many African countries, new customers need a form of identification, payment slip, letter of reference, and proof of residence before being able to open an account. Compare these requirements with those of many non-African countries, where only one or two of these documents are required (Beck, Demirgüç-Kunt, and 2006). The documents can be hard to obtain. In Nigeria, passports are issued only for approved travel purposes. Driver licenses are available only to drivers, and proof of a registered residential address excludes the population living in rural areas and in informal settlements (Truen and others 2005). The requirement for proof of formal income excludes all but government officials and employees of medium and large enterprises. Anti-money-laundering legislation can have a profound impact on access, by tightening documentation requirements and preventing innovative financial institutions from working around these traditional identification requirements. Chamberlain and Walker (2005) estimate that 35 percent of adults in Namibia and 30 percent in South Africa are not able to provide proof of their physical address, as required by anti-money-laundering legislation. The situation is even worse in low-income Swaziland, where 75 percent of adults do not have a verifiable address.

Finally, there is the barrier of inappropriate product features. Bank accounts with all the bells and whistles might be not only too costly but also inappropriate for large numbers of Africans, who need only simple transaction or savings accounts. Checking accounts and built-in overdraft facilities can lead to overindebtedness, especially for individuals who have irregular income and spending needs. Recently, banks across the continent have come up with simpler transaction accounts, partly owing to political pressures. The Mzansi account in South Africa, introduced with the financial charter, resulted in 1.3 million new accounts over nine months, a 10 percent increase in the "banked" population. Banks in Kenya, Uganda, and other countries have introduced new account types, as we discuss in more detail in chapter 4.

Many financial services are not only costly and unsuitable for low-income customers, but also of low quality. According to firm-level surveys, it takes five days to clear a check in South Africa and Uganda, and seven days in Mozambique—longer than the time for an international wire transfer. In most Latin American countries, by contrast, it takes two days.

Affordability, eligibility, and product appropriateness barriers are lower for nonbank financial intermediaries that cater to lower-income households. These intermediaries range from post office savings banks to credit unions and other financial cooperatives to other formal and semiformal microfinance providers. Accordingly, it is to these intermediaries that most African households have resort.

Enterprises Place High Value on Better Financial Services

If a single survey statistic justifies a development focus on finance, it is this finding: more African enterprises report that access to and the cost of finance are major constraints on the operation and growth of their firms than do entrepreneurs in other regions (figure 2.19).[26] This finding comes from firm-level surveys that have enabled us to assess firms' financing constraints and patterns since the early 1990s. Here we rely on the most recent efforts, the World Bank's Investment Climate Assessment (ICA) surveys, which also enable international benchmarking of African firms.

The financing patterns of firms in Africa show some similarities to, but also some striking differences from, those of firms in other regions, as can be observed in figure 2.20. African firms finance about 68 percent of their investment needs with internal funds, more than firms in Latin America and Asia, but less than firms in the Middle East and North Africa and in Europe and Central Asia. Firms in Africa finance a smaller share of investment with bank credit than do firms in East Asia and Latin America, but a larger share than do firms in the Middle East, Europe and Central Asia,

FIGURE 2.19
Financing Obstacles across Regions

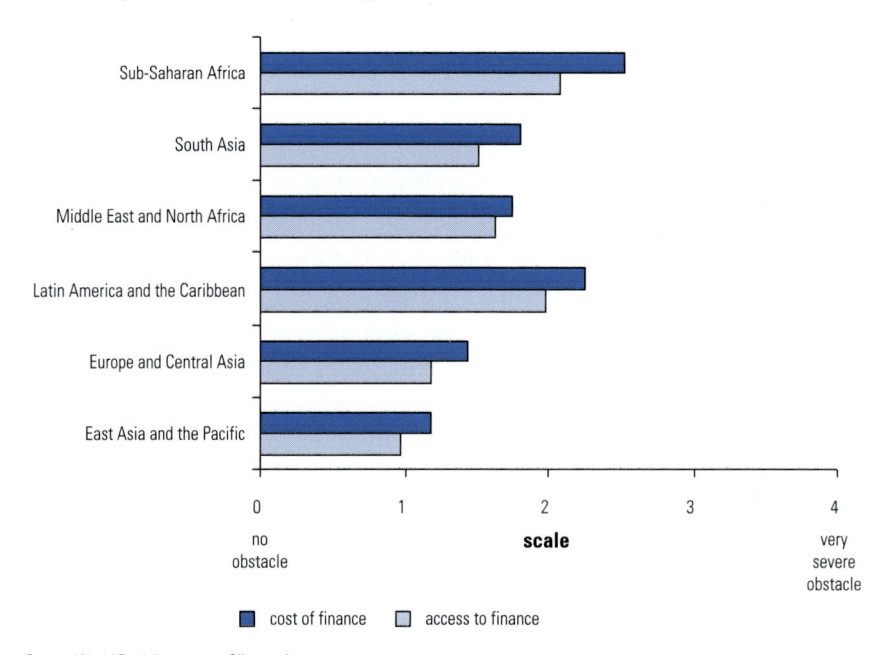

Source: World Bank Investment Climate Assessment surveys.

Note: The figure shows mean ratings for surveyed firms of access to and cost of finance as obstacles to business operation and growth. Ratings were on a five-point scale: 0 = no obstacle, 1 = minor obstacle, 2 = moderate obstacle, 3 = major obstacle, and 4 = very severe obstacle.

FIGURE 2.20
Sources of Financing for Investment across Regions

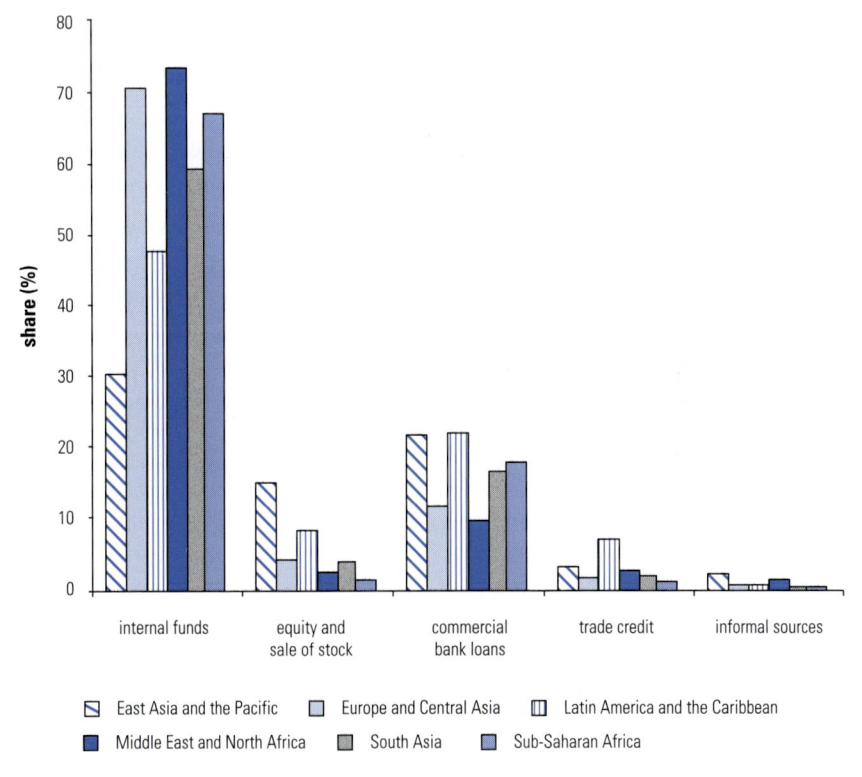

	East Asia and the Pacific	Europe and Central Asia	Latin America and the Caribbean
	Middle East and North Africa	South Asia	Sub-Saharan Africa

Source: World Bank Investment Climate Assessment Surveys.

Note: The figure shows mean shares of different sources of funds for financing new investments by manufacturing firms.

and South Asia. However, firms in Africa finance less investment with equity finance than do firms in any other region—most likely reflecting the underdevelopment of capital markets—and they finance less investment with trade finance than firms in any other region, which might reflect low levels of trust.

The low reliance on trade credit might seem surprising because supplier credit has often been seen as a substitute for bank credit (Fisman and Love 2003). Small firms, in particular, can benefit from trade credit from large firms if the large firms have access to bank finance. Furthermore, the reliance of trade credit relationships on soft information and their link with real transactions should make trade credit especially appealing in an environment so hostile to formal banking credit. Trade credit should be more appropriate, because it is a more flexible arrangement than formal banking relationships in the face of unexpected shocks. The degree to which domestic trade credit at the small scale is confined to networks largely working within particular ethnic communities, partly as a response to the difficult business environment (Eifert, Gelb, and Ramachandran 2006), is touched on below.

As elsewhere, small firms in Africa use fewer formal external financing sources than do large firms (Beck, Demirgüç-Kunt, and Levine 2004). Interestingly, the lack of demand for formal external finance does not vary significantly across firm size (see table 2.6). But firm size eases financing constraints, which leads to the probability that firms' unmet credit demand increases as one moves from large to medium-size to small to micro firms.

Previous research using ICAs has pointed to a large share of firms that do not apply for credit. Researchers have inferred a lack of credit demand by firms—especially small firms. Digging deeper into reasons firms have not applied, however, yields a very different picture. Table 2.6 lists the percentages for three categories of firms; first, firms that applied for and received a loan; second, a group of firms with no demand for loans; and third, a group of firms that is credit constrained—that is, that either applied for a loan and were rejected or did not apply because they did not have sufficient collateral, the application process was too difficult, interest rates were too high, or they simply expected to be rejected. Including this last group of entrepreneurs who are involuntarily excluded from the credit market in the category of entrepreneurs who applied for a loan and were rejected not only reduces the share of enterprises with no demand for credit, but also makes credit-constrained firms the largest group among the small firms.

TABLE 2.6
Credit Demand and Constraints across African Enterprises

	Small enterprises	Medium enterprises	Large enterprises
Received loan (%)	24.8	32.0	55.6
No credit demand (%)	34.0	39.8	32.5
Credit constrained[a] (%)	41.2	28.2	11.9

Source: World Bank's Investment Climate Assessment surveys.

Note: Calculations are based on surveys from Kenya, Madagascar, Senegal, and Uganda. Small enterprises have fewer than 25 employees, medium have 26 to 100, and large have more than 100.
a. Includes firms that applied for a loan and were rejected and firms that did not apply because they (a) did not have sufficient collateral, (b) found the application process too difficult, (c) found interest rates too high, or (d) expected to be rejected.

Beyond the observation that smaller firms have less access to financial services, many observers of firm finance in Africa have commented on the phenomenon of the missing middle: medium and large firms can access formal financial institutions, while microfirms often have access to MFIs (Kaufmann 2005; Sacerdoti 2005). But microfirms that are growing have difficulty expanding because MFIs are not able to expand lending (because of lack of funds or regulatory limits on maximum loan amounts), and banks and finance companies do not consider microfirms formal enough to extend credit to them. Collateral and documentation requirements often lie at the core of the reluctance of banks to extend loans to this segment of firms.

One of the problems faced by many enterprises in countries in Sub-Saharan Africa, as in many other developing countries, is high collateral requirements—often over 100 percent. On average, 83 percent of firms in Sub-Saharan Africa must supply lenders with collateral or a deposit, a proportion similar to that in other regions of the world. Lack of sufficient collateral is widely cited as a reason for not applying for or for being refused credit. In the median African country, firms that must offer collateral must supply 135 percent of the loan value. This figure is lower than in the Middle East and North Africa and in Europe and Central Asia, but it is substantially higher than in East and South Asia.

Numerous financial products available in advanced economies are largely absent in the African environment. Where this lack cannot be explained by the broader environmental issues, including the security of property rights, it may be due to a lack of scale. In some cases, technical fixes, such as specific legislation or an improved information environment, could help. This last consideration is especially pertinent for those products that could potentially compensate for other harder-to-correct weaknesses in the environment, especially for those small firms in the missing middle.

Leasing is an efficient financing tool for small and medium enterprises because it relies on the underlying asset and the cash flows it generates as collateral rather than on the enterprise's and the owner's wealth. Leasing has developed in some African countries, often jump-started with assistance from the International Finance Corporation, but it is often still hampered by tax complications or regulatory uncertainty because of the lack of specific legislation. Although leasing has the advantage that the lessor (lender) owns the leased equipment, this benefit does not always translate into speedy recovery in the case of delinquency, owing to the complexities of court procedures, which are often compounded by judicial inefficiency, if not corruption.

Factoring—which is not a lending technique, strictly speaking—involves the purchase of accounts receivables by the lender or factor. In small enterprises with accounts receivable from large reputable enterprises, this financing technique is attractive because it does not rely on information about the borrower, but the obligor.

In interpreting survey findings, it is important to recognize that the firms surveyed in the ICAs are mostly formal firms in the manufacturing sector. In particular, firms engaged in agriculture—so crucial to current economic well-being across most of Africa (figure 2.21)—are underrepresented. It is clear that access to credit and other financial services is even more restricted in agriculture than in other sectors, and more restricted in rural settings than in urban ones. Much agricultural activity,

FIGURE 2.21
Share of Agriculture across Countries

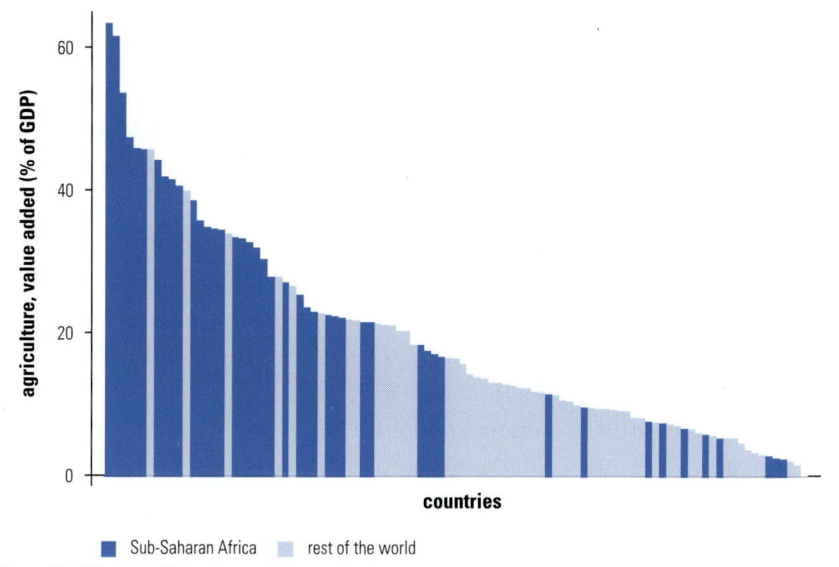

Source: World Bank's World Development Indicators database.

Note: The figure shows the contribution of agriculture (value added) to GDP in 99 countries. African countries are shown in color. All data are for 2005.

especially subsistence agriculture with staple crops, does not lend itself easily to traditional loan products. It requires innovative solutions, as discussed in chapter 4. But even cash crop farmers have a hard time securing external financing because of frequent crop failure and price volatility.

As in household finance, informality is often a major hurdle in accessing formal financial sources, especially in the absence of formal documentation of ownership claims over immovable assets that could be used as collateral. Contract claims cannot be enforced against firms that are not formally registered. Informal economic activity is also disproportionately important in Africa (figure 2.22).[27] There can be no doubt that this sector too is starved of formal finance, having access to it only indirectly (for example, through assistance from friends and relatives—including public servants who access bank credit through salary loans).

FIGURE 2.22
Share of Informal Economic Activities across Countries

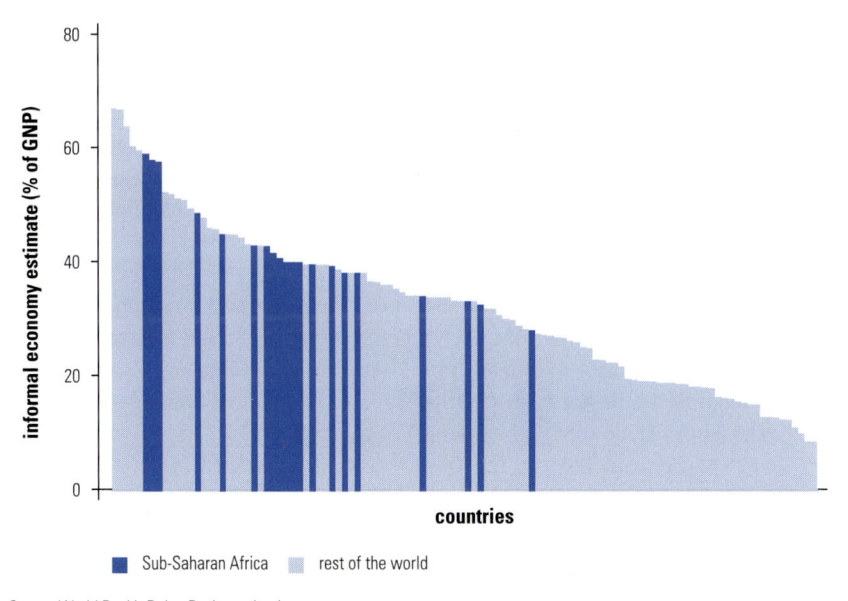

Source: World Bank's Doing Business database.

Note: The figure shows estimates of the informal economy for 110 countries. African countries are shown in color. All data are for 2005.

Notes

1. Throughout this book, *Africa* refers to Sub-Saharan Africa.
2. An intriguing recent discovery is that high poverty seems to be associated with low subsequent national investment rates, but only in countries with low levels of financial depth (Lopez and Serven 2005).
3. However, one should not overlook the limitations of both indicators. Both are measures of size; they do not indicate the efficiency with which financial services are delivered or the quality of those services. Also, both are measures of financial aggregates and, as such, do not give any indication of the penetration of financial services to different agents in the economy—an issue to which we will come back later.
4. Even if an Africa dummy is not statistically significant, examination of the pattern of outliers is meaningful.
5. The low financial depth, despite moderate inflation, in the two CFA franc monetary unions—Communauté Financière d'Afrique (West Africa) and Coopération Financière en Afrique Centrale (Central Africa)—has been long observed. The relative openness of the capital account and a fear of devaluation were once posited as explanations, though neither explanation has as much force now as it would have had in the years before the devaluation of 1994. This study uses the term *CFA zone* to refer to both unions.
6. The level of offshore deposits might also be related to factors unrelated to capital flight, such as use by multinational enterprises or exporters. However, the level of capital flight might be understated by the level of offshore deposits because it does not include capital flight through nonbank channels.
7. In the following, we will use margins (the net interest revenue relative to total earning assets) rather than spreads (the difference between lending and deposit rates) owing to better data availability. Margins are generally lower than spreads because they exclude interest that has not been paid on nonperforming loans.
8. The other main components are loan-loss provisions and noninterest income (such as fees). Thus (approximately), before tax profits = net interest margin + noninterest income – overhead costs – loan-loss provisions.
9. The data used here are for the period 2000 to 2004 and include data on 2,157 banks from 110 countries, including 174 banks from 20 African countries.
10. In 1994, the price level in the Democratic Republic of Congo (then Zaire) increased by a factor of 240.
11. The custom in many English Common Law countries of a general lien against all assets of a borrower also helps bind the borrower to a specific lender, especially given the high registration costs of such liens.
12. It is remarkable that the big-three banks in Nigeria managed to retain as high a share as they did, given the proliferation of state (provincial) government-owned banks from the 1960s on and of private commercial and merchant banks in the late 1980s (Brownbridge and Harvey 1998). The 2005 consolida-

tion will likely lower the effective market power of the big three even if it does not affect their combined market share by much.
13. For instance, half the stocks listed on the Namibian stock exchange are also listed on the Johannesburg exchange (a fact whose origins lie in the precise formulation of Namibian exchange controls, which have allowed fund investment in what are primarily South African companies, provided they are locally listed; see Moss 2003). Five other exchanges—those in Botswana, Ghana, Malawi, and Nigeria, and Zambia's Lusaka exchange—also have primary or secondary listings of one or two firms that are listed in Johannesburg. The largest company listed on the Ghana exchange, AngloGold Ashanti, has its primary listing in Johannesburg and is listed on six other exchanges; most of the trading in AngloGold Ashanti occurs on the New York Stock Exchange. There are also cross-listings between the East African exchanges.
14. Some exchanges have listed firms that have not issued any new securities; market valuation of firms can also increase without the firms raising any new funds.
15. These concepts are spelled out in World Bank (2006).
16. Such rules refer both to the maximum percentage of a company's equity allowed to be controlled by any one foreign investor (5 or 10 percent in exchanges such as those of Botswana, Ghana, Malawi, Tanzania, and Zimbabwe) and to ceilings on the total percentage of foreign ownership of the share (or at least on foreign ownership of the free float). These ceilings are 49 percent in Malawi and Zimbabwe, 55 percent in Botswana, 60 percent in Tanzania (which did not allow foreign portfolio investment in listed equities before 2004), 74 percent in Ghana, and 75 percent in Kenya, for example. There are no particular restrictions of foreign ownership of shares in Mauritius, Uganda, or Zambia.
17. The reluctance of domestic investors to commit themselves to sizable stakes is exemplified by the flotation of Ghana's Produce Buying Company in 2000, which failed to raise the expected funds from the general private sector, leaving the social security fund holding a much higher share (49 percent) than the 20 percent originally envisaged. Moss (2003) documents the risk factors that were probably in the minds of investors.
18. The issue was greatly oversubscribed, and the shares went to a premium of 326 percent on the issue price in the first day's trading. The number of applicants exceeded 250,000—two and a half times the previous number of registered shareholders in the market.
19. With the exception of those in Mauritius, Namibia, and South Africa.
20. For comparison, housing finance comes to between 15 and 21 percent in Chile, Malaysia, and Thailand and reaches 65 percent in Ireland and 78 percent in the Netherlands.
21. Note that the curve-fitting methodology used to arrive at these estimates was chosen so as to, if anything, err on the high side for countries at the low end, thereby perhaps exaggerating access percentages for some low-income African

countries (Honohan 2006). The overall figure of 20 percent should therefore be taken as an upper estimate.
22. Countries in Africa have some of the lowest telephone penetration rates in the world, whether fixed line or mobile, but mobile penetration is increasing rapidly.
23. There seem to be different pricing models for account services. Some banks seem to rely more on large unremunerated minimum balances, while others rely on large monthly fees. A third model, such as in South Africa, tries to impose individual charges on each account-related service.
24. A sad story is told of a widow in Ghana whose ¢907,000 savings deposit (more than US$100), accumulated from savings earned carrying goods in Accra's Makola market, was completely eroded over a period of two years (2003–05) by annual charges imposed by her bank after they increased the minimum balance requirement on savings deposits (Adabre 2005).
25. The cross-country data are based on survey responses from the largest banks in each country. They are averages for all banks that responded, weighted by their share in the deposit market. Fore more detail see Beck, Demirgüç-Kunt, and Martínez Pería (2006).
26. Although these are subjective assessments, note that Beck, Demirgüç-Kunt, and Levine (2006) find that in countries where firms report greater financing obstacles, industries that depend more on external finance grow relatively more slowly and investment resources are reallocated more slowly as demand changes across industries. Also, Beck, Demirgüç-Kunt, and Maksimovic (2005) find a significant negative impact of financing obstacles on firm growth.
27. On average, more of the economy is informal in Sub-Saharan Africa than in other continents. Schneider (2005) estimates the average share of GDP contributed by the informal sector in 32 Sub-Saharan African countries other than South Africa at 44 percent, compared with 43 percent in Latin America, 40 percent in Central and Eastern Europe and the countries of the former Soviet Union, and 30 percent in Asia. The International Labour Organization (ILO 2002) data (for fewer countries) show the share of informal employment in nonagricultural employment as 78 percent for Sub-Saharan African countries other than South Africa; 65 percent for Asia, 51 percent for Latin America, and 48 percent for North Africa.

CHAPTER 3

Finance for Long-Term Growth: Enriching the Flow of Finance to Transform the Economy

Introduction: Mainstream Financial Institutions

Finance's contribution to growth and stability
This chapter deals with the functioning of mainstream financial institutions as mobilizers of funds, providers of risk management services, and financiers of medium- and large-scale enterprises and government. It is in these ways that finance makes its major contribution to sustained economic growth and stability.

With the prospect of an increased flow of external funds of various forms, the major challenge facing African financial systems is that of absorption. How can policy help ensure that these funds are effectively channeled into productive growth, generating uses in both rural and urban areas?

We begin with banking, noting the endemic high liquidity in much of Africa's banks and considering how this liquidity could be more effectively employed over time. Here, of the quartet of distinctive African environmental factors—scale, informality, governance, and shocks—the last two are especially evident.

A need to improve contract enforcement and transparency of information
An ever-growing body of evidence supports the relevance of a proposition that has been reiterated by modernist observers for decades—namely that

improving information and contract enforcement is important for helping manage idiosyncratic shocks. We show that this proposition is especially important in Africa and also highlight the importance of avoiding overly activist prudential regulations that constrain banking effectiveness without materially improving systemic stability.

Ownership of African banks has been evolving rapidly. The likely effect of the return of the international banks (including, but not limited to, those based in South Africa) is reviewed, as is the growth of regional banks; both are positive developments. Recurrent political interest in state-sponsored development finance institutions (DFIs), by contrast, is unlikely to produce results any more successful than the last wave of such institutions, essentially because of governance problems.

Governments are not the best source of long-term funds—
In particular, government-owned and -operated DFIs are not the most promising sources of long-term resources. Long-term funds can be sourced from pension and social security funds, given the right governance structures, and complemented by a more energetic approach to investment banking by the leading intermediaries. Good allocation of long-term funds will benefit from effective securities markets to help make pricing transparent. The regulatory model of existing African securities markets may not be the most appropriate one, however, at least for the smaller countries, as we will explain: in regulation, the modernist model may have been taken too far. The housing and infrastructure sectors demand longer-term funds with specific and typically more limited risks. We review the prospects for financing each, using new approaches.

—But they do need to provide a stable macroeconomic environment
The last section of the chapter turns to macroeconomic issues, pointing out the need to ensure that government policy does not destabilize wholesale financial markets either through debt management policy or through the response of the monetary authorities to shocks such as those resulting from aid inflows. The potential for further regional integration is briefly explored, highlighting the desirability of focusing efforts on those steps that can help improve governance and those that can help overcome the costs of operating at too small a scale.

Improving the Banking System's Ability to Intermediate Funds

Ensuring Bank Lending Capacity

For the foreseeable future, the bulk of investable funds mobilized by African countries' financial systems will be intermediated by national banking systems. Ensuring that the banking system does a good job of intermediating is crucial to the effectiveness of banking systems; neglecting this sector will mean stagnation.

What can Africans hope to get from their banking systems? Certainly they can get more than just credit. Bundled into the operating methodology of all commercial banks is a range of liquidity, risk reduction, payment, and credit services. Credit is a key ingredient in and a major contributor to the functioning of the economic system. Yet African bankers and their customers complain about inadequate volumes of credit. Both would like to see greater volumes of credit, provided it was going to be profitable. From the points of view of borrowing firms and of farms, better availability of affordable credit would remove a significant constraint to expansion.

So why do African banks not lend enough? By their own accounts, in a remarkable number of African countries it is not a lack of mobilized funds that constrains the bankers. As noted in chapter 2, many African banking systems are rather liquid by international standards. As shown in figure 3.1, this is nothing new. Indeed, the median ratio of liquid assets to lending in the aggregate banking balance sheet of African countries has crept up over the years.

Plotting bank liquidity—here defined broadly to include foreign assets as well as local-currency reserves—against monetary depth—the ratio of broad money to gross domestic product (GDP)—helps identify the countries that are most affected by this endemic excess liquidity. It also puts this information in a perspective that shows that excess liquidity can coexist with very limited investable funds (figure 3.2). The International Monetary Fund (IMF 2006) provides a complementary analysis in terms of required and excess domestic reserves. The systems that have mobilized the most resources are not the ones that experience the most excess liquidity. Indeed, if anything, the downward sloping pattern of the plot suggests that excess liquidity tends to coincide more often with limited monetization: the population is unwilling to save in monetary form, and the banks are unable to lend even the limited resources that they have.[1]

FIGURE 3.1
Liquidity of the Banking System in African Economies

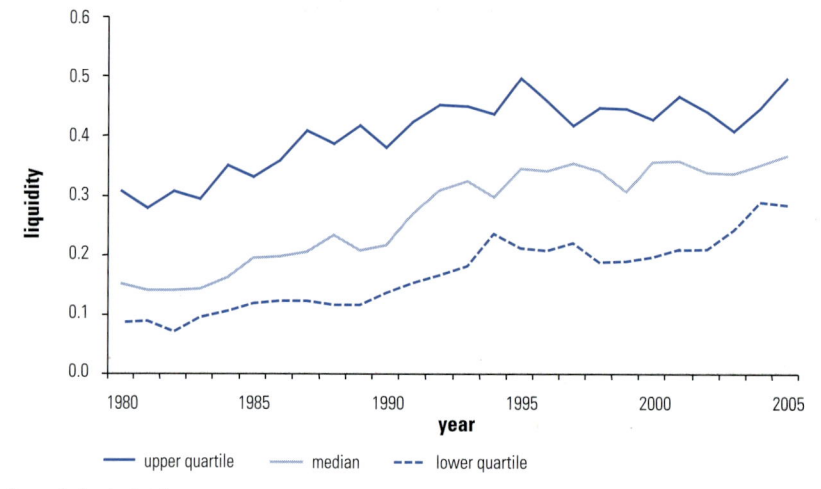

[Line graph showing liquidity from 1980 to 2005, with upper quartile, median, and lower quartile lines. Upper quartile rises from ~0.31 in 1980 to ~0.49 in 2005; median rises from ~0.15 to ~0.36; lower quartile rises from ~0.08 to ~0.28.]

— upper quartile   — median   --- lower quartile

Source: Authors' calculations.

Note: Liquidity is defined as the reserves plus foreign assets of banking institutions divided by the total credit, as in the International Monetary Fund's International Financial Statistics database, lines 20 + 21/(22a..g).

Some of this trend reflects the capital restructuring of failed banks that saw their loan book written down or removed.[2] But it clearly indicates either a problem with generating sufficient satisfactory loan business or a response to perceived liquidity risk. Bankers generally point to the former, though some banks—often foreign-owned ones—are in a position of currency mismatch, having taken more deposits denominated in foreign currency than can prudently be lent out in the local economy (box 3.1). First, and most stridently, bankers complain of a lack of acceptable or "bankable" loan applications. Second, some banks (often the smaller ones) feel constrained by regulatory requirements for diversification of risks: when a single loan must not exceed a quarter of the bank's capital, they find that they do not have enough capital to finance certain large projects. These issues are not new; they have persisted through the past couple of decades. Bankers' avowed inability to lend the resources they have mobilized slows their efforts at mobilization (branches, services) and discourages expansion. We consider both issues in turn, concluding that lack of bankability is likely the more acute and intractable problem. Still, some easily implemented measures on the regulatory side could help.

FIGURE 3.2
African Banks: Financial Depth and Liquidity, 2004

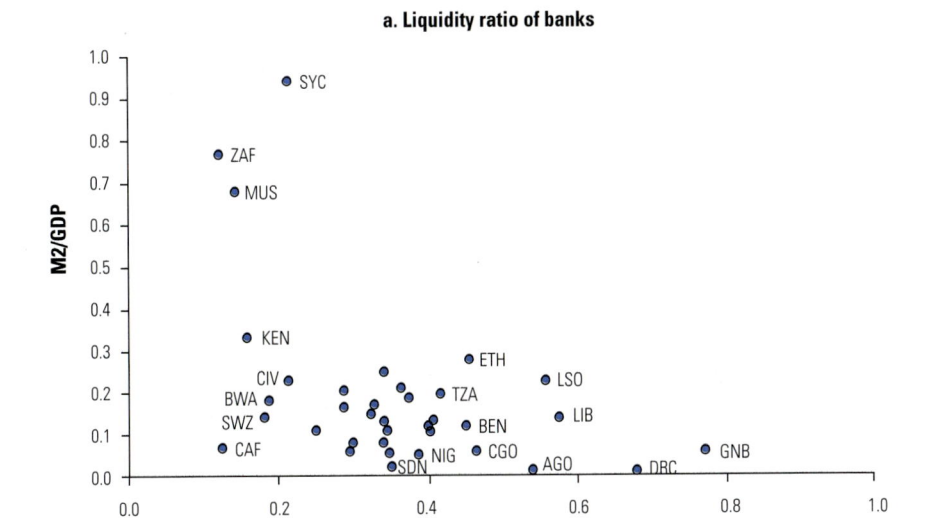

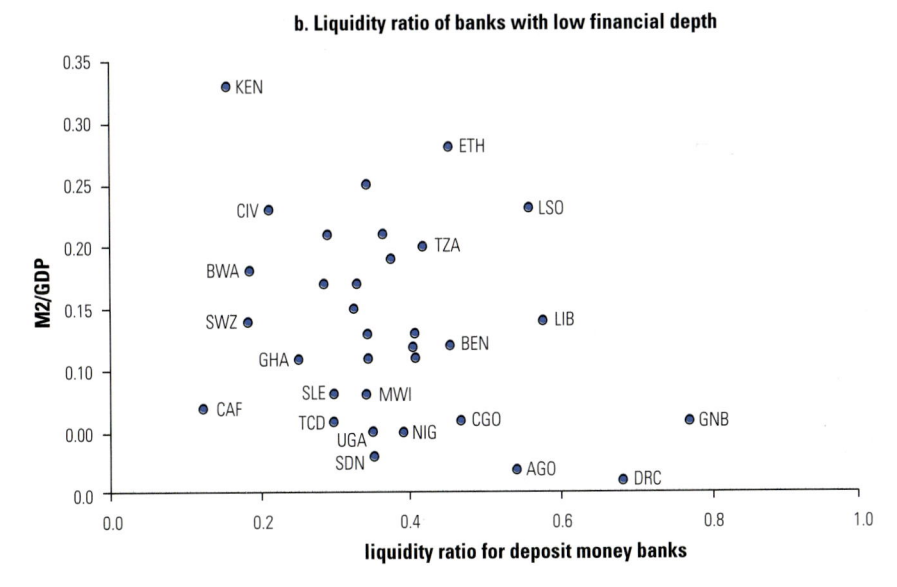

a. Liquidity ratio of banks

b. Liquidity ratio of banks with low financial depth

Source: Authors' calculations.

Note: Country abbreviations are included in the acronym and abbreviations list at the front of the book. *Liquidity* is defined as the reserves plus foreign assets of banking institutions divided by the total credit, as in the International Monetary Fund's International Financial Statistics database, lines 20 + 21/(22a..g). Panel b zooms in on countries with low financial depth.

> ### BOX 3.1
>
> ### Dollarization
>
> The share of bank deposits denominated in foreign currency in African banking systems has risen sharply in recent years. This phenomenon has been relatively unremarked, so policy makers experiencing it in their own country tend to see it as unique to them. In fact, dollarization ratios for the two dozen African countries for which data are available display distribution and growth to similar ratios in other parts of the world (see table).
>
> **Dollarization of Bank Deposits**
> (foreign currency as a percentage of total deposits)
>
> | | Africa (2004 or latest year) | World (2004) | Africa (change since 1994) |
> | --- | --- | --- | --- |
> | Mean | 33.7 | 32.6 | 12.7 |
> | Median | 29.3 | 29.5 | 16.4 |
> | Upper quartile | 44.1 | 47.9 | 16.2 |
> | Lower quartile | 12.8 | 10.4 | 7.1 |
>
> *Sources:* De Nicoló, Honohan, and Ize 2005; Levy-Yeyati 2006.

Information and Contract Enforcement

In contrast to the experience of bankers in advanced economies, where lending is usually more profitable than holding government securities or liquid assets abroad, bankers in Africa have often found lending to be a relatively unprofitable line of business. This trend has been shown, for example, in two detailed recent studies of Nigerian and Ugandan banks (Beck, Cull, and Jerome 2005; Clarke, Cull, and Fuchs 2006). It is easy to see why, generally speaking and in normal times, lending can contribute much more to value added and to the profitability of banks. After all, it is through lending that banks exploit their comparative advantage in credit appraisal and monitoring. Why has it been otherwise in Africa? At times, in some countries, heavy government reliance on domestic borrowing has sent the yield on national government securities so high as to choke off demand from nongovernmental borrowers. But crowding out is far from the whole story and has not occurred in all countries.

> About a third of bank deposits in African countries for which data are available are denominated in foreign currencies. The highest figures recorded are for Liberia (90 percent), the Democratic Republic of Congo (86 percent), Angola (72 percent), and Mozambique (60 percent). For the countries for which data are also available for 1994, there has been an increase of about 1.0 to 1.5 percent per year on average, close also to the worldwide average rate of increase in dollarization. Cross-country research suggests that past inflation and confidence factors are influential in increasing the rate of dollarization. By stabilizing the macroeconomy some countries have managed to reverse dollarization, but overall there has been an upward worldwide trend (De Nicoló, Honohan, and Ize 2005).
>
> Dollarization presents prudential risks and limits the ability of the banks to onlend their mobilized resources in local currency. On average, one of every two dollars mobilized in foreign-currency deposits tends to be invested abroad. But given the perceived exchange rate risks that induce depositors to hold foreign-currency accounts, the alternative is offshore deposits. Outlawing foreign-currency deposits is unlikely to be a preferred option. But any taxes and regulations that favor foreign-currency deposits should be reviewed. For example, Liberia had, until recently, much lower reserve requirements on foreign-currency deposits. And maintenance of a stable

Instead, bankers are unanimous on the two main factors that discourage lending. First is the difficulty of obtaining the information about potential clients that they need to assess those clients' creditworthiness. Second is the difficulty of enforcing creditor rights. Without these two essential ingredients, the banks are left with costly, time-consuming, and unreliable procedures for precredit appraisal and without the comfort of speedy recourse to foreclosure if things go wrong.

Africa is not alone in being deficient in these respects. Indeed, of the six major regions with which the World Bank deals, Sub-Saharan Africa scores third in business confidence in the judicial system and in the World Bank's index of property rights (figure 3.3).[3] And reforms are taking place.

A special commercial court established in Tanzania was greeted with enthusiasm by the business community, though—perhaps inevitably— early achievements were not fully maintained. In Rwanda, the time taken to resolve a dispute fell by 22 percent following the introduction of a specialized court for business, financial, and tax matters (World Bank's Doing

FIGURE 3.3
Business Opinion on Courts and on the Recoverability of Overdue Amounts

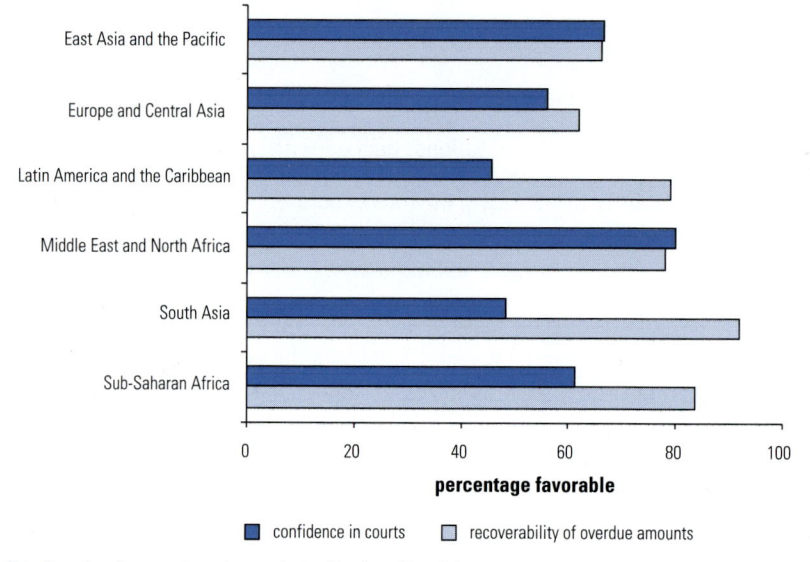

[Bar chart showing percentage favorable for "confidence in courts" and "recoverability of overdue amounts" across six regions: East Asia and the Pacific, Europe and Central Asia, Latin America and the Caribbean, Middle East and North Africa, South Asia, and Sub-Saharan Africa.]

Note: Bars show the percentage of respondents with a favorable opinion.

Source: World Bank's Investment Climate Assessment surveys.

Business database 2006). The idea of a special commercial court is most attractive when it comes to complex commercial cases that require specialist expertise on the part of the relevant judiciary body; the logic of establishing a special court to deal with more routine contract enforcement matters is less compelling.

Procedural changes, many requiring legislation, can represent a more immediate and less costly kind of reform. Here Africa has a relatively poor record, second among the six World Bank regions in number of procedures and in time taken to resolve disputes.[4] For instance, measures to streamline debtor appeals (for example, confining the appeal to matters of law and procedure, not the original evidence) and impose time limits on their filing have been introduced in several African countries. The World Bank's 2006 Doing Business database states, "The time and cost savings allowed more businesses to use the courts. Uganda saw a 62 percent increase in commercial cases filed.... 'We have more faith in the courts now, more trust,' says Musoke, a local businessman. 'The president is now mentioning us in his speeches,' adds a judge in Kampala." Evidently the reforms are believed to improve the enforcement (box 3.2).

BOX 3.2

Points to Look For in an Effective Legal System

A well-functioning legal system is a confluence of modern laws, procedural regulations, and strong institutions, backed with proper enforcement mechanisms.

Laws and Regulations

Whereas the commercial legal frameworks of former colonial powers have been significantly modified in the past half-century, the English Common Law and French Civil Code systems inherited by African countries at independence have rarely been updated. For example, advanced economies have modified their commercial legal frameworks to accommodate the varied types of trading and complex financing arrangements (including concepts such as leasing, securitization, and derivatives trading) that characterize modern and evolving market economies. A particular difficulty for countries with a Civil Code tradition is their inability to take advantage of many new financial instruments, because they have not been able to introduce the Common Law concept of a trust upon which such instruments are based.

To further strengthen their economies, advanced economies have also sought to shift the balance of protections traditionally enjoyed by contracting parties and have evolved different rights and responsibilities for different classes of agents. Realizing the close links between having access to credit and stimulating entrepreneurship, they have sought to ensure that the default risk was minimized through the legal system.

It is time for Africa to incorporate these kinds of changes, appropriately adapted to suit its particular circumstances. For instance, the key agriculture sector could benefit from laws facilitating the use of agricultural products as collateral, such as by introducing the concept of warehousing, and from better price discovery mechanisms for farmers, such as could result from derivative trading in agricultural products. A move toward a streamlined system of conclusive land title registration would add to lenders' confidence in land as collateral, thereby promoting credit flows. In addition, collateral registration procedures need simplification, and the database should

(Box continues on the following page.)

> **BOX 3.2** (*continued*)
>
> be easily accessible so as to assist in prior-charge verification, thereby preventing disputes. Similarly, the introduction of a credit information database would prevent credit arbitrage and would reward honest borrowers.
>
> The threat of insolvency, both corporate and personal, needs to be made real and effective. A specialized approach to insolvency is required. Personal bankruptcy in most countries in Africa is a relic of the early 20th century; corporate insolvency is a part of a companies act that, in most cases, is based on concepts that have not prevailed widely for decades. A mechanism to restructure and rehabilitate viable enterprises with the active participation of the creditor community needs to be adopted.
>
> **Regulatory Institutions and Transparency Requirements**
>
> Increasing penetration of financial services such as banking, insurance, pensions, and microfinance necessitates both an enabling environment for these services to grow and a good regulatory structure to prevent diversion of funds. Unscrupulous elements can exploit the cloak of limited liability to defraud unsuspecting individuals of their hard-earned money. Opacity in the functioning of institutions that access public money and provide public services can lead to disastrous events. Good corporate governance practices, supplemented by proper accounting and auditing principles, are a must, particularly for companies that operate in these sectors. To enable them to highlight weak internal governance in these companies, independent professionals need to be trained through capacity-building efforts. Establishing appropriate disclosure standards and strict, efficient enforce-

As far as credit information is concerned, African countries tend to be behind the rest of the world. Partly this tendency reflects a delayed catch-up to a new wave: worldwide, the proportion of countries with a credit registry jumped from 46 percent in 1988 to 70 percent in 1998 and to 80 percent in 2003; in Africa, the percentage is still just 60 percent. Furthermore, the coverage of the population and the extent of information that registries contain are lower than in other regions—much lower, except for South Africa and its small neighbors (World Bank's Doing Business database 2006). Part of the problem here is the informality of residence and the lack of stable individual identifiers. There are substitutes for a national identity card. Credit registries are

ment procedures should be a priority. The availability of information in the public domain can lead to proper vigilance and quick remedial measures in case problems occur. Strong regulatory institutions can enforce these disclosure standards and other regulations and ensure that the whole system functions well.

Traditional Court System and Enforcement Mechanisms

Quite apart from the necessity of having modern laws, existing legal institutions (as well as new ones) also need adequate staffing and other infrastructure resources. Financial and functional independence from other branches of the government should be encouraged because excessive reliance on the government (often the most significant litigant) usually endangers judicial impartiality.

Despite the growth in the number of legal disputes, legal and judicial institutions have remained static. There has been no corresponding increase in the number of courts or tribunals, or in the number of court personnel to service the courts. Of particular concern are the extreme delays and high levels of frustration encountered in enforcing judgments. An insufficient staff and a lack of incentives to promptly enforce judgments result in the primary relief becoming illusory. Compensation levels have remained low, and there has been little, if any, upgrading of technical skills to keep up with the changing nature of legal disputes. Even the clerical staff needs training on how to keep records and manage excessive caseloads. Without a significant investment in these soft skills, improvements in automation and the introduction of modern case-tracking tools will be wasted.

being built even in anglophone African countries in which they were not traditionally used, such as Kenya and Uganda, and are being expanded to cover all incidents of delinquency in countries that did not cover these issues before.

Bankers have often developed imperfect but workable bilateral arrangements for providing credit references. So they are not always in the forefront of movements to improve credit registries if doing so will entail compulsory sharing of their information with other lenders, even outside the circle of traditional banking. Therefore, although bankers need to be involved in plans for improving credit registries, authorities may need to push beyond the point where bankers want to go.

Property registries, where liens can be recorded and quickly accessed, are also part of the recommended toolkit for facilitating collateralized lending. These registries, too, are something on which many African countries are working, introducing computerized systems that can leapfrog them into quite an efficient system of collateralized lending.

The lack of reliable company accounts is also largely a function of the informality of the economies. Most countries have now adopted the International Financial Reporting Standards (IFRS), so that doctrinal issues are at a minimum. But enforcing prompt filing of reliable accounts and ensuring that the auditing profession is competent and honest are necessarily medium-term projects.

Good information and strong creditor rights are two keys to expanding credit availability. It is clear from increasingly elaborate econometric work, using the extensive cross-country databases maintained by the World Bank, that countries with stronger creditor rights and better credit information enjoy a higher volume of credit (even controlling for other explanatory factors). The borrower benefits through availability when the lender is made secure. Digging deeper, though, we notice that for poor countries, credit information seems more important in influencing the volume of lending than are the legal protections (Djankov, McLiesh, and Shleifer forthcoming). If that is so, it is good news for Africa, because fully reforming legal protections is likely to be a long and drawn-out process in poor countries, at least when it comes to protecting the creditor rights of banks against politically protected borrowers. In fact, in countries with weak creditor rights, coverage of credit registries tends to be better and vice versa: information seems to have emerged as a partial substitute for creditor rights in the countries where such rights were weaker. (This is conspicuously the case in Africa, where countries with a credit registry have an average score of only 1.1 on the World Bank's Doing Business index of creditor rights, whereas those without a credit registry score 3.7 on average.)[5] It leaves open considerable potential for those African countries that still have no credit registries to introduce them—and for those that have them to enhance the extent, quality, and depth of the information collected.

It is not only for medium and large firms that better credit information helps improve credit availability. Indeed, the evidence shows that strengthening this area will yield even greater benefits for micro, small, and medium-scale enterprises (MSMEs) and households (Love and Mylenko 2003). Improving financial access for MSMEs is taken up in greater detail in chapter 4. Some elements of that discussion—notably suggesting that lenders themselves can do more to develop relationship-type lending so as to overcome some of the environmental difficulties—are also relevant for the middle market.

The Role of Prudential Regulation

Could deregulation be another part of the answer to helping increase the flow of credit? To consider this, we need to review why so much attention has been paid in the past few years to upgrading prudential regulation systems.

African financial systems, like most others around the world, experienced widespread banking failures in the 1980s and 1990s. The World Bank's Banking Crisis database records 53 episodes of bank insolvency in 41 African countries since 1980, of which 40 episodes in 32 countries were logged as systemic crises. Many of these events were very costly, whether we measure the effects in terms of the fiscal outlays made to meet depositors' claims (although not all depositors were paid in all cases) or in terms of the subsequent output dip potentially attributable to the crisis. For those events for which data are available, average fiscal costs amounted to 10.6 percent of annual GDP, whereas output losses were estimated at an average of 13.1 percent of GDP (Caprio and others 2005). These figures are all broadly comparable with those recorded in other developing regions.

However, closer familiarity with the nature and evolution of African banking crises reveals that the mix of causes and symptoms was somewhat different from that in other regions. Specifically, while Africa experienced each of the three main syndromes—banking weaknesses attributable to macroeconomic boom and bust, banking weaknesses attributable to bad banking by private banking insiders, and banking weaknesses attributable to government action undermining the solvency of the banks—there were relatively few of the first type and relatively more of the last type. In particular, contrary to what is sometimes suggested, not a single systemic crisis in Africa was caused by maturity mismatches in the banks' portfolios. Even where boom-and-bust cycles (a characteristically Latin American source of crisis) were at work—for example, following the mid-1980s commodity boom in the Union Economique et Monétaire Ouest Africaine (UEMOA) countries—government influences were also at work. Parastatals and firms that had acted as unpaid suppliers to governments and their agencies were prominent in the list of defaulting borrowers.[6] Bad banking was also at work, conspicuously in the major collapses of BCCI

(Bank of Credit and Commerce International, an international banking group headquartered in Luxembourg that successfully mobilized the deposits of wealthy individuals and state enterprises in several African countries before it failed in 1991) and Meridien-BIAO (the successor of the Banque de l'Afrique Occidentale, or BAO, a historic former bank of issue in francophone West Africa, which, when its parent was liquidated, was acquired by an aggressive but unsound banker based in Zambia before collapsing in 1995, affecting numerous countries across western and central Africa, including Swaziland and Equatorial Guinea).[7]

Smaller bank failures in Kenya,[8] Nigeria, and other countries were also associated with insider lending and looting, often involving politically well-connected insiders.[9] But the largest losses related to the nonperforming portfolios of dominant state-owned banks in countries such as Ghana, Tanzania, Uganda, and Zambia and of majority state-controlled banks in Benin, Cameroon, Côte d'Ivoire, Senegal, and other countries of the two African currency unions; in the Democratic Republic of Congo; in Angola and Mozambique; and elsewhere.

Bank regulation and banking supervision can be effective against incompetent or reckless management of a privately owned bank: the banking supervisors act to protect the interests of the depositors and of the wider functioning of the banking and payments system in case failures of such institutions are extensive enough to threaten that system.

By insisting on adequate capitalization, supervisors can also help protect the system against the failure of an international bank. But their abilities in such a case are limited, as witness what happened with the failure of BCCI. Despite formal agreements with the supervisors of such international banks in their home countries, the full strength of the local subsidiary may be exaggerated in its accounts to the extent that some losses or fragilities are hidden in related-party transactions with the parent bank that are opaque to the local supervisor.[10,11]

When it comes to state-owned banks, the role of the supervisor is, in practice, often even weaker. Although the supervisor can point to balance sheet weaknesses of a state-owned bank, if the government is determined to channel the resources of the bank to favored borrowers who do not have the ability or at least the intention to repay, few banking supervision authorities have the political independence to suspend that bank's operations.

Even if limited independence meant that bank supervisors were largely unable to prevent most of the crises in Africa, this may not be the case in the future. The greatly reduced role of state-owned banks in most African countries suggests that any future banking crises are more likely than before to have their roots in boom and bust or in bad banking.[12] Classic techniques of bank supervision may thus be more relevant than they were before. Most African bank supervisory agencies have been upgrading their capacity in recent years. However, that does not mean that every regulatory prudential measure that seems to add to the safety of banks is to be applauded. On the contrary, many such regulations are ineffective and, if they constrain the development of essentially sound risk taking by well-managed banks, could damage growth by far more than any supposed gain in safety (box 3.3).

Undue restrictions on the scope of bank operations can weaken rather than strengthen banks by limiting their profit opportunities. Recent exam-

---

BOX 3.3

Bank Regulation: Avoid Reliance on Extensive Discretionary Powers

Recent research on the effectiveness of prudential regulation questions the unthinking transplantation of practices from rich countries into the very different political and institutional settings that prevail in most countries. Detailed examination of cross-country evidence points to the limited effectiveness—and, in many respects, the counterproductivity—in developing countries of some standard regulatory and supervisory practices. In particular it suggests that too much reliance on discretionary powers given to government officials to keep the banking system safe, sound, and efficient may be misguided. Strikingly, it turns out that countries that grant the largest discretionary powers to their bank supervisors exhibit the most corruption in banking.

Certainly, unthinking application of the Basel II accord is not the way to go for many countries (box 3.4). Instead, in order to have banks that promote social welfare, a country needs political and other institutions that induce its officials to develop policies that maximize social welfare, not the private welfare of officials or bankers. The results also suggest certain practical rules: err on the side of liberality in entry and licensing and in relation to the permitted range of activities. The potential role of market discipline proves to be surprisingly strong, even in poor countries (see Barth, Caprio, and Levine 2005; Beck, Demirgüç-Kunt, and Levine 2006).

ples of such restrictions from the African environment include overuse of collateral requirements, unduly demanding risk concentration rules, and limits on the amount of lending to below-prime borrowers.

In some countries, banks are obliged to fully provision large, uncollateralized loans even if they are performing. For instance, recently Tanzanian regulations required 125 percent collateral for any individual loans larger than 5 percent of the bank's capital. In effect, such uncollateralized lending must be fully financed out of the bank's capital and not at all out of deposits. This practice cannot fail to place a brake on what might otherwise be sound lending backed by a credible projection of cash flow. However, as quantified in chapter 2, collateral requirements seem to be ingrained in African banking practice even where not imposed by regulation. Defenders of high collateral requirements point to the cost and difficulty of recovering even on apparently overcollateralized loans. However valid this consideration may be, it also points to the complementary importance of considerations other than collateral in loan appraisal.

Loan concentration limits can also be too constraining—though they are not always so. In the UEMOA, a single loan can reach 75 percent of the bank's capital before hitting the ceiling; this limit is probably too lenient. But if having as few as 10 loans, each just 10 percent of a bank's capital, is enough to violate aggregate loan concentration limits—as is the case in some other countries—even relatively large banks will have difficulty both in complying with the regulation and in meeting credit needs, even of customers who require no more than the equivalent of just a few million U.S. dollars. Financing large projects without hitting loan concentration ceilings tends to be a problem, particularly in smaller countries with low aggregate financial depth. After all, aggregate bank capital in Rwanda is about US$50 million, in Chad about US$70 million, in Mozambique about US$350 million, and in Tanzania about US$300 million.

Banks have ways around this problem (apart from securing exemptions from the regulatory authorities, a practice that, if widespread, both undermines the coherence of regulation and introduces the sort of regulatory discretion that can lead to corruption). For example, they can form lending consortia with other onshore banks or with offshore banks, including affiliates. However, such collaboration is costly and complicated by exchange controls and other factors. By forcing an excessive degree of information sharing, requirements for such collaboration reduce the incentive for banks to make the effort to determine the creditworthiness of large projects.

In francophone countries, the tradition of obtaining official preapproval of borrowers has been slow to die out. With its origins in the formerly widespread practice of rediscounting a sizable share of banking loans at the central bank, the system of preapproval itself was abolished many years ago. But in the UEMOA, a remnant survives in the form of the rule that at least 60 percent of each bank's portfolio must be loaned to borrowers that have been classified as eligible for refinancing. Because this regulation is not enforced, it may, in practice, be little more than a nuisance, but it is hard to square with a developmental policy. Furthermore, the idea that the banking regulator should pass judgment on the bankability of most borrowers certainly suggests a lack of official confidence in the ability of the banks to do their job.

Banking regulators need to act with restraint, therefore, in fulfilling their remit to keep banking systems safe and sound. Aggressive measures that are likely to constrain the ability of banks to take reasonable and prudent credit risks should be avoided. This is not really a question of accepting materially higher risks of failure; rather it is the avoidance of unnecessarily restrictive precautions. Adoption of the sophisticated versions of the recent Basel II accord on bank regulation is unlikely to help matters: indeed, it would be premature for most African countries (box 3.4). All in all, though, the widespread availability of exemptions and the fact that banks complain only weakly about overregulation suggests that it is not only—or even mainly—a regulatory credit crunch that limits credit growth in Africa.

Ownership and Industrial Structure of the Banking System

If the banking system is going to deliver the credit services so badly needed by African economies, how is it best organized? Are African banking systems too concentrated, too dependent on foreign ownership? Or are there too many small banks? What role should the government play? Here organizational and internationalization issues come to the fore.

Building Strong African Banking Systems

As mentioned in chapter 2, African banking systems are highly concentrated. Studies have shown that liberal entry policies can offset the market power that might otherwise be conferred by concentration (Berger and others 2004). Ensuring an adequate supply of solid banking competitors

> **BOX 3.4**
>
> **Basel II in Africa**
>
> Banking supervisors across Africa are coming under new pressures following the introduction of the new international accord among the bank regulators of advanced economies known as Basel II. There is no official compulsion on regulators in developing countries to adopt the accord, and, indeed, the relatively sophisticated techniques envisaged in parts of the Basel II approach could be quite dangerous if applied in an environment for which the basic data and skills are not available.
>
> For instance, the "standardized" approach to measuring bank capital requirements in Basel II envisages the use of credit rating agencies. These agencies would assign ratings to different borrowers on the basis of the capital required by banks to back loans to such borrowers. It is hard to imagine a credibly independent and authoritative rating industry emerging in small, poor economies. For one thing, there would be little or no market pressure on a rating agency to moderate its ratings, as both bank and borrower would prefer to see a higher rating. An alternative approach in Basel II is to use bankers' own internal rating systems to assign the amount of capital needed. That approach requires the banks to be able to assign credible ratings on the basis of a statistical model of default risk.

has been a constant concern for African banking authorities, especially given the small size of the market.

Bigger financial markets can accommodate competition among large intermediaries. Squaring the circle of competition and scale thus requires financial deepening within countries, as well as more cross-border and regional banking. So far, the degree of competition provided for the main banks by local near-bank institutions is limited; however, they do have stiff competition from offshore banks for large deposits and the best corporate clients.

Changes in bank ownership
The recent pickup in economic growth across the region has contributed to some new entry and expansion in branch numbers. As mentioned in chapter 2, even credit-to-GDP ratios have been picking up. In addition, recent trends in the organization of the banking industry have been affected by

> The data to build such a model do not yet exist in Africa north of the Limpopo River.
>
> Yet international banks, already struggling to meet the new requirements for their home operations, have been urging regulators in developing countries to adopt Basel II in order to harmonize the reporting requirements banks face. Such pressure should be resisted. It is not all that hard for international bankers to prepare returns on the old basis (indeed, reporting to a region-wide regulator would achieve a greater saving, as discussed below). Also, given the complexity of the internal rating models, host regulators could not justify the expense of tooling up to assess the quality of such a model. Above all, if local banks were also allowed to use the more advanced approaches to capital requirements, the difficulty and ambiguity of assessing whether these systems were measuring risk adequately, combined with what is, in practice, a limited degree of political independence of the regulator, would quickly result de facto in a regulatory free-for-all. Although the use of statistical risk models by banks will and should become increasingly widespread in the years ahead, adoption of the advanced capital measurement methods of Basel II should be postponed for the present in Africa.
>
> Africa will likely be affected by the implementation of Basel II in advanced economies, to the extent that it will result in higher capital requirements to back international bank lending to the region, which could constrain access by larger enterprises to offshore borrowing.

three structural changes. First are improvements in international communications (airline connections and telecommunications) in the region, which have facilitated the expansion of regional banks. Second is the bedding down of the reforms that cleaned up the portfolios of long-insolvent banks, many of them state owned, and passed their control to new shareholders. Third is the reemergence of South African banks as investors.

It is unlikely that the new wave of multinational banks in Africa would have occurred without the improvements in communications. The largest such networks so far are Ecobank and the Bank of Africa, both with their roots in the otherwise already integrated UEMOA. Recently, though, both these groups have reached beyond that zone, with the Bank of Africa opening in Kenya and Madagascar and planning an even wider network. Ecobank's proposed joint venture with the larger FirstBank of Nigeria will build scale substantially. Table 3.1 illustrates the range of cross-border banking north of the Limpopo River.

TABLE 3.1
Cross-Border Banking in Africa: Locations of Branches or Subsidiaries of 26 International Banking Groups

Banking group (country)	Angola	Burundi	Benin	Botswana	Burkina Faso	Cameroon	Cape Verde	Central African Rep.	Chad	Comoros	Congo, Rep. of	Côte d'Ivoire	Congo, Dem. Rep. of	Djibouti	Equatorial Guinea	Ethiopia	Gabon	Gambia	Ghana	Guinea	Guinea-Bissau	Kenya	Lesotho
Belgolaise[a] (Belgium)		✓											✓										
Financial Bank (Benin)			✓																				
Finabank (Botswana)																							
Afriland First (Cameroon)						✓									✓								
FOTSO (Cameroon)					✓	✓																	
Cofipa (Côte d'Ivoire)			✓			✓			✓		✓						✓			✓			
BNP Paribas (France)					✓						✓	✓		✓			✓			✓			
Calyon (France)						✓		✓			✓	✓		✓									
SGB (France)			✓		✓	✓		✓	✓		✓				✓				✓	✓			
BGFI (Gabon)											✓				✓		✓						
First International (Gambia)																		✓					
Novobanco (Procredit) (Germany)	✓																						
International Commercial (Ghana)																		✓	✓				
Kenya Commercial (Kenya)																						✓	
BSIC (Libya)			✓		✓			✓	✓									✓	✓	✓	✓		
Ecobank (Mali)			✓		✓	✓	✓	✓	✓		✓	✓							✓	✓		✓	
Capricorn I H (Namibia)				✓																			
Guaranty Trust (Nigeria)																		✓	✓				
Intercontinental (Nigeria)																		✓	✓				
Millennium BCP (Portugal)	✓																						
Bank of Africa (Togo)			✓		✓							✓										✓	
Absa (South Africa)	✓																						
Stanbic (South Africa)				✓							✓	✓	✓						✓			✓	✓
Barclays (United Kingdom)				✓															✓			✓	
Stanchart (United Kingdom)				✓		✓						✓					✓	✓	✓			✓	
Citi (United States)						✓					✓	✓					✓		✓			✓	

Banking group (country)	Liberia	Madagascar	Malawi	Mali	Mauritania	Mauritius	Mozambique	Namibia	Niger	Nigeria	Rwanda	Sao Tome and Principe	Senegal	Seychelles	Sierra Leone	South Africa	Sudan	Swaziland	Tanzania	Togo	Uganda	Zambia	Zimbabwe
Belgolaise[a] (Belgium)					✓					✓	✓								✓	✓	✓		
Financial Bank (Benin)		✓	✓						✓	✓		✓											
Finabank (Botswana)																							
Afriland First (Cameroon)												✓											
FOTSO (Cameroon)												✓											
Cofipa (Côte d'Ivoire)												✓											
BNP Paribas (France)													✓										
Calyon (France)																							
SGB (France)																							
BGFI (Gabon)												✓											
First International (Gambia)	✓														✓								
Novobanco (Procredit) (Germany)																							
International Commercial (Ghana)																							
Kenya Commercial (Kenya)																	✓						
BSIC (Libya)				✓ ✓																			
Ecobank (Mali)	✓																						
Capricorn I H (Namibia)							✓																
Guaranty Trust (Nigeria)										✓													
Intercontinental (Nigeria)							✓			✓													
Millennium BCP (Portugal)							✓ ✓																
Absa (South Africa)		✓							✓														
Stanbic (South Africa)			✓				✓	✓		✓								✓	✓		✓	✓	✓
Bank of Africa (Togo)		✓		✓					✓				✓										
Barclays (United Kingdom)														✓		✓			✓		✓	✓	✓
Stanchart (United Kingdom)										✓					✓	✓		✓	✓		✓	✓	✓
Citi (United States)										✓						✓			✓		✓	✓	✓

Source: Assembled from bank Web sites.

a. Fortis, the new parent of Belgolaise, announced in 2005 that it is winding down the operations of Belgolaise.

Banks based in South Africa have long been heavily involved in the provision of banking services in neighboring countries (Botswana, Lesotho, Namibia, and Swaziland). More recently, Stanbic[13] and, to a lesser extent, Absa have seized opportunities to acquire sizable banks further north. In 2005, UK-based Barclays acquired a controlling stake in Absa; it plans, subject to regulatory approval, to transfer all its African operations to Absa ownership and control. Thus, even if Absa is ultimately controlled by Barclays, two of the three largest banking groups outside South Africa will be run by South African concerns.

The privatization process has been long and drawn out, and it remains incomplete.[14] State-owned commercial banks emerged during the early decades of independence, whether as a result of outright nationalization of existing banks by socialist governments (as in Guinea, Mozambique, Sudan,[15] and Tanzania[16]); as a stand-alone initiative (as in Ghana, Lesotho, and Uganda); or by a process of gradual Africanization of the equity (as in most CFA countries, Kenya, and Nigeria[17]). The collapse of the BCCI and Meridien-BIAO left other governments holding ownership of their local subsidiaries. Increasing disenchantment with the performance of state-owned banks—not only the fiscal costs of meeting unanticipated loan losses but also disappointing functional performance—combined with encouragement from the donor community led most governments to seek to reduce their commercial bank shareholdings and to open the door to new entrants.

They adopted a range of privatization strategies. Transferring the state's shareholding to national social security funds or other parastatal entities was one approach, unlikely to influence governance by much. Another involved selling a minority stake to the general public in an IPO, as in Kenya and Nigeria; even this strategy is a weak form of restraint on management that is still largely appointed by the government. Other partial privatizations also included strategic stakeholders, sometimes with a management contract. In many cases, those stakeholders were the same foreign-owned banks as had been active in colonial times (or their successors), who entered or reentered as strategic investors. Thus, while their African networks are smaller than before, the Société Générale, Crédit Agricole, and BNP Paribas of France are again the main foreign players in the CFA zone, the last two being successors to Crédit Lyonnais and the BCI consortium that were active up to the 1980s.[18] In the anglophone world, Barclays, Standard Chartered, and Standard Bank of South Africa (Stanbic), with Citigroup, are again among the most prominent foreign banks. Portuguese banks have reentered the Angola and Mozambique markets.

Few African governments have stood resolutely against the wave of denationalization. As discussed in chapter 2, in only three countries are most of the banking systems in the hands of the government, whereas in 20 countries foreign shareholders control more than 60 percent of the systems. (Figure 3.4 shows that Africa has gone even further than the rest of the developing world in reducing reliance on government-owned banks and relying on foreign ownership.) Even Ethiopia has permitted the emergence of private—though not foreign-owned—banks. Yet all have displayed a reluctance to cede government ownership and control altogether. In part this unwillingness has been driven by a concern that privatization of large commercial banks that provided essential financial services across the country, including in relatively remote parts, would be followed by closure of the less active and unprofitable branches. The political consequences of extensive layoffs of excess staff members have also been a concern. Broader concerns include the long-term commitment of private owners[19] and their likely responsiveness to matters of national importance. Finally, it is clear that retaining a majority stake of the biggest bank in national hands, even if that stake is diffused among many holders, sometimes remains a political goal for broader ideological reasons.[20]

Scale
The influence of ownership structure depends on the strategies and capacities of the resulting bank management. The goal of cross-border African bank management is to do profitable banking, as distinct from mainly financing existing economic groups in the home country. By sharing certain functions, such banks can also achieve economies of scale, even though for the present groups such as Bank of Africa and Ecobank remain quite small, with little more than US$2 billion in total assets (though the FirstBank-Ecobank combination would have total assets of US$6 billion). Of course, these attributes can be attained by national banks, especially in the larger markets such as those of Nigeria as well as those of Kenya and Tanzania, Cameroon, and (in quieter times) Angola and Côte d'Ivoire.

Achieving scale was also a goal of the Nigerian authorities' decision to impose an exceptionally high minimum capital for banks of ₦25 billion—almost US$200 million. This decision has led to a very dramatic consolidation in the Nigerian banking market, as banks moved to merge and also to

FIGURE 3.4
Patterns of Bank Ownership: Africa and the Rest of the World

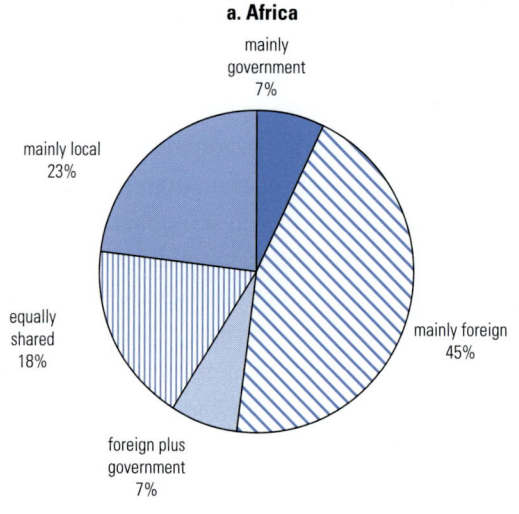

a. Africa

- mainly government 7%
- mainly foreign 45%
- foreign plus government 7%
- equally shared 18%
- mainly local 23%

b. Rest of developing world

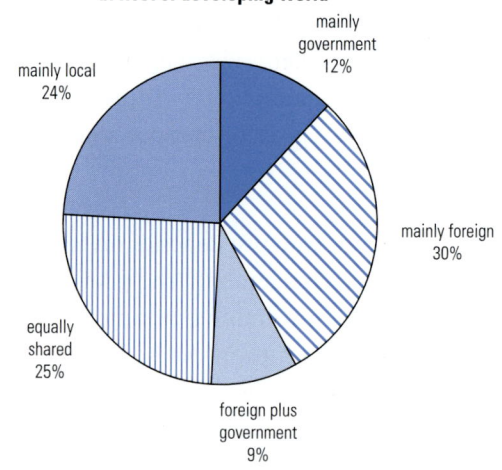

- mainly government 12%
- mainly foreign 30%
- foreign plus government 9%
- equally shared 25%
- mainly local 24%

Source: Authors' estimates based on table 2.3 and the World Bank Regulation and Supervision Survey.

Note: Mainly government controlled, mainly foreign, and *mainly local* mean that more than 60 percent of total assets are held by banks majority owned by the government or majority owned by foreign or local shareholders. *Foreign plus government* means these two categories together hold more than 70 percent. *Equally shared* is a residual category.

raise new capital ahead of the end-2005 deadline. The number of banks—which had expanded substantially in the years of multiple exchange rates to take advantage of special profit opportunities that the regime offered—has shrunk from 89 to 25. An additional side benefit may have been that the shake-up of ownership structures may have led to a realignment of existing centers of economic and financial power in Nigeria, potentially leading banks to focus more on seeking banking profitability than on serving long-established clients and thereby opening the door to hitherto underserved businesses. It is too soon to evaluate the success of the Nigerian experiment: Could it have limited entry unduly? Might the expansion of bank capital lead to a surge of unsound lending? But what is certain is that the future course of banking has been altered, not only in Nigeria but in West Africa as a whole.

Scale is what the large international banks have in plenty, and it should be a dimension from which host countries may benefit with lower costs, if competitive conditions are favorable. Each national subsidiary can draw on an enviable range of head-office services and on financial resources as needed. (Indeed, subsidiaries of the larger international banks increasingly outsource much of what can be automated to their global operations.) But their business models and goals often differ from those of domestic owners. It is clear that banks such as the African subsidiaries of BNP Paribas and Standard Chartered focus especially on serving larger, internationally trading companies and wealthy individuals. They also have important foreign clients trading with Africa. It would take a substantial change in their strategy before they chose to focus, for example, on small and medium-scale enterprises (SMEs).

Client focus
The international evidence suggests that foreign bank entry will not leave SMEs unprovided for; even if the foreign banks do not cater to this segment of firms, the intensified competition for large clients will induce local banks to move downscale (box 3.5). This result is important, because it could be a serious matter if all foreign banks focused mainly on large clients. After all, in some African countries (such as Mozambique and Madagascar) foreign shareholders control almost all commercial banking. But the indications are that the business models and practices of international banks active in Africa vary. Certainly Stanbic and Absa assert that their focus now extends to the full range of banking services and a wide clientele, and their behavior appears to bear this out. Possibly these South African banks see greater commonality between their home market and other parts of Africa. New initiatives in South Africa to reach a lower-income clientele (for example, with the new Mzansi deposit product, dis-

BOX 3.5

Foreign Banks and SME Lending: Evidence from Cross-Country Studies

Foreign bank entry is a controversial issue everywhere. On the one hand, foreign banks are supposed to bring fresh resources, new technologies, and more efficient techniques and new skills to their host banking markets and to induce competitive pressure into the banking systems of their host markets. On the other hand, a larger presence of foreign banks might reduce access to credit, especially for SMEs, because these firms rely more on relationship lending. Furthermore, foreign banks might have less loyalty to their host countries and might withdraw in times of crises or even because of shocks in third countries and in response to global portfolio shifts. Cross-country evidence has confirmed that foreign-owned banks are more efficient than domestic banks in developing countries and that foreign bank entry does, indeed, exert competitive pressure on domestic banks to become more efficient (Claessens, Demirgüç-Kunt, and Huizinga 2001).

The empirical evidence on the effect of foreign bank entry on access to credit has been at worst mixed, if not in fact favorable. On the one hand, borrowers in countries with higher foreign bank presence report lower financing obstacles and are more likely to have access to bank credit (Clarke, Cull, and Martínez Pería 2001). Foreign bank entry helps reduce related lending and its negative effects on resource allocation (Bonin and Imai 2005; Giannetti and Ongena 2005). On the other hand, research on specific developing countries has shown that foreign-owned banks are less likely to lend to more opaque borrowers and rely more on hard rather than soft information (Mian 2006). Also, the short-term benefits of foreign bank presence are not evident in cross-country econometric studies confined to low-income countries—some studies even report negative effects (Detragiache, Gupta, and Tressel 2005).

Although some evidence suggests that foreign banks might have the potential to transmit shocks from their home countries to their host countries, their lending generally does not decline during financial crises in their host countries (Dages, Goldberg, and Kinney 2000; but see Peek and Rosengren 2001). The withdrawal of some foreign banks from Argentina following the crisis of 2001 might be cited as a contrary case, but there it was the arbitrary and uneven government treatment of assets and liabilities denominated in foreign currency that drove the banks out.

cussed further in chapter 4) have also strengthened these banks' understanding of and capacity to serve middle-market customers in the sparsely populated African environment.

It is hard to be definitive about which ownership structures will work best. Although it is comforting to see clear evidence of changed attitudes from the narrow focus all banks had in colonial times (not least in the more extensive use of senior management staff from the region), it would be naive to think that the return of foreign banks is a panacea for African business. Nevertheless, careful analysis of available quantitative evidence suggests that some concerns about privatization and about sales of key banks to foreign owners have been misplaced or at least exaggerated. Even in Nigeria, where the government divested itself of substantial, albeit mostly minority, stakes in some 14 banks in the early 1990s—mainly through public share offerings to Nigerians (a method that has not been very effective in other countries), profitability was turned around fairly quickly. Beck, Cull, and Jerome (2005) find that, although the government appears to have selected the weakest of its banks for privatization through the public sale of shares, the profitability of these banks—which together accounted for half of the system—reached the levels of private banks and did so without shifting the privatized banks' portfolios into government bonds (even though banks that held bonds in those years found them to be more profitable than lending).

The more recent case of Stanbic's purchase of the Uganda Commercial Bank (UCB) shows even more promising features, according to a new study by Clarke, Cull, and Fuchs (2006). Not only has Stanbic, which integrated the former state monopoly bank into its own Ugandan operation, achieved profitability (greatly assisted by the comprehensive recapitalization of the UCB by the government before sale), but more remarkably, only one branch has been closed, and several previously unprofitable branches have been returned to profitability. Furthermore, whereas Stanbic's lending to agriculture was hitherto below even the average for foreign-owned banks (as was UCB's in recent years), post-merger data suggest that the combined operation may have already expanded agricultural lending to a level that, albeit modest, is comparable to that of other foreign-owned banks. There are other positive signs: an SME business development unit was established, and minimum deposit requirements have been drastically lowered. Still, it is too soon to pass definitive judgment on this case.

To be sure, international banks are not in the business for charity. Indeed, examination of the accounts of multinational banks in Sub-Saharan Africa shows that they have much higher returns on assets and equity than do subsidiaries of the same banks in non-African developing countries. This finding can, in part, reflect a risk premium for Africa. But multinational banks in Africa also tend to be more profitable than locally owned banks. Some of this profitability reflects not only superior products, organization, and cost control, but also the benefits of market power. Most administrative controls designed to curb the exercise of market power in banking tend to have a more damaging effect of limiting access than a beneficial one of restraining excessive profits.[21] The only viable solution to overcharging is to ensure a policy environment that not only permits entry[22] but also creates the conditions under which competitors will wish to enter the market to exploit the dynamic profit possibilities of market growth.

Ensuring a competitive environment will remain a challenge, however, especially as the trend toward banking consolidation continues worldwide. In Mozambique, the dominating position of the largest bank is due to the merger of the parents of the two largest banks in their home market of Portugal. And the acquisition by Barclays of Absa, owners of the Tanzanian market leader National Bank of Commerce, has increased bank concentration in that country. It remains to be seen how the exit of Belgolaise will play out, as its regional subsidiaries are absorbed by other owners. However, bearing in mind how small and fragmented the African markets appear to the major international groups, it may well be that future dynamism in competition will come more from African-owned banks expanding across the continent—and not only from Nigeria and South Africa.[23,24]

Populist politics often mobilizes support around hostility to foreign banks, and this hostility can create challenges for political leaders who wish to bring the benefits of foreign bank entry to their countries. The banks also do well to use antennae receptive to political sensitivities. The politics of foreign bank entry in Africa is too little understood, as indeed are other political economy aspects of financial sector reform in Africa. For instance, it may well be that a predominantly locally owned banking system (as in Nigeria) could generate a stronger political constituency for wider governance reform, though there is not enough evidence to support this conjecture.

State-Owned DFIs

An earlier generation of policy makers reached naturally to the creation of state-controlled specialized intermediaries to help channel investable resources into development projects. Some DFIs date back to colonial times, and the rationale for their existence has been the perceived market failures in long-term, agricultural, and small-scale finance. Private institutions see these sectors as costly to service and as offering inadequate returns given the risks. The results of state-owned DFI creation were disappointing, and not only in Africa. Although the crisis of the 1980s brought to light deficiencies in all segments of the financial system, these problems were even more pronounced in the state-owned DFI sector. In addition, funding dried up as international donors had second thoughts about the efficiency and sustainability of many DFIs in channeling funds. State-owned DFIs generally did poorly in reaching the ostensible target market, failed to recover loans, and overall imposed heavy fiscal costs. Part of the problem was political interference, part was poor alignment of incentives, and part was excessive intermediary cost structures. Many have been closed; most were downsized.

But state-owned DFIs—even poorly performing ones—have proved to be tenacious survivors. By no means have they all vanished from the scene. Indeed, more than 60 DFIs operate in Africa today. But in many countries, from Tanzania to Zambia to Mali, state-owned specialized banks have remained in a semifrozen situation, largely illiquid and delivering few services, with their solvency precarious and conditional on support from the government.

Why is it that governments have chosen to continue a half-century-long liaison with DFIs? Partly it is because the perceived gaps in the market, whether for housing finance, industrial development finance, or agricultural finance, are still evident. The authorities' reluctance to take decisive steps to sell or rehabilitate these institutions partly reflects the tension between (a) a continued perception that something needs to be done about the market gaps and (b) the fact that putting banks back onto sound financial footing will entail committing fiscal funds that cannot easily be diverted from other uses. That is why many of these entities remain in a state of suspended animation.

Given that this is clearly an unsatisfactory compromise, which way should governments jump: back into the DFI model but with improvements, or somewhere else? For many years now, the World Bank has been generally discouraging on the matter of state-owned DFIs, a fact that puzzles many given that the World Bank itself can be seen as a state-owned DFI, albeit at a global level, and given the sponsorship by rich country governments of regional and subregional development banks.

In fact, the state-owned DFI model sits most uneasily with contemporary understandings of how market-based financial systems work most effectively. This is essentially because—being conceptualized from a planning perspective—the state-owned DFI model blurs crucial differences: between a loan and a grant, between social and private return, and between the promoters' projections and realistic evaluations. It is one thing to embark on a publicly funded development scheme with full awareness and accounting of the risks and uncertainties involved and with politicians taking responsibility for the outlay of public money. Such an approach fits well in a public finance planning perspective. But a financial institution is established with the intention and expectation that it will be a sustainable and self-financing revolving fund. Adding a mandate to make long-term loans with defined social objectives results in a confusion of roles—and a deferral of evaluation that makes it inherently unlikely that both the financial and social returns will be acceptable. The long terms of the investments and the absence of a secondary market for assessing their evolving value makes manager accountability problematic. Even if doubts about the financial soundness of the investment emerge, it is all too easy for state-owned DFI management to hide behind the smokescreen of social justification. By the time failure becomes evident, those responsible have long since moved on. Thus are the conditions for elite capture created.

Those with experience of state-owned DFIs in Africa or in other regions know that this view is not purely theoretical. One case—Nigeria—is explored in box 3.6. Unfortunately, Nigeria is no exception. The Nigerian snapshot in 2000 could be replicated for numerous countries across the continent. Because these stories are not widely understood or because failures have been wrongly attributed to bad luck, public-spirited people still propose the establishment, rehabilitation, or recapitalization of development banks across Africa. In Nigeria a bill to this effect was introduced in parliament early in 2006.

Proximate reasons for the failure of state-owned DFIs are manifold: exchange rate and other macroeconomic shocks; gross political interference (with pressure not only for specific loan recipients, but also for loan

BOX 3.6

One Country's Experience with State-Owned DFIs

In just one large and well-documented case, the Nigerian DFI sector was found by a Alawode and others (2000) report to present a "relatively dismal financial picture." Available data for seven Nigerian DFIs (the Nigeria Industrial Development Bank, Nigeria Bank for Commerce and Industry, NEXIM, National Economic Reconstruction Fund, Urban Development Bank, Nigeria Education Bank, and Nigerian Agricultural and Credit Bank) in 1997 and 1998 showed

- A combined annual loss of 9 percent of total assets and accumulated losses of 45 percent of total assets (equivalent in 2000 to about US$100 million, despite inflation and currency depreciation)
- Negative net worth of 25 percent of assets (even on the optimistic accounting that was used)
- An average of 78 percent of the loan portfolio not performing (for the four DFIs for which data were available)

Several of the institutions had started up in a vigorous and promising manner, but they made poor loans, charged insufficient interest spreads, incurred excessive foreign exchange risks, and never built a strong credit appraisal culture. As nonperforming loans began to spiral out of control, the availability of cash for new lending began to dry up. Even borrowers that could have repaid had a reduced incentive to do so as the prospects of new loans evaporated. Better-qualified staff left.

- By the late 1990s, the Nigeria Industrial Development Bank had stopped lending to its medium- and large-scale clients, more than half of which were losing money or being liquidated.
- Of the Nigeria Bank for Commerce and Industry's book of loans to SMEs, 98 percent had arrears of payments and essentially all the bank's cash flow was going to pay for staff expenses. Even so, management was planning a new head-office building.
- In the export-promotion bank NEXIM, 99.7 percent of its portfolio was nonperforming within six years of its establishment. Actually, much of

(Box continues on the following page.)

> **BOX 3.6 (*continued*)**
>
> its portfolio had been inherited from the Central Bank of Nigeria, which had provided funds for onlending to several banks that soon became insolvent. As with the National Economic Reconstruction Fund, an Apex institution also providing funds to banks for onlending, the weaker banks were attracted.
>
> - The Urban Development Bank, tasked with providing financing for urban development, failed to mobilize external resources and relied largely on its capital endowment to finance the limited investments it made. These investments were priced at between 2 and 4 percent below commercial rates. Difficulties in recovering discouraged the bank from making further loans or investments beyond the 10 percent of total assets that had been reached by 1997. But the Urban Development Bank retained a sizable staff and four offices, leading to administrative costs equivalent to four dollars per dollar lent.
>
> - Possibly the most disappointing case was that of the Nigeria Education Bank, which, seven years after it was established to help finance the higher education sector, had failed to make a single loan, despite employing 261 staff in 21 offices.
>
> Overall, this experience has been one not only of financial unsustainability but of social failure too: by 2000, the Nigerian DFIs had achieved neither their financial nor their development goals.

forgiveness); and inadequate staff skills, often compounded by decisions to underprice lending. But these reasons all come down to the fundamental ambivalence of the model: is the DFI's goal to make profits as a sustainable, market-driven financial intermediary, or is its goal to achieve specified social or developmental objectives?

A publicly sponsored credit guarantee agency is an idea that is increasingly discussed in development banking circles as an alternative way forward, bypassing what is now the conventional avoidance of new DFIs. Credit guarantees of one sort or another are indeed becoming widespread in the financial systems of advanced economies. They include the securitization of credits by banks and their sale in whole or part (typically with some form of credit guarantee attached) to other banks, nonbank financial institutions such as insurance companies, or other managed funds.[25]

So could this new form of financial technology provide finance for specialized or more risky sectors, where commercial banks seem reluctant to go, or for longer terms than are attractive to commercial banks? The answer to this question needs to be a nuanced one. First, it is important to recognize that many public credit guarantee schemes have embedded hidden subsidies—even Korea's scheme has been losing approximately US$1 billion a year in recent years. To the extent that the repackaging of loans puts them into forms that make them suitable to be held in nonbank portfolios, at home or abroad, then (as in the advanced economies) such schemes could have something to offer. However, it may take the development of a more active secondary market to attract really sizable investments by nonbanks. But a second driver of credit derivatives and the credit guarantee business has been regulatory arbitrage. Risks are transferred from entities such as commercial banks, which are subject to prudential regulation, to entities such as managed funds, specialized credit guarantee companies, and insurance firms, which are less tightly regulated or not regulated at all. If the ultimate holders of risk have deep pockets then this may be all right, but if the failure of the ultimate holders feeds back into the public purse through forced bailouts, then the regulatory arbitrage will prove to have been a costly evasion.

By bringing together different participants in the financial market, some recent experiments with credit guarantee schemes have discovered unexploited investment banking opportunities. The Fonds de Garantie Hypothecaire du Mali (FGHM) was established by local banking insurance and government entities with a simple basic objective: to cross-guarantee mortgage loans. Although that remains its basic business[26]—with an average loan guaranteed of US$23,000 and a total loan book guaranteed of about US$20 million—FGHM has found that its staff's investment banking expertise enables it to get involved in related investment banking-type activities, such as promoting and arranging the sale of a portfolio of mortgage loans. If these initiatives continue to be successful and can be expanded without incurring heavy contingent liabilities for FGHM, perhaps sponsoring and introducing this investment banking expertise into the market will become FGHM's most important social role and chief contribution to financial development in Mali.

But many DFIs have ended up costing the government a multiple of the capital originally injected (because government provided either explicit or implicit guarantees of the DFI's borrowings). Similarly, a guarantee scheme almost automatically triggers very sizable contingent liabilities, in excess of the amount envisaged by the initial explicit investment. The hidden contingent liabilities are far greater than parliament or the general public initially understand. As with state-owned DFIs, the ability to generate these contingent liabilities represents a large honey pot attracting rent seekers.

It is not just that state-owned DFIs failed financially; they also seem generally to have failed to achieve their development goals. Although private sector entities may not have been keen to enter the targeted sectors, they were certainly discouraged from any notion of doing so by the presence of a subsidized competitor. Worse, in many cases no attempt was made to set clear goals for these entities, measure their performance against these goals, and count the cost in a coherent way. For a government operating a DFI now, no exercise is more useful for guiding future policy than undertaking such a cost-benefit review (Yaron, Benjamin, and Charitonenko 1998). As well as informing government decisions directly, a cost-benefit review can have a political economy dynamic. Making the results of these analyses public as a matter of course would provide the basis for a public debate, which could help undermine elite capture of the DFI.

Not all state-owned DFIs have failed in their mission, but the odds of success have been too low. It seems that the DFI model has a good chance of working only if exceptionally strong governance practices and procedures can be maintained and in a responsive and well-informed political environment (box 3.7). This likely explains why more DFI success stories occur in advanced economies, where political, civic, and legal infrastructures to support governance are stronger. Rich countries with strong institutions of governance can afford to risk what is for them relatively small sums on state-owned DFIs. Those countries can absorb prospective losses and deter abuses with the credible threat of sanctions. Multinational development banks, whether at the continental level (such as the African Development Bank) or at the subregional level (such as the East African Development Bank and Development Bank of Southern Africa, or DBSA), also have the advantage of being less dependent on the politics of a single country. But for African countries whose governments are contemplating an expansion of state-owned DFIs, the gamble is unattractive. The scale of potential losses in relation to national income, the poor inherent incentive structures, and the perception that sanctions against abuse are unlikely all make the expected cost-benefit calculation unfavorable for most state-owned DFI initiatives in Africa today. Yet there are some signs of improved

BOX 3.7

Governance Arrangements for DFIs

Examination of the corporate governance practices of some of the most respected public sector financial institutions worldwide suggests a number of features that are worth trying to incorporate in any surviving DFI, so as to reduce the risk of costly failures. Overall, these features aim to establish a level playing field between DFIs and other financial intermediaries, thereby ensuring that the DFI does not gain a privileged position in some segment of the market that could be provided, perhaps more effectively, by others. In particular, all the standard governance requirements for a private company should apply also to any DFI that the government retains. These requirements relate, for example, to the role and responsibility of the board of directors and its various specialized committees (audit, risk management, remuneration) with respect to financial accounting, auditing, and transparency.

Clarity of the function of each public entity is key. There should be a clear administrative separation of responsibilities within government between the exercise of DFI ownership (somebody must be designated the owner's representative), the exercise of ownership functions for state-owned nonfinancial firms, and the setting of relevant private sector development policies. Law and transparent, publicly disseminated regulation should clearly

- Identify and delimit the social and public policy objectives of the DFI—that is, the specific elements of the state's ownership policy

- Define the respective roles, responsibilities, and authorities of the governance bodies of the DFI (owner's representative, board of directors, senior management)

- Provide guidance on how the costs associated with the provision by the DFI of social or public services are to be covered

- Specify the nature of any state obligations to recapitalize or to repay the debts of the DFI

- Provide for adequate transparency and disclosure requirements in regard to the performance of the public policy mandate

(Box continues on the following page.)

> **BOX 3.7** (*continued*)
>
> In addition to the normal financial reporting requirements applicable to any company should be a regular public report on the performance of the DFI in furthering the social and public policy objectives established for it. A performance report requires applying a clear evaluation methodology, using measurable and verifiable social and public policy outcome indicators. It also entails a clear statement of the nature and extent of any state financial assistance, including, for example, subsidies, tax concessions, or guarantees.
>
> Some African DFIs have begun to assess their governance arrangements against these or similar criteria. However, the effectiveness of such procedures depends crucially on a sufficient segment of the public being financially and economically literate, on the ability and willingness of the press to inform public opinion, and on the responsiveness of the political process. These prerequisites are not yet widely present in the region.
>
> *Source:* This text draws on unpublished notes by David Scott.

governance on the continent; perhaps in time the need for health warnings about state-owned DFIs will diminish.

Given that the private market does not function very well in these difficult sectors and yet it seems difficult to reliably overcome the governance and political interference challenges that have marred the performance of so many state-owned DFIs, what is the safest and most promising way forward in African development finance today? Can existing state-owned DFIs be rehabilitated with private ownership participation, diversified lending products, or more dependable sources of local currency? Proponents are already experimenting along these lines. For example, Johannesburg-based DBSA—which has been active in the rehabilitation of DFIs in neighboring countries—is optimistic, even though its management understands that success with these ventures depends crucially on ensuring adequate governance. In some cases, the move to private control has meant a shift toward commercial banking, as with the DFCU Group in Uganda, the Development Bank of Kenya, and, to an extent, Austral Bank in Mozambique. That shift may imply commercial survival of the intermediary but, if taken to extremes, can result in an institution that is a development bank only in name.

More generally, private banks might be willing to enter some of the difficult segments if they are not undercut. Indeed, development banking, in the sense of banking that is focused on longer-term objectives with particular attention to creating social benefit alongside profitability, could be viable for a private investor (or for external development partners, a point taken up again in chapter 4). But in addition, nonbank finance could play a larger role in filling the term- and risk-finance gaps in a sustainable manner.

One good rule of thumb seems to be that publicly financed development banking initiatives are more worth trying if the downside risks are limited. Investment banking services that arrange and broker deals without taking major positions (as in the Mali example) can fill a knowledge gap that undoubtedly exists today in most African financial markets. The limited and manageable subsidies that might be required to launch investment banking firms with such a remit could be well rewarded. This could happen if the firms successfully (a) attract foreign or local venture capital, (b) advise on the financing aspects of public-private partnership (PPP) infrastructure deals, or (c) catalyze market development and new instruments for mortgage finance and, more generally, for bringing together potential providers of long-term or risk finance, at home or abroad, and users—especially in productive sectors that have export potential in the long run.

Term Finance and Risk Finance: Beyond Commercial Banking

The preoccupation with long-term finance that has driven much of the interest in DFIs is not unique to Africa but has been seen down the decades in country after country. Of course not only long-term finance is needed; even export and other trade financing can be scarce and costly in Africa. But there does seem to be evidence that access to medium- and long-term financing enhances firms' growth prospects (Demirgüç-Kunt and Maksimovic 1999). Although we cannot point to much quantitative evidence that the long-term lending situation in Africa is particularly difficult, it is certainly true that long-term finance is far from plentiful. Indeed, in few countries do banks routinely extend loans with maturities beyond three years, even for high-quality borrowers. And, as shown by the survey data reviewed in chapter 2, to the extent that enterprises use the financial system for external financing, it is to banks that they mainly turn.

Yet many productive investment projects, especially in infrastructure, capital goods, or housing stock, are best financed with long-term funds involving maturities of 5, 10, or even 20 years. This is because, although they produce high rates of return and can service and repay significant amounts of debt in the long run, they cannot repay investments out of the cash flows generated within the short-term financing horizons offered in African markets. They require loan repayment profiles that match the long-term cash flow profiles. Of course, some borrowers, finding that lenders will not grant long-term loans, proceed on the assumption that their current borrowing facilities will be rolled over, but all too often the refinancing risks are just too high for the project to go ahead. In housing finance, most middle-class households in Africa could service and repay sufficiently large mortgages to develop adequate housing, if amortization were to be spread over a long enough horizon to reduce monthly mortgage payments to serviceable levels.

It is easy to see why long-term funds may not be as forthcoming as short-term funds. From the perspective of the provider of funds, long-term lending is riskier than short-term lending. Uncertainty and lack of information about the future loom larger. As long as contractual repayments are being met, the long-term lender forgoes the ability to take control or to influence the borrower to take corrective action if the risk of default seems to have increased.

Also, the provider's own liquidity is placed at risk.[27] A bank may recognize that most of its nominally short-term deposits are in practice highly stable, but this stability may depend on macroeconomic conditions. If there is a surge of withdrawals, African banks may not have liquid money markets on which to draw in a hurry. Thus, although the transformation of short-term deposits into longer-term loans is at the heart of conventional banking, the willingness of African banks to push this maturity transformation very far is limited, even where they are not restricted by regulation.

Access to formal risk equity financing is even scarcer. To be sure, retained earnings finance the bulk of working capital needs as well as expansion capital. They are a form of equity, but there is little recourse to public issues, and the organized equity markets are small and inactive and of interest only to a very limited number of large companies, multilaterals, and financial institutions. Private placements are largely on an ad hoc basis. To the extent that other entrepreneurs secure outside equity, it is from such informal sources as relatives, friends, or community members.

Part of the problem for equity finance is the difficulty that the outside equity holder has in monitoring the firm's performance. Perhaps the insiders have found ways to channel much of the true profit of the firm to themselves and their associates, effectively expropriating the outside equity holders of their equity. These monitoring problems are pervasive in equity finance worldwide, but they are worse where information is scarce and unreliable, as in many parts of Africa.

Yet African markets have natural providers of long-term funds and of equity funds. Some are foreign based, and we will have less to say about those. But the elements of the local financial markets have not yet performed in this dimension as they could. Institutional investors, organized securities markets, and certain specific instruments and innovations related to housing and infrastructure finance that can help so far tend to be underprovided in current African conditions. They are briefly reviewed below.

Pension Funds and Other Institutional Investors as Natural Providers of Long-Term Financing

An exception to the general rule that most providers of funds are reluctant to go long-term relates to pension and social security funds. Although such funds are not entirely free of the concerns that discourage other investors, they do have a natural affinity for long-term instruments because the maturity of their liabilities is also long term. Given a rapidly growing population and formal workforce, broad-based social security and government employee pension funds in Africa often have sizable and growing sums that need to be invested for a long term.

At the same time, there is a degree of concern about the actuarial viability of many of these funds. The doubts may relate to the parameters of the underlying schemes, with promised pensions or other benefits that are too generous to be affordable at current rates of contribution. In addition, collecting contributions is not always very effective, and even those who have a very broken contribution record may be able to claim a pension in due course—and if they can, they certainly will. Rising death rates related to AIDS also complicate evaluation of the solvency of pension funds. Depending on death benefits, an increase in early deaths of scheme members may improve or worsen the solvency of the funds; furthermore, death rates may peak in the years ahead, reversing the effect. On the asset side, past investment policies have often seen an erosion of value instead of market-related returns. Investment in low-yielding government securities, losses of real value caused by unexpected inflation, deposits frozen in insolvent commercial or development banks, and other failed investments have been all too common. The poor investment returns often reflected mandates by cash-poor governments and to that extent reflect more a divergence between a stated funding policy and an unfunded reality, not dissimilar to the pay-as-you-go schemes in some advanced economies. Sometimes they reflected other types of poor governance of the funds.

Even a scheme in actuarial deficit, though, is likely to generate substantial surpluses for the next couple of decades in most African countries. Therefore, the effective maturity of its liabilities will be long term. For the present, then, these schemes have sizable sums to invest for the long term; to the extent that these funds are not channeled into funding the government deficit (as they are in the United States and many other countries), they could be available to augment long-term investable funds in the financial market.

An increasing number of social security funds are moving from the defined-benefit model—sometimes unfunded—to a fully funded defined-contribution scheme. One of the expectations of the reformers behind these schemes is that such reform will result in more long-term savings for investment. Yet even when they are being managed at arm's length from the government's fiscal managers, too many of the investable funds of pension and social security schemes are still being placed in short-term bank deposits or short-term government papers. This can be seen, for example, in Senegal and Uganda (see table 2.3). In effect, many countries—and not just in Africa—suffer to a degree from reverse maturity transformation.

The potential for institutional investors to expand the availability of long-term funds is not being realized for various reasons. In some cases, investment restrictions imposed by prudential regulation or policy unduly restrict the scope of pension fund investment policy. Managers of large pension funds do experience pressures from those who seek an easy route to long-term financing of their projects. The challenge is to ensure that governance of these funds is adequate. In advanced financial systems, most of a pension fund's assets can be marked to market, thereby providing interim evaluations of the quality of investment decisions. That is not possible with unlisted equities in a less developed market. Perhaps that is why, when they do move away from bank deposits and government bonds, pension fund managers in many African countries tend to favor property. Property is visible and easier to value than private equity or, indeed, large loans to unlisted companies, let alone more complex instruments such as asset-backed securities. This is where organized securities markets can help anchor and benchmark investment strategies and contribute to the evaluation and maintenance of quality governance.

As well as directly investing, pension funds and others with long-term resources should be willing purchasers of packages of mortgages or mortgage-backed bonds or other long-term instruments arranged by or through intermediaries that do not themselves have long-term resources, such as commercial banks or investment banks. Indeed, the scope for the investment banking skills needed to bridge the gap between pension funds and ultimate borrowers is considerable.

Other forms of institutional and managed funds can also play an increasing role in African term and risk finance over time. The insurance sector in Africa is still small and dominated in almost all countries by nonlife business, with life insurance just beginning to develop. In addition, a number of collective investment schemes have recently been licensed throughout Africa but are not significant market players yet. A handful of foreign institutional investors have been active in African markets and should be seen in a positive light not only because of the investment funds that they import, but also because of the technology transfer that can result from their activities.[28] Experience in other parts of the world suggests that foreign direct or portfolio investors are unlikely to be the most significant contributors to macroeconomic or capital flow volatility. Instead, foreign direct investment (FDI) will be a crucial catalyst in boosting African growth on a sustained basis.[29]

Securities Markets as Catalysts of Long-Term Financing

Organized securities markets could play a key role in facilitating the flow of long-term and risk finance from institutional investors and others to productive enterprises in manufacturing, agribusiness, services, to utilities, and—indirectly—to middle-class house purchasers. But this potential has scarcely been realized to date in Africa.

Despite a considerable pickup in activity, listings, and funds raised in the past few years, it remains true (as described in chapter 2) that, the Johannesburg exchange aside, the 14 exchanges in Sub-Saharan Africa display a low level of equity trading and limited raising of new capital. Nigeria is the most active of the other markets; a flurry of issues there is connected with the increased minimum bank capital. Some of the listed companies have sourced sizable funds for expansion from equity issues, as documented, for example, in Amo Yartey (2006). Overall, though, most of the larger listings in recent years have arisen out of privatizations, tax incentives,[30] mandatory listings for banks, and what might be called vanity listings by multinational or regional firms.

The last category requires explanation. A *vanity listing* is the issue of a relatively small fraction of the equity of a local subsidiary in a context where the parent has no need for the resources that will be raised. Some vanity issuers see such listings as a publicity device, as well as a way of both signaling commitment to the host country and establishing a potential lobby group of local shareholders that may act as political insurance. Other similar listings are a historical legacy: In 2004, Guinness Ghana bought 99.6 percent of Ghana Breweries, but the latter remains a listed company. Local listings allow such firms to offer remuneration to workers in the form of stock (as, for example, with Compagnie Ivoirienne d'Electricité, 69 percent of whose shares are held by a large French utility group). One way or another, foreigners own a sizable proportion of the shares on most of the exchanges, and most of these proportions are strategic stakes. Even in Nigeria, the foreign-owned share is put at just under one-half.

These are reasonable ways for an exchange to begin life. Even vanity issues can provide useful savings vehicles for domestic institutions.[31] But so far, the lack of significant secondary trading in most shares limits the liquidity of shareholdings and means that prices on the exchange are unlikely to represent a reliable indicator of the true value of a block holding of the shares. Besides, most of the shares are effectively locked up in controlling or strategic stakes and are not available for sale.

Bond issues have until recently been few and in some exchanges have required third-party guarantees, with the result that they too do not allow the market to reveal a consensus value on the debt of the issuing company. Although some markets do list medium- and long-term government bonds, in most countries they are still not issued with sufficient regularity to a sufficiently broad investor base or with a sufficiently low perceived default risk to allow the market to establish a reliable yield curve for the national currency (that is, a set of default-free interest rates for different maturities).

In short, the paucity of securities and the lack of trading activity limit the ability of most of these markets to provide a platform for price discovery and benchmarking of other securities. Transaction volumes do not justify investment in technology by either the exchange or member brokers. Limited trading discourages listing and raising money on the exchanges. In a form of vicious circle, the limited number and small size of transactions raise, in turn, transaction costs.

It is in these dimensions that strengthening of the stock markets needs to be envisaged. It may be that too much emphasis has been placed in recent years on building costly regulatory regimes designed to ensure a high level of protection for the retail customer in the secondary market. Such regimes represent a substantial up-front investment, partly in systems and infrastructure but mostly in processes, legislation, regulation, and supervision. Although the technology costs of a basic trading platform have fallen,[32] the more substantial costs and administrative challenges of establishing an operating environment conducive for an exchange have, if anything, increased. These fixed costs make sense in a market with heavy volumes but are not so easy to justify for a start-up market. They lead to high costs, which in turn limit volumes even further. Compliance costs are also potentially high.

The success of the model of regulation that has been adopted depends on a high degree of efficiency in regulation and governance. In the absence of a dependable environment (including accounting standards, supervision, and enforcement), the investment in legislation, regulation, and processes is stranded. The regulatory and judicial regime is not, in many cases, capable of identifying and punishing offenders, and it is therefore likely that compliance is in fact low. Besides, in practice, the main actual and prospective investors in most African equities and bonds are likely to be relatively sophisticated and may not need or benefit much from such protection as the regulatory system can truly provide.

Market architecture should be chosen on the basis of local needs and capacities. It may well be that most African firms would be better served by a lighter regulatory approach, along the lines of "second boards" in advanced economies. The emphasis would be on increasing primary market issuance more than on high-frequency trading efficiency. A lighter regulatory approach, one step beyond the private equity and over-the-counter markets, can work to an extent on the basis of caveat emptor, with the sophistication of analysis resting with the investor.[33] Regulations (for filing, disclosure, and corporate governance) would, of course, exist, but they would be designed with a light touch and chosen in such a way as to be relatively easy to enforce. Some regulators, such as the UK Financial Services Authority (FSA), are already mandated to conduct a benefit-to-cost assessment of all new regulations. And even in the United States, a high-profile committee has recently reported on the need to establish more cost-effective ways of furthering the goals of good governance and transparency, especially in regard to smaller companies (U.S. Securities and Exchange Commission 2006).[34] Similar sentiments should guide African regulation also, but with even greater force.

Several African exchanges—Ghana, Nairobi, Nigeria, and Bourse Régionale des Valeurs Mobilières (BRVM) in West Africa—have multiple listing segments that differ, for example, by permitted ownership concentration and prelisting profit record. The suggestion here is that the second-board model could be the main regulatory approach for small African exchanges rather than being an add-on. Also, in contrast to several second-board markets in advanced economies, which have focused on rapid-growth or high-tech companies, the goal in Africa would be to target small and medium-size companies in general.

Doing so would offer most firms a low-cost market at home. Their offerings on such a market, albeit more lightly regulated, would still appeal to local institutional investors, who would expect a return commensurate with the risks taken. It is not that the tougher requirements are useless—indeed, tighter listing requirements and regulations can increase market liquidity and prices, as has been shown for larger markets. But they result in a compliance cost barrier that shuts out too many African firms that could benefit from outside equity.[35]

For larger companies—able and willing to genuinely establish high governance and transparency standards in order to benefit from a lower cost of capital and to reach a wider international investor clientele—listing on advanced markets such as the Johannesburg or London exchange represents a viable alternative. Mention has been made in chapter 2 of the extent to which larger South African companies have their primary listings in advanced economy exchanges such as those in London, Luxembourg, and Australia.

The migration of the larger companies to international markets is a process that has been experienced worldwide. If such companies raise lower-cost funds abroad, that could leave more funding and more home investor interest for smaller firms that are not at present served. Trading tends to concentrate in the most liquid market, so it is not surprising that the migration of listings can result in lower trading at home of the migrated companies. Indeed, where such migration has happened from previously active markets, some loss of overall liquidity has been observed (Levine and Schmukler 2006). But Africa's exchanges are at a stage from which they can only improve.

This two-tier approach—low-cost local markets for the smaller firms, access to major markets abroad for the larger firms—could be an alternative for or a complement to an expansion of the concept of a regional securities market. The prospect for regional unions of exchanges is discussed later.

Other complementary policies are needed if securities markets are to flourish. They include a stable and predictable tax environment. Furthermore, stock exchange participants will need to start thinking in terms of fostering smaller companies as their future client base by promoting business advisory services. Ultimately, the optimal strategy for developing organized securities markets in Africa will ensure that firms have better access to patient capital. It will not necessarily entail a local securities exchange whose sophistication may act as a barrier to entry for local enterprises in attracting capital.

Long-Term Finance for Housing

Although the lack of well-functioning mortgage markets is far from being the only cause of poor housing quality in Africa, better availability of long-term housing finance could greatly improve housing quality as well as provide a useful outlet for long-term funds. Housing finance can make a lumpy investment into the building, renovation, or expansion of a house more affordable by spreading the costs over time. It can also provide a suitable investment to match the long-term liabilities accumulated by pension funds and insurance companies.

Many middle-class African households have stable and secure incomes and could afford to service long-term mortgages that are sufficient to pay for good housing. Instead, the very limited availability of long-term mortgage finance leaves far too many in the unsatisfactory situation of having to improve their housing only on a "build-as-you-earn" basis, with the inefficiencies and deferrals that that entails.

As documented in chapter 2, most African financial sectors lend very little for housing. If housing finance is available, it is mostly limited to the upper classes and expatriate community. At the other end of the spectrum, as mentioned later, microfinance clients may have access to loans that can be used to improve their housing. It is in the large gap between these two segments that development of the mortgage market can help.

Numerous impediments hold back housing finance in Africa: macroeconomic instability, deficient property rights systems and markets, and lack of proper funding mechanisms. Although damaging for most financial contracts, high inflation is ruinous for the mortgage market. It tends to frontload repayments (with high nominal interest rates required to compensate for expected inflation), making the servicing charges very high in the early years. It can also erode savings and exacerbate financial uncertainty. However, inflation is not the principal barrier to mortgage market development in most African countries today. Long-term finance for housing is typically constrained both on the origination (primary) side and on the funding (secondary) side. Financial institutions are reluctant to extend long maturities to mortgagees because of the weak lending and operational framework. Furthermore, they cannot themselves access long-term financing.[36]

Primary mortgage markets are constrained by inadequate legal and institutional frameworks. Weak legal protection of secured lending and weak enforcement of collateral, incomplete land titles and registration, land transfer restrictions, insufficient credit information on retail borrowers, and lack of building standards and valuation procedures limit the ability of financial institutions to provide long-term finance for housing. In addition, deficiencies in the supply chain often make housing prices unaffordable. In particular, inefficient mechanisms for financing and delivering primary infrastructure make the costs of land development prohibitive. Furthermore, small markets with few transactions reduce the value of collateral and lending costs for banks.

Despite those impediments, lenders in several countries have entered or aggressively expanded the housing finance markets. Banks in South Africa have committed to expanding housing finance to low-income households and have started offering housing finance products targeted to that market. Donor-financed financial institutions, such as the DFCU Group in Uganda, have entered the middle-income housing market. With the aim of stabilizing funding resources, Banques Populaires in Rwanda and Nyesigiso in Mali as well as other microlenders in West Africa have introduced housing-related savings products in the French style.

Another important impediment to long-term housing finance is the lack of long-term resources. Mortgages in most countries, including European countries and the United States, are still funded chiefly through deposit resources. However, this method requires a reasonably stable deposit base and the opportunity for banks to manage liquidity using interbank and repo markets. But there has been increasing interest in employing secondary markets to fund long-term housing loans. One approach is a market in fully securitized mortgage bonds, or at least a market for mortgage-related bonds. Developing an adequate framework for selling and trading securitized mortgage packages is challenging. Given the lack of organized exchanges and the high listing costs and limited trading on such exchanges as do exist, full securitization may be difficult or at least premature in most African countries. Instead, banks and other mortgage originators are likely to achieve similar benefits with lower setup costs by issuing mortgage-related bonds, which are secured by priority claims on the mortgage portfolios on the bank's balance sheet, or similar types of securities. Pension funds and insurance companies would be the prime candidates to purchase such bonds and provide the necessary funding.

Second-tier liquidity facilities, which use proceeds from bond issues (often with partial support and risk sharing by governments or donors) to refinance primary mortgage issuers, have proven an effective alternative for providing long-term finance in many countries. These and other forms of public facility—such as take-out guarantees with adequate financial backing to support long-term funding instruments—can signal government commitment to maintaining a sustainable macroeconomic policy framework. However, if introduced too soon and without adequate governance, they risk generating a dependence of the type familiar from the experience with housing and other DFIs in the past, which conspicuously failed to meet housing finance objectives over the years.

Helping the market develop the necessary funding mechanisms is a more promising approach than previous attempts to provide housing finance directly through state-owned intermediaries. Numerous such institutions (in Cameroon, Rwanda, and Tanzania, for example) have failed both financially as well as in reaching their target clientele. Similarly, creating a funding base through a compulsory savings scheme, as in the case of the Nigerian National Housing Trust Fund, can result in below-market remuneration, nontransparent management of savers' funds, and lengthy borrower waiting lists.

Many households are too poor and lack sufficient creditworthiness to be granted long-term mortgages of sufficient size to pay for a whole house. In such cases, improved step-by-step financing remains a feasible middle course, as discussed in chapter 4. Remittances play an important role in financing housing developments in many African countries. Microlevel surveys in countries such as Ghana and Nigeria suggest that a significant share of remittance flows is channeled into housing construction. Linking remittances with functioning mortgage markets by leveraging them as equity in support of mortgage loans could play an important role in kick-starting housing finance in recipient communities. Developing payment systems and products to provide incentives to make a larger share of informally transmitted remittances available for intermediation in the formal financial system will contribute toward improving the efficiency and effectiveness of remittance finance for housing development.

Innovative Financing Instruments for Infrastructure

The domestic financial system could play a larger role in financing infrastructure, whether by investing in infrastructure-related bonds or by participating in the financing of PPPs in infrastructure.[37] Given their high capital intensity, long time to cost recovery, and relatively predictable cash flows, infrastructure projects provide a natural investment opportunity for long-term savings. By financing infrastructure, local institutional investors can help avoid reverse maturity transformation and improve the risk-return profile of their portfolios.

Local-currency financing of infrastructure may also be a better match for the flow of benefits or service charges, resulting in reduced risk for the lender and a more predictable servicing burden for the provider or user of the infrastructure. Depending on the tariff regime, lower financing costs can ultimately translate into lower user fees.

Depending on whether infrastructure provision is by a public authority, a privately owned utility, or a PPP, a range of financial instruments can be envisaged. Public funding solutions for infrastructure include infrastructure bonds. Depending on the government's general creditworthiness, these could be more attractive than conventional government bonds if backed by a dedicated source of amortization from user fees or earmarked taxes. If a privately owned utility or PPP[38] is involved, unsecured corporate bond issues and initial public share offerings by existing utilities can provide local-currency financing for their domestic costs while equally developing capital markets through new investment opportunities. In addition, securitization of existing utilities' revenues could provide an alternative source of funding in capital markets with a robust legal framework.

The contribution of domestic financial markets to infrastructure finance has been limited to date in Africa. Government and private project sponsors have brought their own financing or have borrowed from international banks. Only a few infrastructure bonds have been floated on domestic capital markets—mainly for the telecommunications sector, where investments can be recovered more quickly, prices are often not regulated, and markets have significant upside potential.

Both sides of the market will need build up relevant investment banking skills if more ambitious domestic financing solutions are to succeed. It may be realistic to begin by funding existing creditworthy utilities before attempting to finance greenfield infrastructure projects.

One problem is the lack of a long-term yield curve against which to establish a realistic price for the bonds. But even more important is the limited ability of banks and institutional investors to analyze, structure, and monitor long-term project risks. Among these risks are a variety of political and regulatory ones. In most African countries, regulatory regimes for infrastructure are incomplete, and future tariff regimes are therefore uncertain. In addition, there may be a high credit risk for projects that depend on government off-take arrangements.[39] Significant technical and commercial losses resulting from fraud, nonpayment, and the absence of metering technologies increase commercial risks. Of course, the whole point of tying the bond to the infrastructure project is to achieve an improved sharing of these risks, but this may be hard to do when the risks are difficult to evaluate.[40]

As with mortgage-related bonds, investors are more reluctant to buy long-term instruments where no liquid securities market provides them with an exit in case they need liquidity. This situation has led to suggestions that a public liquidity facility might be set up to provide a refinancing option with an interest rate cap, mitigating long-term refinancing risk. The facility could also be used for bank loans after an agreed maturity and could equally provide take-out financing for private equity investors after their initial investment horizon. However, such arrangements entail sizable contingent risks for the public authorities and require careful structuring in order to preserve a reasonable balance of risks and to protect the public interest. The application of investment banking and public finance economic evaluation skills in devising and evaluating all such initiatives is crucial if the public interest is to be well served.

Macroeconomic Aspects: Building Confidence and Absorptive Capacity

The ability of national financial systems to function effectively is strongly conditioned by macroeconomic conditions at home and by fiscal pressures on financial markets. And their effectiveness is, or can be, influenced by the wider regional environment, especially where intergovernmental regional cooperation is in place.

Macroeconomic Benefits and Barriers

If current efforts to strengthen the lending ability of domestic financial systems are successful, the incidence of chronic excess banking liquidity will diminish. Furthermore, deeper and more efficient systems will then be able to help economies absorb what could be a growing flow of investable resources from the doubling of aid that has been promised—together with a return onshore of savings now placed offshore—without succumbing to Dutch disease.[41] Instead of simply routing the additional resources that they mobilize into foreign placements or government securities, banks will find it advantageous to onlend them prudently to borrowers whose investment opportunities will spin off wide-ranging benefits to the economy at large. The resulting increase in productive capital will help ensure that the inflows do not create inflationary pressures and that their expansionary effect does not have to be choked off through excessive increases in policy interest rates. The growth effect of such inflows will then be much more lasting.

Indeed, if the effectiveness of financial systems in intermediating funds increases as it should, the relatively low domestic savings rates in Africa and the placement of such large funds both offshore and in foreign-currency deposits onshore will become an increasing constraint (Aryeetey and Udry 2000). After all, most African countries already rely heavily on foreign savings to augment a meager domestic savings rate. The savings ratio (gross domestic savings as a percentage of GDP) for the median African economy has averaged only 8 percent for the past decade, without much sign of an increase. Indeed, in aggregate, foreign transfers and borrowing (mostly aid but also recently including private capital inflows) have financed as much of gross domestic investment as have domestic savings (figure 3.5). In contrast, for low- and middle-income countries across the world as a whole, domestic savings have exceeded domestic investment in every year for the past three decades.

Stabilizing Wholesale Financial Markets

Broad confidence issues permeate all discussion of how to stabilize the performance of wholesale financial markets in Africa. Africans' relatively large external holdings of bank deposits can partly be traced to confidence factors.[42] High yields paid on government bonds denominated in local cur-

FIGURE 3.5
African Countries: Saving and Investment as a Percentage of GDP

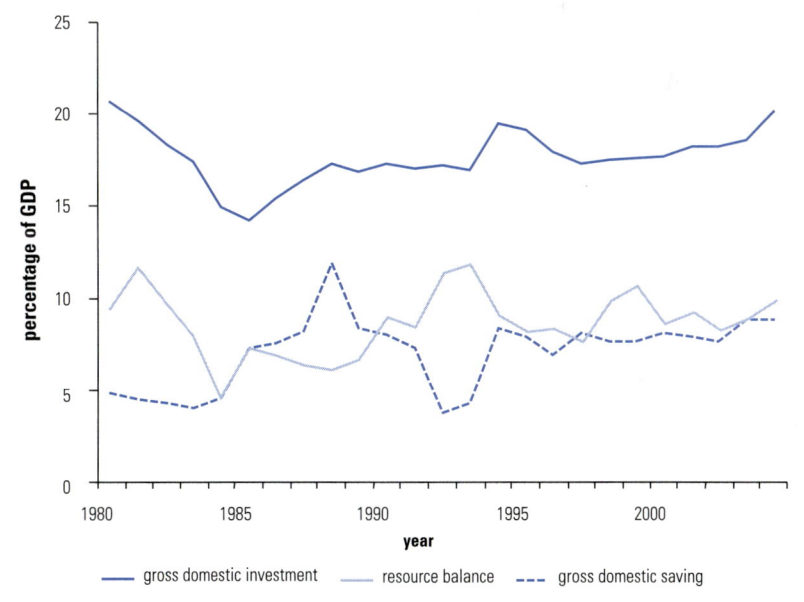

Source: World Bank's World Development Indicators database.

Note: The figure shows the median of African countries. *Resource balance* is the difference between investment and saving.

rency also reflect the fear that repayment difficulties will result in delays, special taxes, or sudden devaluation, as does the growth in the dollarization of bank deposits (see box 3.1).

The perceived systemic risk in African countries is high. It is not only a question of the natural hazards (discussed in chapter 2). Instead, political risk seems to dominate. As just one example of current external perceptions, African countries score an average of 4.5 on a political risk rating scale of 0 to 7 produced by the Belgian export credit agency. This score contrasts with an average of 2.4 for the rest of the world.[43]

The most important lines of solution to these difficulties lie in dimensions that go beyond the scope of this report, covering not only fiscal management but more broadly the functioning of political and social institutions of governance. Nevertheless, a number of relevant elements lie within the scope of financial sector policy. It is appropriate to mention two briefly: management of the domestic government debt and financial policy responses to aid fluctuations.

Management of government debt

Quite apart from its direct impact on government indebtedness, the cost of capital, and vulnerability to shifts in confidence, excessive reliance on domestic government borrowing has a corrosive effect on incentives for banks. It becomes too easy for them to make short-term profits without having to exercise their credit appraisal skills. Thus, such reliance hampers the flow of funds to productive uses. It can also leave banks vulnerable later when rates come down again, resulting in a boom-and-bust cycle. But a coherently planned, moderate, and managed program of government borrowing through the issue of bonds in a transparent market can help build infrastructure that can support private bond issues also.

Investors in African financial markets are typically considered risk averse—a phenomenon long observed (see Austen 1987). Lacking trust in the sustainability of macroeconomic reforms, market participants maintain conservative risk practices. Building confidence in the stabilization of fiscal and macroeconomic policies is a key challenge for reform-oriented policy makers. This learning process benefits from transparent and predictable monetary policy frameworks and clear rules and procedures. Communication of monetary policy targets, provision of reliable market information, and coordination between key government agencies such as the debt management office, central bank, and budget office are crucial steps in preventing unnecessary market shocks and surprises that hinder investor confidence.

Especially in the initial phases, while confidence is still being built, variable rather than fixed interest rates are more likely to appeal to investors in longer-term financing instruments. Long-term infrastructure bonds, discussed previously, can be a very useful means of lengthening maturities.

With confidence increasing, the government debt manager can standardize the bonds that are being traded in the market and concentrate on a few key maturities, establishing a stable and representative yield for the highest-quality bonds at these maturities. This yield can then serve as a reference rate not only for the issuance of private bonds, but also for all sorts of present and future value calculations that are made in the economy. This is what is meant by establishing a yield curve.

In some environments, inflation-indexed instruments could offer attractive protection for pension funds and other long-term investors. Inflation-indexed instruments are most useful where borrower cash flows or security provide a natural inflation hedge like real estate, capital investments in the retail sector, or infrastructure products with strong local cash flows.

Surges in aid and other external flows

The promised doubling of overall aid to Africa will present absorption challenges that can be tackled successfully only if the structural strengthening of domestic financial systems is achieved. Furthermore, the flows are unlikely to increase in a smooth manner. Aid has already been a quite volatile element in the balance of payments of African countries. There have been surges in aid flows, often associated with a change of government or policy orientation or with a postconflict situation. Inflow surges in individual countries are likely to become more common with the increased overall flow of aid. These surges can create challenges for aggregate credit policy.

Aid is not the only source of inflow volatility. Export quantities and prices have also caused booms and busts in the past, often poorly managed. The latest of these is now benefiting petroleum-producing African countries. Private capital flows can also be volatile—as seen in particular episodes affecting Kenya and South Africa, for example. Most of Africa has not experienced such episodes, though, reflecting the minor importance of inward portfolio investment stocks.

There is no mechanical rulebook for quantifying the optimal response by the fiscal and especially the monetary authorities to surges in inflows. But the problem is not as mysterious as it is sometimes made out to be. The first question for the monetary authorities can be boiled down to asking whether the surge is likely to be associated with an increase in the demand for real money balances. If it is, this increased demand should not be choked off by aggressive policy. If it is not, then the relaxed monetary conditions that will result from an accommodating approach will likely result in some combination of inflation, currency depreciation, and current account payments deficit. Mechanical adherence to fixed quantitative targets for the monetary and credit aggregates is not an adequate response. More promising is an "inflation-targeting lite" approach, in which active feedback from market developments allows the shifting demand for money function to be accommodated, thereby ensuring avoidance of mistakes on either side. This approach should ensure, on the one hand, that the flows are not oversterilized by interest rates being pushed up, thereby hampering the output and development response, and, on the other hand, that temporary surges are not allowed to splash into unsustainable spending patterns (box 3.8).

Regional Collaboration

We have already mentioned the potential for regional collaboration in banking and insurance supervision and in securities market trading and governance. Other possible areas of collaboration include accounting and auditing, credit information, payments systems, and—of course—a common currency. Initiatives have been taken in all of these areas and more. Some have been up and running for decades, especially in the CFA zone. Three key questions must be asked about each new initiative in this area: Will it reduce transactions costs? Will it increase effectiveness and enhance confidence by effectively increasing the independence of the regional institution from national political pressures? What countries should be included? These questions await definitive answers, but several considerations need to be kept in mind:

- First, some forms of financial service can cross borders without the need for an elaborate supranational or multinational regulatory structure to govern them. The proliferation of cross-border banks in Africa illustrates how market firms may be prepared to negotiate the costs of work-

BOX 3.8

Surges in External Inflows and Implications for Financial Stability

Sudden changes in the level of aid flows or other external flows (such as payment surpluses now being generated for oil-producing countries by the exceptional levels of oil prices) present issues of macroeconomic and monetary management and demand improvements in intermediation capacity.

To the extent that aid flows and oil money are directly spent on imports without adding to domestic demand, no evident macroeconomic consequences may occur. But more generally, if aid money implies an increase in domestic spending, a sustained increase in such flows implies that the rest of the economic system will adjust—in particular, key variables including real interest rates, income, and exchange rates. Literature on the subject is extensive: the issue arises even in a model as simple as that of Mundell and Fleming, as well as in models of the Dutch disease; for a recent analysis applied to low-income countries, see O'Connell and others (2006). Nonetheless, it is not sufficiently widely recognized that these adjustments need to be taken into account in adapting monetary policy to the new equilibrium.

The equilibrium adjustments of real interest rates and real income (increases) and the real exchange rate (appreciation) that will be needed to clear domestic goods, money, and foreign exchange markets in response to a sustained surge in inflows could be sizable. Their size will depend in particular on the marginal propensity to import out of increased income, the price elasticity of imports, and the interest sensitivity of money demand. If either or both of the first two are high—which is likely in many African countries, though precise and reliable estimates are not generally available—the equilibrium changes will be small. Nevertheless, they will have an effect on the demand for real money balances.

From the point of view of monetary and credit policy, clearly the goal should be to accomplish the adjustment without any impact on inflation. Doing so implies, for example, that the planned growth path of nominal monetary aggregates—including the target for reserve money—should be compatible with the preexisting intended path of prices and the new equilibrium money demand.

(Box continues on the following page.)

> **BOX 3.8** (*continued*)
>
> In practice, none of these magnitudes will be known with precision. Nevertheless, an intended (target) path for reserve money, corresponding to the planned inflation rate, and an expected path of interest rate and exchange rate should be calculated in accordance with the best information available. Then, as events unfold, the deviations of actual from expected can be fed back into the model underlying the original forecasts in order to revise the parameters. Higher inflation or a lower-than-expected interest or exchange rate appreciation would signal the need to tighten the reserve money target, and so on. The monetary targets thus need constant attention in case the demand for money and other relevant relationships should prove to be different than what was expected. Mohanty and Turner (2006) and IMF (2006) discuss these issues in the current African context further.

ing in multiple jurisdictions in order to expand their operations into a wider market. These developments may add to the complexity of the supervisor's job, but the point is that they can happen without being pushed by a cooperative international effort by public authorities.

- Second, even when considered together, the economies and financial systems of most groups of African countries are still small. To achieve a deep and efficient financial system, African countries really need to think of integrating more into the global financial system—not just with their neighboring countries. Cooperation among African regulators and financial trade with neighboring countries can be very valuable, and an understanding of regional conditions means that such dealings are the most natural places to start. But they do not fully solve the problems of small scale.

- Third, it could be a mistake to transplant in an unthinking manner ideas that work in the European Union (EU). The smooth functioning of governance and judicial infrastructures that underpin the operations of the EU cannot at present be ensured in all African regions. Furthermore, the delicate balance of power between large and small nations that has been maintained over the years in the EU may be difficult to replicate in several of the African groups. The economic dominance of South Africa in any African group of which it is a member and of Nigeria in the Economic Community of West African States (ECOWAS), for example, presents difficult challenges to effective cooperation given the other countries' fear that they could be swamped by the largest member of a group they join.

Lack of progress in previous initiatives has made many African policy makers somewhat skeptical about new ideas in this sphere. Doubts can best be overcome by selectivity and prioritization in considering new initiatives, placing the emphasis on efforts that both offer the prospect of sizable concrete gains and are politically and organizationally feasible.

Currency unions

Currency unions have been placed firmly on the political agenda. If we include the Common Monetary Area (CMA) arrangement linking the currencies of Lesotho, Namibia, South Africa, and Swaziland along with the two unions of the CFA zone, Africa has three working examples—the survivors of a more numerous set of colonial era relationships. This book is not the place for a full discussion of the common-currency issue. Despite political commitment to single-currency programs (undoubtedly inspired by the European Monetary Union project), most practitioners do not expect further single currencies to become a reality in any short timescale—especially given the diversity of national macroeconomic policy conditions and the inability of most African governments to provide a fully credible commitment to a single currency.[44]

Regulation and supervision

A regional approach seems to offers the most plausible scenario for gains in the area of intermediary regulation and supervision. Given the limited skill base that exists or can be afforded in these highly specialized areas, there must be significant potential benefits from pooling these skills for a multicountry region so that they can be deployed quickly in a crisis to where they are most needed. A multicountry approach also offers some additional political distance or independence. The experiences of the two regional banking commissions and the single regional insurance commission (covering all 13 states) in the CFA franc zone seem to bear this out, at least to some extent. The full potential is not realized even here, given the degree to which some powers related to licensing and sanctions remain at the national level. The Southern African Development Community (SADC) and the Common Market for Eastern and Southern Africa (COMESA) have also taken steps toward harmonizing banking regulation and supervision, but these initiatives have not yet progressed very far. There is also the Eastern and Southern Africa Anti Money Laundering Group (ESAAMLG).

If a regional regulatory approach were extended to allow cross-border banking on the "single passport" principle adopted by the EU, it could enhance bank competition for small member states within the regulatory region. Banks could provide services across borders without incurring all the costs of separate incorporation in each jurisdiction. A single passport is in effect in both CFA zones, but it is not automatic either in theory or in practice. However, the barriers to entry do not seem to discriminate in practice between CFA and non-CFA applicants, thereby avoiding the danger that a regional approach could raise barriers to entry from solid international banks. SADC, in particular, needs to be alert to this danger, considering the importance of South African banks in many SADC countries already and the risk that they could form a lobby to resist the entry of international banks from outside SADC (Jansen and Vennes 2006). Similar arguments may apply even more to capital market regulation, especially since few African countries have or could have capital markets sufficiently large to fully justify the irreducible fixed cost of setting up a regulatory body that complies fully with international standards.

There is the countervailing danger that despite joining a regional association, members will forgo the potential cost savings by insisting on duplication of office facilities in each country (as seems to have happened, to a degree, in the CFA zone). Indeed, there can be diseconomies of regional cooperation also, if there is a multiplication of international representative meetings between the members. The opportunity for achieving operational and functional independence from national governments may also be missed, depending on the appointments and tenure procedures that are adopted.

A degree of harmonization of the legal framework for banking regulation would seem to be a prerequisite for a joint approach to banking supervision. It has also been suggested that such harmonization (for example, of minimum-percentage risk capital requirements) would be required to ensure a competitive, level playing field for foreign-owned and international banks, though this proposition is not so evident.

Securities markets
Recent technological advances have made it easier to link the operations of securities markets. It might be that by forming multicountry regional mar-

kets, existing exchanges could expand their volume of business and the number of market participants. The theoretical attractions are clear: larger markets are more likely to gain from the vertical and horizontal integration of services and products. Regional securities markets could provide larger economies of scale and increase firms' access to debt and equity. From an investor's perspective, regionalization would theoretically offer opportunities to diversify risk by allowing investment in a wider range of instruments and debt and equity issuers. The development of larger markets would encourage the entry of emerging market funds, which provide access to a global pool of savings for equity issuers. A variety of overlapping initiatives, all of which generally promote greater integration of stock exchanges in Africa, are under discussion (see Irving 2005; for East Africa, see Alawode and others 2002).

There is no doubt that cross-border cooperation and technology transfer can be helpful, especially if they help contain operating and regulatory costs. However, the inescapable fixed costs of establishing a simple, small trading platform are no longer very high. And cross-listing (rather than integration) can allow issuers to access a wider pool of investors. Therefore, the main operating advantage of integrating the functioning of securities markets is to improve liquidity on an hour-to-hour and day-to-day basis. But it is not clear how much would be gained in absolute terms even by pooling all the smaller African securities markets: the result would still be a small and illiquid market. Exchange controls operating between participating countries would eliminate most of the short-term liquidity advantage. (Also, bonds quoted in different national currencies might not attract much cross-border investment.)

Indeed, any proposals for regional securities exchanges must deal effectively with exchange control and other restrictions on cross-border investments in the securities. This point may seem obvious, but such restrictions are often imposed for policy and political reasons that will trump the objectives of securities market integration, and their resolution must be a prerequisite. If the time is not ripe for a general liberalization, limited forms of liberalization—allowing, for example, long-term investments by approved institutional investors—can be a viable halfway measure.

The success of the Bourse Régionale des Valeurs Mobilières in Abidjan has been modest. Cross-border investment using the market has been growing, but volumes are still small. Ivorian firms still dominate the equity board,[45] and it is not clear whether the overall operating costs (of the exchange and its regulation and supervision) are lower than they would have been had Senegal, say, opted for a stand-alone exchange. In the other CFA zone (Communauté Economique et Monétaire de l'Afrique Centrale, or CEMAC), plans for a regional exchange have not received uniform acceptance.[46]

More regionalization is likely to produce gains, but they would not all require an elaborate regionally adopted solution. Indeed, the technical, legal, and administrative efforts required for governments to establish and maintain a jointly controlled and fully integrated multilateral regional exchange (even if exchange control issues were overcome) suggest that less costly step-by-step solutions should have a higher priority. Each element of potential regionalization can be considered as a module. What is the best way to achieve regional economies of scale, liquidity, and risk pooling? Outsourcing to a common service provider for some services might be more effective than insisting on building a new, jointly owned multinational provider. For instance, back-office clearing and settlement services might be efficiently provided to a number of different exchanges by a single entity, even if those exchanges remained otherwise unlinked. Hammering out common regional software and technology standards might be unnecessary when satisfactory existing standards can be taken off the shelf.

Again, the use of linked trading platforms across several countries can be envisaged even if regulation and supervision remains national. A small country could exploit the existence of a well-functioning exchange in a larger neighbor, thereby bringing the advantages of better technology to the home market at lower cost.[47] This hub-and-spoke approach is much less demanding of political and administrative coordination than the multilateral approach, and it could be seen as a potentially promising path toward wider market integration. It can be designed in such a way as to prevent the danger of medium-size companies from poorer countries getting lost among the numerous listings on the larger exchanges. However, it does nothing to restrain the dominance of a small number of exchanges, which can seem unattractive for noneconomic reasons.

Cross-market listings in different countries are another, more limited, alternative to full regionalization. Such listings are already being tried, for example, with the cross-listing of Nairobi-based East African Breweries and Kenya Airways in Dar es Salaam and on the Uganda exchange. An available alternative for larger companies seeking a wider and more liquid market is simply to cross-list on a large international exchange, whether that of Johannesburg or elsewhere. Use of this option will certainly continue to grow.

It is instructive in this context to see the extent to which consolidation of the larger European securities markets is being driven more by private than by government initiative, through mergers and takeovers between existing firms that operate exchanges and related services. There is intergovernmental action in the EU to harmonize and coordinate regulation of these markets, but with exchange controls long since removed, government action has tended to follow rather than lead market integration in this sphere.

Legal framework and accounting
A common set of commercial laws is already in place in the CFA franc zone and could perhaps be achieved in the East African Community, where the member states share the English Common Law tradition. But a comprehensive unification of business law in a wider regional grouping that covers both countries with a Civil Code tradition and those with a Common Law tradition seems a rather remote prospect. Instead, legal harmonization efforts are better directed at more limited initiatives to draft certain framework laws to govern and help facilitate other cooperative arrangements in finance. In contrast, there seems more to be gained, at low risk and low cost, in seeking collaborative arrangements for accounting and auditing. There will be some efficiencies of shared learning and possibilities for cross-border auditing. And a region that has set up a common framework for adoption of the IFRS presents no barriers to further integration in the rest of the continent.

Supplementing the specific cooperative initiatives that may be adopted in these fields, a policy of "thinking regionally, but moving first to deliver the national prerequisites" is likely to be beneficial. This thinking is already embodied in the various macroeconomic and budgetary goals that have been set in African regional groups that aim to create or preserve a common currency and an economic union. It can also guide reforms in other areas (including payments) where cross-country collaborative projects are not yet active.

Notes

1. The Democratic Republic of Congo in the early 2000s is a good example here: civil war eroded monetization, and the banks placed much of their resources abroad. Equatorial Guinea is a good illustration of the limited absorptive capacity of a banking system in the face of large inflows—in this case of oil-related receipts.

2. The trend may in part reflect required reserves, though the monetary authorities' choice of required reserves can be influenced by the actual level of the bank's desired reserves, notably if the authorities wish to limit the emergence of sizable excess reserves. Anyway, while required reserves are high in several countries, a majority of African countries do have sizable excess reserves (IMF 2006).
3. If the survey had been confined to bankers, the responses might have been more critical. Furthermore, things are not so good when it comes to overdue payments, which are reported by 84 percent of African businesses—second only to South Asia. But this finding may be best interpreted as an indication of the informality of payment practices rather than of enforcement per se.
4. It also has the second-highest overall recovery cost, if this cost is expressed as a percentage of per capita income.
5. However, the correlation between credit registry coverage (numbers covered as a share of population) and creditor rights across countries in Africa is significantly positive at +0.61, essentially because large household-level credit registries are largely confined to South Africa and its small neighbors.
6. Azam, Biais, and Dia (2004) discuss the UEMOA banking crisis of the 1980s in terms of a model in which government interference could continue to influence the incentives of international bankers after a crisis.
7. Ironically, it was the ill-fated Meridien-BIAO that became the first private bank to be licensed in Tanzania, in 1991, after a quarter-century of state-monopoly banking.
8. Interestingly, in Kenya resolution of the events of the late 1990s involved large depositors taking considerable losses in some banks, as a result of conversion of part of their deposits to equity as a condition of the bank's survival.
9. Good accounts for the anglophone countries appear in Brownbridge and Harvey (1998). They describe, for instance, the Nigerian experience: liberalization after 1986 resulted in numerous entrants seeking the privileged access to rationed foreign exchange or the opportunity to indulge in looting and insider lending. Most of a previous wave of public sector banks (owned by provincial governments) were in distress by the early 1990s. The three biggest banks, each with a venerable history, survived better. They too had accumulated sizable nonperforming loans, perhaps 40 percent of their total lending, by the mid-1990s, but they stayed afloat thanks to their high liquidity and the overall lack of competitive pressure in the market, which allowed high margins on performing business. Another useful overview of African bank failures is contained in Daumont, Le Gall, and Leroux (2004).
10. One partial success story that illustrates the problems is the abortive first privatization attempt of the Uganda Commercial Bank to a company registered in Malaysia. That company proved to be a front for persons that were deemed unsuitable by the Ugandan authorities and who proceeded to self-lend on a large scale (Clarke, Cull, and Fuchs 2006).
11. Sometimes incentive can work in the opposite direction, with the strength of the local subsidiary flattered in the accounts for tax purposes.

12. An additional threat to be considered is the impact of HIV/AIDS, which adds costs and presents a variety of default and underwriting risks where the epidemic is severe. At the same time, financial intermediaries can be well placed to measure and manage these risks. See Kalavakonda (2005) and Magill (2003).
13. This is the name under which Standard Bank of South Africa (until 1987 a subsidiary of Standard Chartered Bank) operates in several other African countries. In 2000, Stanbic acquired the African operations of ANZ Grindlays, successor to the National Bank of India (but the main Kenya operations of the National Bank of India had become Kenya Commercial Bank).
14. The World Bank's Privatization database records 39 banking privatizations in Africa between 1988 and 2003, with total proceeds coming to US$329 million. A further 50 nonbank financial sector privatizations—many in the insurance sector—for US$100 million are recorded. See Senbet and Otchere (2006) for a critical view of the postprivatization profitability performance of African banks.
15. The tone of the letter received by the director of Barclays in Khartoum suggests a very polite takeover: "According to Revolutionary Council decision dated 25th May, 1970, Banks in the Sudan have been nationalized. Barclays Bank is now called State Bank for Foreign Trade. . . . You are therefore requested to report to your office at 10 a.m. tomorrow morning . . . in order to hand over your work. . . . Board of Directors of State Bank for Foreign Trade extend their thanks to the services you rendered in this country and wish you a pleasant future" (Ackrill and Hannah 2001).
16. In Tanzania, the operations of all seven existing private banks were merged into the new National Bank of Commerce.
17. In Nigeria, it is interesting to note that foreign banks were reluctant to accede to local incorporation. Barclays insisted on removal of the international brand when its shareholding in what became Union Bank of Nigeria was reduced to 20 percent as part of government policy. Contrast this reaction with the modern concern that fly-by-night foreign bankers will use their international brand name to build business, while limiting their exposure by hiding behind local incorporation.
18. Senegal's Compagnie Bancaire de l'Afrique Occidentale has assumed the 150-year heritage of the other colonial French bank, the BAO, whose travails in the 1990s are mentioned later.
19. The recent decision by the Dutch group Fortis to dispose of the Belgolaise network indicates that such concerns are not entirely unfounded.
20. For example, a ceiling of 49 percent was placed on the stake in Tanzania's NMB (National Microfinance Bank), which was acquired in 2005 by the consortium led by Rabobank and (prospectively) on Rabobank's share in Zambia's ZNCB (Zambia National Commercial Bank), though in both cases further share sales to nationals are planned.
21. Requiring accurate publication of charges is an exception. It can be a valuable consumer protection measure, albeit one that is only moderately effective in improving competition.

22. Entry, that is, of credible institutions with adequate capital and fit and proper management. The need for new entrants cannot absolve the regulators from due diligence. And there has to be some caution about embryonic proposals in the context of the World Trade Organization to have countries bind themselves to accepting entry of a bank licensed in any jurisdiction.
23. In the past those seeking to build stable banking systems sometimes advocated formal deposit insurance. However, cross-country research strongly suggests that unintended incentive side effects of formal schemes mean that their introduction is likely to be counterproductive in countries with weak overall governance institutions (Demirgüç-Kunt and Kane 2002). Only five such schemes are fully in operation in Africa today.
24. Only a few African countries (mainly Kenya, Malawi, and Zimbabwe) have made significant commitments binding themselves under the General Agreement on Trade in Services to permit market access in financial services. Given the risk that unsound entrants from poorly regulated foreign countries may take advantage of such commitments where host country supervisory capacity is weak, this caution is probably well founded. It is solid and well-managed banks whose entry should be encouraged.
25. The somewhat ambiguous term risk mitigation is sometimes used in this context where risk shifting would be more accurate. If credit guarantee schemes shift some of the risk to parties who are able to contribute to risk assessment or for whom the assumption of risk can act as a hedge in their portfolio, then there is a real gain. But if the motivation for the transaction is to benefit from a hidden subsidy or a flaw in prudential regulation, then risk is not being mitigated in the system as a whole and may in fact be amplified.
26. Although the guarantee company does some appraisal diligence on the loans guaranteed, this business may be partly a regulatory arbitrage.
27. Long-term lending at fixed interest cannot safely be funded by short-term deposits, given the repricing risk, a risk that can be very high in periods of macroeconomic volatility. This problem can be overstated, though, inasmuch as most borrowers will accept a floating interest rate as the price of getting security of funding for a term. Banks are increasingly aware of the need to ensure that this repricing is written into the contract and that the formula is a fair and transparent one.
28. Several such funds have been active in Africa including Actis (http://www.act.is) and Equator's Africa Growth Fund (http://www.mbendi.co.za). There may be some prospect in the future for deeper international engagement in risk sharing through such mechanisms as international credit derivatives.
29. Although the spinoff benefits for the poor of some FDI, especially some mining investment, can be questioned, there is no doubt that inward FDI already has and will increasingly have a positive effect on firm productivity and national economic growth. Analysis of microlevel data on firms shows sizable productivity gains from FDI into Africa (Moss, Ramachandran, and Shah 2004). At the macro level, FDI inflows, unlike capital market integration generally, are strongly associated with African growth (Collins 2004).

30. Even if no funds are raised and if the listed shares attract little or no trading.
31. One possible example: Tanzania Breweries, the largest firm on the Dar es Salaam stock exchange, with a market capitalization of close to US$400 million and a dividend yield of more than 11 percent. Its principal shareholders, accounting for 94 percent of the total, are South African Breweries, 53 percent; East African Breweries, 20 percent; Unit Trust of Tanzania, 6 percent; Treasury Registrar, United Republic of Tanzania, 4 percent; International Finance Corporation, 4 percent; Public Service Pensions Fund, 3 percent; Umoja Fund, 2 percent; Parastatal Pensions Fund, 1 percent; and National Social Security Fund, 1 percent.
32. And, in any case, traditional nonelectronic callover trading methods, if efficiently organized—as in Dar es Salaam, for example—can be fully adequate for the volume of local trading and the small number of listings.
33. Second-board markets in advanced economies make different and, in some respects, lower demands on the issuer (lower, for example, in regard to having a track record of profitability, a minimum market capitalization, and a minimum number of shareholders; higher sometimes in regard to disclosure). Of course, the costs of going or staying public depend not only on regulations (in a narrow sense) but also on capital market architecture and industry efficiency. The experience of the AIM (Alternative Investment Market) in London(http://www.londonstockexchange.com/en-gb/products/companyservices/ourmarkets/aim_new) in seeking to minimize these costs for listing firms is instructive. The key is to adapt rules on corporate governance and disclosure in a pragmatic and appropriate manner and to remove regulations that are unenforceable in the local environment. For example, it might be useful to follow the AIM in placing the primary responsibility for much of the compliance with regulations on the "nominated adviser," the financial intermediary bringing the firm to market (Grose and Friedman 2006). With governance issues largely devolved to the nominated adviser, AIM does not require (a) any minimum number of shares to be in public hands, (b) any trading record or minimum market capitalization, or (c) any prior shareholder approval for acquisitions (except reverse takeovers). Legal theory underlying the idea of adapting financial regulation to local conditions is discussed in Pistor and Xu (2002).
34. Considering that, by smaller companies, the U.S. committee means those with a market capitalization of less than US$787 million, it is clear that these considerations are relevant for virtually all African enterprises.
35. Even minimal transparency requirements can frighten off potential listers. Moss (2003) suggests that this was one reason Ghana Telecom was not listed in the late 1990s after the sale of a strategic stake to Telekom Malaysia. Transparency to the market also implies transparency to others, including government. Moss also argues that owners of firms often have reason to be reluctant to make this commitment.
36. Akuffo (2006) provides an interesting account illustrating the difficulty of establishing mortgage finance on a scale commensurate with national housing

needs. He describes the gradual mutation of an intermediary that was originally intended as the basis of a sustainable housing finance system in Ghana, with innovative product design, into a commercial bank initiating fewer than 100 mortgages a year and keeping just 30 percent of its assets in mortgage loans.

37. Africa's experience with private participation in infrastructure is well reviewed in Nellis (2005).
38. PPPs in infrastructure trigger further financing alternatives. A well-designed PPP embodies the idea that each party should bear the risks that it is equipped to manage at least cost. For example, the private sector could bear construction, commercial, and financial risks, while the public sector bears political, regulatory, and legal risks. Demand risk is frequently shared because it is influenced both by regulatory policies and by market conditions. However, experience with PPPs in Africa has shown that the actual transfer of risks to the private party is often limited while private sector returns are high, suggesting a limited capacity of governments to negotiate such transactions effectively. If the benefit of a PPP is to exceed its cost (by comparison with public provision), attention needs to be paid in particular to avoiding large contingent liabilities through, for example, guarantees.
39. Investor confidence could be strengthened by an enhanced approach to the planning of public investment spending, including (a) a rigorous and transparent approach to macroeconomic tradeoffs between social expenditure and capital investment in infrastructure; (b) systematic economic and financial cost-benefit analysis as a basis for project selection and prioritization for investment; (c) targeting of areas that cannot be financed by the private sector; (d) institutional structures and capacity to analyze, structure, and negotiate options for private participation; and (e) a transparent and fiscally prudent approach to potential government support in PPPs, such as direct subsidies or guarantees. In addition, further progress in regulatory reforms is required to reduce regulatory risk and move toward long-term financial sustainability of infrastructure sectors.
40. There have been suggestions that, in order to boost market development, international financial institutions or other donors might (a) step in to provide complementary funding, such as project equity or subordinated debt finance, where private markets fail and (b) provide partial guarantees to the providers of infrastructure finance against, for example, regulatory risk. Once again, it requires a balancing act to ensure that such interventions actually support market development rather than create a dependency.
41. Or they could help economies absorb sharply increasing revenues from natural resources, as has recently been occurring in Angola, Chad, the Republic of Congo, Equatorial Guinea, Mozambique, and Nigeria.
42. Evidently this applies even to those external holdings that arise because of the need to hold cash collateral against import shipments.
43. Other export credit insurance agencies have broadly similar ratings. The same agency's commercial risk index, running from 0 to 2, places the average African country at 1.83, compared with 1.18 for the rest of the world.

44. There have been numerous proposals for currency unions in Africa besides those currently in operation in the CFA franc zone (Fielding 2006) and in the CMA of southern Africa. Indeed, as far back as 1963, a common currency for the whole of Africa was an objective of the Organization of African Unity, and it remains a long-term goal of the African Union. Probably the most active current proposals are for the East African Community (EAC), which consists of Kenya, Tanzania, and Uganda, with the likely future membership of Burundi and Rwanda), which aims for monetary union as early as 2010, and the West African Monetary Zone (WAMZ), which consists of Gambia, Ghana, Guinea, Nigeria, and Sierra Leone, with the future planned membership of Liberia. The EAC aims for monetary union as early as 2010, and the WAMZ now aims for monetary union by December 2009. Later, there might be a merger of the UEMOA and WAMZ currencies to achieve the longstanding objective (since 1975) of an ECOWAS monetary union. Although the institutional arrangements for a monetary union could act as an agency of restraint (Stasavage 2000), this can be undermined by fiscal pressures and, as Masson and Pattillo (2005) have argued, divergent policy interests between prospective members could make joining costly for many. The potential gains in intraunion trade are not likely to be large. The EU experience has underlined just how much can be achieved in terms of financial integration without a monetary union, while showing that a single currency can contribute to financial efficiencies (Honohan and Lane 2001).
45. Although the Bank of Africa has joined Senegal's Sonatel as a non-Ivorian equity issuer, the bond market has a wider country representation. In addition to the West African Development Bank and the governments of Burkina Faso, Côte d'Ivoire, and Senegal, bonds are listed from state-owned utilities in Benin and Senegal and from other issuers from Burkina Faso, Côte d'Ivoire, and Mali.
46. The fact of a common currency gives the BRVM bond market a huge advantage relative to other regional projects covering multicurrency country groups. Only if the bonds are denominated in the same currency can there be any question of a common yield curve.
47. The electronic links between the Namibia and Johannesburg exchanges are an illustration. Indeed, the Johannesburg stock exchange has been encouraging a wider use of its technology—though so far others have been cautious about ceding leadership to Johannesburg.

CHAPTER 4

Finance for All

Introduction: Access to Formal Financial Services

Fewer than 20 percent of African adults have an account with a formal or semiformal financial intermediary. However one may wish to measure it, finance for all is still a rather distant goal. This is as true for the savings and payment systems as it is for credit and lending. This chapter examines what steps need to be taken to increase this share—because it must increase if small and medium-scale enterprises (SMEs) and the poor are to benefit from modern financial technology.

An increased emphasis on the formal sector over the informal sector
To be sure, many more Africans have recourse to informal finance for both household and enterprise needs. It is not to diminish the importance of these networks to confine the present discussion to the formal financial sector. The existence of an extensive population of informal financial entities represents an important background for formal intermediaries. In particular, it should not be thought that microfinance institutions (MFIs) as we know them today provide a perfect substitute for the services generated by informal and traditional financial arrangements in much of Africa. However, as African economies modernize and grow, the formal financial sector will increase its relative and absolute importance in serving African households and firms (box 4.1). Access to formal financial services is an

BOX 4.1

Ignoring Informal Finance?

Africa enjoys a vibrant informal finance sector, ranging from shaky *susu* collectors in the marketplaces of Monrovia, to sizable rotating savings and credit schemes in Nairobi, which embody complex but effective incentive designs that have intrigued economic theorists, to *njangi* (tontines) in Yaoundé patronized by the upper-middle classes and processing sizable sums. The vigor of informal systems of intermediation in Africa is documented by numerous studies (Anderson and Baland 2002; Aryeetey and others 1997a, 1997b). When all types, formal and informal, are taken into consideration, perhaps 80 percent of the population has dealings with some form of financial intermediary, even if it is just a money collector or suitcase banker. In addition, as is the case worldwide, friends, relations, and business contacts provide important elements of financial support to SMEs.

Some scholars have assigned a deeper role to informal finance in African societies, discussing, for example, the distinctive role of ROSCAs in mediating interpersonal relationships—a function that has little resemblance to the performance of the formal financial system (Rowlands 1995). Udry (2000) provides some reflections on the wider role of social networks in understanding African economic activity.

That this book does not focus much on informal finance does not imply that it is unimportant or, indeed, that it will not survive the modernization process of which we speak. To be sure, the MFI revolution has, to a degree, built on the experience of these informal structures, and at the bottom end, some of the smallest licensed MFIs have little to distinguish them from informal arrangements.

At the smallest scale, formal and informal intermediaries will continue to function side by side for the foreseeable future—though the formal ones will tend to pull ahead. But the real effectiveness of formal finance lies in its ability to provide a wider range of services at a larger scale and offer a pooling of risks that cannot be attained by the informal sector.

area in which considerable progress can be envisaged in the years ahead. New technology, in terms of both financial engineering and information and communications technology (ICT), can be brought to bear on the problem. Some of the financial technologies discussed are not really new, even in Africa, but have not been applied as extensively as they could be.

Microfinance can service the financial needs of the poor—
The microfinance revolution has given MFIs the confidence to provide deposit and lending services to poor people. Different MFIs use different methodologies, and each claims special advantages for its techniques. Regardless, it is clear that, given the will and management skills, this sector can reach out to the low-income strata of the population in much of Africa—sometimes even without any subsidy, although the high interest rates that are often involved (even when far below moneylender rates) can limit borrowing to the most high-yielding uses of capital.[1] Here the challenge is to achieve scale and reach remote areas without losing management control of costs[2] and of loan appraisal quality.

—And also of SMEs
But this chapter addresses not only the needs of the very poor. With such huge swathes of the economy excluded in practice from access to financial services, attention needs to be paid to what may be described as the middle market. Small or even medium-size firms with credit needs of several thousand U.S. dollars may, given the state of many African economies, be on the margins of informality. They are not in a position to maintain proper business accounts. They are poorly catered to by banks, whose procedures presume a greater degree of formality. Farmers above the subsistence level are often in the same situation.

Good management is more important than organizational model
Who will deliver these enhanced services to these market segments? A proliferation of formal and semiformal intermediaries[3]—more than a thousand across Africa—is currently engaged in microfinance of one form or another. They vary enormously in scale, sophistication, and organizational design.

Advocates of mutuality sometimes argue that cooperatives should take the lead in delivering finance for all. This view has been implicit in the legislative framework in effect in the Union Economique et Monétaire Ouest

Africaine (UEMOA) countries of West Africa. Others argue that the economies of scale and scope of multiservice banks will ultimately give them an unbeatable cost advantage in catering to the majority. The fact that intermediaries representing a wide variety of organizational models have been successful in Africa argues against any dogmatic view either way on this point. At present, diversity and experimentation in organizational structure and business strategies seem to offer the best prospect for broader outreach. What are needed above all are improved management and cost control, as well as a greater awareness of the business opportunities by commercial financiers, who have hitherto neglected the "bottom of the pyramid."

The broader financial policy environment also needs to be conducive to the expansion of microfinance. Ensuring sufficient competition to spur intermediaries into finding ways of safely serving a wider clientele—as well as ensuring that unnecessary regulations do not prevent such efforts—is a key requirement. Among the most important regulatory issues in this context are those relating to interest ceilings. Abuses of predatory lending are better tackled through policies of transparency and codes of practice with regard to lending procedures. South Africa has been a leader in the development and enforcement of such policies. At the same time, lenders cannot be complacent about costs that prevent them from reaching a wider market through lower interest rates. In addition, the higher the interest rates are, the greater the threat of a political backlash that would impose damagingly low ceilings.

In this chapter, all of the quartet of distinctive African environmental factors—scale, informality, governance, and shocks—are in evidence. Many of the microfinance innovations that have been seen worldwide and have been applied in Africa are specifically adapted to dealing with issues of scale and informality and also have application to certain governance issues. So far as shocks are concerned, though, microeconomic or idiosyncratic risk, rather than systemic risk, is most relevant for this chapter; paradoxically, microfinance may be more robust in the face of national systemic risk than in the face of local shocks.

In all cases, the key to ensuring access for smallholders and the poor is the use of innovative financial engineering and modern technology, combined with ruthless attention to low cost. Although some of this effort can be profitable, it is likely for the foreseeable future that at least some of the necessary energy and enthusiasm will have to come from public-spirited activists whose job satisfaction comes from the social value of what they are achieving, rather than assurance that they are earning their opportunity wage in the global financial market. The modernist model alone will not be enough.

Technology and Financial Engineering

Many of the products conventionally offered by banks and even by MFIs in Africa are ill adapted to poor customers' needs. Sometimes the mismatch is painfully obvious, and the solution straightforward. Inflexible regular savings schedules are inappropriate for poor households with volatile cash flows. The same is true of overly flexible transactions accounts that allow costly overdrafts to be triggered inadvertently. Likewise, loan repayment schedules that do not take account of crop cycles are a poor match for smallholder farmers. Although many African intermediaries have developed a product mix that recognizes these problems, too many others have not. It must be stressed that, as much as one must look to novel solutions using the potential of innovative modern technology, long-established and proven financial technologies that can greatly improve financial access for poor people are often not yet in place in Africa. Correcting this situation will require training and outreach. By moving beyond what is generally established, modern technology offers some possibilities for leapfrogging some of the obstacles placed by slow-adjusting infrastructures and other African environmental challenges (Ivaturi 2006).

What kinds of innovations might work well for Africa? Evidently they need to be able to cope with some of the barriers that have been discussed; in addition, they need to have low unit costs. Innovations whose major cost relates to their initial development and other fixed costs, with very low marginal costs per transaction or per new customer engaged, offer important prospects for expanding access to financial services at the bottom of the pyramid.

Some examples already exist in Africa and elsewhere of the use of electronic or financial technologies to meet specific financial access problems. These examples show the potential and the limitations of solutions developed so far. They share some common features: the electronic accumulation, processing, and dissemination of information; the use of cell-phone and other telecommunications technology to bridge distance and isolation problems; and risk pooling through the use of observable correlates for individual risk. Each of these features is associated with relatively low marginal unit costs; however, their setup costs are often considerable.

Credit Innovations

Although many practitioners have rightly reminded us of the importance of other dimensions of financial service access, policy discussions inevitably return to credit. Improvements in the credit environment can be expected from the range of meso-level policy innovations flagged in chapter 3. Improving the stock and usability of collateral is a clear priority. Some steps in this direction, including the improvement of laws governing leasing, hire-purchase, and factoring, can achieve much even without very effective judicial performance or wider governance improvements. Building effective title registries—adapted to local conditions and local concepts of user rights (Fleisig and de la Peña 2003)—helps the process of making collateralized borrowing available. Indeed, if borrowing is collateralized by exportable commodities or if the borrower has a subsupply contract from, say, a multinational mining corporation, credit can be easy to obtain in Africa. But what if neither believable numbers nor good collateral (direct or indirect) are present? What then can the would-be lender do to help appraise creditworthiness? What else is possible, other than to use collateral?

The first subsection here looks at four techniques that seek to do answer these questions.[4] These are clearly part of the modernist agenda. The second subsection asks what is possible when reliance on an individual creditworthiness appraisal cannot be avoided, as is the case with much SME credit.

Techniques for reducing credit risk

In this subsection, we review four credit problems or financing gaps (ranging from agricultural inputs to construction of low-income housing) that have found solutions in parts of Africa. A key question here is whether the modernist agenda does it all: increasing reliance on automated credit approval systems based on verifiable information including accurate, inexpensive, and comprehensive credit registries; speedy enforcement of unbiased court judgments; and so forth. Or is there also a necessary and effective activist agenda that can help?

Experiences from African farm finance suggest that both dimensions may be necessary.[5] Take the examples of contract farming and warehouse receipts finance. Both credit technologies are as old as finance itself, and both seek to resolve issues that are of considerable practical relevance. Expanding both has been high on many agencies' agendas for strengthening farm finance in Africa for several years (Kloeppinger-Todd 2005). Contract farming fits with the modernist agenda, with its credit aspects requiring no more than the basic legal infrastructures combined with private efforts. Indeed, specific legislation may not be required, as has been seen in Uganda. By contrast, warehouse receipts financing for small farmers does not get established without active specific intervention by a sponsor—though sometimes a private bank will find it advantageous to fill that role.

Credit associated with contract farming. In regions where export commodities are farmed on a smallholder basis, underuse of fertilizers is a well-known and longstanding problem to which solutions have been sought for generations. Cash credit for fertilizers (or other inputs) for smallholders is unavailable in eastern and central Africa. But wholesalers, exporters, and processors want to secure a reliable supply of the commodities to ensure that they can operate their facilities profitably. Over the years, in most African countries, private merchants have become the dominant suppliers of fertilizer on credit, as part of a contract farming arrangement, with the credit to be repaid out of the proceeds of the harvest (which are to be sold to the creditor).[6] The benefit to the farmer is increased productivity; the potential downside is the possibly high cost of credit concealed in a low product price offered at harvest. The benefit of the arrangement for the merchant is the prospect of a good supply of product; the risk is that the smallholder might sell the crop on the side to another merchant and default on the loan.[7]

In practice, the arrangement often works well, when times are good. An International Fund for Agricultural Development study (Ruotsi 2003) found that, in the three countries studied, only the cotton supply chain in Mozambique exhibited evidence of market-power abuse by the lender. The lender had been granted a monopoly on cotton purchase in this case as a way of reducing the problem of side sales. One innovative way of limiting the risk of opportunist side sales is for the loan to be made to a cooperative of smallholders. Their collective interest in maintaining the arrangement from year to year is likely more stable than that of any one of their members, and collectively they can exploit small-group dynamics to keep members in line—though this approach has not always worked out well in practice. But reflecting further on this supply-chain credit arrangement reveals that it is rather limited in terms of the range of financial services offered to the farmer, as noted by Pearce (2003). Besides, the amounts of credit are rather small. About half a million smallholders in Kenya use such an arrangement for tea, but the average loan is only about US$30—a sum whose main value may be as a catalyst encouraging a more comprehensive shift to higher-value crops and methods of production.

Farmers seeking to take advantage of predictable seasonal price fluctuations. An alternative to the contract farming model has the farmer, or farmers' cooperative, financing inputs independently of the supply chain and selling the product directly onto the market. In this case, however, the farmer may be at the mercy of price fluctuations around the time of the harvest, unless credit is available to allow the timing of the sale to be optimized. Warehouse receipt finance—a technique that has been known for millennia but is still insufficiently used in Africa, despite numerous successful examples—can form the basis of a solution to this problem. By storing grain of verified quality in an approved independent warehouse, the farmer can offer considerably greater security to the lender.

But getting this kind of arrangement up and running for small farmers is not automatic. Because of scale issues, no group of small farmers will be able to do it on its own. Participation by large as well as small farmers will be essential to reach a viable scale. Then the warehouse operator also needs to establish creditworthiness—perhaps by being part of a warehouse network operating with peer review as a self-regulatory organization. The contract needs to be drawn up in a way that ensures that the banker really does have the semiautomatic security (grain is not released unless the loan is repaid; grain passes to ownership of the bank in case of delinquency) that the approach envisages. Experiences in Ghana and Zambia, for example, have shown how these issues—especially that of scale—have been decisive in making the difference between warehouse finance schemes that are viable and work well for small farmers and those that are not viable (Onumah 2003). Here, then, although the financial technology is very old, a degree of activism is still required by some sponsor who can generate the coordinated action that will be involved.

Two more examples, showing the effectiveness and the limitations of the modernist approach, come not from rural finance but from the cities: from the world of the salaried worker, a part of African society that is growing and will likely become much more important in the future, and from housing finance for low-income households. In one case, banks rely on the formality of their dealings with the employer to generate a surrogate for collateral; in the other case, a misguided modernist attempt to ensure housing quality backfired on what could have been a useful dimension to microcredit.

Salary loans. Low- and middle-income families with secure income often cannot capitalize their future earnings. Salary loans (another technique that has a long history but whose use has exploded in several African countries) can represent one limited but useful component of the solution to this problem. Technology is at work here too, in that electronic payroll administration makes this solution available and cost-effective for the credit provider. The bank—often one of the large international banks, which entered this market drawing on rapidly growing and profitable experience in South Africa—arranges for the loan to be repaid as a first claim on the salary check. These schemes are popular with employees and therefore with their employers. The loans can be put to multiple uses. They can help finance housing improvements and other consumer needs. In addition, it is said that they have also been used to provide seed capital for income-generating activities by other household members (with the primary borrower—the salaried member of the family—effectively acting as the guarantor of the actual beneficiary of the loan). In this way, at least some of the urban salary loans can find their way to funding small business income-generating investments even in rural areas, for example.

There are drawbacks. The bank has a quasi-monopoly position relative to the workers in each establishment. This situation may be contributing to what appear to be exceptionally high interest rates on such loans in some countries—perhaps resulting in supernormal profits, though this supposition awaits a thorough analysis. Regardless of whether the rates could be lower, the demand is high, and borrowers seem glad of the opportunity.

Progressive housing microloans. Classical mortgage finance is out of reach of the poor in most African countries. For one thing, they generally do not have formal title to the land on which they live. Also, they do not have the regular income that a classic mortgage lender would like to see before extending a multiyear loan for a sum sufficient to build even a small house. But without credit, the poor may have to wait for several years of saving before they can make even modest improvements. Instead of reliance on a one-time loan, a progressive financing strategy is the preferred solution being explored by many microlenders wishing to use credit to improve housing for the poor. Progressive financing is, of course, how homes get built in the absence of any credit. The addition of credit allows a more substantial home to be built more quickly. Familiar characteristics of modern microcredit are employed. The first loan may be small and for a short term, but progressively larger and longer loans are made as the creditworthiness of the borrower is established more reliably. The main difference from a conventional microloan is that the term can go out to three or even four years. Break-even lending interest rates can also be lower, reflecting the fact that recovery of loan-processing costs is spread over the longer term.

As often is the case with microcredit, reliance is not placed on collateral; instead, such loans are typically offered only to those who have already established a credit history with the lender. Even if the borrower does not have formal title, as long as he or she has a de facto security of tenure the loan will not go to waste. As with housing finance at a higher level of income, success also hinges on a number of complementary actors, including local authorities, on whom the provision of basic infrastructure services such as water, electricity, and roads likely devolve. A 2002 study in Kenya found that building codes drawn up on the assumption that each housing unit would be built all in one go had the effect of making progressive construction illegal. Thus, a well-intentioned regulation, designed to protect the purchaser from incompetent or unscrupulous developers, had the unintended side effect of inhibiting improvements to the shelter of the poor, because it failed to recognize the impossibility for many to finance all-at-once construction (Brown and others 2002).

Relationship lending to small enterprises: How it can be done in Africa
The four examples in the previous subsection refer to techniques that, one way or another, economize on the need to make a costly customized creditworthiness assessment or to carry out borrower monitoring and follow-up (in several cases by tying the loan to an associated real transaction). An alternative approach—perhaps underused today by formal intermediaries in Africa in their dealings with the middle market—is relationship lending.

By limiting themselves to financing the large and collateralized borrowers, could banks be missing out on a lucrative market?[8] Admittedly, the profitability in Africa of relationship banking with SME borrowers (as distinct from microlending) is uncertain. Hence, it may be that this type of lending should be seen as part of the activist agenda, likely to be sponsored by donors or in the public interest, rather than with a view solely to the financial bottom line.[9]

Observation of the conduct of intrafirm credit business in Africa throws light on some aspects of the environment that need to be taken into account if formal finance is to deepen its engagement with the middle market. After all, intrafirm credit represents a large share of firm financing. Thanks to a thorough analysis of a set of enterprise surveys in seven African countries (Biggs and Srivastava 1996; Bigsten and others 1999, 2003; Fafchamps 2004), we know quite a lot about this market (see appendix).[10] Thus, lenders in the African middle market use a multidimensional evaluation of creditworthiness in making the loan or credit sale, looking at the borrower's capacity, business links, reputation, and character, and using soft or qualitative information where hard data are not available. This approach can be seen as not too far from the recommendations of banking textbooks, but gathering information is especially time consuming and costly and presupposes that the lender is embedded in the local economy. Intrafirm relationship lending in Africa also uses a flexible enforcement strategy, embodying the concept of the excusable default, with the borrower not being pursued for repayment unless and until he or she has the capacity to repay (Fafchamps 2004).[11,12]

Can the modern African bank find better ways of acquiring more of this kind of information about their middle-market SME customers? Those that do can look forward not only to profitable lending, but also to having made a major contribution to the societies in which they operate. It is evident that the public authorities should be extra careful not to stifle such efforts by, for example, adopting regulations that insist on exaggerated levels of collateral or on preapproval of most clients by the central bank or banking regulator (as discussed in chapter 3).

Information, Insurance, and Risk Management Innovations

Although many types of financial product can help reduce or hedge risks,[13] formal insurance schemes or other specific hedges go further than credit or savings, potentially spreading the cost not just over time but—by pooling the risk—over many other agents, including those who are more able to bear it.¹⁴ Reducing the net effect of these risks can help increase average consumption over time as well as reduce its variance. But information problems of moral hazard and adverse selection, as well as administrative costs, hamper the viability of formal insurance products for poor households.¹⁵

The management of risk in rain-fed agriculture, on which a large majority of Africans depend in one way or another, has proved particularly challenging.¹⁶ Not only is it inherently risky, but the classic approaches of risk mitigation and insurance are both difficult to implement. Farmers use multiple approaches to risk management, including loss mitigation techniques (for example, intercropping, production mix, pest and disease control, water management) and reliance on savings. Agricultural insurance tends to be more effective in protecting farmers against infrequent and extreme losses, whereas loss mitigation techniques are more effective against frequent and small losses.

In addition to increasing farmer welfare directly, risk management instruments can facilitate access to agricultural credit at better terms as they increase the creditworthiness of farmers and other agents of the agricultural sector. To the extent that farm-level risk management instruments contribute to the overall financial stability of the agribusiness sector, indirect benefits in terms of credit availability may be realized at other levels of the agribusiness marketing chain. In principle, the first requirement for risk management is information: identifying, measuring, and tracking¹⁷ the risky conditions facing the insured person. This information is often hard to obtain: those who know it will not care to tell.

The overall experience of government-sponsored all-perils crop insurance has been financially disappointing almost everywhere, with claims and administrative costs constantly exceeding premiums. This situation reflects consistent underestimation of the catastrophic risks involved in agriculture, as well as uncontrolled moral hazard and adverse selection. Furthermore, it has not been popular with small farmers, with most of the uptake coming from (and subsidy going to) large farmers.

A new wave of initiatives being piloted in Africa using recent technological and conceptual innovations seeks to design insurance around risks that are important to farmers while remaining relatively easy to evaluate and verify and having limited moral hazard. Initial experience with weather insurance in Malawi is promising (box 4.2), though it remains to be seen just how effective such initiatives will prove when scaled up. A pilot initiative promoted by CRDB Bank in Tanzania seeks to provide price-risk insurance to farmer and processor cooperatives (box 4.3). One lesson is that mainstream banks or other experienced intermediaries are needed to provide the link with global financial markets for reinsuring the tail or catastrophic end of the risks. From the users' point of view, a crucial—and sometimes decisive—deficiency of many such schemes is the scale of basis risk—for example, the lack of perfect correlation between the rainfall observed at the weather station and that experienced by the insured farmer (Binswanger and van den Brink 2005).

Deposit and Payments Innovations

Although somewhat overshadowed by a popular focus on microcredit, all who closely study the coping behaviors of poor people at first hand can see that the poor need simple and reliable savings and payments mechanisms before they need loans. Income receipts and spending needs do not generally coincide; household income that cannot be reliably saved at low cost may be dissipated; and the accumulation of sufficient funds to buy in bulk, or to buy durables or high-value items, largely depends on savings.[18] Transmitting money to family members in remote parts of the country and receiving remittances from family members abroad are also key financial needs for most households.

The challenge for financial service providers is hardly related to creditworthiness at all.[19] Instead, the main challenge is to drive down unit transactions costs sufficiently. That is not easy in many parts of Africa, given the remoteness of bank offices and the tiny individual sums involved in the transactions of poor households.

Some mainstream financial intermediaries have not been interested in this market. The astronomically high minimum balances and high minimum transaction charges some banks insist on are clearly intended to discourage a mass market for which the bank finds no place in its business model.[20] But the use of innovative product design and modern technology has allowed other intermediaries to find ways of making this kind of business pay. As these innovators scale up, the larger players begin to reassess whether they could also share in the newly discovered profitability.

Several examples illustrate how financial innovations or communications technology can work in Africa to solve the problems of remoteness and small scale. The increasing demand for low-cost and convenient prod-

BOX 4.2

Pilot Weather-Based Insurance in Malawi

Most agriculture in Malawi is rain fed. Malawi also suffers from the cumulative effects of repeated droughts, land degradation, and—in some areas—flooding. Repeated droughts force rural households to deplete assets and engage in negative coping strategies; in addition, they create a continual state of food insecurity for the most vulnerable households. In addition to the ex post impacts of drought, the risk of a drought event also has significant impacts on the growth of the agricultural sector by slowing on-farm investment and participation in higher-risk, higher-return productive activities. Drought risk further stifles investment by farmers in higher-value crops because households cannot access credit to purchase such inputs as seed and fertilizer. Banks carry the same risks as their agricultural clients, so they hesitate to invest in agriculture because of potential default during a weather event or losses of revenue associated with low prices.

Traditional insurance has been tried on a small scale in Malawi in recent years, when a number of Malawian insurance companies introduced a multiperil crop insurance product. But after suffering considerable losses caused by moral hazard and high administrative costs in the first year of business, the insurance companies chose to get out of the business. After that experience, Malawian insurers were apprehensive about getting involved in offering agricultural insurance, but they were also interested to see how an alternative to the traditional multiperil policy would work.

The National Association of Small Farmers (NASFAM) is working with farmers to develop marketing channels for value added goods and encouraging its member farmers, who are organized into in clubs of 15 to 20, to become more invested in higher-return activities. NASFAM has attributed the low productivity of Malawian farmers to a lack of both access to credit and quality inputs; in the first year, it chose groundnut as a pilot crop because of its resistance to drought and its growth potential in Malawi.

Groundnut farmers had little access to the credit needed to purchase groundnut seed and traditionally relied on local seed, if any, for production. Many NASFAM farmers had shown interest in planting with certified groundnut seed in order to improve revenues. Certified seed, while more costly, has a number of benefits over local seed, such as a higher resistance to such diseases as fungal infections, which can destroy a crop. In addition, certified seed can be marketed as a named variety of groundnut seed rather then as a generic version.

The groundnut growing cycle has three distinct phases: establishment and vegetative growth, flowering and pod formation, and pod filling and maturity. Agronomic research data for each district, as well as farmers' experience, allow determination of the cumulative rainfall required in each growth phase to achieve a partial crop and avoid water stress. These rainfall trigger points have been made the basis of the insurance contract.

Because these weather contracts could mitigate the weather risk associated with lending to farmers, two banks, Opportunity International Bank of Malawi (OIBM) and Malawi Rural Finance Corporation (MRFC), agreed to lend farmers the money necessary to purchase certified seed if the farmers bought weather insurance. As of March 2006, 892 of NASFAM's farmers borrowed an average of about US$40 each to pay for the seed, including about US$3 each for insurance. The loan agreements stipulate that the bank will be the first beneficiary if there is a payout from the insurance. In addition, NASFAM, which will purchase the majority of the groundnut production from the participating farmers, has agreed to pay the first proceeds from the sale of the produce to the bank. If there is no drought, the farmers will benefit from selling the higher-value production. The participating farmers received information and training on the project jointly from NASFAM, OIBM, and MRFC, to make sure that they fully understood the costs and benefits before contracting for the product.

One issue that arose early during the pilot season was poor germination rates for the seeds. These rates were attributed to the poor quality and rotten seed purchased from the seed provider, not to deficit rainfall. This issue highlighted the fact that weather insurance is a limited protection against yield risk for banks. Once the problem was recognized, NASFAM worked with the seed provider to distribute additional seed to those farmers whose germinations rates were low. Despite this issue, both lenders and the other participants in the pilot—farmers, NASFAM, the insurance association—were reportedly eager to scale up the program in future years.

> **BOX 4.3**
>
> **Price Risk Insurance in Tanzania**
>
> Because marketing practices require them to set prices for farmers early on in the season, intermediaries such as cooperatives and processors in the coffee and cotton sectors of Tanzania are exposed to substantial price risk for six to eight months, during the time that these export commodities are being harvested, purchased, processed, and sold. Intermediary organizations that do not understand or manage this exposure have suffered large-scale trading losses, which resulted in their inability to meet debt obligations.
>
> Local banks that lend to these organizations recognize that these financial exposures are very high. So far, the banks' response to this risk has been to manage it by charging high interest rates (12–14 percent) or curtailing lending when world market prices are moving in adverse directions (Bryla and others 2003). Recently, however, CRDB Bank in Tanzania initiated a new program to improve risk management for the bank and for borrowing clients by offering to intermediate hedging transactions using New York Board of Trade futures and options contracts. CRDB Bank has a strong incentive to actively implement improved risk management practices, because the bank understands well the risks that borrowers are carrying—sometimes better than the borrowers themselves. And unlike the cooperatives, a local bank can be an attractive client for the multinational banks and brokerage houses that offer hedging products. The local Tanzanian bank can then offer its borrowers customized risk management contracts that help manage the intraseasonal price exposure and reduce the risk of trading losses for cooperatives and ginners. Ultimately, improved risk management practices at this level will improve the financial strength of the sector as a whole and reduce the risk of vulnerability to commodity price movements.

ucts proves that a client base exists for deposits and payments products. That demand has pushed providers to come up with innovative ways of reaching out to these untapped markets. They have combined technology and financial innovation to lower unit costs and to reach the poor in sparsely populated areas (Cracknell 2004; Global Development Research Center 2003; Truen and others 2005).

Mobile banking reinvented

For a variety of reasons, Kenya's Equity Bank receives deserved prominence among those interested in outreach to the poor. One reason is its practical reintroduction of a relatively simple technology brought up to date: the mobile banking unit. The bank is doubling its number of vans and expects to have 100 in operation by the end of 2006. Each van is equipped with laptops that have telecommunications links to a fixed branch, allowing the van to provide a wide range of banking services.[21] One mobile unit visits each location once a week at a preset time. Already by mid-2003, two-thirds of loans outstanding were to clients served through mobile banking units (Wright 2005).

Equity Bank has also been creative in terms of providing savings products to respond to the needs of lower-income groups with small savings, as is reflected in its sizable excess of savings mobilized over loans extended (a relatively unusual feature among MFIs). Among its products is a contractual savings product called *jijenge*, designed to provide a disciplined savings mechanism that allows clients to save for predictable life events, with an emergency loan facility that allows the saver quick access to an emergency loan for up to 90 percent of the value of the amount in the savings account. The product design also gives the client the flexibility to set up a customized savings plan whereby he or she determines the length of the contract and the frequency of payments.

Smart cards

Teba Bank of South Africa has long been an innovator in saving and payments mechanisms, beginning with its handling of wage payments for migrant workers in the South African mines.[22] Its Bank A-Card project is intended to use the existing cell-phone network to provide low-cost, entry-level, electronic banking services to low-income and underserved communities in poor and urban areas of South Africa. The user purchases a stored-value card, which can subsequently be topped up. The stored value can be used to pay for goods and services electronically. When a purchase is made, the amount is automatically deducted from the stored value and transferred to the merchant. The Bank A-Card has the functionality of a smart card and can be accepted at all point of sale (PoS) outlets that currently accept ordinary debit cards (DFID and FDCF 2004). This approach substitutes cellular technology for much more expensive fixed lines, using a simple, cost-effective wireless terminal that can be placed in shops frequented by low-income clients. Simple magnetic-stripe debit cards allow for registration of accounts and purchases, cash-back functions, transfers to other accounts, recharges of call time, and third-party payments.

A more sophisticated use of smart cards is exemplified in the Remote Transaction System (RTS) being piloted by three microfinance institutions in Uganda. The RTS also uses a robust ICT solution to reach a greater percentage of the population in rural areas.[23] The RTS allows processing of loan payments, savings deposits, withdrawals, and transfers. At the front end, the technology solution comprises a PoS device equipped with a smart card reader, a printer for generating receipts, and cellular networking capabilities. Each client or client group uses a smart card and personal identification number to authenticate and authorize transactions. At the back end, the RTS includes a server that captures and retains all PoS transactions and connects to each participating MFI's management information system and the accounting systems of all participating institutions (Kam and Tran 2005).

Following this pilot, the MFIs have been rethinking their business processes in order to exploit the full potential of the RTS. Without such a rethink, overlaying the new technology might merely add cost and complexity. The technology has challenged the limits of local physical infrastructure (erratic telephone connectivity, unreliable electricity sources) and the literacy of customers. Furthermore, the pilot showed that the cost associated with building the infrastructure to support this enabling technology would have been too high for the MFIs to incur on their own and that only through shared infrastructures and common standards can the costs of providing financial assistance to a dramatically larger client base can be realized (Firpo 2005). However, the fixed costs having been incurred, the consortium has released RTS as a solution available to developers without a license fee. Here again, we see the logic of both the modernist agenda—using the most advanced technologies available—and the activist agenda, pro bono innovators incurring a fixed cost that can lead to benefits for other smaller MFIs with limited resources and for their customers.

Cell-phone banking
A growing number of African countries enjoy cell-phone banking, which has considerable potential outreach given the rapid expansion of cell-phone use—although it still may not reach the poorest. The value of cell-

phone banking appears highest where the physical presence of well-functioning banking institutions is weakest—as, for example, in the Democratic Republic of Congo. The payments system introduced by Celpay there and in Zambia illustrates how such systems work.[24] The product allows a subscriber to use a cell phone to pay bills, an important innovation in a country where few people have credit or debit cards and carrying cash can be dangerous. To make a payment, the subscriber sends a text message with the details to Celpay, which then returns a text message to the subscriber's cell phone asking for a personal identification number (PIN) to confirm the transaction. Once that is done, Celpay transfers the money between the participants' bank accounts.

The system already has 2,000 users in Zambia, each making several transactions per month. The recipient typically pays Celpay between 1 and 2 percent of the value of the transaction in commission. PIN verification ensures that the system is secure and that both payer and payee receive confirmation of the transaction with a unique reference number; full details of all transactions are available online. The product is simple to use for anyone who knows how to send an SMS (short message service) text message. A registered Celpay user must deposit money into a Celpay account; spending by cell phone can then commence. The user's remaining balance can also be checked by cell phone (Wood and de Cleene 2004).

Lessons from the innovations

These examples illustrate the potential of mobile phones, satellite phones, portable computers, and smart cards in overcoming remoteness and processing-cost barriers to providing payments and making deposits (and sometimes other financial services). They also illustrate a more client-oriented approach to savings product design. If the financial intermediary is focused on reaching the poor, it can easily overcome other barriers—such as the reluctance of poor people to approach an intermediary for fear of being treated with disrespect.

But experience has also shown the sizable setup costs. Piloting was important in nearly all these cases in order to refine the model before rolling it out to a wider clientele. The pilot phase involved interviews with the clients and helped the providers understand clients' needs and preferences. Their views were reflected as much as possible in the product redesign, even though it generally entailed additional investments and training of staff to adapt the intermediaries' working methods. The up-front costs of these innovations and the risk that the scale of uptake will be too low are among the barriers that have slowed progress here. Though all these schemes have the air of modernity about them, they also require a degree of activism by the pioneers in attempting the initial innovations—which may not have been remunerated quickly in many cases.

A long-neglected area: International remittances

Despite considerable recent interest in international remittances generally and efforts to define best practices (Isern, Deshpande, and van Doorn 2005; CPSS and World Bank 2006), the study of international remittances to Africa remains in its infancy (Pearce and Seymour 2005; Sander and Maimbo 2003, 2004). The identified flow of remittances into Africa (through formal channels) jumped from US$1.2 billion in 1994 to US$4.3 billion in 2004 and may have reached US$8 billion in 2005. Three countries—Nigeria, Sudan, and Uganda—account for three-fourths of these measured flows (and the top 17 countries—including all with US$10 million or more—account for more than 97 percent). Even this sizable sum is thought to greatly underestimate total flows—perhaps by about half.[25] As shown in table 4.1, several sizable countries regularly receive inflows in excess of 5 percent of their GDP.[26]

Data are especially lacking on remittances between developing countries, which are relatively more prevalent in Africa than elsewhere: a sizable data collection effort is needed here (World Bank 2005). Indeed, the dynamic and complex patterns of migration in Africa, which create the need for remittances, are themselves not well understood. There has been a feminization of migration, a diversification of migration destinations, a transformation of labor flows into commercial migration, and brain drain from the region. Completing this picture are trafficking in human beings, the changing map of refugee flows, and the increasing role of regional economic organizations in fostering free flows of labor (for a detailed discussion, see Adepoju 2004). Untangling the policy implications for remittance flows of these multifaceted migration characteristics is methodologically challenging.

While the prominence of remittances on the continent continues to grow, the outreach and quality of the financial sector infrastructure for remittances largely remain weak. Compared with some of the technologi-

TABLE 4.1
Remittances: Top Sub-Saharan Recipients

Recipient country	US$ million	Percentage of GDP[a]	Year of last observation
Lesotho	223.0	29.2	2004
Cape Verde	92.1	15.2	2003
Guinea-Bissau	21.3	6.8	2003
Uganda	306.1	5.8	2004
Sudan	1,401.2	5.7	2004
Senegal	448.2	5.4	2003
Togo	128.3	3.9	2003
Mali	138.9	3.5	2003
Benin	49.5	3.2	2003
Nigeria	2,272.7	2.6	2004
Burkina Faso	43.6	1.9	2001
São Tomé and Príncipe	0.6	1.2	2002
Sierra Leone	24.6	0.9	2004
Ghana	82.3	0.8	2004
Mozambique	2.5	0.6	2004
Ethiopia	133.4	0.5	2004
Niger	11.5	0.5	2003

Sources: World Bank's World Development Indicators database, except for Lesotho, data from the United Nations Conference on Trade and Development database Handbook of Statistics 2005.

a. Average 2000–02 flows as percentage of 2001 GDP.

cal solutions discussed above, remittances appear a poor relation but one that could be transformed. The cost of remittances between industrial and developing countries appears to be higher to Africa than to other regions (Hernández-Coss, Egwuagu, and Josefsson 2006). To date, most formal remittances use long-established, speedy, and reliable—but still rather costly—services by money transfer operators (MTOs)[27] such as Western Union and its competitors.[28]

For too long, financial and monetary policies and regulations have created barriers to the flow of remittances and their effective investment (box 4.4). Foreign exchange controls, bureaucratic account opening and cash withdrawal procedures, and limited rural branch networks contribute to an ongoing preference for informal methods of transferring funds. Wide gaps between official and parallel market exchange rates have also encouraged the use of informal channels, as have other explicit or implicit taxes. And for migrants forced to migrate illegally, informal methods are often the only option.

BOX 4.4

Improving the Remittances Situation

Overall, Africa's formal remittance infrastructure's potential is not being maximized. The region remains largely cash dominated. In particular, the proportion of the rural poor who have access to formal banking services, let alone formal payments systems, remains very low. An improved remittance infrastructure on the continent would make advances in five areas (CPSS and the World Bank 2006):

- Transparency and consumer protection
- Payment system infrastructure
- Legal and regulatory framework
- Market structure and competition
- Governance and risk management practices

The market for remittance services should be transparent and have adequate consumer protection. Recently, the UK Department for International Development and the Banking Code Standards Board commissioned a survey on money transfer products offered to members of the diaspora in the United Kingdom in order to address this lack of information and transparency. A number of primary UK remittance destinations were chosen for the survey, including Ghana, Kenya, and Nigeria. Better information on money transfer services should not only help remitters choose a service that best meets their needs, but also promote healthy competition between money transfer providers—competition that reduces the cost and improves the service for remittance senders (Isern, Deshpande, and van Door 2005; Pearce and Seymour 2005).

Improvements to payment system infrastructure that have the potential to increase the efficiency of remittance services should be encouraged. The choice of remittance method is determined by several factors, including ease (methods with less paperwork and documentation requirements were preferred); familiarity (often the remittance method used is the method used by parents and grandparents or recommended by friends and family); cost (although participants had little precise knowledge of cost structures, their perceptions of which methods were cheapest tended to be accurate); speed (of particular importance when the remittance is intended to meet an emergency need); risk tolerance (for theft or other losses; participants claimed to become more risk averse as the size of the remittance increased); and access (how easy it is for the recipient to reach the delivery point). In South Africa, for example, sending by means of a taxi driver is cheap, there are no forms to fill in, and the unbanked can access this means easily. The method is used extensively for both domestic and cross-border remittances and with equal likelihood by both blue- and white-collar workers. Participants also believed that the post office had a much better rural distribution network than the banks and was comparable to the bank in terms of safety and speed (Truen and others 2005).

Remittance services should be supported by a sound, predictable, nondiscriminatory, and proportionate legal and regulatory framework in relevant jurisdictions. Current licensing regulations for money transfer services center on foreign exchange trading. For smaller money transfer operators and informal services, regulations often are opaque and hard to access; compliance may be unaffordable. To be in a better position to review and enhance the regulatory frameworks used in Africa, we must improve our understanding not only of African remittance markets, but also of the business models that make nonbank transfer services attractive to client segments elsewhere in the world and of how those models are licensed and regulated. A facilitative framework in which licensing requirements were adjusted to reflect actual needs for transparency and for management of foreign exchange exposure could greatly enhance the availability and outreach of basic financial services, including money transfers.

Competitive market conditions, including appropriate access to domestic payments infrastructures, should be fostered in the remittance industry. For example, in the absence of a functioning banking system, money transfer companies in Somalia have had an impressive history since the fall of the government in 1991. The market functions very efficiently, providing quick and inexpensive services to all parts of Somalia. The remittance flows through these companies provide subsistence and essential services for families in Somalia. They also facilitate international trade and domestic commerce, even in the remote parts of the country, and finance domestic investment in businesses, community services, construction, and real estate. The principal challenge for government, once it is fully established, will

(Box continues on the following page.)

> **BOX 4.4** *(continued)*
>
> be to find a way to take full advantage of the dynamics of this part of the financial system for the benefit of the Somali private sector while combating the reputational risks of an unregulated industry.
>
> Remittance services should be supported by appropriate governance and risk management practices. As is the case for the payments industry generally, the international remittance industry faces legal, financial, operational, fraud, and reputational risks. In establishing risk control measures, remittance service providers should conduct risk-level assessments to ensure that proposed risk control measures are appropriate to the level of the risks and the size of the business generally. Therefore, money transfer operations need significant investment in skilled human capital (Isern, Deshpande, and van Doorn 2005). New operators need to train staff or hire specialized staff for customer relations and back-office functions. Information systems must be capable of managing the volume of anticipated transfers, ensuring transaction security, possibly interfacing with other transfer operators, and generating reports to comply with regulations (such as anti-money-laundering legislation).

Organization: Who Needs to Do What?

From the examples provided, it is evident that some of the technology-driven innovations that can help improve financial access in Africa can be and are being spontaneously implemented by market intermediaries in some countries. It is likely that more will come from private initiative in the future (not least through the rollout of what has worked in one country, including through the activities of banks, MFIs, and others that are active in more than one country). However, given the fragmentation of national African markets and the small scale of the individual transaction or relationship, the prospective rate of return on the necessary fixed-cost investments in financial technology can seem too low to the private entrepreneur—especially in the generally adverse climate for private investment in Africa, as discussed in chapter 1. Furthermore, several of them have collective action issues (the investment not being worth making unless several intermediaries do it at the same time). The following discussion addresses the question of how this logjam can be broken, whether by donors; by governments at local, national, or transnational levels; by individual banks or associations of private financiers; or by associations of users (as, for example, with mutual credit insurance).

A major theme running through this discussion is the need for adequate governance, in particular where the activist agenda is in play. Activists are not restrained by immediate market pressures; they have chosen to plow money and effort into endeavors that the market has declined. To be even reasonably confident that these efforts and resources will not be wasted or subverted, the sponsoring agency must have good governance. It could be a private entity with deep pockets, likely combined with a social conscience; it could be charitable or donor agencies. National or local governments are not, in present conditions, the most suitable candidates to sponsor an activist agenda in the financial sector.

Diversity of Organizational Models in African Microfinance

One of the most striking features of the recent and ongoing expansion of the microfinance movement in Africa is the proliferation of different types, in terms of financial technology applied, organizational structure, degree of formality and regulation, and clientele. The diversity seems wider than in other regions. Not only that, but the relative importance of different models—even of formal microfinance—differs widely from country to country.

As Robinson (2006, 15–16), reviewing available evidence for Africa, puts it:

> Regardless of their history or institutional form, however, large-scale financially self-sufficient institutions with responsible ownership, skilled governance and management, knowledge of the market, and commitment to microfinance best practices—and a corporate culture emphasizing training, incentives, transparency, efficiency, and accountability—are found clustered at one end of this continuum. The majority of microfinance clients are also clustered at this end. At the other end are the many microfinance providers that lack most or all of these crucial elements. The middle ground is home to numerous positive efforts and to multiple obstacles.

Quantifying the relative importance in outreach of different sizes and types of provider is an inexact science. For one thing, the number of providers is very large. As far as the formal and semiformal sectors are concerned, the most comprehensive database is that prepared by the Consultative Group to Assist the Poor (CGAP) (Christen, Rosenberg, and Jayadeva 2004),[29] which has more than 800 African entries, even though networks of cooperatives and credit unions are assigned only one entry each (as is the Nigerian community bank system). However, the 44 largest entities (by number of accounts) account for about 80 percent of the client base across Africa, fully justifying Robinson's statement that the "microfinance industry in Africa is becoming dominated by large, mature financial institutions and federations with wide outreach" (Robinson 2006, 16). Each of these entities caters for at least 100,000 clients (table 4.2). As with the full list, the top 44 include a wide range of different types of entities: state-owned banks, including postal savings banks; privately owned banks; cooperative savings and credit institutions; and nongovernmental organizations (NGOs).

TABLE 4.2
Large Financial Intermediaries and Networks in Africa Ranked by Outreach

Country	Name of institution	Type	Number of accounts
South Africa	Post Bank	Postal bank	2,100,000
Zimbabwe	People's Own Savings Bank	Savings bank	1,695,000
Kenya	Kenya Post Office Savings Bank (KPOSB)	Postal bank	1,636,000
Ghana	Rural and Community Banks	Banks	1,200,000
Niger	Caisse Nationale d'Epargne	Postal bank	1,124,000
Nigeria	Community Banks	Unit banks	1,000,000
Tanzania	Tanzania Postal Bank	Postal bank	954,000
Kenya	Kenya Union of Savings & Credit Co-operatives (KUSCCO)	Credit union or cooperative	952,000
Côte d'Ivoire	Caisse d'Epargne et des Cheques Postaux (CECP)	Postal bank	828,000
Cameroon	Caisse d'Epargne Postale	Postal bank	700,000
Tanzania	National Microfinance Bank	Bank	670,000
South Africa	Teba Bank	Bank	649,000
Madagascar	Caisse d'Epargne	Postal bank	574,000
Rwanda	Banques Populaires	Credit union or cooperative	385,000
Benin	Fédération des Caisses d'Epargne et de Crédit Agricole Mutuel (FECECAM)	Credit union or cooperative	378,000
Burkina Faso	Caisse Nationale d'Epargne	Postal bank	363,000
Benin	Caisse Nationale d'Epargne	Postal bank	350,000
Côte d'Ivoire	Fédération Nationale des Coopératives d'Epargne et de Crédit de Côte d'Ivoire (FENACOOPEC-CI)	Credit union or cooperative	291,000

FINANCE FOR ALL 165

TABLE 4.2 (*continued*)

Country	Name of institution	Type	Number of accounts
Botswana	Savings Bank	Postal bank	287,000
Nigeria	Countrywomen's Association (COWAN)	NGO	270,000
Uganda	Centenary Rural Development Bank	Bank	251,000
Burkina Faso	Fédération des Caisses Populaires	Credit union or cooperative	248,000
Mauritius	Postal Savings Bank	Postal bank	245,000
Sudan	Savings & Social Development Bank	Savings bank	230,000
Ethiopia	Dedebit Credit and Savings Institution	Nonbank financial intermediary	221,000
Ethiopia	Amhara Credit and Savings Institution	Nonbank financial intermediary	216,000
Namibia	Postal Savings Bank	Postal bank	209,000
Senegal	Caisse Nationale de Crédit Agricole	Agricultural bank	205,000
Malawi	Savings Bank	Postal bank	204,000
Cape Verde	Caixa Económica de Cabo Verde	Savings bank	200,000
Togo	Caisse d'Epargne du Togo	Postal bank	200,000
Senegal	Caisse Nationale d'Epargne	Postal bank	197,000
Gabon	Caisse Nationale d'Epargne	Postal bank	175,000
Kenya	Equity Bank	Bank	173,000
Malawi	Malawi Rural Finance Company	Nonbank financial intermediary	166,000
Niger	Mata Masu Dubara CARE	NGO	162,000
Nigeria	FADU (Farmers' Development Union)	Nonbank financial intermediary	156,000
Ethiopia	Credit Unions	Credit union or cooperative	150,000
Cameroon	Cameroon Cooperative Credit Union League (CAMCCUL)	Credit union or cooperative	149,000
Tanzania	Savings and Credit Cooperatives	Credit union or cooperative	137,000
Togo	Faîtière des Unités Coop (FUCEC)	Credit union or cooperative	133,000
Sudan	Agricultural Bank of Sudan	Agricultural bank	125,000
Uganda	Postbank Uganda	Postal bank	122,000
Mali	Kafo Jiginew	Credit union or cooperative	115,000

Source: Revised by the authors using data from Peachey and Roe 2005 and Christen, Rosenberg, and Jayadeva 2004.

Note: The table includes intermediaries or networks with an outreach objective and with more than 100,000 accounts or customers. It overstates access to the extent that some accounts are dormant: the proportion of dormant accounts in post offices is often very high. The Ghana Association of Rural Banks network is still a fairly loose organization. The Nigeria community banks are not grouped into any formal network.

In interpreting table 4.2, one must recognize that the number of accounts is a most imperfect measure of outreach.[30] Many accounts, especially it seems at postal savings banks, are dormant and thus contribute little to welfare. (As few as 10 percent of the accounts at Uganda's postal savings bank are thought to be active.) Then again, the range of services available from different types of intermediaries differs widely.

These points need to be borne in mind when observing that overall almost half the accounts recorded in the CGAP database for Africa (as augmented) are at savings or postal banks. This figure is about the same as reported for the developing world as a whole. But the breakdown of the other half is quite different in Africa, where various forms of credit cooperatives and NGOs both account for a much higher percentage (20 percent and 10 percent, respectively) than is found in the rest of the world (figure 4.1). However, these shares vary sharply across Africa. In 11 of the 42 African countries in the database, savings and postal banks report more than three-fourths of the accounts; nonbank MFIs have more than three-fourths of the accounts in 16 countries. This finding displays the contrasting mix of organization forms that are observed in African countries.[31]

FIGURE 4.1
Share of Cooperatives, NGOs, Savings, and Other Banks in Providing Access

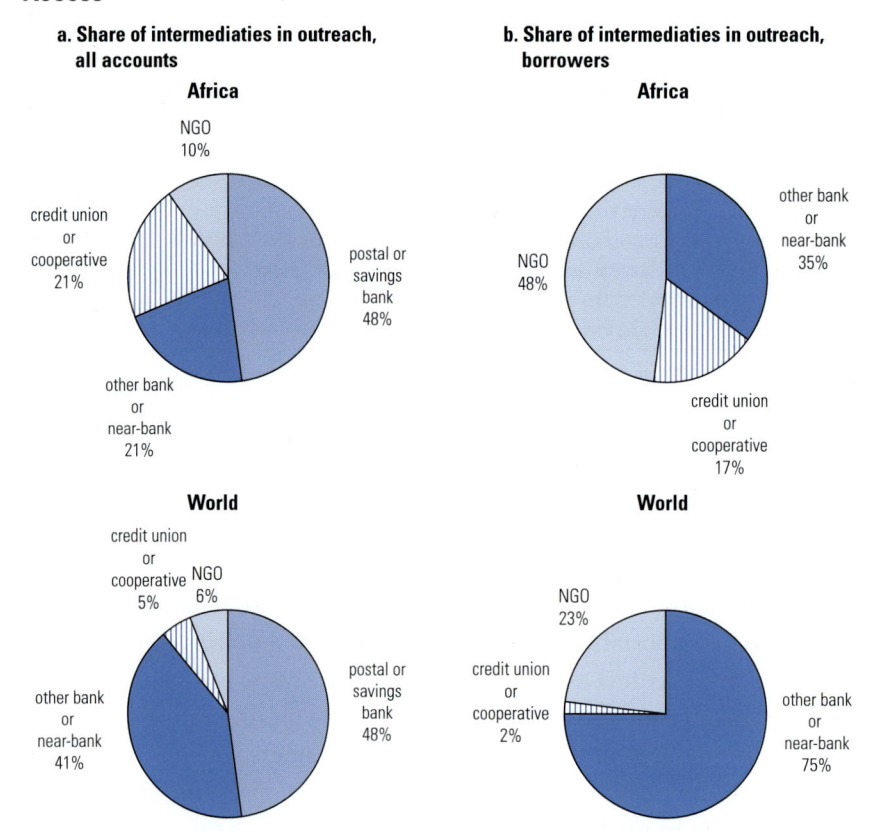

a. Share of intermediaties in outreach, all accounts

Africa
- NGO 10%
- credit union or cooperative 21%
- postal or savings bank 48%
- other bank or near-bank 21%

World
- credit union or cooperative 5%
- NGO 6%
- postal or savings bank 48%
- other bank or near-bank 41%

b. Share of intermediaties in outreach, borrowers

Africa
- NGO 48%
- other bank or near-bank 35%
- credit union or cooperative 17%

World
- NGO 23%
- credit union or cooperative 2%
- other bank or near-bank 75%

Source: Revised by the authors using data from Peachey and Roe 2005 and Christen, Rosenberg, and Jayadeva 2004.

Looking at loan accounts, one notes that here, too, the relative importance of cooperatives and NGOs is much higher in Africa (figure 4.1). This finding raises two questions: Is there something special about the mutual model in Africa? Could banks play a bigger role?[32]

Different Forms of Mutuality

Elements of mutuality[33] contribute strongly to an effective credit culture and to information flows that strengthen credit appraisal and credit discipline. These processes are arguably stronger for relatively small groups and hence, in practice, for small-scale intermediation. They are especially advantageous in informal environments and where external enforcement of credit contracts cannot be ensured. Their strengths thus seem particularly well adapted to environments that are widely experienced in Africa.

Mutuality in African microfinance is observed both in lending and in governance of the intermediary. These are not closely correlated. Whereas some commercial banks and donor-controlled MFIs sometimes use group lending techniques, many cooperative or mutual savings and credit institutions in Africa rely on individual loans but collective governance.

Variations in group lending have been found effective in different environments and in relation to different types of clients. Increasingly, the leading microlenders no longer confine themselves to a single lending model. As just one example, the international NGO CARE promotes an eclectic mix of techniques. For urban and periurban areas, small groups of four to six people are formed.[34] Larger "village" groups of 20 or more are used in rural areas.[35] Another model used by CARE for low-capacity groups, usually women, in remote areas is designed to stimulate and educate these groups to achieve self-organization, with a savings and credit association depending entirely on accumulating the group's own savings (Allen 2002). MFIs across Africa practice many variants of these techniques, differing in contract design as well as in group size.[36]

At the other end of the spectrum, other MFIs favor individual-based loans, seeing them as more flexible and responsive to each borrower's evolving needs than group lending, which can proceed only at the pace of the slowest developer. Procredit/IPC exemplifies this approach. The fact that it has secured banking licenses in several countries illustrates how close its model is to traditional banking—even though with a focus on smaller and lower-income borrowers and therefore with the need to emphasize cost control. Many mutually owned MFIs also make individual-responsibility loans—indeed, this is the classic credit union model.

The distinction being made here is not hard and fast. For instance, in a credit union, individual borrowers are linked through their participation in the ownership of the cooperative, albeit in a much weaker way than can be implied by participation in a group or cross-guaranteed loan. Mutual guarantee associations blur the distinction even more.

Group or individual lending?
Which model is best? For lending, there is little evidence to suggest that either group or individual lending clearly dominates (Cull and Giné 2004).[37] For instance, reliance by group lenders on peer pressure may not always work. In agriculture, the group may be faced with a common or at least covariant risk. Some borrowing farmer groups have colluded to misrepresent their ability to repay—see Binswanger and van den Brink (2005), whose proposal for a sophisticated and coherent community-based structure for coping with the complex risks and incentive problems faced in rural finance deserves more attention that it has yet received.

Perhaps the persistence of a multiplicity of models means that different models work best in different environments. But such a Panglossian conclusion may not be warranted. Survival of the fittest is unlikely to prevail quickly in the social lending sector, which is often donor aided and in which institutions generally have a management team motivated by social concerns. Persons with the multidimensional management skills required to fill a top position in an MFI typically have the qualifications to secure a very highly paid job in the financial service industry in an advanced economy. They stay in African microfinance because of their social motivation. This complicates the comparative evaluation of MFI models, because even an inferior model can be made to work and to survive against the odds if supported by the efforts of able and highly motivated managers. Furthermore, while a growing number of MFIs are reporting profits, others are still kept afloat in practice by donor funds (sometimes in the form of cheap loans and equity, rather than grants). Although donors will not back a losing model indefinitely (and some exits unprofitable MFIs have already exited), their behavior can prolong its life.

The success of cooperatives: Mirage or miracle?
A common misconception among nonspecialists is to suppose that mutuals systematically cater to poorer clients and make smaller loans. The aver-

age loan size for the cooperatives in the sample of African MFIs studied by Lafourcade and others (2005) was about US$500, or about 120 percent of national gross national income (GNI) per capita, well above the average of US$300 for the sample as a whole.[38] Even though this finding suggests that cooperatives cater to a less poor clientele on average, cooperatives report a lower return on assets at 0.4 percent, compared with more than 2 percent for the rest. Social or statutory ceilings on lending interest rates likely contribute: unregulated MFIs have much higher unit costs but more than recover those costs on financial revenue.[39]

Bearing in mind that formal savings and credit cooperatives are, in Stuart Rutherford's (1999) colorful phrase, supercharged rotating savings and credit associations (ROSCAs), it would nonetheless likely be a mistake to assume that the cooperative form is particularly focused on higher-income groups. If data on informal ROSCAs were included, the average loan size for this wider definition of cooperatives would be much lower.

Despite reliance on mutualist ideas of solidarity and social capital, the cooperative model is not immune to failure resulting from malfeasance or insouciance. One problem can be the difficulty of coping with external funding, compromising the self-reliance on which cooperatives are supposedly built. The failure in 1998 of the largest network of cooperatives in Benin, FECECAM (Fédération des Caisses d'Epargne et de Crédit Agricole Mutuel), illustrates this. In that case, among the many lessons learned was "the realization by the network that rapid growth under the impulse of lines of credit at the expense of good financial management can jeopardize an institution's sustainability" (Ouattara 2003, 11–12). Endemic management and portfolio weaknesses have been noted also in East Africa, where the savings and credit cooperative (SACCO) mutualist model may be losing out to other institutional forms.

Furthermore, the mutualist glue that holds the model together in good times may dissolve suddenly if there are adverse shocks, with members deciding not to repay if the institution is seen as likely to be unable to make future loans. The recent case of mutual guarantee associations (MGAs) in Madagascar is a case in point.[40] The MGAs had been developed at the instigation of the national ministry of agriculture, livestock, and fisheries as a way of facilitating the extension of agricultural credit from the multinational Bank of Africa in parts of Madagascar where no mutualist credit institutions were active. However, the crisis of 2002 brought a collapse in farm-gate prices and an inability by some to make repayments, which escalated into a general collapse of credit discipline, with even the organizing committee members of MGAs refusing to repay (Bennett and others 2005). Once again, postmortems identified a failure to embed the solidaristic principles that are presupposed by the mutualist model: for example, the overstrong role of the ministry in promoting the scheme and the lack of understanding by the farmer groups of their collective responsibilities. The collapse uncovered other deficiencies: for instance, loan approval processes that were so cumbersome that the loan was sometimes made too late to meet the agricultural input need for which it had been earmarked (such loans tended to be consumed, resulting in repayment difficulties).

Cooperatives, with their "one person, one vote" governance principle, are not inherently suited to a setup of disparity in resources among members. They may not be well adapted to absorbing external capital funds. Such drawbacks have contributed to the decision of the larger UK mutual financial institutions to convert to the joint-stock corporate structure. In contrast, though, many European mutuals have managed to innovate in corporate structure to get around these limitations. Already there are examples of such innovation in Africa, also. For example, Crédit Mutuel in Senegal launched a regional bank, BIMAO (Banque des Institutions Mutualistes d'Afrique de l'Ouest), that allows it to accept equity (as well as facilitating the provision of other banking services). What were until recently loose confederations of locally based savings and credit cooperatives in West Africa (such as Nyesigiso and Kafo Jiginew in Mali) have, while retaining mutuality, greatly centralized decision making in the national central offices of the networks.[41] Kenya's Cooperative Bank, initially established as a department in the ministry of cooperatives, evolved to become a kind of apex for Kenyan cooperatives as well as a stand-alone licensed bank.

As the power of the central office of the network grows, so the degree to which the member cooperatives are—in practice—being governed by the individual members diminishes. There is an interesting convergence of governance with the network of some 120 rural and community banks in Ghana. These commercial banks (with some restrictions on activities and geographic scope) are not mutual entities, but they formed an association in 1981 which, in turn, established in 2001 the ARB Apex Bank—now acting as a kind of head office (Andah 2005; Steel and Andah 2003).[42, 43] It is not evident that a cooperative member of one of the large networks in Mali or one of the Kenyan cooperatives has a greater tie or is more responsive to the local area in which it operates than is a locally owned rural bank in Ghana.

All in all, governments would be unwise to insist on the mutual organizational form, thereby shutting out the potential offered by other MFI sponsors. Legislative changes under way in the UEMOA have begun to reflect this view by dropping the presumption that MFIs will have a mutualist governance; hitherto MFIs that are not cooperatives have been able to apply for only a temporary five-year license (Lolila-Ramin 2005).

Mainstream Banks: Will Their Role Be Direct or as Wholesalers?

Following successes in microfinance by banks in other regions and the licensing as banks of a handful of African entities focused on SMEs and lower-income borrowers, some observers have suggested that the future for microfinance might lie with banks. If this proposition is intended to refer to the large international banks, it is far from clear that they will have an easy path to tread. Some of them do not have it as part of their business model. Others claim to have a retail strategy reaching further down the income scale and to micro, small, and medium-scale enterprises (MSMEs), but it is unclear just how far down this scale they can realistically hope to go.[44]

In this regard, all eyes are on South Africa and the response of the banks and other leading financial institutions to the expectation that they can and should do more to achieve an inclusive financial system in that country.[45] It is a good testbed: the major banks are solid and skillful, the broader economic environment relatively strong. Yet access for the poor remains limited. Solutions that prove to be effective and financially viable in South Africa may be adaptable to the rest of the continent, after some of the setup and experimentation costs are incurred in South Africa.

Essentially the problem lies in unit costs. Catering for the small transaction costs involved in dealing with the poor can be prohibitively expensive for large international banks. The salaries they pay to their well-educated and well-trained staff members, needed because of the sophistication and complexity of some of their products (and the need for layers of review and control), make anything that involves personal intervention very costly. Technology can dramatically reduce per transaction costs, thereby offering a countervailing force, but putting the technology into effect in a sparsely populated region can also be prohibitively costly if the volume of transactions is not large enough. For example, the per transaction charges made by South African banks even for the low-cost Mzansi accounts (equivalent to more than US$0.50 for an ATM withdrawal and US$0.35 for a PoS withdrawal or purchase) are affordable by lower-middle-income South Africans but are likely too expensive for the average Mozambican. To what extent banks can drive their costs further down to achieve greater outreach is unclear.

What can be envisaged, however, is a wholesaling function for large banks—to help get funding, as well as more sophisticated products, into the market. Already banks are acting as wholesale suppliers of mobilized resources to MFIs and cooperatives in several countries and, of course, they are the main conduit to the payments system. There have been some disappointing failures on the part of specialized lenders financed by banks—the case of Unibank and Saambou in South Africa is discussed in Rust (2002)—but some promising cases also.[46] The failures have partly reflected overconfidence on the part of the funds supplier about the information and management capacity of the primary lender. A particular difficulty arises in creating such links where the primary lender is donor aided, has little capital, or has finances so shaky that commercial lenders require a donor guarantee, which tends to defeat some of the purpose of the exercise. Fortunately, a growing number of solid MFIs do attract commercial bank lending without guarantees (Isern and Porteous 2005).

We have already mentioned the need for banks or other internationally active intermediaries to create the link with international reinsurance or bond markets needed to make some forms of agriculture-related insurance work by laying off the catastrophic end of the risk. Other forms of partnerships between mainstream banks and microfinance entities can be envisaged.

More generally, commercial banks could benefit from close links with MFIs. For example, lacking a formal credit record, small-scale or microentrepreneurs whose credit needs have outgrown the group-lending techniques of microfinance are unlikely to be able to access credit from a commercial bank where they are not known, unless there are some information or cofinancing arrangements between MFIs and banks.

Moving a notch down in scale from the large international banks, the prospects and, indeed, practice of microfinance engagement by local banks are considerably greater. It depends in part on the banks' missions and business models. Such entities as Centenary Rural Development Bank (CERUDEB) in Uganda; Equity Bank and K-Rep in Kenya; CRDB Bank and Akiba Bank in Tanzania, Banque Nationale de Développement Agricole (BNDA) in Mali; Malawi Rural Finance Corporation (MFRC) in Malawi; Afriland Bank, BICEC, and Union Bank in Cameroon; and CNCA in Senegal have shown in different ways that licensed commercial banks in Africa can be effective in microfinance on a substantial scale. These are either microfinance or development specialists focused on a single country, but others such as the Bank of Africa and Ecobank, both present in multiple jurisdictions, are also increasingly involved in small-scale finance.

The National Microfinance Bank (NMB) in Tanzania represents a unique experiment in seeking to build on existing formal structures to reach a wider market. The NMB was carved out of the government-owned National Bank of Commerce when it was being recapitalized and privatized to Absa of South Africa. The NMB was established with a wide branch network—95 branches, of which all but 6 are outside Dar es Salaam—and an extensive deposit business. It had new systems, developed under management contract, with a focus on servicing households and MSME clients. Recently, partly privatized to a consortium led by Rabobank, the bank is gradually beginning to expand its loan portfolio.

Another promising model has been put into effect in Benin and Chad by Financial Bank (a banking group whose international dimension builds on the longstanding migration links between Chad and the coast) and in Zimbabwe by Kingdom Bank. It is the creation of a microfinance subsidiary that might ultimately be spun off into a freestanding unit. The differences in operating procedures and business culture can make this solution attractive (Isern and Porteous 2005; Kloeppinger-Todd 2005).

Commercial banks are not the only large, formal sector institutions that will play a part in increasing access in Africa. Post offices have already been mentioned. Post offices date back to the early colonial era and now vary considerably across Africa in the degree to and the success with which they offer financial services (World Bank and ING Bank forthcoming). The largest post office—that of Nigeria—does not currently offer financial services.

Many postal banks have lacked a customer focus, and some have not been well managed in even more serious ways—a common problem being lack of control over recording of liabilities in situations where passbooks are the legal record. Some have been left in an illiquid state by the government, with disastrous consequences for their ability to honor even the most basic financial contracts, such as repaying the depositor promptly.

But other African postal services have turned the corner and are displaying a promising dynamism. Where they are well managed, they have a considerable natural advantage to exploit their extensive locational network, as well as their information technology capacity to offer simple financial products (savings, payments) to poor customers. They are often the largest single provider of financial services in the country—for example, the Nampost in Namibia claims a 50 percent share of savings customers by number and about 13 percent by value; it has 190 offices across the country. In Benin, the total value of postal checking (CCP, or *compte chèque postal*) and postal saving (CNE, or *caisse nationale d'épargne*) accounts comes to the equivalent of more than half of bank deposits. As well as internal payments, often including the giro system, several offer international payments using the network of Western Union or other MTOs. Ensuring that they are not blocked from admission to the national payments system can help reduce the cost of retail payments.

Moving on to offering credit is being considered in a few cases. This is something that runs up against the political pressures discussed earlier, and it cannot be encouraged unhesitatingly. Some postal banks have been spun off from the post office proper, following the successful experience of a few European countries. However, this experiment has not always been successful, and it risks both increasing costs and undermining the built-in advantages that motivate the use of the post office as a financial service provider to begin with. Some spinoffs—such as that in Kenya, which serves an estimated 1.6 million savers—have concentrated their activities on a much smaller set of offices (about 70 in Kenya), without exploiting the full range of postal outlets (of which there are 900 in Kenya).

Large chains of goods retailers also enjoy some of the same advantages mentioned for the post office, although they do not typically have quite as broad a network of offices. Some African retailers have become interested in diversifying into offering some financial services to a broad clientele. Depository and payments services will, again, be their first products. Supermarket chains are beginning to show an interest in acquiring a limited banking license, which will enable them to offer such services.

Role of Governments: Consistency, Modesty, Regulatory Style

Competition, infrastructure, coordination
As we have discussed, government is often not itself the best-placed entity to deliver financial services (not least because of credibility and gover-

nance issues). Although some of the innovative institutions mentioned elsewhere in this chapter are state owned, these are exceptions that prove the rule. Nevertheless, in numerous ways, government actions can help enhance the quality and outreach of services. In addition to policy for prudential regulation, these actions can be grouped under the headings of promoting competition, providing infrastructure and other public goods, and coordinating.

For competition, maximizing the range of reliable providers and avoiding unnecessary cost impositions on suppliers are two central guiding principles. To take just one example, when the government needs to make payments in remote areas, putting that contract up for competitive tender rather than automatically continuing to use traditional channels can help build scale for new internal payments technologies and spur innovation.

Numerous dimensions of infrastructure, both hard and soft, that the financial sector needs will be provided only with government involvement. At the most basic level, political stability and physical security are fundamental to the ability of the financial system to operate. Many other infrastructural investments, such as those aimed at improvements in education[47] and in transport infrastructure, are needed also by dimensions of economic and social development. Electronic ICT in particular is crucial for enabling many financial innovations.

The meso-level infrastructures for finance, especially legal and informational infrastructures (discussed in chapter 3), remain relevant when it comes to finance for all. Accounting standards and practice, bankruptcy law, recourse to the courts to recover collateral—these infrastructures will all make important contributions. A clear and supportive legal basis for leasing, factoring, and hire-purchase is a particular low-cost reform that unlocks sizable possibilities. Both this and the creation of effective title registries and credit registries can be relevant for improving access to small-scale borrowing. The design and technology of national payments systems are relevant insofar as they help or hinder the competitive provision of low-cost retail payment services at the small scale. (For instance, interchange fees for card transactions that are set at a uniform per item rate can preclude their use by poor people.)

One classic type of public service that is very relevant for the effectiveness of finance is the public provision of small business development—in particular, agricultural extension.[48] These services are not always provided in the most effective way, and it may often be more effective to have them delivered by the private sector, even if subsidized by the state. However, it is clear that there is too little knowledge of basic business methods and, in particular, of ways of making the most of existing financial services. Performance of publicly subsidized business development services is relatively easy to monitor quickly, so that governments can ensure that they are getting value for money. Such evaluations should be carried out on a regular basis.[49]

Helping improve financial literacy is also important in ensuring that the poor make good use of the expanding opportunities and do not suffer from bad financial choices, including overborrowing. Financial literacy efforts can also, perhaps, yield dividends by laying the foundation for efforts to nurture norms for honoring financial contracts.

The introduction of new technology in finance has been pioneered by activist market participants, including NGOs, supported by donor funds and, in some cases, by government budgetary funds. The innovators have worked best when sponsored by agencies with strong governance that helped ensure that they would not be sidetracked from their goals. Policy makers need to understand these innovations to make sure that they do not inadvertently block them through regulation or undercut them with unsustainable and costly subsidies that chill market development without achieving their goal on any significant scale. Market participants will not explore such innovation unless the market is contestable. In short, policy needs to be designed so as to smooth the way for activists.

Even if governance weaknesses mean that a directly involved activist agenda in the financial sector cannot be recommended for most African government agencies, they can act as a broker or facilitator—"knocking heads together" to ensure that activist efforts by others are pooled or coordinated if this means that they could be more effective. Working with industry associations, the government can have an important role to play in overcoming coordination failures that hinder the adoption of shared market standards and financial market infrastructure, such as the establishment of credit bureaus or standardized mortgage contracts to facilitate securitization.

But it is harder for African governments to use policy levers successfully to exert pressure on private providers that are purely profit seeking and have no social goals to push outreach and financial access much beyond the point of profitability. In contrast to the situation in advanced economies, where a degree of legislative or moral pressure on financial intermediaries can be effective and is in practice used to reduce financial exclusion, most African governments cannot assume that this is a viable or sensible way to proceed. To the extent that the problem is getting access percentages up from 10 or 20 percent (in contrast to advanced economies, where the challenge is to reduce exclusion from 10 or 15 percent), the tools and the time frames for achieving different goals need to be realistic. For one thing, given the small size of their markets, African governments have limited economic leverage on mainstream banks in a competitive environment. Too many impositions and the banks will downsize or exit the market.[50] As usual, South Africa provides an exception, with the banks there launching the Msanzi product at least partly to deflect political pressure. Indeed, even if the leverage of other governments remains modest, the South African case, if it continues to prove successful, now offers a focal point for moral suasion: if banks can reach out more effectively in South Africa, why not elsewhere on the continent?

Regulatory model
In addition to working proactively to create the conditions under which providers of financial services can work effectively, governments also strongly influence developments through the model of prudential regulation that they create. A degree of consensus exists about the main elements of a regulatory model for microfinance (Christen and others 2003), and African central banks have been at the fore in gaining acceptance for and putting in place a coherent regulatory framework for microfinance.[51] Yet certain important ambiguities remain. The proliferation of small MFIs, whether cooperative, NGO-sponsored, or coming from other private initiatives, has created a bottleneck for regulators. In several countries, it has become clear that many are poorly managed and are struggling financially; this is undoubtedly also true elsewhere. This situation presents a dilemma for the regulator. On the one hand, small MFIs can hardly present systemic risks, especially if they do not take deposits. On the other hand, the relatively small scale of much terrorism financing means that small size does not preclude the use of an MFI for this purpose.

One overriding principle therefore seems important in guiding regulatory design in regard to MFIs, namely that regulation should not choke off initiative and outreach, especially in remote areas.[52] A sense of proportion is needed with regard to fears of systemic distress and terrorism financing, with anti-money-laundering and combating the financing of terrorism

(AML–CFT) regulations adapted to the scale and functioning of each class of intermediary, as proposed in Isern, Deshpande, and van Doorn (2005). Only the largest deposit-taking MFIs need to be actively supervised for prudential reasons by the banking regulator. In this regard, for most countries, size should be measured by the number of depositing clients. More limited arrangements can be envisaged for the rest. Despite their recent growth and a tendency to concentration in the sector, arguably in no African country does any MFI have a balance sheet sufficiently large that its failure would entail contagion that would cause a wider financial sector meltdown.[53] Focusing on institutions with a large number of clients—and only on those that take deposits—is simply a rational allocation of limited supervisory resources to protect the interests of a large number of clients and also thereby protect social stability.

A new style emerging in Africa is to place MFIs that have sufficiently large capital in a separate regulatory category. The idea is that members of this class are at a scale with which the banks and the central bank can do business. They are more closely supervised than the other MFIs but may be allowed a broader range of activities (perhaps including a wider geographic spread for their lending and deposit-taking activities, permission to deal in foreign exchange, or permission to make larger individual loans). The idea of this additional tier is that these institutions—not having the capital or expertise to carry out the full range of banking services safely—cannot safely be allowed the full freedom of a banking license, yet are too big to be bypassed by prudential regulation.[54] Should this trend toward regulatory emphasis on larger institutions signal the death knell for smaller MFIs? Not yet. It is possible that, in time, one or two models of MFI will emerge as dominant. However, for the present, evidence is insufficient to allow one to conclude that, given the current economic and social environment in Africa, any one of the models has decisive disadvantages or merits.

To be sure, it is unlikely that an MFI sector that has wide outreach and is financially sustainable will in the long run be formed of small institutions. As is clear from econometric analyses of MFI sustainability, scale will prove essential for cost control (Honohan 2004). But the experimental stage that we observe implies that some potential giants of the future are now starting small. If we do not yet really know which model will dominate in the end, we cannot know which types of MFI deserve to grow.[55] The diversity of models in play at present likely facilitates product and process innovation. Given the current state of our knowledge, the fact that the industry is still young, and how essential experimentation will continue to be in the search for successful and sustainable formulas for African conditions, it would be unwise to legislate prematurely for uniformity or to insist from the outset on large scale.

Regulators tend to be hostile to small institutions, and their suspicion is often justified. No fewer than 250 small MFIs were closed in Cameroon following the explosive growth of 1996 to 1999, though 85 percent of the sector remained informal or unregulated. But it was the largest network, FECECAM, that failed in Benin. So closing small entities is no guarantee of safety going forward.

For smaller MFIs, the ambitions of the regulators should be adapted to their means. Keeping an ear to the ground and visiting MFIs on a spot-check basis and in response to rumors or suspicions of which they become aware is as much as the supervisor of the smaller MFIs can hope to do. In many cases, the deficiencies reflect inadequate basic business and book-keeping skills: certainly improvements in financial transparency are badly needed. Identifying capacity-building needs and helping to provide them are two of the most fruitful functions of the supervisor.

Networks of cooperatives, credit unions, and rural banks, such as the Apex Bank of the Ghana Association of Rural Banks, already find it in their collective interest to employ inspectors who visit member MFIs on a regular basis to inspect and advise in a collegial manner. The incentive to do this will remain high as long as MFIs are neither explicitly nor implicitly covered by deposit insurance. Arranging that the official supervisor of the smaller MFIs, working with these networks and apex institutions, can draw in times of need on the staff resources of the main bank regulator will help ensure that any emerging crises can be met with adequate skills. Not all MFIs will be saved by this pragmatic approach, but the benefits in improved focus and cost saving will outweigh the costs, if any.

This more selectively targeted approach to supervision should be matched by a refocusing of regulation. Although it may be hard to design enforceable antimonopoly and consumer protection regulations, these goals should begin to receive greater attention. As well as raising prices, the introduction of technological innovations can be blocked by incumbents, especially with technologies that involve network effects such as the payments system. Furthermore, undue mechanical restrictions on the design and range of products that can be offered by banks and MFIs will stifle innovation that could promote outreach.[56] Artificial rules about the classification of loans; excessive liquidity requirements; ownership restrictions (until recently, no individual private entity could own more than 20 percent of a bank in Uganda); and usury laws and other forms of interest ceilings can constrain banks and make MFIs reluctant to convert to banks, thereby limiting the range of services they can offer their clients.

Interest ceilings are particularly problematic. Although financial specialists universally agree on the damaging social effects of constraining ceilings on bank lending rates, the attempt to control rates has a recurrent populist attraction. Recent draft legislation in Kenya would, for example, have capped bank lending rates at 400 basis points above treasury bill rates, a measure that would have excluded a very large fraction of the potential borrowing market. Nigeria operates a ceiling at a similar level—400 basis points above the minimum rediscount rate—according to the mandatory "guide to bank charges" promulgated by the Central Bank of Nigeria (Charitonenko 2005).[57] The ceiling on bank lending rates in the CEMAC (Communauté Economique et Monétaire de l'Afrique Centrale) zone is currently 15 percent. Even the relatively high 27 percent usury ceiling for MFIs (18 percent for banks) in the UEMOA countries represents a constraint for MFIs in that region and is much lower than the rates of 50 to 80 percent per year that lenders in South Africa have commonly charged on small loans. To be sure, removal or relaxation of usury laws can be politically delicate. The approach adopted by the South African authorities, allowing registered lenders to charge higher rates (while leaving the usury ceilings on the books), had the merit of allowing greater transparency of high-rate lending and potentially preventing predatory lending practices while opening the door to effective microlending (Helms and Reille 2004).

Role of Donors: Resources, Innovation, Independence

Where do external donors fit in? First, of course, they can bring technology, human, and financial resources. Apart from capacity building and other institutional strengthening, donors can be sources of innovation and entrepreneurship. In addition, by exploiting their independence from local interest groups, they may be able to inject a degree of insulation from political pressure and serve to a degree as agencies of restraint. As such, they can venture further down the activist road than it is safe for governments to go. This is also true of a growing group of external providers of funds to microfinance and financial sector development generally (grants, loans, guarantees, equity); they are outside the traditional donor group and may have a more commercial motivation.[58,59]

Numerous examples of these elements have been cited throughout this chapter. Another illustration comes from the equity stakes taken by the International Finance Corporation (IFC) and other donors in small banks and MFIs in Africa. The donors too are affected by scale problems in this regard, especially where (as with the IFC) investments are intended to be remunerative. The equity stakes are small in financial value and cannot easily repay the inevitable minimum administrative costs involved in evaluating and monitoring them. It thus becomes important to supplement the purely financial engagement with an adequate budget for staff costs, while refining ways of evaluating the contribution of these costs to national development.

But the donors must be careful. Their scale often makes them like an elephant in the garden; when they move, locals may be trampled. How can they assist while maintaining incentives for private financial service providers to build their own technology and expand their market supply? How can they ensure that the costs of the assistance are limited to budgeted aid amounts? By now some of the most common causes of damaging side effects and of budget overruns are well known to donors and recipients, with subsidized interest rates topping the list of distortions.

Not all the new ideas in this area are wholly trouble free. For example, loan guarantee schemes are increasingly popular. It is important that they do not become just a covert way of providing sizable de facto interest subsidies to projects with what is in reality a high, but unacknowledged, default risk.[60] To the extent that the guarantee will not be called for several years, even unsuccessful schemes of this type can seem to be well performing for quite a while. The design of the guarantee can reduce the distortion, for example, if the guarantee applies to the first loss only and is not open ended.

Less fraught are such enabling interventions as—to draw on the recommendations of Pearce (2003)—brokering links between private sector participants, promoting farmers' associations, offering technical farm extension advice, and providing basic business development services. By funding setup costs as opposed to marginal costs, these kinds of intervention can avoid the most damaging distortions.

Innovative approaches to solving the problem of choosing which supplier should benefit from a proposed subsidy (perhaps having a competition in which alternative suppliers bid for the subsidy) need to be explored in finance as in other sectors. Indeed, the role of donors, including international financial intermediaries, in enhancing the flow of credit to small-scale borrowers is a delicate issue, given that donor sponsorship often drove the expansion of failing development finance institutions (DFIs) in the past. Most are keen not to repeat the errors of the past. Perhaps one way is to take a more engaged approach to the design and evaluation of onlending projects, to try to ensure that such projects are not undermined by favoritism in lending by the sublenders. This calls for increased efforts in capacity building and, in particular, attention to institutional design.

Finally, donors need to look at conditions in their own countries, notably with regard to international remittances. Do regulatory measures need to be taken to help ensure that the market for sending remittances to Africa is competitive and provides reliable services at low cost? The European Commission has been successful in driving improved international retail payments technologies and in ensuring lower consumer prices for these payments in the context of the European single currency. Could these ideas be extended to remittances toward Africa?

Notes

1. Porteous (2006a) discusses the failure of MFI interest rates to decline over time.
2. Data from http://www.mixmarket.org show that for the 57 elite African MFIs that report the relevant data to the MIX database, the average administrative cost per borrower in 2003 was US$129 (median of US$58). With such high unit costs, it is hard for MFIs to make small loans without relying on explicit or implicit subsidies. Nevertheless, there are indications that reliance on subsidies is falling. More MFIs are now reporting profitability, and with funders shifting to loans and equity, donor grants are not as common (Lafourcade and others 2005).
3. Here we include registered cooperatives and credit-only nongovernmental organizations as well as deposit-taking firms.
4. For financiers and their customers who prefer to deal only in products that comply with the more strict interpretations of Sharia law, a different set of innovations is appropriate. Islamic scholars are continuously refining Sharia-compliant products to achieve overall functionality comparable to that of interest-based finance and conventional insurance. Though growing, the use of these products in Africa remains very limited. The Web site of the Harvard Law School Islamic Finance Project is a valuable resource on this topic: http://ifp.law.harvard.edu.

5. For overall discussion of current issues in rural finance, see Kloeppinger-Todd (2005), Nagarajan and Meyer (2005), and Zeller (2003). At a more technical level, an authoritative and up-to-date survey of the economics of rural finance in developing countries, with numerous references to African studies, is in Conning and Udry (forthcoming).
6. Private merchants have taken on this role because parastatals have withdrawn in many countries. A late government entrant into this activity was that of Kenya in 1992, which displaced sugar factories as supplier of inputs on credit to smallholders in the sugar sector; the results were not sustainable, with heavy write-offs, and the government retreated after about a decade.
7. Because input loans are generally a small fraction of the value of output subsequently purchased, lenders can find even high default rates tolerable. Note that the risk of side sales is essentially confined to commodities whose supply chain does not have a natural constriction point.
8. Boot and Schmeits (2005) argue that (even though it has been diminishing in importance in advanced countries, except for the very largest deals) relationship banking remains at the heart of the competitive advantage of banks.
9. Not only underperforming economies rely on this type of relationship lending. Allen, Qian, and Qian (2005) and Allen and others (2006) note the importance of informal credit arrangements of this type in the rapidly growing Chinese and Indian economies.
10. The more recent wave of World Bank-sponsored investment climate surveys is also beginning to be analyzed in microeconometric analysis; see Eifert, Gelb, and Ramachandran (2006) and Moss, Ramachandran, and Shah (2004). Based on these surveys, Investment Climate Assessment reports have already been completed for a dozen African countries: Benin, Eritrea, Ethiopia, Kenya, Madagascar, Mali, Mauritius, Senegal, South Africa, Tanzania, Uganda, and Zambia, with Malawi soon to appear (http://www.enterprisesurveys.org/ICAs.aspx).
11. The excusable default concept is successfully applied also by one of the world's most effective development banks, Thailand's Bank for Agriculture and Agricultural Cooperatives (Townsend and Yaron 2001); see also Conning and Udry (forthcoming).
12. Credit networks of this type are widely observed to be confined within ethnic groups—reflecting an additional coping strategy of lenders in a difficult business environment. Ethnically limited credit networks restrict the opportunities for growth and productivity improvement (Eifert, Gelb, and Ramachandran 2006); to advocate greater use of relationship lending is in no way to advocate such limitations.
13. A savings account with a financial intermediary is a way of providing some insulation to the flow of household consumption in the event of an emergency. Hit by some losses or an urgent spending need (for medicine, funerals, and the like), a household will not escape the loss in total net present value terms, but temporary consumption compression can be avoided. If the household has access to emergency credit, that too will help.

14. International financial markets in insurance, commodity derivatives, and other products can be directly accessed only by very large entities such as governments. For example, during the food crisis of 2005 to 2006, the government of Malawi implemented an innovative approach to financial risk management of the food security response by purchasing a customized over-the-counter call option, based on South African Futures Exchange (SAFEX) quotations, to cap the price of maize imports. More challenging is making such risk management available widely through the economy.
15. Informal but well-organized insurance arrangements also exist, notably for funeral costs in Africa; see Dercon and others (2004).
16. The emphasis here on agricultural insurance should not hide the presence of other types of microinsurance in Africa. Life cover is often bundled with microcredit. Burial societies, often promoted by funeral companies, are particularly widespread in southern Africa. A variety of microinsurance schemes have emerged for health care, often managed on mutualist principles but often also involving the active participation of health providers, requiring the sponsorship and support of donors. They are sometimes linked with microfinance—indeed, emergency loans have sometimes displaced health microinsurance as the preferred response to health risks. See McCord and Osinde (2003) for East Africa and Louis (2006) for an interesting francophone case study. A valuable set of case studies, including several from Africa, can be found at http://www.microinsurancecentre.org. See also Preker, Scheffler, and Bassett (2006).
17. For example, tracking crop prices allows farmers to time the sale of produce. Farmers often do not know and therefore cannot get fair market prices. Internet technology can help (for example, the info kiosks piloted by PRIDE-Kenya's Drumnet scheme, which could ultimately be expanded to link into payments or even credit services).
18. Following Rutherford (2001), it is convenient to distinguish among three different types of eventuality for which savings are made by poor people: first, to deal with lumpy requirements of predictable life-cycle events (births, deaths, marriages, school fees, old age, and so on) and to cope with the timing mismatch between income receipts (for example, seasonal harvest receipts or the proceeds of the sale of an animal); second, to meet emergencies (sickness, injury, loss of employment, war, flood, and the like); and third, for opportunities (starting a business, acquiring assets, or buying radios, televisions, and so on). Life-cycle events are fairly predictable and liquidity of savings is not a major concern. By contrast, the need to finance emergencies requires liquid savings products. Even if households have the discipline to save at home to meet the diverse needs for lump sums of money at some point, saving at home is not a reliable mechanism. The money stored at home is susceptible to being dissipated in less valuable spending that arises in day-to-day household expenses, demands from relatives, or theft. The problem of losses of savings is documented for Uganda by Wright and Muteesassira (2001). They found that 99 percent of clients saving in the informal sector report losing some of their

savings; on average they lost 22 percent of the amount they had saved in the preceding year. A valuable collection of papers on financial saving mechanisms in Africa is in Wright (2003). Note, however, that precautionary savings in nonfinancial forms are important in Africa, as has been shown by extensive literature; a recent example is Kazianga and Udry (2005).

19. Checking accounts and credit cards represent payment technologies that do entail credit and that may not be as suitable for the poor as savings accounts and debit cards.
20. The pronounced inequality of living standards may have contributed here, because some banks competitively pursued the higher margins attainable from the upper echelons by offering high service quality and ambience not compatible with a crowded mass-market banking hall. Once such banks acknowledge the potential profitability of the mass market, though, they may continue to segment the market by offering exclusive luxurious physical facilities to customers with large balances.
21. Instead of mobile units, Botswana Saving Bank's electronic passbook for savers (which reduces fraud and speeds services) uses a low-cost ATM system and point-of-sale machines placed in selected post offices countrywide. It also relies on live telecommunications-a satellite system that provides much-improved geographic coverage throughout that vast and very sparsely populated country.
22. Long before the introduction of Mzansi accounts by a wider range of South African banks in the context of the Financial Sector Charter, Teba Bank had developed a low-fee, interest-bearing savings account targeted to low-income, predominantly unbanked and underbanked residents in rural South Africa.
23. The system was designed by a team originally convened by Hewlett-Packard and including representatives from ACCION International, Biz Credit, FINCA International, Grameen Technology Center, Freedom from Hunger, Global eChange, and PRIDE AFRICA (Firpo 2005).
24. South Africa-Wizzit, MTN (Mobile Telephone Networks), and Standard Bank-and Kenya-Vodafone MPesa-also have cell-phone banking. There are some differences in functionality (such as the ability to work across different cell-phone networks) and in pricing and target market (Porteous 2006b).
25. For instance, there are no recent data for Cameroon, Côte d'Ivoire, the Democratic Republic of Congo, or Kenya, to take just the largest missing countries.
26. In addition to remitting funds to relatives at home, emigrants may place deposits on their own account in the banking system of their home country. Cape Verde's emigrant deposit scheme is the most remarkable example here, with such deposits (up until recently subsidized) amounting to 40 percent of M2 (Karpowicz 2006).
27. The potential for some steady remittance flows to form the basis for a favorable credit rating is largely lost when the funds flow to a cash point, as with MTOs, in contrast to being sent to a recipient's bank or MFI account.
28. One supplier, Ikobo, has expanded its debit card-based remittance technology to several African countries. This service allows senders to top up remotely a

Visa debit card that has been sent to the recipient, who can immediately withdraw the money from ATMs in African cities. The service seems to be slightly cheaper than the MTOs. Top-up call time codes for some African cell-phone networks can also be purchased in the United Kingdom and other centers (and communicated by phone to the recipient). (Within Africa, call time can sometimes be transferred between user accounts for a small fee.)

29. The database of the CGAP has been augmented by Peachey and Roe (2005), who added more savings banks. The data presented in this study also incorporate some additional refinements, including those suggested by Honohan (2006).
30. The overall household access percentage estimates presented in chapter 2 use a nonlinear function of account numbers that should help reduce the biases mentioned here.
31. Interestingly, the aggregate ratio of MFI deposits to loans is much higher (at 72 percent) in Africa than elsewhere. In other words, the net role of external funds in financing the sector is smaller in Africa.
32. Robinson (2006, 16) reviews the available evidence on the financial performance of leading African providers of microfinance: "Whether specialist organizations or multipurpose institutions, these microfinance providers are generally commercially funded and financially self-sufficient. They tend to have substantial assets and high loan repayment rates. And except for NGOs, their savings accounts typically outnumber their outstanding loans." She also notes that, by comparison with the very low per capita national income, staff salaries at African providers are exceptionally high in international comparisons, though this is offset by much higher productivity as measured by number of clients per staff member.
33. The principles of mutuality are sometimes listed as democracy, participation, solidarity, autonomy, and liability. Case studies of African mutual financial institutions include Ouattara, Gonzalez-Vega, and Graham (1999).
34. The traditional small-group approach, entailing forced lending and a highly regimented repayment schedule, has been criticized for imposing unnecessary transactions costs. Also, although group members may progress to larger loan sizes if the whole group repays on time, the model does not cater to varied evolution of client needs over time.
35. FINCA and ACCION pioneered the village banking model. Sometimes the model relies partly on existing village authority structures for its governance.
36. See Basu, Blavy, and Yulek (2004) for a useful overview.
37. A recent statistical examination of the accounts of several hundred MFIs across the world suggests some interesting regularities (Cull, Demirgüc-Kunt, and Morduch 2005). Firms that use individual-based loans (in contrast to village-based lenders and those making group loans) tend to make larger loans. Only in the case of these individual-based lenders is revenue sensitive to interest rates. There is a positive relationship between labor cost and profitability but, again, only for the individual-based lenders, suggesting that they benefit from spending more on screening and monitoring while group- and village-based institutions do not. Given that individual-based lenders are able to exploit

scale economies by making larger loans to their more creditworthy clients, it is not surprising that their portfolio is weighted toward less poor individuals.
38. Interestingly, the US$300 figure is a higher percentage (89 percent) of per capita GNI than the average observed in Asia, Latin America, or the Middle East and North Africa. This partly reflects the lower income levels in Africa. But some African MFIs make extremely small loans. The average loan size for ASSOPIL (Association pour la Promotion des Initiatives Locales) in Benin and for Bessfa RB in Ghana is US$35 and US$37, respectively. That both are profitable and large MFIs is due to their very high productivity—more than 1,000 borrowers per staff member in the case of ASSOPIL.
39. An instructive finding of Lafourcade and others (2005, figure 8) is that operating expenses represent a much higher proportion of total assets in southern Africa and the Indian Ocean area than is the case in the rest of Africa. Perhaps staff costs are disproportionately higher in the former subregions when compared with the average scale of loans.
40. MGAs (following the postwar continental European model) have begun to emerge in some African countries (De Gobbi 2003). Sometimes sponsored by banks, sometimes by business associations, and sometimes with concrete support from governments, MGAs are a way for groups of SMEs to exploit their special knowledge of members' creditworthiness to guarantee members' borrowings from banks and other financial intermediaries.
41. Other networks of mutuals began with a strong center, as in the case of PAMECAS in Senegal, which, as reflected in the old name that gave it its acronym (Projet d'Appui aux Mutuelles d'Epargne et de Crédit au Sénégal), began as a donor-sponsored effort.
42. Among other things, the ARB Apex Bank operates a very effective retail payments system for the rural banks.
43. Somewhat surprisingly, there seems to be no corresponding apex institution yet for the 700 Nigerian community banks (Charitonenko 2005).
44. If most mainstream financial intermediaries were to embrace the principles of sustainable finance, their contribution would be stronger. For a detailed and inspiring advocacy of this position for Africa, see Wood and de Cleene (2004).
45. In October 2003, responding to actual or anticipated political pressure, South Africa's financial institutions adopted the Black Economic Empowerment Charter, including measures that will make banking services more accessible to low-income households—notably a simplified deposit account—the Mzansi account-offering lower charges and no overdraft facilities (unplanned use of which can prove disastrously costly for the poor). Some of the techniques that have been adopted to give effect to this charter are beginning to find their way into other parts of Africa.
46. In an interesting experiment that might seem to clash with its somewhat conservative image, Barclays Bank has recently piloted an initiative in Ghana to make microloans to susu collectors for onlending to the collectors' clients. The Ghana Cooperative Susu Collectors Association, the self-regulated apex body of the susu collectors, identified 100 of its 4,000 members for the pilot and car-

ried out preliminary screening of those borrowers. The Ghana Microfinance Institutions Network (GHAMFIN) facilitated capacity building for the susu collectors and a basic financial skills education program targeted to those who would be the ultimate borrowers. Noting that Ghana's susu collectors reflect a £75 million economy (equivalent to almost 2 percent of GDP) "thriving below the traditional banking radar," a Barclays news release implies that the program could be profitable at scale.

47. Education and investment in human capital are essential if financial technologies are to be adopted. Codified knowledge, like a credit-scoring or a mortgage-lending tool, requires significant levels of complementary human capital and tacit knowledge, such as ICT literacy, as well as an adequate organizational and management capacity.

48. A contrasting example illustrating the damaging effects of some well-intended government policies is the case of free provision of fertilizer by the government to selected maize farmers in Zambia, which fatally undermined an otherwise promising market-based fertilizer credit scheme (Ruotsi 2003).

49. Value-for-money calculations require considering not only the likely effectiveness of proposed spending (taking into account moral hazard and other potentially adverse unintended side effects), but also the opportunity cost (the value of alternative uses of public funds).

50. The oft-discussed Indian experiment of the late 1970s and 1980s, when banks wishing to expand in the cities were obliged to match this growth with an expansion of their rural branch network (Burgess and Pande 2004), is a case in point. In few African cities is the prospect of opening an additional urban branch a sufficiently attractive proposition to induce a banker to open also in a rural area: such a policy risks backfiring and reducing branches and access overall.

51. Among the most active have been the central banks of Ethiopia, Gambia, Kenya, Tanzania, Uganda, and the two CFA unions.

52. An interesting case study of these concerns appears in Chiumya (2006).

53. Even as nationally dominant an institution as FECECAM, with close to half a million beneficiaries, had deposits amounting to only about 7 percent of bank deposits in the latest year. This is not to imply that institutions with an MFI focus are negligible in terms of total liabilities. For instance, the following are among the top seven intermediaries in their countries, measured by total deposits: FECECAM (Benin); Faîtière des Unités Coop, or FUCEC (Togo); Fédération Nationale des Coopératives d'Epargne et de Crédit, or FENACOOPEC (Côte d'Ivoire); Crédit Mutuel (Senegal); Kafo Jiginew and Nyesigiso (Mali); Réseau des Caisses Populaires du Burkina, or RCPB (Burkina Faso); Cameroon Cooperative Credit Union League, or CAMCCUL, and Union Bank (Cameroon); and Bank of Africa (Madagascar). Many large MFIs also have substantial loans from banks.

54. Proposals in South Africa for two new tiers of restricted core and narrow banks have a somewhat similar motivation, though driven more by a perception that

existing minimum capital requirements for banks were a barrier to new entry in retail banking for low-income clients. The minimum capital required of the proposed new categories of bank would be smaller, at R 50 million and R 10 million, respectively, compared with the minimum for a full service bank of R 250 million. Essentially, in addition to providing transactions services, core banks would be allowed to take deposits and make secured loans; narrow banks would only take deposits. The helpfulness of such elaborate regulatory refinements in facilitating viable and socially useful entry would depend on national circumstances (FinMark Trust 2005).

55. Many African MFI regulators have become uneasy about the proliferation of small moneylenders masquerading under the name of MFIs but operating in the traditional manner of informal moneylenders everywhere. As in the past, the existence of a ready market for the services of these moneylenders reflects the limitations of formal finance.

56. Electronic and cell-phone-based innovations in particular raise important regulatory questions that are well discussed in Porteous (2006b), who stresses the desirability of regulatory openness to innovation and regulatory certainty to give innovators the confidence to make the initial investment. With parts of Africa close to the technological frontier in some aspects of these developments, this area is likely to be a rapidly evolving one for advanced economy regulators also.

57. See the Central Bank of Nigeria's circular dated April 23, 2004, available at http://www.cenbank.org/out/circulars/bsd/2004/bsd-02-2004.pdf.

58. An important example of the new entrants in this field is the Investment Climate Facility for Africa (http://www.investmentclimatefacility.org), a joint endeavor involving several national governments as well as some major multinational business groups. Working with the support of the African Union in the context of the Africa Peer Review Mechanism process set up by the New Partnership for Africa's Development, the facility has financial markets as one of its eight priority areas and is explicitly set up with a view to exploiting this potential.

59. As far as microfinance is concerned, 11 key principles have been endorsed by the Group of Eight, all 33 CGAP donor members, and many others: view them at http://www.cgap.org/portal/site/CGAP/menuitem.64c03ec40a6d295067 808010591010a0. Collectively agreed guidelines for microfinance donors are set out at http://www.cgap.org/portal/binary/com.epicentric.contentmanagement.servlet.ContentDeliveryServlet/Documents/donorguidelines.pdf.

60. Some donors (for example, the U.S. Agency for International Development) have been using business development schemes (for example, one being carried out by Chemonics in Uganda) in coordination with their loan guarantee program, with the goal of bringing projects to the point where the risks are both lower and more easily calculated. It will be interesting to see how successful this model proves to be.

CHAPTER 5

Policy Choices in Current Conditions

Introduction: The Vision

Appropriate affordable and sustainable financial services
The previous chapters have offered a vision of how financial systems in African countries could evolve over the years ahead—a financial sector delivering a more appropriate, affordable, and sustainable package of the services needed by African economies and societies. This evolution means more financial intermediaries that are backed by solid and reputable owners, have skilled management, and compete energetically and imaginatively for business on the basis of strict attention to cost control and knowledge of the local market and conditions. It also means an environment relevant to sound finance—the supporting infrastructures, legal and informational, for property rights that can support financial contracts.

Some of the services are needed by modern firms producing at high levels of productivity for an international as well as a domestic market. Only if the number and size of these firms grow can African economies hope both to absorb the growing numbers of young people entering the labor force in the years ahead[1] and to generate adequate incomes to lift them from absolute poverty.

Financial systems will also be needed to provide services at a small scale to meet the needs of low-income households, microenterprises, and subsistence and smallholder farming securely and at an affordable cost. These services (together with specific improvements in other sectors) will contribute to the ability of the poor to ensure that the new generation has the health and education to participate fully in the opportunities created by the growing modern sector.[2]

There is no need to choose between growth and services
The dichotomy between financial services for growth and those for outreach was clear enough in the past in terms of which institutions catered to which market. But increasingly the dividing line has become blurred, and this trend will continue. One reason is the middle market of small- and medium-scale enterprises that now function at the margins of the formal economy and that are often treated by banks as informal and unbankable entities. These enterprises must increasingly move upscale in terms of their business practices—including their accounting and their engagement with the official sphere—eventually graduating into a higher league of productivity and competitiveness. Another is that increasing awareness of the profit potential at the bottom of the pyramid will result in formal intermediaries moving downscale even as microfinance specialists grow up with their clients. Thus, as has already begun to happen in some countries, some microfinance institutions (MFIs) will become banks and some banks will become market leaders in catering to low-income groups. Meanwhile, the emergence of strong financial intermediaries whose goal is to seek out profitable and secure uses for their funds will offer energetic entrepreneurs a way of securing the finance needed for their growth without having to seek political patronage or a disadvantageous alliance with incumbents.

Governments are better equipped to enable market functioning than to participate in it
Although this vision sees a major role for private activity—reflecting a view that finance is a sector that is uniquely sensitive to adverse and unintended side effects of misconceived government and political intervention—government has a major policy role in seeing that this vision is accomplished. As this report has stressed throughout, the most rewarding task for government is not to try to substitute for the market but instead to enable and encourage market functioning by building the overall environment and the specific meso-level infrastructures needed by market participants. The activities of donors are often important in influencing the

shape of government policies, at least at the technical level, and they, too, need to consider how to contribute to the achievement of the vision.

From Vision to Policy

The goal of this study has been to present a considered review of the challenges and opportunities for financial sector policy in African countries. By now it will be clear that the approach adopted does not lead to a brief checklist of easily accomplished items to be implemented. Any checklist can appear both depressingly long and full of hard-to-accomplish elements.

Indeed, most African countries have, in the past couple of decades, been reforming fundamental banking and central banking laws, as well as their counterparts underpinning the insurance and securities markets. Some of these countries have enacted laws defining and clarifying the operation of mutual funds, leasing companies, and wholesale payments systems, among others, so that the relevant intermediaries can do business without fear that lack of legal certainty will result in unexpected consequences. Legislation underpinning the modern use of collateral and governing insolvency has also been on the agenda, as of course has the whole vexed area of ownership and rights over the use of land. All these efforts are essential to improve legal certainty, without which financial contracts become too risky for all parties.

Meanwhile, regulatory structures have had to be designed and staffed with adequately trained professionals, not only for banks but also for microfinance institutions, whose solvency their clients have little chance of evaluating. Failing banks have had to be restructured, recapitalized, and placed under reputable management and ownership.

All these measures have been necessary and have in most cases only been partially accomplished. Each step has been partly technical, but most have also involved tactical and political choices. Should entry be blocked to give breathing space for incumbents to consolidate? Should entities controlled by nationals be given preference over foreigners in the hope that they might act in the national interest? Is finance so sensitive that everything must be built to the most complex prevailing standards, or are shortcuts permissible and desirable? The reasoning of this report does suggest answers, or at least an orientation to such tactical questions.

Thus, a three-stranded common thread runs through the policy discussion of this report.

- First, while not neglecting to build for the long term, *shortcuts* can be taken that will allow African financial systems to deliver the most essential services faster, without compromising on stability and efficiency.

- Second, openness must be maintained to what the *outside world* can offer, whether in the form of regional cooperation at the policy level or the provision of services by foreign institutions.

- Third, the value of approaching policy with attention to *inclusiveness* as a goal must be understood.

Shortcuts

The bedrock of any coherent vision of what an African financial system should aspire to is certainly defined in large part by what has been achieved in advanced economies,[3] building on solid legal and information foundations. What has been referred to previously as the modernist agenda is what is needed for the long term. Fleshing out that agenda and helping make it a reality over time are what external advisers (including the World Bank) spend most of their time discussing with policy makers. And rightly so. Many of the elements take a long time to put in place. That is not only why making a start on them is important but also why seeking the shortcuts and ensuring that quick-yielding measures receive sufficient priority are important.

The suggestion that information infrastructures may yield greater benefits than legal reform in low-income countries with sizable governance deficits is an example of such a shortcut involving choices and prioritization as between different elements of the modernist agenda.

Another example is in the idea that regulation of securities markets might be more successful in most African markets if it begins with the lighter regulatory touch typical of second-board markets in advanced economies. Likewise, avoidance of the complexities that would be introduced by most variants of the Basel II capital framework for bank regulation is suggested for now. More generally, the desirability of adapting regulatory structures to local needs and capacities is something that needs to be acknowledged more than it has been, though it must not, of course, be an excuse for a semideliberate opening of loopholes that could reintroduce the carelessness and self-dealing that have caused many intermediary failures in the past.

Most of the activist agenda can be seen as a shortcut, for which advanced financial systems have less need (though even these suffer from market failures requiring correction, as has been mentioned). The prominence of the activist agenda is thus likely to subside over time as structural weaknesses are progressively corrected. For the moment, though, getting an effective financial system is a struggle, not something that will happen of its own accord.

But strengthening governance is crucial where activism is being tried. If state-owned development finance institutions (and credit guarantee schemes) have failed for lack of adequate governance in the past, one must be alert to the danger that social security funds, newly encouraged to contribute to the provision of long-term and risk finance, could slip down the same path if their good governance is not ensured.

External Agency

At several points in the discussion, we have argued that external agencies can make up for what is lacking at home. They can offer improved governance through their relative independence from national political pressures. They can offer risk pooling and avoid the diseconomies of small national scale. They can bring technology and help build human capital. This argument applies to regional organizations, to foreign-owned financial intermediaries and markets, and to donors.

Exploring the potential benefits of internationalization, whether regional or global, should be a requirement for policy design in any aspect of finance for African countries. Can the sought-for improvement be achieved more effectively or more cheaply through some form of outsourcing or through regional cooperation? *Foreign* does not necessarily mean *good*, even in finance, and the potential downsides, whether in terms of the sizable coordination costs involved in regionalization or the excessive macroeconomic volatility that might be introduced by premature capital account liberalization, must be carefully calculated. But in many—if not most—cases, the benefits easily outweigh the costs, and many objections (such as the fear that locals will not learn the relevant skills if services are being provided by foreign institutions) prove on examination to be groundless. Managing populist doubts here is a challenge for advisers and even more so for national politicians.

Inclusiveness

Though it may not seem so, conventional financial reform is a potentially radical undertaking, which may be subversive of incumbent interests as it transforms the economy and society by giving opportunities to all. Who can doubt that some such transformation is needed in most African economies today? A society in which all have a clear stake in underwriting sustained economic growth—both the existing elites, who craft policy, and the poor, whose horizons can be substantially lifted only by the assurance of a reasonable share in expanded general prosperity—is the only type of society that will prosper in the decades ahead. Inclusiveness is therefore also a criterion against which policy stances must be evaluated.

Facilitating the extension of microfinance to a wider clientele requires the action not just of the government in ensuring that innovators are not hampered by uncalled-for rules but also of sponsors and intermediaries. The latter must innovate to reduce unit costs and to meet the barriers of scale and remoteness, but they must also ensure that successful innovations are sustained and scaled up, thereby helping achieve inclusiveness by avoiding the syndrome of repeated small-scale initiatives that run out of steam because follow-up is less glamorous than trailblazing.

Inclusiveness is also generated by ensuring a sufficient population of competitive service providers. Otherwise incumbents will restrict themselves to those customers that are easiest to serve. Instead of protecting incumbents from new entrants, many—though not all—African policy makers have wisely been welcoming entry by reputable service providers.

Where Should Government Begin?—Two Attainable Goals

As every country that has participated in the World Bank–International Monetary Fund Financial Sector Assessment Program (FSAP)[4] is well aware, bringing legal and regulatory structures into compliance with best practice—as defined by international regulatory bodies and expert opinion—can be a daunting task. Indeed, for many countries, limited administrative resources mean the task is impossible to accomplish within a short time frame. The task implies more than just adjusting laws and more than accomplishing institutional changes (within court systems, registries, and the like). It can also involve political upheaval because of the power shifts that might result. So prioritization is necessary. There are two

Boost Credit Flows by Strengthening Registries and Streamlining Court Procedures

Given the frequent coexistence of high liquidity and a credit crunch—with bankers in some countries actively discouraging deposits, a lowering of deposit rates, and a widening of spreads—improving the conditions that will help increase the flow of credit to the middle market could be the top priority for many African economies. One dimension to the solution is more innovative use of lending technologies, some of which have been discussed in chapter 4. But much of that lies in the hands of the intermediaries themselves. What can government do? Given the greater freedom now allowed in the determination of interest rates in many African countries and the much lower rates of inflation that now prevail, financial repression and macroeconomic instability may no longer be top of the list of the barriers to increased bank lending—although this situation could change and requires continued vigilance by policy makers. Instead, a number of other needed steps loom larger, several of which have already been alluded to in chapter 3. Taking these steps will help both stability of the financial system and development.

The functioning of registries—of land, of claims on movable assets, of credit records—needs improvement almost everywhere. In many cases, this improvement includes enacting supporting legislation. Closely related are the special pieces of legislation needed to underpin leasing and an expansion of the mortgage market. These too deserve to be considered early on. Some African countries have recently embarked on vigorous efforts along these lines, and an opportunity will soon exist to take stock at a nuts-and-bolts level of the degree of success here (as in other specific areas) to learn from such an evaluation about what works best in African conditions; carrying out such a stock-taking soon is on the World Bank's agenda.

Improving court procedures is, of course, more challenging. In particular, where corruption infects the courts, progress toward effective reform will be slow. But some simple procedural changes can help. The inefficient court procedures behind which delinquent borrowers (that could, but will not, repay) hide can be dismantled—again often requiring legislation and more. The quality of court judgments may be improved by training and perhaps by instituting a special commercial court.

This task is not trivial. Populist opposition to any pro-creditor reforms is likely to be stirred up by vested interests, and the reforms are unlikely to be enacted without vigorous and skilled political championship. Packaging such reforms with a national strategy for expanding the coverage of microfinance could be one way of building consensus around this aspect of the modernist agenda.[5]

Establish Independent Supervision

A politically dependent supervisory agency can be worse than useless, not least by protecting inefficient incumbents from competition. For example, at present, the laws on banking and central banking in many African countries do not give the monetary authority or the banking regulator sufficient operational independence from politicians—and from the banks—to do a good job. The importance of such independence was not yet evident when these laws—often modeled ultimately on since-revised laws of the United Kingdom or France—were enacted.[6]

Yet too much discretionary power in the hands of the banking regulator also can be damaging, and independence of the monetary authority presupposes a free press and an informed public opinion. Accountability is a necessary companion of independence. Accountability, in turn, requires a clear understanding of the goals of the regulator (as with the monetary authority). These goals should envisage facilitating entry of solid intermediaries, thereby enhancing competition. If systemic crises are to be avoided, creating the conditions for greater reliance on market discipline as a complement to official supervision is likely to yield the best results.

If they are to be independent, the banking regulator and the monetary authority need to have commensurate skills and administrative capacity. Here is a delicate balance. In the case of the bank regulator, the marginal benefit of having an additional trained and experienced supervisory staff can seem small in the years between crises, but the value of having one to head off an incipient crisis, or to deal with a crisis when it hits, is high. That is one reason for advocating regional cooperative arrangements in bank regulation (as discussed above). As for the monetary authority, the central bank of many African countries seems to be the best-resourced agency, typically because of the nature of its balance sheet and its ability to dip into seigniorage to cover administrative costs. On the one hand, these resources are sometimes used to create a center of excellence for guiding a wide range of financial policy, not just monetary policy. On the other hand, some of these institutions might have exercised more moderation in their office-building programs. Other central banks labor under the burden of having absorbed the cost of a banking or fiscal crisis and no longer enjoy financial independence, let alone operational or policy independence.

As for the regulation of nonbank finance, a lighter touch to capital market regulation may be appropriate for many African countries. And although insurance and pensions are increasingly important, the complexity of insurance accounting and the still small size of the insurance market argue for recognizing that it may not be feasible to staff the insurance regulator's office to a level that would ensure a high probability that abuses will be forestalled; caveat emptor must remain important for this sector.

The design of prudential regulation for microfinance has become quite a fraught issue in recent years, despite consensus on some principles. The main problems seem to be the diversity and multiplicity of MFIs and a tendency for newly established regulators to overreach and micromanage. Two presumptions may be useful to guide policy in most African countries: (a) non-deposit-taking MFIs do not require prudential regulation and (b) delegated monitoring to umbrella institutions of networks of mutuals or cooperatives can help reduce the central burden of supervision to a practical level. Finally, regulatory design needs to recognize that banks (moving downmarket) and MFIs (moving upmarket) will increasingly compete in the middle market. Regulation of the two in markets where they are both active should be conducive to a healthy competition between them.

Contrasting Initial Conditions

Given the diversity of initial conditions in different African countries, will one size fit all in policy design? Yes and no: yes, insofar as the goal is relying heavily on a self-sustaining, market-driven financial system to make many of the major allocative decisions in the economy; no, in that transplanting some specific practices (such as Basel II's new method for calculating bank capital) into an environment lacking key prerequisites would be a mistake—and also in that priorities will be different for Africa and between different countries within Africa, depending on initial conditions.

Thus, although all African countries face similar issues to a greater or lesser extent, the relative weight to be attached to different aspects will depend on local conditions. For instance, just five different country characteristics immediately point to the different priorities that need to inform the design and timing of policy reforms:[7]

- Postconflict countries
- Sparsely populated countries
- Small countries
- Oil-rich countries
- Countries with critical mass

Postconflict Countries

The resilience of some financial transactions in states whose governments have been overwhelmed by conflict has been remarked upon by some as an illustration of the resilience of the private financial sector and its ability to deliver some services even without the support of the state.[8] But for the most part, the effective range of the formal financial sector in conflict-ridden countries typically shrinks to a limited geographic zone, as up-country branches of banks are abandoned. Most banks indeed collapse altogether or teeter on the brink of insolvency, their liquidity dependent on monetary financing of the government's deficit. The currency notes deteriorate physically and have to compete with the introduction of a parallel or forged currency by insurgent groups.

Among the priorities for the new government is the reestablishment of credibility of the currency, supported by a fair, consistent, and transparent treatment of the problems of preexisting currency notes and by a coherent and credible macroeconomic and monetary policy framework.[9]

Reentry of bankers of substance will present several different challenges. Some of the old bankers will have left for good, but others may wish to reenter, even though their old banks had failed. Can they be considered fit and proper?

The chaos may have created an opportunity for shady transactions to be routed through what was left of the financial system, and even the perception that this could be so, will mean that AML–CFT (anti-money-laundering and combating the financing of terrorism) procedures will have to be put in place earlier than otherwise if this proves necessary to reestablish the country's banking links with international correspondents.

The domestic payments system is likely to require reconstruction from bottom up. If security is still questionable in up-country locations and no bank branches exist yet, the government will have difficulty in making payments, including to its employees. Post offices may not yet be functioning, and in their absence no alternative may exist to having the central bank provide check-cashing facilities on a temporary basis. Eventually, banks will return to the main outlying towns, especially if they are offered a realistic fee for cashing government checks. Electronic payments using mobile-phone technology—which is likely to be one of the first services reaching a wide geographic coverage—and points of sale in a handful of stores in the larger towns may prove feasible at a relatively early date. (The legal texts that would be desirable to place electronic payments on a secure basis may not be strictly necessary to underpin this system at first but will be needed in due course.)[10]

Sparsely Populated Countries

The many sparsely populated countries in Africa display some similarities to postconflict countries in terms of communications difficulties. Here too, then, electronic retail payments and mobile telephony offer a great opportunity. To ensure that these technologies are exploited, policy makers must avoid lock-in to a particular limited technology (some of the systems now being rolled out are a lot more capable than others) or to systems that cannot communicate with each other, to enact the legislation that will make banks and others that use these systems feel secure in their rights, and to remove unneeded banking regulations that might impede the adoption of these technologies.

Many African countries are in the process of introducing highly secure, speedy, and effective wholesale payments systems. The effort should not stop there; indeed, improving retail payments effectiveness is a higher priority for many African countries.

A distributed architecture of the financial system is likely to be an essential feature of sparsely populated countries, though this feature depends on how the population is actually distributed. In some countries, like Chad or Niger, large parts of the country are almost totally uninhabited, with most of the population concentrated in or near a relatively small number of centers. In time, the network of viable bank branches conceivably could blanket these centers. In Tanzania, by contrast, the population is scattered across a large number of isolated settlements. The bulk of the population there will remain as at present—quite far from a bank branch.[11] This situation means that access for a large fraction of the population can be only through MFIs or some form of agencies. The role of governments in smoothing the way for such arrangements is not only regulatory. Ingenuity will be needed to ensure that any subsidies they choose to provide—or the contracts for effecting government payments in rural areas—are designed in a way that offers a level playing field, so that the most efficient financial service providers will end up delivering each aspect of the service. This system may well result in a distributed architecture, with larger institutions such as banks, MFI-network umbrella organizations, or the post office taking the contract and subcontracting parts of it to rural agencies, including MFIs.

Small Countries

Small size presents a somewhat different set of tradeoffs. Here the inability to exploit economies of scale onshore and the tendency of the few providers to exploit monopoly power naturally point to sourcing services—both market and regulatory—offshore. These countries need some way of overcoming the diseconomies of insufficient scale, including the lack of competition between different financial service providers. Policy makers will want to err on the side of increased openness to entry from reputable foreign financial service providers, even if they are clearly going to rely heavily on their parent companies abroad for shared technology, management, and back-office and even credit-approval services.

An alliance with a nearby securities exchange, possibly aiming at the creation of a satellite of the foreign exchange, will also be worth exploring if the country does not have its own—and even if it does. This arrangement can raise exchange control issues for both countries to the extent that dealings on the satellite exchange could be used to export funds, but these issues will become less and less important as reliance on exchange controls diminishes.

The smaller the country, the more attractive regional cooperation on prudential regulation of banks and other intermediaries becomes, and outsourcing these functions to multinational organization can be a very viable solution. To an extent, these advantages of outsourcing have long been recognized by small African countries as different as Guinea-Bissau and Lesotho. But the potential has not yet been altogether fulfilled.

Oil-Rich Countries

Several African countries have been enjoying a sizable boom in the value of oil exports. For the smaller countries in this group, the effects on paper are astonishing. Indeed, Equatorial Guinea may have had the second-highest per capita gross domestic product in the world in 2005. Yet the rest of the economy has little enough to show for these gains. To be sure, the local banks are doing well out of fees charged on international transfers associated with the oil business, even though most of that business is financed offshore. Financial sector policy can have a role both in limiting the Dutch-disease effects of overvaluation that have been seen elsewhere with oil booms and as a mechanism for channeling some of these resources into the financing of productive investment—which in turn can help increase productivity and output in the nonoil sector.

Apart from monetary and exchange rate policy, the issues here are those of the governance of public funds, such as pension and social security funds writ large. These, more than banking or stock exchange issues, will assume priority in the minds of financial sector policy makers.

Countries with Critical Mass

A few African countries have the scale to consider providing a wider range of services onshore and putting in place a more comprehensive administrative and regulatory framework. Policy makers can be more ambitious in the nature and form of their policy initiatives. Kenya and Nigeria have joined South Africa in this category now, and the discussion would be also relevant for some others, increasingly so over time.

The ability of financial sector policy makers in larger economies to strike a distinctive policy note and hold to it has been most dramatically illustrated by the capital adequacy ruling of the Central Bank of Nigeria.[12] This experience shows several features of larger financial systems:

- First, the ability to be innovative and to design policies that are relevant to national needs without frightening away the major participants. In a smaller market, most banks would have chosen to exit the market rather than put up so much capital, but the franchise value of a bank license—its potential profitability—means that Nigerian banks complied.

- Second, the value of a domestic stock market, even in a matter that was primarily for banking. For all the belittling of Africa's stock markets that one hears, the Nigerian stock exchange did manage to raise about US$3 billion toward the recapitalization of the banks. The banks might have had difficulty in raising such funds if they had to rely on a private equity market and might have paid a lot more in fees and in information discount if they had listed on the Johannesburg or London exchange. Once again, the limitations of a small exchange are relative.

- Finally, the role of an active public debate among financial sector specialists and the policy-aware public. Not only was the policy floated first for discussion before being finalized, but also it was extensively and freely debated in the public media. This kind of transparency and consultation in policy formation may not result in as vigorous or informative a debate in smaller countries, but it is a costless and valuable approach.

These reflections emphasize how financial sector policy makers can be more ambitious and comprehensive in their policy formulation. These steps include efforts to improve competitiveness and to sanction abuses of market conduct regulation. (In smaller economies, regulators often do not have an effective way of ensuring that profit-reducing regulations are really enforced: the prospect of lower profits may merely trigger exit.)

Thus, larger countries can be the pioneers in upgrading the market conduct of financial intermediaries and markets. The formation or reactivation of consumer and producer consultative groups could help in the design of such policies. These policies could include not only the market conduct rules that should underpin a well-functioning stock exchange but also regulations designed to curb predatory lending and to promote access of lower-income groups to financial services. Here, recently enacted legislation and the financial sector charter in South Africa offer an interesting model. The adaptation and application of such legislation north of the Limpopo River could begin in the larger economies, and it should have at least a demonstration effect everywhere.

* * *

A combination of modernism and activism, each tempered by an awareness of the limitations of the institutional preconditions in most African countries, will do best in guiding the move toward stronger and more effective financial systems. These limitations include the stretched administrative resources of governments and the weakness of governance institutions, such as institutions of financial oversight. These limitations imply that highly complex regulatory designs are unlikely to be operated effectively and that hands-on government involvement in credit allocation, or generally in the ownership of financial intermediaries, is more likely to be subverted in favor of special interests.

Delivering the infrastructures for the modernization agenda while ensuring that the door is left open for activists—local or foreign, profit-seeking or charitable—is the main agenda for government and its agencies. The agenda is demanding, not only because of its technical complexity and the need to respond to changes in the international environment, but also because it lacks the kind of dramatic initiative that helps secure political support.

Nevertheless, persistence and ingenuity will be repaid given the central importance, for achieving development goals, of making finance work for Africa.

Notes

1. According to United Nations projections, the population in age groups 15 to 59 in Sub-Saharan Africa will grow from 401 million in 2005 to 514 million in 2015 and 656 million in 2025. Although the absolute increases continue to grow, the rate of growth decade by decade has already peaked (at almost 34 percent in the decade ending in 1995).
2. At present, almost one-third of the more than 80 million children in the 10 to 14 age group in Sub-Saharan Africa (excluding South Africa) work in the labor force.
3. To argue that modern finance represents a relatively coherent long-term objective for African financial sector policy makers is not to deny that advanced financial systems have experienced failure. Most advanced economies experienced severe banking collapses in the 1980s or 1990s, resulting in a new emphasis on capital adequacy. The misleading information provided to stock exchange participants and other customers by prominent financial firms in the late 1990s and early 2000s has led to a series of high-profile indictments and extensive regulatory change.

4. Twenty African countries (plus the Communauté Économique et Monétaire de l'Afrique Centrale union) have already participated in the FSAP since 2000. Three countries have already had follow-up assessments.
5. Although the seemingly high interest rates necessarily charged by microfinance companies risks being a stumbling block here, MFIs need to attend to their public image as they expand their coverage, or they too could become unpopular.
6. Anti-money-laundering and combating of financing of terrorism laws and arrangements are being modernized in many countries under international pressure to improve financial integrity.
7. A sixth category—offshore centers—applies only to Mauritius, the Seychelles, and perhaps Cape Verde at present and will not be discussed further here.
8. The case of Somalia is often mentioned, though some other aspects of the economy were considerably more resilient than the financial sector (see Mubarak 2003; Nenova and Harford 2004).
9. Addison, Le Billon, and Murshed (2001) and Addison and others (2005) provide overviews of the issues, with examples from African experiences, including those of Angola, Burundi, the Democratic Republic of Congo, the Republic of Congo, Eritrea, Ethiopia, Liberia, Rwanda, and Somalia.
10. A valuable literature survey of postconflict microfinance is in Nagarajan and McNulty (2004).
11. Although there are 200 bank branches in Tanzania, the mean distance (over all rural households) to the nearest bank branch is 38 kilometers.
12. The policy was announced by Charles Soludo, executive governor of the Central Bank of Nigeria, within a month of his appointment in 2004. He described it as "preliminary thoughts on the major elements of the reforms by the CBN [Central Bank of Nigeria]" on which comments and suggestions of the committee of bankers were solicited "before we finalize them." But the main features were maintained, even to extent of the timetable and the banking consolidation (every bank with a capital of at least the equivalent of about US$200 million—an exceptionally high figure by international standards). See http://www.cenbank.org/documents/speeches.asp.

APPENDIX

African Relationship Lending

Intrafirm credit represents a large fraction of firm financing, especially for small firms and others with limited access to bank finance. Successful credit providers in Africa recognize the continuing importance of a relationship model of credit. Such lenders rely on (a) multidimensional evaluations of creditworthiness in making the loan or credit sale and (b) flexible enforcement (Fafchamps 2004; see also Biggs and Shah 2006).

Credit Appraisal

Acquiring information is time consuming and costly. It also presupposes that the lender is embedded in the local economy. First, the lender needs to know about the borrower's ability to deliver high-quality goods and services to the market. Then the lender needs to know whether the borrower has a good business reputation and would be reluctant to lose it (see box A.1).[1] And last, the lender needs to know if the borrower's ethical character and ability to dissimulate make it unlikely that the borrower will conceal a capacity to repay.

Modern credit-scoring techniques implicitly include some indicators that are correlated with those characteristics, even though they are only very indirectly correlated, on the basis of past repayment record, and are not at the level of detail accumulated by painstaking, face-to-face observation of the borrower in multiple economic and social interactions. The most important

> **BOX A.1**
>
> **Reputation**
>
> Reputation is a widely discussed aspect of credit within tightly knit communities. Scholars of contemporary and historical businesses have explored the ways in which a poor payment record of one member of even a far-flung network of merchants can be reported and result in ostracism from the whole group (Greif 1993). By reporting a default, an aggrieved creditor spreads the bad reputation of the delinquent; the threat of this happening amplifies the costs of default and reduces its incidence.
>
> These reputation networks are generally formed of people with a common ethnicity—Lebanese and Syrian in many countries of West Africa, Asante in Ghana, and others. At the same time, it is commonly observed that foreign firms find it difficult to deal with African firms and find them generally unreliable, and several studies find stronger credit channels within rather than across ethnicities.
>
> This issue has led some people to believe that trust and reputation are inherently ethnically based and that they have no likely or beneficial place in a pluralist financial system. However, it is important to not overstate the role of ethnicity in underlying effective credit flows in Africa. Indeed, the role of ethnicity in supporting credit and other business relationships is often misunderstood. It is not a question of ethnic solidarity. Social networks in Africa are not coterminous with ethnic groups. Ethnic business networks are much smaller than the ethnicities—they are historically created subgroups, not ethnically determined subgroups.

source of this kind of information is the history of successful exchanges. Once trust has been built in this way, it represents a valuable bilateral relationship that can underpin future lending. Reflecting this trust, surprisingly lengthy credit relationships predominate in African markets (Fafchamps 2004).

Enforcement

Having made the loan, lenders find that enforcement proves to be deliberately flexible in the business environment prevailing in most African countries. In the interfirm credit market studied by Fafchamps (2004) and his collaborators, lenders recognize that many uncertainties (weather or transport difficulties are two of the most common) can affect borrowers' ability to repay on time. Nonculpable delays or excusable breaches of contract are therefore automatically excused. Lenders don't regard a delay of even a few weeks to be at all significant. Indeed, in especially uncertain environments, no specific repayment date may be specified. Even after the due date, lenders wait for payment. And a delay does not imply a high probability of nonpayment: typically 80 or 90 percent of delayed interfirm payments eventually come in.

Eventually, when there is a prospect of being repaid, the lender will take some actions. In few African countries does this problem often involve recourse to courts or lawyers (Fafchamps 2004, table 4.5).[2] Instead, when repayment seems possible, the lender will begin to harass or closely monitor the borrower, often turning up on market day or payday, when the borrower might be more likely to have liquidity, to see if the ability to repay has improved. Renegotiation of the loan is also possible at this stage.

Lenders and traders also report other forms of sanction for slow payers. Borrowers cannot expect to get the best deals or priority deliveries when certain goods are scarce. The business relationship is thus a form of business collateral. Ensuring its maintenance is an incentive for debtors to repay. This relationship, of course, suggests and requires a degree of monopoly power for the lender, pointing to the social cost of a credit system that is built on such a costly structure of information gathering.

Notes

1. For centuries, some societies and ethnic groups have cultivated a practice of publicizing and punishing defaults among their members. Some such conventions may partly explain the higher degree of intraethnic group credit observed in some African countries (Fisman 2003).
2. An exception was found for Zimbabwe when it was studied in the mid-1990s. The existence of a relatively efficient court system there did encourage greater use. Interestingly, there were more breaches of contract noted in Zimbabwe, suggesting that the availability of enforcement through courts encouraged more adventurous lending, which led to more breaches.

Bibliography

Acemoglu, Daron, Simon Johnson, and James Robinson. 2001. "The Colonial Origins of Comparative Development: An Empirical Investigation." *American Economic Review* 91 (5): 1369–401.

Ackrill, Margaret, and Leslie Hannah. 2001. *Barclays: The Business of Banking 1690–1996*. Cambridge, UK: Cambridge University Press.

Adabre, Jonathan. 2005. "Bank 'Robs' Woman of Her Widow's Mite." *Public Agenda,* October 10, 2005. http://www.ghanaweb.com/public_agenda/article.php?ID=4351.

Addison, Tony, Philippe Le Billon, and S. Mansoob Murshed. 2001. "Finance in Conflict and Reconstruction." *Journal of International Development* 13 (7): 951–64.

Addison, Tony, Alemayehu Geda, Philippe Le Billon, and S. Mansoob Murshed. 2005. "Reconstructing and Reforming the Financial System in Conflict and Post-Conflict Economies." *Journal of Development Studies* 41 (4): 704–18.

Adepoju, Aderanti. 2004. "Changing Configurations of Migration in Africa." Migration Policy Institute, Washington, DC. http://www.migrationinformation.org/feature/display.cfm?ID=251.

Aghion, Philippe, Peter Howitt, and David Mayer-Foulkes. 2005. "The Effect of Financial Development on Convergence: Theory and Evidence." *Quarterly Journal of Economics* 120 (1): 173–222.

Akuffo, Asare. 2006. "HFC's Pioneering Role and Rationale for Conversion to Full Banking Activities: Sustainability of Specialised Lenders." Paper presented at the World Bank conference on Housing Finance in Emerging Markets, Washington, DC, March 15–17.

Alawode, Abayomi, Tadashi Endo, Yongbeom Kim, and Cally Jordan. 2002. "Capital Market Integration in the East African Community." Financial Sector Study, World Bank, Washington, DC.

Alawode, Abayomi, Paul Murgatroyd, Salomon Samen, Don McIsaac, Carlos Cuevas, Alain Laurin, Fatouma Ibrahima Wane, Loic Chiquier, and Miguel Navarro-Martin. 2000. "Nigeria: Financial Sector Review." Economic Sector Report 29941, World Bank, Washington, DC.

Allen, Franklin, Rajesh Chakrabarti, Sankar De, Jun Qian, and Meijun Qian. 2006. "Financing Firms in India." Working Paper 06-08, Wharton Business School Financial Institutions Center, University of Pennsylvania, Philadelphia. http://fic.wharton.upenn.edu/fic/papers/06/p0608.htm.

Allen, Franklin, Jun Qian, and Meijun Qian. 2005. "Law, Finance, and Economic Growth in China." *Journal of Financial Economics* 77 (1): 57–116.

Allen, Hugh. 2002. "CARE International's Village Savings and Loan Programmes in Africa: Microfinance for the Rural Poor That Works." CARE International, Atlanta, GA. http://www.microfinancegateway.com/content/article/detail/32767.

Amo Yartey, Charles. 2006. "The Stock Market and the Financing of Corporate Growth in Africa: The Case of Ghana." IMF Working Paper 06/201, International Monetary Fund, Washington, DC.

Andah, David Obu. 2005. "Regulation, Supervision, and Access to Micro-finance: The Case of Ghana." Essay on Regulation and Supervision 10, Microfinance Regulation and Supervision Resource Center and IRIS Center, University of Maryland, College Park, MD. http://www.microfinancegateway.com/files/27045_file_Ghana.pdf.

Anderson, Siwan, and Jean-Marie Baland. 2002. "Economics of Roscas and Intrahousehold Resource Allocation." *Quarterly Journal of Economics* 117 (3): 963–95.

Arnold, Guy. 2005. *Africa: A Modern History*. London: Atlantic Books.

Artadi, Elsa V., and Xavier Sala-i-Martin. 2003. "The Economic Tragedy of the XXth Century: Growth in Africa." NBER Working Paper 9865, National Bureau of Economic Research, Cambridge, MA.

Aryeetey, Ernest, Hemamala Hettige, Machiko Nissanke, and William F. Steel. 1997a. "Financial Market Fragmentation and Reforms in Ghana, Malawi, Nigeria, and Tanzania." *World Bank Economic Review* 11 (2): 195–218.

———. 1997b. "Financial Market Fragmentation and Reforms in Sub-Saharan Africa." Technical Paper 356, World Bank, Washington, DC.

Aryeetey, Ernest, and Lemma Senbet. 2004. "Essential Financial Market Reforms in Africa." Technical Publication 63, Institute of Statistical, Social, and Economic Research, University of Ghana, Accra.

Aryeetey, Ernest, and Christopher Udry. 1999. "Rural Household Asset Choice in Ghana." Yale University, New Haven, CT.

———. 2000. "Saving in Sub-Saharan Africa." CID Working Paper 38, Center for International Development, Harvard University, Cambridge, MA.

Austen, Ralph. 1987. *African Economic History: Internal Development and External Dependency*, Portsmouth, NH: Heinemann.

Azam, Jean-Paul. 2004. "Poverty and Growth in the WAEMU after the 1994 Devaluation." Research Paper 2004/19, United Nations University–World Institute for Development Economics Research, Helsinki.

Azam, Jean-Paul, Robert Bates, and Bruno Biais. 2005. "Political Predation and Economic Development." CEPR Discussion Paper 5062, Centre for Economic Policy Research, London.

Azam, Jean-Paul, Bruno Biais, and Magueye Dia. 2004. "Privatization versus Regulation in Developing Countries: The Case of West African Banks." *Journal of African Economies* 13 (3): 361–94.

Azam, Jean-Paul, Augustin Fosu, and Njuguna S. Ndung'u. 2002. "Explaining Slow Growth in Africa." *African Development Review* 14 (2): 177–220.

Barth, James R., Gerard Caprio Jr., and Ross Levine. 2005. *Rethinking Bank Regulation: Till Angels Govern*. New York: Cambridge University Press.

Basu, Anupam, Rodolphe Blavy, and Murat Yulek. 2004. "Microfinance in Africa: Experience and Lessons from Selected African Countries." IMF Working Paper 04/174, International Monetary Fund, Washington, DC.

Beck, Thorsten. 2006. "Creating an Efficient Financial System: Challenges in a Global Economy." Policy Research Working Paper 3856, World Bank, Washington, DC.

Beck, Thorsten, Robert Cull, and Afeikehna Jerome. 2005. "Bank Privatization and Performance: Empirical Evidence from Nigeria." *Journal of Banking and Finance* 29 (8–9): 2355–79.

Beck, Thorsten, and Augusto de la Torre. 2006. "The Basic Analytics of Access to Financial Services." Policy Research Working Paper 4026, World Bank, Washington, DC.

Beck, Thorsten, Aslı Demirgüç-Kunt, and Ross Levine. 2004. "Finance, Inequality, and Poverty." Policy Research Working Paper 3338, World Bank, Washington, DC.

———. 2006. "Bank Supervision and Corruption in Lending." *Journal of Monetary Economics* 53 (8): 2131–63.

Beck, Thorsten, Aslı Demirgüç-Kunt, and Vojislav Maksimovic. 2005. "Financial and Legal Constraints to Firm Growth: Does Firm Size Matter?" *Journal of Finance* 60 (1): 137–77.

Beck, Thorsten, Aslı Demirgüç-Kunt, and María Soledad Martínez Pería. 2005. "Reaching Out: Access to and Use of Banking Services across Countries." Policy Research Working Paper 3754, World Bank, Washington, DC, and *Journal of Financial Economics* forthcoming.

———. 2006. "Banking Services for Everyone? Barriers to Bank Access around the World." Policy Research Working Paper 4079, World Bank, Washington, DC.

Beck, Thorsten, and Ross Levine. 2005. "Legal Institutions and Financial Development." In *Handbook of New Institutional Economics*, ed. Claude Ménard and Mary Shirley, 251–78. Dordrecht, Netherlands: Springer.

Beck, Thorsten, Ross Levine, and Norman Loayza. 2000. "Finance and the Sources of Growth." *Journal of Financial Economics* 58 (1–2): 261–300.

Bennett, Jake, Saidja Drentje, Mark Pickens, and Cari Widmyer. 2005. "Bank of Africa and Mutual Guarantee Associations in Madagascar: Analysis and Recommendations." Columbia Business School, New York.

Berg, Elliot, K. Y. Amoako, Rolf Gusten, Jacob Meerman, and Gene Tidrick. 1981. *Accelerated Development in Sub-Saharan Africa*. Report 3358, Washington, DC: World Bank.

Berger, Allen, Aslı Demirgüç-Kunt, Ross Levine, and Joseph Haubrich. 2004. "Introduction: Bank Concentration and Competition: An Evolution in the Making." *Journal of Money, Banking, and Credit* 36 (3, part 2):433–51.

Besley, Tim. 1995. "Property Rights and Investment: Evidence from Ghana." *Journal of Political Economy* 103 (5): 903–37.

Biggs, Tyler, and Manju Kedia Shah. 2006. "African Small and Medium Enterprises, Networks, and Manufacturing Performance." Policy Research Working Paper 3855, World Bank, Washington, DC.

Biggs, Tyler, and Pradeep Srivastava. 1996. "Structural Aspects of Manufacturing in Sub-Saharan Africa: Findings from a Seven Country Enterprise Survey." World Bank Africa Technical Paper 346, World Bank, Washington, DC.

Bigsten, Arne, Paul Collier, Stefan Dercon, Marcel Fafchamps, Bernard Gauthier, Jan Willem Gunning, Anders Isaksson, Abena Oduro, Remco Oostendorp, Cathy Pattillo, Måns Söderbom, Michael Sylvain, Francis Teal, and Albert Zeufack. 1999. "Investment in Africa's Manufacturing Sector: A Four Country Panel Data Analysis." *Oxford Bulletin of Economics and Statistics* 61 (4): 489–512.

Bigsten, Arne, Paul Collier, Stefan Dercon, Marcel Fafchamps, Bernard Gauthier, Jan Willem Gunning, Abena Oduro, Remco Oostendorp, Cathy Pattillo, Måns Söderbom, and Albert Zeufack. 2003. "Credit Constraints in Manufacturing Enterprises in Africa." *Journal of African Economies* 12 (1): 104–25.

Binswanger, Hans P., and Rogier van den Brink. 2005. "Credit for Small Farmers in Africa Revisited: Pathologies and Remedies." *Savings and Development* 29 (3): 275–92.

Bonin, John, and Masami Imai. 2005. "Soft Related Lending: A Tale of Two Korean Banks." Wesleyan Economics Working Paper 2005-011, Department of Economics, Wesleyan University, Middletown, CT.

Boot, Arnoud, and Anjolein Schmeits. 2005. "The Competitive Challenge in Banking." Working Paper 2005-08, Amsterdam Center for Law and Economics, University of Amsterdam, Amsterdam.

Boyd, John H., Ross Levine, and Bruce D. Smith. 2001. "The Impact of Inflation on Financial Sector Performance." *Journal of Monetary Economics* 47 (2): 221–48.

Brown, Warren, Kimberly Tilock, Nthenya Mule, and Ezra Anyango. 2002. "The Enabling Environment for Housing Microfinance in Kenya." Cities Alliance Shelter Finance for the Poor Series, Issue 4, Cities Alliance, Washington, DC. http://www.citiesalliance.com.

Brownbridge, Martin, and Charles Harvey, with Augustine Fritz Gockel. 1998. *Banking in Africa: The Impact of Financial Sector Reform since Independence*. Oxford, UK: James Curry.

Bryla, Erin, Julie Dana, Ulrich Hess, and Panos Varangis. 2003. "The Use of Price and Weather Risk Management Instruments." Paper presented at the United States Agency for International Development–World Council of Credit Unions conference on Paving the Way Forward for Rural Finance: An International Conference on Best Practices, Washington, DC, June 2–4. http://www.basis.wisc.edu/rfc/.

Buchs, Thierry, and Johan Mathisen. 2004. "Banking Competition and Efficiency in Ghana." Paper presented at the Development Policy Research Unit–Trade and Industrial Policy Strategies–Cornell University Forum on African Development and Poverty Reduction: The Macro-Micro Linkage, Cape Town, South Africa, October 13–15.

Burgess, Robin, and Rohini Pande. 2004. "Do Rural Banks Matter? Evidence from the Indian Social Banking Experiment." CEPR Discussion Paper 4211, Centre for Economic Policy Research, London.

Calderisi, Robert. 2006. *The Trouble with Africa*. New York: Palgrave Macmillan.

Caprio, Gerard, Daniela Klingebiel, Luc Laeven, and Guillermo Noguera. 2005. "Banking Crisis Database." In *Systemic Financial Crises*, ed. Patrick Honohan and Luc Laeven, 307–40. Cambridge, UK: Cambridge University Press.

Carbó, Santiago, Edward P. M. Gardener, and Philip Molyneux. 2005. *Financial Exclusion*. Basingstoke, U.K.: Palgrave Macmillan.

Celpay. 2006. "Comment Fonctionne Celpay?" Celpay, Kinshasa, Democratic Republic of Congo. http://www.celpay.com/fonct.html.

Chamberlain, Doubell, and Richard Walker. 2005. "Measuring Access to Transaction Banking Services in the Southern African Customs Union: An Index Approach." Johannesburg: Genesis.

Charitonenko, Stephanie. 2005. "The Nigerian Legal and Regulatory Framework for Microfinance: Strengths, Weaknesses, and Recent Developments." Essay on Regulation and Supervision 8, Microfinance Regulation and Supervision Resource Center and IRIS Center, University of Maryland, College Park, MD. http://microfinancegateway.com/files/25979_file_Nigeria.pdf.

Chiumya, Chiara. 2006. "The Regulation of Microfinance in Zambia." Essay on Regulation and Supervision 18, Microfinance Regulation and Supervision Resource Center and IRIS Center, University of Maryland, College Park, MD. http://www.microfinancegateway.com/files/32237_file_Zambia.pdf.

Christen, Robert Peck, Timothy R. Lyman, and Richard Rosenberg. 2003. *Microfinance Consensus Guidelines: Guiding Principles on Regulation and Supervision of Microfinance*. Washington, DC: Consultative Group to Assist the Poor.

Christen, Robert Peck, and Douglas Pearce. 2005. "Managing Risks and Designing Products for Agricultural Microfinance: Features of an Emerging Model." Occasional Paper 11, Consultative Group to Assist the Poor, Washington, DC.

Christen, Robert Peck, Richard Rosenberg, and Veena Jayadeva. 2004. "Financial Institutions with a Double Bottom Line: Implications for Microfinance." Occasional Paper 8, Consulatative Group to Assist the Poor, Washington, DC.

Christensen, Jacob. 2004. "Domestic Debt Markets in Sub-Saharan Africa." Working Paper 04/46, International Monetary Fund, Washington, DC.

Claessens, Stijn, Aslı Demirgüç-Kunt, and Harry Huizinga. 2001. "How Does Foreign Bank Entry Affect Domestic Banking Markets?" *Journal of Banking and Finance* 25: 891–911.

Claessens, Stijn, and Luc Laeven. 2004. "What Drives Bank Competition? Some International Evidence." *Journal of Money, Credit, and Banking* 36 (3, part 2): 563–83.

Clark, Robert A. 1998. *Africa's Emerging Securities Markets: Developments in Financial Infrastructure*. Westport, CT: Quorum Books.

Clarke, George R. G., Robert Cull, and Michael Fuchs. 2006. "Bank Privatization in Sub-Saharan Africa: The Case of Uganda Commercial Bank." World Bank, Washington, DC.

Clarke, George R., Robert Cull, and María Soledad Martínez Pería. 2006. "Foreign Bank Participation and Access to Credit across Firms in Developing Countries." *Journal of Comparative Economics* 34 (4): 774–95.

Collier, Paul, and Jan Willem Gunning. 1999a. "Explaining African Economic Performance." *Journal of Economic Literature* 37 (1): 64–111.

———. 1999b. "Why Has Africa Grown Slowly?" *Journal of Economic Perspectives* 12 (3): 3–22.

Collier, Paul, Anke Hoeffler, and Catherine Pattillo. 2004. "Africa's Exodus: Capital Flight and the Brain Drain as Portfolio Decisions." *Journal of African Economies* 13 (2): ii15–54.

Collins, Susan. 2004. "International Financial Integration and Growth in Developing Countries: Issues for Africa." *Journal of African Economies* 13 (4, Suppl. 2): ii55–94.

Commission for Africa. 2005. *Our Common Interest*. Glasgow, Scotland: Commission for Africa.Commission for Africa. 2005. *Our Common Interest*. Glasgow, Scotland: Commission for Africa.

Conning, Jonathan, and Christopher Udry. Forthcoming. "Rural Financial Markets in Developing Countries." In *The Handbook of Agricultural Economics Vol. 3: Agricultural Development: Farmers, Farm Production, and Farm Markets*, ed. Robert E. Evenson, Prabhu Pingali, and T. P. Schultz, eds. Amsterdam: Elsevier. http://urban.hunter.cuny.edu/~conning/papers/Rural_Finance.pdf.

CPSS (Committee on Payment and Settlement Systems) and World Bank. 2006. *General Principles for International Remittance Services: Consultative Report.* Washington, DC: CPSS and World Bank. http://www.bis.org/publ/cpss73.pdf.

Cracknell, David. 2004. "Electronic Banking for the Poor: Panacea, Potential, and Pitfalls." MicroSave, Nairobi. http://www.microsave.org/.

Cuevas, Carlos E., and Klaus P. Fischer. 2006. "Cooperative Financial Institutions: Issues in Governance, Regulation, and Supervision." Working Paper 82, World Bank, Washington, DC.

Cull, Robert, Aslı Demirgüç-Kunt, and Jonathan Morduch. 2005. "Contract Design and Microfinance Performance: A Global Analysis." World Bank, Washington, DC, and *Economic Journal* forthcoming.

Cull, Robert, and Xavier Giné. 2004. "Literature Review on Access to Finance for SME and Low-Income Households." World Bank, Washington, DC.

Dages, Gerard, Linda Goldberg, and Daniel Kinney. 2000. "Foreign and Domestic Bank Participation in Emerging Markets: Lessons from Mexico and Argentina." *Federal Reserve Bank of New York Economic Policy Review* 6 (3): 17–36.

Daumont, Roland, Françoise Le Gall, and François Leroux. 2004. "Banking in Sub-Saharan Africa: What Went Wrong?" IMF Working Paper 04/55, International Monetary Fund, Washington, DC.

De Gobbi, Maria Sabrina. 2003. "Mutual Guarantee Associations for Small and Micro-Entrepreneurs: Lessons Learned from Europe and Africa." *African Development Review* 15 (1): 23–34.

Demirgüç-Kunt, Aslı, and Ed Kane. 2002. "Deposit Insurance around the World: Where Does It Work?" *Journal of Economic Perspectives* 16 (2): 175–95.

Demirgüç-Kunt, Aslı, Luc Laeven, and Ross Levine. 2004. "Regulations, Market Structure, Institutions, and the Cost of Financial Intermediation." *Journal of Money, Credit, and Banking* 36 (3): 593–622.

Demirgüç-Kunt, Aslı, and Vojislav Maksimovic. 1999. "Institutions, Financial Markets, and Firm Debt." *Journal of Financial Economics* 54 (3): 295–336.

De Nicoló, Gianni, Patrick Honohan, and Alain Ize. 2005. "Dollarization of Bank Deposits: Causes and Consequences." *Journal of Banking and Finance* 29 (7): 1697–727.

Dercon, Stefan, Daniel Ayalew, and Madhur Gautam. 2005. "Property Rights in a Very Poor Country: Tenure Insecurity and Investment in Ethiopia." Working Paper 21, Global Poverty Research Group, Oxford, UK. http://www.gprg.org/pubs/workingpapers/pdfs/gprg-wps-021.pdf.

Dercon, Stefan, Tessa Bold, Joachim De Weerdt, and Alula Pankhurst. 2004. "Group-Based Funeral Insurance in Ethiopia and Tanzania." Oxford Centre for the Study of African Economies Working Paper 2004-27, Oxford University, Oxford, UK.

Detragiache, Enrica, Poonam Gupta, and Thierry Tressel. 2005. "Finance in Lower Income Countries: An Empirical Exploration." IMF Working Paper 05/167,

International Monetary Fund, Washington, DC.

DFID (UK Department for International Development) and FDCF (Financial Deepening Challenge Fund). 2004. "FDCF Support for the Use of Technology to Improve Operational Infrastructure for Product and Service Delivery." DFID/FDFC Theme Paper 3: Technology to Improve Delivery, DFID, London.

Djankov, Simeon, Caralee McLiesh, and Andrei Shleifer. Forthcoming. "Private Credit in 129 Countries." *Journal of Financial Economics*. http://www.doingbusiness.org/documents/private_credit_jan23.pdf.

Dussault, Gilles, Pierre Fournier, Alain Letourmy, and Alexander Preker, eds. 2006. *Health Insurance in Francophone Africa*. Report 37149. Washington, DC: World Bank, Washington, DC.

Easterly, William, and Ross Levine. 1997. "Africa's Growth Tragedy: Policies and Ethnic Divisions." *Quarterly Journal of Economics* 112 (2):103–25.

Eaton, Charles, and Andrew Shepherd. 2001. "Contract Farming: Partnerships for Growth." Agricultural Services Bulletin 145, Food and Agriculture Organization, Rome. http://www.fao.org/documents/show_cdr.asp?url_file=//docrep/004/y0937e/y0937e00.htm.

Eboue, Chicot, and Ray Barrell. 2004. "Fast Tracking the African Monetary Cooperation Program: A Joint Report." Paper presented at the African Association of Central Banks, Entebbe, Uganda, May 18.

Eifert, Benn, Alan Gelb, and Vijaya Ramachandran. 2006. "Business Environment and Comparative Advantage in Africa: Evidence from the Investment Climate Data." In *Annual World Bank Conference on Development Economics 2006: Growth and Integration*, ed. François Bourguignon and Boris Pleskovic, 195–234. Washington, DC: World Bank.

Elbadawi, Ibrahim A., and Benno J. Ndulu, eds. 1995. *Contemporary Economic Issues Vol. 6: Economic Development in Sub-Saharan Africa*. London: Palgrave.

Fafchamps, Marcel. 2004. *Market Institutions in Sub-Saharan Africa: Theory and Evidence*. Cambridge, MA: MIT Press.

Fielding, David, ed. 2006. *Macroeconomic Policy in the Franc Zone*. London: Palgrave Macmillan.

FinMark Trust. 2005. "Themes Arising from the Southern African Workshop on Tiered Banking Regulation." FinMark Trust, Marshalltown, U.K. http://www.finmarktrust.org.za/documents/2005/JANUARY/Themes_Tiered.pdf.

Firpo, Janine. 2005. "Banking the Unbanked: Technology's Role in Delivering Accessible Financial Services to the Poor." SEMBA Consulting, Oakland, CA. http://www.sevaksolutions.org/docs/Banking%20the%20Unbanked.pdf.

Fisman, Raymond J. 2003. "Ethnic Ties and the Provision of Credit: Relationship-Level Evidence from African Firms." *Advances in Economic Analysis and Policy* 3 (1): 1211. http://www.bepress.com/bejeap/advances/vol3/iss1/art4.

Fisman, Raymond, and Inessa Love. 2003. "Trade Credit, Financial Intermediary

Development, and Industry Growth." *Journal of Finance* 58: 353–74.

Fleisig, Heywood W., and Nuria de la Peña. 2003. "Legal and Regulatory Requirements for Effective Rural Financial Markets." Paper presented at the United States Agency for International Development–World Council of Credit Unions conference on Paving the Way Forward for Rural Finance: An International Conference on Best Practices. Washington, DC, June 2–4. http://www.basis.wisc.edu/rfc/.

Fosu, Augustin Kwasi, and Stephen A. O'Connell. 2006. "Explaining African Economic Growth: The Role of Anti-Growth Syndromes." In *Annual World Bank Conference on Development Economics 2006: Growth and Integration*, ed. François Bourguignon and Boris Pleskovic, 31–66. Washington, DC: World Bank.

Frankiewicz, Cheryl. 2004. *Information Technology as a Strategic Tool for Microfinance in Africa*. Toronto: Calmeadow. http://www.africapfund.com/site/IMG/pdf/2004_IT_Seminar_Report-2.pdf.

Fuchs, Michael, and Sonia Plaza. 2006. "Sub-regional Financial Integration in Africa." World Bank, Washington, DC.

Gallardo, Joselito, Michael Goldberg, and Bikki Randhawa. 2006. "Strategic Alliances to Scale Up Financial Services in Rural Areas." Working Paper 76, World Bank, Washington, DC.

Gelb, Alan, Ali A. G. Ali, Tesfaye Dinka, Ibrahim Elbadawi, Charles Soludo, and Gene Tidrick. 2000. *Can Africa Claim the 21st Century*. Report 20469, Washington, DC: World Bank.

Genesis Analysis. 2003. *African Families, African Money: Bridging the Money Transfer Divide*. Johannesburg: FinMark Trust.

Gennaioli, Nicola, and Ilia Rainer. 2005. "The Modern Impact of Precolonial Centralization in Africa." Institute for International Economic Studies, Stockholm, Sweden. http://www.iies.su.se/~nicola/Africa.pdf.

Ghirmay, Teame. 2004. "Financial Development and Economic Growth in Sub-Saharan African Countries." *African Development Review* 16 (3): 415–32.

Giannetti, Mariassunta, and Steven Ongena. 2005. "Financial Integration and Entrepreneurial Activity: Evidence from Foreign Bank Entry in Emerging Markets." SITE Working Paper 05/02, Stockholm Institute of Transition Economics, Stockholm.

Gonzalez-Vega, Claudio. 2003. "Deepening Rural Financial Markets: Macroeconomic, Policy, and Political Dimensions." Paper presented at the United States Agency for International Development–World Council of Credit Unions conference on Paving the Way Forward for Rural Finance: An International Conference on Best Practices. Washington, DC, June 2-4. http://www.basis.wisc.edu/rfc/.

Greif, Avner. 1993. "Contract Enforceability and Economic Institutions in Early Trade: The Maghribi Traders' Coalition." *American Economic Review* 83 (3): 525–48.

Grose, Claire, and Felice B. Friedman. 2006. "Promoting Access to Primary Equity

Markets: A Legal and Regulatory Approach." Policy Research Working Paper 3892, World Bank, Washington, DC.

Helms, Brigit, and Xavier Reille. 2004. "Interest Rate Ceilings and Microfinance: The Story So Far." Occasional Paper 9. Consultative Group to Assist the Poor, Washington, DC.

Henry, J. A. 2003. *The First Hundred Years of the Standard Bank*. Oxford, UK: Oxford University Press.

Hernández-Coss, Raúl, Chinyere Egwuagu, and Martin Josefsson. 2006. *The UK-Nigeria Remittance Corridor*. Washington, DC: World Bank and UK Department for International Development.

Hess, Ulrich, Erin Bryla, and John Nash. 2005. *Rural Finance Innovations: Topics and Case Studies*. Report 32726-GLB, World Bank, Washington, DC.

Honohan, Patrick. 2004. "Financial Development, Growth, and Poverty: How Close Are the Links." In *Financial Development and Economic Growth: Explaining the Links*, ed. Charles Goodhart, 1–37. London: Palgrave.

———. 2006. "Household Financial Assets in the Process of Development." Policy Research Working Paper 3965, World Bank, Washington, DC.

Honohan, Patrick, and Philip Lane. 2001. "Will the Euro Trigger More Monetary Unions in Africa?" In *The Impact of EMU on Europe and the Developing Countries*, ed. Charles Wyplosz, 315–38. New York: Oxford University Press.

Honohan, Patrick, and Stephen A. O'Connell. 1997. "Contrasting Monetary Regimes in Africa." IMF Working Paper 97/64, International Monetary Fund, Washington, DC.

ILO (International Labour Office). 2002. *Decent Work and the Informal Economy*. Report VI of the International Labour Conference, 90th Session. Geneva: ILO. http://www.ilo.org/public/english/employment/infeco/download/report6.pdf.

IMF (International Monetary Fund). 2004. "MFD Technical Assistance to Recent Post-Conflict Countries." International Monetary Fund, Washington, DC.

———. 2006. *Regional Economic Outlook: Sub-Saharan Africa*. Washington, DC: International Monetary Fund.

IMF (International Monetary Fund) and World Bank. 2005. *Financial Sector Assessment: A Handbook*. Washington DC: IMF. http://www.imf.org/external/pubs/ft/fsa/eng/index.htm.

Inanga, Eno L. 2001. "Financial Sector Reforms in Sub-Saharan Africa." In *Contemporary Economic Issues Vol. 6: Economic Development in Sub-Saharan Africa*, ed. Ibrahim Elbadawi and Benno J. Ndulu, 205–31. London: Palgrave.

Irving, Jacqueline. 2005. "Regional Integration of Stock Exchanges in Eastern and Southern Africa: Progress and Prospects." IMF Working Paper 05/122, International Monetary Fund, Washington, DC.

Isern, Jennifer, Rani Deshpande, and Judith van Doorn. 2005. "Crafting a Money

Transfers Strategy: Guidance for Pro-Poor Financial Service Providers." Occasional Paper 10, Consultative Group to Assist the Poor, Washington, DC.

Isern, Jennifer, and David Porteous. 2005. "Commercial Banks and Microfinance: Evolving Models of Success." Focus Note 28, World Bank and Consultative Group to Assist the Poor, Washington, DC.

Isern, Jennifer, David Porteous, Raúl Hernández-Coss, and Chinyere Egwuagu. 2005. "AML/CFT Regulation: Implications for Financial Service Providers That Serve Low-Income People." Focus Note 29, World Bank and Consultative Group to Assist the Poor, Washington, DC.

Ivaturi, Gautam. 2006. "Using Technology to Build Inclusive Financial Systems." Focus Note 32, World Bank and Consultative Group to Assist the Poor, Washington, DC.

Jansen, Marion, and Yannick Vennes. 2006. "Liberalizing Financial Services Trade in Africa: Going Regional and Multilateral." Working Paper ERSD-2006-03, World Trade Organization, Geneva.

Jones, Christine W., and Miguel A. Kiguel. 1994. *Adjustment in Africa: Reforms Results and the Road Ahead*. World Bank Policy Research Report 12852. New York: Oxford University Press.

Kalala, Jean-Pierre Muimana, and Alpha Ouedraogo. 2001. "Savings Products and Services in the Informal Sector and Microfinance Institutions: The Case of Mali and Benin." MicroSave, Nairobi, Kenya. http://www.microsave.org.

Kalavakonda, Vijayasekar. 2005. "HIV/AIDS: Financial Sector Issues." World Bank, Washington, DC.

Kam, Matthew, and Tu Tran. 2005. "Lessons from Deploying the Remote Transaction System with Three Microfinance Institutions in Uganda." Paper presented at the United Nations Industrial Development Organization–University of California at Berkeley conference Bridging the Divide, Berkeley, CA, April 21–23.

Karpowicz, Izabela. 2006. "Determinants of Emigrant Deposits in Cape Verde." IMF 06/132, International Monetary Fund, Washington, DC.

Kaufman, Daniel, Aart Kraay, and Massimo Mastruzzi. 2004. "Governance Matters III: Governance Indicators for 1996–2002." *World Bank Economic Review* 18 (2): 253–87.

Kaufmann, Celine. 2005. "Financing SMEs in Africa." Development Centre Policy Insights 7, Organisation for Economic Co-operation and Development, Paris.

Kazianga, Harounan, and Christopher Udry. 2006. "Consumption Smoothing? Livestock, Insurance, and Drought in Rural Burkina Faso." *Journal of Development Economics* 79 (2): 413–46.

Kempson, Elaine. 2006. "Policy Level Response to Financial Exclusion in Developed Economies: Lessons for Developing Countries." Paper presented at the World Bank–Brookings Institute conference Access to Finance: Building Inclusive Financial Systems, Washington, DC, May 30–31.

Kirsten, Marié. 2006. "Policy Initiatives to Expand Financial Outreach in South Africa." Paper presented at the World Bank–Brookings Institute conference Access to Finance: Building Inclusive Financial Systems, Washington, DC, May 30–31. http://www.dbsa.org/document/pdevtoday/Policy%20Initiatives%20to%20expand%20outreach%20-%20Marié%20Kirsten.doc.

Kloeppinger-Todd, Renate, with Anne Ritchie. 2005. *Meeting Development Challenges: Renewed Approaches to Rural Finance.* Washington, DC: World Bank.

Kpodar, Kangni. 2005. "Le Développement Financier et la Croissance: l'Afrique Subsaharienne Est-elle Marginalisée?" *African Development Review* 17 (1): 106–37.

Kula, Olaf, and Elisabeth Farmer. 2004. "Mozambique Rural Financial Services Study." microCase Study 1, Accelerated Microenterprise Advancement Project, Washington, DC. http://www.microlinks.org.

Lafourcade, Anne-Lucie, Jennifer Isern, Patricia Mwangi, and Matthew Brown. 2005. "Overview of the Outreach and Financial Performance of Microfinance Institutions in Africa." Microfinance Information eXchange, Washington, DC. http://www.mixmarket.org/medialibrary/mixmarket/Africa_Data_Study.pdf.

Landell-Mills, Pierre, Ramgopal Agarwala, and Stanley Please. 1989. "Sub-Saharan Africa from Crisis to Sustainable Growth: A Long-term Perspective Study." Economic Policy Paper 8209, World Bank, Washington, DC.

Lensink, Roberta, Nielsa Hermes, and Victor Murinde. 1998. "The Effect of Financial Liberalization on Capital Flight in African Economies." *World Development* 26 (7): 1349–68.

Levine, Ross. 2005. "Finance and Growth: Theory and Evidence." In *Handbook of Economic Growth*, vol. IA, ed. Philippe Aghion and Steven Durlauf, 865–934. Amsterdam: Elsevier.

Levine, Ross, and Sergio Schmukler. 2006. "Internationalization and Stock Market Liquidity." *Review of Finance* 10 (1): 153–87.

Levy-Yeyati, Eduardo. 2006. "Financial Dollarization: Evaluating the Consequences." *Economic Policy* 21 (45): 61–118.

Lolila-Ramin, Zahia. 2005. "Regulation and Supervision of MFIs in the West African Monetary Union: How the PARMEC Law Impedes Access to Finance for SMEs and the Poor." Essay on Regulation and Supervision 5, Microfinance Regulation and Supervision Resource Center and IRIS Center, University of Maryland, College Park, MD. http://www.microfinancegateway.org/files/25522_file_PARMEC.pdf.

Lopez, Humberto, and Luis Serven. 2005. "Too Poor to Grow?" World Bank, Washington, DC.

Louis, Olivier. 2006. "Association d'Entraide des Femmes, Benin." Good and Bad Practices Case Study 22, CGAP Working Group on Microinsurance, World Bank Secretariat, Washington, DC. http://www.microfinancegateway.com/content/article/detail/31893.

Love, Inessa, and Nataliya Mylenko. 2003. "Credit Reporting and Financing Constraints." Policy Research Working Paper 3142. World Bank, Washington, DC.

Magill, John H. 2003. "HIV/AIDS and Rural Microfinance—A Matter of Survival." Paper presented at the United States Agency for International Development–World Council of Credit Unions conference on Paving the Way Forward for Rural Finance: An International Conference on Best Practices. Washington DC, June 2–4. http://www.basis.wisc.edu/rfc/.

Marchat, Jean-Michel, Jean-Paul Azam, George Clarke, Magueye Dia, Philippe Alby, and Mouhssine Afifi. 2005. *Mali: Une Évaluation du Climat des Investissements*. Economic Sector Report. Washington, DC: World Bank.

Masson, Paul R., and Catherine Pattillo. 2005. *The Monetary Geography of Africa*. Washington, DC: Brookings Institution Press.

McCord, Michael J., and Sylvia Osinde. 2003. "Reducing Vulnerability: The Supply of Health Microinsurance in East Africa." MicroSave, Nairobi. http://www.microinsurancecentre.org.

Meredith, Martin. 2005. *The State of Africa: A History of Fifty Years of Independence*. London: Free Press.

Meyer, Richard L., Richard Roberts, and Adam Mugume. 2004. *Agricultural Finance in Uganda: The Way Forward*. Kampala: Financial Systems Development.

Mian, Atif. 2006. "Distance Constraints: The Limits of Foreign Lending in Poor Economies." *Journal of Finance* 61 (3): 1465–505.

Mohanty, M. S., and Philip Turner. 2006. "The Global Economy and Africa: The Challenges of Increased Financial Inflows." In *Central Banks and the Challenge of Development*, 27–43. Basel, Switzerland: Bank for International Settlements.

Montiel, Peter J. 1996. "Financial Policies and Economic Growth: Theory, Evidence, and Country-Specific Experience from Sub-Saharan Africa." *Journal of African Economies* 5 (3 Suppl.): 65–98.

Moss, Todd J. 2003. *Adventure Capitalism: Globalization and the Political Economy of Stock Markets in Africa*. Houndsmills, UK: Palgrave Macmillan.

Moss, Todd J., Vijaya Ramachandran, and Manju Kedia Shah. 2004. "Is Africa's Skepticism of Foreign Capital Justified? Evidence from East African Firm Survey Data." Working Paper 41, Center for Global Development, Washington, DC.

Mubarak, Jamil. 2003. "A Case of Private Supply of Money in Stateless Somalia." *Journal of African Economies* 11 (3): 309–25.

Nagarajan, Geetha, and Michael McNulty. 2004. "Microfinance amid Conflict: Taking Stock of Available Literature." Microreport 1, Accelerated Microenterprise Advancement Project, Washington, DC. http://www.microlinks.org/ev_en.php?ID=3949_201&ID2=DO_TOPIC.

Nagarajan, Geetha, and Richard L. Meyer. 2005. "Rural Finance: Recent Advances and Emerging Lessons, Debates, and Opportunities." Working Paper AEDE-WP-0041-05, Department of Agricultural, Environmental, and Development Economics, Ohio State University, Columbus, OH. http://aede.osu.edu/resources/docs/pdf/GLRUDSWE-YARD-4P14-F4YHR47SMU2X0U77.pdf.

Ncube, Mthuli, and Lemma W. Senbet. 1997. "Perspective on Financial Regulation and Liberalization in Africa under Incentive Problems and Asymmetric Information." *Journal of African Economies* 6 (1): 29–88.

Ndikumana, Léonce, and James K. Boyce. 2002. "Public Debts and Private Assets: Explaining Capital Flight from Sub-Saharan African Countries." PERI Working Paper 32, Political Economic Research Institute, University of Massachusetts, Amherst, MA.

Ndulu, Benno J., Armand Atomate, Michele de Nevers, Mamadou Woury Diallo, Poul Engberg-Pedersen, Navin Girishankar, Nidhi Khattri, Pamela Khumbah, Ita Mary Mannathoko, Haruna Mohammed, Mark Nelson, Michael Sarris, and Yongmei Zhou. 2005. *Building Effective States, Forging Engaged Societies*. Report 37709. Washington, DC: World Bank.

Nellis, John. 2003. "Privatization in Africa: What Has Happened? What Is to Be Done?" Working Paper 25, Center for Global Development, Washington, DC.

———. 2005. "The Evolution of Enterprise Reform in Africa: From State-owned Enterprises to Private Participation in Infrastructure—and Back?" FEEM Working Paper 117, Fondazione Eni Enrico Mattei, Milan, Italy. http://ssrn.com/abstract=828764.

Nenova, Tatiana, and Tim Harford. 2004. "Anarchy and Invention: How Does Somalia Cope without Government?" Public Policy for the Private Sector Note 280, World Bank, Washington, DC.

Nissanke, Machiko, and Ernest Aryeetey. 1998. *Financial Integration and Development: Liberalization and Reform in Sub-Saharan Africa*. London: Routledge.

———. 2006. "Institutional Analysis of Financial Market Fragmentation in Sub-Saharan Africa: A Risk-Cost Configuration Approach." Research Paper 2006/87, United Nations University–World Institute for Development Economics Research, Helsinki.

Nunn, Nathan. 2005. "Slavery, Institutional Development, and Long-Run Growth in Africa, 1400–2000." International Trade Working Paper 0411007, EconWPA, Washington University in St. Louis, MO. http://www.econ.ubc.ca/nnunn/empirical_slavery.pdf.

O'Connell, Stephen, Christopher Adam, Edward Buffie, and Catherine Pattillo. 2006. "Managing External Volatility: Central Bank Options in Low-Income Countries." In *Monetary Policy in Emerging Markets and Other Developing Countries*, ed. Nicoletta Batini. New York: Nova Science Publishers.

Onumah, Gideon E. 2003. "Improving Access to Rural Finance through Regulated Warehouse Receipt Systems in Africa." Paper presented at the United States Agency for International Development–World Council of Credit Unions conference on Paving the Way Forward for Rural Finance: An International Conference on Best Practices. Washington, DC, June 2–4. http://www.basis.wisc.edu/rfc/.

Ouattara, Korotoumou. 2003. "Microfinance Regulation in Benin: Implications of the PARMEC Law for Development and Performance of the Industry." Africa Region Working Paper 50, World Bank, Washington, DC. http://www.worldbank.org/afr/wps/wp50.pdf.

Ouattara, Korotoumou, Claudio Gonzalez-Vega, and Douglas H. Graham. 1999. "Village Banks, Caisses Villageoises, and Credit Unions: Lessons from Client-Owned Microfinance Organizations in West Africa" Occasional Paper 2523, Department of Economics and Sociology, Ohio State University, Columbus, OH.

Peachey, Stephen, and Alan Roe. 2005. "Access to Finance, Measuring the Contribution of Savings Banks." World Savings Bank Institute, Brussels, Belgium.

Pearce, Douglas. 2003. "Buyer and Supplier Credit to Farmers: Do Donors Have a Role to Play?" Rural Finance Innovation Case Study, Consultative Group to Assist the Poor, Washington, DC.

Pearce, Douglas, and Victoria Seymour. 2005. "Summary of the 'Sending Money Home' Project—Remittances to Developing Countries from the U.K." UK Department for International Development, London. http://www.sendmoneyhome.org/Contents/summary.html.

Peek, Joe, and Eric Rosengren. 2001. "Japanese Banking Problems: Implications for Southeast Asia." Working Paper 121, Central Bank of Chile, Santiago.

Piesse, Jenifer, and Bruce Hearn. 2005. "Regional Integration of Equity Markets in Sub-Saharan Africa." *South African Journal of Economics* 73 (1): 36–53.

Pistor, Katherina, and Chenggang Xu. 2002. "Incomplete Law: A Conceptual and Analytical Framework—And Its Application to the Evolution of Financial Market Regulation." Working Paper 204, Columbia Law School, Columbia University, New York.

Porteous, David. 2006a. "Competition and Microcredit Interest Rates." Focus Note 33. World Bank and Consultative Group to Assist the Poor, Washington, DC.

———. 2006b. "The Enabling Environment for Mobile Banking in Africa." UK Department for International Development, London. http://www.bankablefrontier.com/assets/ee.mobil.banking.report.v3.1.pdf.

Preker, Alexander S., Richard M. Scheffler, and Mark C. Bassett. 2006. *Private Voluntary Health Insurance in Development: Friend or Foe*. Washington, DC: World Bank.

Rajan, Raghuram G., and Luigi Zingales. 2003. *Saving Capitalism from the Capitalists*. New York: Crown Business.

Rioja, Felix, and Neven Valev. 2004a. "Does One Size Fit All? A Reexamination of the Finance and Growth Relationship." *Journal of Development Economics*. 74 (2): 429–47.

———. 2004b. "Finance and the Sources of Growth at Various Stages of Economic Development." *Economic Inquiry* 42 (1): 127–40.

Robinson, Marguerite S. 2006. "Microfinance in Sub-Saharan Africa." Draft chapter for *The Microfinance Revolution*. Vol. 3. Forthcoming. Washington, DC: World Bank.

Rowlands, Michael. 1995. "Looking at Financial Landscapes: A Contextual Analysis of ROSCAs in Cameroon." In *Money-Go-Rounds: The Importance of ROSCAs for Women*, ed. Shirley Ardener and Sandra Burman, 111–24. Oxford, UK: Berg.

Ruotsi, Jorma. 2003. *Agricultural Marketing Companies as Sources of Smallholder Credit in Eastern and Southern Africa: Experiences, Insights and Potential Donor Role*. Rome: International Fund for Agricultural Development. http://www.ifad.org/rural finance/policy/pf.pdf.

Rust, Kecia. 2002. "Competition or Co-operation? Understanding the Relationship between Banks and Alternative Lenders in the Low-Income Housing Finance Sector." Occasional Paper 4, Housing Finance Resource Programme, Johannesburg.

Rutherford, Stuart. 1999. "Savings and the Poor: The Methods, Use, and Impact of Savings by the Poor of East Africa." MicroSave, Nairobi. http://www.microfinancegateway.org/redirect.php?mode=link&id=3595.

———. 2001. *The Poor and Their Money*. New York: Oxford University Press.

Sacerdoti, Emilio. 2005. "Access to Bank Credit in Sub-Saharan Africa: Key Issues and Reform Strategies." IMF Working Paper 05/166, International Monetary Fund, Washington, DC.

Sachs, Jeffrey. 2005. *The End of Poverty: Economic Possibilities for Our Time*. New York: Penguin.

Sala-i-Martin, Xavier. 2006. "The World Distribution of Income: Falling Poverty and ... Convergence, Period." *Quarterly Journal of Economics* 121 (2): 351–97.

Sander, Cerstin, and Samuel Munzele Maimbo. 2003. "Migrant Labor Remittances in Africa: Reducing Obstacles to Developmental Contributions." Africa Region Working Paper 64, World Bank, Washington, DC.

———. 2004. "Migrant Remittances in Africa: A Regional Perspective." In *Remittances: Development Impact and Future Prospects*, ed. Dilip Ratha and Samuel Munzele Maimbo, 53–80. Washington, DC: World Bank.

Schneider, Friedrich. 2005. "Shadow Economies around the World: What Do We Know?" *European Journal of Political Economy* 21 (3): 598–642.

Senbet, Lemma W., and Isaac Otchere. 2006. "Financial Sector Reforms in Africa: Perspectives on Issues and Policies." In *Annual World Bank Conference on Development Economics 2006: Growth and Integration*, ed. François Bourguignon and Boris Pleskovic, 81–120. Washington, DC: World Bank.

Silva Lopes, Paulo. 2005. "The Disconcerting Pyramids of Poverty and Inequality of Sub-Saharan Africa." IMF Working Paper 05/47, International Monetary Fund, Washington, DC.

Singh, Ajit. 1999. "Should Africa Promote Stock Market Capitalism?" *Journal of International Development* 11 (3): 343–65.

Skees, Jerry R. 2003. "Risk Management Challenges in Rural Financial Markets: Blending Risk Management Innovations with Rural Finance." Paper presented at the United States Agency for International Development–World Council of Credit Unions conference on Paving the Way Forward for Rural Finance: An International Conference on Best Practices, Washington, DC, June 2-4. http://www.basis.wisc.edu/rfc/.

Stasavage, David. 2000. "The Franc Zone as a Restraint." In *Investment and Risk in Africa*, ed. Paul Collier and Catherine Pattillo, 275–304. Basingstoke, UK: Macmillan.

Steel, William F., and David Obu Andah. 2003. "Rural and Micro Finance Regulation in Ghana: Implications for Development and Performance of the Industry." Africa Region Working Paper 49, World Bank, Washington, DC. http://www.worldbank.org/afr/wps/wp49.pdf.

Stiglitz, Joseph, and Andrew Weiss. 1981. "Credit Rationing in Markets with Imperfect Information." *American Economic Review* 71 (3): 393–410.

Strand, Håvard, Lars Wilhelmsen, Nils Petter Gleditsch, and Mikael Eriksson. 2004. *Armed Conflict Dataset Codebook Version 3.0.* Oslo: International Peace Research Institute. http://prio.no/page/Publication_details//9429/44449.html?PHPSESSID=95442c397e3cfd90f3e3b2f6ba3747d9.

Sundararajan, V., Abayomi A. Alawode, Mathew Jones, and Martin Cihak, eds. 2005. *Financial Sector Assessment: A Handbook.* Washington, DC: World Bank and International Monetary Fund. http://www.imf.org/external/pubs/ft/fsa/eng/index.htm.

Temple, Jonathan. 1998. "Initial Conditions, Social Capital, and Growth in Africa." *Journal of African Economies* 7 (3): 309–47.

Townsend, Robert M., and Jacob Yaron. 2001. "The Credit Risk-Contingency System of an Asian Development Bank." *Economic Perspectives* (Q III): 31–48. http://www.chicagofed.org/publications/economicperspectives/2001/3qepart3.pdf.

Truen, Sarah, Richard Ketley, Hennie Bester, Ben Davis, Hugh-David Hutcheson, Kofi Kwakwa, and Sydney Mogapi. 2005. *Supporting Remittances in Southern Africa: Estimating Market Potential and Assessing Regulatory Obstacles.* Johannesburg: Genesis.

Udry, Christopher. 2000. "Remarks." Paper presented at the Opportunities in Africa: Micro-evidence on Firms and Households Conference, Centre for the Study of African Economics, University of Oxford, Oxford, UK, April 9–10. http://www.csae.ox.ac.uk/conferences/2000-OiA/pdfpapers/udry.PDF.

U.S. Securities and Exchange Commission. 2006. *Final Report of the Advisory Committee on Smaller Public Companies to the U.S. Securities and Exchange Commission.* Washington, DC: U.S. Securities and Exchange Commission. http://www.sec.gov/info/smallbus/acspc/acspc-finalreport_discdraft_041806.pdf.

Widner, Jennifer A. 2000. "The Courts as a Restraint: The Experience of Tanzania, Uganda and Botswana." In *Investment and Risk in Africa*, ed. Paul Collier and Catherine Pattillo, 219–42. Basingstoke, U.K.: Macmillan.

Wood, Christina, and Sean de Cleene. 2004. *Sustainability Banking in Africa*. Johannesburg: African Institute of Corporate Citizenship. http://www.unepfi.org/fileadmin/publications/atf/sustainable_banking_africa_2004.pdf.

World Bank. 1984. *Towards Sustained Development in Sub-Saharan Africa*. Washington, DC: World Bank.

———. 1986. *Financing Adjustment with Growth in Sub-Saharan Africa*. Washington, DC: World Bank.

———. 2005. *Global Economic Prospects Report 2006*. Washington, DC: World Bank.

———. 2006. "Equity Market Indicators: A Primer." Financial Sector Indicators Note 3, World Bank, Washington, DC.

World Bank and ING Bank. Forthcoming. "Worldwide Landscape of Postal Financial Services: Africa." In *The Role of Postal Networks in Expanding Access to Financial Services*. Washington, DC: World Bank.

Wright, Graham A. N., ed. 2003. *Savings in Africa: Remembering the Forgotten Half of Microfinance*. Nairobi: MicroSave. http://www.microfinancegateway.org/files/3452_file_Savings_in_Africa_Remembering_the_forgotten_half_of_microfinance.pdf.

———. 2005. "Designing Innovative Products, Processes, and Channels for the Promotion of Microfinance." Conference paper. Nairobi: MicroSave http://www.microsave.org.

Wright, Graham A. N., and Leonard Muteesassira. 2001. "The Relative Risks to the Savings of Poor People." *Small Enterprise Development* 12 (3): 33–45.

Yaron, Jacob, McDonald Benjamin, and Stephanie Charitonenko. 1998. "Promoting Efficient Rural Financial Intermediation." *World Bank Research Observer* 13 (2): 147–70.

Zeller, Manfred. 2003. "Models of Rural Financial Institutions." Paper presented at the United States Agency for International Development–World Council of Credit Unions conference on Paving the Way Forward for Rural Finance: An International Conference on Best Practices. Washington DC, June 2–4. http://www.basis.wisc.edu/rfc/.

Index

Boxes, figures, maps, notes, and tables are indicated by b, f, m, n, and t, respectively.

Abidjan stock exchange. *See* Bourse Régionale des Valeurs Mobilières
Absa, 92, 95, 98
access to finance, 57–58, 58f, 59f, 60m
   constraint to firms, 61–62
   services, 142–143
account types, 143
accountability, 198
accounting, 131
activist reform agenda, 11–12, 163, 176, 195
administrative framework, 203
adverse selection, 150
affordability of services, 59–60, 73, 191–192
Africa Peer Review Mechanism, 189n
African Development Bank, 104
African economic development, 23n, 24n, 205n
African Economic Research Consortium (AERC), 23n, 24n
African Union, 137n, 189n
agricultural extension, 175–176
agricultural insurance, 152b–153b, 172, 184n
agriculture, 5, 13, 66–67, 66f, 79b, 97, 145, 150, 168, 169. *See also* farm finance
aid absorption, 123–124, 125b–126b
Alternative Investment Market, 135n
AngloGold Ashanti, 69n
Angola, 40
anti-money-laundering and combating the financing of terrorism (AML-CFT), 61, 177–178, 200–201, 206n
ARB Apex Bank (Ghana), 170, 179, 187n

229

Bank of Africa, 89, 93, 169
Bank of Credit and Commerce International (BCCI), 83–84, 92
bankability, lack of, 74
banking systems, 40f, 41, 87–88
bankruptcy, 80b
banks, 9–10, 15, 18, 63, 70n, 76.
    See also post office savings banks; state-owned banks
  access, 57–58, 59, 60
  asset composition, 34f
  branch locations, 90t–91t
  cell-phone, 1–2, 156–157, 185n, 186n
  characteristics, 32–33, 39–40
  concentration, 41, 87–88
  consolidation, 93–94
  credit registries, 81
  cross-border, 90t–91t, 124, 126
  depth, 26–32
  direct or wholesale, 171–174
  efficiency, 33, 36, 41
  entry, 134n
  failures, 83
  foreign-owned, 15, 36, 93, 96b, 98
  lending capacity, 73–74
  liquidity, 74f, 75f, 120
  loan maturities, 56
  mobile, 155
  operating costs, 36–37, 38, 187n
  ownership, 42, 43t, 44m, 72, 94f
    changes, 88–89, 92–93
  profitability, 36, 37t
  regulation, 85b, 86, 127–128, 202–203
  regulators, 198
  supervision, 17, 84–85
Banque Ouest Africaine de Développement (BOAD), 54
Banques Populaires (Rwanda), 116
Barclays, 92, 98, 133n, 187n
Basel II accord, 87, 88b, 89b, 194
basis risk, 151
BCCI. *See* Bank of Credit and Commerce International (BCCI)
Belgolaise, 98
Benin, 137n, 169, 174
Black Economic Empowerment Charter, 187n
BNP Paribas, 92, 95
bonds, 54, 112, 137n
  government borrowing, 122
  infrastructure, 119
borrowing challenges, 19
Botswana Savings Bank, 185n
Bourse Régionale des Valeurs Mobilières (BRVM), 50, 129–130, 137n
Burkina Faso, 137n
business development, 175–176, 189n

Cameroon, 50, 179
Cape Verde, 185n
capital adequacy, 203–204
capital flight, 29, 68n
capital markets, 47–48. *See also* securities markets
CARE International, 167
cell-phone banking, 1–2, 155, 156–157, 185n, 186n
Celpay, 157

CEMAC. *See* Communauté Economique et Monétaire de l'Afrique Centrale
Central Bank of Nigeria, 102b, 180, 206n
CFA zones, 92, 128, 130
CGAP. *See* Consultative Group to Assist the Poor
Chad, 173, 201
Citigroup, 93
Civil Code, 45b–46b, 48m, 49f, 79b, 131
civil strife, 43, 44
client focus, 95, 97–98
coffee, 154b
collaboration, 126–131, 202–203
collateral, 86, 144
commercial court, 77–78, 78f
commercial laws, 131
Common Law, 45b–46b, 48m, 49f, 68n, 79b, 131
Common Market for Eastern and Southern Africa (COMESA), 127–128
Communauté Economique et Monétaire de l'Afrique Centrale (CEMAC), 130
competition, 98, 133n, 142, 198
   among banks, 88, 128
   government role, 175
   in small countries, 202
confidence factors, 121–122, 123, 136n
Congo, Democratic Republic of, 40, 46b, 68n, 131n, 157
Consultative Group to Assist the Poor (CGAP), 164, 165–166

consumer protection regulations, 179
contract enforcement, 8b, 18, 71–72, 77–78, 79b
contract farming, 145
cooperation, 16, 22, 195
Cooperative Bank (Kenya), 170
cooperatives, 166, 166f, 168–171
Côte d'Ivoire, 57, 84, 93, 137n
cotton, 145
court procedures, improvements, 197
court systems, 81b
CRDB Bank (Tanzania), 151, 154b
credit, 27, 63, 64, 82, 166, 166f, 197–198
   access, 17, 96b
   affordability, 73
   appraisal, 207–208
   culture, 167
   demand and constraints, 64t
   depth, 29
   innovations, 144–149
   outreach difficulties, 19–20
   rationing, 33
Crédit Agricole, 92
credit guarantee schemes, 102, 103, 134n
credit information database, 80b
credit insurance agencies, 136n
credit market, interfirm, 209
Crédit Mutuel (Senegal), 170
credit rating agencies, 88b
credit registries, 80, 81, 132n, 175
   strengthening, 197
credit unions, 164, 168
creditor rights, 82, 132n
creditworthiness, 18, 148, 149

crop insurance, 150, 152b
cross-border banking, 90t–91t, 93, 124, 126
crowding out, 76
currency credibility, 200
currency mismatch, 74
currency unions, 16, 127, 137n

DBSA. *See* Development Bank of Southern Africa
debt instruments, issuing, 54
debtor appeals, 78
default, 183n, 209n
delinquency, 81, 132, 209
deposit insurance, 134n
deposits, 17, 27, 76b, 33f. *See also* offshore deposits
 innovations, 151
deregulation, 83
Development Bank of Southern Africa (DBSA), 106
development banking. *See* development finance institutions
development finance institutions (DFIs), 57, 72, 99–100, 102–104, 106–107
 governance, 105b–106b
 Nigeria, 101b–102b
 reporting requirements, 106b
DFCU Group (Uganda), 116
discretionary power, 85b, 198
dispute resolution, 78
documentation requirements, 60, 89b
dollarization, 76b–77b
donor roles, 180–182
drought risk, 152b
Dutch disease, 120, 125b, 203

East African Breweries, 130
East African Community (EAC), 137n
East African Development Bank (EADB), 54
Ecobank, 89, 93
Economic Community of West African States (ECOWAS) monetary union, 137
economic growth, 23n, 30, 30f, 120–121
economic stability, 71
economies of scale, 202
electronic banking services, 155
electronic technologies, 143–144, 185n
eligibility for accounts, 60
employment, 70n
enforcement, 81b, 208–209. *See also* contract enforcement
enterprise finance, 61–62, 64, 64t, 65, 66, 73, 107, 135n, 148, 149, 171, 207
entrepreneurs, 2
environment, 5–6, 72, 98, 142, 192–193
Equatorial Guinea, 131n, 203
Equity Bank (Kenya), 155
equity financing access, 108–109
equity markets, 24n, 48, 52
Ethiopia, 93
ethnic diversity and power, 47b
European Commission, payments policy, 182
external agencies, 195

factoring, 66

farm finance, 141, 145–146, 150, 152b–153b, 154b, 169–170, 181, 184n, 188n. *See also* agriculture
FDI. *See* foreign direct investment
Fédération des Caisses d'Epargne et de Crédit Agricole Mutuel (FECECAM), 169, 179, 188n
fees, 59–60
fertilizer, 145, 188n
FGHM. *See* Fonds de Garantie Hypothecaire du Mali (FGHM)
Financial Bank (Benin-Chad), 173
financial depth, 3f, 25–26, 34f, 75f
  banking, 26–32
  in CFA franc monetary unions, 68n
  private credit and GDP, 35m
  variation across countries, 31–32
financial development, 44–45, 45b–46b, 50f
financial literacy, 176
financial reform, 22–23, 196
Financial Sector Assessment Program (FSAP), 196
financial sector goals, 12–14
financial services, 14, 19–20, 61, 143
Financial Services Authority (FSA), 114
financial systems, 2, 5, 13, 23n, 126, 191
  comparisons, 25–26
  failures, 205
  foundations, 7, 8b–9b
  intermediation, 120–121

low population countries, 201–202
financing for specialized sectors, 103
financing gaps, 144
financing obstacles, 62f
financing patterns of firms, 62–63
financing sources, 63f, 64
FirstBank of Nigeria, 89
Fonds de Garantie Hypothecaire du Mali (FGHM), 103
foreign banks, 15, 36, 93, 96b, 98
foreign direct investment (FDI), 134n
foreign ownership rules, 69n
formal financial sector, 14–17, 139, 141, 200
Fortis, 133n
FSAP. *See* Financial Sector Assessment Program

Gabon 50,
gender gap, 60
General Agreement on Trade in Services, 134n
Ghana, 54, 136n, 170
  Produce Buying Company, 69n
Ghana Breweries, 112
Ghana Microfinance Institutions Network (GHAMFIN), 188n
Ghana Telecom, 135n
governance, 3–4, 6, 110, 163
  across countries, 39f
  and the activist agenda, 176, 195
  DFIs, 105b–106b
  ethnic diversity, 47b
government, 18, 54, 56, 175
  curbing profit seeking, 176–177

debt management, 122–123
ensuring stable environment, 10, 72
infrastructure support, 175, 192–193, 205
legal and regulatory compliance, 196–197
policy environment, 2–3
regionalization of exchanges, 130
reluctance to give up ownership, 93
groundnuts, 152b–153b
group lending, 167, 168, 186n
growth, 2–3, 12–14, 71, 192
 and financial depth, 3f
 firm constraints, 61–62
growth project, 23n, 24n
Guinea-Bissau, 203
Guinness Ghana, 112

hedges, 149–150
HIV/AIDS, 109, 133n
housing finance, 56, 69n, 108, 115–118
 microloans, 147–148
hub-and-spoke approach, 130
human capital, 13–14, 188n

ICA. *See* Investment Climate Assessment
IFC. *See* International Finance Corporation
IFRS. *See* International Financial Reporting Standards
iKobo money transfer, 185n–186n
inclusiveness, 196

income relationship to financial depth, 27, 28
India, branching policy, 188n
individual lending, 167, 168, 186n
inequality gap, 24n
inequality of living standards, 185n
inflation, 28, 40, 116
inflation-indexed instruments, 123
informal economy, 6, 67, 67f, 70n
informal financial sector, 26, 139, 140b, 141
information infrastructure, 194
infrastructure, 13, 15, 108, 136n
 financing instruments, 118–120
 government support, 175, 192–193, 205
 remittances, 158–159
initial public offerings (IPOs), 54
innovation in financial services, 143–144, 157–158
input loans, 183n
instability, 40, 44–45
insurance, 16, 55, 111, 184n, 199
 agriculture, 172
 crop, 150, 152b
 deposit, 134n
 portfolio composition, 55t
insurance schemes, 149–150
integration, 16
interest ceilings, 11, 142, 180
interest rate margins, 33, 36–42, 37f, 38t
interest rates, 20, 21b, 33, 35f
interfirm credit market, 209
intermediaries, 61, 99, 188n, 204
 outreach, 164, 164t–165t
intermediation, 29, 36, 120–121
 capacity, 125b

INDEX

informal systems, 140b
median spreads, 41–42
International Finance Corporation (IFC), 181
International Financial Reporting Standards (IFRS), 82
International Fund for Agricultural Development, 145
intrafirm credit, 207
investment, 16, 63f, 108, 110, 121f
investment banking, 103, 107, 111
Investment Climate Assessment (ICA) surveys, 62, 183n
Investment Climate Facility for Africa, 189n
investors, 122, 136n
IPOs. *See* initial public offerings
Islamic finance, 182n
issuing activity, 54

judiciary improvements, 18

Kafo Jiginew (Mali), 170
Kenya, 132n, 170, 183n
  lending rates, 180
  postal bank, 174
Kenya Airways, 130
Kenya Commercial Bank, 133n
Kenya Electricity Generating Company, 54
Kingdom Bank (Zimbabwe), 173

land ownership, 19, 148
land registries, 82, 197
land tenure, 24n
leasing, 65–66
legal issues, 15, 79b–81b, 131, 175, 193, 196–197

legal tradition, 45b
lenders, specialized, 172
lending, 19, 76, 77, 120, 180
  capacity, 73–74
  group and individual, 167, 168, 186n
  long-term, 134n
  SMEs, 96b
  uncollateralized, 86
  volume of, 82
Lesotho, 203
Liberia, 77b
liquid liabilities, ratio to GDP, 27, 28f, 31f
liquidity, 74f, 74fn, 75f, 129
  excess, 73, 120
  risk, 108
liquidity facilities, 117, 119
listings, 69n, 130, 135n
  primary, 49
  vanity, 112
loan concentration limits, 86
loan guarantee schemes, 181
long-term financing, 16, 56, 107–109
  housing, 115–118
  pension funds, 109–111
  securities markets, 111–115
long-term resources, lack of, 117
low population countries, 201–202

macroeconomic policy, 8b, 120–124
Madagascar, 169
maize, 184n, 188n
Malawi, 150, 152b–153b, 184n
Malawi Rural Finance Corporation (MRFC), 153b

Mali, 103, 170
management of service delivery, 141–142
Maputo stock exchange, 53
market development, 136n
market failure, correcting, 11
market size, 17–18
Mauritius, 28, 41
Meridien-BIAO, 84, 92, 132n
MGAs. *See* mutual guarantee associations
micro, small, and medium-scale enterprises (MSMEs), 82–83
microentrepreneurs, 2
microfinance, 1, 20b, 141, 171, 186n, 196
  by banks, 172–173
  household finance, 57
  models, 163–167
  outreach, 21b
  regulatory model, 177
microfinance institutions (MFIs), 140b, 168, 171, 172
  conversion to bank, 180
  group lending, 167
  regulators, 189n
  supervision, 178–179
  unit costs, 182n
microinsurance, 150–151, 152b–154b, 184n
microloans, 147–148, 187n
middle market, 141, 149, 192, 197
migration, 114, 158
mobile-phone technology, 201. *See also* cell-phone technology
models, piloting, 157
modernist reform agenda, 7–10, 12, 144, 194
  examples, 147
  microfinance, 21b
monetary depth, 28
monetary instability, 40
monetary reserve requirements, 132n
monetary targets, 126b
monetary volatility, 43
money transfer operators (MTOs), 174
money transfer products, 160b, 162b
money transfer services' regulations, 161b
moral hazard, 150
mortgage bonds, 111, 117
mortgage finance, 103, 115, 135n–136n
  expansion obstacles, 56–57
  microloans, 147–148
mortgage market constraints, 116
Mozambique, 53, 56, 61, 98, 145
MFRC. *See* Malawi Rural Finance Corporation
MSMEs. *See* micro, small, and medium-scale enterprises
MTOs. *See* money transfer operators
mutual guarantee associations (MGAs), 169, 170, 187n
mutuality forms, 167–171
mutuality principles, 186n
Mzansi account, 61, 172, 187n

Namibia, 61, 69n, 174
Nampost (Namibia), 174
National Association of Small Farmers (NASFAM) (Malawi), 152b, 153b

National Bank of Commerce (Tanzania), 98, 133n
National Economic Reconstruction Fund (Nigeria), 102b
National Microfinance Bank (NMB) (Tanzania), 133n, 173
New Partnership for Africa's Development, 189n
New York Board of Trade, 154b
NEXIM (Nigeria), 101b
NGOs. *See* nongovernmental organizations
Niger, 201
Nigeria, 15, 54, 60, 97, 132n, 133n
  bank market share, 68n–69n
  capital adequacy ruling, 203–204
  consolidation of banking market, 93–94
  DFIs, 100, 101b–102b
  interest ceilings, 180
Nigeria Bank for Commerce and Industry, 101b
Nigeria Education Bank, 102b
Nigeria Industrial Development Bank, 101b
Nigerian National Housing Trust Fund, 117
NMB. *See* National Microfinance Bank
nonbank finance, 46–48, 199
nongovernmental organizations (NGOs), 166, 166f
Nyesigiso (Mali), 116–117

offshore deposits, 28–29, 33f, 68n
  dollarization, 77b
oil exports, 123, 203

operating costs, 36–37, 38, 38t, 39, 187n
Opportunity International Bank of Malawi (OIBM), 153b
Organization of African Unity, 137n
organizational models, 141–142, 163–167
outreach, 17–20, 21b, 164, 164t–165t, 166f, 192
  measuring, 165
  to poor, 157
ownership, 19, 97
  banks, 42, 43t, 44m, 88–89, 92–93
  patterns, 94f

PAMECAS (Senegal), 187n
payments technologies, 185n
payments innovations, 151
payments systems, 175, 201
pension funds, 55, 55t, 109–111
petroleum exports, 123, 203
point of sale (POS) transactions, 155–156, 201
policy, 4–7, 23n, 71, 115, 125b, 142
  building confidence, 122–123
  design, 199, 200, 204
  enacting, 193–194
  ensuring stable environment, 2–3, 72
  formal financial sector, 14–17
  profit seeking, 176–177
political disruption, 43, 44
political risk, 122
population effects on communication, 201

post office savings banks, 57, 165, 166
post offices, 173–174
poverty, 12–14, 24n, 141–143, 147–148, 151, 157
PPPs. *See* public-private partnerships
price risk insurance, 151, 154b
pricing of account services, 70n
private capital flows, 123
private credit, 27, 29f, 30, 30f
    colonial conditions, 50f
    financial depth, 35m
    legal origin, 49f
    ratio to GDP, 32f
private property rights, 45b
privatization, 1, 92, 93, 97
Procredit/IPC, 167
product features, barriers, 61
product variations, 143
profitability, 98
property registries, 82, 197
property rights protection, 37–38
property title, 19, 148
public-private partnerships (PPPs), 118, 136n

quality of financial services, 61

Rabobank, 133n
refinancing risk, 119
reform, 1–2, 7–12, 193, 196
    contract enforcement, 18
    financial sector, 22–23
    social security funds, 110
regional collaboration, 124–131, 202–203
registries, strengthening, 197–198

regulation, 179, 189n, 202–203
    banks, 83–84, 85, 85b, 86
    loans, preapproval requirement, 87
    nonbank, 103, 199
    regional, 127–128
    securities markets, 113–114, 194
regulators, 189n, 198
regulatory arbitrage, 134n
regulatory compliance, 196–197
regulatory framework, 203
regulatory institutions, 80b
regulatory model, 177–180
regulatory requirements for lending, 74
related party lending, 24n
relationship lending, 19, 148–149, 183
remittances, 158–159, 160b–162b, 182, 185n
    housing finance, 118
    recipients, 159t
remote populations, outreach, 202
Remote Transaction System (RTS), 156
repayments, past due, 209
reporting requirements, 89b, 106b
repricing risk, 134n
reputation, 208b
reserve money, 125b
resource mobilization, 17
resources, lack of long-term, 117
reverse maturity transformation, 110
risk management, 134n, 136n, 150, 184n
risk pooling, 150

risks, 9b
rotating savings and credit association (ROSCA), 140b, 169
Rwanda, 77

SADC. *See* Southern African Development Community
salary loans, 147
savings, 2, 121f, 184n–185n
savings and credit cooperatives (SACCOs). *See* cooperatives
savings institutions, contractual, 48
savings rate, 17, 29, 120–121
scale, 6, 93–95, 202, 203–205
second-board markets, 135n
secondary market liquidity, 51
secondary trading, 112
securities markets, 16, 26, 51f 129, 194. *See also* stock exchanges
  long-term financing, 111–115
  regional collaboration, 128–131
  risk finance, 107–109
  South Africa (Johannesburg), 48–49
Senegal, 110, 130, 133n, 137n, 170, 187n
settler mortality, 50f
Seychelles, 28
Sharia law, 182n
shocks, 6, 18, 43, 44
  insulation from, 183n
  transmission, 96b
  violence, 45
side sales, 183
single passport principle, 128
small and medium-scale enterprises (SMEs), 95, 96b, 141, 192
small-scale finance, 14

smart cards, 155–156
social change, 4
social security funds, 109, 110
Société Générale, 92
Somalia, 206n
South Africa, 116, 171, 172, 177, 187n, 188n–189n
Southern African Development Community (SADC), 127–128
stability, macroeconomic, 8b, 71, 72, 125b–126b
Stanbic, 92, 95, 97, 133n
Standard Bank of South Africa, 133n
Standard Chartered, 92, 95
state-owned banks, 11, 15, 84–85, 92
stock exchanges, 10, 48–54, 113, 129, 137n. *See also* securities markets
  capitalization and value traded, 51f
  creating satellites, 202
  development comparison, 53f
  funds raised, 204
  list of, 52t
  pricing, 54
  transaction volume, 52
Sudan, 133n
sugar, 183n
supervision, 17, 127–128, 198–199
  banks, 84–85
  MFIs, 178–179
supplier credit, 63
Swaziland, 60
systemic risk, 122
Tanzania, 31–32, 98, 132n, 133n, 154b, 173, 202, 206n
Tanzania Breweries, 135n

Teba Bank (South Africa), 155
technology, 143–144, 176, 189n
   for sparsely populated countries, 201–202
   remittances, 185n–186n
   salary loans, 147
   transaction costs, 171–172
telephone penetration rates, 70
term finance, 56–57, 107–109
text messaging, 157
title registries, 175
trade credit, 63
transaction costs, 171–172, 186n
transparency, 9b, 71–72, 80b, 135n
transplantation, 10, 126
transportation networks, 59
trust, 208, 208b

Uganda, 56, 61, 78, 110, 156
Uganda Commercial Bank (UCB), 97, 132n
Union Bank of Nigeria, 133n
Union Economique et Monétaire Ouest Africaine (UEMOA), 50, 141–142, 171

banking crisis, 83, 132
   interest ceilings, 180
unit costs, 151, 154, 171–172, 182n
usury laws, 180
utilities, 118–119

vanity listing, 112
volatility, 43–45

warehouse finance, 145, 146
weather insurance, 150, 152b–153b
West African Monetary Zone (WAMZ), 137n
Western Union, 174
wholesale financial markets, 121–124
wholesaling, banks, 172
World Bank, 83, 100

Zambia, 188n
Zambia National Commercial Bank, 133n
Zimbabwe, 40, 209n

ECO-AUDIT
Environmental Benefits Statement

The World Bank is committed to preserving endangered forests and natural resources. The Office of the Publisher has chosen to print *Making Finance Work for Africa* on 50% recycled paper including 25% post-consumer recycled fiber in accordance with the recommended standards for paper usage set by the Green Press Initiative, a nonprofit program supporting publishers in using fiber that is not sourced from endangered forests. For more information, visit www.greenpressinitiative.org.

Saved:

- 17 trees
- 1,025 lbs. of solid waste
- 6,192 gallons of water
- 1,889 lbs. of net greenhouse gases
- 12 million BTUs of total energy

green press
INITIATIVE

Abb. 26:
Wasserbadbrennerei mit seitlich angebrachtem Verstärker (C. Carl)

Abb. 27:
Wasserbadbrennerei mit Helm, Blase mit Rührwerk, zum zweimaligen Brennen (E. und J. Gürtner)

direkt in die Blase eingebauten Heizschlangen. Diese bergen jedoch beim Abtrieb von Maischen die Gefahr des Anbrennens in sich; außerdem sind sie schlecht zu reinigen. Gegen die Herstellung von Feinbrand mit solchen Dampfschlangenheizungen bestehen allerdings keine Bedenken.

In der Schweiz sind **fahrbare Hafenbrennereien** noch recht verbreitet. Dabei handelt es sich mit wenigen Ausnahmen um eigentliche Dampfbrennereien mit zwei oder drei Kesseln von 200–600 Litern Inhalt. In der Regel bestehen sie aus einer Verstärkerkolonne und einem Dephlegmator, einem Kühler und Zubehör (Dampfkessel, Kran usw., Abb. 18, Seite 53).

Die Arbeitsweise kann etwa folgende sein: Beheizung des ersten Hafens; der Alkohol wird im Verstärker (Glockenböden mit Dephlegmator) angereichert und dann kondensiert. Sobald die Gradstärke auf etwa 40% vol sinkt, wird der zweite Hafen geheizt, wobei die Dämpfe des ersten, zum Teil schon entgeisteten Hafens durch den zweiten Hafen geleitet werden. Nun wird weiter destilliert, bis der Alkoholgehalt des Destillates erneut auf ca. 40% vol gesunken ist. Jetzt heizt man den dritten Hafen an, schaltet den entgeisteten ersten Hafen aus und leitet die Dämpfe des zweiten durch den dritten Hafen usw. Die Vorläufe werden jeweils abgetrennt.

Kontinuierliche **Mostdestillierapparate**, auch Kolonnenbrennereien genannt, werden von obstverarbeitenden Betrieben zur Herstellung von Trinkbranntweinen aus Gärmost und Wein verwendet (Abb. 19, Seite 54). Arbeitsweise einer solchen Anlage: zuerst wird der Gärmost im Dephlegmator (3) auf ca. 65 °C und durch die Schlempe im Vorwärmer (8) auf 75–85 °C vorgewärmt. Anschließend erfolgt die Weiterleitung auf den obersten Glockenboden der Maischekolonne (1), wo der Most von Boden zu Boden fließt und dabei kontinuierlich entgeistet wird. Die entstehenden verunreinigten Alkohol/Wasser-Dämpfe gelangen in die Lutterkolonne (2), während der entgeistete Most die Maischekolonne über den Schlemperegler (8) verläßt. Im Dephlegmator (3) werden die Dämpfe zum größten Teil kondensiert; die leichtflüchtigen Verunreinigungen gelangen in den Aldehydkühler (4), wo sie kondensiert und in die Aldehydpfeife (5) geleitet werden. Dort wird ein geringer Teil als Vorlauf abgezogen; der Rest fließt auf den obersten Boden der Lutterkolonne zurück. Über einen Laugentrichter (10) läßt sich ein Übermaß an flüchtiger bzw. schwefliger Säure in der Kolonne neutralisieren.

Das fertige Destillat (Alkoholgehalt ca. 70% vol) wird normalerweise dem drittobersten Boden der Lutterkolonne entnommen und über den Endkühler (7) zum Abnahmetank geleitet. Der entgeistete Lutter verläßt die Lutterkolonne kontinuierlich über den Lutterregler (9). Maische- und Lutterkolonne werden direkt und indirekt mit Dampf beheizt.

2.3 Verstärkungseinrichtungen

Mit den klassischen, aus Blase, Helm, Geistrohr und Kühler bestehenden Brennapparaten (Abb. 14, 16, 27) lassen sich nur niederprozentige Destillate gewinnen (Rauhbrand), welche einer zweiten Destillation (Feinbrand) unterworfen werden müssen.
Der Grund für diese beschränkte Anreicherung liegt darin, daß solche Apparate – vom Helm mit sehr geringer Wirkung einmal abgesehen – keine Verstärkungseinrichtungen aufweisen. Im Prinzip werden die durch Erhitzung des Brennguts gebildeten, mit Alkohol angereicherten Dämpfe nach Passieren des Geistrohrs im Kühler verflüssigt (**Gleichstromdestillation,** Abb. 28a). Bis zum Beginn des 19. Jahrhunderts war es nur durch mehrmalige Destillation möglich, hochprozentige Destillate herzustellen. Erst *Pistorius* gelang es um 1815 unter Verwendung von hintereinandergeschalteten Blasen und Verstärkerteilen, in einem Arbeitsgang über 80prozentige Destillate zu gewinnen.

Im Verlaufe der letzten Jahrzehnte hat in der Obstbrennerei – vor allem aus wirtschaftlichen Gründen – die Destillation im einmaligen Abtrieb unter Verwendung von speziellen Verstärkern immer mehr Eingang gefunden. Die bessere Anreicherung des Alkohols gelingt deshalb, weil die entstehenden Dämpfe im Gegensatz zur Gleichstromdestillation nur teilweise als Destillat abgenommen, teilweise aber in die Blase zurückgeführt werden. Dabei kommt es zu einem intensiven Stoff- und Wärmeaustausch zwischen dem zurückfließenden Kondensat und den aufsteigenden Dämpfen (**Gegenstromdestillation,** Abb. 28b). Solche

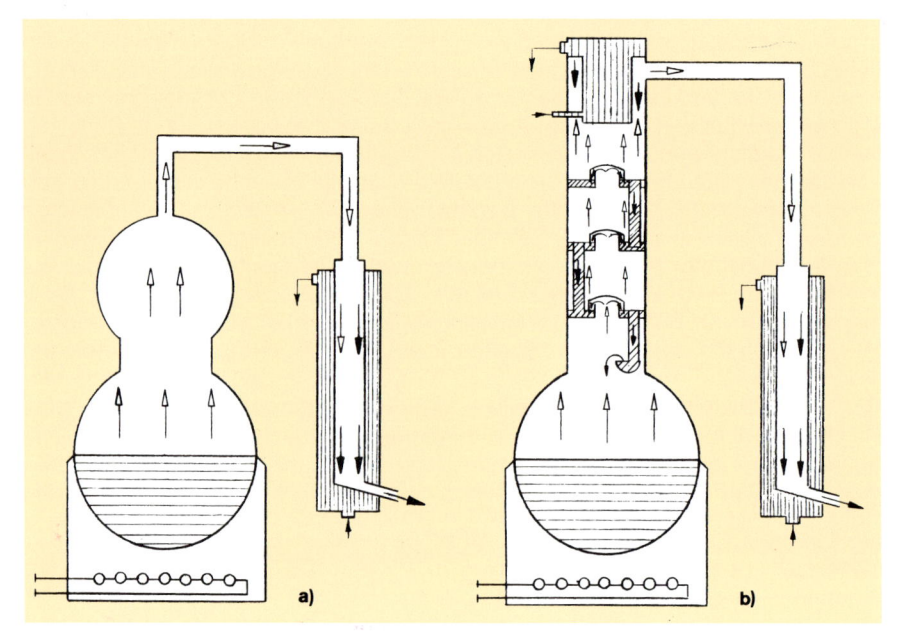

Abb. 28: Prinzip der Gleichstrom– (a) und Gegenstromdestillation (b)
(⟶ Dämpfe ⟶ Kondensat)

Verstärker bestehen meist aus 2–4 Glockenböden und einem Dephlegmator; sie können sowohl über (Abb. 20, 21, 23) als auch neben der Blase (Abb. 22, 24–26) angeordnet sein.

Dephlegmatoren sind als Wasserkasten- oder Röhrendephlegmatoren ausgelegt, wobei auch Kombinationen dieser beiden Typen möglich sind. Der Wasserkastendephlegmator besteht im wesentlichen aus einem zylindrischen Gefäß mit Kühlwasserzufluß und -abfluß, welches den aufsteigenden Dämpfen nur wenig Platz läßt und deswegen eine teilweise Kondensation bewirkt (Abb. 28b). Beim Röhrendephlegmator werden die Dämpfe durch zahlreiche parallele Röhren geleitet, welche ihrerseits von einem zylindrischen Behälter mit Kühlwasserzufluß und -abfluß umgeben sind. Es sind auch Dephlegmatoren mit Stufenregelung erhältlich; ihre Wirkung ist vom Befüllungsgrad abhängig.

Seit einigen Jahren werden auch Brenngeräte angeboten, bei welchen an verschiedenen Stellen des Verstärkerteils (oder auch im Geistrohr) ein wahlweise zuschaltbarer Cyanidabscheider (»Katalysator«) eingebaut ist. Dieser besteht aus Kupfer-Lamellen oder -füllkörpern mit großer Oberfläche, welche für einen zusätzlichen, intensiven Kontakt mit den passierenden Dämpfen sorgt (Abb. 29). Dadurch wird die in den Dämpfen enthaltene Blausäure weitgehend als Kupfer/Cyanid-Komplex gebunden und gelangt somit nicht ins Destillat. Auf diese Weise besteht ein geringeres Risiko erhöhter Ethylcarbamat(EC)-Gehalte, da Blausäure als Vorläufersubstanz zur Bildung von EC praktisch nicht zur Verfügung steht (s. F.3.3). Um wirksam zu bleiben, muß die Katalysatoroberfläche jedoch regelmäßig gereinigt werden (s. Abschnitt 5).

Dem Brenner kommt nun die Aufgabe zu, je nach Rohstoffart und Beschaffenheit der Maische zu entscheiden, in welchem Ausmaß er die Verstärkungseinrichtungen einsetzen soll, um ein optimales Destillat zu erhalten. Konkret bedeutet dies die Ausschaltung eines oder mehrerer Böden sowie die Regulierung der Kühlwassertemperatur und damit des Rücklaufs im Dephlegmator oder Vorkühler. Grundsätzlich werden Geiste und Kräuterextrakte ohne Verwendung von Glockenböden, Vorkühler und Dephlegmator gebrannt. Bei dieser Art von Destillation wird ja bereits ein rektifizierter und höherprozentiger Alkohol mitverwendet, so daß auf die Abscheidung von Fuselöl weitgehend verzichtet werden kann. Rohstoffe wie Weinhefe, Trester und Obstwein erfordern dagegen den Einsatz aller Verstärkungseinrichtungen. Vor allem bei Steinobst (Kirschen!), aber auch bei Williams werden zwecks Aromaschonung höchstens 1–2 Glockenböden in Betrieb genommen, während der Dephlegmator mit reduzierter Wirkung gefahren wird (wo möglich nur teilweise gefüllt oder anstelle von Kaltwasser beispielsweise mit Kühlwasser von 35 °C). Selbstverständlich kann die Wirkung des Verstärkers auch während der Destillation nachreguliert werden.

2.4 Geistrohr

Mit Geistrohr bezeichnet man die Verbindung zwischen dem Helm bzw. Verstärker und dem Kühler. Die früher noch aus Kupfer oder verzinntem Kupfer gefertigten Geistrohre werden heute nur noch aus Edelstahl hergestellt. Bei Verwendung älterer Brennapparate können sowohl Kupfer als auch Zinn von den aus stichigen Maischen herrührenden Essigsäuredämpfen aufgelöst werden, so daß es nach dem Ablösen von Zinn (innert Jahresfrist) zur Bildung von

Sprüharm (rotierend) zur Reinigung

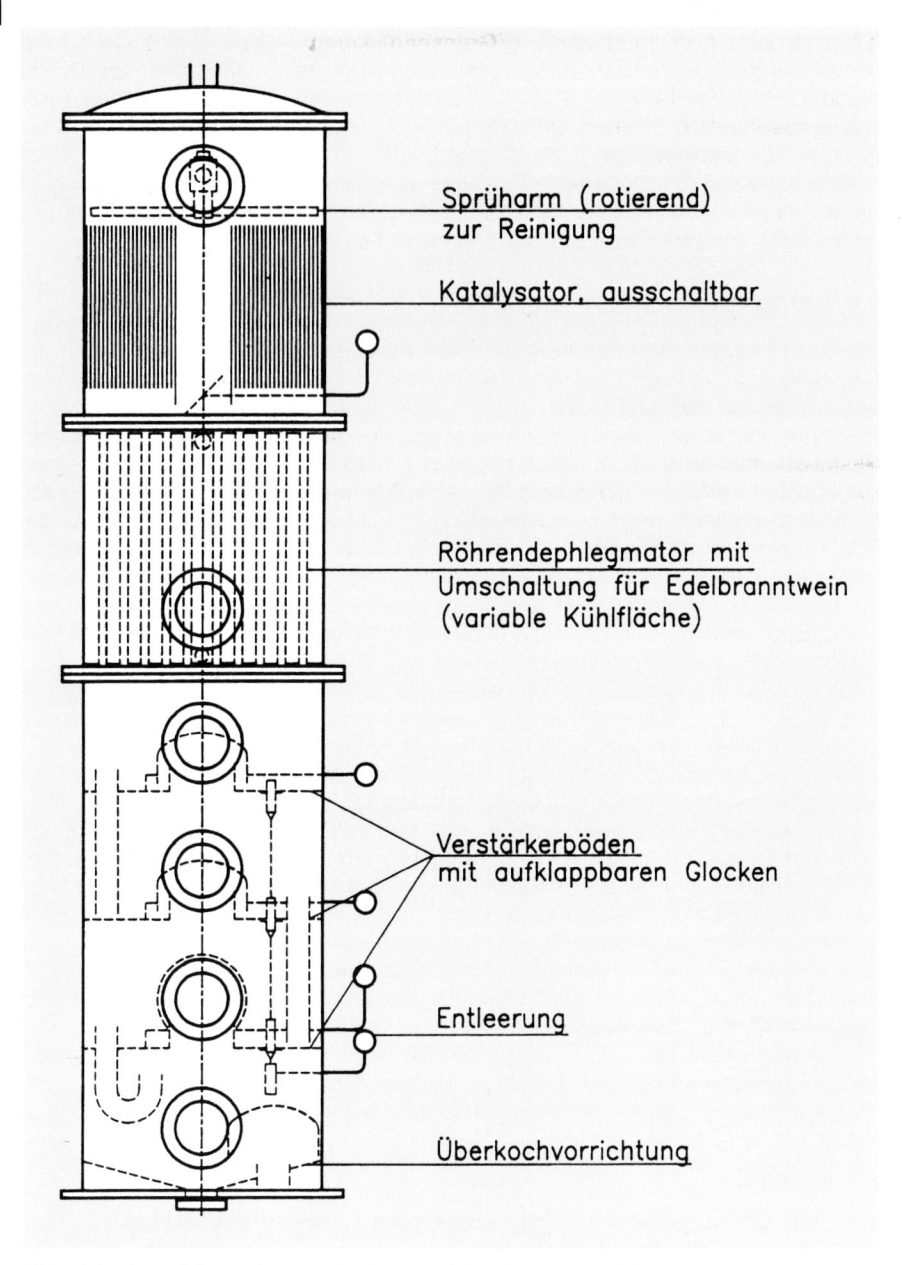

Katalysator, ausschaltbar

Röhrendephlegmator mit Umschaltung für Edelbranntwein (variable Kühlfläche)

Verstärkerböden mit aufklappbaren Glocken

Entleerung

Überkochvorrichtung

Abb. 29: Verstärker mit integriertem, wahlweise zuschaltbarem Cyanidabscheider (System Holstein)

giftigem basischem Kupferacetat (Grünspan) kommt. Diese grünblauen Ausscheidungen gelangen in das Destillat und geben nicht selten zu Beanstandungen Anlaß (s. F.2.1.2). Neben Essigsäure kann auch schweflige Säure, aus eingebrannten Weinen und Gärmosten stammend, auf verzinnte Kupferrohre korrodierend wirken.
Bei der Montage des Geistrohrs (aus Edelstahl!) am Verstärker (aus Kupfer!) ist darauf zu achten, daß Kupfer und Stahl durch nichtleitendes Material getrennt werden, da sich sonst eine elektrochemische Kontaktkorrosion einstellt.

2.5 Kühler und Spiritusablauf (Vorlagen)

Die Ausführungen über den Werkstoff für das Geistrohr gelten sinngemäß auch für Kühler und Vorlagen. Generell sollten die **absteigenden Teile des Brennapparates aus Edelstahl** sein.
Die Wahl eines geeigneten Kühlers hängt weitgehend von der verwendeten Destilliervorrichtung ab. So findet man bei einfachsten Geräten den **Schlangenkühler**, welcher durch einen Wasserbehälter geführt wird. Solche Kühler sind meist noch aus Kupfer, manchmal auch aus gewöhnlichem Flußstahl gefertigt, so daß es hier wiederum zu Grünspan- bzw. Rostbildung kommen kann.

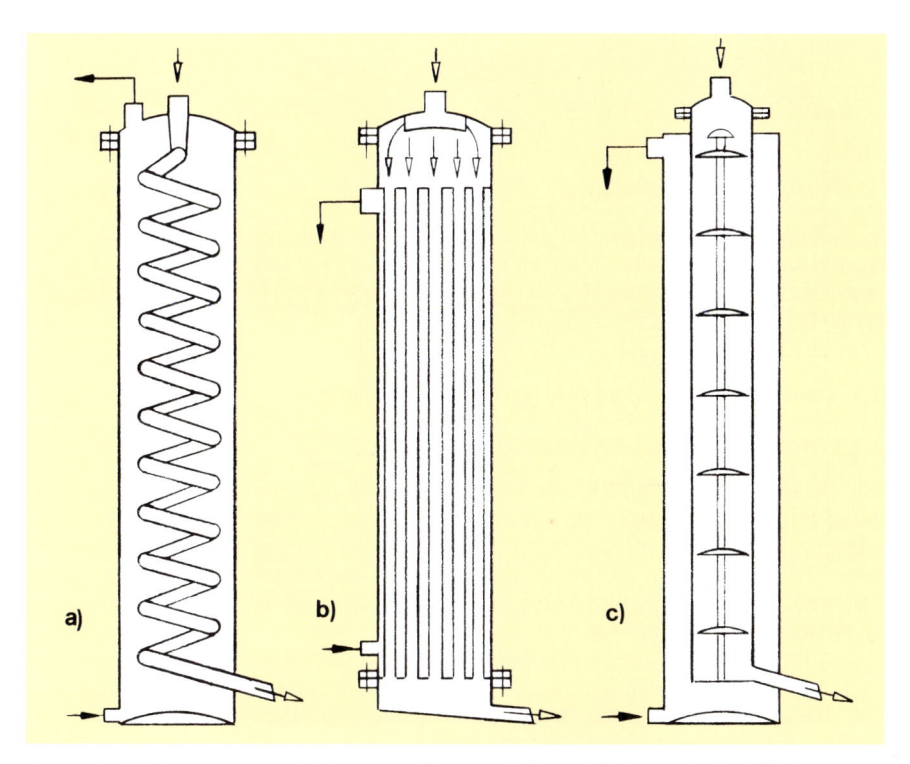

Abb. 30: Kühlertypen (a Schlangenkühler, b Röhrenkühler, c Tellerkühler,
⟶ Kühlwasser, ⟶ Dampfzutritt bzw. Kondensatablauf)

Zudem ist die Reinigung von Schlangenkühlern erschwert, was sie trotz ihrer guten Kühlwirkung zusätzlich disqualifiziert. **Röhrenkühler** aus Edelstahl finden in der Obstbrennerei immer mehr Eingang. Sie bestehen aus wasserumspülten Rohrbündeln, welche oben und unten zu Kammern zusammengefaßt werden. Die Reinigung solcher Kühler ist problemlos (s. Abschnitt 5). **Tellerkühler** nehmen eine Mittelstellung zwischen den im Verschwinden begriffenen Schlangenkühlern und den geschätzten Röhrenkühlern ein. Auch sie sind leicht zu reinigen und weisen eine gute Kühlleistung auf (Abb. 30).

Der Kühlwasserfluß sollte bei allen Typen von unten nach oben, d. h. im **Gegenstrom** erfolgen. Damit wird eine bessere Kühlleistung erreicht. Das Kühlerende ist mit einer »Vorlage« aus Edelstahl auszurüsten, welche es gestattet, Menge, Temperatur, Gradstärke sowie Klarheit, Geruch und Geschmack des ablaufenden Destillates zu kontrollieren. Im Handel werden auch Vorlagen mit automatischer Vor- und Nachlaufabscheidung angeboten. Zur Verhinderung von Alkoholverlusten sollte die Vorlage mit einer Glasglocke überdeckt werden. Es empfiehlt sich insbesondere, die Destillattemperatur gut zu überwachen und gegebenenfalls die Kühlung zu verstärken, da bei höheren Temperaturen bedeutende Verdunstungsverluste in Kauf zu nehmen wären. Aus dem gleichen Grunde ist es angezeigt, das verwendete Auffanggefäß (z.B. Korbflasche) mit einem geeigneten Gegenstand abzudecken.

3 Destillationstechnik

Je nachdem, ob Brenngeräte mit oder ohne Verstärkungseinrichtung zur Verfügung stehen, erfolgt die Herstellung von Obstbränden über ein- oder zweimalige Destillation. Beide Verfahren sind heute üblich; der Trend geht aber eindeutig in Richtung eines einmaligen Abtriebs.

3.1 Destillation ohne Verstärkungseinrichtung

3.1.1 Herstellung von Rauhbrand (Lutter)

Die Blase wird zu 65–75% mit Maische gefüllt und verschlossen. Bei Hefegeläger empfiehlt es sich, die Blase nur zur Hälfte zu füllen (Schäumen!). Dickflüssige, bei direkter Befeuerung zum Anbrennen neigende Maischen, aber auch Trester werden (je nach Konsistenz) mit 20–40% Wasser verdünnt. Obsttrestern, welche eine geringe Alkoholausbeute liefern, setzt man vorteilhafterweise 20% Rauhbrand zu.

Das Aufheizen des Brenngutes soll so erfolgen, daß die letzten 10 Grade des unter dem Siedepunkt liegenden Temperaturbereichs langsam durchlaufen werden, womit man zu starkem Schäumen vorbeugt. Empfehlenswert ist auch die Verwendung sogenannter Antischaum-Mittel in Dosierungen von 2–5 g/hl Maische. Nach dem Anlaufen der ersten Destillatanteile kann die Heizleistung etwas gesteigert werden.

Zu Beginn der Destillation weist der Rauhbrand einen Alkoholgehalt von 40–60% vol auf. Nach gut zwei Stunden sinkt die Alkoholstärke in der Vorlage auf 2–3% vol ab*. Zu diesem Zeitpunkt wird der Brennvorgang abgebrochen; ein weiteres Destillieren des noch in der Schlempe verbliebenen, äußerst geringen Alkoholanteils würde sich schon der Heizkosten wegen nicht mehr lohnen. Zudem ergäbe sich eine unnötige Verdünnung des Destillates. Vielfach wird der Fehler gemacht, daß die Rauhbranddestillation allzu stark forciert wird. Abgesehen von der Schädigung des Aromas werden durch den großen Anteil an überdestillierendem Wasser unnötig viele wasserdampfflüchtige Komponenten, z.B. höhere Alkohole und Fettsäuren, mitgerissen.
Bei der Rauhbranddestillation gibt es weder Vor- noch Nachlaufabscheidung. Es resultiert ein relativ unreines Destillat mit einem Alkoholgehalt von 17–25% vol. Fehler, die von einer schlechten Gärung des Rohmaterials herrühren, lassen sich von geübten Brennern bereits erkennen. Abgesehen von einer ungewöhnlich tiefen Alkoholausbeute (unvollständige Gärung, Mannitstich) können Essigstich, Acroleinbildung oder hohe SO_2-Konzentrationen bereits wahrgenommen werden. Von Fall zu Fall ist deshalb zu entscheiden, ob sich beim Umbrennen des Rauhbrands eine Behandlung aufdrängt (s. F.3) oder ob das Produkt verworfen werden soll.

3.1.2 Herstellung von Feinbrand

Mit der Destillation des Rauhbrandes zum Feinbrand wird einerseits eine **Verstärkung des Alkoholgehaltes**, anderseits aber auch eine **Reinigung** bezweckt.
Je nach Blaseninhalt werden zwei bis vier Rauhbrände zusammen destilliert. Um eine erfolgreiche Abscheidung unerwünschter Komponenten zu erreichen, muß die Destillation von Feinbrand bedeutend behutsamer geschehen als beim Rauhbrand. So soll insbesondere das Anlaufen des Destillats nur **tropfenweise** erfolgen. Die ersten Anteile werden separat aufgefangen und als **Vorlauf** gesammelt. In der Regel liegt diese Menge bei **1 – 1,5 l pro hl Rauhbrand**. Eine differenzierte Feststellung des Umschaltzeitpunktes ist möglich, wenn das anfallende Destillat in Fraktionen zu je 200 ml aufgefangen und fortwährend auf die Vorlaufsnote hin degustiert (verkostet) wird. Bei Destillaten aus qualitativ beeinträchtigten Maischen kann es mitunter nötig werden, bis zu 2,5 l Vorlauf abzunehmen, bei einwandfreiem Rohmaterial genügen vielfach 0,5 l. Im Vorlauf erfolgt unter anderem die Anreicherung der leichterflüchtigen Komponenten Acetaldehyd und Essigester, welche beide einen scharfen und brennenden Geruch aufweisen. In Zweifelsfällen kann auch ein einfacher Vorlauftest durchgeführt werden, welcher auf einer Farbreaktion der Aldehyde beruht (s. G.12). Mitunter stellt sich im Vorlauf auch eine Trübung ein. Ihr Verschwinden darf aber keinesfalls als Kriterium für das Umstellen auf Mittellauf genommen werden.

Während der Dauer des Anlaufens von **Mittellauf** darf die Destillation ebenfalls nicht forciert werden, denn die Abtrennung der störenden Fuselöle ist nur dann in ausreichendem Maße gewährleistet, wenn das Gleichgewicht der Alkohol/

---

* Da die Alkoholkontrolle an der Vorlage relativ ungenau ist, empfiehlt es sich, mit Hilfe eines Lutterprobers (Meßbereich 0–10% vol) eine Kontrollmessung des in einem 100-ml-Standzylinder gesammelten Destillates vorzunehmen (s. G.4.1.1).

Wasser-Dämpfe nicht zu stark gestört ist. Mit der Zeit sinkt der Alkoholgehalt des Mittellaufes. Noch bevor sich eine Trübung einstellt, wird das Destillat in einem anderen Gefäß aufgefangen. Als Anhaltspunkt für das Umstellen auf Nachlauf dient die Anzeige des Vorlage-Alkoholometers. So soll etwa bei Kirschen nicht unter 55% vol, bei Williams und Zwetschgen nicht unter 45% vol gebrannt werden. Zusätzlich zu diesen beiden Kriterien (Klarheit, Alkoholgehalt) ist auch dem **Degustationsbefund** gebührend Beachtung zu schenken. Die bei tieferem Alkoholgehalt vermehrt überdestillierenden Anteile an Fuselölen, höheren Fettsäuren und deren Ester verleihen dem Branntwein einen faden Charakter (»Blasengeschmack«). Werden derartige Veränderungen beobachtet, so ist in jedem Fall auf Nachlauf umzustellen. Der Alkoholgehalt des Mittellaufes beträgt 60–70% vol. Nicht bewährt hat sich das Verfahren, die Umstellung auf Nachlauf erst bei einem durchschnittlichen Alkoholgehalt des Feinbrandes von 45% vol vorzunehmen. Solche Destillate wirken meistens fuselig und kratzend.

Das Abdestillieren des **Nachlaufs** kann forciert werden; mengenmäßig fällt etwa ein Viertel des Rauhbrandes als Nachlauf an. Der durchschnittliche Alkoholgehalt schwankt zwischen 15 und 25, bei Stein- und Kernobst sowie bei Geisten eher zwischen 20 und 25% vol. Die mengenmäßige Verteilung der Feinbrandfraktionen von 100 l Zwetschgenrauhbrand sieht etwa folgendermaßen aus:

1–2 l	Vorlauf (75% vol)
30 l	Mittellauf (60–65 % vol)
20–25 l	Nachlauf (20–25 % vol)
40–45 l	Blasenrückstand (0,1–0,3 % vol).

Bei den mit einfachen Brenngeräten gewonnenen Obstbränden erscheinen – dies im Gegensatz zur Destillation mit Verstärkungseinrichtung – die höheren Alkohole vermehrt im Mittellauf. Obwohl diese Substanzen zum Teil als aromagebende, typische Komponenten zu betrachten sind, kann ein Übermaß die Harmonie des Destillats empfindlich stören (Kratzen im Gaumen, metallähnlicher Belagston). Es empfiehlt sich deshalb, eher zu früh als zu spät auf Nachlauf umzustellen. Nicht nachahmenswert ist die leider vielfach praktizierte Methode, die gesammelten Vor- und Nachläufe dem nächsten Brand wieder zuzusetzen. Die damit verbundene Beeinträchtigung widerspricht nämlich dem durch die Feindestillation angestrebten Reinigungszweck. Am besten werden Vor- und Nachläufe gesammelt und nach einer entsprechenden Behandlung (Kohleschönung, Esterspaltung, s. F.3.2.6) unter erneuter, großzügiger Abtrennung von Vor- und Nachlauf umgebrannt. Der so gewonnene Mittellauf kann den Destillaten in kleinen Mengen zugesetzt werden. Die Verschnittmenge ist durch Vorproben zu ermitteln. Der anfallende Nachlauf ist zu verwerfen.

In verschiedenen Gegenden haben sich **lokale Varianten** der Rauh- und Feinbranddestillation eingebürgert. Ein Verfahren zur Kirschgewinnung besteht beispielsweise darin, daß die Blase zu einem Drittel mit Maische und zu zwei Dritteln mit Rauhbrand gefüllt wird. Nach Abtrennung von Vorlauf destilliert man bis auf 45–48% vol, was zum trinkfertigen Produkt führt. Anschließend erfolgt der Abtrieb des Nachlaufs, der nun mit neuem Rauhbrand und Maische wie vorstehend beschrieben gebrannt wird.

3.2 Destillation mit Verstärkungseinrichtung

Früher herrschte die Auffassung, daß nur gewöhnliche Branntweine aus minderwertigem Obst im einmaligen Abtrieb hergestellt werden sollten, während zur Gewinnung von Spezialitäten dem zeit- und energieaufwendigeren Rauh/Feinbrandverfahren aus Qualitätsgründen der Vorzug zu geben sei. In den letzten Jahren sind jedoch die mit Verstärkern ausgerüsteten Brennhäfen sowohl funktionstechnisch als auch von der Materialseite her maßgeblich verbessert worden, so daß sich die im einmaligen Abtrieb gewonnenen Destillate eher positiv von den in herkömmlicher Weise gebrannten unterscheiden. Voraussetzung ist allerdings, daß die zur Verfügung stehenden Verstärkerelemente der Art und dem Zustand des Brennguts entsprechend eingesetzt werden (s. 2.3). Der Mittellauf ergibt nach Herabsetzen mit Wasser direkt den trinkfertigen Obstbrand. Das Destillat läuft mit ca. 80% vol an. Es empfiehlt sich, vorerst langsam zu destillieren und die Kühlung im Dephlegmator vorübergehend zu drosseln, damit unerwünschte leichtflüchtige Komponenten in den ersten Vorlaufanteilen konzentriert und gegebenenfalls abgetrennt werden können. Die Ausführungen über Vorlaufabtrennung im vorstehenden Abschnitt gelten sinngemäß. Ausgehend von sauber geführten Gärungen – was insbesondere für angesäuerte bzw. enzymbehandelte Kirschenmaischen zutrifft – kann die Abtrennung von Vorlauf sehr gering gehalten werden. Entscheidend ist auch hier die degustative Beurteilung der ersten Destillatfraktionen.

Beim einmaligen Abtrieb liegt der Alkoholgehalt sowohl des Mittel- als auch des Nachlaufs höher als beim Rauh/Feinbrandverfahren (65–70 bzw. 25–30% vol). Zeit- und Brennstoffersparnis wirken sich kostensenkend aus. Die Destillation selbst ist einfach. Durch den Einbau von automatischen Kühlwasserregulierungen (der Kühlwasserzulauf wird über die Kühlwasserablauftemperatur des Dephlegmators gesteuert) wird die Bedienungsperson entlastet, so daß ein einzelner Brenner gleichzeitig mehrere Brenngeräte überwachen kann. Dieses rationellere Arbeiten ist denn auch der Grund dafür, warum immer mehr Betriebe auf das Brennen mit Verstärkergeräten umstellen. Die Destillation wird abgebrochen, wenn das ablaufende Destillat in der Vorlage noch ca. 5–10% vol aufweist. Der zu diesem Zeitpunkt in der Blase noch vorhandene Alkohol kann praktisch vernachlässigt werden; er fällt ausbeutemäßig nicht mehr ins Gewicht. Den anfallenden Nachlauf verwertet man sinngemäß wie in Abschnitt 3.1.2 beschrieben.

4 Gewinnung von speziellen Spirituosen

4.1 Himbeergeist

100 kg frische oder aufgetaute Himbeeren zerstampfen und mit ca. 40 Litern Trinksprit übergießen (bei aromareichen Sorten, besonders bei Waldhimbeeren, kann der Trinkspritanteil erhöht werden). Ansatz nach gutem Umrühren in möglichst vollständig gefülltem, gut verschlossenem Behälter aus Glas, Steingut oder Edelstahl stehen lassen. Zur Gewinnung des besten Aromas genügt eine Extraktionsdauer von 24 Stunden; bei hermetisch verschlossenen Behältern schadet auch eine Standzeit von einigen Tagen nichts. Standzeiten über mehre-

re Monate sind hingegen zu vermeiden (Gefahr der Bildung einer unerwünschten, kernigen Note). Vor der Destillation werden pro 100 Liter Maische 50 l Wasser zugegeben.
Mit Trinksprit angesetzte Himbeeren werden ohne Verstärker gebrannt, wobei im allgemeinen das Abtrennen von Vorlauf nicht erforderlich ist. Das Umstellen auf Nachlauf erfolgt bei 45% vol. Die Nachlaufmenge selbst ist wesentlich kleiner als bei der Destillation vergorener Maischen. Ausgebrannte Maischen können nochmals angesetzt werden: 100 kg mit 20 l Trinksprit überziehen, 24 Stunden stehen lassen und vor der Destillation den Nachlauf aus dem ersten Brand zugeben. Das resultierende Destillat hat aber an Aroma eingebüßt und sollte nur noch im kleinen Verschnitt nachgenommen werden.
Himbeergeist kommt mit einem Mindestalkoholgehalt von 37,5% vol in den Handel*. In der Schweiz erhält der trinkfertige Himbeergeist vielfach einen Zusatz von Zucker, pro Liter z.B. 6–8 g Fructose, womit eine Verbesserung der Geschmacksharmonie zu erzielen ist.

4.2 Wacholder

Zur **gärungslosen** Verarbeitung werden 20 kg Wacholderbeeren zuerst leicht zerquetscht und dann mit 100 l 30prozentigem Trinkalkohol angesetzt. Nach einer Standzeit von ca. 12 Stunden (wiederholtes Umrühren des Ansatzes ist empfehlenswert) kann ohne Verstärkung destilliert werden. Dort, wo noch Wacholdermaischen **vergoren** werden (s. B.2.7.3), erfolgt die Destillation im zweimaligen Abtrieb. Die vergorene Maische brennt man zunächst unter Ausschaltung aller Verstärkungseinrichtungen und ohne Abtrennung von Vor- und Nachlauf. Der Rauhbrand (trüber Lutter) wird pro 100 l mit 5–10 l Wasser und 1 kg Magnesia (Magnesiumoxid) versetzt und über Kieselgur filtriert (s. E.3). Eventuell abgeschiedenes Öl ist vor der Magnesiabehandlung abzuschöpfen bzw. während der Rauhbranddestillation mit einer Florentiner Flasche zu sammeln. Beim Feinbrennen wird bereits bei 65% vol auf Nachlauf umgestellt. Störende Geschmacksstoffe und Öle lassen sich so am besten beseitigen. Über die im Zusammenhang mit Wacholderspirituosen verwendeten Bezeichnungen und Begriffe s. Kapitel I.

4.3 Kräuterspirituosen

Als Ausgangsmaterial dient ein gut rektifiziertes Destillat mit möglichst neutralem Charakter. Nach Einfüllen in den Brennhafen wird soviel Wasser zugesetzt, daß der Blaseninhalt ca. 30% vol aufweist. Die im Fachhandel erhältlichen Kräutermischungen hängt man nun auf einem Siebboden oder -korb in die Blase. Sie können auch direkt dem Brenngut zugesetzt oder in Leinensäcke verpackt in die Blase gehängt werden. Pro 100 Liter Brenngut sind etwa 1–5 kg Kräuter erforderlich (Empfehlungen der Kräuterlieferanten beachten!). Die optimale Dosierung läßt sich über die Degustation des einmal hergestellten Destillates bestimmen. Die Destillation erfolgt am besten mit Hilfe eines Feinbrenngerätes.

---

* Angaben über Mindestalkoholgehalte von Spirituosen in Kap. M.

Des öfteren werden Kräuterdestillate direkt aus Obstwein oder -maische im einmaligen Abtrieb gewonnen. Nach unseren Erfahrungen resultieren aber bessere Qualitäten, wenn die Herstellung unter Verwendung eines ohne Kräuterzusatz erhaltenen Rauhbrands erfolgt. Man hüte sich auch, defekte Spirituosen (schlechte Hefe- oder Drusendestillate, acroleinstichige oder buttersäurehaltige Produkte) zu »verwerten«. Das Resultat wird in den seltensten Fällen befriedigend ausfallen.

Das Destillat (Alkoholgehalt ca. 70% vol) wird zuerst mit enthärtetem Wasser auf ca. 37% vol herabgesetzt. Die entstandene Trübung läßt sich nach Kühlstellen durch Filtration beseitigen (s. E.3). Das weitgehend klare Filtrat kann nun mit hochprozentigem Alkohol auf 42% vol eingestellt werden.

5 Reinigung und Unterhalt der Brennapparaturen

Neue oder lange nicht mehr benützte Brenngeräte gleich welcher Bauart sind vor der Inbetriebnahme mehrmals auszukochen. Zu diesem Zweck füllt man die Blase bis zum Überlaufen an der Füllöffnung mit Wasser. Nach dem Verschließen wird das Wasser ohne Kühlung abdestilliert. Den am Kühlerende austretenden Dampf leitet man mittels eines Schlauches in einen Abwasserschacht oder ins Freie. Wo vorhanden, sind anschließend die Böden zu entleeren.

Grundsätzlich sind die Brenngeräte nach Betriebsschluß täglich mit Wasser zu reinigen. Bei einer laufenden Reinigung ist die Erhaltung einer blanken und damit wirksamen Kupferoberfläche am problemlosesten. Stark verschmutzte Blasen und Helme, wie sie beispielsweise nach Hefebrand anzutreffen sind, werden unter Zusatz von geeigneten Reinigungsmitteln (z.B. 1 kg Soda oder P3 pro Blasenfüllung) gründlich ausgebürstet. Das Geistrohr läßt sich innen am besten mit einer Flaschenbürste säubern. Diese wird mit zwei Schnüren mehrere Male hin und her geführt. In gleicher Weise erfolgt die Reinigung von Röhrenkühlern, während die schwer zugänglichen Schlangenkühler unten verschlossen und während einer Stunde mit heißer Sodalösung gefüllt werden. In allen Fällen ist anschließend ein **erschöpfendes Rückspülen mit kaltem Wasser erforderlich** (Spülwasser mit Universal-Indikatorpapier auf Laugenreste überprüfen!). Auch im Anschluß an die Destillation von aromareichem Brenngut (Wacholder, Kräuter usw.) ist ein Ausdämpfen der Brennanlage bis zur völligen Geruchsneutralität unumgänglich. Vor dem Abbrennen teurer Rohstoffe (Kirschen, Williams) empfiehlt es sich, einen gewöhnlichen Obstwein zu destillieren.

Sind Cyanidabscheider vorhanden (s. 2.3), halte man sich grundsätzlich an die Reinigungsempfehlungen des Brennapparate-Herstellers. Bewährt haben sich Reinigungsmittel, die zur Entfettung von Metallen geeignet sind, z.B. P3-Saxin. Die Frage, wie oft ein Cyanidabscheider gereinigt werden soll, läßt sich nicht allgemeingültig beantworten. Ausschlaggebend sind die Blausäuregehalte der Destillate, die auch selbst ermittelt werden können (s. G.13).

Beim alljährlichen Zerlegen der Brennapparate sind Haupt- und Dephlegmationskühler auf Kalkansatz zu prüfen und nötigenfalls mit 10 prozentiger Ameisensäure zu behandeln (nach dem Auflösen der Krusten sofort wässern!). Gelegentlich sind »unerklärliche« Alkoholverluste auf undichte Stellen im Kühler zurückzuführen. Es empfiehlt sich deshalb, Verschraubstellen und Schweißnähte – eventuell sogar unter Vornahme einer Druckprobe – einer genauen

Prüfung zu unterziehen. In Zweifelsfällen sollte man das den Kühler verlassende Wasser auf einen allfälligen Alkoholgehalt hin untersuchen lassen.
Für die Reinigung der äußeren Kupferteile (Blase, Verstärkeraufsatz) hat sich eine 10prozentige Citronensäure-Lösung bestens bewährt. Diese wird auf die noch warmen Teile aufgetragen und nach kurzer Einwirkungszeit gründlich mit kaltem Wasser abgespült. Zur Außenreinigung der Geräteteile aus Edelstahl genügen meist schwach alkalische oder synthetische Mittel. Wasserflecken lassen sich allenfalls mit etwas Essig entfernen. Wichtig ist, daß Edelstahl nicht mit kratzendem Material (Drahtbürsten, Stahlwolle) »behandelt« wird (s. auch B.1.2).

6 Verwertung der Schlempen

Die **Verfütterung** der als Blasenrückstand anfallenden Schlempen ist mancherorts üblich, deswegen aber nicht weniger problematisch. Zum einen weisen Obstschlempen (Ausnahme: Topinambur) einen wesentlich tieferen Eiweißgehalt auf als Kartoffel- oder Getreideschlempen, so daß ihr Futterwert eher bescheiden ist. Zum andern enthalten sie relativ hohe Anteile an Fruchtsäuren, wodurch sie sich nur in beschränkten Gaben verfüttern lassen; andernfalls wäre mit Verdauungsstörungen zu rechnen. Schlempen aus essigstichigen oder angesäuerten Maischen eignen sich überhaupt nicht für die Verfütterung. In gewissen Gegenden der Schweiz verbietet zudem das Milchregulativ die Verwertung von Obsttrestern zu Futterzwecken. Wenn überhaupt, sollten die verderbsanfälligen Obstschlempen nur in frischem Zustand verfüttert werden.
Wo dies möglich ist, können Obstschlempen entweder direkt oder mit Jauche vermischt als **Düngemittel** auf die Felder ausgetragen werden, wobei die örtlichen Verhältnisse (Boden, Grundwasser) zu beachten sind. Erfahrungsgemäß kann ein Hektar Land pro Jahr bis zu 100 m^3 Schlempe ohne Beeinträchtigung aufnehmen. Wichtig ist, daß die Schlempe nach Beendigung des Brennprozesses direkt im Hafen durch Zugabe von gelöschtem Kalk oder Natronlauge **neutralisiert** wird (das Vermischen kann durch direkte Dampfeinleitung erfolgen). In der Regel werden zur Neutralisation von 100 l Schlempe

> 600 g gelöschter Kalk (Calciumhydroxid)
> oder 1,6 l 30prozentige Natronlauge

benötigt. Die Kontrolle des pH-Wertes (Richtwert pH 8; zulässiger Bereich pH 6,5–9) ist mit Universal-Indikator vorzunehmen (s. G.5.1). Zur Vermeidung von Geruchsimmissionen empfiehlt es sich, die Schlempe unmittelbar nach dem Aufbringen in den Boden einzuarbeiten. Als Alternative ist auch eine Kompostierung auf dem Miststock in Erwägung zu ziehen.
Kommt eine landwirtschaftliche Verwertung der Schlempen – aus welchen Gründen auch immer – nicht in Frage, ist die Möglichkeit einer **Ableitung in eine Kanalisation mit ARA-Anschluß** abzuklären. Die Ableitung von Abwässern unterliegt der Bewilligungspflicht; zudem müssen Abwässer bezüglich ihrer Zusammensetzung innerhalb festgelegter Grenzkonzentrationen liegen. Die behördlichen Anordnungen sind in jedem Falle zu befolgen. Grundsätzlich sollen die Schlempen vorgängig neutralisiert und Feststoffe (Fruchtfleisch, Steine) zurückgehalten werden.

D ALTERUNG VON SPIRITUOSEN

1 Allgemeines

Frisch gewonnene Destillate wirken im allgemeinen degustativ unfertig und unharmonisch. Eine sofortige Herabsetzung (Verdünnung) auf Trinkstärke ist deshalb nicht zu empfehlen; vielmehr besagt eine alte Regel, daß hochprozentige Spirituosen zunächst während einiger Zeit auf dem Dachboden aufbewahrt werden sollten, und zwar in Flaschen, welche mit aufgeschlitzten Korken verschlossen sind. Auf diese Weise wird zwei für die Alterung wesentlichen Voraussetzungen Rechnung getragen: zum einen fördert der **Luftkontakt**, genauer die Reaktion mit Sauerstoff, die oxidative Veränderung von Substanzen, zum andern werden solche Umsetzungen durch **Wärmeeinwirkung** beschleunigt*. Die »Alterung« von Spirituosen ist hier also durchaus positiv zu werten; man versteht darunter Abbau- und Umwandlungsvorgänge von unerwünschten Stoffen in solche, die geruchlich und geschmacklich angenehmer und feiner wirken.
Der Alterungsvorgang verläuft bei Obstbränden wie Williams, Kirsch- und Zwetschgenwasser anders als z.B. bei Cognac und Calvados (Apfelweindestillat mit Faßlagerung). Der Hauptunterschied liegt darin, daß bei der Faßlagerung auch die aus dem Eichenholz stammenden Bestandteile (Lignin, phenolische Verbindungen, Polysaccharide, Mineralstoffe) teils in neue, angenehm riechende Komponenten übergeführt werden bzw. als Katalysatoren bei solchen Vorgängen beschleunigend wirken. Vielfach werden neue Säuren gebildet, der pH-Wert sinkt im Laufe der Zeit und die Ester- und Acetalgehalte nehmen zu (s. Abschnitt 2). Nicht alle Destillate zeigen unter Wärme- und Sauerstoffeinfluß gleiches Verhalten. So ist bei Williams die Alterung mit einem frühzeitigen Abfallen des Buketts (Ranzigwerden, d.h. Verharzen der etherischen Öle) verbunden, so daß hier auf eine forcierte Reifung verzichtet werden sollte. Ähnliches gilt für die Obstgeiste: zur Erhaltung des Aromas ist hier eine Lagerung im Dunkeln bei Temperaturen unterhalb 15 °C empfehlenswert.
Zusammenfassend sei festgehalten, daß sich für Calvados-ähnlichen Apfelbrand, Marc und Weindestillat am besten eine kurzfristige Lagerung in Eichenholz bewährt. Anstelle der Lagerung in Eichenholzfässern kann auch eine solche in Edelstahltanks, Email- oder Glasbehältern (nicht aber in Kunststofftanks!) vorgenommen werden, sofern man den Destillaten Limousinspäne zugibt.
Kirsch-, Pflaumen- und Zwetschgendestillate werden zwecks Alterung in nur teilweise gefüllten und nicht hermetisch verschlossenen Glas-Ballonflaschen oder Tanks im Dunkeln an einem warmen Ort gelagert.
Rasch aufeinanderfolgende Temperaturschwankungen sind der Alterung nicht förderlich. Durch gelegentliches Einblasen von Luft und **kurzes** Eintauchen eines blanken Kupferbleches kann der Alterungsprozeß beschleunigt werden. Destillate, die mittels moderner Brennapparaturen im einmaligen Abtrieb und bei nicht forcierter Brenntechnik gewonnen werden, wirken in der Regel bereits recht harmonisch. Unter diesen Voraussetzungen ist eine 1–2monatige Lagerung als ausreichend zu betrachten.

---

* Nach einer Faustregel verdoppelt sich die Geschwindigkeit einer chemischen Reaktion bei einer Temperaturerhöhung um 10 °.

2 Wichtige Alterungsvorgänge

2.1 Oxidationen

Bekanntestes Beispiel für einen Oxidationsvorgang im Alltag ist die Rostbildung. Dabei reagiert Eisen mit Luftsauerstoff unter Bildung von Eisen/Sauerstoff-Verbindungen, welche andere Eigenschaften als die Ausgangsstoffe aufweisen. Destillate enthalten ebenfalls Substanzen, welche mit Sauerstoff reagieren können. Solche Vorgänge werden als **oxidative Alterung** bezeichnet. Versuchen wir uns zuerst ein Bild über die ungefähre chemische Zusammensetzung eines Destillats zu machen. Neben den Hauptkomponenten (Ethylalkohol, Wasser) finden wir vor allem Methanol (aus dem Pektin stammend), eine ganze Reihe von höheren Alkoholen wie Propyl-, Butyl- und Isobutylalkohol sowie Amylalkohole. Von den Aldehyden kommt Acetaldehyd in allen Destillaten vor. An niederen (d.h. kurzkettigen) Fettsäuren kennen wir Essig-, Propion- und Buttersäure, an höheren Fettsäuren z. B. Capron- und Caprinsäure. Vor allem Aldehyde, aber auch Alkohole können durch Sauerstoff oxidiert werden. Beispiele:

– **Oxidation von Acetaldehyd**

Acetaldehyd ist leicht oxidierbar; durch Reaktion mit Sauerstoff entsteht Essigsäure:

$$CH_3CHO \quad + \quad O \quad \rightarrow \quad CH_3COOH$$
Acetaldehyd　　　Sauerstoff　　　Essigsäure

– **Oxidation von Ethylalkohol**

Vor allem bei der Faßlagerung kann sich unter Mitwirkung von Katalysatoren auch folgende Reaktion abspielen:

$$C_2H_5OH \quad + \quad O \quad \xrightarrow[\text{z.B. Eisen, Kupfer}]{\text{Katalysator}} \quad CH_3CHO \quad + \quad H_2O$$
Ethylalkohol　Sauerstoff　　　　　　　　　　　Acetaldehyd　　　Wasser

Acetaldehyd wird anschließend zu Essigsäure oxidiert, s. oben.

2.2 Veresterungen

Ester sind Reaktionsprodukte von Alkoholen und Säuren; als Nebenprodukt wird Wasser gebildet. In Destillaten entstehen größere Mengen Essigsäureethylester (Essigester):

$$C_2H_5OH \quad + \quad CH_3COOH \quad \rightarrow \quad CH_3COOC_2H_5 \quad + \quad H_2O$$
Ethylalkohol　　Essigsäure　　　　　Essigester　　　　　Wasser

Veresterungen sind prinzipiell zwischen allen Alkoholen und Säuren möglich. Wie vollständig sie ablaufen, hängt neben der Anfangskonzentration der Reaktionspartner auch von Temperatur, Lagerdauer und pH-Wert ab. Da die entstehenden Ester meistens aromatisch und fruchtig riechen, verlieren die frischen Destillate mit der Lagerung ihre herbe, kratzende Note. Veresterungsvorgänge sind umkehrbar; so läßt sich beispielsweise Essigester durch Einwirkung von

Lauge in Ethylalkohol und Essigsäure spalten (»Verseifung«). Dieser Umstand wird bei der Behandlung von Destillaten mit überhöhtem Estergehalt ausgenützt (s. F.3.1.2).

2.3 Acetalisierungen

Bei der Reaktion von Alkoholen mit Aldehyden entstehen Acetale. So reagieren z.B. Acetaldehyd und Ethylalkohol in Gegenwart von wenig Säure zu Acetaldehyd-diethylacetal, einer fruchtig, blumig riechenden Substanz:

$$CH_3CHO + 2\,C_2H_5OH \rightarrow CH_3CH(OC_2H_5)_2 + H_2O$$

Acetaldehyd   Ethylalkohol   Acetaldehyd-diethylacetal   Wasser

Auf diese Weise läßt sich außerhalb des Oxidationsprozesses ein weiterer Anteil des stechend riechenden Acetaldehyds abbauen und in eine ansprechende Bukettkomponente überführen. Übrigens kann Acetaldehyd auch durch Zusammenlagerung teilweise zu Paraldehyd umgesetzt werden (unlöslich, fällt aus).

3 Künstliche Alterung

An Vorschlägen für ein rascheres Alterungsverfahren hat es seit jeher nie gefehlt. In der Literatur sind unzählige Verfahren zu finden, die sich beispielsweise der oligodynamischen Methode (Zusatz von kolloidalem Silber) oder physikalischer Hilfsmittel wie Ultraschall und Ultraviolettstrahlung bedienen. Die ebenfalls vorgeschlagene Ozonisierungsmethode soll jedoch öfters zu einer unangenehmen Geschmacksnote führen. Ein allgemein anwendbares Verfahren hat sich bis heute in der Praxis nicht durchsetzen können, umso mehr, als die meisten dieser künstlichen Alterungsmethoden gar nicht zugelassen sind. Die Lagerung der hochprozentigen Destillate während einigen Wochen oder Monaten sowie gelegentliche Luftzufuhr sind nach wie vor die bewährtesten Mittel, um zu harmonischen Erzeugnissen zu gelangen.

E FERTIGSTELLUNG DER DESTILLATE

1 Herabsetzung auf Trinkstärke

Die meisten Destillate (Mittelläufe) weisen einen über der Trinkstärke von 38–45 % vol liegenden Alkoholgehalt auf und müssen nach erfolgter Lagerung herabgesetzt, d. h. mit Wasser verschnitten werden. Das zu verwendende Wasser hat dabei zwei Hauptanforderungen zu genügen:

– **Geruchs- und Geschmacksneutralität** (der Charakter des Destillats darf in keiner Weise beeinflußt werden)

– **möglichst geringer Gehalt an Härtebildnern** (Calcium, Magnesium), welche in der trinkfertigen Spirituose zu Trübungen führen könnten, s. F.2.1.1.

Möglich wäre die Verwendung von frisch destilliertem Wasser; aus Kostengründen (Energieverbrauch!) wird jedoch zumeist anderen Enthärtungsverfahren der Vorzug gegeben. Im Prinzip eignet sich auch Regenwasser, vorausgesetzt, daß es wirklich geschmacksneutral und auch frei von Fremdstoffen ist. In der Praxis hat sich die Enthärtung mit Ionenaustauscherharzen als gangbare Methode erwiesen (s. 1.2). Die für die Herabsetzung auf einen bestimmten Alkoholgehalt benötigte Verschnittwassermenge läßt sich in einfacher Weise anhand einer Tabelle ermitteln (s. 1.3).

1.1 Bestandteile des Leitungswassers

Wenn Quell- oder Leitungswasser erhitzt wird, fallen bei Temperaturen ab 60 °C wasserunlösliche, sich an den Innenwänden von Erhitzungsgefäßen und Rohrleitungen festsetzende Substanzen aus (»Kesselstein«). Den Hauptbestandteil dieser Ablagerungen bildet der Kalk (Calciumcarbonat, $CaCO_3$). Daneben lassen sich auch noch Magnesiumcarbonat ($MgCO_3$), Gips (Calciumsulfat, $CaSO_4$) sowie Spuren anderer Salze nachweisen. Diese Substanzen stammen aus den Gesteinsschichten, die das Wasser vor der Fassung durchflossen hat, sind also natürlichen Ursprungs. Bei der Kesselsteinbildung läuft hauptsächlich folgender Vorgang ab:

$$Ca(HCO_3)_2 \xrightarrow{\text{erhitzen}} CaCO_3 + CO_2 + H_2O$$

Calciumhydrogencarbonat (wasserlöslich) — Calciumcarbonat (praktisch unlöslich, fällt aus) — Kohlendioxid (Gas) — Wasser

Der Gehalt an Calcium- und Magnesiumsalzen wird als **Wasserhärte** (Gesamthärte) bezeichnet. Ein Maß für die Wasserhärte ist der deutsche Härtegrad (°d). 1 °d entspricht einem Calciumoxid (CaO)-Gehalt von 10 mg/l. In der Schweiz sind auch französische Härtegrade (°f) gebräuchlich. Offiziell wird die Wasserhärte in Millimol/Liter (mmol/l) angegeben. Die Beurteilung der Wasserhärte kann anhand folgender Tabelle vorgenommen werden:

Tab. 2: Beurteilung der Wasserhärte

Gesamthärte in mmol/l	Gesamthärte in °f	Gesamthärte in °d	Bezeichnung
0–0,7	0–7	0–4	sehr weich
0,7–1,5	7–15	4–8	weich
1,5–2,5	15–25	8–14	mittelhart
2,5–3,2	25–32	14–18	ziemlich hart
3,2–4,2	32–42	18–24	hart
4,2–	42–	24–	sehr hart

Für die Herabsetzung von Destillaten kommt grundsätzlich nur sehr weiches Wasser mit einer Härte von höchstens 4 °d in Frage. Der Härtegrad kann mit einem im Handel gebrauchsfertig erhältlichen Reagenziensatz festgestellt werden (s. G.7). Die bei Verwendung von nicht oder nur unzureichend enthärtetem Wasser auftretenden Trübungen bilden sich nur sehr langsam, so daß selbst eine Filtration, auch nach kurzfristiger Kühllagerung, nicht zur erwünschten vollständigen Abtrennung der Härtebildner führen würde. Trübungen können aber nicht nur durch hartes Wasser, sondern auch durch etherische Öle bedingt sein (s. F.2.2).

1.2 Methoden der Wasserenthärtung

In der Praxis existieren mehrere Verfahren, welche die Entfernung mineralischer Bestandteile aus dem Leitungswasser bezwecken. Eine sogenannte **Vollentsalzung**, wie sie durch Destillation oder durch kombinierte Anwendung von Kationen- und Anionenaustauschern erreicht werden kann, ist für die Belange der Obstbrennerei nicht erforderlich. Für die Verwendung als Verschnittwasser genügt eine **Teilentsalzung**, d. h. die Eliminierung der eigentlichen Härtebildner Calcium und Magnesium. Falls das Kühlwasser der Brennapparatur enthärtet werden muß (bei mäßiger Kühlung kann der Kühlwasserablauf ohne weiteres Temperaturen von 60–65 °C erreichen), empfiehlt sich eine Zugabe von Natriumpolyphosphaten (ca. 1–2 g pro m^3) mittels Schleusenvorrichtung oder Dosierpumpe. Dabei kommt es zwar nicht zur Entfernung der Härtebildner, doch werden diese in eine auch bei 65 °C noch wasserlösliche Form gebracht, so daß Kalkablagerungen im Kühler ausbleiben. Weitere Enthärtungsmethoden, wie die forcierte Kesselsteinbildung durch Erhitzen oder die Verwendung niederschlagsbildender Chemikalien (Calciumhydroxid, Soda) haben in der Obstbrennerei keine praktische Bedeutung. Im folgenden soll auf die Teilentsalzung mit Kationenaustauschern eingegangen werden.

1.2.1 Ionenaustauscher

Die Herauslösung von Mineralsalzen aus den Gesteinsschichten erfolgt in Form von elektrisch geladenen Teilchen, den Ionen. Man unterscheidet Ionen mit elektrisch positiver (Kationen) und solche mit elektrisch negativer Ladung (Anionen)*.

Beispiel:
Kochsalz (Natriumchlorid) zerfällt in wässeriger Lösung in Natrium- und Chloridionen:

$$NaCl \xrightarrow{\text{in wässer. Lösung}} Na^+ + Cl^-$$

Kochsalz (fest)   Natrium-Kationen   Chlorid-Anionen
                             (positiv geladen)   (negativ geladen)

Analog dazu liegen auch die Härtebildner Calcium (Ca) und Magnesium (Mg) in Leitungswasser als Kationen vor. Durch **Kationenaustauscher** können sie aus dem Wasser entfernt werden.

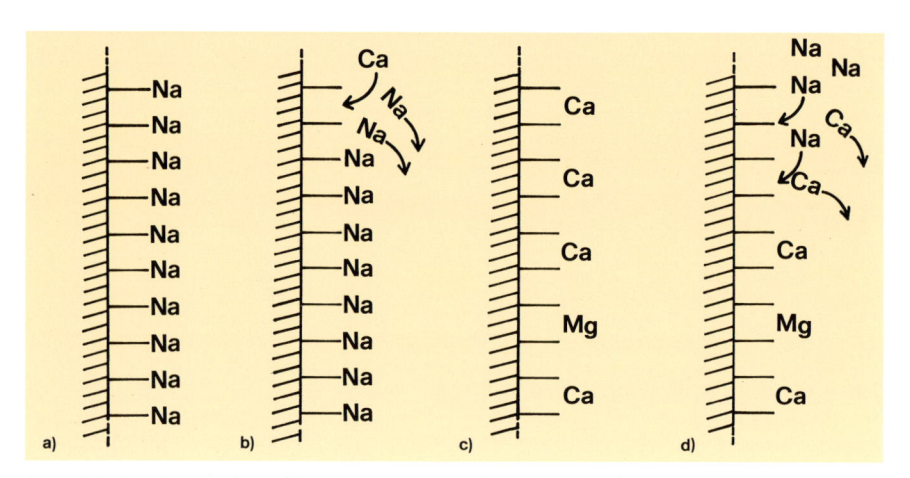

Abb. 31: Funktion eines Kationenaustauschers (s. Text)

Kationenaustauscher sind wasserunlösliche, körnige Kunstharze oder Silikate, welche an aktiven Stellen leicht abspaltbare Kationen, z.B. Natrium-Ionen, enthalten (Abb. 31a).
Nun wird das zu enthärtende Wasser mit dem Austauscherharz in Kontakt gebracht (meist im Durchlaufverfahren). Dabei werden die Calcium- bzw. Magnesium-Ionen an den aktiven Stellen festgehalten und dafür die Natrium-Ionen freigesetzt. Aus Gründen der elektrischen Ladung sind pro Ca- bzw. Mg-Ion zwei aktive Stellen erforderlich (Abb. 31b). Die nun im Wasser anstelle der Härtebildner enthaltenen Na-Ionen bilden keine schwerlöslichen Salze und können demnach im herabgesetzten Destillat auch nicht zu Ausscheidungen führen.

---

* Das Vorhandensein von Ionen in wässeriger Lösung läßt sich an der Erhöhung der elektrischen Leitfähigkeit erkennen. Destilliertes, d.h. salzfreies Wasser leitet den elektrischen Strom praktisch nicht.

Das Austauscherharz ist im Prinzip solange verwendbar, bis sämtliche aktiven Stellen durch Härtebildner besetzt sind (Abb. 31 c). In der Praxis wird jedoch nicht so lange zugewartet (s. 1.2.2). Da der Austauschvorgang umkehrbar ist, kann das Harz durch einen Überschuß an Na-Ionen regeneriert werden. Dieser Vorgang ist beliebig oft wiederholbar (Abb. 31 d).

1.2.2 Praktische Hinweise

Für Kleinbetriebe mit relativ geringem Bedarf an Verschnittwasser sind im Handel komplette Durchlaufenthärter erhältlich, welche wenige Liter Austauscherharz enthalten. Ihren schematischen Aufbau zeigt Abb. 32. Einlauf A kann direkt mit der Wasserleitung verbunden werden.

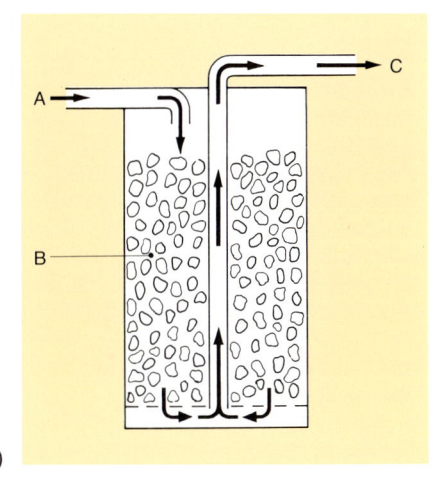

Abb. 32: Schema eines Durchlaufenthärters
A Einlauf (Leitungswasser)
B Austauscherharz
C Ablauf (enthärtetes Wasser)

Die mit einem bestimmten Austauschervolumen erzielbare Verschnittwassermenge richtet sich vor allem nach dem Härtegrad des Leitungswassers, welcher vor der ersten Inbetriebnahme einer Enthärtungsvorrichtung ermittelt werden muß (s. G.7). Auf diese Weise kann abgeschätzt werden, wann die Regenerierung fällig ist. Man beachte die Angaben der Hersteller betreffend Inbetriebnahme, Austauscherkapazität und Regenerierung der Anlage! In Tab. 3 ist an einem Beispiel der Zusammenhang zwischen Härtegrad und erzielbarer Verschnittwassermenge dargestellt:

Tab 3: Erzielbare Weichwassermenge in Abhängigkeit von der Wasserhärte. Kationenaustauscher: 3 l Lewatit (Bayer)

Härte des Leitungswassers			Weichwassermenge
5°d	9°f	0,9 mmol/l	2400 l
10	18	1,8	1200
15	27	2,7	800
20	36	3,6	600
30	54	5,4	400
40	72	7,2	300

Es empfiehlt sich auf jeden Fall, die Resthärte des ablaufenden Wassers vor dem Verschnitt zu prüfen. Bei einem Härtegrad über 4 °d können Calcium- bzw. Magnesiumtrübungen auf der Flasche nicht mit Sicherheit ausgeschlossen werden. Für die Gewährleistung einer einwandfreien Enthärtung sind folgende Punkte zu beachten:

– **Durchlaufgeschwindigkeit:** Für einen vollständigen Kationenaustausch sollten folgende Durchlaufmengen pro Minute eingehalten werden (Richtwerte):

Rohrdurchmesser	Liter/min
8 cm	2
10 cm	3
12 cm	4,5
15 cm	7

– **Austauscherkapazität:** Sobald das Wasser nicht mehr vollständig enthärtet wird, muß das Austauscherharz mit Kochsalzlösung regeneriert werden. Zur Regenerierung benötigt man pro Liter Austauscherharz ca. 500 g Kochsalz, gelöst in 2 l Wasser. Diese Lösung wird durch den Einlauf geleitet (Abb. 33). Nach Zulauf von zwei Dritteln wird die Einleitung für ungefähr 10 Minuten unterbrochen; dann füllt man den Rest ein und wartet erneut 10 Minuten. Man vergewissere sich durch eine Wasserhärte-Bestimmung (s. G.7) von der Vollständigkeit der Regenerierung! Gegebenenfalls muß erneut Kochsalzlösung eingeleitet werden, bis im Ablauf keine Härtebildner mehr nachweisbar sind. Abschließend wird wieder die Wasserleitung mit dem Einlauf verbunden und solange Wasser mit der üblichen Geschwindigkeit durchgeleitet, bis der Kochsalzgeschmack im Ablauf verschwunden ist. Der Enthärter ist wieder betriebsbereit.

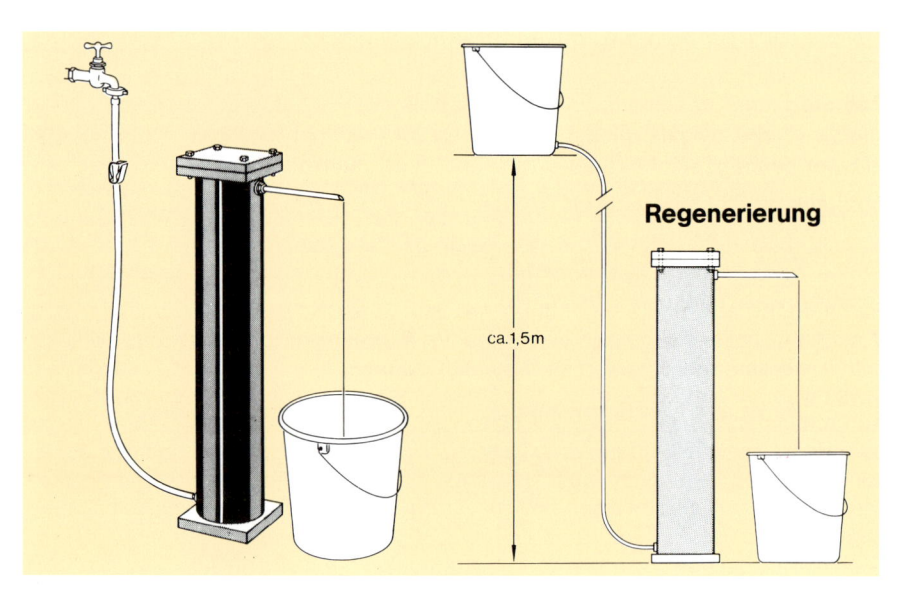

Abb. 33: Wasserenthärtung im Kleinbetrieb

– **Verunreinigungen:** Schmutzbestandteile des verwendeten Wassers beziehungsweise der für die Regenerierung verwendeten Kochsalzlösung können mit der Zeit die Austauscherkapazität beeinträchtigen. In solchen Fällen empfiehlt sich eine Behandlung mit verdünnter Salzsäure. Zu diesem Zweck wird das Austauscherharz aus der Säule in einen Kunststoffeimer geleert und mit dem doppelten Volumen an 0,5 prozentiger Salzsäure übergossen. Nach einer Einwirkungszeit von ca. 5 Minuten gießt man die überstehende Säure ab und spült das Harz mehrmals mit Wasser, bis das Spülwasser einen pH-Wert von 5–6 aufweist (Kontrolle s. G.5). Anschließend kann das Harz in die Säule zurückgegeben und in gewohnter Weise regeneriert werden. Bei sehr starker Verschmutzung ist es angezeigt, das Harz zu ersetzen.

1.3 Ermittlung der Verschnittwassermenge

Werden Alkohol und Wasser in beliebigem Verhältnis miteinander vermischt, so ist das Volumen der Mischung geringer als die Summe der beiden Einzelvolumen. Diese Erscheinung wird **Kontraktion*** genannt; sie ist der Grund dafür, daß man zur Ermittlung der erforderlichen Verschnittwassermenge anhand der Alkoholkonzentration in % vol auf eine Tabelle angewiesen ist (das Resultat der üblichen Mischungsrechnung wäre zu ungenau). Aus Tabelle H.2 läßt sich bei bekannter Alkoholkonzentration eines Destillates (Bestimmung siehe G.4) diejenige Wassermenge entnehmen, die benötigt wird, um 100 l dieses Destillates auf die gewünschte Trinkstärke einzustellen.

Beispiel:

Um 100 l eines Destillates mit 69% vol auf 40% vol herabzusetzen, werden **75 l** Wasser benötigt; für eine Herabsetzung von 69% vol auf 44% vol sind es 59 l (direkt aus Tabelle H.2 ablesbar).
Für beliebige Branntweinmengen ist der entsprechende Tabellenwert umzurechnen.

Beispiel:

Um 24 l eines Destillates mit 74% vol auf 42% vol herabzusetzen, werden **19 l** Wasser benötigt, für 120 l desselben Destillates sind es **95 l**.
Berechnung: Tabellenwert für 100 l von 74 auf 42% vol: **79,2 l**.

für 24 l: $79{,}2 \cdot \dfrac{24}{100} = 19$ l; für 120 l: $79{,}2 \cdot \dfrac{120}{100} = 95$ l

Für nicht in der Tabelle enthaltene Alkoholkonzentrationen kann die benötigte Verschnittwassermenge aus benachbarten Tabellenwerten näherungsweise ermittelt werden. Im allgemeinen empfiehlt es sich, den Verschnitt zunächst mit etwas weniger als der berechneten Wassermenge vorzunehmen und nach einer Kontrollbestimmung noch eine Feinkorrektur durchzuführen. Wichtig ist in jedem Fall eine vollständige Vermischung; auch sollten der zu verdünnende Alkohol und das Verschnittwasser dieselbe Temperatur aufweisen. Gelegentlich wird auch einer stufenweisen Herabsetzung mit Zwischenlagerung der Vorzug gegeben.

---

* Die Kontraktion ist am größten, wenn ungefähr gleiche Raumteile Alkohol und Wasser vermischt werden (s. auch Kapitel K).

2 Kühllagerung

Auch bei Verwendung von einwandfrei enthärtetem Verschnittwasser können in herabgesetzten Destillaten verschiedenartige Trübungen auftreten (s. F.2). Der Grund hierfür liegt in der schlechteren Löslichkeit gewisser Inhaltsstoffe bei tieferem Alkoholgehalt. Da die Löslichkeit außerdem in der Kälte abnimmt, werden die herabgesetzten Destillate während einiger Zeit einer Kühllagerung unterzogen. Damit ist gewährleistet, daß Trübungsbildner weitgehend ausgeschieden und durch anschließende Filtration abgetrennt werden können. Nachtrübungen auf der Flasche sind somit nicht mehr zu befürchten, vorausgesetzt natürlich, daß diese später nicht bei noch tieferen Temperaturen aufbewahrt werden.

Lagertemperaturen zwischen 0 und −10 °C haben sich in der Praxis für die Ausscheidung von Trübungen als geeignet erwiesen. Bei 0 °C muß mit ca. 14 Tagen gerechnet werden, während bei −10 °C nur etwa die Hälfte dieser Zeit erforderlich ist (Richtwerte!). Noch tiefere Temperaturen sind nicht zu empfehlen, da die Destillate zunehmend viskoser werden und eine Filtration erschwert, wenn nicht gar verunmöglicht wird. Bei Kühltemperaturen über dem Gefrierpunkt ist hingegen eine vollständige Ausscheidung nicht in allen Fällen gewährleistet. Wichtig ist, daß auch die der Kühllagerung folgende Filtration bei der entsprechenden Temperatur vorgenommen wird, da bei Erwärmung ein Teil der ausgeschiedenen Stoffe wieder in Lösung gehen und somit das Filter passieren könnte. Zur Kühlung kleinerer Spirituosenmengen stellt man die Gebinde (z.B. Glas-Ballonflasche) am besten in eine Tiefkühltruhe. Im Winter ist bei entsprechend tiefen Außentemperaturen eine Kühllagerung auch im Freien möglich.

3 Filtration

Für die Filtration kleinerer Spirituosenmengen haben sich vor allem Trichter- und Zylinderfilter sowie Schichtenfilter mit Handpumpe bewährt.

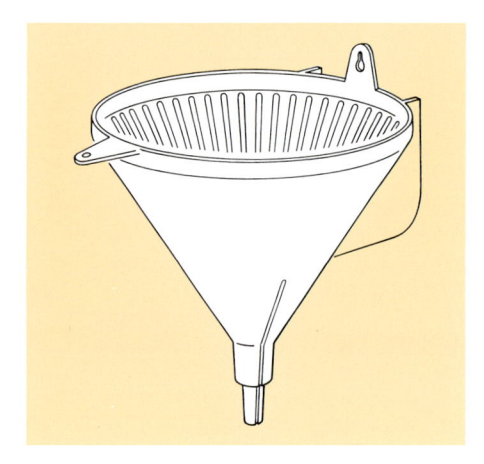

Abb. 34: Trichterfilter

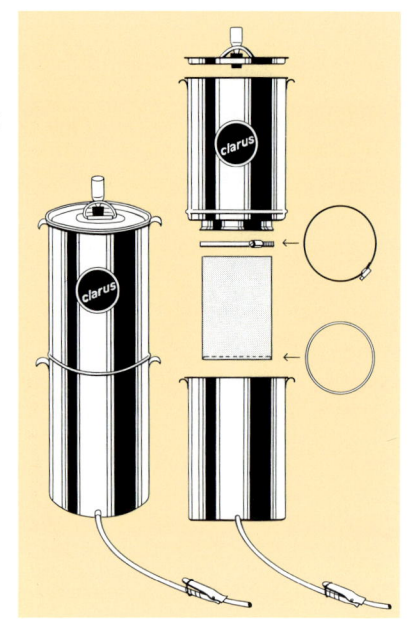

Abb. 35: Zylinderfilter

Bei **Trichterfiltern** werden Faltenfilter verschiedener Durchlässigkeitsgrade verwendet. Es leuchtet ein, daß ihre Leistung umso größer ist, je mehr Filterfläche ausgenützt wird. Dies läßt sich in einfacher Weise mit folgender Anordnung erreichen (Abb. 36): Die Ballonflasche wird so aufgestellt, daß sich das Ende ihres **schräg angeschnittenen Ablaufschlauches** etwa auf der Höhe des Trichterrandes innerhalb des Faltenfilters befindet. Die **Ballonflasche muß mit einem Gummistopfen absolut luftdicht verschlossen und zu Beginn der Filtration vollständig gefüllt sein.** Auf diese Weise läuft aus dem dauernd offenen Schlauch nur soviel Flüssigkeit nach, wie abfiltriert wird. Sobald der Flüssigkeitsspiegel die Schlauchmündung erreicht, hört die Zufuhr auf. Ein Überlaufen des Filters ist unmöglich, und eine Beaufsichtigung erübrigt sich. Die Methode ist besonders vorteilhaft für die Filtration bei Temperaturen unter 0 °C.

Durch Anschwemmen eines **Filterhilfsstoffes** (z. B. Seitz-Supra-Theorit 5, asbestfrei) läßt sich die Filtrationsschärfe erhöhen. Das Filterpulver wird einem Teil des zu klärenden Destillates beigefügt und solange gut verrührt, bis keine Klumpen mehr sichtbar sind. Um eine optimale Filtrationswirkung zu erreichen, empfiehlt es sich, das Gemisch während ca. 20 Minuten aufquellen zu lassen. Anschließend gießt man den Ansatz in einem Zug auf das Filter, damit sich eine gleichmäßige Schicht ausbilden kann. Als Trägermaterial kommen Filz- und Kunststoffsäcke, aber auch Filterpapier in Frage; neben den bereits erwähnten Trichterfiltern eignen sich also vor allem **Zylinderfilter** für die Anschwemmfiltration. Das zunächst noch trübe Filtrat wird auf das Filter zurückgegeben, bis es blank abläuft. Detaillierte Angaben, wie über Art und Dosierung des zu verwendenden Filterhilfsstoffes, Stundenleistung usw. entnehme man der vom Hersteller mitgelieferten Bedienungsanleitung.

Es sei nochmals darauf hingewiesen, daß man die **Filtration möglichst bei der entsprechenden Kühllagertemperartur** vornehmen soll. Nur so ist gewährleistet, daß nicht wieder ein Teil der ausgeschiedenen Stoffe in Lösung geht. Wichtig ist auch, daß das Filter nicht trockenläuft, da sonst mit einer Zerstörung (Abrutschen, Aufreißen) der angeschwemmten Filterschicht gerechnet werden müßte. Nach Beendigung der Filtration oder bei Erschöpfung des Filters ist dieses mit Wasser zu spülen, bevor es getrocknet bzw. wiederverwendet wird. Leider werden mit asbestfreien Filterhilfsmitteln nicht immer gleich gute Filtrationsergebnisse erzielt wie mit asbesthaltigen, die heute nicht mehr benutzt werden dürfen. Für höhere Ansprüche an die Klarheit der Filtrate kommen auch Schichtenfilter mit Motorpumpe (Abb. 37) oder Kerzenfilter (Abb. 38) in

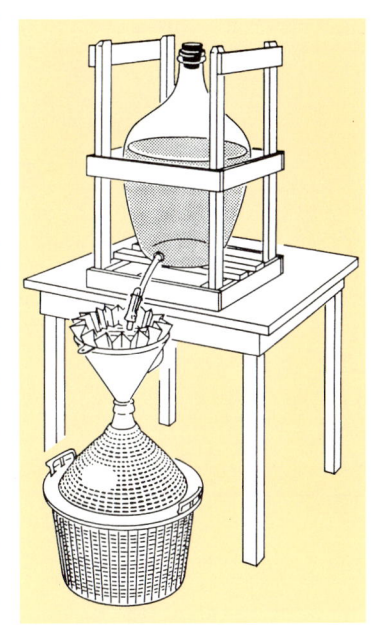

Abb. 36:
Automatische Filtration
(s. Text)

Frage. Bei letzteren ist zu erwähnen, daß das Filtermaterial leicht Aromastoffe absorbiert, was besonders nach Filtration aromaintensiver Destillate (z. B. Hefebrand, Williams) auffällt. Zur Verhinderung von Aromaverschleppungen bei Produktewechsel ist ein besonders gründliches Spülen angezeigt (s. F. 3. 3).
Spirituosen mit hohem Gehalt an etherischen Ölen, wie Wacholder-, Williams- oder Kräuterdestillate, werden vor der Kühllagerung vorzugsweise auf ungefähr 5% vol unter Trinkstärke eingestellt. Nach der bei Kühllagertemperatur vorgenommenen Filtration kann man den Alkoholgehalt mit einem gut rektifizierten Destillat gleicher Provenienz heraufsetzen (s. auch F.2.2).

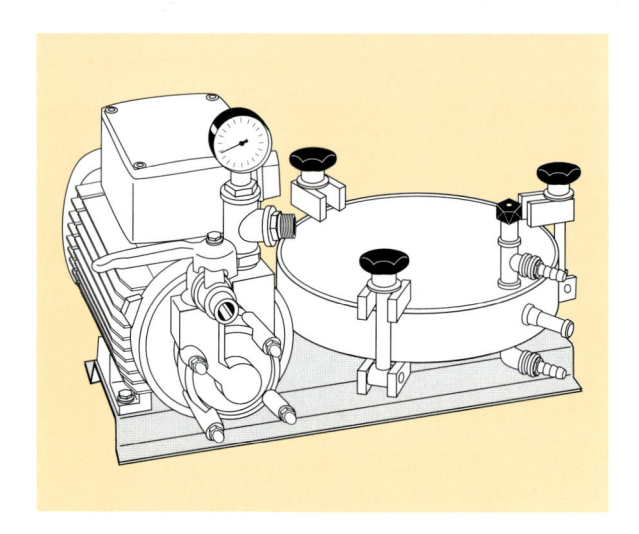

Abb. 37:
Schichtenfilter mit Motorpumpe

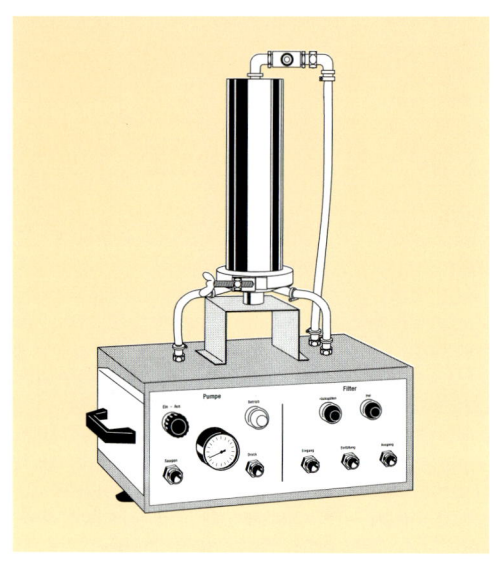

Abb. 38: Kerzenfilter

4 Abfüllung

Die Abfüllung der fertiggestellten Spirituosen bietet im allgemeinen keine besonderen Schwierigkeiten. Wie bei allen Getränken, kommen nur einwandfrei gereinigte, gut ausgespülte Flaschen in Frage (Spülwasser gut abtropfen lassen). Zwar besteht des hohen Alkoholgehaltes wegen keine Gefahr einer mikrobiellen Infektion, dafür sind mechanische Verunreinigungen wie Staub oder Glassplitter in den klaren, farblosen Destillaten besonders leicht zu erkennen. Dies bedeutet, daß auch fabrikneu angelieferte Flaschen auf Verschmutzung zu kontrollieren sind und gegebenenfalls ausgespült bzw. ausgeblasen werden sollten. Bei Kleinstmengen können der Abfüllvorgang und das Verschließen der Flaschen selbstverständlich im reinen Handbetrieb erfolgen. Im einfachsten Fall genügt eine Ablaßgarnitur, bestehend aus Schlauch und Quetschhahn, für den Untenanstich (Abb. 39). Für den Obenanstich eignet sich ein Heber mit manueller Druckerzeugung (Abb. 40).

Für den Klein- und Mittelbetrieb sind im Fachhandel eine Anzahl halbautomatischer Abfüllvorrichtungen erhältlich, mit denen trotz ihrer Einfachheit respektable Leistungen von mehreren hundert Flaschen pro Stunde erreicht werden können (Abb. 42). Ähnliches gilt für das Verschließen der Flaschen, beispielsweise mit Drehverschluß (Abb. 41).

Bei der Abfüllung ist zu beachten, daß das Volumen temperaturabhängig ist. Weicht die Temperatur der abzufüllenden Spirituose von der Eichtemperatur der Flasche ab, so ist dies entsprechend zu berücksichtigen (s. Korrekturtabelle H.5).

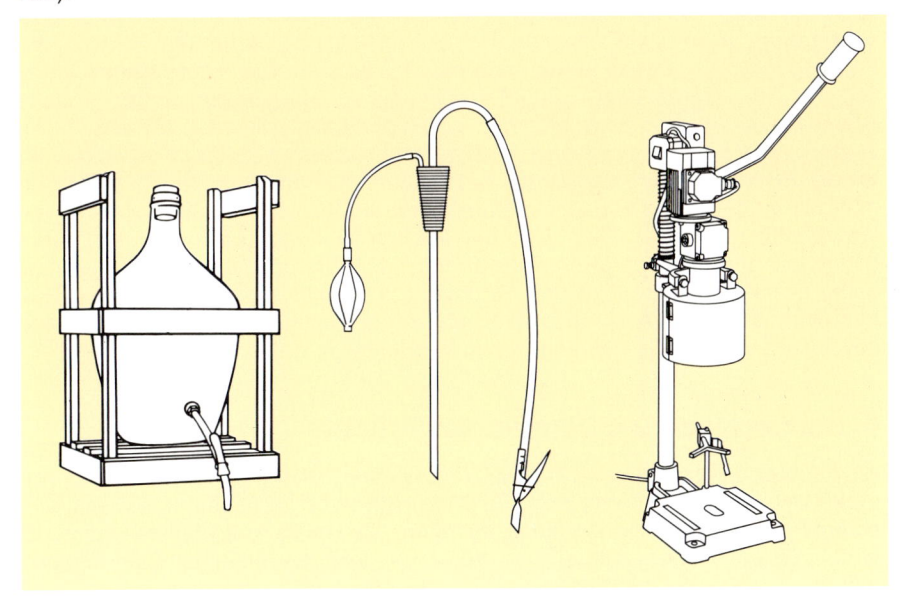

Abb. 39:
Ablaßgarnitur
für den Untenanstich

Abb. 40:
Druckheber für den
Obenanstich

Abb. 41:
Flaschenverschließmaschine
für Drehverschlüsse

Abb. 42: Vakuumfüller

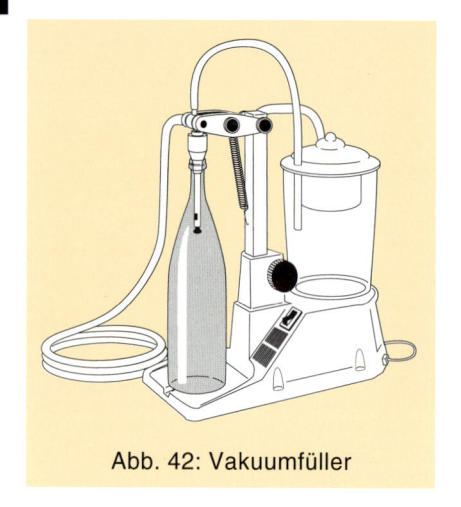

5 Verwendung von Zusatzstoffen

Die Verwendung von »Bonificateurs« im weitesten Sinne, d. h. Zusätzen zur Verbesserung und Abrundung der geruchlichen, geschmacklichen und farblichen Eigenschaften von Spirituosen, nimmt insbesondere bei der Likörherstellung einen breiten Raum ein. In der Spezialitätenbrennerei sind ihrer Verwendung naturgemäß engere Grenzen gesetzt. So darf in der Schweiz der Extraktgehalt von Obstbränden maximal 10 g/l betragen (Ausnahmen siehe M.3.3). Dort, wo Zusätze erlaubt sind, werden beispielsweise alkoholische Pflanzenauszüge, Zuckerarten oder Zuckercouleur verwendet. So erhält Williams häufig einen Zusatz von 4–8 g Fruchtzucker (Fructose) pro Liter. Es würde zu weit führen, an dieser Stelle näher auf die einschlägigen Bestimmungen einzugehen. Als wichtiges Beispiel sei lediglich die Behandlung von Weindestillat erwähnt. Hier wird die klassische Lagerung in Eichenfässern (Cognac!) häufig durch die Aufbewahrung über Eichenholzspänen ersetzt (s. auch D.1). Zur geschmacklichen Abrundung dienen beispielsweise Kaltextrakte aus Nuß- oder Mandelschalen. Rezepte zur Behandlung von Weindestillaten sowie zur Likörbereitung finden sich in Kapitel N.

6 Haltbarmachung eingelegter Früchte

Als beliebte Spezialitäten gelten Spirituosen, welche die dem Rohmaterial entsprechenden Früchte enthalten (z.B. Williamsbirnen). Nicht selten läßt man diese am Baum in die Flaschen hineinwachsen. Die Haltbarkeit solcher Früchte ist allerdings bei Alkoholgehalten um 40% vol nicht gewährleistet (der Alkoholgehalt sinkt ohnehin mit der Zeit, s. M.3.1); es muß im allgemeinen mit baldigen Bräunungserscheinungen gerechnet werden.

Haltbarkeitsverlängernd wirkt sich natürlich ein höherer Alkoholgehalt aus (ca. 45% vol); zusätzlich haben sich folgende Maßnahmen als vorteilhaft erwiesen:

- Flaschen mit eingewachsenen Früchten mit ca. 1prozentiger schwefliger Säure füllen und eine Stunde stehen lassen
- Früchte erschöpfend mit enthärtetem Wasser spülen; gut abtropfen lassen
- Destillat mit 1 g Ascorbinsäure (Vitamin C) pro Liter versetzen und bis zum vollständigen Auflösen umrühren
- Destillat einfüllen (Frucht muß ganz eintauchen)
- vor dem Verschließen Flasche kurz evakuieren (z.B. mit Wasserstrahlpumpe, s. Abb. 43). Treten bei den Früchten Luftblasen aus, Flasche sofort wieder belüften. Vorgang 2–3mal wiederholen
- Flasche in üblicher Weise verschließen.

In der Praxis kann es mitunter vorkommen, daß die in den Flaschen befindlichen Früchte einige Zeit gelagert werden müssen, bis das zum Auffüllen verwendete Destillat zur Verfügung steht. Als haltbarkeitsverlängernd hat sich in diesem Falle ein vollständiges Eintauchen der Früchte in eine Lösung erwiesen, welche pro Liter 10 g Citronensäure, 1 g Ascorbinsäure und 0,1 g SO_2 (= 2 ml 5prozentige Lösung) enthält. Auf diese Weise ist eine mehrmonatige Lagerung ohne wesentlichen Qualitätsverlust möglich. Eine alternative Methode besteht darin, die Flaschen während 2–3 Monaten mit 60%igem Alkohol zu füllen und so die Früchte haltbarer zu machen.

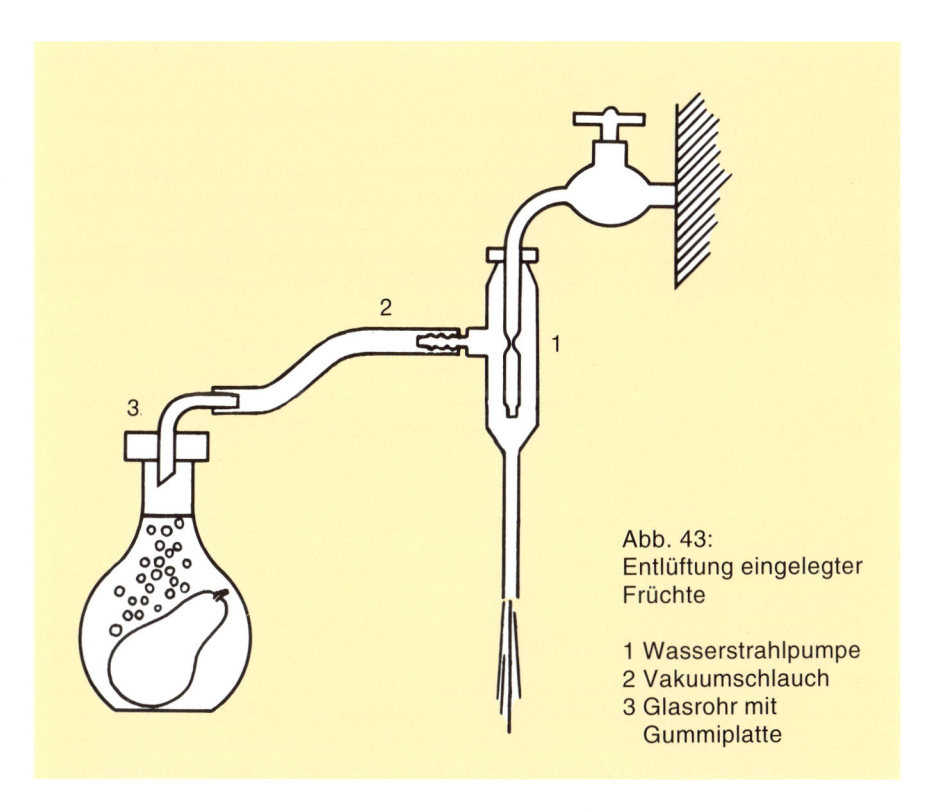

Abb. 43:
Entlüftung eingelegter Früchte

1 Wasserstrahlpumpe
2 Vakuumschlauch
3 Glasrohr mit Gummiplatte

F FEHLER

1 Allgemeines

Unzählig sind die Branntweinproben, welche infolge sichtbarer, geruchlicher oder geschmacklicher Unzulänglichkeiten beanstandet werden müssen. Darunter fallen nicht nur die eigentlichen **Fehler**, sondern auch **Mängel** wie zum Beispiel Aromaschwäche oder zuwenig ausgeprägter Sortencharakter. Nicht selten wird dann die Schuld einseitig dem Rohmaterial bzw. dessen Lieferanten in die Schuhe geschoben, obgleich die Ursachen auch bei der Verarbeitung liegen können. Zwar darf die Bedeutung der Rohstoffqualität als erste Voraussetzung zur Gewinnung sauberer und typischer Destillate keinesfalls unterschätzt werden (s. auch A.1), doch zeigt sich in der Praxis, daß fehlerhafte Destillate noch häufiger auf unterlassene oder wenig geeignete Maßnahmen beim Einmaischen, auf unsaubere Gärführung oder auf ungünstige Destillationsbedingungen zurückzuführen sind, um nur die wichtigsten Ursachen zu nennen.
Auf viele dieser Fehler wurde bereits in den vorstehenden Kapiteln im Zusammenhang mit den entsprechenden Verarbeitungsschritten hingewiesen, doch erscheint es zweckmäßig, sie an dieser Stelle zusammenzufassen, auf ihre Ursachen und ihre Behandlung sowie – nicht zuletzt! – auch auf vorbeugende Maßnahmen zu ihrer Verhütung einzugehen. Zu diesen Maßnahmen gehört auch die Verbesserung fehlerhafter Maischen. Es sei jedoch vorausgeschickt, daß sich nicht jeder Fehler erfolgreich beseitigen läßt. Der Einsatz entsprechender Behandlungsmittel zeitigt mitunter nur eine teilweise Verbesserung (evtl. Verschnitt vornehmen!); in gewissen Fällen bleibt der Erfolg auch versagt.
Des öftern ist die Entfernung fehlerhafter Geruchs- und Geschmackskomponenten mit einer Verminderung erwünschter Aromabestandteile verbunden, so daß die optimale Dosierung des Behandlungsmittels (häufig Aktivkohle) in **Vorversuchen** ermittelt werden muß. Eine Ideallösung zur Fehlerbeseitigung existiert nicht; meist muß ein Kompromiß gefunden werden. Den geringsten Aufwand an Zeit (und Geld) erfordern natürlich jene Destillate, welche dank einwandfreiem Rohmaterial und sachgemäßer Verarbeitung ohne weitere »Rettungsmaßnahmen« abgefüllt werden können. Das Sprichwort »Vorbeugen ist besser als heilen« hat gewiß auch hier seine Berechtigung.

2 Sichtbare Fehler

2.1 Metalltrübungen

2.1.1 Trübungen durch Härtebildner

Weiße Flocken oder ein weißer Bodensatz sind in nahezu allen Destillaten zu erwarten, welche mit gewöhnlichem oder unvollständig enthärtetem Leitungswasser herabgesetzt wurden. Diese Trübungen bestehen aus Calcium- oder Magnesiumsalzen (s. E.1.1). Häufig handelt es sich um eine Calciumsulfat-

(Gips)-Ausscheidung, welche unter dem Mikroskop an den nadelförmigen Kristallen zu erkennen ist (Abb. 44). Die natürlichen Härtebildner des Wassers sind in alkoholischen Lösungen praktisch unlöslich. Leider erfolgt aber ihre Ausscheidung nur allmählich, so daß selbst eine Filtration, auch nach kurzfristiger Kühllagerung, keine Garantie gegen allfällige Nachtrübungen bildet.

Abb. 44:
Calciumsulfat-Kristalle
(Vergrößerung ca. 400 x)

Unannehmlichkeiten werden vermieden, wenn für das Herabsetzen **enthärtetes Wasser** verwendet wird. Leitungswasser eignet sich ohne Enthärtung nur bis maximal 4°d zum Verschnitt.
Die **Beseitigung** der Härtebildner könnte selbstverständlich durch Umbrennen und anschließendes Herabsetzen mit enthärtetem Wasser erfolgen. Einfacher ist eine Behandlung mit saurem Kationenaustauscher (z.B. Dowex 50 W x 8, H-Form) nach vorgängigem Abfiltrieren der bereits ausgeschiedenen Trubteile. Dieses in der Schweiz seit langem praktizierte Verfahren beeinträchtigt das Aroma in keiner Weise und kann wie die Wasserenthärtung (s. E.1.2) durchgeführt werden. Auch kleinere Spirituosenfilter eignen sich dazu. Das einzusetzende Austauschervolumen beträgt ca. 1% des zu behandelnden Destillats. In Zweifelsfällen wende man sich an die Fachinstitute.

2.1.2 Schwermetalltrübungen

Auch diese Fehler sind relativ häufig anzutreffen. Sie äußern sich in den verschiedensten Erscheinungsformen, die von leichten **Verfärbungen** bis zu starken **Trübungen** reichen. Im Gegensatz zu den stets weißen, durch Härtebildner verursachten Ausscheidungen treten Schwermetalltrübungen in verschiedenen **Farben** auf. Ursprünglich klare, farblose Destillate können sich bei entsprechenden Lagerbedingungen (Licht- oder Sauerstoffeinfluß) verfärben und trüben, wobei auch **Farbänderungen** möglich sind. Alle diese Erscheinungen lassen sich auf die Anwesenheit der Schwermetalle (genauer: Schwermetall-Ionen) **Kupfer** und **Eisen** zurückführen, welche mit verschiedenen Bindungspartnern schwerlösliche Verbindungen eingehen. Zusätzlich können erhöhte Schwermetallgehalte auch zu degustativen Beeinträchtigungen führen (s. 3.2.1). In erster Linie ist also dafür zu sorgen, daß keine Schwermetalle in das Destillat gelangen. Aber auch eine erhöhte Konzentration der erwähnten Bindungspartner (vor allem Essigsäure und schweflige Säure) muß vermieden werden. Hier ist vor allem die Untersuchung der Maische vor dem Abbrand wichtig, um entsprechende Gegenmaßnahmen treffen zu können (s. G.6 und G.9).

Als **Hauptgründe** für die unerwünschte Schwermetallaufnahme sind zu nennen:

– **Lagerung** der Destillate in Behältern mit blanken Kupfer- oder Eisenteilen.

– **Destillation** auf Brennvorrichtungen mit schlecht verzinnten Kupfer- oder schadhaften Eisenkühlern. Besonders essigstichige Maischen oder solche mit erhöhten SO_2-Gehalten liefern aggressive Dämpfe, welche im Verlaufe ihrer Kondensation im Kühler Metall-Ionen herauszulösen vermögen.

– **Verschnitt** mit eisenhaltigem Wasser.

Eisentrübungen bilden sich oft erst bei intensiver Luftberührung, wobei die gelben, schwammigen Ausscheidungen allmählich eine braune Farbe annehmen. Besonders zu erwähnen sind die schwarzen Eisen/Gerbstoff-Verbindungen, die dem Destillat, sei es in gelöster oder ungelöster Form, eine unansehnliche Farbe verleihen. Voraussetzung hierfür ist neben dem erwähnten Eisengehalt auch die Anwesenheit von Gerbstoffen, welche bei der Lagerung in Eichenholzfässern (Weinbrand, Marc) in das Destillat gelangen. Ähnliches geschieht bei liegender Lagerung von klaren, mit Korken verschlossenen Spirituosen. Durch das Einpressen des ungeschützten Stopfens werden gerbstoffartige Korkinhaltsstoffe herausgelöst und führen bei Anwesenheit von Eisen wiederum zu derselben Erscheinung.

Unter Lichteinfluß entstehen in kupferhaltigen Destillaten bei gleichzeitiger Anwesenheit von schwefliger Säure rötliche **Cuprosulfit**-Ausscheidungen. Ihre Bildung ist reversibel, d.h. sie verschwinden im Dunkeln, können aber nach kurzer Belichtung wieder in die unlösliche Form übergehen. In sauren, aus essigstichigen Maischen gewonnenen Destillaten beobachtet man gelegentlich auch blaue bis blaugrüne Trübungen, zum Teil in Form von kleinen Kügelchen, die auf Kupfer/Fettsäure-Verbindungen zurückzuführen sind. In einer ersten Phase kommt es zur Bildung von Kupferacetat, anschließend zu Umsetzungen mit höheren Fettsäuren, die in jedem Destillat vorkommen.

Zur **Vorbeugung** gegen Schwermetallausscheidungen ist grundsätzlich jede Berührung des Branntweins mit blanken Eisen- oder Kupferteilen zu vermeiden. Defekte Geräte müssen repariert oder durch geeignetere ersetzt werden. In Zweifelsfällen sollte man im Destillat einen Eisen- und/oder Kupfernachweis durchführen (s. G. 11).

Zur **Behandlung** von Schwermetalltrübungen stehen zwei Verfahren zur Verfügung:

– **Umdestillieren** auf einer geeigneten Anlage, gegebenenfalls nach vorheriger Abstumpfung der Säuren (s. G.5). Die salzartigen Ausscheidungen verbleiben in der Blase.

– Behandlung mit saurem **Kationenaustauscher** (s. 2.1.1).

Ein weiteres Verfahren, die Schönung mit Calciumphytat, kann nicht vorbehaltlos empfohlen werden, da es bei Anwendung dieses Mittels gelegentlich zu Nachtrübungen kommt. Außerdem ist seine Wirkung auf die Entfernung von Eisen-Ionen beschränkt.

2.2 Durch etherische Öle, Fuselöle und Terpene bedingte Trübungen

Im Gegensatz zu den Metalltrübungen handelt es sich hier um Ausscheidungen, welche durch natürliche Inhaltsstoffe bedingt sind. Sie treten im Moment der Herabsetzung hochprozentiger Destillate auf und lassen sich auch nach längerer Kühllagerung kaum zum Absetzen bringen.

Etherische Öle sind Gemische von Verbindungen unterschiedlichster chemischer Zusammensetzung, die an der Aromabildung in der unvergorenen Frucht beteiligt sind. Dort finden sie sich zusammen mit Terpenen, Fetten und Wachsen. Im Gegensatz zu den fetten Ölen, wie z. B. Rapsöl, die ebenfalls aus Pflanzenteilen isoliert werden, hinterlassen etherische Öle auf Papier keinen bleibenden Fettfleck. In reiner Form sind sie in hochprozentigem Alkohol gut, in verdünnten Destillaten eher schlecht löslich. Bei relativ hohen Gehalten an etherischen Ölen und Terpenen werden Ausscheidungen beim Herabsetzen des Alkoholgehaltes nicht zu umgehen sein. Besonders reich an solchen Komponenten sind Wacholder-, Williams-, Hefe- und Kräuterdestillate.

Bei den **Fuselölen** handelt es sich um Nebenprodukte der alkoholischen Gärung. In erster Linie gehören die aus Aminosäuren gebildeten höheren Alkohole zu dieser Gruppe; daneben sind auch höhere Fettsäuren und deren Ester zu erwähnen. Die Siedetemperaturen der höheren Alkohole liegen über jenem von Ethylalkohol (78,3 °C); mit den üblichen Brenngeräten gelangt jedoch ein Großteil des Fuselöls infolge seiner Wasserdampfflüchtigkeit ins Destillat und kann nur teilweise im Nachlauf angereichert werden.

Wegen ihrer schlechten Löslichkeit in Wasser führen auch Fuselöle beim Herabsetzen zu Ausscheidungen und bewirken zusätzlich einen bitterherben Nachgeschmack.

Terpene sind, wie bereits erwähnt, Begleitstoffe der etherischen Öle. Sie setzen sich vorwiegend aus ketten- oder ringförmigen Kohlenwasserstoffen und ihren Sauerstoffderivaten zusammen. In der Pflanze kommt ihnen die Aufgabe zu, die etherischen Öle einzuschließen und am raschen Verdunsten zu hindern. Durch Sonnenlicht, Sauerstoff und Wärme gehen Terpene leicht in harzige Produkte über, welche einen unangenehmen, ranzigen Geruch aufweisen. In niederprozentigem Alkohol sind sie praktisch unlöslich und führen deshalb stets zu Trübungen. Eine besondere Eigenschaft der Terpene liegt darin, daß sie in der Kälte rasch zu Ausscheidungen führen, die aber beim Erwärmen wieder verschwinden. Etherische Öle und Terpene lassen sich leicht voneinander unterscheiden. Die ersteren geben sich an der Bildung von Öltröpfchen zu erkennen, welche sich als »Fettaugen« an der Oberfläche zusammenballen, während Terpene an ihrer bläulich-milchigen Opaleszenz erkannt werden.

Destillate, welche zu den oben beschriebenen Trübungen neigen, werden mit enthärtetem Wasser auf Trinkstärke herabgesetzt und während einer Woche kühl gelagert. Unter Verwendung von speziellen Schönungsmitteln, deren Art und Menge in Vorversuchen zu ermitteln ist, lassen sich die Ausscheidungen besser abtrennen. Nachfolgend einige bewährte Schönungsmittel:

Schönungsmittel	Dosierung (Richtwerte)
Magnesiumoxid	100–1000 g/hl
Kieselgur*	200– 300 g/hl
Bentonit	150 g/hl

Die Schönungen werden so durchgeführt, daß die benötigten Hilfsstoffe in einigen Litern des zu behandelnden Destillats verrührt und dann zur Hauptmenge gegeben werden. Nach ca. 14 tägiger Kühllagerung und mehrmaligem Durchmischen kann filtriert werden.

In manchen Fällen genügt es auch, die Destillate auf ca. 5% vol unter die für den Ausstoß vorgesehene Gradstärke herabzusetzen. Nach Kühlstellen und Zusatz von Filterhilfsmittel wird blank filtriert und mit hochrektifiziertem Alkohol auf Trinkstärke eingestellt.

2.3 Verfärbungen

Abgesehen von schwermetallbedingten Destillatfärbungen, die häufig als Vorstufe von Trübungen auftreten, kommt es gelegentlich zu ungewollten Verfärbungen infolge Holzfaß-Lagerung. Diese lassen sich am besten durch **Umbrennen** beseitigen, wobei die Destillate vorgängig mit Leitungswasser auf 20–30% vol herabzusetzen sind. Eine Kohleschönung mit 10–20 g Farbkohle/hl, z. B. Clarocarbon F oder Granucol FA, sollte nur dann vorgenommen werden, wenn aufgrund von Vorproben feststeht, daß die zur Entfärbung erforderliche Kohlemenge keine allzu gravierenden Aromaverluste nach sich zieht. Eine gewisse Beeinträchtigung wird allerdings kaum zu vermeiden sein, auch wenn man den Kontakt mit dem Schönungsmittel auf ca. 1 Tag beschränkt.

3 Geruchs- und Geschmacksfehler

3.1 Mikrobiell bedingte Fehler

Recht häufig trifft man in Destillaten Geruchs- und Geschmacksfehler an, die auf **Fehlgärungen**, d.h. unerwünschte mikrobielle Tätigkeit zurückzuführen sind. Die dabei entstehenden Produkte wie Essigsäure oder Buttersäure wirken qualitätsvermindernd und können in größeren Mengen ein Destillat bis zur Ungenießbarkeit verderben. Da die Wiederherstellung solcher Spirituosen – wenn überhaupt möglich – immer mit einem gewissen Aufwand verbunden ist, lohnt sich eine sachgemäße Maischebehandlung in jedem Fall (s. insbesondere B.1.3 und 2.2). Nachstehend sind die wichtigsten unerwünschten Mikroorganismen mit den vorzukehrenden Abwehrmaßnahmen zusammengefaßt (in Klammern die entsprechenden Abschnitte).

Kahmhefen sind in jeder Maische anzutreffen. Da sie sauerstoffbedürftig sind, können sie sich erst nach dem Abklingen der Gärung vermehren (Wegfall der Gärgas-Schutzwirkung). Man erkennt sie als zusammenhängende Haut bzw. Hautfetzen auf der Maischeoberfläche. Als Hauptnachteil fällt in Betracht, daß sie eine Reihe von organischen Substanzen, so auch den Ethylalkohol, zersetzen, womit die **Ausbeute vermindert** wird. Vereinzelte Kahmhefearten ver-

---

* Vor Gebrauch wässern!

mögen auch Zucker und Säuren in die ranzig riechende Buttersäure umzuwandeln. Abhilfe: Gärtrichter verwenden (B.1.3), Behälter nach abgeschlossener Gärung spundvoll und luftdicht verschlossen halten (B.3.6.2).
Apiculatus-Hefen (wilde Hefen) finden sich ebenfalls in jeder Maische. Neben ihrem geringen Gärvermögen (dieses wird bei 5-6 % vol unterbunden) erzeugen sie **erhöhte Mengen an flüchtigen Säuren;** auch sind sie nicht in der Lage, Rohrzucker (Saccharose) zu vergären, da ihnen das dazu erforderliche Enzym fehlt. Abhilfe: Reinhefe-Gärung (B.3.2).
Schimmelpilze lassen sich an der Bildung von weißen, grünen oder schwarz gefärbten Rasen auf der Maischeoberfläche erkennen. Noch häufiger ist ihr Auftreten in feuchten Kellern und in leeren, schlecht gereinigten Holzfässern und Schläuchen. Es sind auch immer wieder giftige Stoffwechselprodukte einiger Schimmelpilzarten ins Gespräch gekommen. Abhilfe: Geeignetes Rohmaterial verwenden (A.1), Maischebehälter gut reinigen, nötigenfalls desinfizieren (B.1.2) und nach abgeschlossener Gärung spundvoll halten (B.3.6.2).

Essigbakterien sind uns als unerwünschte »Bewohner« von Obst- und Traubenweinen zur Genüge bekannt. Während sie bei der Weinbereitung mit einer angemessenen Schwefelung in Schach gehalten werden können, finden sie in relativ säurearmen Frucht- und Beerenmaischen einen idealen Nährboden. Die Essigbakterien führen den Alkohol der Maischen in **Essigsäure** über. Luftsauerstoff und Wärme beschleunigen diesen Vorgang. In der Praxis führen essigstichige Maischen zu empfindlichen **Alkoholverlusten.** So wird beispielsweise der Alkoholgehalt einer 10 g/l flüchtige Säuren aufweisenden Maische um nahezu 1% vol vermindert. Abhilfe: Ausschluß von Luftsauerstoff, spundvollhalten der Behälter nach abgeschlossener Gärung, Kühllagerung der Maischen zwischen Gärende und Destillation, Ansäuerung (B.2.2).

Milchsäurebakterien sind in der Natur an verschiedenen spontan ablaufenden Vorgängen beteiligt. Während ihre Tätigkeit etwa bei der Sauerkrautgärung, der Silageherstellung oder der Spezialitätenkäserei erwünscht ist, können gewisse Arten der Gattungen Lactobacillus und Pediococcus im Brennereigewerbe umfangreichen Schaden anrichten. Schon während der Gärung werden Glucose und andere Zucker in das Hauptprodukt **Milchsäure**, aber auch in weitere unerwünschte Komponenten wie Essigsäure und Mannit zerlegt. Nach *Schwarz* und *Malsch* sollen in Kirschenmaischen bis zu 17 g Milchsäure, 5,6 g Essigsäure und 30 g Mannit pro Liter gefunden worden sein. Neben der nicht zu vernachlässigenden **Alkoholeinbuße** fällt bei den durch Milchsäurestich verdorbenen Maischen vor allem noch eine empfindliche Qualitätseinbuße der daraus gewonnenen Destillate ins Gewicht. Ein erschwerender Umstand bei der Verhinderung milchsäurestichiger Maischen liegt darin, daß die Milchsäurebakterien - im Gegensatz zu den Essigbakterien! – nicht unbedingt auf den Luftsauerstoff angewiesen sind, so daß selbst in spundvollen und mit Gärtrichter versehenen Behältern die Zersetzung weitergehen kann.
Dasselbe gilt auch für die **Buttersäurebakterien**, welche vorwiegend Buttersäure bilden, wegen ihrer relativen Säureempfindlichkeit aber glücklicherweise seltener vorkommen. Ebenfalls vorwiegend bei höheren pH-Werten kann das Gärungsnebenprodukt Glycerin durch gewisse Mikroorganismen, z.B. Milchsäurebakterien, in eine Vorstufe des Reizstoffs **Acrolein** umgewandelt werden.

Ein besonders großes Risiko besteht diesbezüglich bei Maischen aus unsauberem Rohmaterial (s. 3.1.5).
Zusammenfaßend läßt sich festhalten, daß einer unerwünschten Bakterientätigkeit mit folgenden Maßnahmen begegnet werden kann:
- sauberes, evtl. gewaschenes Rohmaterial verwenden (kein Hagelobst oder Tropfsaft)
- Maischen ansäuern
- Gärtrichter aufsetzen
- Behälter nach Gärende auffüllen und
- kühl lagern.

3.1.1 Essigstich

Destillate mit »reinem« Essigstich sind in der Praxis kaum anzutreffen, da die Essigsäure (flüchtige Säure) mit dem Alkohol unter teilweiser Esterbildung weiterreagiert. In beschränktem Umfang ist die Esterbildung ein erwünschter und zur Erzielung eines ausgeglichenen Aromas auch notwendiger Vorgang (s. D.2.2). Destillate mit einem Übermaß an flüchtiger Säure und Ester lassen sich in der Regel am stechenden, lösungsmittelähnlichen Geruch (»Nagellackentferner«) sowie am beißenden, sauren Geschmack erkennen. Ihre Behandlung wird im nächsten Abschnitt ausführlich beschrieben. In **leichten Fällen**, d. h. bei nur geringfügig erhöhtem Gehalt an flüchtigen Säuren, kann das Destillat nach dem Herabsetzen auf Trinkstärke einer Schönung mit Magnesiumoxid im Ausmaß von 300–500 g/hl unterzogen werden. Es ist dabei gründlich mit dem Schönungsmittel zu vermischen. Nach 6 Stunden (gelegentliches Umrühren ist empfehlenswert) wird vom Trub abgezogen. Eine solche Behandlung hat sich auch dann als günstig erwiesen, wenn es darum geht, gewisse unsaubere Geschmackskomponenten ohne Beeinträchtigung des spezifischen Sortencharakters aus dem Getränk zu entfernen.

Essigstichige **Maischen**, wie sie besonders bei Kirschen noch häufig vorkommen, werden am besten unmittelbar vor dem Abbrennen einer teilweisen Neutralisation unterzogen. Das einfachste Verfahren besteht darin, der Maische kohlensauren Kalk (Calciumcarbonat) zuzusetzen. Dieser wird mit Wasser zu einem dünnen Brei verrührt und anschließend gründlich mit der Maische vermischt. Dabei entweicht freigesetztes Kohlendioxidgas unter starkem Schäumen, und zwar solange, als Säuren in der Maische vorhanden sind. Als Beispiel sei die Neutralisation von Essigsäure angeführt:

$$2\ CH_3COOH\ +\ CaCO_3\ \longrightarrow\ Ca(CH_3COO)_2\ +\ H_2O\ +\ CO_2 \uparrow$$

Essigsäure — Kalk — Calciumacetat — Wasser — Kohlendioxid (gasförmig)

Eine Überneutralisation ist mit diesem Produkt nicht zu befürchten. Als Faustregel merke man sich, daß zum Abbinden von 10 g/l Gesamtsäure (berechnet als Äpfelsäure) pro 100 Liter Maische 700 g kohlensaurer Kalk erforderlich sind. In Zweifelsfällen kann eine Bestimmung der titrierbaren Säuren vorgenommen werden (s. G.8). Fehlen die Einrichtungen zur genauen Ermittlung des Säuregehaltes, so kann man sich dadurch behelfen, daß der Maische solange vom Kalkbrei zugemischt wird, als ein Aufschäumen zu beobachten ist. Man achte darauf, daß der Behälter, in dem die Neutralisation erfolgt, nur zu ca. 70% gefüllt

ist, damit beim Schäumen keine Verluste entstehen. Ein allzu starkes Schäumen läßt sich auch durch Zugabe von Silicon-Antischaum im Ausmaß von ca. 3 ml/hl Maische unterbinden.
Bei einem anderen Neutralisationsverfahren werden die vorhandenen Säuren zu ca. 90% mit gelöschtem Kalk (Calciumhydroxid) abgebunden (pH 5,6–5,8). Da es sich dabei um ein »stärkeres« Mittel handelt, ist streng darauf zu achten, daß eine Überneutralisation vermieden wird (Kontrolle mit Spezial-pH-Indikatorpapier, s. G.5). Im Anschluß an die Neutralisation ist sofort zu destillieren (Gefahr bakterieller Tätigkeit!)

3.1.2 Erhöhter Estergehalt

Ursache eines erhöhten Estergehaltes ist immer eine stichige Maische, auf deren Neutralisation vor dem Abbrennen – aus welchen Gründen auch immer – verzichtet wurde. Dadurch gelangt ein Übermaß an flüchtigen Säuren (größtenteils Essigsäure) ins Destillat, was zu einer teilweisen Umsetzung mit dem ohnehin im Überschuß vorhandenen Ethylalkohol führt (s. D.2.2). Der so gebildete Essigester ist also kein unmittelbares Produkt bakterieller Tätigkeit (geringere Mengen entstehen auch schon während der Gärung).
Zur Behandlung der resultierenden fehlerhaften Destillate nützt man den Umstand aus, daß Veresterungsvorgänge im alkalischen Bereich, d.h. bei Vorhandensein eines Laugenüberschusses, umkehrbar sind. Dies bedeutet, daß der entstandene Ester wieder in die Ausgangsstoffe (Alkohol und Säure) umgewandelt wird. Nach teilweiser Neutralisation der zurückgebildeten Säure kann umgebrannt werden. Da ein zu hoher Estergehalt besonders häufig bei Kirschbränden anzutreffen ist, wird an dieser Stelle eine Arbeitsvorschrift für die **Behandlung von 50–65%igem Kirsch** angegeben, welche sich unter Berücksichtigung der entsprechenden Estergehalte auch auf andere Destillate übertragen läßt.

Prinzip des Verfahrens

Je nach Estergehalt werden vom defekten Destillat 20 oder mehr Prozent mit Lauge auf pH 5,6–5,8 eingestellt, separat destilliert und später mit der behandelten Hauptmenge vermischt. Die Hauptmenge des fehlerhaften Destillates wird nach Verdünnen vollständig neutralisiert und hierauf mit einem Überschuß an Natronlauge versetzt. Anschließend erfolgt die Esterspaltung durch zweistündiges Erwärmen auf 75°C. Nach Ansäuerung auf pH 5,6–5,8 kann in gewohnter Weise destilliert werden.

Erforderliches Material

Natronlauge, ca. 30%: im Handel erhältlich oder selbst herstellen durch Auflösen von 1 kg festem Natriumhydroxid in Wasser und Auffüllen auf 2,5 l (**Vorsicht:** Schutzbrille und Gummihandschuhe tragen!).
Natronlauge, ca. 15%: Herstellung durch Verdünnung von 1 Liter 30%iger Lauge mit 1 Liter Wasser.
Phosphorsäure, ca. 15%: Herstellung durch Mischen von 1,5 Liter käuflicher 84%iger Phosphorsäure mit 7 Litern Wasser (**Vorsicht,** Schutzbrille und Gummihandschuhe!).
Universalindikator, pH-Bereich 1–10.
Spezialindikator, pH-Bereich 4,0–7,0.

Ausführung

- Bei Verdacht auf erhöhten Säure- und Estergehalt (stechender, lösungsmittelähnlicher Geruch, beißender saurer Geschmack) Ester-Bestimmung vornehmen (s. G.10) oder vornehmen lassen. Resultat in mg Essigester (Ethylacetat) pro 100 ml reinen Alkohol (mg/dl r.A.).
- Falls Estergehalt erhöht (600 mg/dl r.A. oder darüber), den fraglichen Posten in **zwei Teile A und B** aufteilen:

Estergehalt in mg/dl r.A.	Teil A (%)	Teil B (%)
600	50	50
1000	30	70
1500	25	75
2000	20	80

- **Teil A** auf 20–30% vol herabsetzen, mit 15%iger Natronlauge unter Rühren auf pH 5,6–5,8 einstellen (mit Spezialindikator kontrollieren, s. G.5) und anschließend umbrennen
- **Teil B** (z. B. 100 l oder halbes Blasenvolumen) in die Brennblase füllen, mit der gleichen Menge Wasser versetzen und mischen
- 15%ige Natronlauge unter Rühren solange zusetzen, bis pH-Wert 7,0 erreicht ist (mit Universalindikator kontrollieren)
- herabgesetzten, neutralisierten Teil B gemäß nachstehender Tabelle mit ausreichendem **Laugenüberschuß** versetzen (die angegebenen Mengen genügen für einen maximalen ursprünglichen Alkoholgehalt von 65% vol). Gut umrühren. Kontrolle: Universalindikator muß dunkelblaue Farbe aufweisen!

	erforderliche Lauge pro 100 l unverdünnten Teil B (vor Gebrauch auflösen bzw. verdünnen)	
Estergehalt in mg/dl r.A.	festes Natriumhydroxid	od. 30%ige Natronlauge
600	180 g	0,45 l
1000	300 g	0,75 l
1500	450 g	1,13 l
2000	600 g	1,50 l

- Blaseninhalt während 2 Stunden auf 75°C erhitzen. Um das Überdestillieren von Alkohol zu verhindern, wird das Kühlwasser im Dephlegmator voll aufgedreht. Über den Helm legt man zudem vorteilhafterweise Tücher, die mit kaltem Wasser besprützt werden.
- nach dem Abkühlen des Blaseninhaltes unter gutem Mischen mit 15%iger Phosphorsäure bis pH 5,6–5,8 ansäuern (mit Spezialindikator kontrollieren)
- in gewohnter Weise unter Abtrennung von Vor- und Nachlauf destillieren
- resultierendes Destillat mit separat behandeltem Teil A vermischen. Eventuell erneut Ester- und Säuregehalt kontrollieren bzw. kontrollieren lassen.

3.1.3 Buttersäurestich

Buttersäurestichige Trester und Williamsbirnen-Maischen treten vor allem bei warmer Witterung und hohen pH-Werten (Säurearmut) auf. Die daraus gewonnenen Destillate erinnern in Geruch und Geschmack an ranzige Butter, was auf die Bildung von Buttersäure, Valeriansäure, Capronsäure und deren Ester zu-

rückzuführen ist. Die Wiederherstellung solcher Destillate ist in der Regel mit Schwierigkeiten verbunden; dagegen kann mit einer vorsorglichen Maischeansäuerung eine ausreichende Schutzwirkung erzielt werden.
Destillate, die einen deutlichen Buttersäurefehler aufweisen, werden mit 500 g gelöschtem Kalk (Calciumhydroxid) pro hl versetzt, mit Leitungswasser auf ca. 20% vol verdünnt und während einer Stunde im Brennhafen am Rückfluß (d.h. ohne Abnahme von Destillat) gekocht. Dabei soll das Kühlwasser am Verstärker voll aufgedreht sein; der Helm ist zusätzlich mit Wasser zu besprühen. Nach dem Abkühlen wird der pH-Wert mit 15%iger Phosphorsäure (s. 3.1.2) auf 6,5 eingestellt und die Destillation in üblicher Weise unter Vor- und Nachlaufabtrennung vorgenommen. Erfahrungsgemäß sind die resultierenden Destillate nun weitgehend frei von unerwünschten Komponenten, verhalten sich aber geruchlich und geschmacklich zu neutral, so daß sie im Verschnitt nachgenommen werden müssen.

3.1.4 Milchsäurestich

Obgleich die durch unerwünschte Mikroorganismen (v.a. Lactobacillus-Arten) gebildete Milchsäure bei der Destillation in der Maische bzw. im Brennsaft verbleibt, können die entsprechenden Destillate nachteilig verändert sein, und zwar sowohl durch gleichzeitige Bildung von flüchtigen Nebenprodukten der Milchsäuregärung wie z.B. Essigsäure oder Diacetyl als auch durch Entstehung von flüchtigen Estern. Derartige Destillate sind in vielen Fällen nicht konsumfähig und auch nicht wiederherstellbar. Als Behandlungsmethode käme allenfalls eine Esterspaltung mit nachfolgendem Umbrand in Frage (s. 3.1.3), wobei das anfallende Destillat auch in diesem Falle verschnitten werden müßte.

3.1.5 Acroleinstich

Zu Recht gefürchtet ist in Brennereien der Acroleinstich. Die durch bakterielle Tätigkeit gebildete Substanz Hydroxypropionaldehyd zerfällt infolge Hitzeeinwirkung beim Brennvorgang in den Reizstoff Acrolein, welcher trotz seines tiefen Siedepunktes von 52 °C in allen Destillatfraktionen erscheint und somit nur unvollständig als Vorlauf abgetrennt werden kann. Durch die aggressive, tränengasartige Wirkung dieser Substanz wurde schon mancher Brenner zum Verlassen des Raumes gezwungen. Der durch diverse Bakterienarten (z.B. Lactobacillus brevis) verursachte Fehler kann bei den meisten Destillaten auftreten. Bekannt sind vornehmlich acroleinstichige Williams-, Mostobst- und Beerenbrände, die auf unsauberes, mit Erde verschmutztes Rohmaterial zurückzuführen sind. Maischen und Brennsäfte mit extrem hohen pH-Werten sind besonders gefährdet. In solchen Fällen sind häufig noch eine ganze Reihe weiterer unerwünschter Mikroorganismen anwesend, so daß die Destillate zusätzlich zum Acroleinstich noch andere Fehler aufweisen.
Da in Maischen und Mosten nicht Acrolein, sondern dessen Vorstufe vorliegt, ist vor dem Brennen eine Gefährdung nicht ohne weiteres erkennbar. Besteht ein diesbezüglicher Verdacht, so empfiehlt es sich, durch einen **Vorversuch** (Probedestillation, Geruchsprobe!) abzuklären, ob ein acroleinstichiges Destillat zu

erwarten ist. Nötigenfalls können auch die Dienste eines Fachlabors in Anspruch genommen werden. Nach *Rüdiger* soll sich das Überdestillieren von Acrolein durch Zusatz von 1 kg Calciumhydroxid/hl Maische wesentlich vermindern lassen. Leider wird durch diesen massiven Eingriff das Destillat stark beeinträchtigt (Laugengeschmack); auch eine anschließende Kohlebehandlung führt zu keiner befriedigenden Lösung. Am besten werden acroleinverdächtige **Maischen** gleich nach der Gärung unter Abtrennung eines besonders großen Vorlaufs auf Rauhbrände verarbeitet. Nach sofortiger Herabsetzung auf 25% vol (falls erforderlich) und Zugabe von Natronlauge bis pH 6,5 kann der Feinbrand erfolgen. Das auf Trinkstärke herabgesetzte Destillat ist dann während 6 Monaten zu lagern und darf nur noch geklärt, aber nicht mehr destilliert werden. Acrolein hat nämlich die Eigenschaft, im Verlaufe der Lagerung zu polymerisieren, wodurch auch seine unerwünschte Reizwirkung allmählich verschwindet. Es muß aber betont werden, daß sich Acrolein, einmal im Destillat vorhanden, ohne Beeinträchtigung der Qualität kaum mehr vollständig beseitigen läßt.

Eine Behandlungsmöglichkeit für acroleinstichige **Feinbrände** besteht darin, pro hl 400 g Calciumhydroxid zuzusetzen und mit Wasser auf 20–30% vol zu verdünnen. Nach ca. 24 Stunden wird filtriert, mit 15%iger Phosphorsäure (s. 3.1.2) auf pH 6,5 eingestellt und unter Vor- und Nachlaufabtrennung umgebrannt. Gut bewährt hat sich bei Williams auch das Verfahren, das Destillat auf 70 °C zu erwärmen, dann während je einer Stunde reinen Sauerstoff und anschließend Stickstoff durchzuleiten. Ein gewisser Alkohol- und Aromaverlust ist dabei in Kauf zu nehmen (degustativ überprüfen, evtl. Verschnitt vornehmen). Bei sauberer, guter Gärführung (Gärstockungen verhindern!) unter Einsatz der Ansäuerungsmethode (bei Brennsäften auch Schwefelung) ist das Auftreten des Acroleinstichs nicht zu befürchten.

3.1.6 Schwefelwasserstoffehler (Böckser)

Geruch und Geschmack nach faulen Eiern ist vielfach bei Drusen- und Hefe-, nicht selten auch bei Tresterdestillaten anzutreffen. Der Grund für diese Qualitätsminderung ist in der Bildung von **Schwefelwasserstoff** (H_2S) zu suchen. Dieses unangenehm riechende Gas entsteht während der Gärung durch Reduktion hauptsächlich aus elementarem Schwefel (z.T. von schwefelhaltigen Spritzmitteln herrührend) oder durch Zersetzung von Hefeeiweiß. Langes Lagern der Maischen begünstigt die H_2S-Bildung. Dort, wo noch Holzfässer verwendet werden, ist darauf zu achten, daß der Einbrand mit nichttropfenden Schwefelschnitten erfolgt; die Fässer müssen trocken sein. Keinesfalls darf elementarer Schwefel abtropfen oder infolge unvollständiger Verbrennung nachträglich an den Faßwänden kondensieren.

Im Verlaufe der Destillation gelangt der leichtflüchtige Schwefelwasserstoff in das Destillat, wo er sich mit Alkohol (Ethylalkohol) zu Ethylmercaptan umsetzt, welches noch widerlicher riecht und selbst in geringen Mengen zu einer Beeinträchtigung des Buketts führt. Durch Luftkontakt wird Ethylmercaptan in das ebenfalls unangenehm riechende, schwerflüchtige Disulfid übergeführt. Die Entstehung dieser Schwefelverbindungen läßt sich formelmäßig wie folgt zusammenfassen:

element. Schwefel S $\xrightarrow{\text{Hefe}}$ H_2S
Reduktion Schwefelwasserstoff

H_2S + C_2H_5OH $\longrightarrow$ C_2H_5SH + H_2O
Schwefelwasserstoff Ethylalkohol   Ethylmercaptan Wasser
          (Sdp. 37 °C)

C_2H_5SH + C_2H_5SH $\xrightarrow[\text{Oxidation}]{\text{Luftsauerstoff}}$ $C_2H_5S\text{-}SC_2H_5$
Ethylmercaptan   Disulfid (Sdp. 154 °C)

Eine Wiederherstellung solcher fehlerhafter Destillate ist nicht immer möglich. Am ehesten dürfte eine Verbesserung mit einem silberchloridhaltigen Präparat (z.B. Sulfidex) im Ausmaß von ca. 100 g/hl zu erreichen sein. Die Kontaktzeit mit dem unlöslichen Pulver beträgt 3–10 Tage; das Destillat ist von Zeit zu Zeit zu rühren. Nach der Behandlung muß es durch Filtration geklärt werden. Das Auftreten von Mercaptanböcksern läßt sich verhindern, wenn die Destillation der Maischen in Kupfer-Apparaturen vorgenommen wird. Als Alternative oder bei stark schwefelwasserstoffhaltigen Maischen und Brennsäften empfiehlt es sich, diese mit 1 Liter 10%iger Kupfersulfat-Lösung pro 400-Liter-Blase zu übergießen. Der Anwesenheit von Kupfer und Kupfer-Ionen ist es zuzuschreiben, daß Schwefelwasserstoff in Form von nichtflüchtigem Kupfersulfid abgebunden werden kann. In gleicher Weise wirken natürlich auch zusätzliche Kupferflächen (Cyanidabscheider, s. C.2.3).

3.2 Nicht mikrobiell bedingte Fehler

3.2.1 Metallgeschmack

Die Ursachen des Metallgeschmacks von Destillaten, welcher sich meistens in einer kratzenden, bitterherben Note äußert, wurden bereits bei den Trübungen behandelt (s. 2.1.2). An dieser Stelle sei lediglich wiederholt, daß zur Wiederherstellung ein Umbrennen oder eine Ionenaustauscher-Behandlung erforderlich ist. In Zweifelsfällen kann ein Kupfer- oder Eisennachweis vorgenommen werden (s. G.11). Mitunter führt auch eine unerwünschte Aluminium- oder Zinkaufnahme zu degustativen Beeinträchtigungen (5 mg Aluminium/l wirken bereits bitter).

3.2.2 Steingeschmack

Der Steingeschmack findet sich in vielen Steinobstdestillaten. Nicht selten vermag er sogar das eigentliche Sortenbukett zu überdecken. Die Ursache ist eine zu weitgehende Beschädigung der Steine. Dabei wird Amygdalin frei, welches enzymatisch in Glucose, Benzaldehyd und die giftige Blausäure gespaltet wird. Die beiden letztgenannten Komponenten sind (unterschiedlich) flüchtig und erinnern in Geruch und Geschmack an bittere Mandeln. Destillate in Zweifelsfällen von einem Fachlabor untersuchen lassen! Der Blausäuregehalt kann auch selbst ermittelt werden (s. G.13).
Zwecks Verhütung ist darauf zu achten, daß der **Anteil an zerstörten Steinen beim Einmaischen möglichst gering** gehalten wird (s.a. B.2.7.2). Ein baldiges

Abbrennen der vergorenen Maischen hilft ebenfalls, den Steingeschmack zu verringern. Ein Zuviel an Benzaldehyd kann durch einen geringen Zusatz an schwefliger Säure (50 ml 5 %ige SO_2 pro 100 l Destillat) abgebunden werden, sofern nicht mehr destilliert wird. Ein Zusatz von Silbernitrat (10 g pro 100 l Destillat) fällt Blausäure als unlösliches Silbercyanid aus. Nach Abfiltrieren des Niederschlags muß umgebrannt werden.

3.2.3 Herber Beigeschmack

Dieser Fehler ist auf die Mitverarbeitung von Stielen und/oder Blättern oder zu starkes Aufschließen zurückzuführen (Bildung von Hexanol). Er tritt vornehmlich bei Kirsch- und Wacholderdestillaten auf. Mit einer Kohlebehandlung (20-100 g pro hl, Vorproben!) kann eine teilweise Verbesserung erzielt werden. Der Kontakt mit der Kohle ist auf 24 Stunden zu beschränken.

3.2.4 Brenzliger Geschmack

Bei direkter Befeuerung von Brennblasen kann es, insbesondere in dickflüssigen Maischen und Trestern, zu **lokalen Überhitzungen** (Anbrennen) kommen. Die dabei gebildeten Zersetzungsprodukte, z.B. Furfural, verleihen dem Destillat einen brenzligbitteren Geschmack, welcher sich kaum mehr entfernen läßt. Immerhin führt auch hier eine Kohlebehandlung zu einer teilweisen Verbesserung des Produkts.

3.2.5 Schwefeldioxidfehler

Geruch und Geschmack nach schwefliger Säure treten hauptsächlich bei der Destillation von stark mit Schwefeldioxid (SO_2) behandelten Brennsäften und Weinen auf. Maischen sollten ohnehin nicht geschwefelt werden, da mit der Ansäuerung ein zweckmäßigeres Verfahren zur Verfügung steht (s. B.2.2). SO_2-haltige Destillate lassen sich durch **Umbrennen** nach vorgängiger teilweiser Neutralisation vollumfänglich wiederherstellen. Dabei wird das Destillat zuerst auf 20–30% vol herabgesetzt und dann mit 15%iger Natronlauge auf einen pH-Wert von 5,6–5,8 gebracht. Auch stark geschwefelte Maischen können unmittelbar vor dem Abbrennen auf diesen pH-Wert eingestellt werden.
In ähnlicher Weise verfährt man mit stark geschwefelten Brennsäften. Hier ist der pH-Wert unmittelbar vor dem Brennen auf ca. 5,2 einzustellen. Bei Kolonnenbrennereien, wo das Lutterwasser nicht in die Maische(Saft)-Kolonne zurückgeführt wird, kann die Neutralisation auch in der Kolonne erfolgen. Wenn der Brennsaft nach der Gärung weniger als 70 mg Gesamt-SO_2 pro l aufweist, darf auf eine Neutralisation verzichtet werden (Bestimmung des Gesamt-SO_2-Gehaltes s. G.9).

3.2.6 Vor- und Nachlauffehler

Vorlauf- oder fuseliger Nachlaufgeschmack ist auf unzweckmäßige Bedienung der Brennereianlage zurückzuführen: ungeachtet der unterschiedlichen Beschaffenheit der Maischen werden immer die gleichen Vor- und Nachlaufanteile abgeschieden. Der erfahrene Brenner weiß aber, daß jeder Ansatz in der Blase seine spezifischen Merkmale besitzt. So kann bei einwandfreien Maischen der Vorlaufanteil geringer gehalten oder sogar ganz weggelassen werden, während

bei stechend riechendem Vorlauf (Acrolein, Aldehyde, Ester) erst später auf Mittellauf umzuschalten ist. Nur eine gute **organoleptische Überwachung** des Brennvorganges, allenfalls ergänzt durch einen einfach durchzuführenden Vorlauftest, wird zu fehlerfreien Destillaten führen (s. C.3.1.2 bzw. G.12).
Der sicherste Weg zur Wiederherstellung solcher fehlerhafter Destillate besteht in einem **Umbrand** nach vorgängiger Herabsetzung auf Trinkstärke, wobei der Zeitpunkt zum Umschalten auf Mittel- bzw. Nachlauf durch stetige Verkostung der anfallenden Destillatfraktionen ermittelt werden muß.
Gesammelte **Vorläufe** lassen sich nach geeigneter Behandlung ebenfalls noch verwerten. Dazu sind sie mit dem gleichen Volumen Wasser zu verdünnen und pro l unverdünnten Vorlauf mit 20 g Natriumhydroxid zu versetzen. Nach zweistündigem Kochen am Rückfluß (s. 3.1.3) wird mit 15%iger Phosphorsäure auf pH 6,5 eingestellt und unter Abtrennung von Vor- und Nachlauf umgebrannt. Meistens muß man den Mittellauf noch einer Kohlebehandlung (1 kg/hl) unterziehen. Das neutrale, aber weitgehend gereinigte Produkt kann in kleinen Anteilen im Verschnitt nachgenommen werden.

3.3 Andere Fehler und Mängel

Außer den bereits genannten Fehlern sind noch einige weitere zu erwähnen, die in der Brennereipraxis aber im allgemeinen weniger häufig angetroffen werden oder teilweise umstritten sind. Ihre Ursachen sind selten eindeutig zu eruieren; ebensowenig kann in jedem Fall eine taugliche Verbesserungsmethode empfohlen werden. Auch massive Schönungen mit Kohle oder Magnesiumoxid (1–2 kg pro hl) sind nicht immer erfolgreich, selbst dann nicht, wenn man durch diese Behandlung einen empfindlichen Bukettverlust in Kauf nimmt. Führen Schönungsvorproben oder ein Umbrand solcher fehlerhafter Destillate nicht zur gewünschten Verbesserung, so könnte allenfalls in Zusammenarbeit mit einem Fachlabor eine Lösung gesucht werden.

Transport oder Lagerung von Maischen und Destillaten in ungeeigneten beziehungsweise schlecht gereinigten Behältern verursachen mehr oder weniger definierbare Fehltöne, die in Geruch und Geschmack an Teer-, Petrol-, Kunststoff- oder Schimmelkomponenten erinnern. Es sei in diesem Zusammenhang daran erinnert, daß nicht jedes zur Maischelagerung geeignete Behältermaterial auch für hochprozentige Destillate verwendet werden darf (s. D.1). Auch der Kontakt mit nicht lebensmittelechten Schläuchen (Transport von Spirituosen in Gaststätten!) hat schon beträchtliche Schäden verursacht. Mitunter verleihen Trichloranisol-haltige Korken der abgefüllten Spirituose einen **Korkgeschmack,** falls die Flaschen liegend gelagert werden. Fässer, die mit Pentachlorphenol-haltigen Imprägnierungsmitteln behandelt wurden, können dem Destillat ebenfalls einen korkgeschmackähnlichen Fehlton vermitteln.
Aromaschwache Destillate resultieren nicht nur bei Verwendung von unreifem Obst; auch unsaubere Gärungen, allzu hohe Säure- und/oder Enzymdosierungen sowie zu starke Kühlung beim Brennen können zu diesem Mangel führen. Nicht zuletzt ist die Auswahl geeigneter Obstsorten von ausschlaggebender Bedeutung für die Aromaintensität. Noch zu erwähnen sind Destillate mit »**Doppelaroma**«, in denen die Aromakomponenten zweier Obstarten erkennbar

sind. Auch dieser Fehler kann verschiedene Ursachen haben: möglicherweise wurde das Brenngerät beim Wechsel auf andere Maischen nicht genügend gereinigt (Verstärkerböden entleeren und mit warmem Wasser rückspülen!), oder ein Anschwemm- bzw. Schichtenfilter wurde weiter verwendet. Auch bei Kerzenfiltern ist ein regelmäßiges Rückspülen mit hochprozentigem Alkohol und warmem Wasser angezeigt, um Aromaverschleppungen vorzubeugen.

Stinkender **Geruch nach Schnupftabak** wird vornehmlich bei Kernobst- und Zwetschgendestillaten beobachtet. Als Ursache vermutet man bakterielle Stoffwechselprodukte. Eine wirksame Methode zur Behebung dieses Spirituosenfehlers existiert bislang nicht. Ähnliches gilt für **Sauerkrautstich** und **Mannitstich**, welche nach Milchsäuregärungen auftreten können. Beim ebenfalls mikrobiell bedingten **Kartoffelkellergeschmack**, der auf Pyrazine zurückzuführen ist, läßt sich mit einer Kohlebehandlung (z.b. 200 g Granucol Bi/hl) eine Verbesserung erzielen.

Weniger in degustativer als in gesundheitlicher Hinsicht sind in den letzten Jahren **Spirituosen mit erhöhten Ethylcarbamat(EC)-Gehalten** diskutiert worden. Ende 1985 wurden zuerst in Nordamerika, dann auch in Europa, besonders in Steinobstdestillaten Gehalte bis zu mehreren mg/l dieser aufgrund von Tierversuchen als kanzerogen bezeichneten Substanz gefunden. Auch in anderen fermentierten Lebensmitteln wie Bier, Wein, Brot oder Joghurt ist EC nachzuweisen. Die Entstehung von Ethylcarbamat bzw. deren Verhinderung sowie die Entfernung von EC aus Destillaten waren und sind in mehreren Ländern Gegenstand intensiver Forschungsarbeiten. Von den diskutierten Bildungswegen dürfte in Steinobstbränden die Entstehung aus Blausäure, Carbonylverbindungen (z.B. Diacetyl) und Alkohol die wichtigste sein. Nachträglich stellte sich heraus, daß EC auch nach der Destillation durch Lichteinwirkung gebildet werden kann. Die Frage, ob EC für den Menschen in den zur Diskussion stehenden Konzentrationen überhaupt schädlich sei, kann nicht abschließend beantwortet werden. Dessen ungeachtet wurden in der Zwischenzeit zahlreiche Destillations- und Behandlungsmethoden vorgeschlagen und überprüft.

Erfolgversprechende und auch in der Praxis mit vertretbarem Aufwand realisierbare Ansätze zur **Verhinderung erhöhter EC-Gehalte** bestehen beispielsweise in der Verwendung besonderer Cyanidabscheider bei der Destillation (s. C.2.3) sowie einer ausreichenden Vor- und Nachlaufabscheidung (Umschaltung von Mittel- auf Nachlauf bei spätestens 55% vol, s. C.3.1.2). Versuche von *Luz* mit Kirschenmaischen zeigten überdies, daß die auch von uns seit Jahren empfohlenen Maischebereitungsmaßnahmen (einwandfreies Rohmaterial, saubere, verschlossene Behälter, kein verzögertes Einmaischen, Verwendung von Trokkenreinzuchthefe, Ansäuerung usw.) die besten Voraussetzungen für niedrige EC-Gehalte sind. Außerdem erwies sich bei Kirschenmaischen eine mehrmonatige Maischelagerung bei Raumtemperatur als vorteilhaft. Dies setzt allerdings eine strikte Einhaltung der vorerwähnten Bedingungen sowie eine regelmäßige Kontrolle der Maischen voraus, was in der Praxis nicht immer möglich sein dürfte. Zudem scheint sich diese Maßnahme nicht bei allen Steinobstmaischen in gleicher Weise auszuwirken, so daß im Zweifelsfall einer tieferen Lagertemperatur (10–12 °C) der Vorzug zu geben ist.

3.4 Übersichtstabellen

Tab. 4: Mikrobiell bedingte Fehler

Bezeichnung	Auswirkung	Ursache(n)	Behandlung
Acroleinstich	Geruch stechend, tränengasähnlich	Maischeinfektion (bakterielle Glycerinzersetzung)	Destillat längere Zeit lagern; Spezialbehandlungen
Buttersäurestich	Geruch nach ranziger Butter, Fuß-Schweiß	warme Witterung hohe pH-Werte	verseifen, umbrennen, Verschnitt
Essigstich	saurer Geschmack, Geruch nach Essig, evtl. Ester	schlechte Gärung; stichige Maische (Luftzutritt, zu lange Lagerung)	Magnesiumoxid (in leichten Fällen); Neutralisation/Umbrand
Estergeruch	Geruch nach Nagellack, Verdünner	stichige Maische, Spontangärung	verseifen, ansäuern und umbrennen
Schwefelwasserstofffehler (Böckser)	riecht und schmeckt nach faulen Eiern	element. Schwefel, S-haltige Spritzmittel, Hefezersetzung	Sulfidex; Destillation auf Kupferapparat/Kupfersulfat
Sauerkrautstich	Geruch nach Sauerkraut	Milchsäuregärung	----
Kartoffelkellergeschmack	muffiger Kellerton	schlechtes Rohmaterial, ungünstiger Gärverlauf	Kohlebehandlung

Tab. 5: Fehler chemischer Art

Bezeichnung	Auswirkung	Ursache(n)	Behandlung
Kalkausscheidung	weiße Flocken, Bodensatz	hartes Verschnittwasser (Ca, Mg)	umbrennen oder Ionenaustauscher
Kupfertrübung	blaue Flocken oder blaue Kügelchen	Kupferaufnahme aus Brenngerät (Kühler)	umbrennen oder Ionenaustauscher
Eisentrübung	gelblich-braune Ausscheidungen	Kontakt mit Eisenteilen; eisenhalt. Verschnittwasser	umbrennen oder Ionenaustauscher
organische Trübungen	»Fettaugen«, milchige Opaleszenz (beim Herabsetzen)	höhere Alkohole, Fettsäuren, Terpene (natürl. vorkommend)	Kühllagerung mit Schönungsmittel, Kühlfiltration
Vor- und Nachlauffehler	Geruch stechend (Aldehyd, Ester); Geschmack fuselig	allzu schematische Vor- und Nachlaufabtrennung	umbrennen
Schwefeldioxidfehler	Geruch nach SO_2	hohe SO_2-Gaben zu Maische oder Most	neutralisieren, umbrennen
Steingeschmack	Geschmack nach bitteren Mandeln	zuviel Steine zerschlagen; zu lange Maischelagerung	Spezialbehandlungen (SO_2, Silbernitrat)
Metallgeschmack	bitterer Geschmack, Belag auf Zunge	Metallaufnahme (Eisen, Kupfer, Zink)	umbrennen oder Ionenaustauscher

G BETRIEBSKONTROLLE

1 Allgemeines

Auch im Kleinbetrieb kommt der Überwachung des Produktionsablaufs wesentliche Bedeutung zu. Neben der **degustativen** Beurteilung, welche dem erfahrenen Brenner Aufschluß über Qualität sowie eventuell zu treffende Maßnahmen gibt, ist auch der **analytischen** Untersuchung von Maischen und Destillaten Beachtung zu schenken. In Anbetracht der Tatsache, daß die wenigsten Kleinbrenner über eine Fachausbildung oder eine Laboreinrichtung verfügen, hat sich die analytische Betriebskontrolle in einem entsprechend einfachen Rahmen zu halten. Im Fachhandel sind Meßgeräte und Reagenziensätze erhältlich, mit denen sich die allerwichtigsten Bestimmungen ohne Schwierigkeiten ausführen lassen. Dazu gehören die Bestimmungen von

- **Extrakt** (Maischen, Moste)
- **Alkoholgehalt** (Maischen, Moste, Destillate, Liköre)
- **pH-Wert** (Maischen, Moste, Destillate)
- **flüchtigen Säuren** (Maischen, Moste) sowie
- **Wasserhärte** (Kühl- und Verschnittwasser).

Mit einem geringen Mehraufwand kann jeder interessierte Brenner noch weitere, je nach Problemstellung erforderliche Analysen selbst durchführen, z.B.

- **titrierbare Säuren** (Maischen, Moste, Destillate)
- **schweflige Säure** (Moste, Destillate)
- **Ester** (Destillate)
- **Schwermetallnachweis** (Destillate)
- **Vorlauftest** (Destillatfraktionen)
- **Blausäure** (Destillate).

Selbstverständlich können die entsprechenden Untersuchungen auch in Fachlaboratorien vorgenommen werden. Diese sind gegebenenfalls auch in der Lage, mit aufwendigeren Verfahren (z.B. Gaschromatographie) zusätzliche Inhaltsstoffe wie Acetaldehyd, Methanol, höhere Alkohole oder Ethylcarbamat zu bestimmen. Die erstgenannten Analysenmethoden sollten aber jedem Brenner geläufig sein.

Liegt ein Meßergebnis einmal vor, muß es auch richtig **interpretiert** werden können. Aus dem Extraktgehalt unvergorener Moste und Maischefiltrate lassen sich beispielsweise der Zuckergehalt sowie die zu erwartende Alkoholausbeute abschätzen. Für die Beurteilung des angelieferten Rohmaterials von großem Nutzen sind dabei die **Erfahrungswerte,** welche auch im Kleinbetrieb gesammelt werden sollten. Dasselbe gilt natürlich auch für die Zwischen- und Endprodukte (vgl. Richtwerte in den nachfolgenden Abschnitten sowie in Kapitel M).

2 Probenentnahme und -vorbereitung

Analytische Untersuchungen werden immer an einem **kleinen Bruchteil** des zu prüfenden Postens durchgeführt. Während beispielsweise die aräometrische Extraktbestimmung (s. Abschnitt 3) ein Probenvolumen von ca. 200 ml (Milliliter) voraussetzt, genügen für die refraktometrische Bestimmung wenige Tropfen. Für eine gaschromatographische Untersuchung werden lediglich einige Mikroliter (= tausendstel Milliliter) benötigt. Aus diesem Grunde ist dafür zu sorgen, daß es sich bei der untersuchten Probe auch wirklich um ein für den ganzen Posten repräsentatives **Durchschnittsmuster** handelt. Bei **Destillaten** gibt es diesbezüglich im allgemeinen keine Probleme (nach Zusatz von Verschnittwasser ist allerdings ein gründliches Vermischen erforderlich!). **Maischen** sind dagegen vor jeder Probenentnahme gut durchzustoßen, damit das Verhältnis zwischen Saft und Fruchtteilen in der entnommenen Probe jenem im Gärbehälter entspricht.

Maischen können infolge ihres Feststoffanteils nicht direkt untersucht werden, weil dadurch die Messung verfälscht oder gar verunmöglicht wird. Die entnommene Probe (ca. 0,5–1 Liter) muß deshalb filtriert werden, wobei ganze Früchte (z.B. Kirschen, Zwetschgen) vorgängig noch zu zerkleinern sind. Das Filtrat soll möglichst klar ablaufen; die ersten, meist trüben Anteile sind auf das Filter zurückzugießen. Nötigenfalls ist die Filtration zu wiederholen. Das weitgehend klare Filtrat kann für die verschiedenen Untersuchungen eingesetzt werden (s. nachfolgende Abschnitte).

Für die Filtration von Maischen haben sich in der Praxis **Trichterfilter** bewährt, beispielsweise die Poly-Fix-Filter, welche mit Papier-Faltenfiltern beschickt werden und auch für die Filtration von Destillaten Verwendung finden (s. E.3).

3 Extrakt

Unter »Extrakt« (auch Trockensubstanz genannt) versteht man im weitesten Sinne alle in einem Obsterzeugnis enthaltenen löslichen Stoffe, welche sich beim Abdestillieren des wässerig-alkoholischen Anteils nicht verflüchtigen. Darunter fallen Zucker, Fruchtsäuren, Mineral- und eiweißartige Stoffe, um nur die wichtigsten Komponenten zu erwähnen (s. auch A. 2). Der Extraktgehalt stellt eine unentbehrliche Beurteilungsgrundlage sowohl für unvergorene als auch für vergorene Maischen und Moste dar (s. 3.3). Er läßt sich in einfacher Weise aräometrisch oder refraktometrisch ermitteln (s. 3.1 und 3.2). Da im Obst der Extraktgehalt hauptsächlich durch den Anteil an vergärbaren Zuckern bestimmt wird, kann daraus mit recht guter Näherung die voraussichtliche Alkoholausbeute berechnet werden (s. 3.4).

3.1 Aräometrie

Ein Aräometer, auch Senkwaage oder Spindel genannt, besteht aus einem hohlen, am unteren Ende beschwerten Glasschwimmkörper, an dessen oberem Ende ein dünnes, mit Ableseskala versehenes Rohr angebracht ist (Abb. 45).

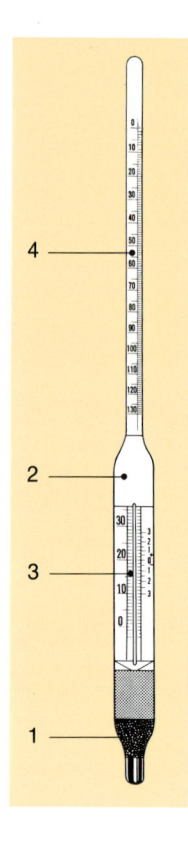

Genauere Aräometer weisen meistens im unteren Teil ein Thermometer auf. Zur Vornahme einer Messung wird das Aräometer in die Probelösung eingetaucht. Je nach Extraktgehalt wird es mehr oder weniger tief einsinken, da ein Körper in einer Flüssigkeit genau soviel an Gewicht verliert, wie die von ihm verdrängte Flüssigkeit wiegt **(Prinzip von Archimedes)**. In einer extraktarmen, d.h. spezifisch leichten Flüssigkeit taucht ein Aräometer also tiefer ein als in einer extraktreicheren. Da bekanntlich die räumliche Ausdehnung von Flüssigkeiten temperaturabhängig ist, muß sich eine aräometrische Messung immer auf eine bestimmte **Normaltemperatur** beziehen. Bei Meßtemperaturen, welche von der Normaltemperatur abweichen, ist deshalb eine Korrektur des Ablesewertes erforderlich (s. Arbeitsanleitung).

Als Extraktspindeln sind in der Brennereipraxis vor allem das **Saccharometer** sowie die Mostwaage im Gebrauch.

Daneben werden auch Dichtewaagen oder Aräometer mit Doppelskala verwendet. Leider ist es bis heute nicht gelungen, sich auf ein allgemein anerkanntes Einheitsverfahren zur Extraktbestimmung festzulegen. In Tab. 6 werden die beiden in der Obstbrennerei verbreitetsten Aräometertypen vorgestellt.

Abb. 45: Aräometer (1: Ballast, 2: Schwimmkörper, 3: Temperaturskala, 4: Ableseskala, hier z.B. für Mostgewicht)

Tab. 6: Aräometertypen zur Extraktbestimmung in Mosten und Maischen

Bezeichnung	Saccharometer	Mostwaage*
Normaltemperatur	20°C	20°C
Anzeige	in Prozent (%), d.h. Anzahl g Saccharose pro 100 g Lösung	in Mostgraden (°), d.h. (rel. Dichte − 1) x 1000
Meßbereich (Teilung)	-1 – 25% (0,2%) oder -1 – 7% (0,1%)	0–130° (1°)

* Die sogenannten »Oechslewaagen« beziehen sich meistens auf eine Normaltemperatur von 17,5°C (in der Schweiz 15°C). Für den Praktiker ist der Unterschied zwischen Most- und Oechslegraden allerdings nicht gravierend (das Mostgewicht bei 20°C liegt etwa 0,5° höher als das Oechslegewicht bei 17,5°C, also innerhalb der Meßgenauigkeit). Trotzdem wäre es im Sinne einer Vereinheitlichung zu begrüßen, wenn die Oechslewaagen den Mostwaagen weichen würden.

Für die Aräometrie benötigt man außerdem einen sogenannten **Spindelzylinder** von ausreichender Höhe und Weite. Das Aräometer muß in der Probelösung mit genügend Spielraum schwimmen können. Steht eine ebene Unterlage zur Verfügung, so genügt ein Standzylinder, andernfalls wäre einer kardanischen Aufhängung der Vorzug zu geben (Abb. 46).

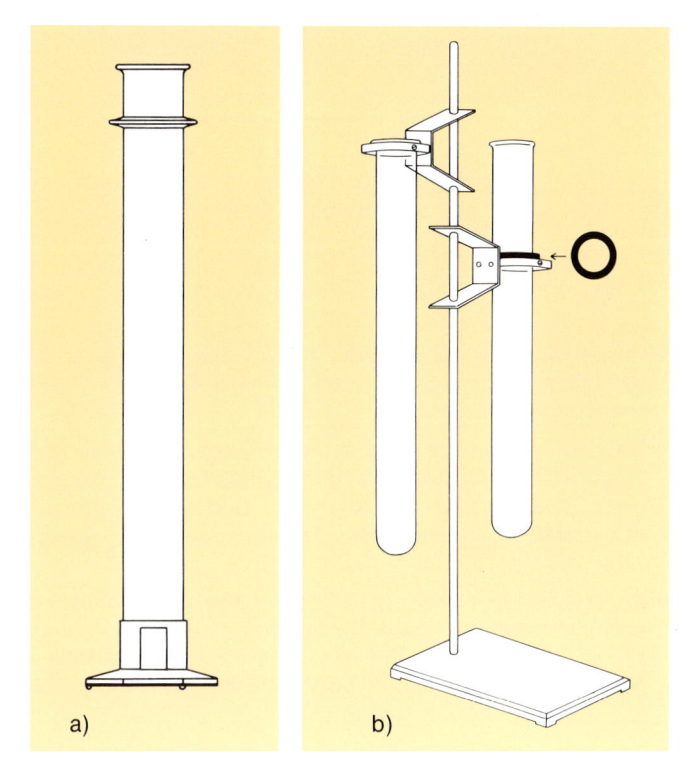

Abb. 46:
Spindelzylinder
a: Standzylinder
b: Zylinder mit kardanischer Aufhängung

Merkpunkte und Arbeitsanleitung

- Aräometer liefern nur einwandfreie Resultate, wenn sie intakt, sauber und fettfrei sind. Instrument jeweils nach Gebrauch gründlich mit Wasser reinigen. Zum Abtrocknen ein fusselfreies Tuch verwenden.
- Aräometer vor Hitze und Kälte, vor Stoß und Fall schützen. Gefährlich ist auch ein harter Aufprall auf den Zylinderboden bei unsachgemäßer Einbringung des Aräometers.
- Auch Spindelzylinder müssen sauber gehalten werden (besonders gefährlich sind Fettfilme an den Innenwandungen). Sie sind sofort nach Gebrauch ausgiebig zu spülen und mit der Mündung nach unten zum Trocknen aufzuhängen (Abtropfgestell).
- Der Durchmesser des Spindelzylinders sollte wesentlich größer sein als der Durchmesser des Aräometer-Schwimmkörpers, damit das Instrument genügend Spielraum nach allen Seiten hat. Häufig werden zu enge Spindelzylinder verwendet.

G

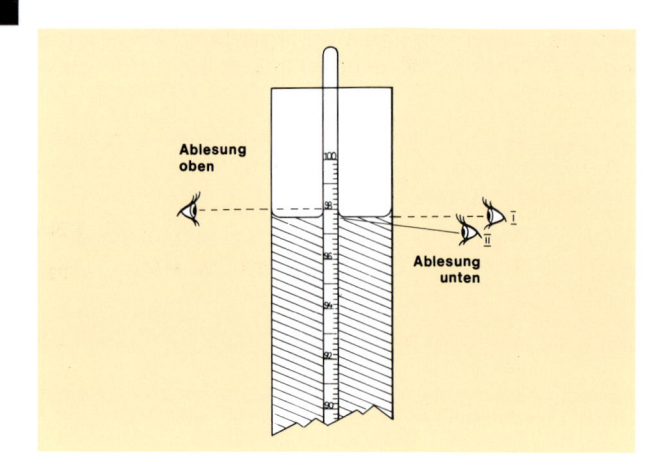

Abb. 47: Ablesung des Aräometers

- Die Untersuchungsflüssigkeit soll frei von Feststoffen sein und keine Schichtenbildung aufweisen. Deswegen Flüssigkeit vorher filtrieren und einwandfrei mischen (s. Abschnitt 2).

- Man fasse das Instrument an der Stengelspitze und führe es langsam in die Flüssigkeit ein, bis es frei und lotrecht schwimmt. Aräometer in der Flüssigkeit nicht auf- und abpendeln lassen, da sonst der Stengel über den Meniskus hinaus benetzt und durch den entstehenden Flüssigkeitsfilm das Gewicht des Aräometers unzulässig erhöht würde.

- Am Aräometer haftende Luftblasen beeinflussen die Genauigkeit der Messung. Werden Luftblasen am Aräometer festgestellt, Instrument aus der Flüssigkeit herausziehen und vorsichtig erneut eintauchen, bis die Luftbläschen verschwunden sind. Auch durch vorsichtiges Rotieren des Aräometers lassen sich anhängende Luftblasen ablösen.

- Die Temperatur der Untersuchungsprobe weicht häufig von der Temperatur des Aräometers ab, besonders wenn sie aus kalten Lagerräumen in wärmere Untersuchungsräume gebracht wird. Bei offensichtlichen Temperaturdifferenzen Aräometerwert erst ca. 1–2 Minuten nach dem Eintauchen des Instruments ablesen. Für ganz exakte Messungen müssen sowohl Probe als auch Aräometer Raumtemperatur haben.

- Aräometerwerte müssen richtig abgelesen werden. Aräometer ohne aufgedruckte Ablesevorschrift sind stets auf »**Ablesung unten**« justiert. Auf »Ablesung oben« justierte Instrumente müssen durch den Aufdruck »Ablesung oben« gekennzeichnet sein. Abb. 47 veranschaulicht richtiges Ablesen der Aräometer. Für »Ablesung unten« gibt es zwei Ablesemöglichkeiten.

- Die **Eichung** eines Aräometers ist die amtliche Garantie dafür, daß die Abweichung an keiner Stelle der Aräometer-Skala größer ist als ein Teilstrich. Jedes Aräometer hat einen fertigungsbedingten Eigenfehler. Bei der Eichung der Instrumente wird auf Wunsch und gegen Gebühr die Abweichung der Instrumentenanzeige gegenüber dem Idealwert an jedem der Prüfpunkte festgestellt und in ein »Fehlerverzeichnis« eingetragen. Die Berücksichtigung des Fehlerverzeichnisses gewährleistet ein Höchstmaß an Genauigkeit bei aräometrischen Untersuchungen.

Temperaturkorrektur: Weicht die am Thermometer abgelesene Temperatur der Probelösung von der Normaltemperatur ab, so muß das abgelesene Resultat korrigiert werden. Dies geschieht entweder

– mittels der am Thermometer angebrachten **Korrekturskala** (die allerdings nur Mittelwerte angeben kann), oder, falls eine solche fehlt, durch

– **Faustregeln:**
beim **Saccharometer** pro Grad über bzw. unter Normaltemperatur 0,06% zubzw. abzählen
bei der **Mostwaage** pro Grad über bzw. unter Normaltemperatur 0,2° zu- bzw. abzählen

Beispiel:
Bei der Extraktbestimmung in einem Kirschenmaischefiltrat liest man an der Saccharometerskala 17,2% ab; die Temperatur der Probelösung beträgt 15°C. Normaltemperatur (NT) = 20°C
Abweichung von der Normaltemperatur: 20–15 = 5 Grad **unter** NT
Korrektur: 5 x 0,06 = 0,3 % müssen vom abgelesenen Wert **abgezogen** werden; der korrigierte Extraktgehalt beträgt also 17,2–0,3 = **16,9%.**

– Genauer kann die Temperaturkorrektur nur mit Hilfe eigentlicher **Korrekturtabellen** erfolgen.

3.2 Refraktometrie

Bei der Refraktometrie handelt es sich um eine optische Meßmethode, wobei die **Konzentrationsabhängigkeit der Lichtbrechung** zur Extraktbestimmung ausgenützt wird. Die in der Praxis verwendeten Hand-Refraktometer weisen meist eine Ableseskala auf, welche sich wie beim Saccharometer auf wässerige Zuckerlösungen (g Saccharose pro 100 g Lösung) bezieht. Verbreitet sind auch Meßgeräte mit Doppelskala (Zucker-%/Mostgewicht). Da auch die Lichtbrechung temperaturabhängig ist, muß die Refraktometeranzeige bei einer von der NT (20°C) abweichenden Meßtemperatur noch korrigiert werden (s. Arbeitsanleitung).

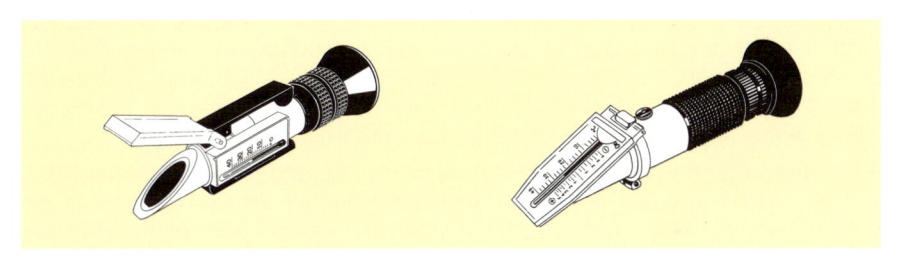

Abb. 48: Hand-Rekfraktometer

Für die Messung werden nur einige Tropfen Saft oder Maischefiltrat benötigt. Umso mehr ist darauf zu achten, daß es sich bei der untersuchten Flüssigkeit um ein gutes **Durchschnittsmuster** handelt. Nötigenfalls sind mehrere Messungen durchzuführen. Während Aräometer sowohl vor als auch nach der Gärung zur Extraktmessung eingesetzt werden können, ist bei der refraktometrischen Untersuchung alkoholhaltiger, d.h. in Gärung befindlicher oder vergorener Flüssigkeiten Vorsicht geboten (s. 3.3.2).

Arbeitsanleitung
Die Messung wird nach der zum verwendeten Refraktometer gehörenden Bedienungsanleitung vorgenommen. Im allgemeinen verfährt man folgendermaßen:

- Untersuchungslösung möglichst klar filtrieren (s. Abschnitt 2)
- Ableseskala unter Anpeilung einer guten Lichtquelle auf individuelle Sehschärfe einstellen
- Deckel aufklappen, 2–3 Tropfen destilliertes Wasser von 20°C auf die Meßprismenfläche geben, Deckel wieder zuklappen
- Lichtquelle anpeilen, anhand der Grenzlinie hell/dunkel Nullpunkt überprüfen, eventuell Korrektur vornehmen
- Deckel aufklappen, Prismenfläche mit feuchtem Tuch sorgfältig reinigen
- 2–3 Tropfen der Probelösung auf die Meßprismenfläche bringen, Deckel wieder zuklappen
- Lichtquelle anpeilen, Ablesung vornehmen (Grenzlinie hell/dunkel).

Bemerkungen
1. Zur Erzielung einer kontrastreichen Grenzlinie sind wenig gefärbte, blanke Lösungen im durchfallenden, stark gefärbte Lösungen im reflektierten Licht zu messen. Dies geschieht je nach verwendetem Gerät durch Drehung des Refraktometers in der Längsachse um 180° oder durch Verwendung spezieller Lichteintrittsöffnungen.
2. Nach jeder Messung sind Meßprismenfläche und Deckel-Unterseite mit einem feuchten, fusselfreien Tuch gründlich zu reinigen und vollständig zu trocknen. Zur Vermeidung von Kratzern, die das Meßgerät unbrauchbar machen könnten, ist jede Berührung der Glasteile mit harten Gegenständen zu unterlassen.
3. Es ist streng darauf zu achten, daß Hand-Refraktometer nicht unter fließendem Wasser oder im Wasserbehälter abgespült werden, da eindringendes Wasser Schäden am Instrument verursachen würde.
4. Das Refraktometer sollte trocken und gut gereinigt bei Raumtemperatur aufbewahrt werden.

Temperaturkorrektur: Als **Faustregel** merke man sich, daß bei Meßtemperaturen, die von der Normaltemperatur abweichen, pro Grad über bzw. unter 20°C 0,07% zu- bzw. 0,06% abzuzählen sind. Genauere Korrekturen lassen sich anhand spezieller Korrekturtabellen vornehmen, in welchen auch die verschiedenen Konzentrationen berücksichtigt sind. Einen Auszug aus einer solchen Tabelle, welcher die in der Obstbrennerei üblichen Bereiche abdeckt, zeigt Tab. 7:

Tab. 7: Temperaturkorrektur für die refraktometrische Extraktbestimmung

Temperatur °C	Konzentrationsbereiche			
	5%	10%	15%	20%
5	−0,75	−0,80	−0,85	−0,90
6	−0,71	−0,76	−0,80	−0,85
7	−0,67	−0,72	−0,75	−0,79
8	−0,63	−0,67	−0,71	−0,74
9	−0,58	−0,62	−0,66	−0,68
10	−0,54	−0,58	−0,61	−0,64
11	−0,49	−0,53	−0,55	−0,58
12	−0,45	−0,48	−0,50	−0,52
13	−0,40	−0,42	−0,44	−0,46
14	−0,35	−0,37	−0,39	−0,40
15	−0,29	−0,31	−0,33	−0,34
16	−0,24	−0,25	−0,26	−0,27
17	−0,18	−0,19	−0,20	−0,21
18	−0,13	−0,13	−0,14	−0,14
19	−0,06	−0,06	−0,07	−0,07
20	0	0	0	0
21	+0,07	+0,07	+0,07	+0,07
22	+0,13	+0,14	+0,14	+0,15
23	+0,20	+0,21	+0,22	+0,22
24	+0,27	+0,28	+0,29	+0,30
25	+0,35	+0,36	+0,37	+0,38
26	+0,42	+0,43	+0,44	+0,45
27	+0,50	+0,52	+0,53	+0,54
28	+0,57	+0,60	+0,61	+0,62
29	+0,66	+0,68	+0,69	+0,71
30	+0,74	+0,77	+0,78	+0,79

Beispiel:
Bei einer Meßtemperatur von 12°C wird in einer Zwetschgenmaische ein Extraktgehalt von 16,1% gemessen. Der korrigierte Wert beträgt 16,1−0,5 = **15,6%**.

3.3 Interpretation der Meßergebnisse

3.3.1 Unvergorene Säfte und Maischen

Die Zuckergehalte von Brennereirohstoffen unterliegen erfahrungsgemäß gewissen Schwankungen, die neben dem Reifegrad auch durch Faktoren wie Sorte, Klima, Jahrgang und Bodenverhältnisse bedingt sind (s. A. 1). Dasselbe gilt natürlich noch vermehrt für die Extraktgehalte, da der unvergärbare Extraktanteil ebenfalls keine feste Größe ist. Trotzdem lassen sich für die verschiedenen Rohstoffe gewisse Schwankungsbreiten angeben, innerhalb welcher sich die Extraktgehalte normalerweise bewegen (Tab. 8). Damit wird dem Brenner eine erste Beurteilung erleichtert; zusätzlich wird er natürlich seine eigenen Erfahrungswerte hinzuziehen können. Darüber hinaus läßt sich aus dem Extraktgehalt unvergorener Maischen und Moste die zu erwartende Alkoholausbeute ermitteln (s. 3.4).

Tab. 8: Extraktgehalte unvergorener Maischen (nach *Pieper, Bruchmann* und *Kolb*). Die Angaben beziehen sich auf das Maische**filtrat**. Sie decken sich weitgehend mit eigenen und aus schweizerischen Großbetrieben stammenden Werten.

Rohstoffe	Zucker-%	Mostgewicht
Äpfel, Birnen	12–17	48–68
Williamsbirnen	10–14	40–56
Kirschen	13–22	52–88
Zwetschgen	10–20	40–80
Pflaumen	10–15	40–60
Himbeeren, Heidelbeeren, Brombeeren	8–10	32–40
Holunderbeeren	8–11	32–44
Topinambur	14–16	56–64

3.3.2 Vergorene Säfte und Maischen

Bedingt durch die Umwandlung der Zucker in die Hauptprodukte Alkohol und Kohlendioxid, sinkt der Extraktgehalt im Verlaufe der Gärung. Der nach Gärende meßbare Extraktgehalt, auch **Vergärungsgrad** genannt, wird durch den Gehalt an unvergärbaren Maischeinhaltsstoffen bestimmt. So erhöht beispielsweise der unvergärbare Zuckeralkohol **Sorbit** den Extraktgehalt von Steinobstmaischen nicht unwesentlich. In Kirschen mit einem Sorbitanteil von ca. 40 g/l macht dies etwa 2% aus. Mit 0,5–1% tragen aber auch die Fruchtsäuren an den

Tab. 9: Extraktgehalte vergorener Maischen (nach *Pieper, Bruchmann* und *Kolb*, ergänzt durch eigene Werte). Die Angaben beziehen sich auf das Maische**filtrat**.

Rohstoffe	Zucker-%	Mostgewicht
Äpfel	1–3 (2–6)*	4–12
Birnen	1,5–4 (3–8)	6–16
Williamsbirnen	2,5–4 (4–8)	10–16
Kirschen	3–6 (6–10)	12–24
Zwetschgen	2–5 (5–8)	12–20
Pflaumen	2–3	8–12
Himbeeren, Heidelbeeren, Brombeeren	1–2	4–8
Holunderbeeren	3–5	12–20
Topinambur	1	4

* Angaben in Klammern sind refraktometrisch ermittelte Werte. Sie liegen erfahrungsgemäß höher als die aräometrisch erhaltenen und sind, weil stark vom jeweiligen Alkoholgehalt abhängig, auch weniger zuverlässig.

Vergärungsgrad bei. In Tabelle 9 sind die Vergärungsgrade der wichtigsten Brennereirohstoffe zusammengestellt. Größere Abweichungen von diesen Werten können auf eine Gärstockung zurückzuführen sein. In solchen Fällen ist es angezeigt, eine **Prüfung auf Endvergärung** vorzunehmen (s. B. 3.6.1). Grundsätzlich bestünde auch die Möglichkeit, eine Zuckerbestimmung durchzuführen oder durchführen zu lassen. Es gilt dabei aber zu beachten, daß nicht jeder chemisch ermittelte Zuckergehalt auch dem tatsächlich vorhandenen Zucker entspricht, da weitere unvergärbare Substanzen, wie z.b. Galakturonsäure, miterfaßt werden. Genauere Resultate lassen sich nur mit aufwendigeren Methoden erhalten, was sich aber für die Praxis kaum lohnt.

3.4 Ermittlung der voraussichtlichen Alkoholausbeute

Bereits vor der Gärung kann sich jeder Brenner ein Bild über die zu erwartende Alkoholausbeute machen. Zwei verschiedene Verfahren stehen ihm dabei zur Verfügung:
– Berechnung mittels **Näherungsformel** (s. 3.4.1)
– **Graphisches Verfahren** (s. 3.4.2).
Beiden Methoden gemeinsam ist die Verwendung von **Erfahrungswerten,** wobei es sich im ersten Fall um allgemeines Zahlenmaterial und im zweiten um betriebsintern gesammelte Daten handelt. Beide Möglichkeiten haben ihre Vorteile; es darf aber nicht eine absolute Übereinstimmung mit den tatsächlich erhaltenen Ausbeuten erwartet werden, da die äußeren Bedingungen (Rohmaterial, Gärverlauf) nie genau dieselben sind.

3.4.1 Berechnung mittels Näherungsformel

Ausgangsgröße ist der aräometrisch gemessene **Extraktgehalt E.** Das mit der Mostwaage erhaltene Mostgewicht muß durch 4 geteilt werden (genauere Umrechnung mittels Tab. H. 4):

$$\text{Extraktgehalt} = \frac{\text{Mostgewicht}}{4}$$

Beispiel: 48° = 12%

a) **Zuckergehalt Z:** Dazu ist der Extraktgehalt um den nichtvergärbaren Anteil (= **Nichtzuckerstoffe NZ**) zu vermindern:

$$\text{Zuckergehalt} = \text{Extraktgehalt} - \text{Nichtzuckerstoffe}$$

Der Anteil an Nichtzuckerstoffen ist von der Obstart abhängig und beträgt nach *Nosko*

- ca. 2,5% bei Filtraten/Mosten aus Äpfeln
- ca. 3,5% bei Filtraten/Mosten aus Birnen, Brombeeren, Heidelbeeren und Himbeeren
- ca. 4% bei Filtraten aus Zwetschgen
- ca. 5% bei Filtraten aus Kirschen.

Beispiel: Der Extraktgehalt eines Birnenmaischefiltrates beträgt 14%. Nichtzuckerstoffe (s. oben) = 3,5% → Zuckergehalt = **10,5%**.

b) **Alkoholausbeute (bezogen auf Maischefiltrat):** Theoretisch entstehen aus 100 kg Zucker ca. 51 kg, d.h. 64,5 l Alkohol (s. A. 2.1). Unter Praxisbedingungen rechnet man dagegen mit einer Ausbeute von 56 l reinem Alkohol pro 100 kg Zucker. Daraus ergibt sich der **Ausbeutefaktor 0,56**, welcher mit dem Zuckergehalt zu multiplizieren ist, um die auf das Maischefiltrat bezogene Alkoholausbeute zu erhalten:

> Alkohol pro 100 l Most/Filtrat = Zuckergehalt x 0,56

Beispiel: Der Zuckergehalt einer Kirschenmaische beträgt 15,2%. Damit ist eine Alkoholausbeute von 15,2 x 0,56 = **8,5 l** reinem Alkohol pro 100 l Maischefiltrat zu erwarten.

c) **Alkoholausbeute (bezogen auf Maische):** Aus praktischen Gründen kann die Extraktmessung nur in einem weitgehend trub- und feststofffreien Filtrat erfolgen. Alle bisher berechneten Größen beziehen sich deshalb auf Most oder Maischefiltrat. Um die Alkoholausbeute direkt auf die Maische beziehen zu können, muß ihr **Tresteranteil**, d.h. der Gehalt an wasserunlöslichen Bestandteilen wie Kerne, Steine, Schalen usw. bekannt sein. Natürlich ist auch der Tresteranteil von der Obstart abhängig; besonders hoch liegt er begreiflicherweise beim Steinobst. Für die wichtigsten Brennereirohstoffe existieren Richtwerte:

Rohstoffe	Tresteranteil in %	Tresterfaktor T
Äpfel	6–8%	0,94–0,92
Birnen	8–10%	0,92–0,90
Zwetschgen	11–12%	0,89–0,88
Kirschen	15–16%	0,85–0,84

Der aus dem Tresteranteil in % berechnete **Tresterfaktor T** ist diejenige Zahl, mit welcher die auf 100 l Maischefiltrat bezogene Ausbeute multipliziert werden muß, um die auf 100 l Maische bezogene Ausbeute zu erhalten:

> Alkohol pro 100 l Maische = Alkohol pro 100 l Maischefiltrat x T

Beispiel: Birnenmaische mit einer Alkoholausbeute von 5,6 l/100 l Maischefiltrat. Auf 100 l Maische bezogen beträgt die Ausbeute 5,6 x 0,9 = **5,04 l r.A**. (Angenommener Tresteranteil von 10%).

Zusammengefaßt lassen sich die Berechnungsschritte a) – c) wie folgt formulieren:

> voraussichtliche Alkoholausbeute pro 100 l Maische = (E–NZ) x 0,56 x T

Die entsprechenden Werte für Nichtzuckerstoffe (NZ) und Tresterfaktor (T) sind den unter a) bzw. c) gemachten Angaben zu entnehmen.

Beispiel: Der Extraktgehalt eines Kirschenmaischefiltrates beträgt 21,4%; die Werte für NZ und T sind 5% bzw. 0,85. Die voraussichtliche Alkoholausbeute pro 100 l Maische beträgt

$$(21{,}4-5) \times 0{,}56 \times 0{,}85 = \mathbf{7{,}8\ l.}$$

3.4.2 Graphisches Verfahren

Diese Methode stützt sich auf die Analysenzahlen eines einzelnen Brennereibetriebes. Durch die im Laufe der Jahre zusammengetragenen Analysenwerte für **Extraktgehalt** und **Alkoholausbeute** (Bestimmung s. Abschnitt 4) kann eine Graphik erstellt werden (s. Abb. 49). Die resultierenden Meßpunkte werden näherungsweise durch eine Gerade charakterisiert. Je mehr Meßwerte zur Verfügung stehen, desto verläßlicher ist eine Ermittlung der voraussichtlichen Ausbeute möglich. Auf diese Weise kann den spezifischen Verhältnissen des einzelnen Betriebs (verarbeitete Sorten, Klimaverhältnisse) besser Rechnung getragen werden. Selbstverständlich ist für jede einzelne Rohstoffart eine solche Graphik zu erstellen.

Beispiele (in der Graphik eingezeichnet):

a) bei einem Extraktgehalt von 16% ist eine Alkoholausbeute von **6,9 l r. A./100 l** Maischefiltrat zu erwarten.

b) entsprechender Erwartungswert für 12%: **4,8 l r.A.**

Der Graphik ist außerdem zu entnehmen, daß bei mittleren Extraktgehalten eine genauere Voraussage möglich ist als bei hohen oder tiefen Werten.

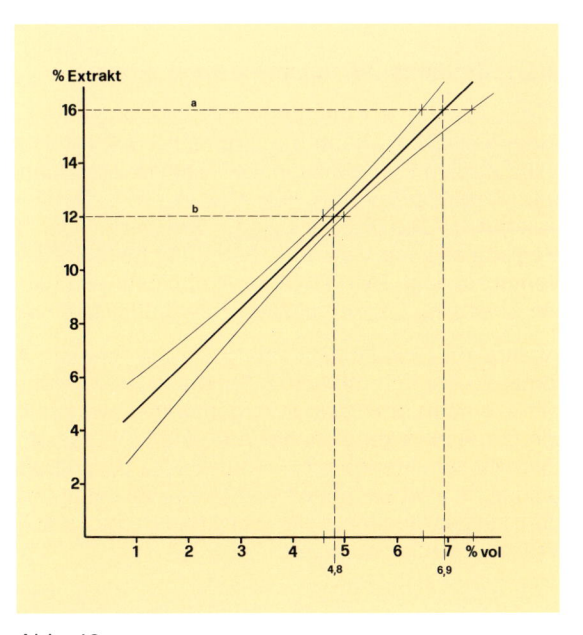

Abb. 49:
Abhängigkeit der Alkoholausbeute vom Extraktgehalt bei Williamsbirnen (nach *Nosko*)

4 Alkohol

Neben der Extraktbestimmung nimmt die Ermittlung des Alkoholgehaltes in der Betriebskontrolle eine zentrale Stellung ein. Dies gilt für Destillate und Destillatfraktionen ebenso wie für vergorene Maischen und Moste. Von den verschiedenen Bestimmungsmethoden eignen sich für die Brennereipraxis in erster Linie **Aräometrie** (s. 4.1) und **Ebullioskopie** (s. 4.2). Bei sachgemäßer Ausführung liefern sie trotz ihrer Einfachheit ausreichend genaue Resultate.

Die Angabe des Alkoholgehaltes erfolgt in der Praxis vorwiegend in »**Volumenprozenten**« (übliche Abkürzungen % vol oder Vol.%), d. h. **Anzahl Liter reinen Alkohols in 100 Litern Probelösung*** (Maischefiltrat, Most, Lutterwasser, Destillat). Da diese Angabe temperaturabhängig ist, muß eine **Bezugstemperatur** festgelegt werden. Diese liegt sowohl in der Schweiz als auch in Deutschland bei **20°C**. Damit entfallen früher übliche, teilweise aus anderen Einheiten umgerechnete Bezugstemperaturen (15°C; 15,56°C). Entsprechende Meßgeräte sind auch nicht mehr eichfähig. Die Umwandlung von Volumenprozenten in andere Gehaltsangaben wie Massenprozent** (Abkürzung % mas) oder Gramm pro Liter (Abkürzung g/l) kann anhand der Tabelle H. 3 vorgenommen werden.

4.1 Aräometrie

4.1.1 Bestimmung in extraktfreien Proben

Die in Abschn. 3.1 gegebenen Erläuterungen zur Aräometrie gelten sinngemäß auch hier. Direkt kann die aräometrische Alkoholbestimmung allerdings nur in extraktfreien Probelösungen (Destillate, Destillatfraktionen, Lutterwasser) erfolgen. Streng genommen liefert sie nur in ausschließlich Alkohol und Wasser enthaltenden Gemischen exakte Resultate; der Einfluß allfällig vorhandener Begleitstoffe wie Methanol, Ester und höhere Alkohole wird in der Praxis jedoch vernachlässigt. Extrakthaltige Probelösungen (Maischefiltrate, Moste, Destillate mit Zusätzen, Liköre) müssen zuerst destilliert werden (s. 4.1.2).

Analog zur Extraktbestimmung müssen genaue Alkoholspindeln (auch Alkoholometer genannt) mit einem Thermometer versehen sein, damit gegebenenfalls eine Temperaturkorrektur vorgenommen werden kann. Selbstverständlich deckt ein genaues Alkoholometer nur einen Teil der Volumenprozentskala ab (Spindeln mit dem Meßbereich von 0–100% vol und entsprechend grober Skaleneinteilung, d. h. Abstufungen von 1–2% vol sind höchstens für Näherungsmessungen zu gebrauchen). Die Einstellung der Destillate auf Trinkstärke erfordert Präzisions-Alkoholometer.

---

* Streng genommen müßte bei der auf ein Gesamtvolumen bezogenen Angabe von Alkoholkonzentration gesprochen werden.

** Die Bezeichnung »Massenprozent« ersetzt die früher übliche Bezeichnung »Gewichtsprozent« (Gew.%).

G

Vorschlag zur Alkoholometer-Ausstattung einer Brennerei:

– **Vorlage-Alkoholometer** 0–100% vol, 0–85% vol;

– einfache **Thermo-Alkoholometer:**

Type	0–100% vol	20°C
Type	0– 85% vol	20°C
Type	30– 85% vol	20°C

– **eichfähige und geeichte Thermo-Alkoholometer,**
insbesondere für die Einstellung auf Trinkstärke:

Type 35–50% vol 20°C, in 0,2% geteilt
Type 35–45 und
Type 40–50% vol 20°C, in 0,1% geteilt, Euro-Klasse II
Type 35–40
Type 40–45 und
Type 45–50% vol 20°C, in 0,1% geteilt, Euro-Klasse III und DIN 12803,
(diese Instrumente für 200ml Destillat und die Bereiche von 0–5% vol bis 95–100 bzw. 98–103% vol sind obligatorisch für die Bundesmonopolverwaltung und die nachgeordneten Stellen, z.B. Zoll, auch Wirtschaftskontrolldienst)

Zur Messung benötigt man außerdem passende, genügend weite **Spindelzylinder** (s. 3.1). Die Durchführung der Messung erfolgt in gleicher Weise wie bei der Extraktbestimmung. Es sei nochmals nachdrücklich darauf hingewiesen, daß für präzise Meßergebnisse nicht nur geeichte, sondern auch peinlich saubere Meßgeräte unbedingte Voraussetzung sind. **Insbesondere ist darauf zu achten, daß Spindel, Spindelzylinder sowie sämtliche mit der Probelösung in Berührung kommenden Gefäße fettfrei sind.** Nötigenfalls ist eine Reinigung mit Sodalösung vorzunehmen. Anschließend wird mit hochprozentigem Alkohol gespült. Selbstverständlich muß auch die Untersuchungslösung fettfrei sein (eine auf der Lösung schwimmende Fettschicht würde die Oberflächenspannung und somit die Eintauchtiefe verändern, d. h. zu ungenauen Resultaten führen).

Temperaturkorrektur: Weicht die Meßtemperatur von der Normaltemperatur (20°C) ab, so zeigt das Alkoholometer einen falschen, »scheinbaren« Alkoholgehalt an, der sich je nach Konzentrationsbereich mehr oder weniger stark vom richtigen, »wahren« Gehalt unterscheidet. In Abb. 50 wird dieser Zusammenhang für den in erster Linie interessierenden Bereich von 30...60% vol anhand einiger Beispiele dargestellt: Die beträchtliche Temperaturabhängigkeit der aräometrischen Alkoholbestimmung fällt dabei sofort ins Auge. In diesem Bereich gilt folgende **Faustregel:**

Für Meßtemperaturen, die von der Normaltemperatur abweichen, sind pro Grad über bzw. unter 20°C 0,4% vol ab- bzw. hinzuzuzählen.

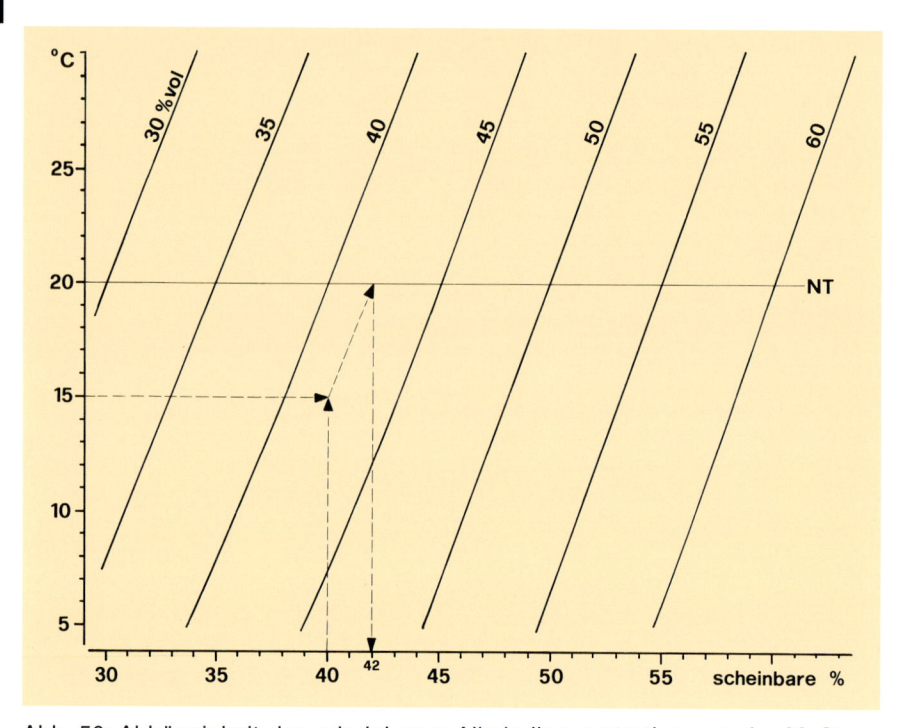

Abb. 50: Abhängigkeit der scheinbaren Alkoholkonzentration von der Meßtemperatur

Beispiel: Bei einer Temperatur von 15°C werden 40 »scheinbare« % vol gemessen. Der »wahre« Alkoholgehalt liegt (20−15) x 0,4% vol höher, d.h. er beträgt 42% vol. Diese Lösung wird auch auf graphischem Wege erhalten (in der Abb. gestrichelt eingezeichnet).

Für eine **exakte Temperaturkorrektur** ist hingegen die Verwendung einer eigentlichen **Korrekturtabelle** erforderlich. In Tafel 1 der Amtlichen Alkoholtafeln der BRD ist die Temperaturabhängigkeit der Alkoholometer-Ablesung für den gesamten Konzentrationsbereich (Abstufungen von 0,1 % vol) bei Meßtemperaturen von 0...30°C (Abstufungen von 0,2 Grad) wiedergegeben. Tabelle H.1 umfaßt den für die Brennereipraxis besonders wichtigen Bereich.

4.1.2 Bestimmung in extrakthaltigen Proben

In extrakthaltigen Probelösungen wird die aräometrische Alkoholbestimmung verfälscht, da Extraktstoffe die Dichte erhöhen. Dies führt zu einer entsprechend geringeren Eintauchtiefe, d.h. zur Anzeige eines geringeren Alkoholgehaltes. Aus diesem Grunde muß vor der aräometrischen Bestimmung eine **Destillation** vorgenommen werden. Das resultierende Destillat ist dabei mit destilliertem Wasser auf das ursprüngliche Volumen zu ergänzen. Dieses Verfahren ist selbstverständlich nicht nur bei vergorenen Mosten und Maischen (Berechnung der Alkoholausbeute), sondern auch bei extrakthaltigen Spirituosen anzuwenden (s. Beispiel).

Beispiel:
Williams mit einem Extraktgehalt von 4,5 g/l (Zusatz von Fructose)
Aräometrische Alkoholbestimmung direkt: 53,4% vol
Aräometrische Alkoholbestimmung nach vorgängiger Destillation: 54,1% vol

Eine genaue Alkoholbestimmung in extrakthaltigen Probelösungen setzt voraus, daß das Volumen sowohl vor als auch nach der Destillation exakt abgemessen werden kann. Dies würde sowohl geeichte Meßkolben als auch eine Vorrichtung zur Einstellung der Eichtemperatur (meistens 20°C) erfordern (Wasserbad). Da gerade letztere einem Brennereibetrieb im Normalfall nicht zur Verfügung steht, anderseits eine genaue Abmessung dickbreiiger Maischen ohnehin mit Schwierigkeiten verbunden ist, wird nachstehend eine vereinfachte Arbeitsvorschrift angegeben. Sie liefert brauchbare Ergebnisse, ohne allerdings die Präzision einer Referenzmethode zu erreichen, was ja in der Praxis auch nicht erforderlich ist. Die zur Destillation benötigte Apparatur ist in Abb. 51 dargestellt:

Es bedeuten

1: Destillierkolben (500 ml, evtl. 1000 ml Inhalt), dazu passender

2: Destillieraufsatz

3: Schlangenkühler (Länge ca. 25 cm), mit Zu- und Ablauf für Kühlwasser

4: Vorlage (Meßkolben mit 200, bzw. 250 ml Inhalt)

5: Gasbrenner (oder Spiegelbrenner)

6: Stativ

7: Asbestdrahtnetz (erübrigt sich bei Verwendung eines Spiegelbrenners)

Weiteres Material:

Meßzylinder (Inhalt 500 ml)

Spritzflasche für dest. Wasser

Siedesteine

Silicon-Antischaumlösung

Alkoholometer (Meßbereich je nach Probe)

Spindelzylinder, dazu passend

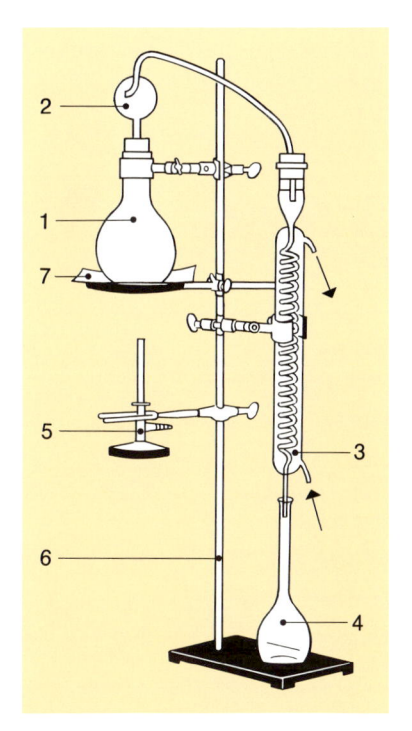

Abb. 51: Destillationsvorrichtung

G

Arbeitsanleitung

- Durchschnittsmuster herstellen (besonders wichtig bei Maischen: nach gutem Umrühren mehrere Liter entnehmen und vor dem Abmessen nochmals vermischen, s. Abschn. 2)
- Probe nötigenfalls durch genügend langes Stehenlassen auf Raumtemperatur bringen (ca. 20°C)
- Probe abmessen (erforderliche Menge und Art des Meßgefäßes s. Tab. 10)
- Gegebenenfalls Wasser zusetzen (s. Tab. 10), gut vermischen
- Inhalt des Meßgefäßes vollständig in den Destillierkolben überführen (Meßgefäß dreimal mit je ca. 20 ml Wasser ausspülen und Spülwasser jedesmal in den Destillierkolben geben)
- 5-8 Siedesteine und bei Maischen 2-3 Tropfen Antischaumlösung zugeben
- Destillierkolben gasdicht an den Destillieraufsatz anschließen
- Vorlagekolben (Inhalt s. Tab. 10) mit ca.10 ml destilliertem Wasser füllen und so unter den Kühler stellen, daß das Kühlerende ins Wasser taucht. Im Falle von Spirituosen empfiehlt es sich zudem, den Vorlagekolben in ein Eis/Wasser-Gemisch zu stellen
- Kühlwasser einschalten
- langsam, unter guter Kühlung destillieren: nachdem ca. 40 ml Destillat aufgefangen wurden, Vorlage so stellen, daß das Kühlerende etwas unter der Eichmarke liegt
- nachdem ca. drei Viertel (bei Spirituosen mindestens vier Fünftel) der Vorlage gefüllt sind, Destillation abbrechen und Kolben unter Abspülen des Kühlerendes mit destilliertem Wasser bis nahe zur Marke füllen; Inhalt gut vermischen
- Vorlage verschlossen während einiger Zeit stehen lassen, bis der Inhalt Raumtemperatur aufweist (ca. 20°C), anschließend

Tab. 10: Angaben zur Arbeitsanleitung (alle Volumenangaben in ml)

Probe	Abzumessende Menge	Meßgefäß (Volumen)	Wasserzusatz (ohne Spülw.)	Vorlagevolumen	Ausbeutefaktor*
Spirituosen (extrakthaltig)	200	Meßkolben (200)	–	200	–
Most	300	Meßzylinder (500)	–	200	0,67
Dünnflüssige Maische	200	Meßzylinder (500)	50	200	–
Dickflüssige Maische	200	Meßzylinder (500)	150	200	–
Dickbreiige Maische	200	Meßzylinder (500)	250	250	1,25

* wird nur benötigt, falls die abgemessene Probemenge nicht mit dem Vorlagevolumen übereinstimmt.

- Kolbeninhalt mit destilliertem Wasser genau bis zur Marke füllen und nochmals gut vermischen
- Destillat in den Spindelzylinder geben und aräometrische Alkoholbestimmung ausführen (s. 4.1.1).

Berechnung der Alkoholausbeute von Maischen und Mosten

a) Abgemessene Probemenge stimmt mit dem Vorlagevolumen überein: Der ermittelte wahre Alkoholgehalt des Destillates (in % vol) entspricht der Alkoholausbeute in l reinem Alkohol pro 100 l Most bzw. Maische.

b) Abgemessene Probemenge stimmt mit dem Vorlagevolumen nicht überein: Der ermittelte wahre Alkoholgehalt multipliziert mit dem **Ausbeutefaktor** ergibt die Alkoholausbeute in l reinem Alkohol pro 100 l Most bzw. Maische.

Beispiel: 300 ml Most wurden in eine Vorlage von 200 ml Inhalt destilliert. Wahrer Alkoholgehalt des Destillates: 7,9% vol. Ausbeutefaktor gem. Tabelle: 0,67. Ausbeute = 7,9 x 0,67 = **5,3 l r.A./100 l** Most.

4.2 Ebullioskopie

Die Alkoholbestimmung mittels Ebullioskop beruht auf der Messung der Siedetemperatur einer Probelösung. Diese liegt umso tiefer, je höher der Alkoholgehalt ist. Das in der Praxis verbreitete Ebullioskop nach Malligand (s. Abb. 52) erlaubt die Bestimmung von Alkoholgehalten bis max. 20% vol, da in diesem Bereich eine besonders ausgeprägte Abhängigkeit der Siedetemperatur vom Alkoholgehalt besteht. Anstelle einer Temperaturskala ist das Thermometer mit einer Volumenprozenteinteilung versehen, so daß das Resultat direkt abgelesen werden kann. Von Vorteil ist außerdem der geringe Bedarf an Probemenge (ca. 40 ml) und Zeit (wenige Minuten). Da die Siedetemperatur auch von den Extraktstoffen beeinflußt wird, eignet sich diese Methode in erster Linie zur Bestimmung der Ausbeute, also für zuckerarme, praktisch vollständig vergorene Moste und Maischen. Wegen der Druckabhängigkeit der Siedetemperatur muß das Gerät vor der Bestimmung mit Wasser geeicht werden.

Arbeitsanleitung

a) Eichung:
- Kochgefäß bis zur unteren der beiden im Inneren angebrachten Ringmarken mit destilliertem Wasser füllen
- Thermometeraufsatz vorsichtig aufschrauben
- mit Spritbrenner erhitzen, bis der Quecksilberfaden des Thermometers endgültig stehen bleibt
- Nullpunkt der verschiebbaren Skala genau auf den Endpunkt des Quecksilberfadens einstellen; Skala mittels Rändelschraube fixieren

b) Messung:
- Kochgefäß zweimal mit der zu untersuchenden Probe (Most, Maische**filtrat**, s. Abschn. 2) ausspülen und anschließend bis zur oberen der beiden im Inneren angebrachten Ringmarken füllen

- Thermometeraufsatz vorsichtig aufschrauben
- Kühler mit kaltem Wasser füllen und aufschrauben
- mit Spritbrenner erhitzen, bis der Quecksilberfaden des Thermometers endgültig stehen bleibt
- Alkoholgehalt (in % vol) sofort ablesen.

Bemerkungen: 1. Das Aufsetzen des Kühlers ist bei der Eichung nicht erforderlich, da das reine Wasser beim Entweichen von Wasserdampf seine Siedetemperatur nicht verändert. Hingegen muß das Kühlwasser vor jeder Messung erneuert werden, um ein Entweichen von Alkoholdämpfen zu verhindern. 2. Eine erneute Eichung mit Wasser ist erforderlich, wenn sich der Barometerstand verändert hat.

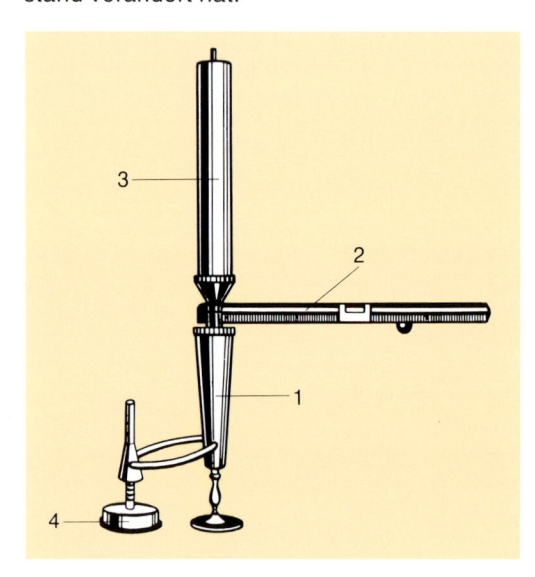

Es bedeuten

1: Kochgefäß

2: Thermometer mit Volumenprozentskala

3: Kühler

4: Spritbrenner

Abb. 52: Ebullioskop nach Malligand

Berechnung der Alkoholausbeute
Bei Mosten entspricht der abgelesene Alkoholgehalt der Ausbeute in l r.A./100 l. Hingegen bezieht sich bei Maischen das abgelesene Resultat auf das **Filtrat** (eine direkte Bestimmung in der Maische ist nicht möglich). Zur Umrechnung auf Maische ist man auf den von der Obstart abhängigen **Tresterfaktor T** angewiesen (s. 3.4.1). Die Formel lautet: Alkoholausbeute = abgelesener Alkoholgehalt x T.

4.3 Interpretation der Meßergebnisse

Weichen die ermittelten Alkoholausbeuten wesentlich von den erwarteten (s. 3.4) ab, so sollten die möglichen Gründe eines Alkoholverlustes sorgfältig abgeklärt werden (Fehlgärungen, unvollständige Gärung, undichte Behälter usw.). Zudem ist es wichtig, die Ausbeutezahlen nach Rohmaterial, Jahrgang und anderen Kriterien zu ordnen. Damit verschafft sich jeder Praktiker ein Bild über die Verhältnisse im eigenen Betrieb. Als Beispiel ist in Tab. 11 eine Auswahl von Ausbeutezahlen der Eidg. Alkoholverwaltung zusammengestellt.

Tab. 11: **Mittlere Alkoholausbeute aus 100 kg Rohstoffen**[1]
(aus den statistischen Angaben der Eidg. Alkoholverwaltung 1993)

Rohstoffe	Liter 100% vol	Rohstoffe	Liter 100% vol
Äpfel	4,5–5,5	Weintrauben	6–9
Birnen	4,1–4,7	Traubentrester	3,5–4,5
Williamsbirnen	3,5–4	Wein	8–11
Quitten	2,5–3	Weinhefen	5,5–6,5
Obstwein	5–6	Weinresten	7–10
Hefe, Trubsatz	4,5–5,5		
Kernobsttrester	3,3–4	Erdbeeren	3–4
		Brombeeren	2–3
Aprikosen	3,5–4	Heidelbeeren	3–4
Kirschen	5,5–6,5	Himbeeren	2–3
Weichselkirschen	4–5	Holunder	2,5–3
Mirabellen	6–7	Johannisbeeren	3,5–4,5
Pfirsiche	3,5–4	Wacholder	10–12
Pflaumen	4,5–5,5	Cassis	3,5–4,5
Reineclauden	4,5–5		
Zwetschgen	4,8–5,5	Enzianmaische	2–3
Schlehen	3–3,5	Enzianwurzeln	4–5

[1] Die mittleren Ausbeutezahlen können je nach dem Jahrgang, dem Reifegrad, der Sorte und Herkunft der Früchte und der daraus gewonnenen Erzeugnisse höher oder niedriger ausfallen

5 pH-Wert

Der pH-Wert als Maß für den sauren Charakter wässeriger Lösungen ist in der Obstbrennerei aus zwei Gründen von Bedeutung: Zum einen ist die Tätigkeit von Mikroorganismen wie Hefen und Bakterien pH-abhängig und kann deshalb durch Verschiebung des pH-Wertes gefördert oder unterbunden werden (s. B.2.2).

Zum anderen besteht ein Zusammenhang zwischen dem pH-Wert und dem Verhältnis freie/gebundene Säuren einer Lösung. Betrachten wir zum Beispiel verdünnte Essigsäure: die Lösung reagiert sauer, d.h. ihr pH-Wert liegt tiefer als jener einer neutralen Lösung (pH = 7, s. Abb. 53). Außerdem weist sie den typischen Essiggeruch auf, was bedeutet, daß Essigsäure in freier Form vorliegt. Erhöhen wir nun den pH-Wert durch Zugabe von Lauge, so erhöht sich auch der Anteil der in gebundener Form vorhandenen Säure. Wie Tab. 12 entnommen werden kann, ist Essigsäure bei pH 7 (Neutralpunkt) zu mehr als 99% abgebunden, was man unschwer am Verschwinden des Essiggeruchs erkennen kann.

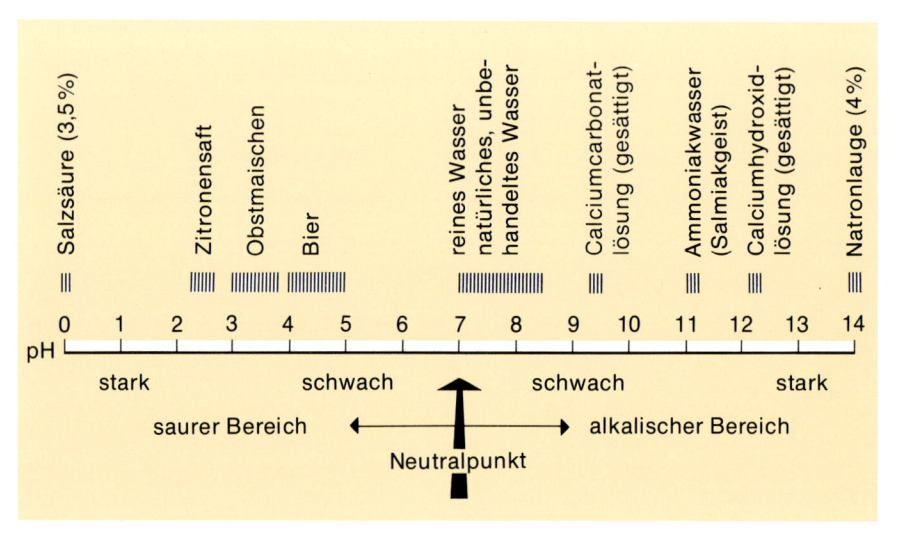

Abb. 53: pH-Skala mit Beispielen

Praktisch ergibt sich daraus für den Brenner die Möglichkeit, Maischen und Destillate mit einem zu hohen Gehalt an flüchtigen Säuren (Essigsäure, schweflige Säure) **vor** dem Ab- oder Umbrand mit Lauge zu behandeln. Damit werden die Säuren in ihre nichtflüchtige Form übergeführt und können somit auch nicht ins Destillat gelangen. Eine vollständige Neutralisation ist dabei weder nötig noch empfehlenswert, da ein gewisser Säuregehalt in Branntweinen normal ist. Über die Abhängigkeit des freien bzw. gebundenen Anteils der Essigsäure vom pH-Wert orientiert Tab. 12.

5.1 Bestimmung mit Indikatoren

Indikatoren sind Farbstoffe, die je nach dem pH-Wert der Lösung, in welcher sie enthalten sind, ihre Farbe ändern können. Am einfachsten erfolgt die pH-Messung mittels **Indikatorpapier** oder **Indikatorstäbchen** aus Kunststoff.

Tab. 12: Anteile der freien bzw. gebundenen Essigsäure (wässerige Lösung) in Abhängigkeit vom pH-Wert (hervorgehoben ist der für die Brennereipraxis besonders wichtige Bereich).

pH-Wert	Anteil an gebundener Essigsäure (%)	Anteil an freier Essigsäure (%)
2,0	0,2	99,8
3,0	1,7	98,3
4,0	14,8	85,2
4,76	50,0	50,0
5,0	63,5	36,5
5,2	73,4	26,6
5,4	**81,4**	**18,6**
5,6	**87,4**	**12,6**
5,8	**91,6**	**8,4**
6,0	94,6	5,4
6,5	98,2	1,8
7,0	99,4	0,6
8,0	99,9	0,1

Diese sind mit einem Indikatorgemisch versehen und werden kurz in die zu untersuchende Flüssigkeit eingetaucht. Anhand des gebildeten Farbtons sowie einer Reihe von Vergleichsfarben läßt sich nun mit guter Näherung auf den pH-Wert der Probelösung schließen. Für die Belange der Obstbrennerei genügen z. B. Indikatorstäbchen mit Abstufungen von 0,2–0,3 pH-Einheiten vollauf (Meßbereiche 2,5–4,5 bzw. 4,0–7,0). Allgemein verwendbar und in vielen Fällen nützlich sind Universal-Indikatorstäbchen für den gesamten pH-Bereich von 0–14 (Abstufung eine pH-Einheit).

Wichtig: Indikatorstäbchen bzw. -papiere (im Handel sind z. B. Packungen zu 100 Stück, Abreißheftchen oder Rollen) sind zum **einmaligen Gebrauch** bestimmt. Sie müssen **trocken** und **vor Dämpfen geschützt** aufbewahrt werden.

5.2 Elektrometrische Bestimmung

Exakter, als dies mit Indikatoren möglich ist, kann der pH-Wert nur mit einer speziellen Meßvorrichtung bestimmt werden. Diese besteht aus Meßgerät und der in die Probelösung einzutauchenden Elektrode (s. Abb. 54). Dort, wo ein solches zur Verfügung steht, halte man sich genau an die vom Hersteller mitgelieferte Bedienungsanleitung. Es sind auch batteriebetriebene Geräte im Taschenformat erhältlich. Im Prinzip gliedert sich die Bestimmung wie folgt:

a) Eichung: Diese erfolgt mit zwei Pufferlösungen, wobei die eine im Neutralbereich, die andere im Meßbereich (z. B. pH 4–5) liegen soll. Die Eichung ist täglich vor der ersten Messung durchzuführen.

b) Messung: Elektrode in die Probelösung eintauchen, entsprechenden Meßbereich wählen und pH-Wert bei konstanter Anzeige ablesen.

Wichtig: Zur Aufbewahrung ist die Elektrode in die vom Hersteller vorgeschriebene Elektrolyt-Lösung einzutauchen. Man beachte auch die Mindestfüllhöhe der Bezugselektroden-Flüssigkeit.

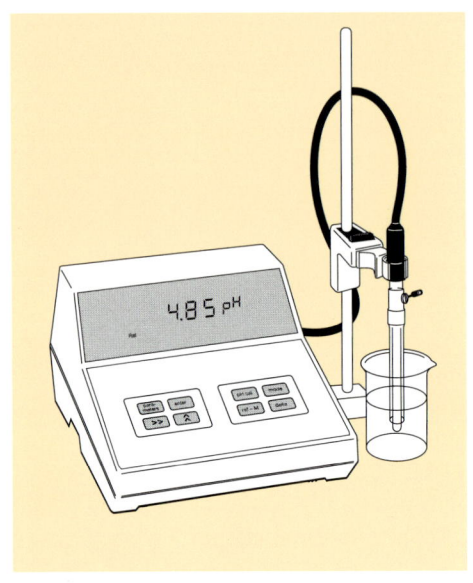

Abb. 54: pH-Meßgerät mit Elektrode

6 Flüchtige Säuren

Als »flüchtige Säuren« bezeichnet man die Gesamtheit aller mit Wasserdampf flüchtigen organischen Säuren. Zur Hauptsache handelt es sich dabei um Essigsäure, daneben liegen auch geringe Mengen an Ameisen- und Propionsäure vor. Vergorene Maischen mit einem erhöhten Gehalt an flüchtigen Säuren lassen auf unerwünschte Bakterientätigkeit schließen; sie sind deshalb als gefährdet zu betrachten und zuerst abzubrennen. Bei deutlich essigstichigen Maischen ist zudem unmittelbar vor dem Abbrennen eine teilweise Neutralisation vorzunehmen (s. F. 3.1.1).

Flüchtige Säuren in g/l Maischefiltrat	Beurteilung	Maßnahmen
unter 2 g/l	normal	keine
2–4 g/l	leicht erhöhte flüchtige Säuren	Maische nicht länger lagern bzw. leicht neutralisieren
über 4 g/l	erhöhte flüchtige Säuren; Gefahr erhöhter Esterbildung	neutralisieren und sofort brennen!

Die Bestimmung der flüchtigen Säuren kann in einfacher Weise mit dem **Flüchtigsäuremesser** (Abb. 55) vorgenommen werden. Dieser ist im Fachhandel mit allem erforderlichen Zubehör (inkl. Reagenzien) erhältlich.

Arbeitsanleitung
- Kühler vor jeder Bestimmung aus der an dem oberen Flüssigkeitsstutzen angeschlossenen Vorratsflasche mit kaltem Wasser füllen (angewärmtes Wasser nach jeder Bestimmung am unteren Stutzen mit Quetschhahn in der zweiten Flasche auffangen) oder bei entsprechender Untersuchungskapazität kontinuierlich kühlen (in diesem Falle wird das Kühlwasser über den unteren Stutzen zugeführt und über den oberen Stutzen abgeleitet)
- am Ventil Leitungswasser in die Spezialpipette bis zur obersten Ringmarke aufsaugen (dabei Quetschhahn drücken) und Spezialpipette auf das Destillierrohr aufsetzen

Es bedeuten

1: Spezialpipette

2: Destillierrohr mit

3: Wasserkühler

4: Destillierkolben

5: Spiritusbrenner

6: Vorratsflasche mit Kühlwasser

7: Flüchtigsäure-Meßzylinder (Vorlage)

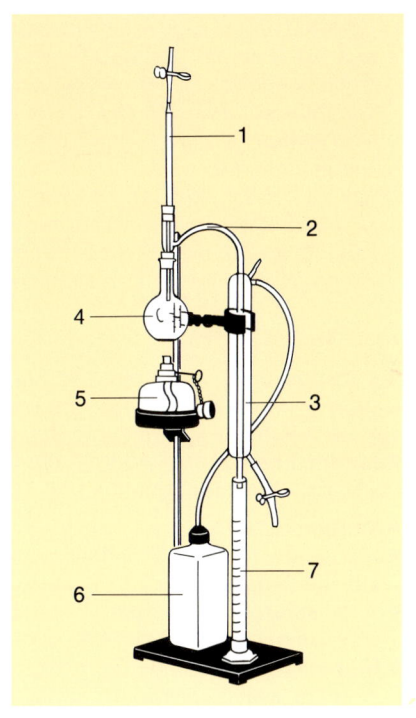

Abb. 55: Flüchtigsäuremesser

- 5,0 ml Maischefiltrat (s. Abschn. 2) in den Destillierkolben pipettieren
- 1 Löffel Siedegemisch und 1 Tropfen Antischaum-Lösung beifügen
- Destillierkolben an den Siliconstopfen des Destillierrohrs anschließen
- Flüchtigsäure-Meßzylinder unter Kühler stellen
- Spritbrenner anzünden und so unter Destillierkolben bringen, daß der Abstand des Dochtes vom Boden des Kolbens ca. 3 cm beträgt. Destillieren. Hat das Destillat die erste Ringmarke des Flüchtigsäure-Meßzylinders erreicht, Quetschhahn der Pipette drücken und Wasser bis zur nächsttieferen Ring-

marke in den Destillierkolben auslaufen lassen, weiterdestillieren bis zur zweiten Ringmarke des Meßzylinders, Quetschhahn der Pipette erneut drücken und Wasser bis zur nächsten Ringmarke der Pipette ausfließen lassen, weiterdestillieren bis zur dritten Ringmarke des Meßzylinders, restliches Wasser aus der Pipette in den Destillierkolben entleeren und bis zur Nullmarke des Meßzylinders weiterdestillieren. Sobald Nullmarke erreicht ist, Flüchtigsäure-Meßzylinder entfernen und Spritbrenner ausschwenken oder löschen
- 1 Tropfen Indikator-Lösung zum Destillat im Meßzylinder geben
- aus Tropfflasche unter Schwenken des Meßzylinders 0,01 N Natronlauge zusetzen, bis die entstehende hellrote Färbung der Flüssigkeit ca. 1/2 Minute bestehen bleibt
- am Flüchtigsäure-Meßzylinder den Gehalt der untersuchten Probe in g flüchtigen Säuren/l ablesen.

Bemerkungen:
1) 0,01 N Natronlauge ist nicht lagerstabil. Sie sollte in 4-Wochen-Intervallen aus 0,1 N Natronlauge zubereitet werden. Man pipettiere 10,0 ml 0,1 N Natronlauge in einen 100-ml-Meßkolben, fülle destilliertes Wasser genau bis zur Ringmarke nach und mische den Ansatz gut. Er wird anschließend in die Vorratsflasche für 0,01 N Lauge entleert. Auf der Vorratsflasche das Herstelldatum notieren.
2) Bei zu hohen Gehalten an flüchtigen Säuren muß das Maischefiltrat im 100-ml-Meßkolben verdünnt werden (z.B. 50 ml Maischefiltrat mit Wasser auf 100 ml verdünnen = Verdünnungsfaktor 2). Das abgelesene Resultat ist mit dem Verdünnungsfaktor zu multiplizieren.

7 Wasserhärte

Auf die negativen Auswirkungen bei der Verwendung von zu hartem Verschnittwasser wurde bereits hingewiesen (s. F. 2.1.1). Die Kontrolle von Verschnittwasser auf Resthärte erfolgt mit einem gebrauchsfertig im Fachhandel erhältlichen **Reagenziensatz** (Aquamerck Wasserhärtebestimmung). Dieser besteht aus Meßgefäß, Indikatortabletten und Titrierlösung.

Arbeitsanleitung
- Meßgefäß mehrmals mit dem zu untersuchenden Wasser spülen und dann bis zur Strichmarke füllen
- 1 Indikatortablette zugeben und Zerfall durch kreisendes Umschwenken beschleunigen (Indikatortablette ist nicht vollständig löslich)
- Beurteilung anhand der Färbung:

Färbung	Wasserhärte (°d)	Beurteilung/Maßnahmen
grün	0	Das untersuchte
graugrün	0,02	Wasser ist als
grauviolett	0,05	Verschnittwasser
rotviolett	0,1	geeignet
rot	höher als 0,1	– Endgültige Beurteilung erst nach Titration (s. unten) – Austauscher regenerieren (s. E. 1.2.2)

● Ist die Untersuchungslösung deutlich rot gefärbt, Titrierlösung **tropfenweise** zugeben, bis der **Farbumschlag nach grün** erfolgt. **Wichtig:** Tropfpipette senkrecht halten und Meßgefäß nach jedem Tropfen umschwenken. **Tropfen zählen.**

Die Härte des untersuchten Wassers (°d) entspricht der **Tropfenzahl** (für die Umrechnung in französische Härtegrade gilt: 1°d = 1,79°f). Als Verschnittwasser ist nur sehr weiches Wasser (0–4°d bzw. 0–7°f) geeignet.

8 Titrierbare Säuren

Unter »titrierbaren Säuren« (auch Gesamtsäure) versteht man die Gesamtheit der vorhandenen **freien** Säuren, mit Ausnahme von Kohlensäure. Letztere ist vor der Bestimmung durch kräftiges Schütteln aus der Probelösung zu entfernen. Die Bestimmung der titrierbaren Säuren in essigstichigen **Maischen** dient zur Ermittlung der für die Neutralisation ungefähr **bereitzustellenden** Laugenmenge. Diese läßt sich anhand des Gehaltes an titrierbaren Säuren (berechnet als Wein-, Äpfel- oder Essigsäure) nachfolgender Tabelle entnehmen. **Die Einstellung des pH-Wertes auf 5,6–5,8 ist mit Indikatorpapier oder -stäbchen zu kontrollieren.**

Tab. 13: Neutralisation von Säuren. Die angegebenen Laugenmengen beziehen sich auf 1 hl (100 l) je Gramm titrierbare Säuren/l

titr. Säuren berechnet als	Ätznatron NaOH	Natronlauge NaOH 32%	gelöschter Kalk $Ca(OH)_2$	kohlensaurer Kalk $CaCO_3$
Weinsäure	50 g	110 ml	45 g	60 g
Äpfelsäure	55 g	125 ml	50 g	70 g
Essigsäure	60 g	140 ml	55 g	80 g

Beispiel: 4,5 hl einer stichigen Kirschenmaische müssen gebrannt werden. Der Gehalt an titrierbaren Säuren (berechnet als Essigsäure) beträgt 12,5 g/l. Wieviel kohlensaurer Kalk ($CaCO_3$) ist zur Abstumpfung der Säuren ungefähr erforderlich?

Lösung: Zuerst Tabellenwert suchen (Essigsäure/kohlensaurer Kalk) → **80 g.**
Gesuchte Menge = Tabellenwert x Anzahl hl x titr. Säuren
= 80 g x 4,5 x 12,5
= **4500 g** oder 4,5 kg.

In **Destillaten** entspricht der Gehalt an titrierbaren Säuren weitgehend der vorhandenen Essigsäure. Erhöhte Werte sind über einen Verschnitt oder durch Abstumpfen der Säure auf pH 5,6 mit anschließendem Umbrand zu korrigieren. Die erforderliche Laugenmenge ist dabei in oben angegebener Weise zu ermitteln. Oft genügt es auch, nur einen Teil des Destillates zu behandeln und mit dem nicht behandelten Anteil in geeigneter Weise zu verschneiden (s. F.3.1.2).

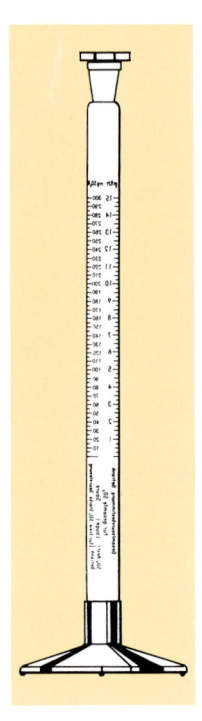

Zur Bestimmung der titrierbaren Säuren eignet sich der aus der Weinanalytik bekannte **Titrovin-Zylinder** (Abb. 56), welcher außerdem für die Bestimmung der schwefligen Säure eingesetzt werden kann (s. Abschnitt 9). Die zur Titration verwendete **Blaulauge** (Natronlauge mit Indikator) ist gebrauchsfertig im Fachhandel erhältlich.

Wichtig: Die **Skala** des Meßzylinders bezieht sich auf **Weinsäure**. Für die Angabe als Essig- oder Äpfelsäure ist der abgelesene Wert mit den Faktoren 0,8 bzw. 0,9 zu multiplizieren.

Arbeitsanleitung

- Probelösung nötigenfalls durch kräftiges Schütteln von Kohlensäure befreien
- Titrovin-Zylinder mit dem zu untersuchenden Maischefiltrat bzw. Destillat ausspülen
- Probe bis zum untersten Strich der **roten** Skala (Nullmarke) einfüllen
- Titrovin-Blaulauge tropfenweise zusetzen, wobei die Lösung jeweils durch langsames Umkippen des mit Gummistopfen verschlossenen Zylinders zu vermischen ist
- nach dem Farbumschlag Zylinder auf horizontale Unterlage stellen und Gesamtsäuregehalt an der **roten** Skala ablesen (Angabe in Gramm Weinsäure pro Liter untersuchte Probe)
- nötigenfalls Umrechnungen vornehmen.

Abb. 56: Titrovin-Zylinder zur Bestimmung der titrierbaren Säuren

9 Schweflige Säure

In Brennsäften übersteigt der Gehalt an schwefliger Säure die kritische Grenze bei der üblichen SO_2-Dosierung normalerweise nicht; hingegen kann stark geschwefeltes Brenngut (z. B. zugekaufte Obstweine und Weine, ausländische Williamsmaischen usw.) zu geruchlich und geschmacklich beeinträchtigten Destillaten führen. Zur Vorbeugung empfiehlt es sich, die gesamte schweflige Säure zu bestimmen und im Falle von höher als 60–70 mg SO_2/l liegenden Werten vor dem Abbrand eine Neutralisation vorzunehmen (s. F. 3.2.5).

Die Bestimmung der gesamten schwefligen Säure läßt sich ebenfalls im **Titrovin-Zylinder** durchführen (s. Abschnitt 8). An Reagenzien werden zusätzlich Titrovin-Lauge, -Säure und -Jodat/Jodidlösung benötigt.

Arbeitsanleitung

- Titrovin-Zylinder mit der zu untersuchenden Probelösung (Brennsaft, Maischefiltrat) ausspülen
- Probe bis zur untersten **gelben** Strichmarke einfüllen
- Titrovin-Lauge bis zur **grünen** Strichmarke über der Anschrift »Lauge« einfüllen; Inhalt durch langsames Umkippen des Zylinders mischen
- nach ca. 10 Minuten Titrovin-Säure bis zum untersten Strich (Nullmarke) der **gelben** Skala einfüllen, Inhalt mischen

- sofort tropfenweise Jodat/Jodidlösung zugeben. Nach jeder Zugabe Zylinderinhalt unter Vermeidung von Schaumbildung durchmischen (Gummistopfen aufsetzen)
- nach dem Farbumschlag (Blaufärbung der Lösung bleibt während mindestens 10 Sekunden bestehen) Zylinder auf horizontale Unterlage stellen und Gesamt-SO_2-Gehalt an der **gelben** Skala ablesen (Angabe in mg SO_2 pro Liter untersuchte Probe).

Hinweis: Die Methode eignet sich für helle oder farbschwache Probelösungen. Für die Untersuchung stark gefärbter Proben genügt es oft, eine Verdünnung mit Wasser vorzunehmen (z. B. 1 Teil Probe und 1 Teil Wasser; Verdünnungsfaktor 2). Das abgelesene Resultat ist mit dem Verdünnungsfaktor zu multiplizieren. Läßt sich der Farbumschlag auch nach Vornahme einer Verdünnung nicht eindeutig feststellen, empfiehlt es sich, die Probelösung zuerst mit Aktivkohle zu entfärben (1 Teelöffel Aktivkohle pro 100 ml Probe, schütteln und filtrieren).

10 Ester

Die Kenntnis des Estergehaltes erlaubt es im Falle von erhöhten Werten, geeignete Verbesserungsmaßnahmen vorzunehmen (s. F. 3.1.2). Die zur Bestimmung erforderliche Apparatur ist in Abb. 57 dargestellt.

Es bedeuten

1: Stehkolben (200 ml Inhalt) mit Schliff, dazu passender

2: Kugelkühler (Länge ca. 30 cm), mit Zu- und Ablauf für Kühlwasser; Befestigung mit Stativ

3: Dreibein mit Drahtnetz

4: Gasbrenner (auch Spritbrenner kann verwendet werden)

Weiteres Material:

1 Pipette (50 ml)

2 Titrationsbüretten (50 ml), mit 0,1-ml-Einteilung

2 Trichter zum Einfüllen der Reagenzien

2 Becherglaser (100 ml), als Auffangbehälter für Büretteninhalt

3 Stative mit Befestigungsklammern (für Kühler und Büretten)

Reagenzien:

(gebrauchsfertig im Fachhandel erhältlich)

Natronlauge, 0,1 N
Schwefelsäure, 0,1 N
Phenolphthalein-Lösung, 1%ig in Alkohol
Siedesteine

Abb. 57: Apparatur zur Esterbestimmung

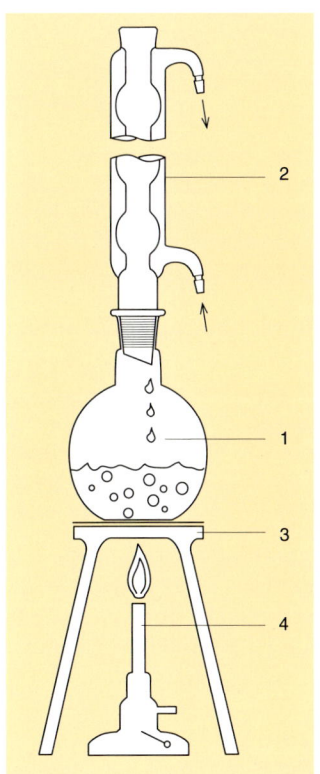

G

Arbeitsanleitung
- 50,0 ml der zu untersuchenden Spirituose in den Stehkolben pipettieren und einige Tropfen Phenolphthalein-Lösung zugeben
- unter ständigem Umschwenken des Kolbens aus der Bürette soviel Natronlauge zugeben, bis der Kolbeninhalt schwach rosa gefärbt ist (Kolben vor eine weiße Unterlage halten!)
- Kolbeninhalt mit einem genau bemessenen Überschuß an Natronlauge versetzen (siehe Bemerkung am Schluß). Der Kolbeninhalt färbt sich tiefrot
- einige Siedesteine zusetzen und Kolben gasdicht (Schliff) an den Kühler anschließen
- Kühlwasser einschalten
- Kolbeninhalt mit Gas- oder Spritbrenner erwärmen und während 30 Minuten leicht sieden lassen (rote Färbung muß bestehen bleiben)
- nach dem Abkühlen Kühler entfernen und unter stetigem Umschwenken des Kolbens Schwefelsäure aus der Bürette zugeben, bis die Rotfärbung verschwindet und nur noch ein schwaches Rosa sichtbar ist (gleicher Farbton wie vor Zugabe des Laugenüberschusses)
- an der Bürettenskala Säureverbrauch auf 0,1 ml genau ablesen.

Bemerkung: Die Menge des Laugenüberschusses ist dem zu erwartenden Estergehalt anzupassen. Sie beträgt bei normalen Estergehalten für

Weinbrand	8–10 ml
Kernobstbranntwein	ca. 15 ml
Kirsch, Zwetschgenwasser, Williams	20–30 ml

Die Laugenmenge soll so bemessen sein, daß zur Rücktitration mindestens 3 ml, möglichst aber nicht mehr als 10 ml Schwefelsäure verbraucht werden. Verschwindet im Verlaufe der Kochdauer die Rotfärbung (zu geringer Laugenüberschuß), so muß die Bestimmung mit einer größeren Laugenmenge wiederholt werden (erhöhter Estergehalt!).

Berechnung des Estergehaltes

$$\text{Estergehalt, in mg Essigester pro 100 ml r. A.} = \frac{1762 \times (a-b)}{A}$$

wobei

a = vorgelegter Überschuß an 0,1 N Natronlauge
b = zur Rücktitration verbrauchte 0,1 N Schwefelsäure
A = Alkoholgehalt des Destillates (in % vol).

Beispiel: Bestimmung des Estergehaltes in einem degustativ an Nagellack erinnernden Kirschwasser (Alkoholgehalt 51,1 % vol)
vorgelegter Überschuß an 0,1 N Natronlauge: a = 40,0 ml
zur Rücktitration verbrauchte 0,1 N Schwefelsäure: b = 3,7 ml

$$\text{Estergehalt} = \frac{1762 \times (40,0-3,7)}{51,1} = \mathbf{1252 \text{ mg}/100 \text{ ml r.A.}}$$

Der Kirsch muß behandelt werden!

11 Nachweis von Eisen, Kupfer und Zink

Die Anwesenheit von Eisen, Kupfer und – seltener – Zink ist in Destillaten immer wieder Ursache von Trübungen und Verfärbungen. Der **Nachweis** dieser Schwermetalle kann direkt in dem auf **ca. 30 % vol** verdünnten Destillat vorgenommen werden. Das dazu benötigte Reagenz läßt sich in einfacher Weise durch Auflösen einer Messerspitze (ca. 1 g) **Kaliumhexacyanoferrat** (gelbes Blutlaugensalz) in 100 ml enthärtetem Wasser herstellen. Nachweisreaktionen: wenige Milliliter des zu untersuchenden Destillats mit ca. 5 Tropfen Kaliumhexacyanoferrat-Reagenz versetzen und umschwenken.

Blaufärbung ist ein Beweis für die Anwesenheit von **Eisen**,
Rotfärbung weist auf **Kupfer** hin, während eine
grau-weiße Flockung auf **Zink** schließen läßt.

Bleibt die Untersuchungslösung auch nach längerem Stehenlassen leicht gelblich gefärbt (Eigenfarbe des Reagenz), so ist das Destillat weitgehend frei von Schwermetallen. Kleinere Konzentrationen könnten allenfalls mit empfindlicheren Methoden nachgewiesen werden.

Das Ausmaß einer Schwermetallaufnahme läßt sich mit einiger Übung an der Trübungs- bzw. Färbungsintensität erkennen. Hilfreich sind zu diesem Zweck auch die im Fachhandel erhältlichen **Teststäbchen** für Eisen, Kupfer oder Zink, welche in gleicher Weise wie die Indikatorstäbchen zur pH-Messung kurz in das Destillat getaucht werden. Der Schwermetallgehalt kann hierauf mit Hilfe einer Farbskala abgeschätzt werden.

12 Vorlauftest

Eine ausreichende Vorlaufabtrennung zu Beginn der Destillation gehört mit zu den wichtigen Voraussetzungen für die Gewinnung einwandfreier Mittelläufe. Auf der anderen Seite ist es nicht notwendig, immer die gleiche Vorlaufmenge abzutrennen. Die degustative Überwachung des Brennvorgangs hilft mit, den dem Brenngut angepaßten, optimalen Zeitpunkt zum Umschalten auf Mittellauf zu erkennen (s. C.3.1.2). Dies setzt aber auch einige Erfahrung voraus.
In Zweifelsfällen kann die Ermittlung der Vorlaufmenge auch anhand eines gebrauchsfertig im Fachhandel erhältlichen Vorlaufabtrennungs-Tests erfolgen. Dieser beruht auf dem Nachweis von Acetaldehyd als typischer Vorlaufkomponente. Dabei wird die Destillatprobe mit drei Reagenzienlösungen vermischt und die sich bildende Farbe mit einer Farbbewertungstafel verglichen. So läßt sich innert 2–3 Minuten nach Entnahme der Probe entscheiden, ob die Vorlaufabtrennung ausreichend sei oder ob mit der Umschaltung auf Mittellauf noch zugewartet werden soll.
Eine detaillierte Arbeitsanleitung liegt jeder Grundausstattung des Tests bei. Die Reagenzien, deren Haltbarkeit beschränkt ist, können separat nachbestellt werden.

13 Blausäure

Steinobstmaischen und deren Destillate können erhöhte Mengen an freier und gebundener Blausäure enthalten. Die Blausäure wird vor allem beim Beschädigen der Steine, aber auch aus intakten Steinen während zu langer Maischelagerung freigesetzt. Beim Brennvorgang geht die flüchtige Blausäure in das Destillat über und kann dort in erhöhten Mengen zu Problemen führen, namentlich

- Steingeschmack, der das typische Fruchtaroma überdeckt (s. F.3.2.2)
- Überschreitung des gesetzlichen Höchstwertes für Blausäure (s. M.1.3)
- Bildung von Ethylcarbamat durch Lichteinwirkung (s. F.3.3).

In der Brennerei ist es daher wichtig, den Blausäuregehalt zu prüfen und mit geeigneten Verfahren, z.B. einem Cyanidabscheider (»Katalysator«, s. C.2.3) eine erhöhte Ethylcarbamat-Bildung zu verhindern. Durch regelmäßige Untersuchung der Destillate läßt sich außerdem entscheiden, wann eine Reinigung der Katalysatoroberfläche fällig ist (s. C.5).

Mit einem gebrauchsfertig im Fachhandel erhältlichen Farbtest läßt sich der Blausäuregehalt von Destillaten rasch und zuverlässig ermitteln. Jedem Testbesteck, welches für etwa 200 Bestimmungen ausreicht, liegt eine ausführliche Arbeitsanleitung bei. Die Reagenzien können separat nachbestellt werden.

H TABELLEN

1 Korrekturtabelle zur Ermittlung des Alkoholgehaltes (Volumenkonzentration) bei 20°C aus der Ablesung des Alkoholometers und der Meßtemperatur

    Ablesebereich: 34,0......................50,9 % vol
    Temperaturbereich: 0,0......................30,0°C

Beispiel: Ablesung (scheinbarer Alkoholgehalt)   37,7 % vol
          Meßtemperatur   14,4°C
          Alkoholgehalt bei 20°C   **40,0 % vol**

Tabelle H.1 ist ein Auszug aus Tafel 1 der Amtlichen Alkoholtafeln der BRD (s. Literaturverzeichnis O.2).

Achtung: Diese Tabelle setzt die Verwendung von bei 20°C geeichten Alkoholometern voraus (vgl. G. 4.1).

Volumenkonzentration bei 20 °C in Prozent

Temp. °C	Anzeige des Alkoholometers in % vol								
	34,0	34,1	34,2	34,3	34,4	34,5	34,6	34,7	34,8	34,9
0,0	42,2	42,3	42,4	42,5	42,6	42,7	42,8	42,9	43,0	43,1
0,2	42,2	42,3	42,4	42,5	42,5	42,6	42,7	42,8	42,9	43,0
0,4	42,1	42,2	42,3	42,4	42,5	42,6	42,7	42,7	42,8	42,9
0,6	42,0	42,1	42,2	42,3	42,4	42,5	42,6	42,7	42,8	42,9
0,8	41,9	42,0	42,1	42,2	42,3	42,4	42,5	42,6	42,7	42,8
1,0	41,8	41,9	42,0	42,1	42,2	42,3	42,4	42,5	42,6	42,7
1,2	41,8	41,8	41,9	42,0	42,1	42,2	42,3	42,4	42,5	42,6
1,4	41,7	41,8	41,9	42,0	42,1	42,1	42,2	42,3	42,4	42,5
1,6	41,6	41,7	41,8	41,9	42,0	42,1	42,2	42,3	42,3	42,4
1,8	41,5	41,6	41,7	41,8	41,9	42,0	42,1	42,2	42,3	42,4
2,0	41,4	41,5	41,6	41,7	41,8	41,9	42,0	42,1	42,2	42,3
2,2	41,3	41,4	41,5	41,6	41,7	41,8	41,9	42,0	42,1	42,2
2,4	41,3	41,4	41,4	41,5	41,6	41,7	41,8	41,9	42,0	42,1
2,6	41,2	41,3	41,4	41,5	41,6	41,7	41,7	41,8	41,9	42,0
2,8	41,1	41,2	41,3	41,4	41,5	41,6	41,7	41,8	41,9	42,0
3,0	41,0	41,1	41,2	41,3	41,4	41,5	41,6	41,7	41,8	41,9
3,2	40,9	41,0	41,1	41,2	41,3	41,4	41,5	41,6	41,7	41,8
3,4	40,8	40,9	41,0	41,1	41,2	41,3	41,4	41,5	41,6	41,7
3,6	40,8	40,9	41,0	41,0	41,1	41,2	41,3	41,4	41,5	41,6
3,8	40,7	40,8	40,9	41,0	41,1	41,2	41,3	41,3	41,4	41,5
4,0	40,6	40,7	40,8	40,9	41,0	41,1	41,2	41,3	41,4	41,5
4,2	40,5	40,6	40,7	40,8	40,9	41,0	41,1	41,2	41,3	41,4
4,4	40,4	40,5	40,6	40,7	40,8	40,9	41,0	41,1	41,2	41,3
4,6	40,3	40,4	40,5	40,6	40,7	40,8	40,9	41,0	41,1	41,2
4,8	40,3	40,4	40,5	40,6	40,6	40,7	40,8	40,9	41,0	41,1
5,0	40,2	40,3	40,4	40,5	40,6	40,7	40,8	40,9	41,0	41,0
5,2	40,1	40,2	40,3	40,4	40,5	40,6	40,7	40,8	40,9	41,0
5,4	40,0	40,1	40,2	40,3	40,4	40,5	40,6	40,7	40,8	40,9
5,6	39,9	40,0	40,1	40,2	40,3	40,4	40,5	40,6	40,7	40,8
5,8	39,8	39,9	40,0	40,1	40,2	40,3	40,4	40,5	40,6	40,7
6,0	39,8	39,9	40,0	40,1	40,2	40,2	40,3	40,4	40,5	40,6
6,2	39,7	39,8	39,9	40,0	40,1	40,2	40,3	40,4	40,5	40,6
6,4	39,6	39,7	39,8	39,9	40,0	40,1	40,2	40,3	40,4	40,5
6,6	39,5	39,6	39,7	39,8	39,9	40,0	40,1	40,2	40,3	40,4
6,8	39,4	39,5	39,6	39,7	39,8	39,9	40,0	40,1	40,2	40,3
7,0	39,3	39,4	39,5	39,6	39,7	39,8	39,9	40,0	40,1	40,2
7,2	39,3	39,4	39,5	39,6	39,7	39,8	39,9	39,9	40,0	40,1
7,4	39,2	39,3	39,4	39,5	39,6	39,7	39,8	39,9	40,0	40,1
7,6	39,1	39,2	39,3	39,4	39,5	39,6	39,7	39,8	39,9	40,0
7,8	39,0	39,1	39,2	39,3	39,4	39,5	39,6	39,7	39,8	39,9
8,0	38,9	39,0	39,1	39,2	39,3	39,4	39,5	39,6	39,7	39,8
8,2	38,8	38,9	39,0	39,1	39,2	39,3	39,4	39,5	39,6	39,7
8,4	38,8	38,9	39,0	39,1	39,2	39,3	39,4	39,5	39,6	39,7
8,6	38,7	38,8	38,9	39,0	39,1	39,2	39,3	39,4	39,5	39,6
8,8	38,6	38,7	38,8	38,9	39,0	39,1	39,2	39,3	39,4	39,5
9,0	38,5	38,6	38,7	38,8	38,9	39,0	39,1	39,2	39,3	39,4
9,2	38,4	38,5	38,6	38,7	38,8	38,9	39,0	39,1	39,2	39,3
9,4	38,4	38,5	38,5	38,6	38,7	38,8	38,9	39,0	39,1	39,2
9,6	38,3	38,4	38,5	38,6	38,7	38,8	38,9	39,0	39,1	39,2
9,8	38,2	38,3	38,4	38,5	38,6	38,7	38,8	38,9	39,0	39,1

Volumenkonzentration bei 20 °C in Prozent

Temp. °C	\	\	\	Anzeige des Alkoholometers in % vol					
	34,0	34,1	34,2	34,3	34,4	34,5	34,6	34,7	34,8	34,9
10,0	38,1	38,2	38,3	38,4	38,5	38,6	38,7	38,8	38,9	39,0
10,2	38,0	38,1	38,2	38,3	38,4	38,5	38,6	38,7	38,8	38,9
10,4	37,9	38,0	38,1	38,2	38,3	38,4	38,5	38,6	38,7	38,8
10,6	37,9	38,0	38,1	38,2	38,3	38,4	38,4	38,5	38,6	38,7
10,8	37,8	37,9	38,0	38,1	38,2	38,3	38,4	38,5	38,6	38,7
11,0	37,7	37,8	37,9	38,0	38,1	38,2	38,3	38,4	38,5	38,6
11,2	37,6	37,7	37,8	37,9	38,0	38,1	38,2	38,3	38,4	38,5
11,4	37,5	37,6	37,7	37,8	37,9	38,0	38,1	38,2	38,3	38,4
11,6	37,4	37,5	37,6	37,7	37,8	37,9	38,0	38,1	38,2	38,3
11,8	37,4	37,5	37,6	37,7	37,8	37,9	38,0	38,1	38,2	38,3
12,0	37,3	37,4	37,5	37,6	37,7	37,8	37,9	38,0	38,1	38,2
12,2	37,2	37,3	37,4	37,5	37,6	37,7	37,8	37,9	38,0	38,1
12,4	37,1	37,2	37,3	37,4	37,5	37,6	37,7	37,8	37,9	38,0
12,6	37,0	37,1	37,2	37,3	37,4	37,5	37,6	37,7	37,8	37,9
12,8	36,9	37,0	37,1	37,2	37,3	37,4	37,5	37,6	37,7	37,8
13,0	36,9	37,0	37,1	37,2	37,3	37,4	37,5	37,6	37,7	37,8
13,2	36,8	36,9	37,0	37,1	37,2	37,3	37,4	37,5	37,6	37,7
13,4	36,7	36,8	36,9	37,0	37,1	37,2	37,3	37,4	37,5	37,6
13,6	36,6	36,7	36,8	36,9	37,0	37,1	37,2	37,3	37,4	37,5
13,8	36,5	36,6	36,7	36,8	36,9	37,0	37,1	37,2	37,3	37,4
14,0	36,5	36,6	36,7	36,8	36,9	37,0	37,1	37,2	37,3	37,4
14,2	36,4	36,5	36,6	36,7	36,8	36,9	37,0	37,1	37,2	37,3
14,4	36,3	36,4	36,5	36,6	36,7	36,8	36,9	37,0	37,1	37,2
14,6	36,2	36,3	36,4	36,5	36,6	36,7	36,8	36,9	37,0	37,1
14,8	36,1	36,2	36,3	36,4	36,5	36,6	36,7	36,8	36,9	37,0
15,0	36,0	36,1	36,2	36,3	36,4	36,5	36,6	36,7	36,8	36,9
15,2	36,0	36,1	36,2	36,3	36,4	36,5	36,6	36,7	36,8	36,9
15,4	35,9	36,0	36,1	36,2	36,3	36,4	36,5	36,6	36,7	36,8
15,6	35,8	35,9	36,0	36,1	36,2	36,3	36,4	36,5	36,6	36,7
15,8	35,7	35,8	35,9	36,0	36,1	36,2	36,3	36,4	36,5	36,6
16,0	35,6	35,7	35,8	35,9	36,0	36,1	36,2	36,3	36,4	36,5
16,2	35,6	35,7	35,8	35,9	36,0	36,1	36,2	36,3	36,3	36,4
16,4	35,5	35,6	35,7	35,8	35,9	36,0	36,1	36,2	36,3	36,4
16,6	35,4	35,5	35,6	35,7	35,8	35,9	36,0	36,1	36,2	36,3
16,8	35,3	35,4	35,5	35,6	35,7	35,8	35,9	36,0	36,1	36,2
17,0	35,2	35,3	35,4	35,5	35,6	35,7	35,8	35,9	36,0	36,1
17,2	35,1	35,2	35,3	35,4	35,5	35,6	35,7	35,8	35,9	36,0
17,4	35,1	35,2	35,3	35,4	35,5	35,6	35,7	35,8	35,9	36,0
17,6	35,0	35,1	35,2	35,3	35,4	35,5	35,6	35,7	35,8	35,9
17,8	34,9	35,0	35,1	35,2	35,3	35,4	35,5	35,6	35,7	35,8
18,0	34,8	34,9	35,0	35,1	35,2	35,3	35,4	35,5	35,6	35,7
18,2	34,7	34,8	34,9	35,0	35,1	35,2	35,3	35,4	35,5	35,6
18,4	34,7	34,8	34,9	35,0	35,1	35,2	35,3	35,4	35,5	35,6
18,6	34,6	34,7	34,8	34,9	35,0	35,1	35,2	35,3	35,4	35,5
18,8	34,5	34,6	34,7	34,8	34,9	35,0	35,1	35,2	35,3	35,4
19,0	34,4	34,5	34,6	34,7	34,8	34,9	35,0	35,1	35,2	35,3
19,2	34,3	34,4	34,5	34,6	34,7	34,8	34,9	35,0	35,1	35,2
19,4	34,2	34,3	34,4	34,5	34,6	34,7	34,8	34,9	35,0	35,1
19,6	34,2	34,3	34,4	34,5	34,6	34,7	34,8	34,9	35,0	35,1
19,8	34,1	34,2	34,3	34,4	34,5	34,6	34,7	34,8	34,9	35,0

Volumenkonzentration bei 20 °C in Prozent

Temp. °C	Anzeige des Alkoholometers in % vol								
	34,0	34,1	34,2	34,3	34,4	34,5	34,6	34,7	34,8	34,9
20,0	34,0	34,1	34,2	34,3	34,4	34,5	34,6	34,7	34,8	34,9
20,2	33,9	34,0	34,1	34,2	34,3	34,4	34,5	34,6	34,7	34,8
20,4	33,8	33,9	34,0	34,1	34,2	34,3	34,4	34,5	34,6	34,7
20,6	33,8	33,9	34,0	34,1	34,2	34,3	34,4	34,5	34,6	34,7
20,8	33,7	33,8	33,9	34,0	34,1	34,2	34,3	34,4	34,5	34,6
21,0	33,6	33,7	33,8	33,9	34,0	34,1	34,2	34,3	34,4	34,5
21,2	33,5	33,6	33,7	33,8	33,9	34,0	34,1	34,2	34,3	34,4
21,4	33,4	33,5	33,6	33,7	33,8	33,9	34,0	34,1	34,2	34,3
21,6	33,3	33,4	33,5	33,6	33,7	33,8	33,9	34,0	34,1	34,2
21,8	33,3	33,4	33,5	33,6	33,7	33,8	33,9	34,0	34,1	34,2
22,0	33,2	33,3	33,4	33,5	33,6	33,7	33,8	33,9	34,0	34,1
22,2	33,1	33,2	33,3	33,4	33,5	33,6	33,7	33,8	33,9	34,0
22,4	33,0	33,1	33,2	33,3	33,4	33,5	33,6	33,7	33,8	33,9
22,6	32,9	33,0	33,1	33,2	33,3	33,4	33,5	33,6	33,7	33,8
22,8	32,9	33,0	33,1	33,2	33,3	33,4	33,5	33,6	33,7	33,8
23,0	32,8	32,9	33,0	33,1	33,2	33,3	33,4	33,5	33,6	33,7
23,2	32,7	32,8	32,9	33,0	33,1	33,2	33,3	33,4	33,5	33,6
23,4	32,6	32,7	32,8	32,9	33,0	33,1	33,2	33,3	33,4	33,5
23,6	32,5	32,6	32,7	32,8	32,9	33,0	33,1	33,2	33,3	33,4
23,8	32,5	32,6	32,7	32,8	32,9	33,0	33,1	33,2	33,3	33,4
24,0	32,4	32,5	32,6	32,7	32,8	32,9	33,0	33,1	33,2	33,3
24,2	32,3	32,4	32,5	32,6	32,7	32,8	32,9	33,0	33,1	33,2
24,4	32,2	32,3	32,4	32,5	32,6	32,7	32,8	32,9	33,0	33,1
24,6	32,1	32,2	32,3	32,4	32,5	32,6	32,7	32,8	32,9	33,0
24,8	32,1	32,2	32,3	32,4	32,5	32,6	32,7	32,8	32,9	33,0
25,0	32,0	32,1	32,2	32,3	32,4	32,5	32,6	32,7	32,8	32,9
25,2	31,9	32,0	32,1	32,2	32,3	32,4	32,5	32,6	32,7	32,8
25,4	31,8	31,9	32,0	32,1	32,2	32,3	32,4	32,5	32,6	32,7
25,6	31,7	31,8	31,9	32,0	32,1	32,2	32,3	32,4	32,5	32,6
25,8	31,6	31,7	31,8	31,9	32,0	32,1	32,2	32,3	32,4	32,5
26,0	31,6	31,7	31,8	31,9	32,0	32,1	32,2	32,3	32,4	32,5
26,2	31,5	31,6	31,7	31,8	31,9	32,0	32,1	32,2	32,3	32,4
26,4	31,4	31,5	31,6	31,7	31,8	31,9	32,0	32,1	32,2	32,3
26,6	31,3	31,4	31,5	31,6	31,7	31,8	31,9	32,0	32,1	32,2
26,8	31,2	31,3	31,4	31,5	31,6	31,7	31,8	31,9	32,0	32,1
27,0	31,2	31,3	31,4	31,5	31,6	31,7	31,8	31,9	32,0	32,1
27,2	31,1	31,2	31,3	31,4	31,5	31,6	31,7	31,8	31,9	32,0
27,4	31,0	31,1	31,2	31,3	31,4	31,5	31,6	31,7	31,8	31,9
27,6	30,9	31,0	31,1	31,2	31,3	31,4	31,5	31,6	31,7	31,8
27,8	30,8	30,9	31,0	31,1	31,2	31,3	31,4	31,5	31,6	31,7
28,0	30,8	30,9	31,0	31,1	31,2	31,3	31,4	31,5	31,6	31,7
28,2	30,7	30,8	30,9	31,0	31,1	31,2	31,3	31,4	31,5	31,6
28,4	30,6	30,7	30,8	30,9	31,0	31,1	31,2	31,3	31,4	31,5
28,6	30,5	30,6	30,7	30,8	30,9	31,0	31,1	31,2	31,3	31,4
28,8	30,4	30,5	30,6	30,7	30,8	30,9	31,0	31,1	31,2	31,3
29,0	30,4	30,5	30,6	30,7	30,8	30,9	31,0	31,1	31,2	31,3
29,2	30,3	30,4	30,5	30,6	30,7	30,8	30,9	31,0	31,1	31,2
29,4	30,2	30,3	30,4	30,5	30,6	30,7	30,8	30,9	31,0	31,1
29,6	30,1	30,2	30,3	30,4	30,5	30,6	30,7	30,8	30,9	31,0
29,8	30,0	30,1	30,2	30,3	30,4	30,5	30,6	30,7	30,8	30,9
30,0	30,0	30,1	30,2	30,3	30,4	30,5	30,6	30,7	30,8	30,9

Volumenkonzentration bei 20 °C in Prozent

Temp. °C	Anzeige des Alkoholometers in % vol									
	35,0	35,1	35,2	35,3	35,4	35,5	35,6	35,7	35,8	35,9
0,0	43,2	43,3	43,4	43,5	43,6	43,7	43,8	43,9	43,9	44,0
0,2	43,1	43,2	43,3	43,4	43,5	43,6	43,7	43,8	43,9	44,0
0,4	43,0	43,1	43,2	43,3	43,4	43,5	43,6	43,7	43,8	43,9
0,6	43,0	43,0	43,1	43,2	43,3	43,4	43,5	43,6	43,7	43,8
0,8	42,9	43,0	43,1	43,2	43,2	43,3	43,4	43,5	43,6	43,7
1,0	42,8	42,9	43,0	43,1	43,2	43,3	43,4	43,4	43,5	43,6
1,2	42,7	42,8	42,9	43,0	43,1	43,2	43,3	43,4	43,5	43,6
1,4	42,6	42,7	42,8	42,9	43,0	43,1	43,2	43,3	43,4	43,5
1,6	42,5	42,6	42,7	42,8	42,9	43,0	43,1	43,2	43,3	43,4
1,8	42,5	42,6	42,6	42,7	42,8	42,9	43,0	43,1	43,2	43,3
2,0	42,4	42,5	42,6	42,7	42,8	42,9	42,9	43,0	43,1	43,2
2,2	42,3	42,4	42,5	42,6	42,7	42,8	42,9	43,0	43,1	43,2
2,4	42,2	42,3	42,4	42,5	42,6	42,7	42,8	42,9	43,0	43,1
2,6	42,1	42,2	42,3	42,4	42,5	42,6	42,7	42,8	42,9	43,0
2,8	42,0	42,1	42,2	42,3	42,4	42,5	42,6	42,7	42,8	42,9
3,0	42,0	42,1	42,2	42,3	42,3	42,4	42,5	42,6	42,7	42,8
3,2	41,9	42,0	42,1	42,2	42,3	42,4	42,5	42,6	42,6	42,7
3,4	41,8	41,9	42,0	42,1	42,2	42,3	42,4	42,5	42,6	42,7
3,6	41,7	41,8	41,9	42,0	42,1	42,2	42,3	42,4	42,5	42,6
3,8	41,6	41,7	41,8	41,9	42,0	42,1	42,2	42,3	42,4	42,5
4,0	41,6	41,7	41,7	41,8	41,9	42,0	42,1	42,2	42,3	42,4
4,2	41,5	41,6	41,7	41,8	41,9	42,0	42,1	42,1	42,2	42,3
4,4	41,4	41,5	41,6	41,7	41,8	41,9	42,0	42,1	42,2	42,3
4,6	41,3	41,4	41,5	41,6	41,7	41,8	41,9	42,0	42,1	42,2
4,8	41,2	41,3	41,4	41,5	41,6	41,7	41,8	41,9	42,0	42,1
5,0	41,1	41,2	41,3	41,4	41,5	41,6	41,7	41,8	41,9	42,0
5,2	41,1	41,2	41,3	41,4	41,5	41,5	41,6	41,7	41,8	41,9
5,4	41,0	41,1	41,2	41,3	41,4	41,5	41,6	41,7	41,8	41,9
5,6	40,9	41,0	41,1	41,2	41,3	41,4	41,5	41,6	41,7	41,8
5,8	40,8	40,9	41,0	41,1	41,2	41,3	41,4	41,5	41,6	41,7
6,0	40,7	40,8	40,9	41,0	41,1	41,2	41,3	41,4	41,5	41,6
6,2	40,7	40,8	40,8	40,9	41,0	41,1	41,2	41,3	41,4	41,5
6,4	40,6	40,7	40,8	40,9	41,0	41,1	41,2	41,2	41,3	41,4
6,6	40,5	40,6	40,7	40,8	40,9	41,0	41,1	41,2	41,3	41,4
6,8	40,4	40,5	40,6	40,7	40,8	40,9	41,0	41,1	41,2	41,3
7,0	40,3	40,4	40,5	40,6	40,7	40,8	40,9	41,0	41,1	41,2
7,2	40,2	40,3	40,4	40,5	40,6	40,7	40,8	40,9	41,0	41,1
7,4	40,2	40,3	40,4	40,5	40,5	40,6	40,7	40,8	40,9	41,0
7,6	40,1	40,2	40,3	40,4	40,5	40,6	40,7	40,8	40,9	41,0
7,8	40,0	40,1	40,2	40,3	40,4	40,5	40,6	40,7	40,8	40,9
8,0	39,9	40,0	40,1	40,2	40,3	40,4	40,5	40,6	40,7	40,8
8,2	39,8	39,9	40,0	40,1	40,2	40,3	40,4	40,5	40,6	40,7
8,4	39,7	39,8	39,9	40,0	40,1	40,2	40,3	40,4	40,5	40,6
8,6	39,7	39,8	39,9	40,0	40,1	40,2	40,3	40,4	40,4	40,5
8,8	39,6	39,7	39,8	39,9	40,0	40,1	40,2	40,3	40,4	40,5
9,0	39,5	39,6	39,7	39,8	39,9	40,0	40,1	40,2	40,3	40,4
9,2	39,4	39,5	39,6	39,7	39,8	39,9	40,0	40,1	40,2	40,3
9,4	39,3	39,4	39,5	39,6	39,7	39,8	39,9	40,0	40,1	40,2
9,6	39,3	39,4	39,5	39,6	39,6	39,7	39,8	39,9	40,0	40,1
9,8	39,2	39,3	39,4	39,5	39,6	39,7	39,8	39,9	40,0	40,1

Volumenkonzentration bei 20 °C in Prozent

Temp. °C	Anzeige des Alkoholometers in % vol									
	35,0	35,1	35,2	35,3	35,4	35,5	35,6	35,7	35,8	35,9
10,0	39,1	39,2	39,3	39,4	39,5	39,6	39,7	39,8	39,9	40,0
10,2	39,0	39,1	39,2	39,3	39,4	39,5	39,6	39,7	39,8	39,9
10,4	38,9	39,0	39,1	39,2	39,3	39,4	39,5	39,6	39,7	39,8
10,6	38,8	38,9	39,0	39,1	39,2	39,3	39,4	39,5	39,6	39,7
10,8	38,8	38,9	39,0	39,1	39,2	39,3	39,4	39,5	39,6	39,6
11,0	38,7	38,8	38,9	39,0	39,1	39,2	39,3	39,4	39,5	39,6
11,2	38,6	38,7	38,8	38,9	39,0	39,1	39,2	39,3	39,4	39,5
11,4	38,5	38,6	38,7	38,8	38,9	39,0	39,1	39,2	39,3	39,4
11,6	38,4	38,5	38,6	38,7	38,8	38,9	39,0	39,1	39,2	39,3
11,8	38,4	38,5	38,5	38,6	38,7	38,8	38,9	39,0	39,1	39,2
12,0	38,3	38,4	38,5	38,6	38,7	38,8	38,9	39,0	39,1	39,2
12,2	38,2	38,3	38,4	38,5	38,6	38,7	38,8	38,9	39,0	39,1
12,4	38,1	38,2	38,3	38,4	38,5	38,6	38,7	38,8	38,9	39,0
12,6	38,0	38,1	38,2	38,3	38,4	38,5	38,6	38,7	38,8	38,9
12,8	37,9	38,0	38,1	38,2	38,3	38,4	38,5	38,6	38,7	38,8
13,0	37,9	38,0	38,1	38,2	38,3	38,4	38,5	38,6	38,7	38,8
13,2	37,8	37,9	38,0	38,1	38,2	38,3	38,4	38,5	38,6	38,7
13,4	37,7	37,8	37,9	38,0	38,1	38,2	38,3	38,4	38,5	38,6
13,6	37,6	37,7	37,8	37,9	38,0	38,1	38,2	38,3	38,4	38,5
13,8	37,5	37,6	37,7	37,8	37,9	38,0	38,1	38,2	38,3	38,4
14,0	37,4	37,5	37,6	37,7	37,8	37,9	38,0	38,1	38,2	38,3
14,2	37,4	37,5	37,6	37,7	37,8	37,9	38,0	38,1	38,2	38,3
14,4	37,3	37,4	37,5	37,6	37,7	37,8	37,9	38,0	38,1	38,2
14,6	37,2	37,3	37,4	37,5	37,6	37,7	37,8	37,9	38,0	38,1
14,8	37,1	37,2	37,3	37,4	37,5	37,6	37,7	37,8	37,9	38,0
15,0	37,0	37,1	37,2	37,3	37,4	37,5	37,6	37,7	37,8	37,9
15,2	37,0	37,1	37,2	37,3	37,4	37,5	37,6	37,7	37,8	37,9
15,4	36,9	37,0	37,1	37,2	37,3	37,4	37,5	37,6	37,7	37,8
15,6	36,8	36,9	37,0	37,1	37,2	37,3	37,4	37,5	37,6	37,7
15,8	36,7	36,8	36,9	37,0	37,1	37,2	37,3	37,4	37,5	37,6
16,0	36,6	36,7	36,8	36,9	37,0	37,1	37,2	37,3	37,4	37,5
16,2	36,5	36,6	36,7	36,8	36,9	37,0	37,1	37,2	37,3	37,4
16,4	36,5	36,6	36,7	36,8	36,9	37,0	37,1	37,2	37,3	37,4
16,6	36,4	36,5	36,6	36,7	36,8	36,9	37,0	37,1	37,2	37,3
16,8	36,3	36,4	36,5	36,6	36,7	36,8	36,9	37,0	37,1	37,2
17,0	36,2	36,3	36,4	36,5	36,6	36,7	36,8	36,9	37,0	37,1
17,2	36,1	36,2	36,3	36,4	36,5	36,6	36,7	36,8	36,9	37,0
17,4	36,1	36,2	36,3	36,4	36,5	36,6	36,7	36,8	36,9	37,0
17,6	36,0	36,1	36,2	36,3	36,4	36,5	36,6	36,7	36,8	36,9
17,8	35,9	36,0	36,1	36,2	36,3	36,4	36,5	36,6	36,7	36,8
18,0	35,8	35,9	36,0	36,1	36,2	36,3	36,4	36,5	36,6	36,7
18,2	35,7	35,8	35,9	36,0	36,1	36,2	36,3	36,4	36,5	36,6
18,4	35,7	35,8	35,9	36,0	36,1	36,2	36,3	36,4	36,5	36,6
18,6	35,6	35,7	35,8	35,9	36,0	36,1	36,2	36,3	36,4	36,5
18,8	35,5	35,6	35,7	35,8	35,9	36,0	36,1	36,2	36,3	36,4
19,0	35,4	35,5	35,6	35,7	35,8	35,9	36,0	36,1	36,2	36,3
19,2	35,3	35,4	35,5	35,6	35,7	35,8	35,9	36,0	36,1	36,2
19,4	35,2	35,3	35,4	35,5	35,6	35,7	35,8	35,9	36,0	36,1
19,6	35,2	35,3	35,4	35,5	35,6	35,7	35,8	35,9	36,0	36,1
19,8	35,1	35,2	35,3	35,4	35,5	35,6	35,7	35,8	35,9	36,0

Volumenkonzentration bei 20 °C in Prozent

Temp. °C	\multicolumn{10}{c}{Anzeige des Alkoholometers in % vol}

Temp. °C	35,0	35,1	35,2	35,3	35,4	35,5	35,6	35,7	35,8	35,9
20,0	35,0	35,1	35,2	35,3	35,4	35,5	35,6	35,7	35,8	35,9
20,2	34,9	35,0	35,1	35,2	35,3	35,4	35,5	35,6	35,7	35,8
20,4	34,8	34,9	35,0	35,1	35,2	35,3	35,4	35,5	35,6	35,7
20,6	34,8	34,9	35,0	35,1	35,2	35,3	35,4	35,5	35,6	35,7
20,8	34,7	34,8	34,9	35,0	35,1	35,2	35,3	35,4	35,5	35,6
21,0	34,6	34,7	34,8	34,9	35,0	35,1	35,2	35,3	35,4	35,5
21,2	34,5	34,6	34,7	34,8	34,9	35,0	35,1	35,2	35,3	35,4
21,4	34,4	34,5	34,6	34,7	34,8	34,9	35,0	35,1	35,2	35,3
21,6	34,3	34,4	34,5	34,6	34,7	34,8	34,9	35,0	35,1	35,2
21,8	34,3	34,4	34,5	34,6	34,7	34,8	34,9	35,0	35,1	35,2
22,0	34,2	34,3	34,4	34,5	34,6	34,7	34,8	34,9	35,0	35,1
22,2	34,1	34,2	34,3	34,4	34,5	34,6	34,7	34,8	34,9	35,0
22,4	34,0	34,1	34,2	34,3	34,4	34,5	34,6	34,7	34,8	34,9
22,6	33,9	34,0	34,1	34,2	34,3	34,4	34,5	34,6	34,7	34,8
22,8	33,9	34,0	34,1	34,2	34,3	34,4	34,5	34,6	34,7	34,8
23,0	33,8	33,9	34,0	34,1	34,2	34,3	34,4	34,5	34,6	34,7
23,2	33,7	33,8	33,9	34,0	34,1	34,2	34,3	34,4	34,5	34,6
23,4	33,6	33,7	33,8	33,9	34,0	34,1	34,2	34,3	34,4	34,5
23,6	33,5	33,6	33,7	33,8	33,9	34,0	34,1	34,2	34,3	34,4
23,8	33,5	33,6	33,7	33,8	33,9	34,0	34,1	34,2	34,3	34,4
24,0	33,4	33,5	33,6	33,7	33,8	33,9	34,0	34,1	34,2	34,3
24,2	33,3	33,4	33,5	33,6	33,7	33,8	33,9	34,0	34,1	34,2
24,4	33,2	33,3	33,4	33,5	33,6	33,7	33,8	33,9	34,0	34,1
24,6	33,1	33,2	33,3	33,4	33,5	33,6	33,7	33,8	33,9	34,0
24,8	33,1	33,2	33,3	33,4	33,5	33,6	33,7	33,8	33,9	34,0
25,0	33,0	33,1	33,2	33,3	33,4	33,5	33,6	33,7	33,8	33,9
25,2	32,9	33,0	33,1	33,2	33,3	33,4	33,5	33,6	33,7	33,8
25,4	32,8	32,9	33,0	33,1	33,2	33,3	33,4	33,5	33,6	33,7
25,6	32,7	32,8	32,9	33,0	33,1	33,2	33,3	33,4	33,5	33,6
25,8	32,6	32,7	32,8	32,9	33,0	33,1	33,2	33,3	33,4	33,5
26,0	32,6	32,7	32,8	32,9	33,0	33,1	33,2	33,3	33,4	33,5
26,2	32,5	32,6	32,7	32,8	32,9	33,0	33,1	33,2	33,3	33,4
26,4	32,4	32,5	32,6	32,7	32,8	32,9	33,0	33,1	33,2	33,3
26,6	32,3	32,4	32,5	32,6	32,7	32,8	32,9	33,0	33,1	33,2
26,8	32,2	32,3	32,4	32,5	32,6	32,7	32,8	32,9	33,0	33,1
27,0	32,2	32,3	32,4	32,5	32,6	32,7	32,8	32,9	33,0	33,1
27,2	32,1	32,2	32,3	32,4	32,5	32,6	32,7	32,8	32,9	33,0
27,4	32,0	32,1	32,2	32,3	32,4	32,5	32,6	32,7	32,8	32,9
27,6	31,9	32,0	32,1	32,2	32,3	32,4	32,5	32,6	32,7	32,8
27,8	31,8	31,9	32,0	32,1	32,2	32,3	32,4	32,5	32,6	32,7
28,0	31,8	31,9	32,0	32,1	32,2	32,3	32,4	32,5	32,6	32,7
28,2	31,7	31,8	31,9	32,0	32,1	32,2	32,3	32,4	32,5	32,6
28,4	31,6	31,7	31,8	31,9	32,0	32,1	32,2	32,3	32,4	32,5
28,6	31,5	31,6	31,7	31,8	31,9	32,0	32,1	32,2	32,3	32,4
28,8	31,4	31,5	31,6	31,7	31,8	31,9	32,0	32,1	32,2	32,3
29,0	31,4	31,5	31,6	31,7	31,8	31,9	32,0	32,1	32,2	32,3
29,2	31,3	31,4	31,5	31,6	31,7	31,8	31,9	32,0	32,1	32,2
29,4	31,2	31,3	31,4	31,5	31,6	31,7	31,8	31,9	32,0	32,1
29,6	31,1	31,2	31,3	31,4	31,5	31,6	31,7	31,8	31,9	32,0
29,8	31,0	31,1	31,2	31,3	31,4	31,5	31,6	31,7	31,8	31,9
30,0	31,0	31,0	31,1	31,2	31,3	31,4	31,5	31,6	31,7	31,8

Volumenkonzentration bei 20 °C in Prozent

Temp. °C	Anzeige des Alkoholometers in % vol								
	36,0	36,1	36,2	36,3	36,4	36,5	36,6	36,7	36,8	36,9
0,0	44,1	44,2	44,3	44,4	44,5	44,6	44,7	44,8	44,9	45,0
0,2	44,1	44,1	44,2	44,3	44,4	44,5	44,6	44,7	44,8	44,9
0,4	44,0	44,1	44,2	44,3	44,3	44,4	44,5	44,6	44,7	44,8
0,6	43,9	44,0	44,1	44,2	44,3	44,4	44,5	44,5	44,6	44,7
0,8	43,8	43,9	44,0	44,1	44,2	44,3	44,4	44,5	44,6	44,7
1,0	43,7	43,8	43,9	44,0	44,1	44,2	44,3	44,4	44,5	44,6
1,2	43,6	43,7	43,8	43,9	44,0	44,1	44,2	44,3	44,4	44,5
1,4	43,6	43,7	43,8	43,9	43,9	44,0	44,1	44,2	44,3	44,4
1,6	43,5	43,6	43,7	43,8	43,9	44,0	44,1	44,1	44,2	44,3
1,8	43,4	43,5	43,6	43,7	43,8	43,9	44,0	44,1	44,2	44,3
2,0	43,3	43,4	43,5	43,6	43,7	43,8	43,9	44,0	44,1	44,2
2,2	43,2	43,3	43,4	43,5	43,6	43,7	43,8	43,9	44,0	44,1
2,4	43,2	43,3	43,4	43,4	43,5	43,6	43,7	43,8	43,9	44,0
2,6	43,1	43,2	43,3	43,4	43,5	43,6	43,7	43,7	43,8	43,9
2,8	43,0	43,1	43,2	43,3	43,4	43,5	43,6	43,7	43,8	43,9
3,0	42,9	43,0	43,1	43,2	43,3	43,4	43,5	43,6	43,7	43,8
3,2	42,8	42,9	43,0	43,1	43,2	43,3	43,4	43,5	43,6	43,7
3,4	42,8	42,9	42,9	43,0	43,1	43,2	43,3	43,4	43,5	43,6
3,6	42,7	42,8	42,9	43,0	43,1	43,2	43,2	43,3	43,4	43,5
3,8	42,6	42,7	42,8	42,9	43,0	43,1	43,2	43,3	43,4	43,5
4,0	42,5	42,6	42,7	42,8	42,9	43,0	43,1	43,2	43,3	43,4
4,2	42,4	42,5	42,6	42,7	42,8	42,9	43,0	43,1	43,2	43,3
4,4	42,4	42,4	42,5	42,6	42,7	42,8	42,9	43,0	43,1	43,2
4,6	42,3	42,4	42,5	42,6	42,7	42,8	42,8	42,9	43,0	43,1
4,8	42,2	42,3	42,4	42,5	42,6	42,7	42,8	42,9	43,0	43,1
5,0	42,1	42,2	42,3	42,4	42,5	42,6	42,7	42,8	42,9	43,0
5,2	42,0	42,1	42,2	42,3	42,4	42,5	42,6	42,7	42,8	42,9
5,4	41,9	42,0	42,1	42,2	42,3	42,4	42,5	42,6	42,7	42,8
5,6	41,9	42,0	42,1	42,2	42,3	42,3	42,4	42,5	42,6	42,7
5,8	41,8	41,9	42,0	42,1	42,2	42,3	42,4	42,5	42,6	42,6
6,0	41,7	41,8	41,9	42,0	42,1	42,2	42,3	42,4	42,5	42,6
6,2	41,6	41,7	41,8	41,9	42,0	42,1	42,2	42,3	42,4	42,5
6,4	41,5	41,6	41,7	41,8	41,9	42,0	42,1	42,2	42,3	42,4
6,6	41,5	41,6	41,7	41,7	41,8	41,9	42,0	42,1	42,2	42,3
6,8	41,4	41,5	41,6	41,7	41,8	41,9	42,0	42,1	42,2	42,2
7,0	41,3	41,4	41,5	41,6	41,7	41,8	41,9	42,0	42,1	42,2
7,2	41,2	41,3	41,4	41,5	41,6	41,7	41,8	41,9	42,0	42,1
7,4	41,1	41,2	41,3	41,4	41,5	41,6	41,7	41,8	41,9	42,0
7,6	41,1	41,1	41,2	41,3	41,4	41,5	41,6	41,7	41,8	41,9
7,8	41,0	41,1	41,2	41,3	41,4	41,5	41,6	41,6	41,7	41,8
8,0	40,9	41,0	41,1	41,2	41,3	41,4	41,5	41,6	41,7	41,8
8,2	40,8	40,9	41,0	41,1	41,2	41,3	41,4	41,5	41,6	41,7
8,4	40,7	40,8	40,9	41,0	41,1	41,2	41,3	41,4	41,5	41,6
8,6	40,6	40,7	40,8	40,9	41,0	41,1	41,2	41,3	41,4	41,5
8,8	40,6	40,7	40,8	40,9	41,0	41,0	41,1	41,2	41,3	41,4
9,0	40,5	40,6	40,7	40,8	40,9	41,0	41,1	41,2	41,3	41,4
9,2	40,4	40,5	40,6	40,7	40,8	40,9	41,0	41,1	41,2	41,3
9,4	40,3	40,4	40,5	40,6	40,7	40,8	40,9	41,0	41,1	41,2
9,6	40,2	40,3	40,4	40,5	40,6	40,7	40,8	40,9	41,0	41,1
9,8	40,2	40,3	40,4	40,4	40,5	40,6	40,7	40,8	40,9	41,0

Volumenkonzentration bei 20 °C in Prozent

Temp. °C	\multicolumn{9}{c}{Anzeige des Alkoholometers in % vol}

Temp. °C	36,0	36,1	36,2	36,3	36,4	36,5	36,6	36,7	36,8	36,9
10,0	40,1	40,2	40,3	40,4	40,5	40,6	40,7	40,8	40,9	41,0
10,2	40,0	40,1	40,2	40,3	40,4	40,5	40,6	40,7	40,8	40,9
10,4	39,9	40,0	40,1	40,2	40,3	40,4	40,5	40,6	40,7	40,8
10,6	39,8	39,9	40,0	40,1	40,2	40,3	40,4	40,5	40,6	40,7
10,8	39,7	39,8	39,9	40,0	40,1	40,2	40,3	40,4	40,5	40,6
11,0	39,7	39,8	39,9	40,0	40,1	40,2	40,3	40,4	40,5	40,5
11,2	39,6	39,7	39,8	39,9	40,0	40,1	40,2	40,3	40,4	40,5
11,4	39,5	39,6	39,7	39,8	39,9	40,0	40,1	40,2	40,3	40,4
11,6	39,4	39,5	39,6	39,7	39,8	39,9	40,0	40,1	40,2	40,3
11,8	39,3	39,4	39,5	39,6	39,7	39,8	39,9	40,0	40,1	40,2
12,0	39,3	39,4	39,5	39,6	39,7	39,7	39,8	39,9	40,0	40,1
12,2	39,2	39,3	39,4	39,5	39,6	39,7	39,8	39,9	40,0	40,1
12,4	39,1	39,2	39,3	39,4	39,5	39,6	39,7	39,8	39,9	40,0
12,6	39,0	39,1	39,2	39,3	39,4	39,5	39,6	39,7	39,8	39,9
12,8	38,9	39,0	39,1	39,2	39,3	39,4	39,5	39,6	39,7	39,8
13,0	38,8	38,9	39,0	39,1	39,2	39,3	39,4	39,5	39,6	39,7
13,2	38,8	38,9	39,0	39,1	39,2	39,3	39,4	39,5	39,6	39,7
13,4	38,7	38,8	38,9	39,0	39,1	39,2	39,3	39,4	39,5	39,6
13,6	38,6	38,7	38,8	38,9	39,0	39,1	39,2	39,3	39,4	39,5
13,8	38,5	38,6	38,7	38,8	38,9	39,0	39,1	39,2	39,3	39,4
14,0	38,4	38,5	38,6	38,7	38,8	38,9	39,0	39,1	39,2	39,3
14,2	38,4	38,5	38,6	38,7	38,8	38,9	39,0	39,1	39,2	39,3
14,4	38,3	38,4	38,5	38,6	38,7	38,8	38,9	39,0	39,1	39,2
14,6	38,2	38,3	38,4	38,5	38,6	38,7	38,8	38,9	39,0	39,1
14,8	38,1	38,2	38,3	38,4	38,5	38,6	38,7	38,8	38,9	39,0
15,0	38,0	38,1	38,2	38,3	38,4	38,5	38,6	38,7	38,8	38,9
15,2	38,0	38,1	38,2	38,3	38,3	38,4	38,5	38,6	38,7	38,8
15,4	37,9	38,0	38,1	38,2	38,3	38,4	38,5	38,6	38,7	38,8
15,6	37,8	37,9	38,0	38,1	38,2	38,3	38,4	38,5	38,6	38,7
15,8	37,7	37,8	37,9	38,0	38,1	38,2	38,3	38,4	38,5	38,6
16,0	37,6	37,7	37,8	37,9	38,0	38,1	38,2	38,3	38,4	38,5
16,2	37,5	37,6	37,7	37,8	37,9	38,0	38,1	38,2	38,3	38,4
16,4	37,5	37,6	37,7	37,8	37,9	38,0	38,1	38,2	38,3	38,4
16,6	37,4	37,5	37,6	37,7	37,8	37,9	38,0	38,1	38,2	38,3
16,8	37,3	37,4	37,5	37,6	37,7	37,8	37,9	38,0	38,1	38,2
17,0	37,2	37,3	37,4	37,5	37,6	37,7	37,8	37,9	38,0	38,1
17,2	37,1	37,2	37,3	37,4	37,5	37,6	37,7	37,8	37,9	38,0
17,4	37,1	37,2	37,3	37,4	37,5	37,6	37,7	37,8	37,9	38,0
17,6	37,0	37,1	37,2	37,3	37,4	37,5	37,6	37,7	37,8	37,9
17,8	36,9	37,0	37,1	37,2	37,3	37,4	37,5	37,6	37,7	37,8
18,0	36,8	36,9	37,0	37,1	37,2	37,3	37,4	37,5	37,6	37,7
18,2	36,7	36,8	36,9	37,0	37,1	37,2	37,3	37,4	37,5	37,6
18,4	36,7	36,8	36,9	36,9	37,0	37,1	37,2	37,3	37,4	37,5
18,6	36,6	36,7	36,8	36,9	37,0	37,1	37,2	37,3	37,4	37,5
18,8	36,5	36,6	36,7	36,8	36,9	37,0	37,1	37,2	37,3	37,4
19,0	36,4	36,5	36,6	36,7	36,8	36,9	37,0	37,1	37,2	37,3
19,2	36,3	36,4	36,5	36,6	36,7	36,8	36,9	37,0	37,1	37,2
19,4	36,2	36,3	36,4	36,5	36,6	36,7	36,8	36,9	37,0	37,1
19,6	36,2	36,3	36,4	36,5	36,6	36,7	36,8	36,9	37,0	37,1
19,8	36,1	36,2	36,3	36,4	36,5	36,6	36,7	36,8	36,9	37,0

Volumenkonzentration bei 20 °C in Prozent

Temp. °C	Anzeige des Alkoholometers in % vol								
	36,0	36,1	36,2	36,3	36,4	36,5	36,6	36,7	36,8	36,9
20,0	36,0	36,1	36,2	36,3	36,4	36,5	36,6	36,7	36,8	36,9
20,2	35,9	36,0	36,1	36,2	36,3	36,4	36,5	36,6	36,7	36,8
20,4	35,8	35,9	36,0	36,1	36,2	36,3	36,4	36,5	36,6	36,7
20,6	35,8	35,9	36,0	36,1	36,2	36,3	36,4	36,5	36,6	36,7
20,8	35,7	35,8	35,9	36,0	36,1	36,2	36,3	36,4	36,5	36,6
21,0	35,6	35,7	35,8	35,9	36,0	36,1	36,2	36,3	36,4	36,5
21,2	35,5	35,6	35,7	35,8	35,9	36,0	36,1	36,2	36,3	36,4
21,4	35,4	35,5	35,6	35,7	35,8	35,9	36,0	36,1	36,2	36,3
21,6	35,4	35,5	35,6	35,7	35,8	35,9	36,0	36,1	36,2	36,3
21,8	35,3	35,4	35,5	35,6	35,7	35,8	35,9	36,0	36,1	36,2
22,0	35,2	35,3	35,4	35,5	35,6	35,7	35,8	35,9	36,0	36,1
22,2	35,1	35,2	35,3	35,4	35,5	35,6	35,7	35,8	35,9	36,0
22,4	35,0	35,1	35,2	35,3	35,4	35,5	35,6	35,7	35,8	35,9
22,6	34,9	35,0	35,1	35,2	35,3	35,4	35,5	35,6	35,7	35,8
22,8	34,9	35,0	35,1	35,2	35,3	35,4	35,5	35,6	35,7	35,8
23,0	34,8	34,9	35,0	35,1	35,2	35,3	35,4	35,5	35,6	35,7
23,2	34,7	34,8	34,9	35,0	35,1	35,2	35,3	35,4	35,5	35,6
23,4	34,6	34,7	34,8	34,9	35,0	35,1	35,2	35,3	35,4	35,5
23,6	34,5	34,6	34,7	34,8	34,9	35,0	35,1	35,2	35,3	35,4
23,8	34,5	34,6	34,7	34,8	34,9	35,0	35,1	35,2	35,3	35,4
24,0	34,4	34,5	34,6	34,7	34,8	34,9	35,0	35,1	35,2	35,3
24,2	34,3	34,4	34,5	34,6	34,7	34,8	34,9	35,0	35,1	35,2
24,4	34,2	34,3	34,4	34,5	34,6	34,7	34,8	34,9	35,0	35,1
24,6	34,1	34,2	34,3	34,4	34,5	34,6	34,7	34,8	34,9	35,0
24,8	34,1	34,2	34,3	34,4	34,5	34,6	34,7	34,8	34,9	35,0
25,0	34,0	34,1	34,2	34,3	34,4	34,5	34,6	34,7	34,8	34,9
25,2	33,9	34,0	34,1	34,2	34,3	34,4	34,5	34,6	34,7	34,8
25,4	33,8	33,9	34,0	34,1	34,2	34,3	34,4	34,5	34,6	34,7
25,6	33,7	33,8	33,9	34,0	34,1	34,2	34,3	34,4	34,5	34,6
25,8	33,6	33,7	33,8	33,9	34,0	34,1	34,2	34,3	34,4	34,6
26,0	33,6	33,7	33,8	33,9	34,0	34,1	34,2	34,3	34,4	34,5
26,2	33,5	33,6	33,7	33,8	33,9	34,0	34,1	34,2	34,3	34,4
26,4	33,4	33,5	33,6	33,7	33,8	33,9	34,0	34,1	34,2	34,3
26,6	33,3	33,4	33,5	33,6	33,7	33,8	33,9	34,0	34,1	34,2
26,8	33,2	33,3	33,4	33,5	33,6	33,7	33,8	33,9	34,0	34,1
27,0	33,2	33,3	33,4	33,5	33,6	33,7	33,8	33,9	34,0	34,1
27,2	33,1	33,2	33,3	33,4	33,5	33,6	33,7	33,8	33,9	34,0
27,4	33,0	33,1	33,2	33,3	33,4	33,5	33,6	33,7	33,8	33,9
27,6	32,9	33,0	33,1	33,2	33,3	33,4	33,5	33,6	33,7	33,8
27,8	32,8	32,9	33,0	33,1	33,2	33,3	33,4	33,5	33,6	33,7
28,0	32,8	32,9	33,0	33,1	33,2	33,3	33,4	33,5	33,6	33,7
28,2	32,7	32,8	32,9	33,0	33,1	33,2	33,3	33,4	33,5	33,6
28,4	32,6	32,7	32,8	32,9	33,0	33,1	33,2	33,3	33,4	33,5
28,6	32,5	32,6	32,7	32,8	32,9	33,0	33,1	33,2	33,3	33,4
28,8	32,4	32,5	32,6	32,7	32,8	32,9	33,0	33,1	33,2	33,3
29,0	32,4	32,5	32,6	32,7	32,8	32,9	33,0	33,1	33,2	33,3
29,2	32,3	32,4	32,5	32,6	32,7	32,8	32,9	33,0	33,1	33,2
29,4	32,2	32,3	32,4	32,5	32,6	32,7	32,8	32,9	33,0	33,1
29,6	32,1	32,2	32,3	32,4	32,5	32,6	32,7	32,8	32,9	33,0
29,8	32,0	32,1	32,2	32,3	32,4	32,5	32,6	32,7	32,8	32,9
30,0	31,9	32,0	32,1	32,2	32,3	32,4	32,5	32,6	32,7	32,8

Volumenkonzentration bei 20 °C in Prozent

Temp. °C	\multicolumn{10}{c}{Anzeige des Alkoholometers in % vol}

Temp. °C	37,0	37,1	37,2	37,3	37,4	37,5	37,6	37,7	37,8	37,9
0,0	45,1	45,2	45,3	45,3	45,4	45,5	45,6	45,7	45,8	45,9
0,2	45,0	45,1	45,2	45,3	45,4	45,5	45,5	45,6	45,7	45,8
0,4	44,9	45,0	45,1	45,2	45,3	45,4	45,5	45,6	45,7	45,7
0,6	44,8	44,9	45,0	45,1	45,2	45,3	45,4	45,5	45,6	45,7
0,8	44,7	44,8	44,9	45,0	45,1	45,2	45,3	45,4	45,5	45,6
1,0	44,7	44,8	44,9	44,9	45,0	45,1	45,2	45,3	45,4	45,5
1,2	44,6	44,7	44,8	44,9	45,0	45,1	45,2	45,2	45,3	45,4
1,4	44,5	44,6	44,7	44,8	44,9	45,0	45,1	45,2	45,3	45,4
1,6	44,4	44,5	44,6	44,7	44,8	44,9	45,0	45,1	45,2	45,3
1,8	44,3	44,4	44,5	44,6	44,7	44,8	44,9	45,0	45,1	45,2
2,0	44,3	44,4	44,5	44,6	44,6	44,7	44,8	44,9	45,0	45,1
2,2	44,2	44,3	44,4	44,5	44,6	44,7	44,8	44,8	44,9	45,0
2,4	44,1	44,2	44,3	44,4	44,5	44,6	44,7	44,8	44,9	45,0
2,6	44,0	44,1	44,2	44,3	44,4	44,5	44,6	44,7	44,8	44,9
2,8	44,0	44,0	44,1	44,2	44,3	44,4	44,5	44,6	44,7	44,8
3,0	43,9	44,0	44,1	44,2	44,2	44,3	44,4	44,5	44,6	44,7
3,2	43,8	43,9	44,0	44,1	44,2	44,3	44,4	44,5	44,5	44,6
3,4	43,7	43,8	43,9	44,0	44,1	44,2	44,3	44,4	44,5	44,6
3,6	43,6	43,7	43,8	43,9	44,0	44,1	44,2	44,3	44,4	44,5
3,8	43,5	43,6	43,7	43,8	43,9	44,0	44,1	44,2	44,3	44,4
4,0	43,5	43,6	43,7	43,8	43,8	43,9	44,0	44,1	44,2	44,3
4,2	43,4	43,5	43,6	43,7	43,8	43,9	44,0	44,1	44,1	44,2
4,4	43,3	43,4	43,5	43,6	43,7	43,8	43,9	44,0	44,1	44,2
4,6	43,2	43,3	43,4	43,5	43,6	43,7	43,8	43,9	44,0	44,1
4,8	43,1	43,2	43,3	43,4	43,5	43,6	43,7	43,8	43,9	44,0
5,0	43,1	43,2	43,3	43,4	43,4	43,5	43,6	43,7	43,8	43,9
5,2	43,0	43,1	43,2	43,3	43,4	43,5	43,6	43,7	43,8	43,9
5,4	42,9	43,0	43,1	43,2	43,3	43,4	43,5	43,6	43,7	43,8
5,6	42,8	42,9	43,0	43,1	43,2	43,3	43,4	43,5	43,6	43,7
5,8	42,7	42,8	42,9	43,0	43,1	43,2	43,3	43,4	43,5	43,6
6,0	42,7	42,8	42,9	43,0	43,0	43,1	43,2	43,3	43,4	43,5
6,2	42,6	42,7	42,8	42,9	43,0	43,1	43,2	43,3	43,4	43,4
6,4	42,5	42,6	42,7	42,8	42,9	43,0	43,1	43,2	43,3	43,4
6,6	42,4	42,5	42,6	42,7	42,8	42,9	43,0	43,1	43,2	43,3
6,8	42,3	42,4	42,5	42,6	42,7	42,8	42,9	43,0	43,1	43,2
7,0	42,3	42,4	42,5	42,6	42,6	42,7	42,8	42,9	43,0	43,1
7,2	42,2	42,3	42,4	42,5	42,6	42,7	42,8	42,9	43,0	43,0
7,4	42,1	42,2	42,3	42,4	42,5	42,6	42,7	42,8	42,9	43,0
7,6	42,0	42,1	42,2	42,3	42,4	42,5	42,6	42,7	42,8	42,9
7,8	41,9	42,0	42,1	42,2	42,3	42,4	42,5	42,6	42,7	42,8
8,0	41,9	42,0	42,1	42,1	42,2	42,3	42,4	42,5	42,6	42,7
8,2	41,8	41,9	42,0	42,1	42,2	42,3	42,4	42,5	42,6	42,6
8,4	41,7	41,8	41,9	42,0	42,1	42,2	42,3	42,4	42,5	42,6
8,6	41,6	41,7	41,8	41,9	42,0	42,1	42,2	42,3	42,4	42,5
8,8	41,5	41,6	41,7	41,8	41,9	42,0	42,1	42,2	42,3	42,4
9,0	41,5	41,6	41,6	41,7	41,8	41,9	42,0	42,1	42,2	42,3
9,2	41,4	41,5	41,6	41,7	41,8	41,9	42,0	42,1	42,2	42,2
9,4	41,3	41,4	41,5	41,6	41,7	41,8	41,9	42,0	42,1	42,2
9,6	41,2	41,3	41,4	41,5	41,6	41,7	41,8	41,9	42,0	42,1
9,8	41,1	41,2	41,3	41,4	41,5	41,6	41,7	41,8	41,9	42,0

Volumenkonzentration bei 20 °C in Prozent

Temp. °C	Anzeige des Alkoholometers in % vol								
	37,0	37,1	37,2	37,3	37,4	37,5	37,6	37,7	37,8	37,9
10,0	41,1	41,1	41,2	41,3	41,4	41,5	41,6	41,7	41,8	41,9
10,2	41,0	41,1	41,2	41,3	41,4	41,5	41,6	41,7	41,8	41,8
10,4	40,9	41,0	41,1	41,2	41,3	41,4	41,5	41,6	41,7	41,8
10,6	40,8	40,9	41,0	41,1	41,2	41,3	41,4	41,5	41,6	41,7
10,8	40,7	40,8	40,9	41,0	41,1	41,2	41,3	41,4	41,5	41,6
11,0	40,6	40,7	40,8	40,9	41,0	41,1	41,2	41,3	41,4	41,5
11,2	40,6	40,7	40,8	40,9	41,0	41,1	41,2	41,3	41,3	41,4
11,4	40,5	40,6	40,7	40,8	40,9	41,0	41,1	41,2	41,3	41,4
11,6	40,4	40,5	40,6	40,7	40,8	40,9	41,0	41,1	41,2	41,3
11,8	40,3	40,4	40,5	40,6	40,7	40,8	40,9	41,0	41,1	41,2
12,0	40,2	40,3	40,4	40,5	40,6	40,7	40,8	40,9	41,0	41,1
12,2	40,2	40,3	40,4	40,5	40,6	40,7	40,7	40,8	40,9	41,0
12,4	40,1	40,2	40,3	40,4	40,5	40,6	40,7	40,8	40,9	41,0
12,6	40,0	40,1	40,2	40,3	40,4	40,5	40,6	40,7	40,8	40,9
12,8	39,9	40,0	40,1	40,2	40,3	40,4	40,5	40,6	40,7	40,8
13,0	39,8	39,9	40,0	40,1	40,2	40,3	40,4	40,5	40,6	40,7
13,2	39,8	39,9	40,0	40,1	40,1	40,2	40,3	40,4	40,5	40,6
13,4	39,7	39,8	39,9	40,0	40,1	40,2	40,3	40,4	40,5	40,6
13,6	39,6	39,7	39,8	39,9	40,0	40,1	40,2	40,3	40,4	40,5
13,8	39,5	39,6	39,7	39,8	39,9	40,0	40,1	40,2	40,3	40,4
14,0	39,4	39,5	39,6	39,7	39,8	39,9	40,0	40,1	40,2	40,3
14,2	39,4	39,4	39,5	39,6	39,7	39,8	39,9	40,0	40,1	40,2
14,4	39,3	39,4	39,5	39,6	39,7	39,8	39,9	40,0	40,1	40,2
14,6	39,2	39,3	39,4	39,5	39,6	39,7	39,8	39,9	40,0	40,1
14,8	39,1	39,2	39,3	39,4	39,5	39,6	39,7	39,8	39,9	40,0
15,0	39,0	39,1	39,2	39,3	39,4	39,5	39,6	39,7	39,8	39,9
15,2	38,9	39,0	39,1	39,2	39,3	39,4	39,5	39,6	39,7	39,8
15,4	38,9	39,0	39,1	39,2	39,3	39,4	39,5	39,6	39,7	39,8
15,6	38,8	38,9	39,0	39,1	39,2	39,3	39,4	39,5	39,6	39,7
15,8	38,7	38,8	38,9	39,0	39,1	39,2	39,3	39,4	39,5	39,6
16,0	38,6	38,7	38,8	38,9	39,0	39,1	39,2	39,3	39,4	39,5
16,2	38,5	38,6	38,7	38,8	38,9	39,0	39,1	39,2	39,3	39,4
16,4	38,5	38,6	38,7	38,8	38,9	39,0	39,1	39,2	39,3	39,4
16,6	38,4	38,5	38,6	38,7	38,8	38,9	39,0	39,1	39,2	39,3
16,8	38,3	38,4	38,5	38,6	38,7	38,8	38,9	39,0	39,1	39,2
17,0	38,2	38,3	38,4	38,5	38,6	38,7	38,8	38,9	39,0	39,1
17,2	38,1	38,2	38,3	38,4	38,5	38,6	38,7	38,8	38,9	39,0
17,4	38,1	38,2	38,3	38,4	38,5	38,6	38,7	38,8	38,8	38,9
17,6	38,0	38,1	38,2	38,3	38,4	38,5	38,6	38,7	38,8	38,9
17,8	37,9	38,0	38,1	38,2	38,3	38,4	38,5	38,6	38,7	38,8
18,0	37,8	37,9	38,0	38,1	38,2	38,3	38,4	38,5	38,6	38,7
18,2	37,7	37,8	37,9	38,0	38,1	38,2	38,3	38,4	38,5	38,6
18,4	37,6	37,7	37,8	37,9	38,0	38,1	38,2	38,3	38,4	38,5
18,6	37,6	37,7	37,8	37,9	38,0	38,1	38,2	38,3	38,4	38,5
18,8	37,5	37,6	37,7	37,8	37,9	38,0	38,1	38,2	38,3	38,4
19,0	37,4	37,5	37,6	37,7	37,8	37,9	38,0	38,1	38,2	38,3
19,2	37,3	37,4	37,5	37,6	37,7	37,8	37,9	38,0	38,1	38,2
19,4	37,2	37,3	37,4	37,5	37,6	37,7	37,8	37,9	38,0	38,1
19,6	37,2	37,3	37,4	37,5	37,6	37,7	37,8	37,9	38,0	38,1
19,8	37,1	37,2	37,3	37,4	37,5	37,6	37,7	37,8	37,9	38,0

Volumenkonzentration bei 20 °C in Prozent

| Temp. °C | \multicolumn{10}{c}{Anzeige des Alkoholometers in % vol} |

Temp. °C	37,0	37,1	37,2	37,3	37,4	37,5	37,6	37,7	37,8	37,9
20,0	37,0	37,1	37,2	37,3	37,4	37,5	37,6	37,7	37,8	37,9
20,2	36,9	37,0	37,1	37,2	37,3	37,4	37,5	37,6	37,7	37,8
20,4	36,8	36,9	37,0	37,1	37,2	37,3	37,4	37,5	37,6	37,7
20,6	36,8	36,9	37,0	37,1	37,2	37,3	37,4	37,5	37,6	37,7
20,8	36,7	36,8	36,9	37,0	37,1	37,2	37,3	37,4	37,5	37,6
21,0	36,6	36,7	36,8	36,9	37,0	37,1	37,2	37,3	37,4	37,5
21,2	36,5	36,6	36,7	36,8	36,9	37,0	37,1	37,2	37,3	37,4
21,4	36,4	36,5	36,6	36,7	36,8	36,9	37,0	37,1	37,2	37,3
21,6	36,4	36,5	36,6	36,7	36,8	36,9	37,0	37,1	37,2	37,3
21,8	36,3	36,4	36,5	36,6	36,7	36,8	36,9	37,0	37,1	37,2
22,0	36,2	36,3	36,4	36,5	36,6	36,7	36,8	36,9	37,0	37,1
22,2	36,1	36,2	36,3	36,4	36,5	36,6	36,7	36,8	36,9	37,0
22,4	36,0	36,1	36,2	36,3	36,4	36,5	36,6	36,7	36,8	36,9
22,6	35,9	36,0	36,1	36,2	36,3	36,4	36,5	36,6	36,7	36,8
22,8	35,9	36,0	36,1	36,2	36,3	36,4	36,5	36,6	36,7	36,8
23,0	35,8	35,9	36,0	36,1	36,2	36,3	36,4	36,5	36,6	36,7
23,2	35,7	35,8	35,9	36,0	36,1	36,2	36,3	36,4	36,5	36,6
23,4	35,6	35,7	35,8	35,9	36,0	36,1	36,2	36,3	36,4	36,5
23,6	35,5	35,6	35,7	35,8	35,9	36,0	36,1	36,2	36,3	36,4
23,8	35,5	35,6	35,7	35,8	35,9	36,0	36,1	36,2	36,3	36,4
24,0	35,4	35,5	35,6	35,7	35,8	35,9	36,0	36,1	36,2	36,3
24,2	35,3	35,4	35,5	35,6	35,7	35,8	35,9	36,0	36,1	36,2
24,4	35,2	35,3	35,4	35,5	35,6	35,7	35,8	35,9	36,0	36,1
24,6	35,1	35,2	35,3	35,4	35,5	35,6	35,7	35,8	35,9	36,0
24,8	35,1	35,2	35,3	35,4	35,5	35,6	35,7	35,8	35,9	36,0
25,0	35,0	35,1	35,2	35,3	35,4	35,5	35,6	35,7	35,8	35,9
25,2	34,9	35,0	35,1	35,2	35,3	35,4	35,5	35,6	35,7	35,8
25,4	34,8	34,9	35,0	35,1	35,2	35,3	35,4	35,5	35,6	35,7
25,6	34,7	34,8	34,9	35,0	35,1	35,2	35,3	35,4	35,5	35,6
25,8	34,7	34,8	34,9	35,0	35,1	35,2	35,3	35,4	35,5	35,6
26,0	34,6	34,7	34,8	34,9	35,0	35,1	35,2	35,3	35,4	35,5
26,2	34,5	34,6	34,7	34,8	34,9	35,0	35,1	35,2	35,3	35,4
26,4	34,4	34,5	34,6	34,7	34,8	34,9	35,0	35,1	35,2	35,3
26,6	34,3	34,4	34,5	34,6	34,7	34,8	34,9	35,0	35,1	35,2
26,8	34,2	34,3	34,4	34,5	34,6	34,7	34,8	35,0	35,1	35,2
27,0	34,2	34,3	34,4	34,5	34,6	34,7	34,8	34,9	35,0	35,1
27,2	34,1	34,2	34,3	34,4	34,5	34,6	34,7	34,8	34,9	35,0
27,4	34,0	34,1	34,2	34,3	34,4	34,5	34,6	34,7	34,8	34,9
27,6	33,9	34,0	34,1	34,2	34,3	34,4	34,5	34,6	34,7	34,8
27,8	33,8	33,9	34,0	34,1	34,2	34,3	34,4	34,5	34,6	34,7
28,0	33,8	33,9	34,0	34,1	34,2	34,3	34,4	34,5	34,6	34,7
28,2	33,7	33,8	33,9	34,0	34,1	34,2	34,3	34,4	34,5	34,6
28,4	33,6	33,7	33,8	33,9	34,0	34,1	34,2	34,3	34,4	34,5
28,6	33,5	33,6	33,7	33,8	33,9	34,0	34,1	34,2	34,3	34,4
28,8	33,4	33,5	33,6	33,7	33,8	33,9	34,0	34,1	34,2	34,3
29,0	33,4	33,5	33,6	33,7	33,8	33,9	34,0	34,1	34,2	34,3
29,2	33,3	33,4	33,5	33,6	33,7	33,8	33,9	34,0	34,1	34,2
29,4	33,2	33,3	33,4	33,5	33,6	33,7	33,8	33,9	34,0	34,1
29,6	33,1	33,2	33,3	33,4	33,5	33,6	33,7	33,8	33,9	34,0
29,8	33,0	33,1	33,2	33,3	33,4	33,5	33,6	33,7	33,8	33,9
30,0	33,0	33,1	33,2	33,3	33,4	33,5	33,6	33,7	33,8	33,9

Volumenkonzentration bei 20 °C in Prozent

Temp. °C	Anzeige des Alkoholometers in % vol									
	38,0	38,1	38,2	38,3	38,4	38,5	38,6	38,7	38,8	38,9
0,0	46,0	46,1	46,2	46,3	46,4	46,5	46,6	46,6	46,7	46,8
0,2	45,9	46,0	46,1	46,2	46,3	46,4	46,5	46,6	46,7	46,8
0,4	45,8	45,9	46,0	46,1	46,2	46,3	46,4	46,5	46,6	46,7
0,6	45,8	45,9	45,9	46,0	46,1	46,2	46,3	46,4	46,5	46,6
0,8	45,7	45,8	45,9	46,0	46,1	46,1	46,2	46,3	46,4	46,5
1,0	45,6	45,7	45,8	45,9	46,0	46,1	46,2	46,3	46,4	46,4
1,2	45,5	45,6	45,7	45,8	45,9	46,0	46,1	46,2	46,3	46,4
1,4	45,4	45,5	45,6	45,7	45,8	45,9	46,0	46,1	46,2	46,3
1,6	45,4	45,5	45,6	45,6	45,7	45,8	45,9	46,0	46,1	46,2
1,8	45.3	45,4	45,5	45,6	45,7	45,8	45,9	45,9	46,0	46,1
2,0	45,2	45,3	45,4	45,5	45,6	45,7	45,8	45,9	46,0	46,1
2,2	45,1	45,2	45,3	45,4	45,5	45,6	45,7	45,8	45,9	46,0
2,4	45,1	45,1	45,2	45,3	45,4	45,5	45,6	45,7	45,8	45,9
2,6	45,0	45,1	45,2	45,3	45,4	45,4	45,5	45,6	45,7	45,8
2,8	44,9	45,0	45,1	45,2	45,3	45,4	45,5	45,6	45,6	45,7
3,0	44,8	44,9	45,0	45,1	45,2	45,3	45,4	45,5	45,6	45,7
3,2	44,7	44,8	44,9	45,0	45,1	45,2	45,3	45,4	45,5	45,6
3,4	44,7	44,8	44,8	44,9	45,0	45,1	45,2	45,3	45,4	45,5
3,6	44,6	44,7	44,8	44,9	45,0	45,1	45,1	45,2	45,3	45,4
3,8	44,5	44,6	44,7	44,8	44,9	45,0	45,1	45,2	45,3	45,4
4,0	44,4	44,5	44,6	44,7	44,8	44,9	45,0	45,1	45,2	45,3
4,2	44,3	44,4	44,5	44,6	44,7	44,8	44,9	45,0	45,1	45,2
4,4	44,3	44,4	44,5	44,5	44,6	44,7	44,8	44,9	45,0	45,1
4,6	44,2	44,3	44,4	44,5	44,6	44,7	44,8	44,8	44,9	45,0
4,8	44,1	44,2	44,3	44,4	44,5	44,6	44,7	44,8	44,9	45,0
5,0	44,0	44,1	44,2	44,3	44,4	44,5	44,6	44,7	44,8	44,9
5,2	43,9	44,0	44,1	44,2	44,3	44,4	44,5	44,6	44,7	44,8
5,4	43,9	44,0	44,1	44,1	44,2	44,3	44,4	44,5	44,6	44,7
5,6	43,8	43,9	44,0	44,1	44,2	44,3	44,4	44,5	44,5	44,6
5,8	43,7	43,8	43,9	44,0	44,1	44,2	44,3	44,4	44,5	44,6
6,0	43,6	43,7	43,8	43,9	44,0	44,1	44,2	44,3	44,4	44,5
6,2	43,5	43,6	43,7	43,8	43,9	44,0	44,1	44,2	44,3	44,4
6,4	43,5	43,6	43,7	43,8	43,8	43,9	44,0	44,1	44,2	44,3
6,6	43,4	43,5	43,6	43,7	43,8	43,9	44,0	44,1	44,2	44,2
6,8	43,3	43,4	43,5	43,6	43,7	43,8	43,9	44,0	44,1	44,2
7,0	43,2	43,3	43,4	43,5	43,6	43,7	43,8	43,9	44,0	44,1
7,2	43,1	43,2	43,3	43,4	43,5	43,6	43,7	43,8	43,9	44,0
7,4	43,1	43,2	43,3	43,4	43,5	43,5	43,6	43,7	43,8	43,9
7,6	43,0	43,1	43,2	43,3	43,4	43,5	43,6	43,7	43,8	43,9
7,8	42,9	43,0	43,1	43,2	43,3	43,4	43,5	43,6	43,7	43,8
8,0	42,8	42,9	43,0	43,1	43,2	43,3	43,4	43,5	43,6	43,7
8,2	42,7	42,8	42,9	43,0	43,1	43,2	43,3	43,4	43,5	43,6
8,4	42,7	42,8	42,9	43,0	43,1	43,1	43,2	43,3	43,4	43,5
8,6	42,6	42,7	42,8	42,9	43,0	43,1	43,2	43,3	43,4	43,5
8,8	42,5	42,6	42,7	42,8	42,9	43,0	43,1	43,2	43,3	43,4
9,0	42,4	42,5	42,6	42,7	42,8	42,9	43,0	43,1	43,2	43,3
9,2	42,3	42,4	42,5	42,6	42,7	42,8	42,9	43,0	43,1	43,2
9,4	42,3	42,4	42,5	42,6	42,7	42,8	42,8	42,9	43,0	43,1
9,6	42,2	42,3	42,4	42,5	42,6	42,7	42,8	42,9	43,0	43,1
9,8	42,1	42,2	42,3	42,4	42,5	42,6	42,7	42,8	42,9	43,0

Volumenkonzentration bei 20 °C in Prozent

Temp.	Anzeige des Alkoholometers in % vol								
°C	38,0	38,1	38,2	38,3	38,4	38,5	38,6	38,7	38,8	38,9
10,0	42,0	42,1	42,2	42,3	42,4	42,5	42,6	42,7	42,8	42,9
10,2	41,9	42,0	42,1	42,2	42,3	42,4	42,5	42,6	42,7	42,8
10,4	41,9	42,0	42,1	42,2	42,3	42,4	42,4	42,5	42,6	42,7
10,6	41,8	41,9	42,0	42,1	42,2	42,3	42,4	42,5	42,6	42,7
10,8	41,7	41,8	41,9	42,0	42,1	42,2	42,3	42,4	42,5	42,6
11,0	41,6	41,7	41,8	41,9	42,0	42,1	42,2	42,3	42,4	42,5
11,2	41,5	41,6	41,7	41,8	41,9	42,0	42,1	42,2	42,3	42,4
11,4	41,5	41,6	41,7	41,8	41,9	42,0	42,1	42,1	42,2	42,3
11,6	41,4	41,5	41,6	41,7	41,8	41,9	42,0	42,1	42,2	42,3
11,8	41,3	41,4	41,5	41,6	41,7	41,8	41,9	42,0	42,1	42,2
12,0	41,2	41,3	41,4	41,5	41,6	41,7	41,8	41,9	42,0	42,1
12,2	41,1	41,2	41,3	41,4	41,5	41,6	41,7	41,8	41,9	42,0
12,4	41,1	41,2	41,3	41,4	41,5	41,6	41,7	41,7	41,8	41,9
12,6	41,0	41,1	41,2	41,3	41,4	41,5	41,6	41,7	41,8	41,9
12,8	40,9	41,0	41,1	41,2	41,3	41,4	41,5	41,6	41,7	41,8
13,0	40,8	40,9	41,0	41,1	41,2	41,3	41,4	41,5	41,6	41,7
13,2	40,7	40,8	40,9	41,0	41,1	41,2	41,3	41,4	41,5	41,6
13,4	40,7	40,8	40,9	41,0	41,1	41,2	41,3	41,3	41,4	41,5
13,6	40,6	40,7	40,8	40,9	41,0	41,1	41,2	41,3	41,4	41,5
13,8	40,5	40,6	40,7	40,8	40,9	41,0	41,1	41,2	41,3	41,4
14,0	40,4	40,5	40,6	40,7	40,8	40,9	41,0	41,1	41,2	41,3
14,2	40,3	40,4	40,5	40,6	40,7	40,8	40,9	41,0	41,1	41,2
14,4	40,3	40,4	40,5	40,6	40,7	40,8	40,8	40,9	41,0	41,1
14,6	40,2	40,3	40,4	40,5	40,6	40,7	40,8	40,9	41,0	41,1
14,8	40,1	40,2	40,3	40,4	40,5	40,6	40,7	40,8	40,9	41,0
15,0	40,0	40,1	40,2	40,3	40,4	40,5	40,6	40,7	40,8	40,9
15,2	39,9	40,0	40,1	40,2	40,3	40,4	40,5	40,6	40,7	40,8
15,4	39,9	40,0	40,1	40,2	40,3	40,3	40,4	40,5	40,6	40,7
15,6	39,8	39,9	40,0	40,1	40,2	40,3	40,4	40,5	40,6	40,7
15,8	39,7	39,8	39,9	40,0	40,1	40,2	40,3	40,4	40,5	40,6
16,0	39,6	39,7	39,8	39,9	40,0	40,1	40,2	40,3	40,4	40,5
16,2	39,5	39,6	39,7	39,8	39,9	40,0	40,1	40,2	40,3	40,4
16,4	39,5	39,6	39,7	39,7	39,8	39,9	40,0	40,1	40,2	40,3
16,6	39,4	39,5	39,6	39,7	39,8	39,9	40,0	40,1	40,2	40,3
16,8	39,3	39,4	39,5	39,6	39,7	39,8	39,9	40,0	40,1	40,2
17,0	39,2	39,3	39,4	39,5	39,6	39,7	39,8	39,9	40,0	40,1
17,2	39,1	39,2	39,3	39,4	39,5	39,6	39,7	39,8	39,9	40,0
17,4	39,0	39,1	39,2	39,3	39,4	39,5	39,6	39,7	39,8	39,9
17,6	39,0	39,1	39,2	39,3	39,4	39,5	39,6	39,7	39,8	39,9
17,8	38,9	39,0	39,1	39,2	39,3	39,4	39,5	39,6	39,7	39,8
18,0	38,8	38,9	39,0	39,1	39,2	39,3	39,4	39,5	39,6	39,7
18,2	38,7	38,8	38,9	39,0	39,1	39,2	39,3	39,4	39,5	39,6
18,4	38,6	38,7	38,8	38,9	39,0	39,1	39,2	39,3	39,4	39,5
18,6	38,6	38,7	38,8	38,9	39,0	39,1	39,2	39,3	39,4	39,5
18,8	38,5	38,6	38,7	38,8	38,9	39,0	39,1	39,2	39,3	39,4
19,0	38,4	38,5	38,6	38,7	38,8	38,9	39,0	39,1	39,2	39,3
19,2	38,3	38,4	38,5	38,6	38,7	38,8	38,9	39,0	39,1	39,2
19,4	38,2	38,3	38,4	38,5	38,6	38,7	38,8	38,9	39,0	39,1
19,6	38,2	38,3	38,4	38,5	38,6	38,7	38,8	38,9	39,0	39,1
19,8	38,1	38,2	38,3	38,4	38,5	38,6	38,7	38,8	38,9	39,0

Volumenkonzentration bei 20 °C in Prozent

Temp. °C	Anzeige des Alkoholometers in % vol								
	38,0	38,1	38,2	38,3	38,4	38,5	38,6	38,7	38,8	38,9
20,0	38,0	38,1	38,2	38,3	38,4	38,5	38,6	38,7	38,8	38,9
20,2	37,9	38,0	38,1	38,2	38,3	38,4	38,5	38,6	38,7	38,8
20,4	37,8	37,9	38,0	38,1	38,2	38,3	38,4	38,5	38,6	38,7
20,6	37,8	37,9	38,0	38,1	38,2	38,3	38,4	38,5	38,6	38,7
20,8	37,7	37,8	37,9	38,0	38,1	38,2	38,3	38,4	38,5	38,6
21,0	37,6	37,7	37,8	37,9	38,0	38,1	38,2	38,3	38,4	38,5
21,2	37,5	37,6	37,7	37,8	37,9	38,0	38,1	38,2	38,3	38,4
21,4	37,4	37,5	37,6	37,7	37,8	37,9	38,0	38,1	38,2	38,3
21,6	37,4	37,5	37,6	37,7	37,8	37,9	38,0	38,1	38,2	38,3
21,8	37,3	37,4	37,5	37,6	37,7	37,8	37,9	38,0	38,1	38,2
22,0	37,2	37,3	37,4	37,5	37,6	37,7	37,8	37,9	38,0	38,1
22,2	37,1	37,2	37,3	37,4	37,5	37,6	37,7	37,8	37,9	38,0
22,4	37,0	37,1	37,2	37,3	37,4	37,5	37,6	37,7	37,8	37,9
22,6	37,0	37,1	37,2	37,3	37,4	37,5	37,6	37,7	37,8	37,9
22,8	36,9	37,0	37,1	37,2	37,3	37,4	37,5	37,6	37,7	37,8
23,0	36,8	36,9	37,0	37,1	37,2	37,3	37,4	37,5	37,6	37,7
23,2	36,7	36,8	36,9	37,0	37,1	37,2	37,3	37,4	37,5	37,6
23,4	36,6	36,7	36,8	36,9	37,0	37,1	37,2	37,3	37,4	37,5
23,6	36,5	36,6	36,7	36,8	36,9	37,0	37,1	37,2	37,3	37,4
23,8	36,5	36,6	36,7	36,8	36,9	37,0	37,1	37,2	37,3	37,4
24,0	36,4	36,5	36,6	36,7	36,8	36,9	37,0	37,1	37,2	37,3
24,2	36,3	36,4	36,5	36,6	36,7	36,8	36,9	37,0	37,1	37,2
24,4	36,2	36,3	36,4	36,5	36,6	36,7	36,8	36,9	37,0	37,1
24,6	36,1	36,2	36,3	36,4	36,5	36,6	36,7	36,8	36,9	37,0
24,8	36,1	36,2	36,3	36,4	36,5	36,6	36,7	36,8	36,9	37,0
25,0	36,0	36,1	36,2	36,3	36,4	36,5	36,6	36,7	36,8	36,9
25,2	35,9	36,0	36,1	36,2	36,3	36,4	36,5	36,6	36,7	36,8
25,4	35,8	35,9	36,0	36,1	36,2	36,3	36,4	36,5	36,6	36,7
25,6	35,7	35,8	35,9	36,0	36,1	36,2	36,3	36,4	36,5	36,6
25,8	35,7	35,8	35,9	36,0	36,1	36,2	36,3	36,4	36,5	36,6
26,0	35,6	35,7	35,8	35,9	36,0	36,1	36,2	36,3	36,4	36,5
26,2	35,5	35,6	35,7	35,8	35,9	36,0	36,1	36,2	36,3	36,4
26,4	35,4	35,5	35,6	35,7	35,8	35,9	36,0	36,1	36,2	36,3
26,6	35,3	35,4	35,5	35,6	35,7	35,8	35,9	36,0	36,1	36,2
26,8	35,3	35,4	35,5	35,6	35,7	35,8	35,9	36,0	36,1	36,2
27,0	35,2	35,3	35,4	35,5	35,6	35,7	35,8	35,9	36,0	36,1
27,2	35,1	35,2	35,3	35,4	35,5	35,6	35,7	35,8	35,9	36,0
27,4	35,0	35,1	35,2	35,3	35,4	35,5	35,6	35,7	35,8	35,9
27,6	34,9	35,0	35,1	35,2	35,3	35,4	35,5	35,6	35,7	35,8
27,8	34,8	34,9	35,1	35,2	35,3	35,4	35,5	35,6	35,7	35,8
28,0	34,8	34,9	35,0	35,1	35,2	35,3	35,4	35,5	35,6	35,7
28,2	34,7	34,8	34,9	35,0	35,1	35,2	35,3	35,4	35,5	35,6
28,4	34,6	34,7	34,8	34,9	35,0	35,1	35,2	35,3	35,4	35,5
28,6	34,5	34,6	34,7	34,8	34,9	35,0	35,1	35,2	35,3	35,4
28,8	34,4	34,5	34,6	34,7	34,8	34,9	35,1	35,2	35,3	35,4
29,0	34,4	34,5	34,6	34,7	34,8	34,9	35,0	35,1	35,2	35,3
29,2	34,3	34,4	34,5	34,6	34,7	34,8	34,9	35,0	35,1	35,2
29,4	34,2	34,3	34,4	34,5	34,6	34,7	34,8	34,9	35,0	35,1
29,6	34,1	34,2	34,3	34,4	34,5	34,6	34,7	34,8	34,9	35,0
29,8	34,0	34,1	34,2	34,3	34,4	34,5	34,6	34,7	34,8	34,9
30,0	34,0	34,1	34,2	34,3	34,4	34,5	34,6	34,7	34,8	34,9

Volumenkonzentration bei 20 °C in Prozent

Temp. °C	Anzeige des Alkoholometers in % vol								
	39,0	39,1	39,2	39,3	39,4	39,5	39,6	39,7	39,8	39,9
0,0	46,9	47,0	47,1	47,2	47,3	47,4	47,5	47,6	47,7	47,8
0,2	46,8	46,9	47,0	47,1	47,2	47,3	47,4	47,5	47,6	47,7
0,4	46,8	46,9	47,0	47,0	47,1	47,2	47,3	47,4	47,5	47,6
0,6	46,7	46,8	46,9	47,0	47,1	47,2	47,3	47,3	47,4	47,5
0,8	46,6	46,7	46,8	46,9	47,0	47,1	47,2	47,3	47,4	47,5
1,0	46,5	46,6	46,7	46,8	46,9	47,0	47,1	47,2	47,3	47,4
1,2	46,5	46,6	46,6	46,7	46,8	46,9	47,0	47,1	47,2	47,3
1,4	46,4	46,5	46,6	46,7	46,8	46,8	46,9	47,0	47,1	47,2
1,6	46,3	46,4	46,5	46,6	46,7	46,8	46,9	47,0	47,1	47,1
1,8	46,2	46,3	46,4	46,5	46,6	46,7	46,8	46,9	47,0	47,1
2,0	46,1	46,2	46,3	46,4	46,5	46,6	46,7	46,8	46,9	47,0
2,2	46,1	46,2	46,3	46,4	46,4	46,5	46,6	46,7	46,8	46,9
2,4	46,0	46,1	46,2	46,3	46,4	46,5	46,6	46,6	46,7	46,8
2,6	45,9	46,0	46,1	46,2	46,3	46,4	46,5	46,6	46,7	46,8
2,8	45,8	45,9	46,0	46,1	46,2	46,3	46,4	46,5	46,6	46,7
3,0	45,8	45,9	45,9	46,0	46,1	46,2	46,3	46,4	46,5	46,6
3,2	45,7	45,8	45,9	46,0	46,1	46,2	46,2	46,3	46,4	46,5
3,4	45,6	45,7	45,8	45,9	46,0	46,1	46,2	46,3	46,4	46,5
3,6	45,5	45,6	45,7	45,8	45,9	46,0	46,1	46,2	46,3	46,4
3,8	45,4	45,5	45,6	45,7	45,8	45,9	46,0	46,1	46,2	46,3
4,0	45,4	45,5	45,6	45,7	45,7	45,8	45,9	46,0	46,1	46,2
4,2	45,3	45,4	45,5	45,6	45,7	45,8	45,9	46,0	46,0	46,1
4,4	45,2	45,3	45,4	45,5	45,6	45,7	45,8	45,9	46,0	46,1
4,6	45,1	45,2	45,3	45,4	45,5	45,6	45,7	45,8	45,9	46,0
4,8	45,1	45,1	45,2	45,3	45,4	45,5	45,6	45,7	45,8	45,9
5,0	45,0	45,1	45,2	45,3	45,4	45,4	45,5	45,6	45,7	45,8
5,2	44,9	45,0	45,1	45,2	45,3	45,4	45,5	45,6	45,7	45,8
5,4	44,8	44,9	45,0	45,1	45,2	45,3	45,4	45,5	45,6	45,7
5,6	44,7	44,8	44,9	45,0	45,1	45,2	45,3	45,4	45,5	45,6
5,8	44,7	44,8	44,9	44,9	45,0	45,1	45,2	45,3	45,4	45,5
6,0	44,6	44,7	44,8	44,9	45,0	45,1	45,2	45,2	45,3	45,4
6,2	44,5	44,6	44,7	44,8	44,9	45,0	45,1	45,2	45,3	45,4
6,4	44,4	44,5	44,6	44,7	44,8	44,9	45,0	45,1	45,2	45,3
6,6	44,3	44,4	44,5	44,6	44,7	44,8	44,9	45,0	45,1	45,2
6,8	44,3	44,4	44,5	44,6	44,6	44,7	44,8	44,9	45,0	45,1
7,0	44,2	44,3	44,4	44,5	44,6	44,7	44,8	44,9	45,0	45,0
7,2	44,1	44,2	44,3	44,4	44,5	44,6	44,7	44,8	44,9	45,0
7,4	44,0	44,1	44,2	44,3	44,4	44,5	44,6	44,7	44,8	44,9
7,6	43,9	44,0	44,1	44,2	44,3	44,4	44,5	44,6	44,7	44,8
7,8	43,9	44,0	44,1	44,2	44,3	44,4	44,4	44,5	44,6	44,7
8,0	43,8	43,9	44,0	44,1	44,2	44,3	44,4	44,5	44,6	44,7
8,2	43,7	43,8	43,9	44,0	44,1	44,2	44,3	44,4	44,5	44,6
8,4	43,6	43,7	43,8	43,9	44,0	44,1	44,2	44,3	44,4	44,5
8,6	43,6	43,6	43,7	43,8	43,9	44,0	44,1	44,2	44,3	44,4
8,8	43,5	43,6	43,7	43,8	43,9	44,0	44,1	44,2	44,2	44,3
9,0	43,4	43,5	43,6	43,7	43,8	43,9	44,0	44,1	44,2	44,3
9,2	43,3	43,4	43,5	43,6	43,7	43,8	43,9	44,0	44,1	44,2
9,4	43,2	43,3	43,4	43,5	43,6	43,7	43,8	43,9	44,0	44,1
9,6	43,2	43,3	43,4	43,4	43,5	43,6	43,7	43,8	43,9	44,0
9,8	43,1	43,2	43,3	43,4	43,5	43,6	43,7	43,8	43,9	44,0

Volumenkonzentration bei 20 °C in Prozent

Temp. °C	Anzeige des Alkoholometers in % vol								
	39,0	39,1	39,2	39,3	39,4	39,5	39,6	39,7	39,8	39,9
10,0	43,0	43,1	43,2	43,3	43,4	43,5	43,6	43,7	43,8	43,9
10,2	42,9	43,0	43,1	43,2	43,3	43,4	43,5	43,6	43,7	43,8
10,4	42,8	42,9	43,0	43,1	43,2	43,3	43,4	43,5	43,6	43,7
10,6	42,8	42,9	43,0	43,1	43,1	43,2	43,3	43,4	43,5	43,6
10,8	42,7	42,8	42,9	43,0	43,1	43,2	43,3	43,4	43,5	43,6
11,0	42,6	42,7	42,8	42,9	43,0	43,1	43,2	43,3	43,4	43,5
11,2	42,5	42,6	42,7	42,8	42,9	43,0	43,1	43,2	43,3	43,4
11,4	42,4	42,5	42,6	42,7	42,8	42,9	43,0	43,1	43,2	43,3
11,6	42,4	42,5	42,6	42,7	42,8	42,8	42,9	43,0	43,1	43,2
11,8	42,3	42,4	42,5	42,6	42,7	42,8	42,9	43,0	43,1	43,2
12,0	42,2	42,3	42,4	42,5	42,6	42,7	42,8	42,9	43,0	43,1
12,2	42,1	42,2	42,3	42,4	42,5	42,6	42,7	42,8	42,9	43,0
12,4	42,0	42,1	42,2	42,3	42,4	42,5	42,6	42,7	42,8	42,9
12,6	42,0	42,1	42,2	42,3	42,4	42,5	42,6	42,6	42,7	42,8
12,8	41,9	42,0	42,1	42,2	42,3	42,4	42,5	42,6	42,7	42,8
13,0	41,8	41,9	42,0	42,1	42,2	42,3	42,4	42,5	42,6	42,7
13,2	41,7	41,8	41,9	42,0	42,1	42,2	42,3	42,4	42,5	42,6
13,4	41,6	41,7	41,8	41,9	42,0	42,1	42,2	42,3	42,4	42,5
13,6	41,6	41,7	41,8	41,9	42,0	42,1	42,2	42,3	42,4	42,4
13,8	41,5	41,6	41,7	41,8	41,9	42,0	42,1	42,2	42,3	42,4
14,0	41,4	41,5	41,6	41,7	41,8	41,9	42,0	42,1	42,2	42,3
14,2	41,3	41,4	41,5	41,6	41,7	41,8	41,9	42,0	42,1	42,2
14,4	41,2	41,3	41,4	41,5	41,6	41,7	41,8	41,9	42,0	42,1
14,6	41,2	41,3	41,4	41,5	41,6	41,7	41,8	41,9	42,0	42,1
14,8	41,1	41,2	41,3	41,4	41,5	41,6	41,7	41,8	41,9	42,0
15,0	41,0	41,1	41,2	41,3	41,4	41,5	41,6	41,7	41,8	41,9
15,2	40,9	41,0	41,1	41,2	41,3	41,4	41,5	41,6	41,7	41,8
15,4	40,8	40,9	41,0	41,1	41,2	41,3	41,4	41,5	41,6	41,7
15,6	40,8	40,9	41,0	41,1	41,2	41,3	41,4	41,5	41,6	41,7
15,8	40,7	40,8	40,9	41,0	41,1	41,2	41,3	41,4	41,5	41,6
16,0	40,6	40,7	40,8	40,9	41,0	41,1	41,2	41,3	41,4	41,5
16,2	40,5	40,6	40,7	40,8	40,9	41,0	41,1	41,2	41,3	41,4
16,4	40,4	40,5	40,6	40,7	40,8	40,9	41,0	41,1	41,2	41,3
16,6	40,4	40,5	40,6	40,7	40,8	40,9	41,0	41,1	41,2	41,3
16,8	40,3	40,4	40,5	40,6	40,7	40,8	40,9	41,0	41,1	41,2
17,0	40,2	40,3	40,4	40,5	40,6	40,7	40,8	40,9	41,0	41,1
17,2	40,1	40,2	40,3	40,4	40,5	40,6	40,7	40,8	40,9	41,0
17,4	40,0	40,1	40,2	40,3	40,4	40,5	40,6	40,7	40,8	40,9
17,6	40,0	40,1	40,2	40,3	40,4	40,5	40,6	40,7	40,8	40,9
17,8	39,9	40,0	40,1	40,2	40,3	40,4	40,5	40,6	40,7	40,8
18,0	39,8	39,9	40,0	40,1	40,2	40,3	40,4	40,5	40,6	40,7
18,2	39,7	39,8	39,9	40,0	40,1	40,2	40,3	40,4	40,5	40,6
18,4	39,6	39,7	39,8	39,9	40,0	40,1	40,2	40,3	40,4	40,5
18,6	39,6	39,7	39,8	39,9	40,0	40,1	40,2	40,3	40,4	40,5
18,8	39,5	39,6	39,7	39,8	39,9	40,0	40,1	40,2	40,3	40,4
19,0	39,4	39,5	39,6	39,7	39,8	39,8	39,9	40,1	40,2	40,3
19,2	39,3	39,4	39,5	39,6	39,7	39,8	39,9	40,0	40,1	40,2
19,4	39,2	39,3	39,4	39,5	39,6	39,7	39,8	39,9	40,0	40,1
19,6	39,2	39,3	39,4	39,5	39,6	39,7	39,8	39,9	40,0	40,1
19,8	39,1	39,2	39,3	39,4	39,5	39,6	39,7	39,8	39,9	40,0

H

Volumenkonzentration bei 20 °C in Prozent

Temp. °C	Anzeige des Alkoholometers in % vol									
	39,0	39,1	39,2	39,3	39,4	39,5	39,6	39,7	39,8	39,9
20,0	39,0	39,1	39,2	39,3	39,4	39,5	39,6	39,7	39,8	39,9
20,2	38,9	39,0	39,1	39,2	39,3	39,4	39,5	39,6	39,7	39,8
20,4	38,8	38,9	39,0	39,1	39,2	39,3	39,4	39,5	39,6	39,7
20,6	38,8	38,9	39,0	39,1	39,2	39,3	39,4	39,5	39,6	39,7
20,8	38,7	38,8	38,9	39,0	39,1	39,2	39,3	39,4	39,5	39,6
21,0	38,6	38,7	38,8	38,9	39,0	39,1	39,2	39,3	39,4	39,5
21,2	38,5	38,6	38,7	38,8	38,9	39,0	39,1	39,2	39,3	39,4
21,4	38,4	38,5	38,6	38,7	38,8	38,9	39,0	39,1	39,2	39,3
21,6	38,4	38,5	38,6	38,7	38,8	38,9	39,0	39,1	39,2	39,3
21,8	38,3	38,4	38,5	38,6	38,7	38,8	38,9	39,0	39,1	39,2
22,0	38,2	38,3	38,4	38,5	38,6	38,7	38,8	38,9	39,0	39,1
22,2	38,1	38,2	38,3	38,4	38,5	38,6	38,7	38,8	38,9	39,0
22,4	38,0	38,1	38,2	38,3	38,4	38,5	38,6	38,7	38,8	38,9
22,6	38,0	38,1	38,2	38,3	38,4	38,5	38,6	38,7	38,8	38,9
22,8	37,9	38,0	38,1	38,2	38,3	38,4	38,5	38,6	38,7	38,8
23,0	37,8	37,9	38,0	38,1	38,2	38,3	38,4	38,5	38,6	38,7
23,2	37,7	37,8	37,9	38,0	38,1	38,2	38,3	38,4	38,5	38,6
23,4	37,6	37,7	37,8	37,9	38,0	38,1	38,2	38,3	38,4	38,5
23,6	37,6	37,7	37,8	37,9	38,0	38,1	38,2	38,3	38,4	38,5
23,8	37,5	37,6	37,7	37,8	37,9	38,0	38,1	38,2	38,3	38,4
24,0	37,4	37,5	37,6	37,7	37,8	37,9	38,0	38,1	38,2	38,3
24,2	37,3	37,4	37,5	37,6	37,7	37,8	37,9	38,0	38,1	38,2
24,4	37,2	37,3	37,4	37,5	37,6	37,7	37,8	37,9	38,0	38,1
24,6	37,1	37,3	37,4	37,5	37,6	37,7	37,8	37,9	38,0	38,1
24,8	37,1	37,2	37,3	37,4	37,5	37,6	37,7	37,8	37,9	38,0
25,0	37,0	37,1	37,2	37,3	37,4	37,5	37,6	37,7	37,8	37,9
25,2	36,9	37,0	37,1	37,2	37,3	37,4	37,5	37,6	37,7	37,8
25,4	36,8	36,9	37,0	37,1	37,2	37,3	37,4	37,5	37,6	37,7
25,6	36,7	36,8	36,9	37,0	37,2	37,3	37,4	37,5	37,6	37,7
25,8	36,7	36,8	36,9	37,0	37,1	37,2	37,3	37,4	37,5	37,6
26,0	36,6	36,7	36,8	36,9	37,0	37,1	37,2	37,3	37,4	37,5
26,2	36,5	36,6	36,7	36,8	36,9	37,0	37,1	37,2	37,3	37,4
26,4	36,4	36,5	36,6	36,7	36,8	36,9	37,0	37,1	37,2	37,3
26,6	36,3	36,4	36,5	36,6	36,7	36,8	36,9	37,1	37,2	37,3
26,8	36,3	36,4	36,5	36,6	36,7	36,8	36,9	37,0	37,1	37,2
27,0	36,2	36,3	36,4	36,5	36,6	36,7	36,8	36,9	37,0	37,1
27,2	36,1	36,2	36,3	36,4	36,5	36,6	36,7	36,8	36,9	37,0
27,4	36,0	36,1	36,2	36,3	36,4	36,5	36,6	36,7	36,8	36,9
27,6	35,9	36,0	36,1	36,2	36,3	36,4	36,5	36,6	36,7	36,9
27,8	35,9	36,0	36,1	36,2	36,3	36,4	36,5	36,6	36,7	36,8
28,0	35,8	35,9	36,0	36,1	36,2	36,3	36,4	36,5	36,6	36,7
28,2	35,7	35,8	35,9	36,0	36,1	36,2	36,3	36,4	36,5	36,6
28,4	35,6	35,7	35,8	35,9	36,0	36,1	36,2	36,3	36,4	36,5
28,6	35,5	35,6	35,7	35,8	35,9	36,0	36,1	36,2	36,3	36,4
28,8	35,5	35,6	35,7	35,8	35,9	36,0	36,1	36,2	36,3	36,4
29,0	35,4	35,5	35,6	35,7	35,8	35,9	36,0	36,1	36,2	36,3
29,2	35,3	35,4	35,5	35,6	35,7	35,8	35,9	36,0	36,1	36,2
29,4	35,2	35,3	35,4	35,5	35,6	35,7	35,8	35,9	36,0	36,1
29,6	35,1	35,2	35,3	35,4	35,5	35,6	35,7	35,8	35,9	36,0
29,8	35,1	35,2	35,3	35,4	35,5	35,6	35,7	35,8	35,9	36,0
30,0	35,0	35,1	35,2	35,3	35,4	35,5	35,6	35,7	35,8	35,9

Volumenkonzentration bei 20 °C in Prozent

Temp. °C	Anzeige des Alkoholometers in % vol								
	40,0	40,1	40,2	40,3	40,4	40,5	40,6	40,7	40,8	40,9
0,0	47,9	47,9	48,0	48,1	48,2	48,3	48,4	48,5	48,6	48,7
0,2	47,8	47,9	48,0	48,1	48,1	48,2	48,3	48,4	48,5	48,6
0,4	47,7	47,8	47,9	48,0	48,1	48,2	48,3	48,4	48,4	48,5
0,6	47,6	47,7	47,8	47,9	48,0	48,1	48,2	48,3	48,4	48,5
0,8	47,5	47,6	47,7	47,8	47,9	48,0	48,1	48,2	48,3	48,4
1,0	47,5	47,6	47,7	47,7	47,8	47,9	48,0	48,1	48,2	48,3
1,2	47,4	47,5	47,6	47,7	47,8	47,9	48,0	48,0	48,1	48,2
1,4	47,3	47,4	47,5	47,6	47,7	47,8	47,9	48,0	48,1	48,2
1,6	47,2	47,3	47,4	47,5	47,6	47,7	47,8	47,9	48,0	48,1
1,8	47,2	47,3	47,3	47,4	47,5	47,6	47,7	47,8	47,9	48,0
2,0	47,1	47,2	47,3	47,4	47,5	47,6	47,6	47,7	47,8	47,9
2,2	47,0	47,1	47,2	47,3	47,4	47,5	47,6	47,7	47,8	47,9
2,4	46,9	47,0	47,1	47,2	47,3	47,4	47,5	47,6	47,7	47,8
2,6	46,9	46,9	47,0	47,1	47,2	47,3	47,4	47,5	47,6	47,7
2,8	46,8	46,9	47,0	47,1	47,2	47,2	47,3	47,4	47,5	47,6
3,0	46,7	46,8	46,9	47,0	47,1	47,2	47,3	47,4	47,5	47,5
3,2	46,6	46,7	46,8	46,9	47,0	47,1	47,2	47,3	47,4	47,5
3,4	46,5	46,6	46,7	46,8	46,9	47,0	47,1	47,2	47,3	47,4
3,6	46,5	46,6	46,7	46,8	46,8	46,9	47,0	47,1	47,2	47,3
3,8	46,4	46,5	46,6	46,7	46,8	46,9	47,0	47,1	47,1	47,2
4,0	46,3	46,4	46,5	46,6	46,7	46,8	46,9	47,0	47,1	47,2
4,2	46,2	46,3	46,4	46,5	46,6	46,7	46,8	46,9	47,0	47,1
4,4	46,2	46,3	46,3	46,4	46,5	46,6	46,7	46,8	46,9	47,0
4,6	46,1	46,2	46,3	46,4	46,5	46,6	46,6	46,7	46,8	46,9
4,8	46,0	46,1	46,2	46,3	46,4	46,5	46,6	46,7	46,8	46,9
5,0	45,9	46,0	46,1	46,2	46,3	46,4	46,5	46,6	46,7	46,8
5,2	45,8	45,9	46,0	46,1	46,2	46,3	46,4	46,5	46,6	46,7
5,4	45,8	45,9	46,0	46,1	46,1	46,2	46,3	46,4	46,5	46,6
5,6	45,7	45,8	45,9	46,0	46,1	46,2	46,3	46,4	46,5	46,5
5,8	45,6	45,7	45,8	45,9	46,0	46,1	46,2	46,3	46,4	46,5
6,0	45,5	45,6	45,7	45,8	45,9	46,0	46,1	46,2	46,3	46,4
6,2	45,5	45,6	45,6	45,7	45,8	45,9	46,0	46,1	46,2	46,3
6,4	45,4	45,5	45,6	45,7	45,8	45,9	46,0	46,0	46,1	46,2
6,6	45,3	45,4	45,5	45,6	45,7	45,8	45,9	46,0	46,1	46,2
6,8	45,2	45,3	45,4	45,5	45,6	45,7	45,8	45,9	46,0	46,1
7,0	45,1	45,2	45,3	45,4	45,5	45,6	45,7	45,8	45,9	46,0
7,2	45,1	45,2	45,3	45,4	45,5	45,5	45,6	45,7	45,8	45,9
7,4	45,0	45,1	45,2	45,3	45,4	45,5	45,6	45,7	45,8	45,9
7,6	44,9	45,0	45,1	45,2	45,3	45,4	45,5	45,6	45,7	45,8
7,8	44,8	44,9	45,0	45,1	45,2	45,3	45,4	45,5	45,6	45,7
8,0	44,8	44,9	44,9	45,0	45,1	45,2	45,3	45,4	45,5	45,6
8,2	44,7	44,8	44,9	45,0	45,1	45,2	45,3	45,3	45,4	45,5
8,4	44,6	44,7	44,8	44,9	45,0	45,1	45,2	45,3	45,4	45,5
8,6	44,5	44,6	44,7	44,8	44,9	45,0	45,1	45,2	45,3	45,4
8,8	44,4	44,5	44,6	44,7	44,8	44,9	45,0	45,1	45,2	45,3
9,0	44,4	44,5	44,6	44,7	44,7	44,8	44,9	45,0	45,1	45,2
9,2	44,3	44,4	44,5	44,6	44,7	44,8	44,9	45,0	45,1	45,2
9,4	44,2	44,3	44,4	44,5	44,6	44,7	44,8	44,9	45,0	45,1
9,6	44,1	44,2	44,3	44,4	44,5	44,6	44,7	44,8	44,9	45,0
9,8	44,0	44,1	44,2	44,3	44,4	44,5	44,6	44,7	44,8	44,9

Volumenkonzentration bei 20 °C in Prozent

Temp. °C	Anzeige des Alkoholometers in % vol									
	40,0	40,1	40,2	40,3	40,4	40,5	40,6	40,7	40,8	40,9
10,0	44,0	44,1	44,2	44,3	44,4	44,5	44,6	44,6	44,7	44,8
10,2	43,9	44,0	44,1	44,2	44,3	44,4	44,5	44,6	44,7	44,8
10,4	43,8	43,9	44,0	44,1	44,2	44,3	44,4	44,5	44,6	44,7
10,6	43,7	43,8	43,9	44,0	44,1	44,2	44,3	44,4	44,5	44,6
10,8	43,7	43,8	43,8	43,9	44,0	44,1	44,2	44,3	44,4	44,5
11,0	43,6	43,7	43,8	43,9	44,0	44,1	44,2	44,3	44,4	44,5
11,2	43,5	43,6	43,7	43,8	43,9	44,0	44,1	44,2	44,3	44,4
11,4	43,4	43,5	43,6	43,7	43,8	43,9	44,0	44,1	44,2	44,3
11,6	43,3	43,4	43,5	43,6	43,7	43,8	43,9	44,0	44,1	44,2
11,8	43,3	43,4	43,5	43,6	43,6	43,7	43,8	43,9	44,0	44,1
12,0	43,2	43,3	43,4	43,5	43,6	43,7	43,8	43,9	44,0	44,1
12,2	43,1	43,2	43,3	43,4	43,5	43,6	43,7	43,8	43,9	44,0
12,4	43,0	43,1	43,2	43,3	43,4	43,5	43,6	43,7	43,8	43,9
12,6	42,9	43,0	43,1	43,2	43,3	43,4	43,5	43,6	43,7	43,8
12,8	42,9	43,0	43,1	43,2	43,3	43,4	43,5	43,5	43,6	43,7
13,0	42,8	42,9	43,0	43,1	43,2	43,3	43,4	43,5	43,6	43,7
13,2	42,7	42,8	42,9	43,0	43,1	43,2	43,3	43,4	43,5	43,6
13,4	42,6	42,7	42,8	42,9	43,0	43,1	43,2	43,3	43,4	43,5
13,6	42,5	42,6	42,7	42,8	42,9	43,0	43,1	43,2	43,3	43,4
13,8	42,5	42,6	42,7	42,8	42,9	43,0	43,1	43,2	43,3	43,4
14,0	42,4	42,5	42,6	42,7	42,8	42,9	43,0	43,1	43,2	43,3
14,2	42,3	42,4	42,5	42,6	42,7	42,8	42,9	43,0	43,1	43,2
14,4	42,2	42,3	42,4	42,5	42,6	42,7	42,8	42,9	43,0	43,1
14,6	42,2	42,2	42,3	42,4	42,5	42,6	42,7	42,8	42,9	43,0
14,8	42,1	42,2	42,3	42,4	42,5	42,6	42,7	42,8	42,9	43,0
15,0	42,0	42,1	42,2	42,3	42,4	42,5	42,6	42,7	42,8	42,9
15,2	41,9	42,0	42,1	42,2	42,3	42,4	42,5	42,6	42,7	42,8
15,4	41,8	41,9	42,0	42,1	42,2	42,3	42,4	42,5	42,6	42,7
15,6	41,8	41,9	42,0	42,0	42,1	42,2	42,3	42,4	42,5	42,6
15,8	41,7	41,8	41,9	42,0	42,1	42,2	42,3	42,4	42,5	42,6
16,0	41,6	41,7	41,8	41,9	42,0	42,1	42,2	42,3	42,4	42,5
16,2	41,5	41,6	41,7	41,8	41,9	42,0	42,1	42,2	42,3	42,4
16,4	41,4	41,5	41,6	41,7	41,8	41,9	42,0	42,1	42,2	42,3
16,6	41,4	41,5	41,6	41,7	41,8	41,9	42,0	42,0	42,1	42,2
16,8	41,3	41,4	41,5	41,6	41,7	41,8	41,9	42,0	42,1	42,2
17,0	41,2	41,3	41,4	41,5	41,6	41,7	41,8	41,9	42,0	42,1
17,2	41,1	41,2	41,3	41,4	41,5	41,6	41,7	41,8	41,9	42,0
17,4	41,0	41,1	41,2	41,3	41,4	41,5	41,6	41,7	41,8	41,9
17,6	41,0	41,1	41,2	41,3	41,4	41,5	41,6	41,7	41,8	41,9
17,8	40,9	41,0	41,1	41,2	41,3	41,4	41,5	41,6	41,7	41,8
18,0	40,8	40,9	41,0	41,1	41,2	41,3	41,4	41,5	41,6	41,7
18,2	40,7	40,8	40,9	41,0	41,1	41,2	41,3	41,4	41,5	41,6
18,4	40,6	40,7	40,8	40,9	41,0	41,1	41,2	41,3	41,4	41,5
18,6	40,6	40,7	40,8	40,9	41,0	41,1	41,2	41,3	41,4	41,5
18,8	40,5	40,6	40,7	40,8	40,9	41,0	41,1	41,2	41,3	41,4
19,0	40,4	40,5	40,6	40,7	40,8	40,9	41,0	41,1	41,2	41,3
19,2	40,3	40,4	40,5	40,6	40,7	40,8	40,9	41,0	41,1	41,2
19,4	40,2	40,3	40,4	40,5	40,6	40,7	40,8	40,9	41,0	41,1
19,6	40,2	40,3	40,4	40,5	40,6	40,7	40,8	40,9	41,0	41,1
19,8	40,1	40,2	40,3	40,4	40,5	40,6	40,7	40,8	40,9	41,0

Volumenkonzentration bei 20 °C in Prozent

Temp. °C	Anzeige des Alkoholometers in % vol								
	40,0	40,1	40,2	40,3	40,4	40,5	40,6	40,7	40,8	40,9
20,0	40,0	40,1	40,2	40,3	40,4	40,5	40,6	40,7	40,8	40,9
20,2	39,9	40,0	40,1	40,2	40,3	40,4	40,5	40,6	40,7	40,8
20,4	39,8	39,9	40,0	40,1	40,2	40,3	40,4	40,5	40,6	40,7
20,6	39,8	39,9	40,0	40,1	40,2	40,3	40,4	40,5	40,6	40,7
20,8	39,7	39,8	39,9	40,0	40,1	40,2	40,3	40,4	40,5	40,6
21,0	39,6	39,7	39,8	39,9	40,0	40,1	40,2	40,3	40,4	40,5
21,2	39,5	39,6	39,7	39,8	39,9	40,0	40,1	40,2	40,3	40,4
21,4	39,4	39,5	39,6	39,7	39,8	39,9	40,0	40,1	40,2	40,3
21,6	39,4	39,5	39,6	39,7	39,8	39,9	40,0	40,1	40,2	40,3
21,8	39,3	39,4	39,5	39,6	39,7	39,8	39,9	40,0	40,1	40,2
22,0	39,2	39,3	39,4	39,5	39,6	39,7	39,8	39,9	40,0	40,1
22,2	39,1	39,2	39,3	39,4	39,5	39,6	39,7	39,8	39,9	40,0
22,4	39,0	39,1	39,2	39,3	39,4	39,5	39,6	39,7	39,8	39,9
22,6	39,0	39,1	39,2	39,3	39,4	39,5	39,6	39,7	39,8	39,9
22,8	38,9	39,0	39,1	39,2	39,3	39,4	39,5	39,6	39,7	39,8
23,0	38,8	38,9	39,0	39,1	39,2	39,3	39,4	39,5	39,6	39,7
23,2	38,7	38,8	38,9	39,0	39,1	39,2	39,3	39,4	39,5	39,6
23,4	38,6	38,7	38,8	38,9	39,0	39,1	39,2	39,3	39,4	39,5
23,6	38,6	38,7	38,8	38,9	39,0	39,1	39,2	39,3	39,4	39,5
23,8	38,5	38,6	38,7	38,8	38,9	39,0	39,1	39,2	39,3	39,4
24,0	38,4	38,5	38,6	38,7	38,8	38,9	39,0	39,1	39,2	39,3
24,2	38,3	38,4	38,5	38,6	38,7	38,8	38,9	39,0	39,1	39,2
24,4	38,2	38,3	38,4	38,5	38,6	38,7	38,8	38,9	39,0	39,1
24,6	38,2	38,3	38,4	38,5	38,6	38,7	38,8	38,9	39,0	39,1
24,8	38,1	38,2	38,3	38,4	38,5	38,6	38,7	38,8	38,9	39,0
25,0	38,0	38,1	38,2	38,3	38,4	38,5	38,6	38,7	38,8	38,9
25,2	37,9	38,0	38,1	38,2	38,3	38,4	38,5	38,6	38,7	38,8
25,4	37,8	37,9	38,0	38,1	38,2	38,3	38,4	38,5	38,6	38,7
25,6	37,8	37,9	38,0	38,1	38,2	38,3	38,4	38,5	38,6	38,7
25,8	37,7	37,8	37,9	38,0	38,1	38,2	38,3	38,4	38,5	38,6
26,0	37,6	37,7	37,8	37,9	38,0	38,1	38,2	38,3	38,4	38,5
26,2	37,5	37,6	37,7	37,8	37,9	38,0	38,1	38,2	38,3	38,4
26,4	37,4	37,5	37,6	37,7	37,8	37,9	38,0	38,1	38,2	38,3
26,6	37,4	37,5	37,6	37,7	37,8	37,9	38,0	38,1	38,2	38,3
26,8	37,3	37,4	37,5	37,6	37,7	37,8	37,9	38,0	38,1	38,2
27,0	37,2	37,3	37,4	37,5	37,6	37,7	37,8	37,9	38,0	38,1
27,2	37,1	37,2	37,3	37,4	37,5	37,6	37,7	37,8	37,9	38,0
27,4	37,0	37,1	37,2	37,3	37,4	37,5	37,6	37,7	37,8	37,9
27,6	37,0	37,1	37,2	37,3	37,4	37,5	37,6	37,7	37,8	37,9
27,8	36,9	37,0	37,1	37,2	37,3	37,4	37,5	37,6	37,7	37,8
28,0	36,8	36,9	37,0	37,1	37,2	37,3	37,4	37,5	37,6	37,7
28,2	36,7	36,8	36,9	37,0	37,1	37,2	37,3	37,4	37,5	37,6
28,4	36,6	36,7	36,8	36,9	37,0	37,1	37,2	37,3	37,4	37,5
28,6	36,5	36,6	36,7	36,8	36,9	37,0	37,1	37,2	37,3	37,5
28,8	36,5	36,6	36,7	36,8	36,9	37,0	37,1	37,2	37,3	37,4
29,0	36,4	36,5	36,6	36,7	36,8	36,9	37,0	37,1	37,2	37,3
29,2	36,3	36,4	36,5	36,6	36,7	36,8	36,9	37,0	37,1	37,2
29,4	36,2	36,3	36,4	36,5	36,6	36,7	36,8	36,9	37,0	37,1
29,6	36,1	36,2	36,3	36,5	36,6	36,7	36,8	36,9	37,0	37,1
29,8	36,1	36,2	36,3	36,4	36,5	36,6	36,7	36,8	36,9	37,0
30,0	36,0	36,1	36,2	36,3	36,4	36,5	36,6	36,7	36,8	36,9

Volumenkonzentration bei 20 °C in Prozent

Temp. °C	Anzeige des Alkoholometers in % vol								
	41,0	41,1	41,2	41,3	41,4	41,5	41,6	41,7	41,8	41,9
0,0	48,8	48,9	49,0	49,1	49,2	49,2	49,3	49,4	49,5	49,6
0,2	48,7	48,8	48,9	49,0	49,1	49,2	49,3	49,4	49,4	49,5
0,4	48,6	48,7	48,8	48,9	49,0	49,1	49,2	49,3	49,4	49,5
0,6	48,6	48,6	48,7	48,8	48,9	49,0	49,1	49,2	49,3	49,4
0,8	48,5	48,6	48,7	48,8	48,8	48,9	49,0	49,1	49,2	49,3
1,0	48,4	48,5	48,6	48,7	48,8	48,9	49,0	49,1	49,1	49,2
1,2	48,3	48,4	48,5	48,6	48,7	48,8	48,9	49,0	49,1	49,2
1,4	48,3	48,3	48,4	48,5	48,6	48,7	48,8	48,9	49,0	49,1
1,6	48,2	48,3	48,4	48,5	48,5	48,6	48,7	48,8	48,9	49,0
1,8	48,1	48,2	48,3	48,4	48,5	48,6	48,7	48,8	48,8	48,9
2,0	48,0	48,1	48,2	48,3	48,4	48,5	48,6	48,7	48,8	48,9
2,2	47,9	48,0	48,1	48,2	48,3	48,4	48,5	48,6	48,7	48,8
2,4	47,9	48,0	48,1	48,2	48,2	48,3	48,4	48,5	48,6	48,7
2,6	47,8	47,9	48,0	48,1	48,2	48,3	48,4	48,5	48,5	48,6
2,8	47,7	47,8	47,9	48,0	48,1	48,2	48,3	48,4	48,5	48,6
3,0	47,6	47,7	47,8	47,9	48,0	48,1	48,2	48,3	48,4	48,5
3,2	47,6	47,7	47,8	47,8	47,9	48,0	48,1	48,2	48,3	48,4
3,4	47,5	47,6	47,7	47,8	47,9	48,0	48,1	48,1	48,2	48,3
3,6	47,4	47,5	47,6	47,7	47,8	47,9	48,0	48,1	48,2	48,3
3,8	47,3	47,4	47,5	47,6	47,7	47,8	47,9	48,0	48,1	48,2
4,0	47,3	47,4	47,4	47,5	47,6	47,7	47,8	47,9	48,0	48,1
4,2	47,2	47,3	47,4	47,5	47,6	47,7	47,7	47,8	47,9	48,0
4,4	47,1	47,2	47,3	47,4	47,5	47,6	47,7	47,8	47,9	48,0
4,6	47,0	47,1	47,2	47,3	47,4	47,5	47,6	47,7	47,8	47,9
4,8	47,0	47,0	47,1	47,2	47,3	47,4	47,5	47,6	47,7	47,8
5,0	46,9	47,0	47,1	47,2	47,3	47,3	47,4	47,5	47,6	47,7
5,2	46,8	46,9	47,0	47,1	47,2	47,3	47,4	47,5	47,6	47,7
5,4	46,7	46,8	46,9	47,0	47,1	47,2	47,3	47,4	47,5	47,6
5,6	46,6	46,7	46,8	46,9	47,0	47,1	47,2	47,3	47,4	47,5
5,8	46,6	46,7	46,8	46,9	46,9	47,0	47,1	47,2	47,3	47,4
6,0	46,5	46,6	46,7	46,8	46,9	47,0	47,1	47,2	47,3	47,3
6,2	46,4	46,5	46,6	46,7	46,8	46,9	47,0	47,1	47,2	47,3
6,4	46,3	46,4	46,5	46,6	46,7	46,8	46,9	47,0	47,1	47,2
6,6	46,3	46,4	46,4	46,5	46,6	46,7	46,8	46,9	47,0	47,1
6,8	46,2	46,3	46,4	46,5	46,6	46,7	46,8	46,8	46,9	47,0
7,0	46,1	46,2	46,3	46,4	46,5	46,6	46,7	46,8	46,9	47,0
7,2	46,0	46,1	46,2	46,3	46,4	46,5	46,6	46,7	46,8	46,9
7,4	45,9	46,0	46,1	46,2	46,3	46,4	46,5	46,6	46,7	46,8
7,6	45,9	46,0	46,1	46,2	46,3	46,4	46,4	46,5	46,6	46,7
7,8	45,8	45,9	46,0	46,1	46,2	46,3	46,4	46,5	46,6	46,7
8,0	45,7	45,8	45,9	46,0	46,1	46,2	46,3	46,4	46,5	46,6
8,2	45,6	45,7	45,8	45,9	46,0	46,1	46,2	46,3	46,4	46,5
8,4	45,6	45,7	45,8	45,8	45,9	46,0	46,1	46,2	46,3	46,4
8,6	45,5	45,6	45,7	45,8	45,9	46,0	46,1	46,2	46,3	46,3
8,8	45,4	45,5	45,6	45,7	45,8	45,9	46,0	46,1	46,2	46,3
9,0	45,3	45,4	45,5	45,6	45,7	45,8	45,9	46,0	46,1	46,2
9,2	45,2	45,3	45,4	45,5	45,6	45,7	45,8	45,9	46,0	46,1
9,4	45,2	45,3	45,4	45,5	45,6	45,7	45,8	45,8	45,9	46,0
9,6	45,1	45,2	45,3	45,4	45,5	45,6	45,7	45,8	45,9	46,0
9,8	45,0	45,1	45,2	45,3	45,4	45,5	45,6	45,7	45,8	45,9

Volumenkonzentration bei 20 °C in Prozent

Temp. °C	Anzeige des Alkoholometers in % vol								
	41,0	41,1	41,2	41,3	41,4	41,5	41,6	41,7	41,8	41,9
10,0	44,9	45,0	45,1	45,2	45,3	45,4	45,5	45,6	45,7	45,8
10,2	44,9	45,0	45,1	45,2	45,2	45,3	45,4	45,5	45,6	45,7
10,4	44,8	44,9	45,0	45,1	45,2	45,3	45,4	45,5	45,6	45,7
10,6	44,7	44,8	44,9	45,0	45,1	45,2	45,3	45,4	45,5	45,6
10,8	44,6	44,7	44,8	44,9	45,0	45,1	45,2	45,3	45,4	45,5
11,0	44,5	44,6	44,7	44,8	44,9	45,0	45,1	45,2	45,3	45,4
11,2	44,5	44,6	44,7	44,8	44,9	45,0	45,1	45,2	45,2	45,3
11,4	44,4	44,5	44,6	44,7	44,8	44,9	45,0	45,1	45,2	45,3
11,6	44,3	44,4	44,5	44,6	44,7	44,8	44,9	45,0	45,1	45,2
11,8	44,2	44,3	44,4	44,5	44,6	44,7	44,8	44,9	45,0	45,1
12,0	44,2	44,3	44,4	44,4	44,5	44,6	44,7	44,8	44,9	45,0
12,2	44,1	44,2	44,3	44,4	44,5	44,6	44,7	44,8	44,9	45,0
12,4	44,0	44,1	44,2	44,3	44,4	44,5	44,6	44,7	44,8	44,9
12,6	43,9	44,0	44,1	44,2	44,3	44,4	44,5	44,6	44,7	44,8
12,8	43,8	43,9	44,0	44,1	44,2	44,3	44,4	44,5	44,6	44,7
13,0	43,8	43,9	44,0	44,1	44,2	44,3	44,4	44,4	44,5	44,6
13,2	43,7	43,8	43,9	44,0	44,1	44,2	44,3	44,4	44,5	44,6
13,4	43,6	43,7	43,8	43,9	44,0	44,1	44,2	44,3	44,4	44,5
13,6	43,5	43,6	43,7	43,8	43,9	44,0	44,1	44,2	44,3	44,4
13,8	43,5	43,5	43,6	43,7	43,8	43,9	44,0	44,1	44,2	44,3
14,0	43,4	43,5	43,6	43,7	43,8	43,9	44,0	44,1	44,2	44,3
14,2	43,3	43,4	43,5	43,6	43,7	43,8	43,9	44,0	44,1	44,2
14,4	43,2	43,3	43,4	43,5	43,6	43,7	43,8	43,9	44,0	44,1
14,6	43,1	43,2	43,3	43,4	43,5	43,6	43,7	43,8	43,9	44,0
14,8	43,1	43,2	43,3	43,4	43,5	43,5	43,6	43,7	43,8	43,9
15,0	43,0	43,1	43,2	43,3	43,4	43,5	43,6	43,7	43,8	43,9
15,2	42,9	43,0	43,1	43,2	43,3	43,4	43,5	43,6	43,7	43,8
15,4	42,8	42,9	43,0	43,1	43,2	43,3	43,4	43,5	43,6	43,7
15,6	42,7	42,8	42,9	43,0	43,1	43,2	43,3	43,4	43,5	43,6
15,8	42,7	42,8	42,9	43,0	43,1	43,2	43,3	43,4	43,5	43,6
16,0	42,6	42,7	42,8	42,9	43,0	43,1	43,2	43,3	43,4	43,5
16,2	42,5	42,6	42,7	42,8	42,9	43,0	43,1	43,2	43,3	43,4
16,4	42,4	42,5	42,6	42,7	42,8	42,9	43,0	43,1	43,2	43,3
16,6	42,3	42,4	42,5	42,6	42,7	42,8	42,9	43,0	43,1	43,2
16,8	42,3	42,4	42,5	42,6	42,7	42,8	42,9	43,0	43,1	43,2
17,0	42,2	42,3	42,4	42,5	42,6	42,7	42,8	42,9	43,0	43,1
17,2	42,1	42,2	42,3	42,4	42,5	42,6	42,7	42,8	42,9	43,0
17,4	42,0	42,1	42,2	42,3	42,4	42,5	42,6	42,7	42,8	42,9
17,6	42,0	42,1	42,2	42,2	42,3	42,4	42,5	42,6	42,7	42,8
17,8	41,9	42,0	42,1	42,2	42,3	42,4	42,5	42,6	42,7	42,8
18,0	41,8	41,9	42,0	42,1	42,2	42,3	42,4	42,5	42,6	42,7
18,2	41,7	41,8	41,9	42,0	42,1	42,2	42,3	42,4	42,5	42,6
18,4	41,6	41,7	41,8	41,9	42,0	42,1	42,2	42,3	42,4	42,5
18,6	41,6	41,7	41,8	41,9	42,0	42,1	42,2	42,3	42,4	42,5
18,8	41,5	41,6	41,7	41,8	41,9	42,0	42,1	42,2	42,3	42,4
19,0	41,4	41,5	41,6	41,7	41,8	41,9	42,0	42,1	42,2	42,3
19,2	41,3	41,4	41,5	41,6	41,7	41,8	41,9	42,0	42,1	42,2
19,4	41,2	41,3	41,4	41,5	41,6	41,7	41,8	41,9	42,0	42,1
19,6	41,2	41,3	41,4	41,5	41,6	41,7	41,8	41,9	42,0	42,1
19,8	41,1	41,2	41,3	41,4	41,5	41,6	41,7	41,8	41,9	42,0

Volumenkonzentration bei 20 °C in Prozent

Temp. °C	Anzeige des Alkoholometers in % vol									
	41,0	41,1	41,2	41,3	41,4	41,5	41,6	41,7	41,8	41,9
20,0	41,0	41,1	41,2	41,3	41,4	41,5	41,6	41,7	41,8	41,9
20,2	40,9	41,0	41,1	41,2	41,3	41,4	41,5	41,6	41,7	41,8
20,4	40,8	40,9	41,0	41,1	41,2	41,3	41,4	41,5	41,6	41,7
20,6	40,8	40,9	41,0	41,1	41,2	41,3	41,4	41,5	41,6	41,7
20,8	40,7	40,8	40,9	41,0	41,1	41,2	41,3	41,4	41,5	41,6
21,0	40,6	40,7	40,8	40,9	41,0	41,1	41,2	41,3	41,4	41,5
21,2	40,5	40,6	40,7	40,8	40,9	41,0	41,1	41,2	41,3	41,4
21,4	40,4	40,5	40,6	40,7	40,8	40,9	41,0	41,1	41,2	41,3
21,6	40,4	40,5	40,6	40,7	40,8	40,9	41,0	41,1	41,2	41,3
21,8	40,3	40,4	40,5	40,6	40,7	40,8	40,9	41,0	41,1	41,2
22,0	40,2	40,3	40,4	40,5	40,6	40,7	40,8	40,9	41,0	41,1
22,2	40,1	40,2	40,3	40,4	40,5	40,6	40,7	40,8	40,9	41,0
22,4	40,0	40,1	40,2	40,3	40,4	40,5	40,6	40,7	40,9	41,0
22,6	40,0	40,1	40,2	40,3	40,4	40,5	40,6	40,7	40,8	40,9
22,8	39,9	40,0	40,1	40,2	40,3	40,4	40,5	40,6	40,7	40,8
23,0	39,8	39,9	40,0	40,1	40,2	40,3	40,4	40,5	40,6	40,7
23,2	39,7	39,8	39,9	40,0	40,1	40,2	40,3	40,4	40,5	40,6
23,4	39,6	39,7	39,8	39,9	40,1	40,2	40,3	40,4	40,5	40,6
23,6	39,6	39,7	39,8	39,9	40,0	40,1	40,2	40,3	40,4	40,5
23,8	39,5	39,6	39,7	39,8	39,9	40,0	40,1	40,2	40,3	40,4
24,0	39,4	39,5	39,6	39,7	39,8	39,9	40,0	40,1	40,2	40,3
24,2	39,3	39,4	39,5	39,6	39,7	39,8	39,9	40,0	40,1	40,2
24,4	39,2	39,3	39,4	39,6	39,7	39,8	39,9	40,0	40,1	40,2
24,6	39,2	39,3	39,4	39,5	39,6	39,7	39,8	39,9	40,0	40,1
24,8	39,1	39,2	39,3	39,4	39,5	39,6	39,7	39,8	39,9	40,0
25,0	39,0	39,1	39,2	39,3	39,4	39,5	39,6	39,7	39,8	39,9
25,2	38,9	39,0	39,1	39,2	39,3	39,4	39,5	39,6	39,7	39,8
25,4	38,8	38,9	39,1	39,2	39,3	39,4	39,5	39,6	39,7	39,8
25,6	38,8	38,9	39,0	39,1	39,2	39,3	39,4	39,5	39,6	39,7
25,8	38,7	38,8	38,9	39,0	39,1	39,2	39,3	39,4	39,5	39,6
26,0	38,6	38,7	38,8	38,9	39,0	39,1	39,2	39,3	39,4	39,5
26,2	38,5	38,6	38,7	38,8	38,9	39,0	39,1	39,2	39,3	39,4
26,4	38,4	38,5	38,7	38,8	38,9	39,0	39,1	39,2	39,3	39,4
26,6	38,4	38,5	38,6	38,7	38,8	38,9	39,0	39,1	39,2	39,3
26,8	38,3	38,4	38,5	38,6	38,7	38,8	38,9	39,0	39,1	39,2
27,0	38,2	38,3	38,4	38,5	38,6	38,7	38,8	38,9	39,0	39,1
27,2	38,1	38,2	38,3	38,4	38,5	38,6	38,7	38,8	38,9	39,0
27,4	38,0	38,1	38,3	38,4	38,5	38,6	38,7	38,8	38,9	39,0
27,6	38,0	38,1	38,2	38,3	38,4	38,5	38,6	38,7	38,8	38,9
27,8	37,9	38,0	38,1	38,2	38,3	38,4	38,5	38,6	38,7	38,8
28,0	37,8	37,9	38,0	38,1	38,2	38,3	38,4	38,5	38,6	38,7
28,2	37,7	37,8	37,9	38,0	38,1	38,2	38,3	38,4	38,5	38,6
28,4	37,6	37,7	37,8	38,0	38,1	38,2	38,3	38,4	38,5	38,6
28,6	37,6	37,7	37,8	37,9	38,0	38,1	38,2	38,3	38,4	38,5
28,8	37,5	37,6	37,7	37,8	37,9	38,0	38,1	38,2	38,3	38,4
29,0	37,4	37,5	37,6	37,7	37,8	37,9	38,0	38,1	38,2	38,3
29,2	37,3	37,4	37,5	37,6	37,7	37,8	37,9	38,0	38,1	38,2
29,4	37,2	37,3	37,4	37,6	37,7	37,8	37,9	38,0	38,1	38,2
29,6	37,2	37,3	37,4	37,5	37,6	37,7	37,8	37,9	38,0	38,1
29,8	37,1	37,2	37,3	37,4	37,5	37,6	37,7	37,8	37,9	38,0
30,0	37,0	37,1	37,2	37,3	37,4	37,5	37,6	37,7	37,8	37,9

Volumenkonzentration bei 20 °C in Prozent

Temp. °C	Anzeige des Alkoholometers in % vol								
	42,0	42,1	42,2	42,3	42,4	42,5	42,6	42,7	42,8	42,9
0,0	49,7	49,8	49,9	50,0	50,1	50,2	50,3	50,4	50,5	50,5
0,2	49,6	49,7	49,8	49,9	50,0	50,1	50,2	50,3	50,4	50,5
0,4	49,6	49,7	49,7	49,8	49,9	50,0	50,1	50,2	50,3	50,4
0,6	49,5	49,6	49,7	49,8	49,9	49,9	50,0	50,1	50,2	50,3
0,8	49,4	49,5	49,6	49,7	49,8	49,9	50,0	50,1	50,2	50,2
1,0	49,3	49,4	49,5	49,6	49,7	49,8	49,9	50,0	50,1	50,2
1,2	49,3	49,4	49,4	49,5	49,6	49,7	49,8	49,9	50,0	50,1
1,4	49,2	49,3	49,4	49,5	49,6	49,7	49,7	49,8	49,9	50,0
1,6	49,1	49,2	49,3	49,4	49,5	49,6	49,7	49,8	49,9	49,9
1,8	49,0	49,1	49,2	49,3	49,4	49,5	49,6	49,7	49,8	49,9
2,0	49,0	49,1	49,1	49,2	49,3	49,4	49,5	49,6	49,7	49,8
2,2	48,9	49,0	49,1	49,2	49,3	49,4	49,4	49,5	49,6	49,7
2,4	48,8	48,9	49,0	49,1	49,2	49,3	49,4	49,5	49,6	49,7
2,6	48,7	48,8	48,9	49,0	49,1	49,2	49,3	49,4	49,5	49,6
2,8	48,7	48,8	48,8	48,9	49,0	49,1	49,2	49,3	49,4	49,5
3,0	48,6	48,7	48,8	48,9	49,0	49,1	49,1	49,2	49,3	49,4
3,2	48,5	48,6	48,7	48,8	48,9	49,0	49,1	49,2	49,3	49,4
3,4	48,4	48,5	48,6	48,7	48,8	48,9	49,0	49,1	49,2	49,3
3,6	48,4	48,4	48,5	48,6	48,7	48,8	48,9	49,0	49,1	49,2
3,8	48,3	48,4	48,5	48,6	48,7	48,8	48,8	48,9	49,0	49,1
4,0	48,2	48,3	48,4	48,5	48,6	48,7	48,8	48,9	49,0	49,1
4,2	48,1	48,2	48,3	48,4	48,5	48,6	48,7	48,8	48,9	49,0
4,4	48,1	48,1	48,2	48,3	48,4	48,5	48,6	48,7	48,8	48,9
4,6	48,0	48,1	48,2	48,3	48,4	48,4	48,5	48,6	48,7	48,8
4,8	47,9	48,0	48,1	48,2	48,3	48,4	48,5	48,6	48,7	48,8
5,0	47,8	47,9	48,0	48,1	48,2	48,3	48,4	48,5	48,6	48,7
5,2	47,7	47,8	47,9	48,0	48,1	48,2	48,3	48,4	48,5	48,6
5,4	47,7	47,8	47,9	48,0	48,1	48,1	48,2	48,3	48,4	48,5
5,6	47,6	47,7	47,8	47,9	48,0	48,1	48,2	48,3	48,4	48,5
5,8	47,5	47,6	47,7	47,8	47,9	48,0	48,1	48,2	48,3	48,4
6,0	47,4	47,5	47,6	47,7	47,8	47,9	48,0	48,1	48,2	48,3
6,2	47,4	47,5	47,6	47,7	47,7	47,8	47,9	48,0	48,1	48,2
6,4	47,3	47,4	47,5	47,6	47,7	47,8	47,9	48,0	48,1	48,1
6,6	47,2	47,3	47,4	47,5	47,6	47,7	47,8	47,9	48,0	48,1
6,8	47,1	47,2	47,3	47,4	47,5	47,6	47,7	47,8	47,9	48,0
7,0	47,1	47,2	47,3	47,3	47,4	47,5	47,6	47,7	47,8	47,9
7,2	47,0	47,1	47,2	47,3	47,4	47,5	47,6	47,7	47,7	47,8
7,4	46,9	47,0	47,1	47,2	47,3	47,4	47,5	47,6	47,7	47,8
7,6	46,8	46,9	47,0	47,1	47,2	47,3	47,4	47,5	47,6	47,7
7,8	46,8	46,8	46,9	47,0	47,1	47,2	47,3	47,4	47,5	47,6
8,0	46,7	46,8	46,9	47,0	47,1	47,2	47,3	47,3	47,4	47,5
8,2	46,6	46,7	46,8	46,9	47,0	47,1	47,2	47,3	47,4	47,5
8,4	46,5	46,6	46,7	46,8	46,9	47,0	47,1	47,2	47,3	47,4
8,6	46,4	46,5	46,6	46,7	46,8	46,9	47,0	47,1	47,2	47,3
8,8	46,4	46,5	46,6	46,7	46,8	46,9	46,9	47,0	47,1	47,2
9,0	46,3	46,4	46,5	46,6	46,7	46,8	46,9	47,0	47,1	47,2
9,2	46,2	46,3	46,4	46,5	46,6	46,7	46,8	46,9	47,0	47,1
9,4	46,1	46,2	46,3	46,4	46,5	46,6	46,7	46,8	46,9	47,0
9,6	46,1	46,2	46,3	46,4	46,4	46,5	46,6	46,7	46,8	46,9
9,8	46,0	46,1	46,2	46,3	46,4	46,5	46,6	46,7	46,8	46,9

Volumenkonzentration bei 20 °C in Prozent

Temp. °C	\multicolumn{10}{c}{Anzeige des Alkoholometers in % vol}

Temp. °C	42,0	42,1	42,2	42,3	42,4	42,5	42,6	42,7	42,8	42,9
10,0	45,9	46,0	46,1	46,2	46,3	46,4	46,5	46,6	46,7	46,8
10,2	45,8	45,9	46,0	46,1	46,2	46,3	46,4	46,5	46,6	46,7
10,4	45,8	45,8	45,9	46,0	46,1	46,2	46,3	46,4	46,5	46,6
10,6	45,7	45,8	45,9	46,0	46,1	46,2	46,3	46,4	46,5	46,5
10,8	45,6	45,7	45,8	45,9	46,0	46,1	46,2	46,3	46,4	46,5
11,0	45,5	45,6	45,7	45,8	45,9	46,0	46,1	46,2	46,3	46,4
11,2	45,4	45,5	45,6	45,7	45,8	45,9	46,0	46,1	46,2	46,3
11,4	45,4	45,5	45,6	45,7	45,8	45,9	45,9	46,0	46,1	46,2
11,6	45,3	45,4	45,5	45,6	45,7	45,8	45,9	46,0	46,1	46,2
11,8	45,2	45,3	45,4	45,5	45,6	45,7	45,8	45,9	46,0	46,1
12,0	45,1	45,2	45,3	45,4	45,5	45,6	45,7	45,8	45,9	46,0
12,2	45,1	45,2	45,2	45,3	45,4	45,5	45,6	45,7	45,8	45,9
12,4	45,0	45,1	45,2	45,3	45,4	45,5	45,6	45,7	45,8	45,9
12,6	44,9	45,0	45,1	45,2	45,3	45,4	45,5	45,6	45,7	45,8
12,8	44,8	44,9	45,0	45,1	45,2	45,3	45,4	45,5	45,6	45,7
13,0	44,7	44,8	44,9	45,0	45,1	45,2	45,3	45,4	45,5	45,6
13,2	44,7	44,8	44,9	45,0	45,1	45,2	45,3	45,4	45,4	45,5
13,4	44,6	44,7	44,8	44,9	45,0	45,1	45,2	45,3	45,4	45,5
13,6	44,5	44,6	44,7	44,8	44,9	45,0	45,1	45,2	45,3	45,4
13,8	44,4	44,5	44,6	44,7	44,8	44,9	45,0	45,1	45,2	45,3
14,0	44,4	44,5	44,6	44,6	44,7	44,8	44,9	45,0	45,1	45,2
14,2	44,3	44,4	44,5	44,6	44,7	44,8	44,9	45,0	45,1	45,2
14,4	44,2	44,3	44,4	44,5	44,6	44,7	44,8	44,9	45,0	45,1
14,6	44,1	44,2	44,3	44,4	44,5	44,6	44,7	44,8	44,9	45,0
14,8	44,0	44,1	44,2	44,3	44,4	44,5	44,6	44,7	44,8	44,9
15,0	44,0	44,1	44,2	44,3	44,4	44,5	44,6	44,7	44,8	44,9
15,2	43,9	44,0	44,1	44,2	44,3	44,4	44,5	44,6	44,7	44,8
15,4	43,8	43,9	44,0	44,1	44,2	44,3	44,4	44,5	44,6	44,7
15,6	43,7	43,8	43,9	44,0	44,1	44,2	44,3	44,4	44,5	44,6
15,8	43,7	43,7	43,8	43,9	44,0	44,1	44,2	44,3	44,4	44,5
16,0	43,6	43,7	43,8	43,9	44,0	44,1	44,2	44,3	44,4	44,5
16,2	43,5	43,6	43,7	43,8	43,9	44,0	44,1	44,2	44,3	44,4
16,4	43,4	43,5	43,6	43,7	43,8	43,9	44,0	44,1	44,2	44,3
16,6	43,3	43,4	43,5	43,6	43,7	43,8	43,9	44,0	44,1	44,2
16,8	43,3	43,4	43,5	43,6	43,7	43,8	43,9	44,0	44,1	44,2
17,0	43,2	43,3	43,4	43,5	43,6	43,7	43,8	43,9	44,0	44,1
17,2	43,1	43,2	43,3	43,4	43,5	43,6	43,7	43,8	43,9	44,0
17,4	43,0	43,1	43,2	43,3	43,4	43,5	43,6	43,7	43,8	43,9
17,6	42,9	43,0	43,1	43,2	43,3	43,4	43,5	43,6	43,7	43,8
17,8	42,9	43,0	43,1	43,2	43,3	43,4	43,5	43,6	43,7	43,8
18,0	42,8	42,9	43,0	43,1	43,2	43,3	43,4	43,5	43,6	43,7
18,2	42,7	42,8	42,9	43,0	43,1	43,2	43,3	43,4	43,5	43,6
18,4	42,6	42,7	42,8	42,9	43,0	43,1	43,2	43,3	43,4	43,5
18,6	42,6	42,7	42,8	42,9	43,0	43,0	43,1	43,2	43,3	43,4
18,8	42,5	42,6	42,7	42,8	42,9	43,0	43,1	43,2	43,3	43,4
19,0	42,4	42,5	42,6	42,7	42,8	42,9	43,0	43,1	43,2	43,3
19,2	42,3	42,4	42,5	42,6	42,7	42,8	42,9	43,0	43,1	43,2
19,4	42,2	42,3	42,4	42,5	42,6	42,7	42,8	42,9	43,0	43,1
19,6	42,2	42,3	42,4	42,5	42,6	42,7	42,8	42,9	43,0	43,1
19,8	42,1	42,2	42,3	42,4	42,5	42,6	42,7	42,8	42,9	43,0

Volumenkonzentration bei 20 °C in Prozent

Temp. °C	Anzeige des Alkoholometers in % vol									
	42,0	42,1	42,2	42,3	42,4	42,5	42,6	42,7	42,8	42,9
20,0	42,0	42,1	42,2	42,3	42,4	42,5	42,6	42,7	42,8	42,9
20,2	41,9	42,0	42,1	42,2	42,3	42,4	42,5	42,6	42,7	42,8
20,4	41,8	41,9	42,0	42,1	42,2	42,3	42,4	42,5	42,6	42,7
20,6	41,8	41,9	42,0	42,1	42,2	42,3	42,4	42,5	42,6	42,7
20,8	41,7	41,8	41,9	42,0	42,1	42,2	42,3	42,4	42,5	42,6
21,0	41,6	41,7	41,8	41,9	42,0	42,1	42,2	42,3	42,4	42,5
21,2	41,5	41,6	41,7	41,8	41,9	42,0	42,1	42,2	42,3	42,4
21,4	41,4	41,5	41,6	41,7	41,8	41,9	42,0	42,1	42,2	42,4
21,6	41,4	41,5	41,6	41,7	41,8	41,9	42,0	42,1	42,2	42,3
21,8	41,3	41,4	41,5	41,6	41,7	41,8	41,9	42,0	42,1	42,2
22,0	41,2	41,3	41,4	41,5	41,6	41,7	41,8	41,9	42,0	42,1
22,2	41,1	41,2	41,3	41,4	41,5	41,6	41,7	41,8	41,9	42,0
22,4	41,1	41,2	41,3	41,4	41,5	41,6	41,7	41,8	41,9	42,0
22,6	41,0	41,1	41,2	41,3	41,4	41,5	41,6	41,7	41,8	41,9
22,8	40,9	41,0	41,1	41,2	41,3	41,4	41,5	41,6	41,7	41,8
23,0	40,8	40,9	41,0	41,1	41,2	41,3	41,4	41,5	41,6	41,7
23,2	40,7	40,8	40,9	41,0	41,1	41,2	41,3	41,4	41,5	41,6
23,4	40,7	40,8	40,9	41,0	41,1	41,2	41,3	41,4	41,5	41,6
23,6	40,6	40,7	40,8	40,9	41,0	41,1	41,2	41,3	41,4	41,5
23,8	40,5	40,6	40,7	40,8	40,9	41,0	41,1	41,2	41,3	41,4
24,0	40,4	40,5	40,6	40,7	40,8	40,9	41,0	41,1	41,2	41,3
24,2	40,3	40,4	40,5	40,6	40,7	40,8	40,9	41,0	41,1	41,2
24,4	40,3	40,4	40,5	40,6	40,7	40,8	40,9	41,0	41,1	41,2
24,6	40,2	40,3	40,4	40,5	40,6	40,7	40,8	40,9	41,0	41,1
24,8	40,1	40,2	40,3	40,4	40,5	40,6	40,7	40,8	40,9	41,0
25,0	40,0	40,1	40,2	40,3	40,4	40,5	40,6	40,7	40,8	40,9
25,2	39,9	40,0	40,1	40,2	40,3	40,4	40,5	40,6	40,8	40,9
25,4	39,9	40,0	40,1	40,2	40,3	40,4	40,5	40,6	40,7	40,8
25,6	39,8	39,9	40,0	40,1	40,2	40,3	40,4	40,5	40,6	40,7
25,8	39,7	39,8	39,9	40,0	40,1	40,2	40,3	40,4	40,5	40,6
26,0	39,6	39,7	39,8	39,9	40,0	40,1	40,2	40,3	40,4	40,5
26,2	39,5	39,6	39,7	39,8	39,9	40,0	40,2	40,3	40,4	40,5
26,4	39,5	39,6	39,7	39,8	39,9	40,0	40,1	40,2	40,3	40,4
26,6	39,4	39,5	39,6	39,7	39,8	39,9	40,0	40,1	40,2	40,3
26,8	39,3	39,4	39,5	39,6	39,7	39,8	39,9	40,0	40,1	40,2
27,0	39,2	39,3	39,4	39,5	39,6	39,7	39,8	39,9	40,0	40,1
27,2	39,1	39,2	39,3	39,4	39,6	39,7	39,8	39,9	40,0	40,1
27,4	39,1	39,2	39,3	39,4	39,5	39,6	39,7	39,8	39,9	40,0
27,6	39,0	39,1	39,2	39,3	39,4	39,5	39,6	39,7	39,8	39,9
27,8	38,9	39,0	39,1	39,2	39,3	39,4	39,5	39,6	39,7	39,8
28,0	38,8	38,9	39,0	39,1	39,2	39,3	39,4	39,5	39,6	39,7
28,2	38,7	38,8	38,9	39,0	39,2	39,3	39,4	39,5	39,6	39,7
28,4	38,7	38,8	38,9	39,0	39,1	39,2	39,3	39,4	39,5	39,6
28,6	38,6	38,7	38,8	38,9	39,0	39,1	39,2	39,3	39,4	39,5
28,8	38,5	38,6	38,7	38,8	38,9	39,0	39,1	39,2	39,3	39,4
29,0	38,4	38,5	38,6	38,7	38,8	38,9	39,0	39,1	39,2	39,3
29,2	38,3	38,4	38,5	38,7	38,8	38,9	39,0	39,1	39,2	39,3
29,4	38,3	38,4	38,5	38,6	38,7	38,8	38,9	39,0	39,1	39,2
29,6	38,2	38,3	38,4	38,5	38,6	38,7	38,8	38,9	39,0	39,1
29,8	38,1	38,2	38,3	38,4	38,5	38,6	38,7	38,8	38,9	39,0
30,0	38,0	38,1	38,2	38,3	38,4	38,5	38,6	38,7	38,8	38,9

Volumenkonzentration bei 20 °C in Prozent

Temp. °C	Anzeige des Alkoholometers in % vol									
	43,0	43,1	43,2	43,3	43,4	43,5	43,6	43,7	43,8	43,9
0,0	50,6	50,7	50,8	50,9	51,0	51,1	51,2	51,3	51,4	51,5
0,2	50,6	50,7	50,7	50,8	50,9	51,0	51,1	51,2	51,3	51,4
0,4	50,5	50,6	50,7	50,8	50,9	51,0	51,0	51,1	51,2	51,3
0,6	50,4	50,5	50,6	50,7	50,8	50,9	51,0	51,1	51,2	51,3
0,8	50,3	50,4	50,5	50,6	50,7	50,8	50,9	51,0	51,1	51,2
1,0	50,3	50,4	50,5	50,5	50,6	50,7	50,8	50,9	51,0	51,1
1,2	50,2	50,3	50,4	50,5	50,6	50,7	50,8	50,8	50,9	51,0
1,4	50,1	50,2	50,3	50,4	50,5	50,6	50,7	50,8	50,9	51,0
1,6	50,0	50,1	50,2	50,3	50,4	50,5	50,6	50,7	50,8	50,9
1,8	50,0	50,1	50,2	50,2	50,3	50,4	50,5	50,6	50,7	50,8
2,0	49,9	50,0	50,1	50,2	50,3	50,4	50,5	50,6	50,6	50,7
2,2	49,8	49,9	50,0	50,1	50,2	50,3	50,4	50,5	50,6	50,7
2,4	49,7	49,8	49,9	50,0	50,1	50,2	50,3	50,4	50,5	50,6
2,6	49,7	49,8	49,9	50,0	50,0	50,1	50,2	50,3	50,4	50,5
2,8	49,6	49,7	49,8	49,9	50,0	50,1	50,2	50,3	50,3	50,4
3,0	49,5	49,6	49,7	49,8	49,9	50,0	50,1	50,2	50,3	50,4
3,2	49,4	49,5	49,6	49,7	49,8	49,9	50,0	50,1	50,2	50,3
3,4	49,4	49,5	49,6	49,7	49,7	49,8	49,9	50,0	50,1	50,2
3,6	49,3	49,4	49,5	49,6	49,7	49,8	49,9	50,0	50,1	50,2
3,8	49,2	49,3	49,4	49,5	49,6	49,7	49,8	49,9	50,0	50,1
4,0	49,1	49,2	49,3	49,4	49,5	49,6	49,7	49,8	49,9	50,0
4,2	49,1	49,2	49,3	49,4	49,5	49,5	49,6	49,7	49,8	49,9
4,4	49,0	49,1	49,2	49,3	49,4	49,5	49,6	49,7	49,8	49,8
4,6	48,9	49,0	49,1	49,2	49,3	49,4	49,5	49,6	49,7	49,8
4,8	48,8	48,9	49,0	49,1	49,2	49,3	49,4	49,5	49,6	49,7
5,0	48,8	48,9	49,0	49,1	49,2	49,2	49,3	49,4	49,5	49,6
5,2	48,7	48,8	48,9	49,0	49,1	49,2	49,3	49,4	49,5	49,6
5,4	48,6	48,7	48,8	48,9	49,0	49,1	49,2	49,3	49,4	49,5
5,6	48,5	48,6	48,7	48,8	48,9	49,0	49,1	49,2	49,3	49,4
5,8	48,5	48,6	48,7	48,8	48,9	48,9	49,0	49,1	49,2	49,3
6,0	48,4	48,5	48,6	48,7	48,8	48,9	49,0	49,1	49,2	49,3
6,2	48,3	48,4	48,5	48,6	48,7	48,8	48,9	49,0	49,1	49,2
6,4	48,2	48,3	48,4	48,5	48,6	48,7	48,8	48,9	49,0	49,1
6,6	48,2	48,3	48,4	48,5	48,6	48,6	48,7	48,8	48,9	49,0
6,8	48,1	48,2	48,3	48,4	48,5	48,6	48,7	48,8	48,9	49,0
7,0	48,0	48,1	48,2	48,3	48,4	48,5	48,6	48,7	48,8	48,9
7,2	47,9	48,0	48,1	48,2	48,3	48,4	48,5	48,6	48,7	48,8
7,4	47,9	48,0	48,1	48,2	48,2	48,3	48,4	48,5	48,6	48,7
7,6	47,8	47,9	48,0	48,1	48,2	48,3	48,4	48,5	48,6	48,7
7,8	47,7	47,8	47,9	48,0	48,1	48,2	48,3	48,4	48,5	48,6
8,0	47,6	47,7	47,8	47,9	48,0	48,1	48,2	48,3	48,4	48,5
8,2	47,6	47,7	47,8	47,8	47,9	48,0	48,1	48,2	48,3	48,4
8,4	47,5	47,6	47,7	47,8	47,9	48,0	48,1	48,2	48,3	48,4
8,6	47,4	47,5	47,6	47,7	47,8	47,9	48,0	48,1	48,2	48,3
8,8	47,3	47,4	47,5	47,6	47,7	47,8	47,9	48,0	48,1	48,2
9,0	47,3	47,4	47,4	47,5	47,6	47,7	47,8	47,9	48,0	48,1
9,2	47,2	47,3	47,4	47,5	47,6	47,7	47,8	47,9	48,0	48,0
9,4	47,1	47,2	47,3	47,4	47,5	47,6	47,7	47,8	47,9	48,0
9,6	47,0	47,1	47,2	47,3	47,4	47,5	47,6	47,7	47,8	47,9
9,8	47,0	47,0	47,1	47,2	47,3	47,4	47,5	47,6	47,7	47,8

Volumenkonzentration bei 20 °C in Prozent

Temp. °C	\multicolumn{9}{c}{Anzeige des Alkoholometers in % vol}

Temp. °C	43,0	43,1	43,2	43,3	43,4	43,5	43,6	43,7	43,8	43,9
10,0	46,9	47,0	47,1	47,2	47,3	47,4	47,5	47,6	47,6	47,7
10,2	46,8	46,9	47,0	47,1	47,2	47,3	47,4	47,5	47,6	47,7
10,4	46,7	46,8	46,9	47,0	47,1	47,2	47,3	47,4	47,5	47,6
10,6	46,6	46,7	46,8	46,9	47,0	47,1	47,2	47,3	47,4	47,5
10,8	46,6	46,7	46,8	46,9	47,0	47,1	47,2	47,2	47,3	47,4
11,0	46,5	46,6	46,7	46,8	46,9	47,0	47,1	47,2	47,3	47,4
11,2	46,4	46,5	46,6	46,7	46,8	46,9	47,0	47,1	47,2	47,3
11,4	46,3	46,4	46,5	46,6	46,7	46,8	46,9	47,0	47,1	47,2
11,6	46,3	46,4	46,5	46,6	46,7	46,7	46,8	46,9	47,0	47,1
11,8	46,2	46,3	46,4	46,5	46,6	46,7	46,8	46,9	47,0	47,1
12,0	46,1	46,2	46,3	46,4	46,5	46,6	46,7	46,8	46,9	47,0
12,2	46,0	46,1	46,2	46,3	46,4	46,5	46,6	46,7	46,8	46,9
12,4	46,0	46,1	46,1	46,2	46,3	46,4	46,5	46,6	46,7	46,8
12,6	45,9	46,0	46,1	46,2	46,3	46,4	46,5	46,6	46,7	46,8
12,8	45,8	45,9	46,0	46,1	46,2	46,3	46,4	46,5	46,6	46,7
13,0	45,7	45,8	45,9	46,0	46,1	46,2	46,3	46,4	46,5	46,6
13,2	45,6	45,7	45,8	45,9	46,0	46,1	46,2	46,3	46,4	46,5
13,4	45,6	45,7	45,8	45,9	46,0	46,1	46,2	46,3	46,4	46,4
13,6	45,5	45,6	45,7	45,8	45,9	46,0	46,1	46,2	46,3	46,4
13,8	45,4	45,5	45,6	45,7	45,8	45,9	46,0	46,1	46,2	46,3
14,0	45,3	45,4	45,5	45,6	45,7	45,8	45,9	46,0	46,1	46,2
14,2	45,3	45,4	45,5	45,6	45,7	45,7	45,8	45,9	46,0	46,1
14,4	45,2	45,3	45,4	45,5	45,6	45,7	45,8	45,9	46,0	46,1
14,6	45,1	45,2	45,3	45,4	45,5	45,6	45,7	45,8	45,9	46,0
14,8	45,0	45,1	45,2	45,3	45,4	45,5	45,6	45,7	45,8	45,9
15,0	44,9	45,0	45,1	45,2	45,3	45,4	45,5	45,6	45,7	45,8
15,2	44,9	45,0	45,1	45,2	45,3	45,4	45,5	45,6	45,7	45,8
15,4	44,8	44,9	45,0	45,1	45,2	45,3	45,4	45,5	45,6	45,7
15,6	44,7	44,8	44,9	45,0	45,1	45,2	45,3	45,4	45,5	45,6
15,8	44,6	44,7	44,8	44,9	45,0	45,1	45,2	45,3	45,4	45,5
16,0	44,6	44,7	44,8	44,9	45,0	45,1	45,2	45,3	45,4	45,5
16,2	44,5	44,6	44,7	44,8	44,9	45,0	45,1	45,2	45,3	45,4
16,4	44,4	44,5	44,6	44,7	44,8	44,9	45,0	45,1	45,2	45,3
16,6	44,3	44,4	44,5	44,6	44,7	44,8	44,9	45,0	45,1	45,2
16,8	44,2	44,3	44,4	44,5	44,6	44,7	44,8	44,9	45,0	45,1
17,0	44,2	44,3	44,4	44,5	44,6	44,7	44,8	44,9	45,0	45,1
17,2	44,1	44,2	44,3	44,4	44,5	44,6	44,7	44,8	44,9	45,0
17,4	44,0	44,1	44,2	44,3	44,4	44,5	44,6	44,7	44,8	44,9
17,6	43,9	44,0	44,1	44,2	44,3	44,4	44,5	44,6	44,7	44,8
17,8	43,9	44,0	44,1	44,2	44,3	44,4	44,5	44,6	44,7	44,8
18,0	43,8	43,9	44,0	44,1	44,2	44,3	44,4	44,5	44,6	44,7
18,2	43,7	43,8	43,9	44,0	44,1	44,2	44,3	44,4	44,5	44,6
18,4	43,6	43,7	43,8	43,9	44,0	44,1	44,2	44,3	44,4	44,5
18,6	43,5	43,6	43,7	43,8	43,9	44,0	44,1	44,2	44,3	44,4
18,8	43,5	43,6	43,7	43,8	43,9	44,0	44,1	44,2	44,3	44,4
19,0	43,4	43,5	43,6	43,7	43,8	43,9	44,0	44,1	44,2	44,3
19,2	43,3	43,4	43,5	43,6	43,7	43,8	43,9	44,0	44,1	44,2
19,4	43,2	43,3	43,4	43,5	43,6	43,7	43,8	43,9	44,0	44,1
19,6	43,2	43,3	43,4	43,5	43,6	43,7	43,8	43,9	44,0	44,1
19,8	43,1	43,2	43,3	43,4	43,5	43,6	43,7	43,8	43,9	44,0

Volumenkonzentration bei 20 °C in Prozent

Temp. °C	Anzeige des Alkoholometers in % vol								
	43,0	43,1	43,2	43,3	43,4	43,5	43,6	43,7	43,8	43,9
20,0	43,0	43,1	43,2	43,3	43,4	43,5	43,6	43,7	43,8	43,9
20,2	42,9	43,0	43,1	43,2	43,3	43,4	43,5	43,6	43,7	43,8
20,4	42,8	42,9	43,0	43,1	43,2	43,3	43,4	43,5	43,6	43,7
20,6	42,8	42,9	43,0	43,1	43,2	43,3	43,4	43,5	43,6	43,7
20,8	42,7	42,8	42,9	43,0	43,1	43,2	43,3	43,4	43,5	43,6
21,0	42,6	42,7	42,8	42,9	43,0	43,1	43,2	43,3	43,4	43,5
21,2	42,5	42,6	42,7	42,8	42,9	43,0	43,1	43,2	43,3	43,4
21,4	42,5	42,6	42,7	42,8	42,9	43,0	43,1	43,2	43,3	43,4
21,6	42,4	42,5	42,6	42,7	42,8	42,9	43,0	43,1	43,2	43,3
21,8	42,3	42,4	42,5	42,6	42,7	42,8	42,9	43,0	43,1	43,2
22,0	42,2	42,3	42,4	42,5	42,6	42,7	42,8	42,9	43,0	43,1
22,2	42,1	42,2	42,3	42,4	42,5	42,6	42,7	42,8	42,9	43,0
22,4	42,1	42,2	42,3	42,4	42,5	42,6	42,7	42,8	42,9	43,0
22,6	42,0	42,1	42,2	42,3	42,4	42,5	42,6	42,7	42,8	42,9
22,8	41,9	42,0	42,1	42,2	42,3	42,4	42,5	42,6	42,7	42,8
23,0	41,8	41,9	42,0	42,1	42,2	42,3	42,4	42,5	42,6	42,7
23,2	41,7	41,8	41,9	42,0	42,1	42,2	42,3	42,4	42,5	42,7
23,4	41,7	41,8	41,9	42,0	42,1	42,2	42,3	42,4	42,5	42,6
23,6	41,6	41,7	41,8	41,9	42,0	42,1	42,2	42,3	42,4	42,5
23,8	41,5	41,6	41,7	41,8	41,9	42,0	42,1	42,2	42,3	42,4
24,0	41,4	41,5	41,6	41,7	41,8	41,9	42,0	42,1	42,2	42,3
24,2	41,3	41,4	41,6	41,7	41,8	41,9	42,0	42,1	42,2	42,3
24,4	41,3	41,4	41,5	41,6	41,7	41,8	41,9	42,0	42,1	42,2
24,6	41,2	41,3	41,4	41,5	41,6	41,7	41,8	41,9	42,0	42,1
24,8	41,1	41,2	41,3	41,4	41,5	41,6	41,7	41,8	41,9	42,0
25,0	41,0	41,1	41,2	41,3	41,4	41,5	41,6	41,7	41,8	41,9
25,2	41,0	41,1	41,2	41,3	41,4	41,5	41,6	41,7	41,8	41,9
25,4	40,9	41,0	41,1	41,2	41,3	41,4	41,5	41,6	41,7	41,8
25,6	40,8	40,9	41,0	41,1	41,2	41,3	41,4	41,5	41,6	41,7
25,8	40,7	40,8	40,9	41,0	41,1	41,2	41,3	41,4	41,5	41,6
26,0	40,6	40,7	40,8	40,9	41,0	41,1	41,2	41,3	41,4	41,6
26,2	40,6	40,7	40,8	40,9	41,0	41,1	41,2	41,3	41,4	41,5
26,4	40,5	40,6	40,7	40,8	40,9	41,0	41,1	41,2	41,3	41,4
26,6	40,4	40,5	40,6	40,7	40,8	40,9	41,0	41,1	41,2	41,3
26,8	40,3	40,4	40,5	40,6	40,7	40,8	40,9	41,0	41,1	41,2
27,0	40,2	40,3	40,4	40,5	40,6	40,7	40,9	41,0	41,1	41,2
27,2	40,2	40,3	40,4	40,5	40,6	40,7	40,8	40,9	41,0	41,1
27,4	40,1	40,2	40,3	40,4	40,5	40,6	40,7	40,8	40,9	41,0
27,6	40,0	40,1	40,2	40,3	40,4	40,5	40,6	40,7	40,8	40,9
27,8	39,9	40,0	40,1	40,2	40,3	40,4	40,5	40,6	40,7	40,8
28,0	39,8	39,9	40,0	40,1	40,3	40,4	40,5	40,6	40,7	40,8
28,2	39,8	39,9	40,0	40,1	40,2	40,3	40,4	40,5	40,6	40,7
28,4	39,7	39,8	39,9	40,0	40,1	40,2	40,3	40,4	40,5	40,6
28,6	39,6	39,7	39,8	39,9	40,0	40,1	40,2	40,3	40,4	40,5
28,8	39,5	39,6	39,7	39,8	39,9	40,0	40,1	40,2	40,3	40,4
29,0	39,4	39,5	39,6	39,8	39,9	40,0	40,1	40,2	40,3	40,4
29,2	39,4	39,5	39,6	39,7	39,8	39,9	40,0	40,1	40,2	40,3
29,4	39,3	39,4	39,5	39,6	39,7	39,8	39,9	40,0	40,1	40,2
29,6	39,2	39,3	39,4	39,5	39,6	39,7	39,8	39,9	40,0	40,1
29,8	39,1	39,2	39,3	39,4	39,5	39,6	39,7	39,8	39,9	40,0
30,0	39,0	39,1	39,3	39,4	39,5	39,6	39,7	39,8	39,9	40,0

Volumenkonzentration bei 20 °C in Prozent

Temp. °C	Anzeige des Alkoholometers in % vol									
	44,0	44,1	44,2	44,3	44,4	44,5	44,6	44,7	44,8	44,9
0,0	51,6	51,7	51,8	51,8	51,9	52,0	52,1	52,2	52,3	52,4
0,2	51,5	51,6	51,7	51,8	51,9	52,0	52,1	52,1	52,2	52,3
0,4	51,4	51,5	51,6	51,7	51,8	51,9	52,0	52,1	52,2	52,3
0,6	51,3	51,4	51,5	51,6	51,7	51,8	51,9	52,0	52,1	52,2
0,8	51,3	51,4	51,5	51,6	51,6	51,7	51,8	51,9	52,0	52,1
1,0	51,2	51,3	51,4	51,5	51,6	51,7	51,8	51,9	51,9	52,0
1,2	51,1	51,2	51,3	51,4	51,5	51,6	51,7	51,8	51,9	52,0
1,4	51,1	51,1	51,2	51,3	51,4	51,5	51,6	51,7	51,8	51,9
1,6	51,0	51,1	51,2	51,3	51,4	51,4	51,5	51,6	51,7	51,8
1,8	50,9	51,0	51,1	51,2	51,3	51,4	51,5	51,6	51,7	51,8
2,0	50,8	50,9	51,0	51,1	51,2	51,3	51,4	51,5	51,6	51,7
2,2	50,8	50,9	50,9	51,0	51,1	51,2	51,3	51,4	51,5	51,6
2,4	50,7	50,8	50,9	51,0	51,1	51,2	51,2	51,3	51,4	51,5
2,6	50,6	50,7	50,8	50,9	51,0	51,1	51,2	51,3	51,4	51,5
2,8	50,5	50,6	50,7	50,8	50,9	51,0	51,1	51,2	51,3	51,4
3,0	50,5	50,6	50,7	50,7	50,8	50,9	51,0	51,1	51,2	51,3
3,2	50,4	50,5	50,6	50,7	50,8	50,9	51,0	51,0	51,1	51,2
3,4	50,3	50,4	50,5	50,6	50,7	50,8	50,9	51,0	51,1	51,2
3,6	50,2	50,3	50,4	50,5	50,6	50,7	50,8	50,9	51,0	51,1
3,8	50,2	50,3	50,4	50,5	50,5	50,6	50,7	50,8	50,9	51,0
4,0	50,1	50,2	50,3	50,4	50,5	50,6	50,7	50,8	50,8	50,9
4,2	50,0	50,1	50,2	50,3	50,4	50,5	50,6	50,7	50,8	50,9
4,4	49,9	50,0	50,1	50,2	50,3	50,4	50,5	50,6	50,7	50,8
4,6	49,9	50,0	50,1	50,2	50,2	50,3	50,4	50,5	50,6	50,7
4,8	49,8	49,9	50,0	50,1	50,2	50,3	50,4	50,5	50,6	50,7
5,0	49,7	49,8	49,9	50,0	50,1	50,2	50,3	50,4	50,5	50,6
5,2	49,6	49,7	49,8	49,9	50,0	50,1	50,2	50,3	50,4	50,5
5,4	49,6	49,7	49,8	49,9	50,0	50,0	50,1	50,2	50,3	50,4
5,6	49,5	49,6	49,7	49,8	49,9	50,0	50,1	50,2	50,3	50,4
5,8	49,4	49,5	49,6	49,7	49,8	49,9	50,0	50,1	50,2	50,3
6,0	49,3	49,4	49,5	49,6	49,7	49,8	49,9	50,0	50,1	50,2
6,2	49,3	49,4	49,5	49,6	49,7	49,8	49,8	49,9	50,0	50,1
6,4	49,2	49,3	49,4	49,5	49,6	49,7	49,8	49,9	50,0	50,1
6,6	49,1	49,2	49,3	49,4	49,5	49,6	49,7	49,8	49,9	50,0
6,8	49,0	49,1	49,2	49,3	49,4	49,5	49,6	49,7	49,8	49,9
7,0	49,0	49,1	49,2	49,3	49,4	49,5	49,5	49,6	49,7	49,8
7,2	48,9	49,0	49,1	49,2	49,3	49,4	49,5	49,6	49,7	49,8
7,4	48,8	48,9	49,0	49,1	49,2	49,3	49,4	49,5	49,6	49,7
7,6	48,7	48,8	48,9	49,0	49,1	49,2	49,3	49,4	49,5	49,6
7,8	48,7	48,8	48,9	49,0	49,1	49,2	49,2	49,3	49,4	49,5
8,0	48,6	48,7	48,8	48,9	49,0	49,1	49,2	49,3	49,4	49,5
8,2	48,5	48,6	48,7	48,8	48,9	49,0	49,1	49,2	49,3	49,4
8,4	48,4	48,5	48,6	48,7	48,8	48,9	49,0	49,1	49,2	49,3
8,6	48,4	48,5	48,6	48,7	48,8	48,9	48,9	49,0	49,1	49,2
8,8	48,3	48,4	48,5	48,6	48,7	48,8	48,9	49,0	49,1	49,2
9,0	48,2	48,3	48,4	48,5	48,6	48,7	48,8	48,9	49,0	49,1
9,2	48,1	48,2	48,3	48,4	48,5	48,6	48,7	48,8	48,9	49,0
9,4	48,1	48,2	48,3	48,4	48,5	48,6	48,6	48,7	48,8	48,9
9,6	48,0	48,1	48,2	48,3	48,4	48,5	48,6	48,7	48,8	48,9
9,8	47,9	48,0	48,1	48,2	48,3	48,4	48,5	48,6	48,7	48,8

Volumenkonzentration bei 20 °C in Prozent

Temp. °C	Anzeige des Alkoholometers in % vol									
	44,0	44,1	44,2	44,3	44,4	44,5	44,6	44,7	44,8	44,9
10,0	47,8	47,9	48,0	48,1	48,2	48,3	48,4	48,5	48,6	48,7
10,2	47,8	47,9	48,0	48,1	48,2	48,3	48,3	48,4	48,5	48,6
10,4	47,7	47,8	47,9	48,0	48,1	48,2	48,3	48,4	48,5	48,6
10,6	47,6	47,7	47,8	47,9	48,0	48,1	48,2	48,3	48,4	48,5
10,8	47,5	47,6	47,7	47,8	47,9	48,0	48,1	48,2	48,3	48,4
11,0	47,5	47,6	47,7	47,8	47,9	47,9	48,0	48,1	48,2	48,3
11,2	47,4	47,5	47,6	47,7	47,8	47,9	48,0	48,1	48,2	48,3
11,4	47,3	47,4	47,5	47,6	47,7	47,8	47,9	48,0	48,1	48,2
11,6	47,2	47,3	47,4	47,5	47,6	47,7	47,8	47,9	48,0	48,1
11,8	47,2	47,3	47,4	47,5	47,5	47,6	47,7	47,8	47,9	48,0
12,0	47,1	47,2	47,3	47,4	47,5	47,6	47,7	47,8	47,9	48,0
12,2	47,0	47,1	47,2	47,3	47,4	47,5	47,6	47,7	47,8	47,9
12,4	46,9	47,0	47,1	47,2	47,3	47,4	47,5	47,6	47,7	47,8
12,6	46,9	47,0	47,0	47,1	47,2	47,3	47,4	47,5	47,6	47,7
12,8	46,8	46,9	47,0	47,1	47,2	47,3	47,4	47,5	47,6	47,7
13,0	46,7	46,8	46,9	47,0	47,1	47,2	47,3	47,4	47,5	47,6
13,2	46,6	46,7	46,8	46,9	47,0	47,1	47,2	47,3	47,4	47,5
13,4	46,5	46,6	46,7	46,8	46,9	47,0	47,1	47,2	47,3	47,4
13,6	46,5	46,6	46,7	46,8	46,9	47,0	47,1	47,2	47,3	47,4
13,8	46,4	46,5	46,6	46,7	46,8	46,9	47,0	47,1	47,2	47,3
14,0	46,3	46,4	46,5	46,6	46,7	46,8	46,9	47,0	47,1	47,2
14,2	46,2	46,3	46,4	46,5	46,6	46,7	46,8	46,9	47,0	47,1
14,4	46,2	46,3	46,4	46,5	46,6	46,7	46,8	46,9	47,0	47,0
14,6	46,1	46,2	46,3	46,4	46,5	46,6	46,7	46,8	46,9	47,0
14,8	46,0	46,1	46,2	46,3	46,4	46,5	46,6	46,7	46,8	46,9
15,0	45,9	46,0	46,1	46,2	46,3	46,4	46,5	46,6	46,7	46,8
15,2	45,9	46,0	46,1	46,2	46,3	46,3	46,4	46,5	46,6	46,7
15,4	45,8	45,9	46,0	46,1	46,2	46,3	46,4	46,5	46,6	46,7
15,6	45,7	45,8	45,9	46,0	46,1	46,2	46,3	46,4	46,5	46,6
15,8	45,6	45,7	45,8	45,9	46,0	46,1	46,2	46,3	46,4	46,5
16,0	45,5	45,6	45,7	45,8	45,9	46,0	46,1	46,2	46,3	46,4
16,2	45,5	45,6	45,7	45,8	45,9	46,0	46,1	46,2	46,3	46,4
16,4	45,4	45,5	45,6	45,7	45,8	45,9	46,0	46,1	46,2	46,3
16,6	45,3	45,4	45,5	45,6	45,7	45,8	45,9	46,0	46,1	46,2
16,8	45,2	45,3	45,4	45,5	45,6	45,7	45,8	45,9	46,0	46,1
17,0	45,2	45,3	45,4	45,5	45,6	45,7	45,8	45,9	46,0	46,1
17,2	45,1	45,2	45,3	45,4	45,5	45,6	45,7	45,8	45,9	46,0
17,4	45,0	45,1	45,2	45,3	45,4	45,5	45,6	45,7	45,8	45,9
17,6	44,9	45,0	45,1	45,2	45,3	45,4	45,5	45,6	45,7	45,8
17,8	44,9	45,0	45,1	45,2	45,3	45,4	45,4	45,5	45,6	45,7
18,0	44,8	44,9	45,0	45,1	45,2	45,3	45,4	45,5	45,6	45,7
18,2	44,7	44,8	44,9	45,0	45,1	45,2	45,3	45,4	45,5	45,6
18,4	44,6	44,7	44,8	44,9	45,0	45,1	45,2	45,3	45,4	45,5
18,6	44,5	44,6	44,7	44,8	44,9	45,0	45,1	45,2	45,3	45,4
18,8	44,5	44,6	44,7	44,8	44,9	45,0	45,1	45,2	45,3	45,4
19,0	44,4	44,5	44,6	44,7	44,8	44,9	45,0	45,1	45,2	45,3
19,2	44,3	44,4	44,5	44,6	44,7	44,8	44,9	45,0	45,1	45,2
19,4	44,2	44,3	44,4	44,5	44,6	44,7	44,8	44,9	45,0	45,1
19,6	44,2	44,3	44,4	44,5	44,6	44,7	44,8	44,9	45,0	45,1
19,8	44,1	44,2	44,3	44,4	44,5	44,6	44,7	44,8	44,9	45,0

Volumenkonzentration bei 20 °C in Prozent

Temp. °C	Anzeige des Alkoholometers in % vol									
	44,0	44,1	44,2	44,3	44,4	44,5	44,6	44,7	44,8	44,9
20,0	44,0	44,1	44,2	44,3	44,4	44,5	44,6	44,7	44,8	44,9
20,2	43,9	44,0	44,1	44,2	44,3	44,4	44,5	44,6	44,7	44,8
20,4	43,8	43,9	44,0	44,1	44,2	44,3	44,4	44,5	44,6	44,7
20,6	43,8	43,9	44,0	44,1	44,2	44,3	44,4	44,5	44,6	44,7
20,8	43,7	43,8	43,9	44,0	44,1	44,2	44,3	44,4	44,5	44,6
21,0	43,6	43,7	43,8	43,9	44,0	44,1	44,2	44,3	44,4	44,5
21,2	43,5	43,6	43,7	43,8	43,9	44,0	44,1	44,2	44,3	44,4
21,4	43,5	43,6	43,7	43,8	43,9	44,0	44,1	44,2	44,3	44,4
21,6	43,4	43,5	43,6	43,7	43,8	43,9	44,0	44,1	44,2	44,3
21,8	43,3	43,4	43,5	43,6	43,7	43,8	43,9	44,0	44,1	44,2
22,0	43,2	43,3	43,4	43,5	43,6	43,7	43,8	43,9	44,0	44,1
22,2	43,1	43,2	43,3	43,4	43,5	43,6	43,7	43,8	43,9	44,0
22,4	43,1	43,2	43,3	43,4	43,5	43,6	43,7	43,8	43,9	44,0
22,6	43,0	43,1	43,2	43,3	43,4	43,5	43,6	43,7	43,8	43,9
22,8	42,9	43,0	43,1	43,2	43,3	43,4	43,5	43,6	43,7	43,8
23,0	42,8	42,9	43,0	43,1	43,2	43,3	43,4	43,5	43,6	43,7
23,2	42,8	42,9	43,0	43,1	43,2	43,3	43,4	43,5	43,6	43,7
23,4	42,7	42,8	42,9	43,0	43,1	43,2	43,3	43,4	43,5	43,6
23,6	42,6	42,7	42,8	42,9	43,0	43,1	43,2	43,3	43,4	43,5
23,8	42,5	42,6	42,7	42,8	42,9	43,0	43,1	43,2	43,3	43,4
24,0	42,4	42,5	42,6	42,7	42,8	42,9	43,0	43,1	43,2	43,3
24,2	42,4	42,5	42,6	42,7	42,8	42,9	43,0	43,1	43,2	43,3
24,4	42,3	42,4	42,5	42,6	42,7	42,8	42,9	43,0	43,1	43,2
24,6	42,2	42,3	42,4	42,5	42,6	42,7	42,8	42,9	43,0	43,1
24,8	42,1	42,2	42,3	42,4	42,5	42,6	42,7	42,8	42,9	43,0
25,0	42,0	42,1	42,2	42,3	42,5	42,6	42,7	42,8	42,9	43,0
25,2	42,0	42,1	42,2	42,3	42,4	42,5	42,6	42,7	42,8	42,9
25,4	41,9	42,0	42,1	42,2	42,3	42,4	42,5	42,6	42,7	42,8
25,6	41,8	41,9	42,0	42,1	42,2	42,3	42,4	42,5	42,6	42,7
25,8	41,7	41,8	41,9	42,0	42,1	42,2	42,3	42,4	42,5	42,6
26,0	41,7	41,8	41,9	42,0	42,1	42,2	42,3	42,4	42,5	42,6
26,2	41,6	41,7	41,8	41,9	42,0	42,1	42,2	42,3	42,4	42,5
26,4	41,5	41,6	41,7	41,8	41,9	42,0	42,1	42,2	42,3	42,4
26,6	41,4	41,5	41,6	41,7	41,8	41,9	42,0	42,1	42,2	42,3
26,8	41,3	41,4	41,5	41,6	41,7	41,8	41,9	42,0	42,2	42,3
27,0	41,3	41,4	41,5	41,6	41,7	41,8	41,9	42,0	42,1	42,2
27,2	41,2	41,3	41,4	41,5	41,6	41,7	41,8	41,9	42,0	42,1
27,4	41,1	41,2	41,3	41,4	41,5	41,6	41,7	41,8	41,9	42,0
27,6	41,0	41,1	41,2	41,3	41,4	41,5	41,6	41,7	41,8	41,9
27,8	40,9	41,0	41,1	41,2	41,3	41,5	41,6	41,7	41,8	41,9
28,0	40,9	41,0	41,1	41,2	41,3	41,4	41,5	41,6	41,7	41,8
28,2	40,8	40,9	41,0	41,1	41,2	41,3	41,4	41,5	41,6	41,7
28,4	40,7	40,8	40,9	41,0	41,1	41,2	41,3	41,4	41,5	41,6
28,6	40,6	40,7	40,8	40,9	41,0	41,1	41,2	41,3	41,4	41,5
28,8	40,5	40,6	40,8	40,9	41,0	41,1	41,2	41,3	41,4	41,5
29,0	40,5	40,6	40,7	40,8	40,9	41,0	41,1	41,2	41,3	41,4
29,2	40,4	40,5	40,6	40,7	40,8	40,9	41,0	41,1	41,2	41,3
29,4	40,3	40,4	40,5	40,6	40,7	40,8	40,9	41,0	41,1	41,2
29,6	40,2	40,3	40,4	40,5	40,6	40,7	40,8	40,9	41,0	41,2
29,8	40,2	40,3	40,4	40,5	40,6	40,7	40,8	40,9	41,0	41,1
30,0	40,1	40,2	40,3	40,4	40,5	40,6	40,7	40,8	40,9	41,0

Volumenkonzentration bei 20 °C in Prozent

Temp. °C	Anzeige des Alkoholometers in % vol									
	45,0	45,1	45,2	45,3	45,4	45,5	45,6	45,7	45,8	45,9
0,0	52,5	52,6	52,7	52,8	52,9	53,0	53,1	53,2	53,2	53,3
0,2	52,4	52,5	52,6	52,7	52,8	52,9	53,0	53,1	53,2	53,3
0,4	52,4	52,4	52,5	52,6	52,7	52,8	52,9	53,0	53,1	53,2
0,6	52,3	52,4	52,5	52,6	52,7	52,7	52,8	52,9	53,0	53,1
0,8	52,2	52,3	52,4	52,5	52,6	52,7	52,8	52,9	53,0	53,1
1,0	52,1	52,2	52,3	52,4	52,5	52,6	52,7	52,8	52,9	53,0
1,2	52,1	52,2	52,3	52,3	52,4	52,5	52,6	52,7	52,8	52,9
1,4	52,0	52,1	52,2	52,3	52,4	52,5	52,6	52,6	52,7	52,8
1,6	51,9	52,0	52,1	52,2	52,3	52,4	52,5	52,6	52,7	52,8
1,8	51,8	51,9	52,0	52,1	52,2	52,3	52,4	52,5	52,6	52,7
2,0	51,8	51,9	52,0	52,1	52,1	52,2	52,3	52,4	52,5	52,6
2,2	51,7	51,8	51,9	52,0	52,1	52,2	52,3	52,4	52,5	52,5
2,4	51,6	51,7	51,8	51,9	52,0	52,1	52,2	52,3	52,4	52,5
2,6	51,6	51,6	51,7	51,8	51,9	52,0	52,1	52,2	52,3	52,4
2,8	51,5	51,6	51,7	51,8	51,9	52,0	52,0	52,1	52,2	52,3
3,0	51,4	51,5	51,6	51,7	51,8	51,9	52,0	52,1	52,2	52,3
3,2	51,3	51,4	51,5	51,6	51,7	51,8	51,9	52,0	52,1	52,2
3,4	51,3	51,4	51,4	51,5	51,6	51,7	51,8	51,9	52,0	52,1
3,6	51,2	51,3	51,4	51,5	51,6	51,7	51,8	51,8	51,9	52,0
3,8	51,1	51,2	51,3	51,4	51,5	51,6	51,7	51,8	51,9	52,0
4,0	51,0	51,1	51,2	51,3	51,4	51,5	51,6	51,7	51,8	51,9
4,2	51,0	51,1	51,2	51,3	51,3	51,4	51,5	51,6	51,7	51,8
4,4	50,9	51,0	51,1	51,2	51,3	51,4	51,5	51,6	51,7	51,7
4,6	50,8	50,9	51,0	51,1	51,2	51,3	51,4	51,5	51,6	51,7
4,8	50,7	50,8	50,9	51,0	51,1	51,2	51,3	51,4	51,5	51,6
5,0	50,7	50,8	50,9	51,0	51,1	51,1	51,2	51,3	51,4	51,5
5,2	50,6	50,7	50,8	50,9	51,0	51,1	51,2	51,3	51,4	51,5
5,4	50,5	50,6	50,7	50,8	50,9	51,0	51,1	51,2	51,3	51,4
5,6	50,5	50,5	50,6	50,7	50,8	50,9	51,0	51,1	51,2	51,3
5,8	50,4	50,5	50,6	50,7	50,8	50,9	50,9	51,0	51,1	51,2
6,0	50,3	50,4	50,5	50,6	50,7	50,8	50,9	51,0	51,1	51,2
6,2	50,2	50,3	50,4	50,5	50,6	50,7	50,8	50,9	51,0	51,1
6,4	50,2	50,3	50,3	50,4	50,5	50,6	50,7	50,8	50,9	51,0
6,6	50,1	50,2	50,3	50,4	50,5	50,6	50,7	50,8	50,8	50,9
6,8	50,0	50,1	50,2	50,3	50,4	50,5	50,6	50,7	50,8	50,9
7,0	49,9	50,0	50,1	50,2	50,3	50,4	50,5	50,6	50,7	50,8
7,2	49,9	50,0	50,0	50,1	50,2	50,3	50,4	50,5	50,6	50,7
7,4	49,8	49,9	50,0	50,1	50,2	50,3	50,4	50,5	50,6	50,6
7,6	49,7	49,8	49,9	50,0	50,1	50,2	50,3	50,4	50,5	50,6
7,8	49,6	49,7	49,8	49,9	50,0	50,1	50,2	50,3	50,4	50,5
8,0	49,6	49,7	49,8	49,8	49,9	50,0	50,1	50,2	50,3	50,4
8,2	49,5	49,6	49,7	49,8	49,9	50,0	50,1	50,2	50,3	50,4
8,4	49,4	49,5	49,6	49,7	49,8	49,9	50,0	50,1	50,2	50,3
8,6	49,3	49,4	49,5	49,6	49,7	49,8	49,9	50,0	50,1	50,2
8,8	49,3	49,4	49,5	49,6	49,6	49,7	49,8	49,9	50,0	50,1
9,0	49,2	49,3	49,4	49,5	49,6	49,7	49,8	49,9	50,0	50,1
9,2	49,1	49,2	49,3	49,4	49,5	49,6	49,7	49,8	49,9	50,0
9,4	49,0	49,1	49,2	49,3	49,4	49,5	49,6	49,7	49,8	49,9
9,6	49,0	49,1	49,2	49,3	49,3	49,4	49,5	49,6	49,7	49,8
9,8	48,9	49,0	49,1	49,2	49,3	49,4	49,5	49,6	49,7	49,8

Volumenkonzentration bei 20 °C in Prozent

Temp. °C	Anzeige des Alkoholometers in % vol								
	45,0	45,1	45,2	45,3	45,4	45,5	45,6	45,7	45,8	45,9
10,0	48,8	48,9	49,0	49,1	49,2	49,3	49,4	49,5	49,6	49,7
10,2	48,7	48,8	48,9	49,0	49,1	49,2	49,3	49,4	49,5	49,6
10,4	48,7	48,8	48,9	49,0	49,0	49,1	49,2	49,3	49,4	49,5
10,6	48,6	48,7	48,8	48,9	49,0	49,1	49,2	49,3	49,4	49,5
10,8	48,5	48,6	48,7	48,8	48,9	49,0	49,1	49,2	49,3	49,4
11,0	48,4	48,5	48,6	48,7	48,8	48,9	49,0	49,1	49,2	49,3
11,2	48,4	48,5	48,6	48,7	48,7	48,8	48,9	49,0	49,1	49,2
11,4	48,3	48,4	48,5	48,6	48,7	48,8	48,9	49,0	49,1	49,2
11,6	48,2	48,3	48,4	48,5	48,6	48,7	48,8	48,9	49,0	49,1
11,8	48,1	48,2	48,3	48,4	48,5	48,6	48,7	48,8	48,9	49,0
12,0	48,1	48,2	48,3	48,4	48,4	48,5	48,6	48,7	48,8	48,9
12,2	48,0	48,1	48,2	48,3	48,4	48,5	48,6	48,7	48,8	48,9
12,4	47,9	48,0	48,1	48,2	48,3	48,4	48,5	48,6	48,7	48,8
12,6	47,8	47,9	48,0	48,1	48,2	48,3	48,4	48,5	48,6	48,7
12,8	47,8	47,9	48,0	48,0	48,1	48,2	48,3	48,4	48,5	48,6
13,0	47,7	47,8	47,9	48,0	48,1	48,2	48,3	48,4	48,5	48,6
13,2	47,6	47,7	47,8	47,9	48,0	48,1	48,2	48,3	48,4	48,5
13,4	47,5	47,6	47,7	47,8	47,9	48,0	48,1	48,2	48,3	48,4
13,6	47,5	47,6	47,6	47,7	47,8	47,9	48,0	48,1	48,2	48,3
13,8	47,4	47,5	47,6	47,7	47,8	47,9	48,0	48,1	48,2	48,3
14,0	47,3	47,4	47,5	47,6	47,7	47,8	47,9	48,0	48,1	48,2
14,2	47,2	47,3	47,4	47,5	47,6	47,7	47,8	47,9	48,0	48,1
14,4	47,1	47,2	47,3	47,4	47,5	47,6	47,7	47,8	47,9	48,0
14,6	47,1	47,2	47,3	47,4	47,5	47,6	47,7	47,8	47,9	48,0
14,8	47,0	47,1	47,2	47,3	47,4	47,5	47,6	47,7	47,8	47,9
15,0	46,9	47,0	47,1	47,2	47,3	47,4	47,5	47,6	47,7	47,8
15,2	46,8	46,9	47,0	47,1	47,2	47,3	47,4	47,5	47,6	47,7
15,4	46,8	46,9	47,0	47,1	47,2	47,3	47,4	47,5	47,6	47,7
15,6	46,7	46,8	46,9	47,0	47,1	47,2	47,3	47,4	47,5	47,6
15,8	46,6	46,7	46,8	46,9	47,0	47,1	47,2	47,3	47,4	47,5
16,0	46,5	46,6	46,7	46,8	46,9	47,0	47,1	47,2	47,3	47,4
16,2	46,5	46,6	46,7	46,8	46,9	47,0	47,1	47,2	47,3	47,4
16,4	46,4	46,5	46,6	46,7	46,8	46,9	47,0	47,1	47,2	47,3
16,6	46,3	46,4	46,5	46,6	46,7	46,8	46,9	47,0	47,1	47,2
16,8	46,2	46,3	46,4	46,5	46,6	46,7	46,8	46,9	47,0	47,1
17,0	46,2	46,3	46,4	46,5	46,6	46,7	46,7	46,8	46,9	47,0
17,2	46,1	46,2	46,3	46,4	46,5	46,6	46,7	46,8	46,9	47,0
17,4	46,0	46,1	46,2	46,3	46,4	46,5	46,6	46,7	46,8	46,9
17,6	45,9	46,0	46,1	46,2	46,3	46,4	46,5	46,6	46,7	46,8
17,8	45,8	45,9	46,0	46,1	46,2	46,3	46,4	46,5	46,6	46,7
18,0	45,8	45,9	46,0	46,1	46,2	46,3	46,4	46,5	46,6	46,7
18,2	45,7	45,8	45,9	46,0	46,1	46,2	46,3	46,4	46,5	46,6
18,4	45,6	45,7	45,8	45,9	46,0	46,1	46,2	46,3	46,4	46,5
18,6	45,5	45,6	45,7	45,8	45,9	46,0	46,1	46,2	46,3	46,4
18,8	45,5	45,6	45,7	45,8	45,9	46,0	46,1	46,2	46,3	46,4
19,0	45,4	45,5	45,6	45,7	45,8	45,9	46,0	46,1	46,2	46,3
19,2	45,3	45,4	45,5	45,6	45,7	45,8	45,9	46,0	46,1	46,2
19,4	45,2	45,3	45,4	45,5	45,6	45,7	45,8	45,9	46,0	46,1
19,6	45,2	45,3	45,4	45,5	45,6	45,7	45,8	45,9	46,0	46,1
19,8	45,1	45,2	45,3	45,4	45,5	45,6	45,7	45,8	45,9	46,0

Volumenkonzentration bei 20 °C in Prozent

Temp. °C	Anzeige des Alkoholometers in % vol									
	45,0	45,1	45,2	45,3	45,4	45,5	45,6	45,7	45,8	45,9
20,0	45,0	45,1	45,2	45,3	45,4	45,5	45,6	45,7	45,8	45,9
20,2	44,9	45,0	45,1	45,2	45,3	45,4	45,5	45,6	45,7	45,8
20,4	44,8	44,9	45,0	45,1	45,2	45,3	45,4	45,5	45,6	45,7
20,6	44,8	44,9	45,0	45,1	45,2	45,3	45,4	45,5	45,6	45,7
20,8	44,7	44,8	44,9	45,0	45,1	45,2	45,3	45,4	45,5	45,6
21,0	44,6	44,7	44,8	44,9	45,0	45,1	45,2	45,3	45,4	45,5
21,2	44,5	44,6	44,7	44,8	44,9	45,0	45,1	45,2	45,3	45,4
21,4	44,5	44,6	44,7	44,8	44,9	45,0	45,1	45,2	45,3	45,4
21,6	44,4	44,5	44,6	44,7	44,8	44,9	45,0	45,1	45,2	45,3
21,8	44,3	44,4	44,5	44,6	44,7	44,8	44,9	45,0	45,1	45,2
22,0	44,2	44,3	44,4	44,5	44,6	44,7	44,8	44,9	45,0	45,1
22,2	44,1	44,2	44,3	44,4	44,6	44,7	44,8	44,9	45,0	45,1
22,4	44,1	44,2	44,3	44,4	44,5	44,6	44,7	44,8	44,9	45,0
22,6	44,0	44,1	44,2	44,3	44,4	44,5	44,6	44,7	44,8	44,9
22,8	43,9	44,0	44,1	44,2	44,3	44,4	44,5	44,6	44,7	44,8
23,0	43,8	43,9	44,0	44,1	44,2	44,3	44,4	44,5	44,6	44,7
23,2	43,8	43,9	44,0	44,1	44,2	44,3	44,4	44,5	44,6	44,7
23,4	43,7	43,8	43,9	44,0	44,1	44,2	44,3	44,4	44,5	44,6
23,6	43,6	43,7	43,8	43,9	44,0	44,1	44,2	44,3	44,4	44,5
23,8	43,5	43,6	43,7	43,8	43,9	44,0	44,1	44,2	44,3	44,4
24,0	43,4	43,5	43,7	43,8	43,9	44,0	44,1	44,2	44,3	44,4
24,2	43,4	43,5	43,6	43,7	43,8	43,9	44,0	44,1	44,2	44,3
24,4	43,3	43,4	43,5	43,6	43,7	43,8	43,9	44,0	44,1	44,2
24,6	43,2	43,3	43,4	43,5	43,6	43,7	43,8	43,9	44,0	44,1
24,8	43,1	43,2	43,3	43,4	43,5	43,6	43,7	43,8	43,9	44,0
25,0	43,1	43,2	43,3	43,4	43,5	43,6	43,7	43,8	43,9	44,0
25,2	43,0	43,1	43,2	43,3	43,4	43,5	43,6	43,7	43,8	43,9
25,4	42,9	43,0	43,1	43,2	43,3	43,4	43,5	43,6	43,7	43,8
25,6	42,8	42,9	43,0	43,1	43,2	43,3	43,4	43,5	43,6	43,7
25,8	42,7	42,8	42,9	43,0	43,2	43,3	43,4	43,5	43,6	43,7
26,0	42,7	42,8	42,9	43,0	43,1	43,2	43,3	43,4	43,5	43,6
26,2	42,6	42,7	42,8	42,9	43,0	43,1	43,2	43,3	43,4	43,5
26,4	42,5	42,6	42,7	42,8	42,9	43,0	43,1	43,2	43,3	43,4
26,6	42,4	42,5	42,6	42,7	42,8	42,9	43,0	43,1	43,2	43,3
26,8	42,4	42,5	42,6	42,7	42,8	42,9	43,0	43,1	43,2	43,3
27,0	42,3	42,4	42,5	42,6	42,7	42,8	42,9	43,0	43,1	43,2
27,2	42,2	42,3	42,4	42,5	42,6	42,7	42,8	42,9	43,0	43,1
27,4	42,1	42,2	42,3	42,4	42,5	42,6	42,7	42,8	42,9	43,0
27,6	42,0	42,1	42,2	42,3	42,4	42,6	42,7	42,8	42,9	43,0
27,8	42,0	42,1	42,2	42,3	42,4	42,5	42,6	42,7	42,8	42,9
28,0	41,9	42,0	42,1	42,2	42,3	42,4	42,5	42,6	42,7	42,8
28,2	41,8	41,9	42,0	42,1	42,2	42,3	42,4	42,5	42,6	42,7
28,4	41,7	41,8	41,9	42,0	42,1	42,2	42,3	42,4	42,5	42,6
28,6	41,6	41,7	41,9	42,0	42,1	42,2	42,3	42,4	42,5	42,6
28,8	41,6	41,7	41,8	41,9	42,0	42,1	42,2	42,3	42,4	42,5
29,0	41,5	41,6	41,7	41,8	41,9	42,0	42,1	42,2	42,3	42,4
29,2	41,4	41,5	41,6	41,7	41,8	41,9	42,0	42,1	42,2	42,3
29,4	41,3	41,4	41,5	41,6	41,7	41,8	41,9	42,0	42,2	42,3
29,6	41,3	41,4	41,5	41,6	41,7	41,8	41,9	42,0	42,1	42,2
29,8	41,2	41,3	41,4	41,5	41,6	41,7	41,8	41,9	42,0	42,1
30,0	41,1	41,2	41,3	41,4	41,5	41,6	41,7	41,8	41,9	42,0

Volumenkonzentration bei 20 °C in Prozent

Temp. °C	Anzeige des Alkoholometers in % vol									
	46,0	46,1	46,2	46,3	46,4	46,5	46,6	46,7	46,8	46,9
0,0	53,4	53,5	53,6	53,7	53,8	53,9	54,0	54,1	54,2	54,3
0,2	53,4	53,5	53,5	53,6	53,7	53,8	53,9	54,0	54,1	54,2
0,4	53,3	53,4	53,5	53,6	53,7	53,8	53,9	53,9	54,0	54,1
0,6	53,2	53,3	53,4	53,5	53,6	53,7	53,8	53,9	54,0	54,1
0,8	53,1	53,2	53,3	53,4	53,5	53,6	53,7	53,8	53,9	54,0
1,0	53,1	53,2	53,3	53,4	53,4	53,5	53,6	53,7	53,8	53,9
1,2	53,0	53,1	53,2	53,3	53,4	53,5	53,6	53,7	53,8	53,8
1,4	52,9	53,0	53,1	53,2	53,3	53,4	53,5	53,6	53,7	53,8
1,6	52,9	53,0	53,0	53,1	53,2	53,3	53,4	53,5	53,6	53,7
1,8	52,8	52,9	53,0	53,1	53,2	53,3	53,3	53,4	53,5	53,6
2,0	52,7	52,8	52,9	53,0	53,1	53,2	53,3	53,4	53,5	53,6
2,2	52,6	52,7	52,8	52,9	53,0	53,1	53,2	53,3	53,4	53,5
2,4	52,6	52,7	52,8	52,9	52,9	53,0	53,1	53,2	53,3	53,4
2,6	52,5	52,6	52,7	52,8	52,9	53,0	53,1	53,2	53,3	53,3
2,8	52,4	52,5	52,6	52,7	52,8	52,9	53,0	53,1	53,2	53,3
3,0	52,4	52,4	52,5	52,6	52,7	52,8	52,9	53,0	53,1	53,2
3,2	52,3	52,4	52,5	52,6	52,7	52,8	52,8	52,9	53,0	53,1
3,4	52,2	52,3	52,4	52,5	52,6	52,7	52,8	52,9	53,0	53,1
3,6	52,1	52,2	52,3	52,4	52,5	52,6	52,7	52,8	52,9	53,0
3,8	52,1	52,2	52,3	52,3	52,4	52,5	52,6	52,7	52,8	52,9
4,0	52,0	52,1	52,2	52,3	52,4	52,5	52,6	52,7	52,7	52,8
4,2	51,9	52,0	52,1	52,2	52,3	52,4	52,5	52,6	52,7	52,8
4,4	51,8	51,9	52,0	52,1	52,2	52,3	52,4	52,5	52,6	52,7
4,6	51,8	51,9	52,0	52,1	52,1	52,2	52,3	52,4	52,5	52,6
4,8	51,7	51,8	51,9	52,0	52,1	52,2	52,3	52,4	52,5	52,6
5,0	51,6	51,7	51,8	51,9	52,0	52,1	52,2	52,3	52,4	52,5
5,2	51,6	51,6	51,7	51,8	51,9	52,0	52,1	52,2	52,3	52,4
5,4	51,5	51,6	51,7	51,8	51,9	52,0	52,0	52,1	52,2	52,3
5,6	51,4	51,5	51,6	51,7	51,8	51,9	52,0	52,1	52,2	52,3
5,8	51,3	51,4	51,5	51,6	51,7	51,8	51,9	52,0	52,1	52,2
6,0	51,3	51,4	51,4	51,5	51,6	51,7	51,8	51,9	52,0	52,1
6,2	51,2	51,3	51,4	51,5	51,6	51,7	51,8	51,9	51,9	52,0
6,4	51,1	51,2	51,3	51,4	51,5	51,6	51,7	51,8	51,9	52,0
6,6	51,0	51,1	51,2	51,3	51,4	51,5	51,6	51,7	51,8	51,9
6,8	51,0	51,1	51,2	51,3	51,3	51,4	51,5	51,6	51,7	51,8
7,0	50,9	51,0	51,1	51,2	51,3	51,4	51,5	51,6	51,7	51,8
7,2	50,8	50,9	51,0	51,1	51,2	51,3	51,4	51,5	51,6	51,7
7,4	50,7	50,8	50,9	51,0	51,1	51,2	51,3	51,4	51,5	51,6
7,6	50,7	50,8	50,9	51,0	51,1	51,1	51,2	51,3	51,4	51,5
7,8	50,6	50,7	50,8	50,9	51,0	51,1	51,2	51,3	51,4	51,5
8,0	50,5	50,6	50,7	50,8	50,9	51,0	51,1	51,2	51,3	51,4
8,2	50,4	50,5	50,6	50,7	50,8	50,9	51,0	51,1	51,2	51,3
8,4	50,4	50,5	50,6	50,7	50,8	50,9	51,0	51,0	51,1	51,2
8,6	50,3	50,4	50,5	50,6	50,7	50,8	50,9	51,0	51,1	51,2
8,8	50,2	50,3	50,4	50,5	50,6	50,7	50,8	50,9	51,0	51,1
9,0	50,2	50,2	50,3	50,4	50,5	50,6	50,7	50,8	50,9	51,0
9,2	50,1	50,2	50,3	50,4	50,5	50,6	50,7	50,8	50,9	50,9
9,4	50,0	50,1	50,2	50,3	50,4	50,5	50,6	50,7	50,8	50,9
9,6	49,9	50,0	50,1	50,2	50,3	50,4	50,5	50,6	50,7	50,8
9,8	49,9	50,0	50,0	50,1	50,2	50,3	50,4	50,5	50,6	50,7

Volumenkonzentration bei 20 °C in Prozent

Temp. °C	Anzeige des Alkoholometers in % vol									
	46,0	46,1	46,2	46,3	46,4	46,5	46,6	46,7	46,8	46,9
10,0	49,8	49,9	50,0	50,1	50,2	50,3	50,4	50,5	50,6	50,7
10,2	49,7	49,8	49,9	50,0	50,1	50,2	50,3	50,4	50,5	50,6
10,4	49,6	49,7	49,8	49,9	50,0	50,1	50,2	50,3	50,4	50,5
10,6	49,6	49,7	49,8	49,8	49,9	50,0	50,1	50,2	50,3	50,4
10,8	49,5	49,6	49,7	49,8	49,9	50,0	50,1	50,2	50,3	50,4
11,0	49,4	49,5	49,6	49,7	49,8	49,9	50,0	50,1	50,2	50,3
11,2	49,3	49,4	49,5	49,6	49,7	49,8	49,9	50,0	50,1	50,2
11,4	49,3	49,4	49,5	49,6	49,6	49,7	49,8	49,9	50,0	50,1
11,6	49,2	49,3	49,4	49,5	49,6	49,7	49,8	49,9	50,0	50,1
11,8	49,1	49,2	49,3	49,4	49,5	49,6	49,7	49,8	49,9	50,0
12,0	49,0	49,1	49,2	49,3	49,4	49,5	49,6	49,7	49,8	49,9
12,2	49,0	49,1	49,2	49,3	49,3	49,4	49,5	49,6	49,7	49,8
12,4	48,9	49,0	49,1	49,2	49,3	49,4	49,5	49,6	49,7	49,8
12,6	48,8	48,9	49,0	49,1	49,2	49,3	49,4	49,5	49,6	49,7
12,8	48,7	48,8	48,9	49,0	49,1	49,2	49,3	49,4	49,5	49,6
13,0	48,7	48,8	48,9	49,0	49,0	49,1	49,2	49,3	49,4	49,5
13,2	48,6	48,7	48,8	48,9	49,0	49,1	49,2	49,3	49,4	49,5
13,4	48,5	48,6	48,7	48,8	48,9	49,0	49,1	49,2	49,3	49,4
13,6	48,4	48,5	48,6	48,7	48,8	48,9	49,0	49,1	49,2	49,3
13,8	48,4	48,5	48,6	48,7	48,7	48,8	48,9	49,0	49,1	49,2
14,0	48,3	48,4	48,5	48,6	48,7	48,8	48,9	49,0	49,1	49,2
14,2	48,2	48,3	48,4	48,5	48,6	48,7	48,8	48,9	49,0	49,1
14,4	48,1	48,2	48,3	48,4	48,5	48,6	48,7	48,8	48,9	49,0
14,6	48,1	48,2	48,3	48,4	48,4	48,5	48,6	48,7	48,8	48,9
14,8	48,0	48,1	48,2	48,3	48,4	48,5	48,6	48,7	48,8	48,9
15,0	47,9	48,0	48,1	48,2	48,3	48,4	48,5	48,6	48,7	48,8
15,2	47,8	47,9	48,0	48,1	48,2	48,3	48,4	48,5	48,6	48,7
15,4	47,8	47,9	48,0	48,0	48,1	48,2	48,3	48,4	48,5	48,6
15,6	47,7	47,8	47,9	48,0	48,1	48,2	48,3	48,4	48,5	48,6
15,8	47,6	47,7	47,8	47,9	48,0	48,1	48,2	48,3	48,4	48,5
16,0	47,5	47,6	47,7	47,8	47,9	48,0	48,1	48,2	48,3	48,4
16,2	47,4	47,5	47,6	47,7	47,8	47,9	48,0	48,1	48,2	48,3
16,4	47,4	47,5	47,6	47,7	47,8	47,9	48,0	48,1	48,2	48,3
16,6	47,3	47,4	47,5	47,6	47,7	47,8	47,9	48,0	48,1	48,2
16,8	47,2	47,3	47,4	47,5	47,6	47,7	47,8	47,9	48,0	48,1
17,0	47,1	47,2	47,3	47,4	47,5	47,6	47,7	47,8	47,9	48,0
17,2	47,1	47,2	47,3	47,4	47,5	47,6	47,7	47,8	47,9	48,0
17,4	47,0	47,1	47,2	47,3	47,4	47,5	47,6	47,7	47,8	47,9
17,6	46,9	47,0	47,1	47,2	47,3	47,4	47,5	47,6	47,7	47,8
17,8	46,8	46,9	47,0	47,1	47,2	47,3	47,4	47,5	47,6	47,7
18,0	46,8	46,9	47,0	47,1	47,2	47,3	47,4	47,5	47,6	47,7
18,2	46,7	46,8	46,9	47,0	47,1	47,2	47,3	47,4	47,5	47,6
18,4	46,6	46,7	46,8	46,9	47,0	47,1	47,2	47,3	47,4	47,5
18,6	46,5	46,6	46,7	46,8	46,9	47,0	47,1	47,2	47,3	47,4
18,8	46,5	46,6	46,7	46,8	46,9	47,0	47,1	47,2	47,3	47,4
19,0	46,4	46,5	46,6	46,7	46,8	46,9	47,0	47,1	47,2	47,3
19,2	46,3	46,4	46,5	46,6	46,7	46,8	46,9	47,0	47,1	47,2
19,4	46,2	46,3	46,4	46,5	46,6	46,7	46,8	46,9	47,0	47,1
19,6	46,2	46,3	46,4	46,5	46,6	46,7	46,8	46,9	47,0	47,1
19,8	46,1	46,2	46,3	46,4	46,5	46,6	46,7	46,8	46,9	47,0

Volumenkonzentration bei 20 °C in Prozent

Temp. °C	Anzeige des Alkoholometers in % vol									
	46,0	46,1	46,2	46,3	46,4	46,5	46,6	46,7	46,8	46,9
20,0	46,0	46,1	46,2	46,3	46,4	46,5	46,6	46,7	46,8	46,9
20,2	45,9	46,0	46,1	46,2	46,3	46,4	46,5	46,6	46,7	46,8
20,4	45,8	45,9	46,0	46,1	46,2	46,3	46,4	46,5	46,6	46,7
20,6	45,8	45,9	46,0	46,1	46,2	46,3	46,4	46,5	46,6	46,7
20,8	45,7	45,8	45,9	46,0	46,1	46,2	46,3	46,4	46,5	46,6
21,0	45,6	45,7	45,8	45,9	46,0	46,1	46,2	46,3	46,4	46,5
21,2	45,5	45,6	45,7	45,8	45,9	46,0	46,1	46,2	46,3	46,4
21,4	45,5	45,6	45,7	45,8	45,9	46,0	46,1	46,2	46,3	46,4
21,6	45,4	45,5	45,6	45,7	45,8	45,9	46,0	46,1	46,2	46,3
21,8	45,3	45,4	45,5	45,6	45,7	45,8	45,9	46,0	46,1	46,2
22,0	45,2	45,3	45,4	45,5	45,6	45,7	45,8	45,9	46,0	46,1
22,2	45,2	45,3	45,4	45,5	45,6	45,7	45,8	45,9	46,0	46,1
22,4	45,1	45,2	45,3	45,4	45,5	45,6	45,7	45,8	45,9	46,0
22,6	45,0	45,1	45,2	45,3	45,4	45,5	45,6	45,7	45,8	45,9
22,8	44,9	45,0	45,1	45,2	45,3	45,4	45,5	45,6	45,7	45,8
23,0	44,8	44,9	45,0	45,1	45,2	45,3	45,5	45,6	45,7	45,8
23,2	44,8	44,9	45,0	45,1	45,2	45,3	45,4	45,5	45,6	45,7
23,4	44,7	44,8	44,9	45,0	45,1	45,2	45,3	45,4	45,5	45,6
23,6	44,6	44,7	44,8	44,9	45,0	45,1	45,2	45,3	45,4	45,5
23,8	44,5	44,6	44,7	44,8	44,9	45,0	45,1	45,2	45,3	45,4
24,0	44,5	44,6	44,7	44,8	44,9	45,0	45,1	45,2	45,3	45,4
24,2	44,4	44,5	44,6	44,7	44,8	44,9	45,0	45,1	45,2	45,3
24,4	44,3	44,4	44,5	44,6	44,7	44,8	44,9	45,0	45,1	45,2
24,6	44,2	44,3	44,4	44,5	44,6	44,7	44,8	44,9	45,0	45,1
24,8	44,1	44,3	44,4	44,5	44,6	44,7	44,8	44,9	45,0	45,1
25,0	44,1	44,2	44,3	44,4	44,5	44,6	44,7	44,8	44,9	45,0
25,2	44,0	44,1	44,2	44,3	44,4	44,5	44,6	44,7	44,8	44,9
25,4	43,9	44,0	44,1	44,2	44,3	44,4	44,5	44,6	44,7	44,8
25,6	43,8	43,9	44,0	44,1	44,2	44,3	44,4	44,5	44,7	44,8
25,8	43,8	43,9	44,0	44,1	44,2	44,3	44,4	44,5	44,6	44,7
26,0	43,7	43,8	43,9	44,0	44,1	44,2	44,3	44,4	44,5	44,6
26,2	43,6	43,7	43,8	43,9	44,0	44,1	44,2	44,3	44,4	44,5
26,4	43,5	43,6	43,7	43,8	43,9	44,0	44,1	44,2	44,3	44,4
26,6	43,4	43,6	43,7	43,8	43,9	44,0	44,1	44,2	44,3	44,4
26,8	43,4	43,5	43,6	43,7	43,8	43,9	44,0	44,1	44,2	44,3
27,0	43,3	43,4	43,5	43,6	43,7	43,8	43,9	44,0	44,1	44,2
27,2	43,2	43,3	43,4	43,5	43,6	43,7	43,8	43,9	44,0	44,1
27,4	43,1	43,2	43,3	43,4	43,5	43,6	43,7	43,9	44,0	44,1
27,6	43,1	43,2	43,3	43,4	43,5	43,6	43,7	43,8	43,9	44,0
27,8	43,0	43,1	43,2	43,3	43,4	43,5	43,6	43,7	43,8	43,9
28,0	42,9	43,0	43,1	43,2	43,3	43,4	43,5	43,6	43,7	43,8
28,2	42,8	42,9	43,0	43,1	43,2	43,3	43,4	43,5	43,6	43,7
28,4	42,7	42,8	43,0	43,1	43,2	43,3	43,4	43,5	43,6	43,7
28,6	42,7	42,8	42,9	43,0	43,1	43,2	43,3	43,4	43,5	43,6
28,8	42,6	42,7	42,8	42,9	43,0	43,1	43,2	43,3	43,4	43,5
29,0	42,5	42,6	42,7	42,8	42,9	43,0	43,1	43,2	43,3	43,4
29,2	42,4	42,5	42,6	42,7	42,8	42,9	43,0	43,2	43,3	43,4
29,4	42,4	42,5	42,6	42,7	42,8	42,9	43,0	43,1	43,2	43,3
29,6	42,3	42,4	42,5	42,6	42,7	42,8	42,9	43,0	43,1	43,2
29,8	42,2	42,3	42,4	42,5	42,6	42,7	42,8	42,9	43,0	43,1
30,0	42,1	42,2	42,3	42,4	42,5	42,6	42,7	42,8	42,9	43,0

Volumenkonzentration bei 20 °C in Prozent

Temp. °C	Anzeige des Alkoholometers in % vol									
	47,0	47,1	47,2	47,3	47,4	47,5	47,6	47,7	47,8	47,9
0,0	54,4	54,5	54,6	54,6	54,7	54,8	54,9	55,0	55,1	55,2
0,2	54,3	54,4	54,5	54,6	54,7	54,8	54,9	55,0	55,0	55,1
0,4	54,2	54,3	54,4	54,5	54,6	54,7	54,8	54,9	55,0	55,1
0,6	54,2	54,2	54,3	54,4	54,5	54,6	54,7	54,8	54,9	55,0
0,8	54,1	54,2	54,3	54,4	54,5	54,6	54,6	54,7	54,8	54,9
1,0	54,0	54,1	54,2	54,3	54,4	54,5	54,6	54,7	54,8	54,9
1,2	53,9	54,0	54,1	54,2	54,3	54,4	54,5	54,6	54,7	54,8
1,4	53,9	54,0	54,1	54,2	54,2	54,3	54,4	54,5	54,6	54,7
1,6	53,8	53,9	54,0	54,1	54,2	54,3	54,4	54,5	54,6	54,6
1,8	53,7	53,8	53,9	54,0	54,1	54,2	54,3	54,4	54,5	54,6
2,0	53,7	53,7	53,8	53,9	54,0	54,1	54,2	54,3	54,4	54,5
2,2	53,6	53,7	53,8	53,9	54,0	54,1	54,2	54,2	54,3	54,4
2,4	53,5	53,6	53,7	53,8	53,9	54,0	54,1	54,2	54,3	54,4
2,6	53,4	53,5	53,6	53,7	53,8	53,9	54,0	54,1	54,2	54,3
2,8	53,4	53,5	53,6	53,7	53,7	53,8	53,9	54,0	54,1	54,2
3,0	53,3	53,4	53,5	53,6	53,7	53,8	53,9	54,0	54,1	54,1
3,2	53,2	53,3	53,4	53,5	53,6	53,7	53,8	53,9	54,0	54,1
3,4	53,2	53,2	53,3	53,4	53,5	53,6	53,7	53,8	53,9	54,0
3,6	53,1	53,2	53,3	53,4	53,5	53,6	53,7	53,7	53,8	53,9
3,8	53,0	53,1	53,2	53,3	53,4	53,5	53,6	53,7	53,8	53,9
4,0	52,9	53,0	53,1	53,2	53,3	53,4	53,5	53,6	53,7	53,8
4,2	52,9	53,0	53,1	53,2	53,2	53,3	53,4	53,5	53,6	53,7
4,4	52,8	52,9	53,0	53,1	53,2	53,3	53,4	53,5	53,6	53,6
4,6	52,7	52,8	52,9	53,0	53,1	53,2	53,3	53,4	53,5	53,6
4,8	52,6	52,7	52,8	52,9	53,0	53,1	53,2	53,3	53,4	53,5
5,0	52,6	52,7	52,8	52,9	53,0	53,1	53,1	53,2	53,3	53,4
5,2	52,5	52,6	52,7	52,8	52,9	53,0	53,1	53,2	53,3	53,4
5,4	52,4	52,5	52,6	52,7	52,8	52,9	53,0	53,1	53,2	53,3
5,6	52,4	52,5	52,5	52,6	52,7	52,8	52,9	53,0	53,1	53,2
5,8	52,3	52,4	52,5	52,6	52,7	52,8	52,9	53,0	53,1	53,1
6,0	52,2	52,3	52,4	52,5	52,6	52,7	52,8	52,9	53,0	53,1
6,2	52,1	52,2	52,3	52,4	52,5	52,6	52,7	52,8	52,9	53,0
6,4	52,1	52,2	52,3	52,4	52,5	52,5	52,6	52,7	52,8	52,9
6,6	52,0	52,1	52,2	52,3	52,4	52,5	52,6	52,7	52,8	52,9
6,8	51,9	52,0	52,1	52,2	52,3	52,4	52,5	52,6	52,7	52,8
7,0	51,8	51,9	52,0	52,1	52,2	52,3	52,4	52,5	52,6	52,7
7,2	51,8	51,9	52,0	52,1	52,2	52,3	52,4	52,4	52,5	52,6
7,4	51,7	51,8	51,9	52,0	52,1	52,2	52,3	52,4	52,5	52,6
7,6	51,6	51,7	51,8	51,9	52,0	52,1	52,2	52,3	52,4	52,5
7,8	51,6	51,7	51,7	51,8	51,9	52,0	52,1	52,2	52,3	52,4
8,0	51,5	51,6	51,7	51,8	51,9	52,0	52,1	52,2	52,3	52,4
8,2	51,4	51,5	51,6	51,7	51,8	51,9	52,0	52,1	52,2	52,3
8,4	51,3	51,4	51,5	51,6	51,7	51,8	51,9	52,0	52,1	52,2
8,6	51,3	51,4	51,5	51,6	51,7	51,7	51,8	51,9	52,0	52,1
8,8	51,2	51,3	51,4	51,5	51,6	51,7	51,8	51,9	52,0	52,1
9,0	51,1	51,2	51,3	51,4	51,5	51,6	51,7	51,8	51,9	52,0
9,2	51,0	51,1	51,2	51,3	51,4	51,5	51,6	51,7	51,8	51,9
9,4	51,0	51,1	51,2	51,3	51,4	51,5	51,6	51,6	51,7	51,8
9,6	50,9	51,0	51,1	51,2	51,3	51,4	51,5	51,6	51,7	51,8
9,8	50,8	50,9	51,0	51,1	51,2	51,3	51,4	51,5	51,6	51,7

Volumenkonzentration bei 20 °C in Prozent

Temp. °C	Anzeige des Alkoholometers in % vol								
	47,0	47,1	47,2	47,3	47,4	47,5	47,6	47,7	47,8	47,9
10,0	50,7	50,8	50,9	51,0	51,1	51,2	51,3	51,4	51,5	51,6
10,2	50,7	50,8	50,9	51,0	51,1	51,2	51,3	51,4	51,5	51,5
10,4	50,6	50,7	50,8	50,9	51,0	51,1	51,2	51,3	51,4	51,5
10,6	50,5	50,6	50,7	50,8	50,9	51,0	51,1	51,2	51,3	51,4
10,8	50,5	50,6	50,6	50,7	50,8	50,9	51,0	51,1	51,2	51,3
11,0	50,4	50,5	50,6	50,7	50,8	50,9	51,0	51,1	51,2	51,3
11,2	50,3	50,4	50,5	50,6	50,7	50,8	50,9	51,0	51,1	51,2
11,4	50,2	50,3	50,4	50,5	50,6	50,7	50,8	50,9	51,0	51,1
11,6	50,2	50,3	50,4	50,5	50,5	50,6	50,7	50,8	50,9	51,0
11,8	50,1	50,2	50,3	50,4	50,5	50,6	50,7	50,8	50,9	51,0
12,0	50,0	50,1	50,2	50,3	50,4	50,5	50,6	50,7	50,8	50,9
12,2	49,9	50,0	50,1	50,2	50,3	50,4	50,5	50,6	50,7	50,8
12,4	49,9	50,0	50,1	50,2	50,3	50,3	50,4	50,5	50,6	50,7
12,6	49,8	49,9	50,0	50,1	50,2	50,3	50,4	50,5	50,6	50,7
12,8	49,7	49,8	49,9	50,0	50,1	50,2	50,3	50,4	50,5	50,6
13,0	49,6	49,7	49,8	49,9	50,0	50,1	50,2	50,3	50,4	50,5
13,2	49,6	49,7	49,8	49,9	50,0	50,1	50,2	50,2	50,3	50,4
13,4	49,5	49,6	49,7	49,8	49,9	50,0	50,1	50,2	50,3	50,4
13,6	49,4	49,5	49,6	49,7	49,8	49,9	50,0	50,1	50,2	50,3
13,8	49,3	49,4	49,5	49,6	49,7	49,8	49,9	50,0	50,1	50,2
14,0	49,3	49,4	49,5	49,6	49,7	49,8	49,9	50,0	50,0	50,1
14,2	49,2	49,3	49,4	49,5	49,6	49,7	49,8	49,9	50,0	50,1
14,4	49,1	49,2	49,3	49,4	49,5	49,6	49,7	49,8	49,9	50,0
14,6	49,0	49,1	49,2	49,3	49,4	49,5	49,6	49,7	49,8	49,9
14,8	49,0	49,1	49,2	49,3	49,4	49,5	49,6	49,7	49,8	49,9
15,0	48,9	49,0	49,1	49,2	49,3	49,4	49,5	49,6	49,7	49,8
15,2	48,8	48,9	49,0	49,1	49,2	49,3	49,4	49,5	49,6	49,7
15,4	48,7	48,8	48,9	49,0	49,1	49,2	49,3	49,4	49,5	49,6
15,6	48,7	48,8	48,9	49,0	49,1	49,2	49,3	49,4	49,5	49,6
15,8	48,6	48,7	48,8	48,9	49,0	49,1	49,2	49,3	49,4	49,5
16,0	48,5	48,6	48,7	48,8	48,9	49,0	49,1	49,2	49,3	49,4
16,2	48,4	48,5	48,6	48,7	48,8	48,9	49,0	49,1	49,2	49,3
16,4	48,4	48,5	48,6	48,7	48,8	48,9	49,0	49,1	49,2	49,3
16,6	48,3	48,4	48,5	48,6	48,7	48,8	48,9	49,0	49,1	49,2
16,8	48,2	48,3	48,4	48,5	48,6	48,7	48,8	48,9	49,0	49,1
17,0	48,1	48,2	48,3	48,4	48,5	48,6	48,7	48,8	48,9	49,0
17,2	48,1	48,2	48,3	48,4	48,5	48,6	48,7	48,8	48,9	49,0
17,4	48,0	48,1	48,2	48,3	48,4	48,5	48,6	48,7	48,8	48,9
17,6	47,9	48,0	48,1	48,2	48,3	48,4	48,5	48,6	48,7	48,8
17,8	47,8	47,9	48,0	48,1	48,2	48,3	48,4	48,5	48,6	48,7
18,0	47,8	47,9	48,0	48,1	48,2	48,3	48,4	48,5	48,6	48,7
18,2	47,7	47,8	47,9	48,0	48,1	48,2	48,3	48,4	48,5	48,6
18,4	47,6	47,7	47,8	47,9	48,0	48,1	48,2	48,3	48,4	48,5
18,6	47,5	47,6	47,7	47,8	47,9	48,0	48,1	48,2	48,3	48,4
18,8	47,5	47,6	47,7	47,8	47,9	48,0	48,1	48,2	48,3	48,4
19,0	47,4	47,5	47,6	47,7	47,8	47,9	48,0	48,1	48,2	48,3
19,2	47,3	47,4	47,5	47,6	47,7	47,8	47,9	48,0	48,1	48,2
19,4	47,2	47,3	47,4	47,5	47,6	47,7	47,8	47,9	48,0	48,1
19,6	47,2	47,3	47,4	47,5	47,6	47,7	47,8	47,9	48,0	48,1
19,8	47,1	47,2	47,3	47,4	47,5	47,6	47,7	47,8	47,9	48,0

Volumenkonzentration bei 20 °C in Prozent

Temp. °C	Anzeige des Alkoholometers in % vol									
	47,0	47,1	47,2	47,3	47,4	47,5	47,6	47,7	47,8	47,9
20,0	47,0	47,1	47,2	47,3	47,4	47,5	47,6	47,7	47,8	47,9
20,2	46,9	47,0	47,1	47,2	47,3	47,4	47,5	47,6	47,7	47,8
20,4	46,8	46,9	47,0	47,1	47,2	47,3	47,4	47,5	47,6	47,7
20,6	46,8	46,9	47,0	47,1	47,2	47,3	47,4	47,5	47,6	47,7
20,8	46,7	46,8	46,9	47,0	47,1	47,2	47,3	47,4	47,5	47,6
21,0	46,6	46,7	46,8	46,9	47,0	47,1	47,2	47,3	47,4	47,5
21,2	46,5	46,6	46,7	46,8	46,9	47,0	47,1	47,2	47,3	47,4
21,4	46,5	46,6	46,7	46,8	46,9	47,0	47,1	47,2	47,3	47,4
21,6	46,4	46,5	46,6	46,7	46,8	46,9	47,0	47,1	47,2	47,3
21,8	46,3	46,4	46,5	46,6	46,7	46,8	46,9	47,0	47,1	47,2
22,0	46,2	46,3	46,4	46,5	46,6	46,7	46,8	46,9	47,0	47,1
22,2	46,2	46,3	46,4	46,5	46,6	46,7	46,8	46,9	47,0	47,1
22,4	46,1	46,2	46,3	46,4	46,5	46,6	46,7	46,8	46,9	47,0
22,6	46,0	46,1	46,2	46,3	46,4	46,5	46,6	46,7	46,8	46,9
22,8	45,9	46,0	46,1	46,2	46,3	46,4	46,5	46,6	46,7	46,8
23,0	45,9	46,0	46,1	46,2	46,3	46,4	46,5	46,6	46,7	46,8
23,2	45,8	45,9	46,0	46,1	46,2	46,3	46,4	46,5	46,6	46,7
23,4	45,7	45,8	45,9	46,0	46,1	46,2	46,3	46,4	46,5	46,6
23,6	45,6	45,7	45,8	45,9	46,0	46,1	46,2	46,3	46,4	46,5
23,8	45,5	45,6	45,7	45,8	46,0	46,1	46,2	46,3	46,4	46,5
24,0	45,5	45,6	45,7	45,8	45,9	46,0	46,1	46,2	46,3	46,4
24,2	45,4	45,5	45,6	45,7	45,8	45,9	46,0	46,1	46,2	46,3
24,4	45,3	45,4	45,5	45,6	45,7	45,8	45,9	46,0	46,1	46,2
24,6	45,2	45,3	45,4	45,5	45,6	45,7	45,8	45,9	46,0	46,2
24,8	45,2	45,3	45,4	45,5	45,6	45,7	45,8	45,9	46,0	46,1
25,0	45,1	45,2	45,3	45,4	45,5	45,6	45,7	45,8	45,9	46,0
25,2	45,0	45,1	45,2	45,3	45,4	45,5	45,6	45,7	45,8	45,9
25,4	44,9	45,0	45,1	45,2	45,3	45,4	45,5	45,6	45,7	45,8
25,6	44,9	45,0	45,1	45,2	45,3	45,4	45,5	45,6	45,7	45,8
25,8	44,8	44,9	45,0	45,1	45,2	45,3	45,4	45,5	45,6	45,7
26,0	44,7	44,8	44,9	45,0	45,1	45,2	45,3	45,4	45,5	45,6
26,2	44,6	44,7	44,8	44,9	45,0	45,1	45,2	45,3	45,4	45,5
26,4	44,5	44,6	44,7	44,8	45,0	45,1	45,2	45,3	45,4	45,5
26,6	44,5	44,6	44,7	44,8	44,9	45,0	45,1	45,2	45,3	45,4
26,8	44,4	44,5	44,6	44,7	44,8	44,9	45,0	45,1	45,2	45,3
27,0	44,3	44,4	44,5	44,6	44,7	44,8	44,9	45,0	45,1	45,2
27,2	44,2	44,3	44,4	44,5	44,6	44,7	44,8	44,9	45,1	45,2
27,4	44,2	44,3	44,4	44,5	44,6	44,7	44,8	44,9	45,0	45,1
27,6	44,1	44,2	44,3	44,4	44,5	44,6	44,7	44,8	44,9	45,0
27,8	44,0	44,1	44,2	44,3	44,4	44,5	44,6	44,7	44,8	44,9
28,0	43,9	44,0	44,1	44,2	44,3	44,4	44,5	44,6	44,7	44,8
28,2	43,8	43,9	44,1	44,2	44,3	44,4	44,5	44,6	44,7	44,8
28,4	43,8	43,9	44,0	44,1	44,2	44,3	44,4	44,5	44,6	44,7
28,6	43,7	43,8	43,9	44,0	44,1	44,2	44,3	44,4	44,5	44,6
28,8	43,6	43,7	43,8	43,9	44,0	44,1	44,2	44,3	44,4	44,5
29,0	43,5	43,6	43,7	43,8	43,9	44,0	44,2	44,3	44,4	44,5
29,2	43,5	43,6	43,7	43,8	43,9	44,0	44,1	44,2	44,3	44,4
29,4	43,4	43,5	43,6	43,7	43,8	43,9	44,0	44,1	44,2	44,3
29,6	43,3	43,4	43,5	43,6	43,7	43,8	43,9	44,0	44,1	44,2
29,8	43,2	43,3	43,4	43,5	43,6	43,7	43,8	43,9	44,0	44,1
30,0	43,1	43,3	43,4	43,5	43,6	43,7	43,8	43,9	44,0	44,1

Volumenkonzentration bei 20 °C in Prozent

Temp. °C	Anzeige des Alkoholometers in % vol									
	48,0	48,1	48,2	48,3	48,4	48,5	48,6	48,7	48,8	48,9
0,0	55,3	55,4	55,5	55,6	55,7	55,8	55,9	56,0	56,1	56,2
0,2	55,2	55,3	55,4	55,5	55,6	55,7	55,8	55,9	56,0	56,1
0,4	55,2	55,3	55,4	55,4	55,5	55,6	55,7	55,8	55,9	56,0
0,6	55,1	55,2	55,3	55,4	55,5	55,6	55,7	55,8	55,8	55,9
0,8	55,0	55,1	55,2	55,3	55,4	55,5	55,6	55,7	55,8	55,9
1,0	55,0	55,0	55,1	55,2	55,3	55,4	55,5	55,6	55,7	55,8
1,2	54,9	55,0	55,1	55,2	55,3	55,4	55,4	55,5	55,6	55,7
1,4	54,8	54,9	55,0	55,1	55,2	55,3	55,4	55,5	55,6	55,7
1,6	54,7	54,8	54,9	55,0	55,1	55,2	55,3	55,4	55,5	55,6
1,8	54,7	54,8	54,9	55,0	55,0	55,1	55,2	55,3	55,4	55,5
2,0	54,6	54,7	54,8	54,9	55,0	55,1	55,2	55,3	55,4	55,5
2,2	54,5	54,6	54,7	54,8	54,9	55,0	55,1	55,2	55,3	55,4
2,4	54,5	54,6	54,6	54,7	54,8	54,9	55,0	55,1	55,2	55,3
2,6	54,4	54,5	54,6	54,7	54,8	54,9	55,0	55,0	55,1	55,2
2,8	54,3	54,4	54,5	54,6	54,7	54,8	54,9	55,0	55,1	55,2
3,0	54,2	54,3	54,4	54,5	54,6	54,7	54,8	54,9	55,0	55,1
3,2	54,2	54,3	54,4	54,5	54,6	54,6	54,7	54,8	54,9	55,0
3,4	54,1	54,2	54,3	54,4	54,5	54,6	54,7	54,8	54,9	55,0
3,6	54,0	54,1	54,2	54,3	54,4	54,5	54,6	54,7	54,8	54,9
3,8	54,0	54,1	54,1	54,2	54,3	54,4	54,5	54,6	54,7	54,8
4,0	53,9	54,0	54,1	54,2	54,3	54,4	54,5	54,6	54,6	54,7
4,2	53,8	53,9	54,0	54,1	54,2	54,3	54,4	54,5	54,6	54,7
4,4	53,7	53,8	53,9	54,0	54,1	54,2	54,3	54,4	54,5	54,6
4,6	53,7	53,8	53,9	54,0	54,1	54,1	54,2	54,3	54,4	54,5
4,8	53,6	53,7	53,8	53,9	54,0	54,1	54,2	54,3	54,4	54,5
5,0	53,5	53,6	53,7	53,8	53,9	54,0	54,1	54,2	54,3	54,4
5,2	53,5	53,6	53,6	53,7	53,8	53,9	54,0	54,1	54,2	54,3
5,4	53,4	53,5	53,6	53,7	53,8	53,9	54,0	54,1	54,2	54,2
5,6	53,3	53,4	53,5	53,6	53,7	53,8	53,9	54,0	54,1	54,2
5,8	53,2	53,3	53,4	53,5	53,6	53,7	53,8	53,9	54,0	54,1
6,0	53,2	53,3	53,4	53,5	53,6	53,6	53,7	53,8	53,9	54,0
6,2	53,1	53,2	53,3	53,4	53,5	53,6	53,7	53,8	53,9	54,0
6,4	53,0	53,1	53,2	53,3	53,4	53,5	53,6	53,7	53,8	53,9
6,6	53,0	53,1	53,1	53,2	53,3	53,4	53,5	53,6	53,7	53,8
6,8	52,9	53,0	53,1	53,2	53,3	53,4	53,5	53,6	53,7	53,7
7,0	52,8	52,9	53,0	53,1	53,2	53,3	53,4	53,5	53,6	53,7
7,2	52,7	52,8	52,9	53,0	53,1	53,2	53,3	53,4	53,5	53,6
7,4	52,7	52,8	52,9	53,0	53,1	53,1	53,2	53,3	53,4	53,5
7,6	52,6	52,7	52,8	52,9	53,0	53,1	53,2	53,3	53,4	53,5
7,8	52,5	52,6	52,7	52,8	52,9	53,0	53,1	53,2	53,3	53,4
8,0	52,4	52,5	52,6	52,7	52,8	52,9	53,0	53,1	53,2	53,3
8,2	52,4	52,5	52,6	52,7	52,8	52,9	53,0	53,1	53,1	53,2
8,4	52,3	52,4	52,5	52,6	52,7	52,8	52,9	53,0	53,1	53,2
8,6	52,2	52,3	52,4	52,5	52,6	52,7	52,8	52,9	53,0	53,1
8,8	52,2	52,3	52,4	52,4	52,5	52,6	52,7	52,8	52,9	53,0
9,0	52,1	52,2	52,3	52,4	52,5	52,6	52,7	52,8	52,9	53,0
9,2	52,0	52,1	52,2	52,3	52,4	52,5	52,6	52,7	52,8	52,9
9,4	51,9	52,0	52,1	52,2	52,3	52,4	52,5	52,6	52,7	52,8
9,6	51,9	52,0	52,1	52,2	52,3	52,4	52,4	52,5	52,6	52,7
9,8	51,8	51,9	52,0	52,1	52,2	52,3	52,4	52,5	52,6	52,7

Volumenkonzentration bei 20 °C in Prozent

Temp. °C	Anzeige des Alkoholometers in % vol									
	48,0	48,1	48,2	48,3	48,4	48,5	48,6	48,7	48,8	48,9
10,0	51,7	51,8	51,9	52,0	52,1	52,2	52,3	52,4	52,5	52,6
10,2	51,6	51,7	51,8	51,9	52,0	52,1	52,2	52,3	52,4	52,5
10,4	51,6	51,7	51,8	51,9	52,0	52,1	52,2	52,3	52,4	52,4
10,6	51,5	51,6	51,7	51,8	51,9	52,0	52,1	52,2	52,3	52,4
10,8	51,4	51,5	51,6	51,7	51,8	51,9	52,0	52,1	52,2	52,3
11,0	51,4	51,5	51,5	51,6	51,7	51,8	51,9	52,0	52,1	52,2
11,2	51,3	51,4	51,5	51,6	51,7	51,8	51,9	52,0	52,1	52,2
11,4	51,2	51,3	51,4	51,5	51,6	51,7	51,8	51,9	52,0	52,1
11,6	51,1	51,2	51,3	51,4	51,5	51,6	51,7	51,8	51,9	52,0
11,8	51,1	51,2	51,3	51,4	51,4	51,5	51,6	51,7	51,8	51,9
12,0	51,0	51,1	51,2	51,3	51,4	51,5	51,6	51,7	51,8	51,9
12,2	50,9	51,0	51,1	51,2	51,3	51,4	51,5	51,6	51,7	51,8
12,4	50,8	50,9	51,0	51,1	51,2	51,3	51,4	51,5	51,6	51,7
12,6	50,8	50,9	51,0	51,1	51,2	51,3	51,4	51,4	51,5	51,6
12,8	50,7	50,8	50,9	51,0	51,1	51,2	51,3	51,4	51,5	51,6
13,0	50,6	50,7	50,8	50,9	51,0	51,1	51,2	51,3	51,4	51,5
13,2	50,5	50,6	50,7	50,8	50,9	51,0	51,1	51,2	51,3	51,4
13,4	50,5	50,6	50,7	50,8	50,9	51,0	51,1	51,2	51,3	51,4
13,6	50,4	50,5	50,6	50,7	50,8	50,9	51,0	51,1	51,2	51,3
13,8	50,3	50,4	50,5	50,6	50,7	50,8	50,9	51,0	51,1	51,2
14,0	50,2	50,3	50,4	50,5	50,6	50,7	50,8	50,9	51,0	51,1
14,2	50,2	50,3	50,4	50,5	50,6	50,7	50,8	50,9	51,0	51,1
14,4	50,1	50,2	50,3	50,4	50,5	50,6	50,7	50,8	50,9	51,0
14,6	50,0	50,1	50,2	50,3	50,4	50,5	50,6	50,7	50,8	50,9
14,8	49,9	50,0	50,1	50,2	50,3	50,4	50,5	50,6	50,7	50,8
15,0	49,9	50,0	50,1	50,2	50,3	50,4	50,5	50,6	50,7	50,8
15,2	49,8	49,9	50,0	50,1	50,2	50,3	50,4	50,5	50,6	50,7
15,4	49,7	49,8	49,9	50,0	50,1	50,2	50,3	50,4	50,5	50,6
15,6	49,7	49,8	49,8	49,9	50,0	50,1	50,2	50,3	50,4	50,5
15,8	49,6	49,7	49,8	49,9	50,0	50,1	50,2	50,3	50,4	50,5
16,0	49,5	49,6	49,7	49,8	49,9	50,0	50,1	50,2	50,3	50,4
16,2	49,4	49,5	49,6	49,7	49,8	49,9	50,0	50,1	50,2	50,3
16,4	49,4	49,5	49,6	49,6	49,7	49,8	49,9	50,0	50,1	50,2
16,6	49,3	49,4	49,5	49,6	49,7	49,8	49,9	50,0	50,1	50,2
16,8	49,2	49,3	49,4	49,5	49,6	49,7	49,8	49,9	50,0	50,1
17,0	49,1	49,2	49,3	49,4	49,5	49,6	49,7	49,8	49,9	50,0
17,2	49,1	49,2	49,3	49,4	49,5	49,5	49,6	49,7	49,8	49,9
17,4	49,0	49,1	49,2	49,3	49,4	49,5	49,6	49,7	49,8	49,9
17,6	48,9	49,0	49,1	49,2	49,3	49,4	49,5	49,6	49,7	49,8
17,8	48,8	48,9	49,0	49,1	49,2	49,3	49,4	49,5	49,6	49,7
18,0	48,8	48,9	49,0	49,1	49,2	49,3	49,4	49,4	49,5	49,6
18,2	48,7	48,8	48,9	49,0	49,1	49,2	49,3	49,4	49,5	49,6
18,4	48,6	48,7	48,8	48,9	49,0	49,1	49,2	49,3	49,4	49,5
18,6	48,5	48,6	48,7	48,8	48,9	49,0	49,1	49,2	49,3	49,4
18,8	48,5	48,6	48,7	48,8	48,9	49,0	49,1	49,2	49,2	49,3
19,0	48,4	48,5	48,6	48,7	48,8	48,9	49,0	49,1	49,2	49,3
19,2	48,3	48,4	48,5	48,6	48,7	48,8	48,9	49,0	49,1	49,2
19,4	48,2	48,3	48,4	48,5	48,6	48,7	48,8	48,9	49,0	49,1
19,6	48,2	48,3	48,4	48,5	48,6	48,7	48,8	48,9	49,0	49,1
19,8	48,1	48,2	48,3	48,4	48,5	48,6	48,7	48,8	48,9	49,0

Volumenkonzentration bei 20 °C in Prozent

Temp. °C	Anzeige des Alkoholometers in % vol									
	48,0	48,1	48,2	48,3	48,4	48,5	48,6	48,7	48,8	48,9
20,0	48,0	48,1	48,2	48,3	48,4	48,5	48,6	48,7	48,8	48,9
20,2	47,9	48,0	48,1	48,2	48,3	48,4	48,5	48,6	48,7	48,8
20,4	47,8	47,9	48,0	48,1	48,2	48,3	48,4	48,5	48,6	48,7
20,6	47,8	47,9	48,0	48,1	48,2	48,3	48,4	48,5	48,6	48,7
20,8	47,7	47,8	47,9	48,0	48,1	48,2	48,3	48,4	48,5	48,6
21,0	47,6	47,7	47,8	47,9	48,0	48,1	48,2	48,3	48,4	48,5
21,2	47,5	47,6	47,7	47,8	47,9	48,0	48,1	48,2	48,3	48,4
21,4	47,5	47,6	47,7	47,8	47,9	48,0	48,1	48,2	48,3	48,4
21,6	47,4	47,5	47,6	47,7	47,8	47,9	48,0	48,1	48,2	48,3
21,8	47,3	47,4	47,5	47,6	47,7	47,8	47,9	48,0	48,1	48,2
22,0	47,2	47,3	47,4	47,5	47,6	47,7	47,8	47,9	48,0	48,1
22,2	47,2	47,3	47,4	47,5	47,6	47,7	47,8	47,9	48,0	48,1
22,4	47,1	47,2	47,3	47,4	47,5	47,6	47,7	47,8	47,9	48,0
22,6	47,0	47,1	47,2	47,3	47,4	47,5	47,6	47,7	47,8	47,9
22,8	46,9	47,0	47,1	47,2	47,3	47,4	47,5	47,6	47,7	47,8
23,0	46,9	47,0	47,1	47,2	47,3	47,4	47,5	47,6	47,7	47,8
23,2	46,8	46,9	47,0	47,1	47,2	47,3	47,4	47,5	47,6	47,7
23,4	46,7	46,8	46,9	47,0	47,1	47,2	47,3	47,4	47,5	47,6
23,6	46,6	46,7	46,8	46,9	47,0	47,1	47,2	47,3	47,4	47,5
23,8	46,6	46,7	46,8	46,9	47,0	47,1	47,2	47,3	47,4	47,5
24,0	46,5	46,6	46,7	46,8	46,9	47,0	47,1	47,2	47,3	47,4
24,2	46,4	46,5	46,6	46,7	46,8	46,9	47,0	47,1	47,2	47,3
24,4	46,3	46,4	46,5	46,6	46,7	46,8	46,9	47,0	47,1	47,2
24,6	46,3	46,4	46,5	46,6	46,7	46,8	46,9	47,0	47,1	47,2
24,8	46,2	46,3	46,4	46,5	46,6	46,7	46,8	46,9	47,0	47,1
25,0	46,1	46,2	46,3	46,4	46,5	46,6	46,7	46,8	46,9	47,0
25,2	46,0	46,1	46,2	46,3	46,4	46,5	46,6	46,7	46,8	46,9
25,4	45,9	46,0	46,1	46,2	46,4	46,5	46,6	46,7	46,8	46,9
25,6	45,9	46,0	46,1	46,2	46,3	46,4	46,5	46,6	46,7	46,8
25,8	45,8	45,9	46,0	46,1	46,2	46,3	46,4	46,5	46,6	46,7
26,0	45,7	45,8	45,9	46,0	46,1	46,2	46,3	46,4	46,5	46,6
26,2	45,6	45,7	45,8	45,9	46,0	46,1	46,2	46,4	46,5	46,6
26,4	45,6	45,7	45,8	45,9	46,0	46,1	46,2	46,3	46,4	46,5
26,6	45,5	45,6	45,7	45,8	45,9	46,0	46,1	46,2	46,3	46,4
26,8	45,4	45,5	45,6	45,7	45,8	45,9	46,0	46,1	46,2	46,3
27,0	45,3	45,4	45,5	45,6	45,7	45,8	45,9	46,0	46,1	46,2
27,2	45,3	45,4	45,5	45,6	45,7	45,8	45,9	46,0	46,1	46,2
27,4	45,2	45,3	45,4	45,5	45,6	45,7	45,8	45,9	46,0	46,1
27,6	45,1	45,2	45,3	45,4	45,5	45,6	45,7	45,8	45,9	46,0
27,8	45,0	45,1	45,2	45,3	45,4	45,5	45,6	45,7	45,8	45,9
28,0	44,9	45,0	45,2	45,3	45,4	45,5	45,6	45,7	45,8	45,9
28,2	44,9	45,0	45,1	45,2	45,3	45,4	45,5	45,6	45,7	45,8
28,4	44,8	44,9	45,0	45,1	45,2	45,3	45,4	45,5	45,6	45,7
28,6	44,7	44,8	44,9	45,0	45,1	45,2	45,3	45,4	45,5	45,6
28,8	44,6	44,7	44,8	44,9	45,0	45,1	45,2	45,3	45,4	45,6
29,0	44,6	44,7	44,8	44,9	45,0	45,1	45,2	45,3	45,4	45,5
29,2	44,5	44,6	44,7	44,8	44,9	45,0	45,1	45,2	45,3	45,4
29,4	44,4	44,5	44,6	44,7	44,8	44,9	45,0	45,1	45,2	45,3
29,6	44,3	44,4	44,5	44,6	44,7	44,8	44,9	45,0	45,1	45,3
29,8	44,3	44,4	44,5	44,6	44,7	44,8	44,9	45,0	45,1	45,2
30,0	44,2	44,3	44,4	44,5	44,6	44,7	44,8	44,9	45,0	45,1

Volumenkonzentration bei 20 °C in Prozent

Temp. °C	\multicolumn{9}{c}{Anzeige des Alkoholometers in % vol}

Temp. °C	49,0	49,1	49,2	49,3	49,4	49,5	49,6	49,7	49,8	49,9
0,0	56,2	56,3	56,4	56,5	56,6	56,7	56,8	56,9	57,0	57,1
0,2	56,2	56,3	56,4	56,5	56,6	56,6	56,7	56,8	56,9	57,0
0,4	56,1	56,2	56,3	56,4	56,5	56,6	56,7	56,8	56,9	57,0
0,6	56,0	56,1	56,2	56,3	56,4	56,5	56,6	56,7	56,8	56,9
0,8	56,0	56,1	56,2	56,2	56,3	56,4	56,5	56,6	56,7	56,8
1,0	55,9	56,0	56,1	56,2	56,3	56,4	56,5	56,6	56,7	56,7
1,2	55,8	55,9	56,0	56,1	56,2	56,3	56,4	56,5	56,6	56,7
1,4	55,8	55,9	55,9	56,0	56,1	56,2	56,3	56,4	56,5	56,6
1,6	55,7	55,8	55,9	56,0	56,1	56,2	56,3	56,3	56,4	56,5
1,8	55,6	55,7	55,8	55,9	56,0	56,1	56,2	56,3	56,4	56,5
2,0	55,5	55,6	55,7	55,8	55,9	56,0	56,1	56,2	56,3	56,4
2,2	55,5	55,6	55,7	55,8	55,9	55,9	56,0	56,1	56,2	56,3
2,4	55,4	55,5	55,6	55,7	55,8	55,9	56,0	56,1	56,2	56,3
2,6	55,3	55,4	55,5	55,6	55,7	55,8	55,9	56,0	56,1	56,2
2,8	55,3	55,4	55,5	55,5	55,6	55,7	55,8	55,9	56,0	56,1
3,0	55,2	55,3	55,4	55,5	55,6	55,7	55,8	55,9	56,0	56,0
3,2	55,1	55,2	55,3	55,4	55,5	55,6	55,7	55,8	55,9	56,0
3,4	55,1	55,1	55,2	55,3	55,4	55,5	55,6	55,7	55,8	55,9
3,6	55,0	55,1	55,2	55,3	55,4	55,5	55,6	55,6	55,7	55,8
3,8	54,9	55,0	55,1	55,2	55,3	55,4	55,5	55,6	55,7	55,8
4,0	54,8	54,9	55,0	55,1	55,2	55,3	55,4	55,5	55,6	55,7
4,2	54,8	54,9	55,0	55,1	55,2	55,2	55,3	55,4	55,5	55,6
4,4	54,7	54,8	54,9	55,0	55,1	55,2	55,3	55,4	55,5	55,6
4,6	54,6	54,7	54,8	54,9	55,0	55,1	55,2	55,3	55,4	55,5
4,8	54,6	54,7	54,7	54,8	54,9	55,0	55,1	55,2	55,3	55,4
5,0	54,5	54,6	54,7	54,8	54,9	55,0	55,1	55,2	55,3	55,3
5,2	54,4	54,5	54,6	54,7	54,8	54,9	55,0	55,1	55,2	55,3
5,4	54,3	54,4	54,5	54,6	54,7	54,8	54,9	55,0	55,1	55,2
5,6	54,3	54,4	54,5	54,6	54,7	54,8	54,8	54,9	55,0	55,1
5,8	54,2	54,3	54,4	54,5	54,6	54,7	54,8	54,9	55,0	55,1
6,0	54,1	54,2	54,3	54,4	54,5	54,6	54,7	54,8	54,9	55,0
6,2	54,1	54,2	54,2	54,3	54,4	54,5	54,6	54,7	54,8	54,9
6,4	54,0	54,1	54,2	54,3	54,4	54,4	54,5	54,6	54,7	54,9
6,6	53,9	54,0	54,1	54,2	54,3	54,4	54,5	54,6	54,7	54,8
6,8	53,8	53,9	54,0	54,1	54,2	54,3	54,4	54,5	54,6	54,7
7,0	53,8	53,9	54,0	54,1	54,2	54,3	54,3	54,4	54,5	54,6
7,2	53,7	53,8	53,9	54,0	54,1	54,2	54,3	54,4	54,5	54,6
7,4	53,6	53,7	53,8	53,9	54,0	54,1	54,2	54,3	54,4	54,5
7,6	53,6	53,7	53,7	53,8	53,9	54,0	54,1	54,2	54,3	54,4
7,8	53,5	53,6	53,7	53,8	53,9	54,0	54,1	54,2	54,3	54,4
8,0	53,4	53,5	53,6	53,7	53,8	53,9	54,0	54,1	54,2	54,3
8,2	53,3	53,4	53,5	53,6	53,7	53,8	53,9	54,0	54,1	54,2
8,4	53,3	53,4	53,5	53,6	53,7	53,8	53,8	53,9	54,0	54,1
8,6	53,2	53,3	53,4	53,5	53,6	53,7	53,8	53,9	54,0	54,1
8,8	53,1	53,2	53,3	53,4	53,5	53,6	53,7	53,8	53,9	54,0
9,0	53,1	53,1	53,2	53,3	53,4	53,5	53,6	53,7	53,8	53,9
9,2	53,0	53,1	53,2	53,3	53,4	53,5	53,6	53,7	53,8	53,9
9,4	52,9	53,0	53,1	53,2	53,3	53,4	53,5	53,6	53,7	53,8
9,6	52,8	52,9	53,0	53,1	53,2	53,3	53,4	53,5	53,6	53,7
9,8	52,8	52,9	53,0	53,1	53,2	53,2	53,3	53,4	53,5	53,6

Volumenkonzentration bei 20 °C in Prozent

Temp. °C	Anzeige des Alkoholometers in % vol									
	49,0	49,1	49,2	49,3	49,4	49,5	49,6	49,7	49,8	49,9
10,0	52,7	52,8	52,9	53,0	53,1	53,2	53,3	53,4	53,5	53,6
10,2	52,6	52,7	52,8	52,9	53,0	53,1	53,2	53,3	53,4	53,5
10,4	52,5	52,6	52,7	52,8	52,9	53,0	53,1	53,2	53,3	53,4
10,6	52,5	52,6	52,7	52,8	52,9	53,0	53,1	53,2	53,3	53,3
10,8	52,4	52,5	52,6	52,7	52,8	52,9	53,0	53,1	53,2	53,3
11,0	52,3	52,4	52,5	52,6	52,7	52,8	52,9	53,0	53,1	53,2
11,2	52,3	52,4	52,4	52,5	52,6	52,7	52,8	52,9	53,0	53,1
11,4	52,2	52,3	52,4	52,5	52,6	52,7	52,8	52,9	53,0	53,1
11,6	52,1	52,2	52,3	52,4	52,5	52,6	52,7	52,8	52,9	53,0
11,8	52,0	52,1	52,2	52,3	52,4	52,5	52,6	52,7	52,8	52,9
12,0	52,0	52,1	52,2	52,3	52,4	52,5	52,5	52,6	52,7	52,8
12,2	51,9	52,0	52,1	52,2	52,3	52,4	52,5	52,6	52,7	52,8
12,4	51,8	51,9	52,0	52,1	52,2	52,3	52,4	52,5	52,6	52,7
12,6	51,7	51,8	51,9	52,0	52,1	52,2	52,3	52,4	52,5	52,6
12,8	51,7	51,8	51,9	52,0	52,1	52,2	52,3	52,4	52,5	52,6
13,0	51,6	51,7	51,8	51,9	52,0	52,1	52,2	52,3	52,4	52,5
13,2	51,5	51,6	51,7	51,8	51,9	52,0	52,1	52,2	52,3	52,4
13,4	51,4	51,5	51,6	51,7	51,8	51,9	52,0	52,1	52,2	52,3
13,6	51,4	51,5	51,6	51,7	51,8	51,9	52,0	52,1	52,2	52,3
13,8	51,3	51,4	51,5	51,6	51,7	51,8	51,9	52,0	52,1	52,2
14,0	51,2	51,3	51,4	51,5	51,6	51,7	51,8	51,9	52,0	52,1
14,2	51,2	51,3	51,4	51,5	51,5	51,6	51,7	51,8	51,9	52,0
14,4	51,1	51,2	51,3	51,4	51,5	51,6	51,7	51,8	51,9	52,0
14,6	51,0	51,1	51,2	51,3	51,4	51,5	51,6	51,7	51,8	51,9
14,8	50,9	51,0	51,1	51,2	51,3	51,4	51,5	51,6	51,7	51,8
15,0	50,9	51,0	51,1	51,2	51,3	51,4	51,5	51,6	51,6	51,7
15,2	50,8	50,9	51,0	51,1	51,2	51,3	51,4	51,5	51,6	51,7
15,4	50,7	50,8	50,9	51,0	51,1	51,2	51,3	51,4	51,5	51,6
15,6	50,6	50,7	50,8	50,9	51,0	51,1	51,2	51,3	51,4	51,5
15,8	50,6	50,7	50,8	50,9	51,0	51,1	51,2	51,3	51,4	51,5
16,0	50,5	50,6	50,7	50,8	50,9	51,0	51,1	51,2	51,3	51,4
16,2	50,4	50,5	50,6	50,7	50,8	50,9	51,0	51,1	51,2	51,3
16,4	50,3	50,4	50,5	50,6	50,7	50,8	50,9	51,0	51,1	51,2
16,6	50,3	50,4	50,5	50,6	50,7	50,8	50,9	51,0	51,1	51,2
16,8	50,2	50,3	50,4	50,5	50,6	50,7	50,8	50,9	51,0	51,1
17,0	50,1	50,2	50,3	50,4	50,5	50,6	50,7	50,8	50,9	51,0
17,2	50,0	50,1	50,2	50,3	50,4	50,5	50,6	50,7	50,8	50,9
17,4	50,0	50,1	50,2	50,3	50,4	50,5	50,6	50,7	50,8	50,9
17,6	49,9	50,0	50,1	50,2	50,3	50,4	50,5	50,6	50,7	50,8
17,8	49,8	49,9	50,0	50,1	50,2	50,3	50,4	50,5	50,6	50,7
18,0	49,7	49,8	49,9	50,0	50,1	50,2	50,3	50,4	50,5	50,6
18,2	49,7	49,8	49,9	50,0	50,1	50,2	50,3	50,4	50,5	50,6
18,4	49,6	49,7	49,8	49,9	50,0	50,1	50,2	50,3	50,4	50,5
18,6	49,5	49,6	49,7	49,8	49,9	50,0	50,1	50,2	50,3	50,4
18,8	49,4	49,5	49,6	49,7	49,8	49,9	50,0	50,1	50,2	50,3
19,0	49,4	49,5	49,6	49,7	49,8	49,9	50,0	50,1	50,2	50,3
19,2	49,3	49,4	49,5	49,6	49,7	49,8	49,9	50,0	50,1	50,2
19,4	49,2	49,3	49,4	49,5	49,6	49,7	49,8	49,9	50,0	50,1
19,6	49,1	49,2	49,3	49,4	49,5	49,6	49,7	49,8	49,9	50,0
19,8	49,1	49,2	49,3	49,4	49,5	49,6	49,7	49,8	49,9	50,0

Volumenkonzentration bei 20 °C in Prozent

Temp. °C	Anzeige des Alkoholometers in % vol								
	49,0	49,1	49,2	49,3	49,4	49,5	49,6	49,7	49,8	49,9
20,0	49,0	49,1	49,2	49,3	49,4	49,5	49,6	49,7	49,8	49,9
20,2	48,9	49,0	49,1	49,2	49,3	49,4	49,5	49,6	49,7	49,8
20,4	48,8	48,9	49,1	49,2	49,3	49,4	49,5	49,6	49,7	49,8
20,6	48,8	48,9	49,0	49,1	49,2	49,3	49,4	49,5	49,6	49,7
20,8	48,7	48,8	48,9	49,0	49,1	49,2	49,3	49,4	49,5	49,6
21,0	48,6	48,7	48,8	48,9	49,0	49,1	49,2	49,3	49,4	49,5
21,2	48,5	48,6	48,7	48,9	49,0	49,1	49,2	49,3	49,4	49,5
21,4	48,5	48,6	48,7	48,8	48,9	49,0	49,1	49,2	49,3	49,4
21,6	48,4	48,5	48,6	48,7	48,8	48,9	49,0	49,1	49,2	49,3
21,8	48,3	48,4	48,5	48,6	48,7	48,8	48,9	49,0	49,1	49,2
22,0	48,2	48,3	48,4	48,5	48,6	48,8	48,9	49,0	49,1	49,2
22,2	48,2	48,3	48,4	48,5	48,6	48,7	48,8	48,9	49,0	49,1
22,4	48,1	48,2	48,3	48,4	48,5	48,6	48,7	48,8	48,9	49,0
22,6	48,0	48,1	48,2	48,3	48,4	48,5	48,6	48,7	48,8	48,9
22,8	47,9	48,0	48,1	48,2	48,3	48,4	48,6	48,7	48,8	48,9
23,0	47,9	48,0	48,1	48,2	48,3	48,4	48,5	48,6	48,7	48,8
23,2	47,8	47,9	48,0	48,1	48,2	48,3	48,4	48,5	48,6	48,7
23,4	47,7	47,8	47,9	48,0	48,1	48,2	48,3	48,4	48,5	48,6
23,6	47,6	47,7	47,8	47,9	48,0	48,1	48,2	48,3	48,5	48,6
23,8	47,6	47,7	47,8	47,9	48,0	48,1	48,2	48,3	48,4	48,5
24,0	47,5	47,6	47,7	47,8	47,9	48,0	48,1	48,2	48,3	48,4
24,2	47,4	47,5	47,6	47,7	47,8	47,9	48,0	48,1	48,2	48,3
24,4	47,3	47,4	47,5	47,6	47,7	47,8	47,9	48,0	48,1	48,3
24,6	47,3	47,4	47,5	47,6	47,7	47,8	47,9	48,0	48,1	48,2
24,8	47,2	47,3	47,4	47,5	47,6	47,7	47,8	47,9	48,0	48,1
25,0	47,1	47,2	47,3	47,4	47,5	47,6	47,7	47,8	47,9	48,0
25,2	47,0	47,1	47,2	47,3	47,4	47,5	47,6	47,7	47,8	47,9
25,4	47,0	47,1	47,2	47,3	47,4	47,5	47,6	47,7	47,8	47,9
25,6	46,9	47,0	47,1	47,2	47,3	47,4	47,5	47,6	47,7	47,8
25,8	46,8	46,9	47,0	47,1	47,2	47,3	47,4	47,5	47,6	47,7
26,0	46,7	46,8	46,9	47,0	47,1	47,2	47,3	47,4	47,5	47,6
26,2	46,7	46,8	46,9	47,0	47,1	47,2	47,3	47,4	47,5	47,6
26,4	46,6	46,7	46,8	46,9	47,0	47,1	47,2	47,3	47,4	47,5
26,6	46,5	46,6	46,7	46,8	46,9	47,0	47,1	47,2	47,3	47,4
26,8	46,4	46,5	46,6	46,7	46,8	46,9	47,0	47,1	47,2	47,3
27,0	46,3	46,5	46,6	46,7	46,8	46,9	47,0	47,1	47,2	47,3
27,2	46,3	46,4	46,5	46,6	46,7	46,8	46,9	47,0	47,1	47,2
27,4	46,2	46,3	46,4	46,5	46,6	46,7	46,8	46,9	47,0	47,1
27,6	46,1	46,2	46,3	46,4	46,5	46,6	46,7	46,8	46,9	47,0
27,8	46,0	46,1	46,2	46,3	46,5	46,6	46,7	46,8	46,9	47,0
28,0	46,0	46,1	46,2	46,3	46,4	46,5	46,6	46,7	46,8	46,9
28,2	45,9	46,0	46,1	46,2	46,3	46,4	46,5	46,6	46,7	46,8
28,4	45,8	45,9	46,0	46,1	46,2	46,3	46,4	46,5	46,6	46,7
28,6	45,7	45,8	45,9	46,0	46,1	46,2	46,4	46,5	46,6	46,7
28,8	45,7	45,8	45,9	46,0	46,1	46,2	46,3	46,4	46,5	46,6
29,0	45,6	45,7	45,8	45,9	46,0	46,1	46,2	46,3	46,4	46,5
29,2	45,5	45,6	45,7	45,8	45,9	46,0	46,1	46,2	46,3	46,4
29,4	45,4	45,5	45,6	45,7	45,8	45,9	46,0	46,1	46,2	46,4
29,6	45,4	45,5	45,6	45,7	45,8	45,9	46,0	46,1	46,2	46,3
29,8	45,3	45,4	45,5	45,6	45,7	45,8	45,9	46,0	46,1	46,2
30,0	45,2	45,3	45,4	45,5	45,6	45,7	45,8	45,9	46,0	46,1

Volumenkonzentration bei 20 °C in Prozent

Temp. °C	Anzeige des Alkoholometers in % vol								
	50,0	50,1	50,2	50,3	50,4	50,5	50,6	50,7	50,8	50,9
0,0	57,2	57,3	57,4	57,5	57,6	57,7	57,8	57,8	57,9	58,0
0,2	57,1	57,2	57,3	57,4	57,5	57,6	57,7	57,8	57,9	58,0
0,4	57,1	57,1	57,2	57,3	57,4	57,5	57,6	57,7	57,8	57,9
0,6	57,0	57,1	57,2	57,3	57,4	57,5	57,5	57,6	57,7	57,8
0,8	56,9	57,0	57,1	57,2	57,3	57,4	57,5	57,6	57,7	57,8
1,0	56,8	56,9	57,0	57,1	57,2	57,3	57,4	57,5	57,6	57,7
1,2	56,8	56,9	57,0	57,1	57,2	57,2	57,3	57,4	57,5	57,6
1,4	56,7	56,8	56,9	57,0	57,1	57,2	57,3	57,4	57,5	57,6
1,6	56,6	56,7	56,8	56,9	57,0	57,1	57,2	57,3	57,4	57,5
1,8	56,6	56,7	56,8	56,8	56,9	57,0	57,1	57,2	57,3	57,4
2,0	56,5	56,6	56,7	56,8	56,9	57,0	57,1	57,2	57,3	57,3
2,2	56,4	56,5	56,6	56,7	56,8	56,9	57,0	57,1	57,2	57,3
2,4	56,4	56,4	56,5	56,6	56,7	56,8	56,9	57,0	57,1	57,2
2,6	56,3	56,4	56,5	56,6	56,7	56,8	56,9	57,0	57,0	57,1
2,8	56,2	56,3	56,4	56,5	56,6	56,7	56,8	56,9	57,0	57,1
3,0	56,1	56,2	56,3	56,4	56,5	56,6	56,7	56,8	56,9	57,0
3,2	56,1	56,2	56,3	56,4	56,5	56,6	56,6	56,7	56,8	56,9
3,4	56,0	56,1	56,2	56,3	56,4	56,5	56,6	56,7	56,8	56,9
3,6	55,9	56,0	56,1	56,2	56,3	56,4	56,5	56,6	56,7	56,8
3,8	55,9	56,0	56,1	56,2	56,2	56,3	56,4	56,5	56,6	56,7
4,0	55,8	55,9	56,0	56,1	56,2	56,3	56,4	56,5	56,6	56,7
4,2	55,7	55,8	55,9	56,0	56,1	56,2	56,3	56,4	56,5	56,6
4,4	55,7	55,7	55,8	55,9	56,0	56,1	56,2	56,3	56,4	56,5
4,6	55,6	55,7	55,8	55,9	56,0	56,1	56,2	56,3	56,3	56,4
4,8	55,5	55,6	55,7	55,8	55,9	56,0	56,1	56,2	56,3	56,4
5,0	55,4	55,5	55,6	55,7	55,8	55,9	56,0	56,1	56,2	56,3
5,2	55,4	55,5	55,6	55,7	55,8	55,9	55,9	56,0	56,1	56,2
5,4	55,3	55,4	55,5	55,6	55,7	55,8	55,9	56,0	56,1	56,2
5,6	55,2	55,3	55,4	55,5	55,6	55,7	55,8	55,9	56,0	56,1
5,8	55,2	55,3	55,4	55,4	55,5	55,6	55,7	55,8	55,9	56,0
6,0	55,1	55,2	55,3	55,4	55,5	55,6	55,7	55,8	55,9	56,0
6,2	55,0	55,1	55,2	55,3	55,4	55,5	55,6	55,7	55,8	55,9
6,4	54,9	55,0	55,1	55,2	55,3	55,4	55,5	55,6	55,7	55,8
6,6	54,9	55,0	55,1	55,2	55,3	55,4	55,5	55,6	55,6	55,7
6,8	54,8	54,9	55,0	55,1	55,2	55,3	55,4	55,5	55,6	55,7
7,0	54,7	54,8	54,9	55,0	55,1	55,2	55,3	55,4	55,5	55,6
7,2	54,7	54,8	54,9	55,0	55,0	55,1	55,2	55,3	55,4	55,5
7,4	54,6	54,7	54,8	54,9	55,0	55,1	55,2	55,3	55,4	55,5
7,6	54,5	54,6	54,7	54,8	54,9	55,0	55,1	55,2	55,3	55,4
7,8	54,4	54,5	54,6	54,7	54,8	54,9	55,0	55,1	55,2	55,3
8,0	54,4	54,5	54,6	54,7	54,8	54,9	55,0	55,1	55,2	55,2
8,2	54,3	54,4	54,5	54,6	54,7	54,8	54,9	55,0	55,1	55,2
8,4	54,2	54,3	54,4	54,5	54,6	54,7	54,8	54,9	55,0	55,1
8,6	54,2	54,3	54,4	54,5	54,6	54,6	54,7	54,8	54,9	55,0
8,8	54,1	54,2	54,3	54,4	54,5	54,6	54,7	54,8	54,9	55,0
9,0	54,0	54,1	54,2	54,3	54,4	54,5	54,6	54,7	54,8	54,9
9,2	53,9	54,0	54,1	54,2	54,3	54,4	54,5	54,6	54,7	54,8
9,4	53,9	54,0	54,1	54,2	54,3	54,4	54,5	54,6	54,7	54,8
9,6	53,8	53,9	54,0	54,1	54,2	54,3	54,4	54,5	54,6	54,7
9,8	53,7	53,8	53,9	54,0	54,1	54,2	54,3	54,4	54,5	54,6

Volumenkonzentration bei 20 °C in Prozent

Temp. °C	\multicolumn{10}{c}{Anzeige des Alkoholometers in % vol}

Temp. °C	50,0	50,1	50,2	50,3	50,4	50,5	50,6	50,7	50,8	50,9
10,0	53,7	53,8	53,9	54,0	54,1	54,1	54,2	54,3	54,4	54,5
10,2	53,6	53,7	53,8	53,9	54,0	54,1	54,2	54,3	54,4	54,5
10,4	53,5	53,6	53,7	53,8	53,9	54,0	54,1	54,2	54,3	54,4
10,6	53,4	53,5	53,6	53,7	53,8	53,9	54,0	54,1	54,2	54,3
10,8	53,4	53,5	53,6	53,7	53,8	53,9	54,0	54,1	54,2	54,3
11,0	53,3	53,4	53,5	53,6	53,7	53,8	53,9	54,0	54,1	54,2
11,2	53,2	53,3	53,4	53,5	53,6	53,7	53,8	53,9	54,0	54,1
11,4	53,2	53,3	53,4	53,4	53,5	53,6	53,7	53,8	53,9	54,0
11,6	53,1	53,2	53,3	53,4	53,5	53,6	53,7	53,8	53,9	54,0
11,8	53,0	53,1	53,2	53,3	53,4	53,5	53,6	53,7	53,8	53,9
12,0	52,9	53,0	53,1	53,2	53,3	53,4	53,5	53,6	53,7	53,8
12,2	52,9	53,0	53,1	53,2	53,3	53,4	53,5	53,6	53,7	53,7
12,4	52,8	52,9	53,0	53,1	53,2	53,3	53,4	53,5	53,6	53,7
12,6	52,7	52,8	52,9	53,0	53,1	53,2	53,3	53,4	53,5	53,6
12,8	52,6	52,7	52,8	52,9	53,0	53,1	53,2	53,3	53,4	53,5
13,0	52,6	52,7	52,8	52,9	53,0	53,1	53,2	53,3	53,4	53,5
13,2	52,5	52,6	52,7	52,8	52,9	53,0	53,1	53,2	53,3	53,4
13,4	52,4	52,5	52,6	52,7	52,8	52,9	53,0	53,1	53,2	53,3
13,6	52,4	52,5	52,6	52,7	52,8	52,8	52,9	53,0	53,1	53,2
13,8	52,3	52,4	52,5	52,6	52,7	52,8	52,9	53,0	53,1	53,2
14,0	52,2	52,3	52,4	52,5	52,6	52,7	52,8	52,9	53,0	53,1
14,2	52,1	52,2	52,3	52,4	52,5	52,6	52,7	52,8	52,9	53,0
14,4	52,1	52,2	52,3	52,4	52,5	52,6	52,7	52,8	52,9	53,0
14,6	52,0	52,1	52,2	52,3	52,4	52,5	52,6	52,7	52,8	52,9
14,8	51,9	52,0	52,1	52,2	52,3	52,4	52,5	52,6	52,7	52,8
15,0	51,8	51,9	52,0	52,1	52,2	52,3	52,4	52,5	52,6	52,7
15,2	51,8	51,9	52,0	52,1	52,2	52,3	52,4	52,5	52,6	52,7
15,4	51,7	51,8	51,9	52,0	52,1	52,2	52,3	52,4	52,5	52,6
15,6	51,6	51,7	51,8	51,9	52,0	52,1	52,2	52,3	52,4	52,5
15,8	51,6	51,7	51,8	51,9	51,9	52,0	52,1	52,2	52,3	52,4
16,0	51,5	51,6	51,7	51,8	51,9	52,0	52,1	52,2	52,3	52,4
16,2	51,4	51,5	51,6	51,7	51,8	51,9	52,0	52,1	52,2	52,3
16,4	51,3	51,4	51,5	51,6	51,7	51,8	51,9	52,0	52,1	52,2
16,6	51,3	51,4	51,5	51,6	51,7	51,8	51,9	52,0	52,1	52,2
16,8	51,2	51,3	51,4	51,5	51,6	51,7	51,8	51,9	52,0	52,1
17,0	51,1	51,2	51,3	51,4	51,5	51,6	51,7	51,8	51,9	52,0
17,2	51,0	51,1	51,2	51,3	51,4	51,5	51,6	51,7	51,8	51,9
17,4	51,0	51,1	51,2	51,3	51,4	51,5	51,6	51,7	51,8	51,9
17,6	50,9	51,0	51,1	51,2	51,3	51,4	51,5	51,6	51,7	51,8
17,8	50,8	50,9	51,0	51,1	51,2	51,3	51,4	51,5	51,6	51,7
18,0	50,7	50,8	50,9	51,0	51,1	51,2	51,3	51,4	51,5	51,6
18,2	50,7	50,8	50,9	51,0	51,1	51,2	51,3	51,4	51,5	51,6
18,4	50,6	50,7	50,8	50,9	51,0	51,1	51,2	51,3	51,4	51,5
18,6	50,5	50,6	50,7	50,8	50,9	51,0	51,1	51,2	51,3	51,4
18,8	50,4	50,5	50,6	50,7	50,8	50,9	51,0	51,1	51,2	51,3
19,0	50,4	50,5	50,6	50,7	50,8	50,9	51,0	51,1	51,2	51,3
19,2	50,3	50,4	50,5	50,6	50,7	50,8	50,9	51,0	51,1	51,2
19,4	50,2	50,3	50,4	50,5	50,6	50,7	50,8	50,9	51,0	51,1
19,6	50,1	50,2	50,3	50,4	50,5	50,6	50,7	50,8	50,9	51,0
19,8	50,1	50,2	50,3	50,4	50,5	50,6	50,7	50,8	50,9	51,0

Volumenkonzentration bei 20 °C in Prozent

Temp. °C	\multicolumn{9}{c}{Anzeige des Alkoholometers in % vol}
	50,0	50,1	50,2	50,3	50,4	50,5	50,6	50,7	50,8	50,9
20,0	50,0	50,1	50,2	50,3	50,4	50,5	50,6	50,7	50,8	50,9
20,2	49,9	50,0	50,1	50,2	50,3	50,4	50,5	50,6	50,7	50,8
20,4	49,9	50,0	50,1	50,2	50,3	50,4	50,5	50,6	50,7	50,8
20,6	49,8	49,9	50,0	50,1	50,2	50,3	50,4	50,5	50,6	50,7
20,8	49,7	49,8	49,9	50,0	50,1	50,2	50,3	50,4	50,5	50,6
21,0	49,6	49,7	49,8	49,9	50,0	50,1	50,2	50,3	50,4	50,5
21,2	49,6	49,7	49,8	49,9	50,0	50,1	50,2	50,3	50,4	50,5
21,4	49,5	49,6	49,7	49,8	49,9	50,0	50,1	50,2	50,3	50,4
21,6	49,4	49,5	49,6	49,7	49,8	49,9	50,0	50,1	50,2	50,3
21,8	49,3	49,4	49,5	49,6	49,7	49,8	49,9	50,0	50,1	50,2
22,0	49,3	49,4	49,5	49,6	49,7	49,8	49,9	50,0	50,1	50,2
22,2	49,2	49,3	49,4	49,5	49,6	49,7	49,8	49,9	50,0	50,1
22,4	49,1	49,2	49,3	49,4	49,5	49,6	49,7	49,8	49,9	50,0
22,6	49,0	49,1	49,2	49,3	49,4	49,5	49,6	49,7	49,8	49,9
22,8	49,0	49,1	49,2	49,3	49,4	49,5	49,6	49,7	49,8	49,9
23,0	48,9	49,0	49,1	49,2	49,3	49,4	49,5	49,6	49,7	49,8
23,2	48,8	48,9	49,0	49,1	49,2	49,3	49,4	49,5	49,6	49,7
23,4	48,7	48,8	48,9	49,0	49,1	49,2	49,3	49,4	49,5	49,6
23,6	48,7	48,8	48,9	49,0	49,1	49,2	49,3	49,4	49,5	49,6
23,8	48,6	48,7	48,8	48,9	49,0	49,1	49,2	49,3	49,4	49,5
24,0	48,5	48,6	48,7	48,8	48,9	49,0	49,1	49,2	49,3	49,4
24,2	48,4	48,5	48,6	48,7	48,8	48,9	49,0	49,1	49,2	49,3
24,4	48,4	48,5	48,6	48,7	48,8	48,9	49,0	49,1	49,2	49,3
24,6	48,3	48,4	48,5	48,6	48,7	48,8	48,9	49,0	49,1	49,2
24,8	48,2	48,3	48,4	48,5	48,6	48,7	48,8	48,9	49,0	49,1
25,0	48,1	48,2	48,3	48,4	48,5	48,6	48,7	48,8	48,9	49,0
25,2	48,0	48,2	48,3	48,4	48,5	48,6	48,7	48,8	48,9	49,0
25,4	48,0	48,1	48,2	48,3	48,4	48,5	48,6	48,7	48,8	48,9
25,6	47,9	48,0	48,1	48,2	48,3	48,4	48,5	48,6	48,7	48,8
25,8	47,8	47,9	48,0	48,1	48,2	48,3	48,4	48,5	48,6	48,7
26,0	47,7	47,8	47,9	48,1	48,2	48,3	48,4	48,5	48,6	48,7
26,2	47,7	47,8	47,9	48,0	48,1	48,2	48,3	48,4	48,5	48,6
26,4	47,6	47,7	47,8	47,9	48,0	48,1	48,2	48,3	48,4	48,5
26,6	47,5	47,6	47,7	47,8	47,9	48,0	48,1	48,2	48,3	48,4
26,8	47,4	47,5	47,6	47,7	47,9	48,0	48,1	48,2	48,3	48,4
27,0	47,4	47,5	47,6	47,7	47,8	47,9	48,0	48,1	48,2	48,3
27,2	47,3	47,4	47,5	47,6	47,7	47,8	47,9	48,0	48,1	48,2
27,4	47,2	47,3	47,4	47,5	47,6	47,7	47,8	47,9	48,0	48,1
27,6	47,1	47,2	47,3	47,4	47,5	47,6	47,8	47,9	48,0	48,1
27,8	47,1	47,2	47,3	47,4	47,5	47,6	47,7	47,8	47,9	48,0
28,0	47,0	47,1	47,2	47,3	47,4	47,5	47,6	47,7	47,8	47,9
28,2	46,9	47,0	47,1	47,2	47,3	47,4	47,5	47,6	47,7	47,8
28,4	46,8	46,9	47,0	47,1	47,2	47,3	47,4	47,6	47,7	47,8
28,6	46,8	46,9	47,0	47,1	47,2	47,3	47,4	47,5	47,6	47,7
28,8	46,7	46,8	46,9	47,0	47,1	47,2	47,3	47,4	47,5	47,6
29,0	46,6	46,7	46,8	46,9	47,0	47,1	47,2	47,3	47,4	47,5
29,2	46,5	46,6	46,7	46,8	46,9	47,0	47,1	47,2	47,3	47,5
29,4	46,5	46,6	46,7	46,8	46,9	47,0	47,1	47,2	47,3	47,4
29,6	46,4	46,5	46,6	46,7	46,8	46,9	47,0	47,1	47,2	47,3
29,8	46,3	46,4	46,5	46,6	46,7	46,8	46,9	47,0	47,1	47,2
30,0	46,2	46,3	46,4	46,5	46,6	46,7	46,8	46,9	47,0	47,1

2 Mischungstabelle für die Herabsetzung von Destillaten

Die Tabelle gibt die Anzahl Liter Wasser an, welche zu 100 l des Destillates gleicher Temperatur zuzusetzen sind, um die gewünschte Trinkstärke zu erhalten (Beispiele s. E.1.3).

Alkohol-gehalt (% vol)	34	35	36	37	37,5	38	39	40	41	42	43	44	45	46	47	48	49	50
95	186,8	178,7	171,2	164,0	160,5	157,1	150,7	144,5	138,6	133,0	127,6	122,5	117,6	112,9	108,4	104,1	99,9	96,0
90	170,8	163,2	156,0	149,2	145,9	142,7	136,6	130,8	125,2	119,9	114,7	110,0	105,3	100,9	96,6	92,5	88,5	84,7
85	155,1	147,9	141,1	134,8	131,7	128,6	122,8	117,3	112,0	107,0	102,2	97,7	93,3	89,1	85,0	81,2	77,4	73,9
80	139,6	132,8	126,4	120,4	117,5	114,6	109,2	104,0	99,1	94,3	89,7	85,5	81,3	77,4	73,5	70,0	66,4	63,1
79	136,5	129,8	123,5	117,6	114,7	111,9	106,5	101,4	96,5	91,8	87,3	83,1	79,0	75,1	71,3	67,8	64,3	61,0
78	133,4	126,8	120,5	114,7	111,9	109,1	103,7	98,7	93,9	89,2	84,8	80,6	76,6	72,8	69,0	65,5	62,1	58,8
77	130,3	123,8	117,6	111,8	109,0	106,3	101,0	96,0	91,3	86,7	82,3	78,2	74,2	70,5	66,7	63,3	59,9	56,7
76	127,2	120,8	114,7	109,0	106,2	103,5	98,3	93,4	88,7	84,2	79,9	75,8	71,9	68,2	64,5	61,1	57,8	54,6
75	124,1	117,8	111,8	106,2	103,4	100,7	95,6	90,8	86,1	81,7	77,4	73,4	69,5	65,9	62,2	58,9	55,6	52,4
74	121,0	114,8	108,8	103,3	100,6	97,9	92,9	88,1	83,5	79,2	74,9	71,0	67,1	63,6	60,0	56,7	53,4	50,3
73	117,9	111,8	105,9	100,4	97,7	95,1	90,2	85,5	80,9	76,7	72,4	68,6	64,8	61,3	57,7	54,5	51,2	48,2
72	114,9	108,8	103,0	97,6	95,0	92,4	87,5	82,9	78,4	74,2	70,0	66,2	62,5	59,0	55,5	52,3	49,1	46,1
71	111,8	105,8	100,1	94,7	92,1	89,6	84,8	80,2	75,8	71,6	67,5	63,8	60,1	56,7	53,2	50,0	46,9	43,9
70	108,7	102,8	97,2	91,8	89,3	86,8	82,1	77,6	73,2	69,1	65,1	61,4	57,7	54,4	50,9	47,8	44,7	41,8
69	105,7	99,8	94,3	89,1	86,6	84,1	79,4	75,0	70,7	66,6	62,7	59,0	55,4	52,1	48,7	45,6	42,6	39,7
68	102,6	96,8	91,4	86,2	83,7	81,3	76,7	72,3	68,1	64,1	60,2	56,6	53,0	49,8	46,5	43,4	40,4	37,6
67	99,5	93,8	88,5	83,4	81,0	78,6	74,0	69,7	65,5	61,6	57,8	54,2	50,7	47,5	44,2	41,2	38,3	35,5
66	96,5	90,9	85,6	80,6	78,2	75,9	71,4	67,1	63,0	59,1	55,4	51,9	48,4	45,2	42,0	39,0	36,2	33,4

gewünschter Alkoholgehalt (% vol)

63	87,3	81,9	76,9	72,2	69,9	67,6	63,3	59,3	55,3	51,6	48,0	44,7	41,4	38,3	35,3	32,4	29,7	27,1
62	84,3	79,0	74,0	69,4	67,1	64,9	60,7	56,7	52,8	49,2	45,6	42,3	39,1	36,1	33,1	30,3	27,6	25,0
61	81,2	76,0	71,1	66,5	64,3	62,1	58,0	54,1	50,2	46,7	43,1	39,9	36,8	33,8	30,8	28,1	25,4	22,9
60	78,2	73,0	68,2	63,7	61,5	59,4	55,3	51,5	47,7	44,2	40,7	37,5	34,5	31,5	28,6	25,9	23,3	20,8
59	75,1	70,1	65,4	60,9	58,8	56,7	52,7	48,9	45,2	41,7	38,3	35,2	32,2	29,3	26,4	23,8	21,2	18,7
58	72,0	67,1	62,5	58,1	56,0	53,9	50,0	46,3	42,6	39,2	35,9	32,8	29,8	27,0	24,2	21,6	19,0	16,6
57	69,0	64,1	59,8	55,3	53,2	51,2	47,3	43,7	40,1	36,7	33,5	30,4	27,5	24,7	22,0	19,4	16,9	14,5
56	66,0	61,2	56,7	52,5	50,5	48,5	44,7	41,1	37,6	34,3	31,1	28,1	25,2	22,5	19,8	17,2	14,8	12,4
55	62,9	58,2	53,8	49,7	47,7	45,8	42,0	38,4	35,0	31,8	28,7	25,7	22,9	20,2	17,5	15,1	12,6	10,3
54	59,8	55,2	50,9	46,9	44,9	43,0	39,3	35,8	32,5	29,3	26,3	23,3	20,6	17,9	15,3	12,9	10,5	8,2
53	56,8	52,3	48,0	44,1	42,2	40,3	36,7	33,2	30,0	26,8	23,9	21,0	18,3	15,6	13,1	10,7	8,4	6,2
52	53,8	49,4	45,2	41,3	39,4	37,6	34,1	30,7	27,5	24,4	21,5	18,7	16,0	13,4	10,9	8,6	6,3	4,2
51	50,8	46,4	42,3	38,5	36,7	34,9	31,4	28,1	24,9	21,9	19,1	16,3	13,7	11,1	8,7	6,4	4,3	2,1
50	47,8	43,5	39,5	35,7	33,9	32,2	28,8	25,5	22,4	19,5	16,7	14,0	11,4	8,9	6,5	4,3	2,2	
49	44,8	40,6	36,7	33,0	31,2	29,5	26,2	23,0	19,9	17,1	14,3	11,7	9,1	6,7	4,4	2,2		
48	41,7	37,6	33,8	30,2	28,5	26,8	23,5	20,4	17,4	14,6	11,9	9,3	6,8	4,5	2,2			
47	38,7	34,7	31,0	27,4	25,7	24,1	20,9	17,8	14,9	12,1	9,5	7,0	4,5	2,3				
46	35,7	31,8	28,2	24,7	23,0	21,4	18,3	15,3	12,4	9,7	7,1	4,7	2,3					
45	32,8	28,9	25,3	22,0	20,3	18,7	15,7	12,7	9,9	7,3	4,7	2,3						
44	29,8	26,0	22,4	19,2	17,6	16,0	13,0	10,1	7,4	4,9	2,4							
43	26,8	23,1	19,6	16,4	14,8	13,3	10,4	7,6	5,0	2,5								
42	23,8	20,2	16,8	13,7	12,2	10,7	7,8	5,1	2,6									
41	20,8	17,3	14,0	10,9	9,4	8,0	5,2	2,6										
40	17,8	14,4	11,2	8,2	6,7	5,3	2,6											

3 Alkohol-Umrechnungstabelle für die Gehaltsangabe in Volumenprozent (% vol), Massenprozent (% mas), Gramm pro Liter (g/l) und die Dichte ϱ (g/cm³) entsprechender Alkohol/Wasser-Mischungen bei 20 °C

% vol	% mas	g/l	ϱ (20°C)	% vol	% mas	g/l	ϱ (20°C)
1	0,8	7,9	0,9967	26	21,2	205,2	0,9670
2	1,6	15,8	0,9952	27	22,1	213,1	0,9658
3	2,4	23,7	0,9938	28	22,9	221,0	0,9646
4	3,2	31,6	0,9924	29	23,8	228,9	0,9634
5	4,0	39,5	0,9910	30	24,6	236,8	0,9622
6	4,8	47,4	0,9897	31	25,5	244,7	0,9609
7	5,6	55,2	0,9884	32	26,4	252,6	0,9596
8	6,4	63,1	0,9872	33	27,2	260,5	0,9583
9	7,2	71,0	0,9859	34	28,0	268,4	0,9570
10	8,0	78,9	0,9847	35	28,9	276,2	0,9556
11	8,8	86,8	0,9835	36	29,8	284,1	0,9542
12	9,6	94,7	0,9824	37	30,6	292,0	0,9527
13	10,5	102,6	0,9812	38	31,5	299,9	0,9512
14	11,3	110,5	0,9801	39	32,4	307,8	0,9496
15	12,1	118,4	0,9790	40	33,3	315,7	0,9480
16	12,9	126,3	0,9779	41	34,2	323,6	0,9464
17	13,7	134,2	0,9768	42	35,1	331,5	0,9448
18	14,6	142,1	0,9757	43	36,0	339,4	0,9431
19	15,4	150,0	0,9746	44	36,9	347,3	0,9413
20	16,2	157,9	0,9730	45	37,8	355,2	0,9395
21	17,0	165,7	0,9725	46	38,7	363,1	0,9377
22	17,9	173,6	0,9714	47	39,6	371,0	0,9359
23	18,7	181,5	0,9703	48	40,6	378,8	0,9340
24	19,6	189,4	0,9692	49	41,5	386,7	0,9321
25	20,4	197,3	0,9681	50	42,4	394,6	0,9301

Tab. H. 3

% vol	% mas	g/l	ϱ (20 °C)	% vol	% mas	g/l	ϱ (20 °C)
51	43,3	402,5	0,9282	76	69,0	599,8	0,8701
52	44,3	410,4	0,9261	77	70,0	607,7	0,8675
53	45,3	418,3	0,9241	78	71,2	615,6	0,8648
54	46,2	426,2	0,9221	79	72,3	623,5	0,8620
55	47,2	434,1	0,9199	80	73,5	631,4	0,8593
56	48,2	442,0	0,9178	81	74,6	639,3	0,8565
57	49,1	449,9	0,9157	82	75,8	647,2	0,8536
58	50,1	457,8	0,9135	83	77,0	655,1	0,8507
59	51,1	465,7	0,9113	84	78,2	663,0	0,8478
60	52,1	473,6	0,9091	85	79,4	670,9	0,8448
61	53,1	481,5	0,9069	86	80,6	678,8	0,8418
62	54,1	489,3	0,9046	87	81,8	686,7	0,8388
63	55,1	497,2	0,9023	88	83,1	694,6	0,8356
64	56,1	505,1	0,9000	89	84,4	702,4	0,8325
65	57,2	513,0	0,8976	90	85,7	710,3	0,8292
66	58,2	520,9	0,8953	91	87,0	718,2	0,8258
67	59,2	528,8	0,8929	92	88,3	726,1	0,8223
68	60,3	536,7	0,8905	93	89,7	734,0	0,8188
69	61,3	544,6	0,8880	94	91,0	741,9	0,8152
70	62,4	552,5	0,8856	95	92,4	749,8	0,8114
71	63,5	560,4	0,8830	96	93,8	757,7	0,8074
72	64,6	568,3	0,8805	97	95,3	765,6	0,8033
73	65,6	576,2	0,8780	98	96,8	773,5	0,7989
74	66,7	584,1	0,8754	99	98,4	781,4	0,7942
75	67,8	591,9	0,8728	100	100,0	789,3	0,7893

4 Extrakt-Umrechnungstabelle für die Gehaltsangabe in Massenprozent, Mostgewicht und Gramm pro Liter

Bezugssubstanz: Saccharose; Bezugstemperatur: 20 °C
Zur Ermittlung des Zuckergehaltes von Mosten und Maischefiltraten sind die Nichtzuckerstoffe in Abzug zu bringen (s. G.3.4.1)

%	Mostgewicht	g/l	%	Mostgewicht	g/l	%	Mostgewicht	g/l
0,0	0,0	0	14,0	56,8	148	22,0	91,9	240
1,0	3,9	10	14,2	57,7	150	22,2	92,8	242
2,0	7,8	20	14,4	58,5	152	22,4	93,8	245
3,0	11,7	30	14,6	59,4	155	22,6	94,6	247
4,0	15,7	41	14,8	60,2	157	22,8	95,6	250
5,0	19,7	51	15,0	61,1	159	23,0	96,5	252
6,0	23,7	62	15,2	62,0	161	23,2	97,4	254
7,0	27,7	72	15,4	62,8	164	23,4	98,3	257
7,6	30,2	78	15,6	63,7	166	23,6	99,2	259
7,8	31,0	80	15,8	64,5	168	23,8	100,1	262
8,0	31,8	82	16,0	65,4	170	24,0	101,0	264
8,2	32,6	84	16,2	66,3	173	24,2	101,9	266
8,4	33,4	87	16,4	67,1	175	24,4	102,9	269
8,6	34,3	89	16,6	68,0	177	24,6	103,8	271
8,8	35,1	91	16,8	68,9	180	24,8	104,7	274
9,0	35,9	93	17,0	69,8	182	25,0	105,6	276
9,2	36,7	95	17,2	70,6	184	25,2	106,6	279
9,4	37,5	97	17,4	71,5	186	25,4	107,5	281
9,6	38,4	100	17,6	72,4	189	25,6	108,4	284
9,8	39,2	102	17,8	73,2	191	25,8	109,3	286
10,0	40,0	104	18,0	74,1	193	26,0	110,3	289
10,2	40,9	106	18,2	75,0	196	26,2	111,2	291
10,4	41,7	108	18,4	75,9	198	26,4	112,1	293
10,6	42,5	110	18,6	76,8	200	26,6	113,1	296
10,8	43,3	112	18,8	77,6	202	26,8	114,0	298
11,0	44,2	115	19,0	78,5	205	27,0	114,9	301
11,2	45,0	117	19,2	79,4	207	27,2	115,9	303
11,4	45,8	119	19,4	80,3	210	27,4	116,8	306
11,6	46,7	121	19,6	81,2	212	27,6	117,7	308
11,8	47,5	123	19,8	82,1	214	27,8	118,7	311
12,0	48,4	126	20,0	83,0	217	28,0	119,6	313
12,2	49,2	128	20,2	83,9	219	28,2	120,6	316
12,4	50,0	130	20,4	84,7	221	28,4	121,5	318
12,6	50,9	132	20,6	85,6	223	28,6	122,5	321
12,8	51,7	134	20,8	86,5	226	28,8	123,4	323
13,0	52,6	137	21,0	87,4	228	29,0	124,4	326
13,2	53,4	139	21,2	88,3	230	29,2	125,3	328
13,4	54,3	141	21,4	89,2	233	29,4	126,3	331
13,6	55,1	143	21,6	90,1	235	29,6	127,2	333
13,8	56,0	146	21,8	91,0	238	29,8	128,2	336
14,0	56,8	148	22,0	91,9	240	30,0	129,1	339

5 Volumenveränderung von Alkohol/Wasser-Mischungen in Abhängigkeit von der Temperatur (nach *Schopfer*)

Angegeben sind die Volumenerhöhungen in $^0/_{00}$ (oder ml/l) gegenüber dem Volumen bei 0 °C

Alkoholgehalt		Temperatur (°C)							
% vol	% mas	5	10	15	20	25	30	35	40	50
0	0	−0,1	+0,1	0,7	1,6	2,8	4,2	5,8	7,7	11,8
6,3	5	0	0,4	1,2	2,0	3,2	4,8	6,5	8,4	12,8
12,4	10	0,2	1,0	1,9	3,2	4,7	6,4	8,3	10,6	15,6
18,6	15	0,8	1,9	3,2	4,9	6,9	9,1	11,2	13,6	19,3
24,6	20	1,5	3,2	5,0	7,2	9,5	12,1	14,8	17,6	23,9
30,4	25	2,2	4,3	6,9	9,4	12,5	15,5	18,4	21,9	28,8
36,2	30	2,7	5,6	8,7	11,8	15,2	18,7	22,3	25,9	33,8
41,9	35	3,1	6,5	10,0	13,5	17,1	21,1	25,3	29,3	37,8
47,4	40	3,5	7,2	11,2	15,3	19,2	23,3	27,6	31,9	41,0
52,7	45	3,9	7,7	11,9	16,1	20,4	24,9	29,3	34,0	43,4
57,9	50	4,1	8,1	12,5	17,1	21,5	26,3	31,0	35,8	45,5
62,9	55	4,3	8,3	12,9	17,4	22,0	26,7	31,7	36,4	46,4
67,7	60	4,5	9,0	13,6	18,2	23,0	27,9	32,9	38,1	48,8
72,4	65	4,6	9,2	13,9	18,6	23,6	28,5	33,6	38,7	49,2
77,0	70	4,8	9,4	14,2	19,1	24,3	29,3	34,6	40,2	51,2
85,5	80	5,0	9,7	15,0	20,3	25,5	30,8	36,5	42,0	53,5
93,3	90	5,2	9,9	15,3	20,5	25,9	31,6	37,4	43,4	55,5
100	100	5,4	10,5	16,1	21,7	27,3	33,3	39,2	45,1	57,4

Beispiel: Das Volumen eines Branntweins (ca. 42% vol) nimmt bei einer Temperaturerhöhung von 15 auf 25 °C um 7,1 ml pro l zu (Differenz zwischen entsprechenden Tabellenwerten bilden!)

I BEGRIFFE UND AUSDRÜCKE

Kurze Umschreibung einiger wichtiger Begriffe und Ausdrücke, soweit nicht schon im Textteil darauf eingegangen wurde (Übersicht s. Sachregister). Für nähere Angaben und Definitionen im Wortlaut wird auf die zitierten Gesetzestexte verwiesen.

Absinth

Wermutkräuterdestillat. Enthält das Nervengift Thujon, welches bei chronischem Mißbrauch epileptische Anfälle hervorruft und zu schweren psychischen Schäden (Verblödung) führen kann. Das Herstellen und Inverkehrbringen von Absinth ist in den meisten europäischen Staaten verboten.

Absoluter Alkohol

ist ein nahezu wasserfreier Ethylalkohol mit einer Gradstärke von mindestens 99,8% vol. Verwendung für technische und medizinische Zwecke (s. auch Stichwort »Sprit«).

Alkohol

s. Spezialkapitel K.

Aprikosenbrand

auch Marillenbrand, wird vor allem in Ungarn hergestellt und ist unter dem Namen »Barack Palinka« (spr. Barask) bekannt. Die Lagerung in Eichenfässern verleiht ihm eine hellgoldgelbe Farbe.

Armagnac

Französischer Weinbrand. Geschützte Bezeichnung für das Erzeugnis aus der gleichnamigen Landschaft in der Gascogne (Südfrankreich). Das Armagnac-Brenngerät muß einen kontinuierlichen Zufluß haben und mit doppelter oder dreifach aufeinandergesetzter Brennblase versehen sein. Im Gegensatz zu Cognac (s. dort) wird Armagnac nur einmal gebrannt.

Azeotrop

Gemisch zweier oder mehrerer Flüssigkeiten, dessen Dampf dieselbe Zusammensetzung wie die flüssige Phase aufweist. Ein solches Gemisch läßt sich also durch Destillation nicht in seine Bestandteile zerlegen (keine Anreicherung der leichterflüchtigen Komponente(n) im Dampf). Bekanntestes Beispiel ist das Gemisch Alkohol/Wasser (95,57% mas bzw. 97,2% vol) mit einem sogenannten Minimumsiedepunkt von 78,15°C (reiner A. siedet bei 78,3°C). Absoluter Alkohol (s. dort) läßt sich also nicht allein durch Destillation von Alkohol/Wasser-Gemischen gewinnen; es müssen zusätzlich wasserentziehende Mittel verwendet werden.

Begriffsbestimmungen für Spirituosen

1989 wurden europäische Begriffsbestimmungen für Spirituosen (EG-BegrBest) in Kraft gesetzt (EWG-VO Nr. 1576/89). Zusammen mit nachgeordneten Erlassen, in denen Detailfragen geregelt sind, ersetzen sie die bisherigen einschlägigen Bestimmungen der einzelnen Staaten. Für die Schweiz geltende Bestimmungen finden sich in der Verordnung über Lebensmittel und Gebrauchsgegenstände (Lebensmittelverordnung).

Brand
s. Stichwort »Branntwein«.

Brandy
s. Stichwort »Weinbrand«.

Branntwein
Dieser Begriff hat mehrere Bedeutungen. Während im bisherigen Sprachgebrauch darunter vor allem extraktfreie und extraktarme Spirituosen mit oder ohne Geschmackszutaten zu verstehen waren, also eigentlich die meisten nicht zu den Likören gehörenden Spirituosen, soll im EG-Raum und neuerdings auch in der Schweiz diese Bezeichnung offiziell nur noch für Destillate aus Wein verwendet werden. Für Destillate aus Obststoffen tritt die Bezeichnung »Brand« mit zusätzlicher Nennung der Frucht, z.B. »Birnenbrand«. Für Brände aus Steinobst (z.B. Kirschen und Zwetschgen) ist jedoch auch die Bezeichnung »...wasser« zulässig, s.a. Stichwort »Obstbrand«. Zur monopolrechtlichen Bedeutung des Begriffs s. Kapitel L.

Calvados
Geschützte Bezeichnung für französisches Destillat aus Apfelwein (cidre), welches durch Lagerung in Eichenholzfässern seine Bernsteinfarbe und sein besonderes Bukett erhält. Name vom Departement Calvados (Normandie).

Cartiergrade
In der Schweiz noch gelegentlich von Hausbrennern verwendete Alkoholskala. Cartier-Alkoholometer verfügen über kein Thermometer; sie sind ungenau und nicht eichfähig. Zur amtlichen Feststellung der Gradstärke dürfen sie nicht eingesetzt werden.
Die Beziehung zwischen Cartier- und Volumenprozent-Skala gibt folgende Tabelle wieder:

Cart.-Grade		% vol	Cart.-Grade		% vol	Cart.-Grade		% vol
17	=	38	22	=	57	26	=	68
18	=	43	23	=	60	27	=	71
19	=	47	24	=	63	28	=	73
20	=	51	25	=	66	29	=	75
21	=	54				30	=	78

Cognac
Französischer Weinbrand. Geschützte Bezeichnung für das Erzeugnis genau festgelegter Gebiete der Charente (nördlich von Bordeaux). Als Ausgangsstoff dient unfiltrierter Wein, der ausschließlich aus bestimmten weißen Traubensorten wie Ugni blanc, Colombard und Folle blanche gewonnen wurde. Die Destillation erfolgt in den typischen zwiebelförmigen Cognac-Brennblasen im Rauh/Feinbrand-Verfahren. Wie beim Armagnac (s. dort) sind Lagerungsverfahren und Bezeichnungen genau umschrieben.

Degustation

oder Sinnenprüfung gibt die erste Auskunft über das Aussehen der Untersuchungsprobe, über Vorhandensein und Reinheit der für die vorliegende Spirituose sortentypischen Geruchs- und Geschmacksstoffe sowie über allfällige degustativ wahrnehmbare Fremdzusätze oder Fehler, herrührend von verdorbenen oder ungeeigneten Roh- und Hilfsstoffen, verdorbenen Maischen, Fehlern bei der Herstellung, Lagerung usw. Bei der Prüfung auf Geruch und Geschmack leisten tulpenförmige Degustationsgläser mit eingeschliffenem Deckel oder Cognac-Schwenker gute Dienste. Die Degustation ist bei einer Temperatur von 20–25°C sowohl am Originalprodukt als auch am mit einwandfreiem Trinkwasser auf ca. 30% vol verdünnten Originalprodukt vorzunehmen (s. auch Stichwort »Qualitätsprüfungen«).

Dephlegmation

Durch Kühlung erreichte Teilkondensation eines Gasgemisches; dabei wird der restliche, nicht kondensierte Dampf gegenüber dem Kondensat mit der leichterflüchtigen, d. h. tiefersiedenden Komponente angereichert. Bei Alkohol/Wasser-Dämpfen werden also durch Dephlegmation ein alkoholreicherer Dampf und eine alkoholärmere Flüssigkeit (Phlegma) gewonnen.

Edelbranntwein

Diese früher in den deutschen Begriffsbestimmungen für Erzeugnisse überdurchschnittlicher Qualität vorgesehene Bezeichnung ist in den EG-BegrBest nicht mehr aufgeführt (s. a. Stichwort »Branntwein«).

Enzian

ist ein aus vergorenen Enzianwurzeln mit oder ohne Zusatz von Alkohol gewonnenes Destillat. Zuckerzusatz und Färbung sind unzulässig.

Grappa

ist ein Destillat aus vergorenen Traubentrestern oder aus einer Mischung von vergorenen Traubentrestern und Weindrusen oder Trauben. Bezeichnung für Erzeugnisse Italiens und der Südschweiz. Vielfach wird dem Grappa ein Zweig der Gartenraute (Ruta graveolens) beigefügt.

Himbeergeist

s. Stichworte »Obstgeist« und »Obstbrand«.

Kernobstbranntwein

ist die monopolrechtliche Bezeichnung für das Destillat aus vergorenen Äpfeln und/oder Birnen, aus vergorenen Teilen dieser Früchte oder aus Apfel- oder Birnenwein. Die EG-BegrBest unterscheiden »Obstbrand« (s. dort) und »Brand aus Apfel- oder Birnenwein« (s. a. Stichwort »Calvados«).
Ein Destillat aus vergorenen Quitten gilt in der Schweiz monopolrechtlich nicht als Kernobst-, sondern als Spezialitätenbranntwein und wird von der Alkoholverwaltung auch nicht übernommen.

Kirschbrand

in der Schweiz »Kirschenbrand«, kann auch als »Kirsch« oder als »Kirschwasser« bezeichnet werden (s. a. Stichworte »Branntwein«, »Obstbrand«).

Likör

Spirituose mit einem Mindestzuckergehalt von 100 g/l (Schweiz: 50 g/l) und einem Mindestalkoholgehalt von 15% vol. Der Alkohol muß landwirtschaftlichen Ursprungs sein. Ausnahmen bezüglich Alkohol- und Zuckergehalt sind in den EG-BegrBest geregelt (Beispiele: Mindestalkoholgehalt von Eierlikör 14% vol, Mindestzuckergehalt von Kirschlikör 70 g/l, von Eierlikör 150 g/l), ebenso die Verwendung bzw. der Mindestgehalt gewisser Zutaten (Beispiel: Eierlikör muß mindestens 150 g Eigelb/l enthalten).

Obstbrand

Offizieller Oberbegriff für Spirituosen, die bisher auch als »Obstbranntweine« bezeichnet wurden. Darunter fallen zum einen die Brände aus vergorenen Früchten oder den vergorenen Mosten dieser Früchte, wobei ein Zuckerzusatz unzulässig ist. Die gewonnenen Spirituosen werden unter Voranstellung des Namens der verwendeten Frucht als »...brand« oder »...wasser« bezeichnet. In gewissen Fällen sind auch Kurzformen wie »Kirsch« oder »Williams« möglich. Ebenfalls unter diesen Begriff fallen Destillate aus nicht vergorenen oder nur angegorenen Früchten, die mit neutralem, hochprozentigem Alkohol landwirtschaftlichen Ursprungs überzogen wurden. In diesem Fall ist auch die Bezeichnung »...geist« zulässig, wie z.B. »Himbeergeist«.

Obstgeist

wird aus frischen oder tiefgekühlten Früchten (v.a. Beeren) durch Zugabe von Alkohol und nachfolgende Destillation gewonnen (s. auch Stichwort »Obstbrand«).

Obstwasser

s. Stichwort »Obstbrand«.

Qualitätsprüfungen

von Spirituosen werden von der Deutschen Landwirtschafts-Gesellschaft (DLG) auf freiwilliger Basis durchgeführt mit dem Ziel, die Herstellung und den Absatz hochwertiger Erzeugnisse zu fördern. Die Prüfung umfaßt chemische und physikalische Untersuchungen sowie eine degustative Beurteilung durch Sachverständige. Die neutral, d.h. ohne Kenntnis der Herkunft geprüften Erzeugnisse werden aufgrund der vorgenommenen Untersuchungen eingestuft und gegebenenfalls prämiert. Anmeldeunterlagen sind erhältlich bei DLG, Fachbereich Markt und Ernährung, Eschborner Landstraße 122, 60489 Frankfurt a.M.

Rektifikation

Mehrmalige Destillation einer alkoholhaltigen Flüssigkeit ohne dazwischenliegendes Abfangen von Destillat, wobei der entstehende alkoholreichere Dampf und die alkoholärmere Flüssigkeit im Gegenstrom aneinander vorbeigeführt werden. Zur Erzielung einer optimalen Verstärkungswirkung ist ein möglichst vollständiger Stoff- und Wärmeaustausch zwischen flüssiger und gasförmiger Phase erforderlich. Dies wird in der Praxis durch sogenannte Glockenböden erreicht. Nicht zu vergessen ist der zusätzliche Reinigungseffekt der Rektifikation.

Spirituosen

sind nach den EG-BegrBest alkoholische Flüssigkeiten, die zum menschlichen Verbrauch bestimmt sind, besondere organoleptische Eigenschaften und einen Mindestalkoholgehalt von 15% vol aufweisen. Der in Spirituosen enthaltene Alkohol muß durch Gärung und nachfolgende Destillation aus landwirtschaftlichen Rohstoffen gewonnen sein.

Sprit (Trinksprit)

auch Neutralalkohol genannt, wird in den EG-BegrBest als »Äthylalkohol landwirtschaftlichen Ursprungs« bezeichnet; im Anhang I dieser Bestimmungen sind auch die Anforderungen an diesen festgelegt (Alkoholgehalt z. B. mindestens 96% vol).

Steinhäger

s. Stichwort »Wacholder«.

Synthesealkohol

wird heute hauptsächlich aus Ethylen, einem Nebenprodukt der Erdölverarbeitung, hergestellt. Seine Verwendung zu Genußzwecken ist nicht erlaubt.

Verschnitt

ist in den EG-BegrBest als ein Verfahren definiert, bei welchem einer Spirituose Ethylalkohol landwirtschaftlichen Ursprungs zugesetzt wird.

Wacholder

ist ein Erzeugnis aus der Kategorie »Spirituose mit Wacholder«, welches aus Sprit und/oder Korndestillat unter Zugabe von Wacholderdestillat und/oder Wacholderlutter hergestellt wird. Wacholderdestillat gewinnt man durch Destillation von Wacholderbeeren nach Überziehen mit Alkohol. Wacholderlutter wird das Destillat aus vergorener Wacholderbeermaische genannt (Rauhbrand mit max. 15% vol). »Steinhäger« ist eine geschützte geographische Herkunftsbezeichnung; sein Aroma stammt hauptsächlich aus Wacholderlutter, welcher unter Zusatz von Sprit und/oder Getreidedestillat feingebrannt wurde; daneben darf lediglich eine geringe Menge an Wacholderbeeren zugesetzt werden.

Weinbrand

auch Brandy genannt, ist Weindestillat, welches in Eichenholzbehältern mindestens ein Jahr oder aber mindestens sechs Monate, wenn das Fassungsvermögen der Eichenfässer unter 1000 Litern liegt, gereift ist. S. a. Stichworte »Armagnac« und »Cognac«.

Weingeist

historische Bezeichnung für Alkohol (s. Spezialkapitel K).

Williams

s. Stichwort »Obstbrand«.

Zwetschgenwasser

s. Stichwort »Obstbrand«.

K ALKOHOL

Chemische Formel CH$_3$-CH$_2$-OH oder C$_2$H$_6$O   Molmasse: 46,07

Für das in der Umgangssprache »Alkohol« genannte Gärungsprodukt sind auch die Bezeichnungen Ethylalkohol, Ethanol, Weingeist oder Sprit im Gebrauch. Reiner Alkohol (r.A.) ist eine klare, farblose, würzig riechende und brennend schmeckende, leicht entzündliche Flüssigkeit. In kleinen Mengen läßt sich A. in der Atmosphäre, in Gewässern und im Erdboden nachweisen, d.h. überall dort, wo nasse, zucker- oder stärkehaltige Substanzen durch die allgegenwärtigen Hefezellen vergoren werden. Alkohol findet sich auch im menschlichen Blut (physiologischer Gehalt 0,02–0,03‰) sowie in tierischen Geweben.

1 Physikalische und chemische Eigenschaften

Dichte (20°C): 0,7893 g/cm^3 Siedepunkt: 78,3°C   Schmelzpunkt: –114,5°C

Alkohol verbrennt mit schwach leuchtender Flamme zu Kohlendioxid und Wasser. Der Flammpunkt (d.h. die niedrigste Temperatur, bei der laufend soviel A. verdunstet, daß die Dämpfe zusammen mit Luft ein durch Fremdzündung entflammbares Gemisch ergeben), beträgt 12°C. **Luft/Alkoholdampf-Gemische** sind im Bereich von 3,4–15% vol **explosiv**. Dies gilt es in Brennereien zu beachten, wo laufend A. verdunstet. Da A.dämpfe schwerer als Luft sind, sammeln sie sich am Boden der Räume an. Damit die untere Explosionsgrenze nicht erreicht werden kann, ist für eine ausreichende Lüftung zu sorgen. Größere Sammelgefäße für hochprozentige Destillate sollten ohnehin nicht in unmittelbarer Nähe von Brenngeräten oder offenem Feuer aufgestellt werden und sind gut verschlossen zu halten.

Mit Wasser ist A. in jedem beliebigen Verhältnis mischbar. Das Volumen der Mischung ist jedoch geringer als die Summe der beiden Einzelvolumina vor dem Vermischen **(Kontraktion)**. So ergeben z.B. 50 l reiner A. und 50 l Wasser nicht 100 l Mischung, sondern nur ca. 96,3 l mit 51,9 % vol. Die Kontraktion beträgt demnach 3,7 l (s. auch Tab. 14). Der Mischvorgang ist außerdem mit einer Erwärmung verbunden.

Tab.14: Kontraktion beim Mischen von Alkohol und Wasser

A.gehalt der Mischung (% vol)	100 l der Mischung enthalten Alkohol (l)	Wasser (l)	Kontraktion (l)
10	10	90,7	0,7
20	20	81,7	1,7
30	30	72,7	2,7
40	40	63,4	3,4
50	50	53,7	3,7
53,93	53,93	49,84	3,77
60	60	43,7	3,7
70	70	33,4	3,4
80	80	22,8	2,8
90	90	11,9	1,9

In Tabelle 15 sind die **Gefrierpunkte** von Alkohol/Wasser-Mischungen angegeben. Bei extrakthaltigen Spirituosen liegen die entsprechenden Werte noch tiefer.

Tab. 15 : Gefrierpunkte von Alkohol/Wasser-Mischungen

Alkoholgehalt (% vol)	10	20	30	40	50	60
Gefrierpunkt (°C)	−3,5	−8	−15	−23	−31	−39

2 Physiologische und toxische Wirkungen

Nach der Einnahme gelangt der A. via Magen und Darm rasch ins Blut und von dort in den ganzen Körper, so auch in die Nerven und Hirnzellen. In der Leber wird A. durch Oxidation mit einer Geschwindigkeit von etwa 0,1 g pro kg Körpergewicht und Stunde abgebaut; bei mäßigem Genuß ist somit der größte Teil des Alkohols nach 6–8 Stunden vom Körper verarbeitet oder ausgeschieden (kleine Mengen auch via Atemluft und Harn).
Die Wirkung von A. ist primär von der Dosis abhängig: kleinere Mengen wirken anregend, größere Mengen dagegen berauschend und narkotisierend. Daneben bestehen beträchtliche individuelle Unterschiede (Alter, Geschlecht usw.). Kinder sind besonders empfindlich; die tödliche Dosis für ein 5–6jähriges Kind liegt bei 30 ml A. Frauen haben eine geringere A.toleranz als Männer: während beim Mann in der Regel erst ab täglich 60 ml reinem A. eine Fettleber oder mit der Zeit auch eine irreversible Hepatitis (Leberentzündung) auftritt, die dann zur Zirrhose (Verhärtung und Schrumpfung) führt, sind es bei der Frau schon 20 ml täglich. Außerdem sind alkoholische Getränke umso schädlicher, je höher ihr A.gehalt ist. Branntwein schadet also mehr als Bier (bei gleichen A.mengen). Hinzu kommt, daß der Abbau von A. durch Begleitstoffe wie Fuselöle und Ester verzögert wird. Weitere wirkungsbeeinflussende Faktoren sind der allgemeine Gesundheitszustand, die gleichzeitige Einnahme von Medikamenten, klimatische Verhältnisse sowie die Zeitspanne, in der eine bestimmte A.menge eingenommen wird. Wegen des leichten Übertritts von A. in den Blutkreislauf des Embryos ist auch auf seine teratogene (fruchtschädigende) Wirkung hinzuweisen. A.konsum in der Schwangerschaft ist eine der häufigsten Ursachen der angeborenen Idiotie.
Eine akute Vergiftung durch einmaligen Genuß einer größeren A.menge äußert sich durch Gesichtsrötung, allgemeines Wärmegefühl und Enthemmung. Einem anfänglich erhöhten Bewegungsdrang folgen Ermüdung und Muskelerschlaffung, erschwertes Sprechen, Gleichgewichtsstörungen, und schließlich kann Bewußtlosigkeit mit Atemstillstand eintreten. Schwere Trunkenheit entspricht einem Blutalkoholgehalt von 2–3‰.
Bei fortgesetztem A.mißbrauch kommt es zu einer Beeinträchtigung aller inneren Organe (neben den bereits erwähnten Leberschäden z.B. Verdauungsstörungen und Gefäßkrankheiten) sowie zu psychischen Störungen (Persönlichkeitsveränderungen, intellektueller Abbau).

3 Herstellung, Verwendung und Verbraucher

A. gehört zu den volkswirtschaftlich und technisch wichtigsten Substanzen. Neben seiner Rolle als Genußmittel sind in erster Linie die vielfältigen Anwendungsmöglichkeiten in Labor, Gewerbe und Industrie von Bedeutung. Eine Übersicht mit Anwendungsbeispielen zeigt Tabelle 16:

Tab. 16: Herstellung, Verwendung und Verbraucher von Sprit (nach einer Zusammenstellung der Eidg. Alkoholverwaltung)

	ZUCKERHALTIGE ROHSTOFFE	STÄRKEHALTIGE ROHSTOFFE, HOLZ		ETHYLEN usw.
Herstellung	Gärung Rektifikation	Verzuckerung Gärung Rektifikation		Synthese Rektifikation
SPRIT	TRINKSPRIT	VERBILLIGTER SPRIT	INDUSTRIESPRIT	SEKUNDASPRIT
Verwendung	**Lösungen** Spirituosen Liköre Verschnitte Wermut Essenzen Pharmazeutische Erzeugnisse **Extraktionen** Essenzen Aromen	**Synthese** von chemischen Wirkstoffen für Pharmazeutika, Kosmetika, Chemikalien **Lösungen** Pharmazeutische Erzeugnisse Sirupe, Salben, homöopathische Heilmittel, Tierheilmittel Parfums, Kölnisch Wasser Körperpflegemittel Sprays, Nagellacke **Extraktionen, Fällungen** Drogenextrakte, Leberextrakte Enzyme, Alkaloide, Vitamine Etherische Oele, Pflanzenextrakte, Essenzen, Aromen **Desinfektion, Sterilisation** Hautdesinfektion **Spezielle Reinigungsverfahren** **Reagens**	**Synthese** von Aldehyden, Aminen, Estern, Ethern, Sprengstoffen, Kunststoffen, Heilmitteln, Waschmitteln **Lösungen** Farben, Lacke, Harze, Verdünner, Kunststoffe, photographische Emulsionen, Seifen, Tinten, Bremsöle Umdruckflüssigkeit, Sprays **Extraktionen, Fällungen, Kristallisationen** Pektin, Enzyme, Vitamine, Drogen, Alkaloide, Chem. Verbindungen **Treibstoffzusatz** **Desinfektion, Sterilisation** Chirurg. Instrumente **Reinigung** Maschinen, Uhrenbestandteile, Möbel **Reagens**	**Lösungen** Lacke, Farben, Tinten Verdünner, Klebstoffe Reinigungsmittel **Brennstoff** **Reinigung** Maschinen, Haushalt
Verbraucher	Lebensmittelindustrie Pharm. Industrie Apotheken, Drogerien	Pharmazeutische Industrie Chemische Industrie Elektronikindustrie Apotheken, Drogerien Laboratorien, Spitäler Ärzte, Zahnärzte usw.	Essighersteller Pharmazeutische Industrie Chemische Industrie Lack- und Farbenindustrie Seifen-, Maschinen-, Uhren-, Textilind. Graphisches Gewerbe Apotheken, Drogerien Laboratorien, Spitäler	Chemische Industrie Lack- und Farbenindustrie Möbelindustrie Graphisches Gewerbe Haushalt

L GESETZLICHES

Kurzartikel über die gesetzlichen Grundlagen der Obstbrennerei in Deutschland, der Schweiz und Österreich, unter besonderer Berücksichtigung der Haus- und Kleinbrennerei.

1 Deutschland

von Ministerialrat Jarsombeck, Bonn

Die allgemeinen steuerlichen und monopolrechtlichen Bedingungen für die Herstellung von Branntwein* in der Bundesrepublik Deutschland sind in dem **Gesetz über das Branntweinmonopol** vom 8. April 1922 und seinen Durchführungsverordnungen (Grundbestimmungen, Brennereiordnung, Alkoholverordnung) geregelt. Aufgrund des staatlichen Branntweinmonopols ist der hergestellte Branntwein gemäß § 58 BranntwMonG grundsätzlich ablieferungspflichtig. Ausnahmen gelten u. a. für Branntwein aus Obststoffen und jeglichen Branntwein, der in einer Abfindungsbrennerei hergestellt ist (§ 76 Abs. 1 BranntwMonG).

Die Herstellung des (ablieferungsfreien) Obstbranntweins ist eine Domäne der deutschen Kleinbrennereien. Diese arbeiten entweder unter zollamtlichem Mitverschluß (Verschlußbrennereien) oder unverschlossen und werden dann in einem steuerlichen Pauschalierungsverfahren »abgefunden« – sogenannte Abfindungsbrennereien (§ 57 BranntwMonG i.V.m. § 114 ff Brennereiordnung). Da die Produktion der Verschlußkleinbrennereien mengenmäßig keine Rolle spielt, soll im folgenden im wesentlichen nur von den **Abfindungs**brennereien die Rede sein.

Die ca. 31.000 Abfindungsbrennereien – in diesen Brennereien wurde im Betriebsjahr 1991/92 ca. 60.000, darunter 50.000 hl A. aus Obststoffen erzeugt – sind auf die südlichen Regionen Deutschlands beschränkt mit besonderer Konzentration auf Baden-Württemberg. Ihre Zahl ist nicht beliebig vermehrbar, da für die einzelnen Oberfinanzbezirke sogenannte Grenzzahlen festgelegt sind, die nicht überschritten werden können (§ 119 Brennereiordnung). Unter einer »Abfindungsbrennerei« versteht man eine kleine Destillieranlage, die unter Verzicht auf die sonst vorgeschriebenen amtlichen Verschlüsse (wie Plomben, Zollschlösser u. a.) Branntwein erzeugt und deren (kontingentsmäßig beschränkte) Produktion in einem amtlichen Schätzverfahren pauschal ermittelt wird. Dies geschieht in der Weise, daß für die einzelnen Brennrohstoffe bestimmte **Ausbeutesätze** (§§ 120 ff Brennereiordnung) festgelegt sind, anhand derer in Verbindung mit der eingesetzten Rohstoffmenge die erzeugte Alkoholmenge fiktiv errechnet wird. Das Verfahren ist seit Jahren weitgehend automatisiert: Der Brennereibesitzer ist verpflichtet (§ 168 Brennereiordnung), mindestens fünf Werktage vor dem Beginn des Brennens bei der »Zentralstelle Abfindungsbrennereien bei dem Hauptzollamt Stuttgart-West« eine sog. **Abfindungsanmeldung** abzugeben und hierin Angaben u. a. über Art und Menge der zu brennen-

---

* Unter »**Branntwein**« versteht das Gesetz über das Branntweinmonopol sowohl den hochgrädig destillierten Alkohol (Sprit) als auch das Destillat mit dem typischen auf den Rohstoff hinweisenden Aroma (z. B. Rum, Kirschwasser u. ä.).

den Stoffe zu machen. Hieraus errechnet die EDV-Anlage die maßgebende Menge Branntweins, die der amtlichen Erfassung zugrundezulegen ist.

Es gibt drei Klassen von Abfindungsbrennereien:
Obstabfindungsbrennereien dürfen nur Obst, Beeren, Wein, Weinhefe, Most, Wurzeln oder Rückstände davon verarbeiten (Oststoffe i. S. des § 27 BranntwMonG).

Landwirtschaftliche Abfindungsbrennereien müssen mit einem landwirtschaftlichen Betrieb verbunden sein. Grundsätzlich dürfen nur Kartoffeln oder Getreide gebrannt werden. Darüber hinaus sind aber auch **selbst**gewonnene Oststoffe zur Verarbeitung »im Zwischenbetrieb« zugelassen.

Gewerbliche Abfindungsbrennereien sind in der Rohstoffauswahl grundsätzlich frei; sie verarbeiten überwiegend Oststoffe.

Das gesetzliche Brennkontingent der Abfindungsbrennerei beträgt in der Regel 3 hl A. pro Jahr. Innerhalb der Grenzzahl **neu** zugelassene Obstbrennereien dürfen lediglich 50 l A. aus **selbstgewonnenen** Oststoffen unter Abfindung brennen (§ 116 Brennereiordnung). Lediglich die Obstabfindungsbrennereien haben das Recht, zum Ausgleich von Rekord- und Mißernten innerhalb eines »**Abschnitts**« von zehn Jahren das hierauf entfallende Gesamtkontingent nach freiem Belieben auf die einzelnen Jahre zu verteilen. So könnte z. B. eine Brennerei in einem Jahr mit der Produktion ganz aussetzen, im nächsten Jahr dafür aber das Doppelte brennen.

Es bestehen zwei Möglichkeiten der Branntweinverwertung:

1. Der Brenner vermarktet sein Erzeugnis selbst. In diesem Fall erhält er von der »Zentralstelle Abfindungsbrennen« einen Steuerbescheid. Die Steuer für Branntwein aus Kleinbrennereien ist ermäßigt (§ 131 Abs. 2 BranntwMonG). Der Steuersatz für Branntwein aus Steinobst, Beeren oder Enzianwurzeln beträgt z. Zt. 2.000 DM/hl A. (Regelsatz: 2.550 DM), für Branntwein aus anderen Rohstoffen hingegen 2.175 DM/hl A. Die besondere Ermäßigung für Branntwein aus Steinobst u. a. wird mit den besonders hohen Rohstoffkosten begründet. Die Branntweinproduktion kleinerer Betriebe wird im übrigen nicht nur dann steuerlich begünstigt, wenn sie aus dem Inland stammt. Vielmehr kommen nach § 131 Abs. 2 Satz 3 BranntwMonG auch **ausländische** Brennereien mit einer Jahresproduktion bis zu 10 hl A. in den Genuß der ermäßigten Steuersätze. Kleinbrennereien, z. B. aus der Schweiz und Österreich, die in Deutschland ihre Originalerzeugnisse absetzen wollen, werden insoweit also den deutschen Brennereien gleichgestellt. Dies entspricht den gegenseitigen steuerlichen Diskriminierungsverboten nach Art. 18 der Freihandelsabkommen der EG mit der Schweiz und Österreich vom 22. Juli 1972.

2. Der Brenner liefert den erzeugten Branntwein an die **Bundesmonopolverwaltung für Branntwein** in Offenbach ab. Diese Ablieferungsmöglichkeit (§ 76 Abs. 2 BranntwMonG) besteht jedoch nur für Branntwein aus Kernobst und mehligen Stoffen, scheidet also aus für z. B. Branntwein aus Steinobst, der von den Brennereien ohne Schwierigkeiten selbst vermarktet werden kann. Die Übernahmepreise errechnen sich nach §§ 65, 69, 72 Abs. 2 BranntwMonG. Sie betragen für Kernobstbranntwein z. Zt. das Zweieinhalbfache des Branntweingrundpreises. Dies ist der Preis, der die durchschnittlichen Herstellungskosten in einer 500-hl-Kartoffelbrennerei repräsentiert.

Für beide Verwertungsmöglichkeiten gilt:

Sind die tatsächlichen Rohstoffausbeuten höher als die nach den amtlichen Ausbeutesätzen – was die Regel sein wird –, so verbleibt die sogenannte **Überausbeute** dem Brenner steuerfrei und ohne Verwendungsvorbehalte zur Verfügung. Besondere steuerfreie Mengen für den Hausbedarf sind dem deutschen Branntweinsteuerrecht nicht bekannt.

Neben den Abfindungsbrennern selbst gibt es noch eine weitere – zahlenmäßig beträchtliche – Gruppe von Kleinstherstellern (registriert sind mehr als 700.000 Personen). Es sind dies die sogenannten **Stoffbesitzer** (§ 36 BranntwMonG, § 9 Brennereiordnung), die – gerätebedingt – mit den Abfindungsbrennereien in einer Art Symbiose zusammenarbeiten. Unter Stoffbesitzern versteht man nämlich solche Personen **ohne eigenes Brenngerät**, die **selbstgewonnene** Obststoffe in einer fremden Brennerei brennen. Diese Personen gelten nach deutschem Steuerrecht als Branntweinhersteller und werden deshalb auch Steuerschuldner. Ebenso wie die Abfindungsbrenner, deren Brenngerät sie benutzen (oder benutzen lassen), haben sie vor dem Brennen Abfindungsanmeldungen abzugeben. Ihre steuerlichen und monopolrechtlichen Vergünstigungen entsprechen denen der Abfindungsbrenner, doch ist ihr Erzeugungskontingent auf nur 50 l A. im Jahr festgeschrieben, allerdings dürfen sie auch im »Abschnitt« brennen (§ 41 Abs. 1 BranntwMonG). Es gibt Abfindungsbrennereien, in denen mehrere hundert Stoffbesitzer ihr Obst brennen. Auch in diesem Fall verlangt die deutsche Gesetzgebung, daß das Obst der zahlreichen Besitzer getrennt voneinander gelagert und gebrannt wird (§ 174 Brennereiordnung). Von den eingangs genannten 60.000 hl A. haben im Betriebsjahr 1991/92 Stoffbesitzer mehr als 18.000 hl A. erzeugt.

Die Abfindungsbrennereien sind in der Regel Nebenerwerbsbetriebe. Sie dienen damit der Existenzsicherung kleinbäuerlicher und kleingewerblicher Betriebe (z.B. Wirtshäuser), mittelbar aber auch der Landschaftspflege, weil die lukrative Verwertung von Obst über den Brennkessel zur Erhaltung der Obstbaumbestände beiträgt. Das Abfindungs- und Stoffbesitzerbrennen entlastet den heimischen Obstmarkt um ca. 200.000 t im Jahr.

Neben den Abfindungsbrennern und Stoffbesitzern gibt es noch zwei weitere Gruppen von Obstbranntweinherstellern. Es sind dies die sogenannten **Obstverschlußbrennereien,** die Obstbranntwein unter Zollkontrolle herstellen und voll versteuern müssen, sowie die **Obstgemeinschaftsbrennereien** (§ 37 BranntwMonG). Die letzteren sind genossenschaftlich organisiert mit der Maßgabe, daß pro Genosse aus dessen selbstgewonnenen Obststoffen nicht mehr als 3 hl A. produziert werden. Mit der Schaffung dieses Typs der Verschlußbrennerei hatte der Gesetzgeber die Hoffnung verknüpft, hiermit die zahllosen Stoffbesitzer »einzufangen«. Diese Hoffnung erfüllte sich nicht. 1978 wurden die den Kleinbrennereien entsprechenden steuerlichen Vergünstigungen aufgehoben. Die Obstgemeinschaftsbrennereien haben jedoch weiterhin das Recht, ihren Kernobstbranntwein zu gleichen Preisen wie die Kleinbrenner an das Monopol abzuliefern.

Quellen:
1. Das Gesetz über das Branntweinmonopol und seine Durchführungsverordnungen sowie die zahlreichen Dienstanweisungen sind abgedruckt und auf dem neuesten Stand gehalten in:
»Vorschriftensammlung Bundesfinanzverwaltung – VSF –, Stoffgebiet: Verbrauchsteuern, Abschnitt: Branntweinmonopol und Branntweinsteuer«, Vertrieb: Bundesanzeiger Verlagsgesellschaft mbH, Köln.
2. Hoppe/Heinricht, Kommentar zum Branntweinmonopolgesetz nebst Ausführungsbestimmungen (4 Bände). Verlag der Versuchs- und Lehranstalt für Spiritusfabrikation und Fermentationstechnologie, Berlin.

2 Schweiz

von Sektionschef Bechler, Bern

Bedingt durch die im letzten Jahrhundert überbordende Kartoffelschnaps-Schwemme wurde mit der **Alkoholordnung von 1885/86** erstmals eine Regelung der Alkoholherstellung auf Bundesebene erreicht. Damit verfügten die Behörden über ein wirksames Instrument zur Kontrolle der Kartoffelbrennerei, während die Obstbrennerei vorerst von jeder Überwachung und Besteuerung ausgenommen blieb. Mit der starken Ausdehnung des Mostobstanbaues zu Beginn dieses Jahrhunderts wurde die Schweiz von billigem Obstbranntwein überschwemmt, so daß eine weitergehende Alkoholgesetzgebung geschaffen werden mußte. Grundlage dazu bildete der im Jahre 1930 vom Volk angenommene **Verfassungsartikel 32 bis**, mit welchem der Bund beauftragt wurde, auf dem Wege der Gesetzgebung Vorschriften über die Herstellung, die Einfuhr, die Reinigung, den Verkauf und die fiskalische Belastung gebrannter Wasser* zu erlassen. Damit sollte der Verbrauch von Trinkbranntwein und dementsprechend auch dessen Herstellung und Einfuhr vermindert werden.

Mit dem **Bundesgesetz über die gebrannten Wasser** vom 21. 6. 32 (Alkoholgesetz) sowie dem **Bundesgesetz über die Konzessionierung der Hausbrennerei** vom 23. 6. 44 (Hausbrennereigesetz) wurden die Voraussetzungen geschaffen, den Verbrauch gebrannter Wasser in den Griff zu bekommen. Durch Verfassung und Gesetz steht das Recht zur Herstellung und Reinigung gebrannter Wasser ausschließlich dem Bunde zu **(Monopol)**, wobei aber die Ausübung durch Erteilung von **Konzessionen** Dritten überlassen wird. Die Durchführung des Monopols ist der **Alkoholverwaltung** übertragen, welche über eine

---

* Als **gebrannte Wasser** im Sinne des Alkoholgesetzes gelten in erster Linie Sprit und Branntwein, also durch Destillation gewonnene Erzeugnisse. Beim **Sprit** handelt es sich um hochgrädig destillierten Alkohol, welcher die Eigenschaften (Aroma und Geschmack) der verwendeten Rohstoffe ganz oder fast ganz verloren hat. Sprit wird zur Herstellung von Getränken und Genußmitteln sowie zu pharmazeutisch-kosmetischen und chemisch-technischen Zwecken verwendet. **Branntweine** zum Trinkverbrauch haben wegen der weniger hochgrädigen Destillation ihr typisches Aroma behalten. In der Schweiz wird Kernobst- und Spezialitätenbranntwein hergestellt. Aus dem Ausland werden auch Branntweine wie Whisky, Wodka, Cognac und Rum eingeführt, deren Rohstoffe in der Schweiz nicht gebrannt werden dürfen. Nicht unter die Alkoholgesetzgebung fallen die ausschließlich durch Vergärung gewonnenen alkoholischen Erzeugnisse wie Wein und Bier, vorausgesetzt, daß ihnen weder Sprit noch Branntwein zugemischt wurde. Ist dies der Fall (z. B. bei Wermut), so gelten sie ebenfalls als gebrannte Wasser.

Außendienstorganisation (Kreisinspektoren, örtliche Brennereiaufsichtsstellen) verfügt. Sie hat durch geeignete Maßnahmen für die Einschränkung sowohl des Angebots als auch der Nachfrage zu sorgen. Dazu gehören beispielsweise die Beschränkung der Brennereirohstoffe (ausländisches Kernobst, Rohstoffe aus Zucker, Melasse und Getreide sowie Kartoffeln dürfen nicht gebrannt werden), die Förderung der brennlosen Verwertung (z. B. alkoholfreie Obstsäfte, Kartoffel als Nahrungs- und Futtermittel) ebenso wie die Verminderung der Brennapparate durch freiwilligen Aufkauf. Die Nachfrage wird in erster Linie durch fiskalische Belastung vermindert; aber auch vorbeugende Maßnahmen (Aufklärungs- und Werbetätigkeit) werden ergriffen.

Wie ist nun die Obstbrennerei in der Schweiz organisiert und welche Vorschriften sollte der Branntweinproduzent kennen? Die Antwort auf diese Fragen findet man in erster Linie in der **Vollziehungsverordnung** zum Alkohol- und Hausbrennereigesetz. Als **Branntweinproduzenten** gelten nicht nur die Brenner, sondern auch die sogenannten **Brennauftraggeber,** welche über keinen eigenen Brennapparat verfügen. Sie müssen ihre Rohstoffe bei einem **Lohnbrenner** verarbeiten lassen. Für den Betrieb von Brennereien werden verschiedene **Konzessionen** erteilt:

1. Als **Hausbrenner** gilt, wer einen Landwirtschaftsbetrieb selber bewirtschaftet und ausschließlich Rohstoffe des selbstbewirtschafteten Bodens oder selber gesammeltes Wildgewächs brennt. Die **Hausbrennerkonzession** wird erteilt, wenn der Inhaber eines Brennapparates die Bedingungen für die Anerkennung als Hausbrenner erfüllt. Insbesondere ist zu beachten, daß prinzipiell nur Hausbrennereien konzessioniert werden können, die 1930 anläßlich der Erhebung gemeldet und numeriert worden sind. In der **Konzessionsurkunde** werden die Brennapparate aufgeführt, für welche die Konzession Geltung hat. Standortveränderungen, Umänderungen oder Ersatz eines Brennapparates bzw. einzelner Teile davon sind bewilligungspflichtig; Reparaturen müssen vor ihrer Ausführung gemeldet werden (siehe Konzessionsbedingungen). Die bäuerliche Branntweinerzeugung ist – im Gegensatz zur voll besteuerten gewerblichen Produktion – steuerfrei, soweit sie für den Haushalt und den Landwirtschaftsbetrieb des Produzenten benötigt wird. In bestimmten Fällen ist die Alkoholverwaltung befugt, für diesen sogenannten, **steuerfreien Eigenbedarf** eine Höchstmenge festzusetzen. Dies kann sie insbesondere dann, wenn der Hausbrenner auch eine Ausschankbewilligung für geistige Getränke besitzt oder wenn die beanspruchte Menge steuerfreien Branntweins auf einen Mißbrauch schließen läßt. Der Konzessionsinhaber ist außerdem verpflichtet, alljährlich bei der Brennereiaufsichtstelle eine **Brennkarte** zu beziehen, auf welcher er die vorgeschriebenen Angaben über Branntweinerzeugung, -vorräte sowie über die Verwendung des Branntweins laufend einzutragen hat. Dies gilt sinngemäß auch für den **Hausbrennauftraggeber,** welcher die Brennkarte mit den Rohstoffen dem Lohnbrenner zu übergeben und mit dem Branntwein wieder zurückzunehmen hat. Für die Weitergabe von Kernobst- und Spezialitätenbranntwein an Dritte ist der Brennkarteninhaber steuerpflichtig. Die Vollziehungsverordnung zum Alkohol- und Hausbrennereigesetz befaßt sich speziell im dritten Abschnitt (Art. 37–66) mit Hausbrennern und Hausbrennauftraggebern.

2. Wer Branntwein herstellt, aber die Anforderungen an den Status eines Hausbrenners nicht erfüllt, gilt als **Gewerbebrenner** und ist für den hergestellten Branntwein voll steuerpflichtig, unbekümmert darum, ob er auf gewerblicher Basis oder nur für den Eigenbedarf Branntwein produziert. Für den Betrieb einer Gewerbebrennerei dürfen gemäß Alkoholgesetz Konzessionen nur soweit erteilt werden, als dies den wirtschaftlichen Bedürfnissen des Landes entspricht. Gewerbliche Konzessionen werden erteilt für die
– Herstellung von **Kernobstbranntwein**
– Herstellung von **Spezialitätenbranntwein** und
– für den Betrieb einer **Lohnbrennerei.**
Die für die Konzessionsinhaber geltenden Vorschriften sind in **Pflichtenheften** zusammengefaßt. Für Gewerbebrenner und **gewerbliche Brennauftraggeber** ist außerdem der zweite Abschnitt (Art. 2–36) der obenerwähnten Vollziehungsverordnung maßgebend. Mit der **Besteuerung** befaßt sich der vierte Abschnitt (Art. 67–72), wobei die Höhe der Steuersätze durch besondere Verordnungen des Bundesrates festgesetzt wird. Zur Zeit (1994) beträgt die sogenannte Selbstverkaufsabgabe auf Kernobstbranntwein Fr. 26.– je Liter 100 % Alkohol und die Steuer auf Spezialitätenbranntwein Fr. 21.50 je Liter 100 % Alkohol. Importierte Branntweine werden mit einer sogenannten Monopolgebühr und nach 100 kg brutto fiskalisch belastet, was, je nach Branntweinart, umgerechnet einer Besteuerung von Fr. 32.– bis 58.– je Liter 100% A. entspricht.

Anmerkung

Nach dem geltenden Alkoholgesetz werden die Steuern auf in- und ausländischen Branntweinen unterschiedlich veranlagt (inländische nach Liter 100 % Alkohol, ausländische nach 100 kg brutto). Außerdem sind die Steuersätze für inländische gebrannte Wasser wesentlich tiefer als für ausländische. Bei einem Beitritt zum EWR wäre diese Diskriminierung beseitigt worden.

Bereits im Rahmen der damaligen Konsultationsverfahren wurde der Spirituosenbranche zugesichert, die vorgesehenen Revisionen auch bei einem allfälligen Abseitsstehen der Schweiz nach und nach zu verwirklichen. Ebenso hat der Bundesrat in Beantwortung einer parlamentarischen Anfrage betreffend Besteuerung der Spirituosen ausgeführt, daß es unumgänglich sein werde, die Steuersätze auf inländischen und auf importierten Spirituosen mindestens nach und nach näher zusammenzuführen. Die gegenwärtige Besteuerung von Spirituosen diskriminiere die ausländischen Waren im Handel und stehe darum nicht im Einklang mit den GATT-Bestimmungen. Zur Zeit ist deshalb eine Revision des Bundesgesetzes über die gebrannten Wasser im Gange.

Schwerpunkte der Revision sind die Vereinheitlichung der Bemessungsgrundlagen bei der Besteuerung in- und ausländischer Spirituosen (Hektoliter 100 % vol) sowie die Schaffung eines Einheitssteuersatzes. Die Höhe dieses Satzes wird auf Verordnungsstufe festgelegt. Zur Verminderung des administrativen Aufwands werden gleichzeitig eine Änderung der Kontrolle des Kleinhandels sowie in verschiedenen Bereichen Anpassungen an die geltende Praxis der Alkoholverwaltung vorgeschlagen.

Quellen:
Bundesgesetz über die gebrannten Wasser (Alkoholgesetz) vom 21. Juni 1932.
Bundesgesetz über die Konzessionierung der Hausbrennerei vom 23. Juni 1944.
Vollziehungsverordnung zu diesen beiden Gesetzen vom 6. April 1962
(Stand am 1. Oktober 1989).
Pflichtenhefte der Eidgenössischen Alkoholverwaltung (EAV) für Gewerbebrennereien:
– Pflichtenheft für Lohnbrenner
– Pflichtenheft m. Anhang für Kernobst- und Spezialitätenbrenner.
Broschüren der EAV:
»Die Eidgenössische Alkoholverwaltung«, »Was sind Spirituosen«, »Die Alkoholordnung im Dienste der Volksgesundheit«.
Entwurf zur Botschaft betreffend Änderung des Bundesgesetzes über die gebrannten Wasser (Alkoholgesetz) vom 6. Oktober 1993.

Adresse: Eidg. Alkoholverwaltung, Postfach, 3000 **Bern** 9, Telefon 031 309 12 11

3 Österreich
von Hofrat Univ. Prof. Dipl. Ing. Dr. Weiss, Klosterneuburg

Mit dem Bundesgesetz vom 31. August 1994 (703. Bundesgesetz, mit dem das Gesetz über das Branntweinmonopol an das Gemeinschaftsrecht angepaßt wird; Alkohol-Steuer und Monopolgesetz 1995) wurde in Österreich das Branntweinmonopolgesetz an jenes der Europäischen Union angepaßt. Damit verlieren die Bestimmungen des Branntweinmonopolgesetzes 1922 sowie die damit verbundenen Ausführungsbestimmungen und Verordnungen mit dem Beitritt der Republik Österreich zur Europäischen Union ihre Gültigkeit. Verordnungen auf Grund dieses Bundesgesetzes können bereits von dem seiner Kundmachung folgenden Tag erlassen werden.

Die Herstellung von Branntwein erfolgt entweder in **Verschlußbrennereien** (§ 20ff) oder unter **Abfindung** (§ 55ff). Für den bäuerlichen Produzenten wird in erster Linie die Herstellung von Alkohol unter Abfindung von Bedeutung sein. Dabei werden selbstgewonnene Stoffe auf einem zugelassenen einfachen Brenngerät verarbeitet.

Das Gesetz unterteilt die selbstgewonnenen **alkoholbildenden Stoffe** in

a) Früchte heimischer Arten von Stein- und Kernobst, Beeren, Wurzeln, Getreide und Halmrüben, die der Verfügungsberechtigte als Eigentümer, Pächter oder Nutznießer einer Liegenschaft geerntet hat (die Herstellung von Alkohol unter Abfindung aus Getreide oder Halmrüben ist nur zulässig, wenn diese durch einen Verfügungsberechtigten in einem Bergbauernbetrieb geerntet worden sind und ihm nicht genügend andere alkoholbildende Stoffe zur Verfügung stehen);

b) wild wachsende Beeren und Wurzeln, die der Verfügungsberechtigte gesammelt hat oder sammeln ließ;

c) Produkte, die bei der Verarbeitung von in a) bezeichneten Früchten durch den Verfügungsberechtigten ohne einen Zusatz von Waren, die die Alkoholausbeute erhöhen können, angefallen sind;

d) Produkte, die bei der Verarbeitung von in a) bezeichneten Früchten durch den Verfügungsberechtigten angefallen sind, soweit sie den Bestimmungen des Weingesetzes 1985 entsprechen;

e) Wein im Sinne des Weingesetzes 1985, der bei der Verarbeitung von Weintrauben durch den Verfügungsberechtigten angefallen ist.

Ein **einfaches Brenngerät** besteht aus einer Heizung, einer Brennblase, einem Helm, einem Geistrohr und einer Kühleinrichtung. Nicht gestattet sind:
a) kontinuierlicher Betrieb;
b) Blaseninhalt größer als 150 l (Rauminhalt der Blase ist die Litermenge, die durch Wassereinguß bis zum Überlaufen bei der obersten Füllöffnung ermittelt wird);
c) zum Entleeren der Blase andere Einrichtungen als ein Ablaßhahn oder eine Kippvorrichtung;
d) andere Öffnungen an Brennblase und Helm als Füllöffnungen und Öffnungen zum Geistrohr, zum Ablaßhahn und Schauglas.

Als **Füllraum** der Brennblase gelten 80% ihres Rauminhaltes, wenn der Rauminhalt des Helmes 36% des Rauminhaltes der Brennblase nicht übersteigt. Einfache Brenngeräte können mit folgenden Sondereinrichtungen ausgestattet werden:
– Wasserbad bis 0,5 bar
– Ablaßhahn oder Kippvorrichtung
– Rührwerk
– Rohr, durch das Dampf aus dem Wasserbad in die Brennblase geleitet wird
– Öl-, Gas- oder Elektroheizung
– Ölbad
– Verstärkungsanlagen, die aus nicht mehr als drei Böden und einem Dephlegmator bestehen.

Der Antrag auf **Zulassung** eines einfachen Brenngerätes ist durch dessen Eigentümer schriftlich bei dem Zollamt durchzuführen, in dessen Bereich das Brenngerät aufbewahrt werden soll. Nach einem gesetzlich festgelegten Verfahren erfolgt die bescheidmäßige Zulassung; diese erlischt, wenn am Brenngerät Veränderungen durchgeführt werden.

Auch die **Anmeldung** zur Herstellung von Alkohol unter Abfindung hat fristgerecht (mindestens 5 Werktage vor Brennbeginn) und schriftlich beim zuständigen Zollamt zu erfolgen. Die Anmeldung gilt als Steuererklärung und ist gebührenfrei (Gebührenpflicht entsteht, wenn Sonderwünsche angemeldet werden, z.B. Änderung der Brennfrist). Eine Bewilligung gilt als erteilt, wenn das Zollamt nicht innerhalb von drei Tagen nach Anmeldung einen negativen Bescheid erläßt.

Die Alkoholmenge, die der Steuer unterliegt **(Abfindungsmenge),** und der Zeitraum, der zum Herstellen der Abfindungsmenge erforderlich ist, werden pauschal nach amtlicherseits festgelegten Durchschnittswerten bestimmt. Dem Abfindungsberechtigten steht jährlich eine Erzeugungsmenge von 100 l Alkohol zum ermäßigten Steuersatz von öS 54,– je l Alkohol zu. Er kann jedoch über diese Erzeugungsmenge hinaus jährlich 100 l Alkohol zum Steuersatz von öS 90,– je l Alkohol herstellen. Eine abschnittsweise Abfindung sieht das neue Gesetz nicht mehr vor.

Die erforderliche Zeit zur Herstellung des Alkohols **(Brenndauer)** ist auf eine Folge von Tagen zu verteilen. Unterbrochen kann die Brenndauer durch Sonntage, gesetzliche Feiertage oder Stunden zwischen 18.00 Uhr und 6.00 Uhr werden (in besonderen begründeten Fällen auch in anderer Weise). Das einfache Brenngerät darf vor Beginn der Brennfrist nicht befüllt und muß vor Ablauf der Brennfrist entleert sein. Werden gemischte Maischen angemeldet, so hat die Berechnung nach jener Stoffgattung zu erfolgen, für welche der höchste Ausbeutesatz festgesetzt ist.

Eine endgültige Festlegung der **Ausbeutesätze** (Liter Ethanol je Hekoliter Maische) liegt zum Zeitpunkt der Manuskriptabgabe (1994) noch nicht vor, vorerst gelten folgende:

Kirschen	5,0
Zwetschgen und Mirabellen	5,5
Sonstiges Steinobst	3,0
Kernobst	3,0
Kernobsttrester	1,0
Weinbeeren	4,5
Vogelbeeren und Wacholderbeeren	1,5
Sonstiges Beerenobst	2,0
Traubenweinhefe, flüssig	3,0
Traubenweinhefe, gepreßt	2,0
Obstweinhefe, flüssig oder gepreßt	2,0
Weintrester, vollständig ausgepreßt	1,0
Tresterwein	4,0
Topinamburs	3,5
Enzian und sonstige Wurzeln	2,0

Von jener Alkoholmenge, die im Rahmen eines land- und forstwirtschaftlichen Betriebes in einem Jahr unter Abfindung hergestellt wird, sind für den **Hausbedarf** für den abfindungsberechtigten Landwirt (einschließlich Ehepartner) 15 l Alkohol und für jeden Haushaltsangehörigen, der zu Beginn des Kalenderjahres das 19. Lebensjahr vollendet hat, 6 l Alkohol (bis zu einer Höchstmenge von 51 l Alkohol) in den Bundesländern Tirol und Vorarlberg bzw. 3 l Alkohol (bis zu einer Höchstmenge von 27 l Alkohol) in allen anderen Bundesländern, bestimmt. Landwirt ist, wer einen land- und forstwirtschaftlichen Betrieb als selbständige Wirtschaftseinheit allein oder zusammen mit Haushaltsangehörigen bewirtschaftet und daraus seinen und den Lebensunterhalt seiner Familie zumindest zu einem erheblichen Teil bestreitet. Weiters muß der abfindungsberechtigte Landwirt seinen ordentlichen Wohnsitz am land- und forstwirtschaftlichen Betrieb, der den Mittelpunkt seiner Lebensinteressen darstellt, haben.

Der Abfindungsberechtigte hat die auf die Abfindungsmenge entfallende Steuer selbst zu berechnen **(Selbstberechnung)** und den Steuerbetrag in der Abfindungsanmeldung anzugeben. Steht dem Abfindungsberechtigten eine Steuerbefreiung (s. Hausbedarf) zu, ist vor Berechnung der Steuer von der Abfindungsmenge die steuerfreie Alkoholmenge abzuziehen. Die Steuerschuld entsteht mit Beginn des Brennvorganges und ist bis zum 25. des auf das Entstehen der Steuerschuld folgenden Kalendermonats bei dem zuständigen Zollamt zu entrichten.

Der unter Abfindung hergestellte Alkohol (einschließlich des alkoholsteuerfrei erzeugten Alkohols für den Hausbedarf) darf an folgende Personen veräußert werden:

a) Letztverbraucher (in Kleingebinden mit einem deutlich sichtbaren Vermerk, daß der Inhalt unter Abfindung hergestellt wurde);
b) Gast- und Schankgewerbetreibende (ebenfalls mit Abfindungsvermerk) zum Weiterverkauf im Gast- und Schankbetrieb;
c) Inhaber eines Alkohollagers.

Alle Abfindungsberechtigten haben ein **Überwachungsbuch** zu führen, in dem Art und Menge der zur Herstellung von Alkohol bestimmten alkoholbildenden Stoffe unverzüglich aufzuzeichnen sind. Aus diesem Buch muß zu ersehen sein:
a) Behälter, in denen sich die Waren befinden;
b) Tag, an dem mit der Herstellung von Alkohol begonnen und über die Stoffe verfügt wird;
c) Art der Verfügung über die Stoffe;
d) wenn Alkohol an Inhaber von Alkohollagern abgegeben wird (s. oben), die Alkoholmenge; weiters hat er diese Tatsache dem Zollamt unverzüglich zu melden.

Wer vor Inkrafttreten dieses Gesetzes berechtigt war, Branntwein unter Abfindung mit einer Erzeugungsgrenze von 300 l Weingeist herzustellen, kann, wenn er die Voraussetzungen für die Herstellung von Alkohol unter Abfindung erfüllt, weiterhin 300 l Alkohol herstellen, wenn das Brenngerät nicht vom Aufbewahrungsort weggebracht und ausschließlich von dessen Eigentümer verwendet wird. 300-l-Abfindungsbrenner, denen das Recht zusteht, alkoholbildende Stoffe zuzukaufen, dürfen dies auch weiterhin tun. Ein Zusatzkontingent von 100 l Alkohol zu einem Steuersatz von öS 90,– steht auch den 300-l-Abfindungsbrennern zu.

Verschlußbrennereien sind Teile von Betrieben, in welchen auf verschlußsicheren Herstellungsanlagen unter Steueraussetzung Alkohol durch Destillation oder andere Verfahren gewonnen, gereinigt und anschließend einer üblichen Lagerbehandlung unterzogen werden kann. Das Errichten und Betreiben von Verschlußbrennereien bedarf die Erfüllung einer ganzen Reihe von Erfordernissen, die im Alkohol-Steuer- und Monopolgesetz 1995 aufgelistet sind. Für Kleinproduzenten ist von Interesse, daß auch die Möglichkeit besteht, unter definierten Auflagen, eine Verschlußbrennerei mit einer Jahreserzeugung bis zu 400 l Alkohol zu errichten. Allerdings ist diesen Produzenten das Verbringen oder Verbringenlassen von Alkohol außerhalb des Steuergebietes verboten. Verschlußbrennereien mit einer Jahreserzeugung bis zu 400 l Alkohol haben eine ermäßigte Alkoholsteuer von öS 54.– je l Alkohol zu entrichten.

Werden Destillate in den Verkehr gebracht – das Österreichische Lebensmittelgesetz 1975 versteht unter **Inverkehrsetzung** im Zusammenhang mit Lebensmitteln im allgemeinen jede Tätigkeit, sofern sie »... zu Erwerbszwecken ... geschieht.« – so finden hinsichtlich der Etikettierung die Bestimmungen der **Lebensmittelkennzeichnungsverordnung** 1993 (LMKV 1993) und im Hinblick auf die Produktqualität die Bestimmungen des Österreichischen Lebensmittelbuches, Kapitel B 23 (Spirituosen) Anwendung.

Die LMKV 1993 sieht verpflichtend folgende Kennzeichnungselemente vor:
– Sachbezeichnung (z. B. Österreichischer Qualitätskirschbrand)
– Erzeugername und Firmensitz
– Füllmenge (falls dies nicht auf der Flasche angegeben ist)
– Los
– Alkoholgehalt in Volumenprozenten.

Weiters ist bei Destillaten, die im Abfindungswege hergestellt worden sind, diese Tatsache zu deklarieren.

M ANALYSENZAHLEN

Soweit es möglich ist, verbindliche Grenzwerte aufzustellen, sind in den meisten Staaten die analytischen Anforderungen an Spirituosen auf dem Verordnungswege geregelt. Dies betrifft in erster Linie den Alkoholgehalt, aber auch charakteristische Begleitstoffe, wie Methanol, höhere Alkohole, Säuren und Ester, sowie allfällige Zusätze und Zutaten. Die ständig verbesserten Analysenmethoden bedingen aber auch eine Anpassung bzw. Erweiterung bestehender Grenzwerte. In den nachfolgenden Abschnitten sind die wichtigsten analytischen Anforderungen an Obstbrände und einige andere Spirituosen aufgeführt. Zu beachten ist jedoch, daß diese Bestimmungen recht häufigen Änderungen unterworfen sind. Für nähere Angaben und Definitionen im Wortlaut wird auf die zitierten Gesetzestexte verwiesen.

1 EG-Staaten

1.1 Alkohol

Die **Mindest**alkoholgehalte sind in den **europäischen Begriffsbestimmungen für Spirituosen** (EWG-Verordnung Nr. 1576/89 vom 29. Mai 1989) festgelegt. Beispiele aus Art. 3, Abs. 1:

Branntwein	
Tresterbrand	
Brand aus Obsttrester	
Obstbrand	37,5% vol
Brand aus Apfel- oder Birnenwein	
Enzian	
Grappa	
Brandy/Weinbrand	36% vol

In den einzelnen Mitgliedstaaten können für Spirituosen mit geschützten Herkunftsbezeichnungen höhere Mindestalkoholgehalte gefordert werden (Art. 3, Abs. 2). Beispiele:

Deutschland	Deutscher Weinbrand	
	Fränkischer Obstler	38% vol
	Bayerischer Gebirgsenzian	
	Steinhäger	
	Schwarzwälder Kirschwasser	
	Schwarzwälder Himbeergeist	
	Schwarzwälder Mirabellenwasser	
	Schwarzwälder Williamsbirne	40% vol
	Schwarzwälder Zwetschgenwasser	
	Fränkisches Zwetschgenwasser	
	Fränkisches Kirschwasser	

Frankreich	Cognac Armagnac Marc de Bourgogne Marc d'Alsace Gewürztraminer Calvados Eau-de-vie de poire de Bretagne Eau-de-vie de cidre de Normandie	40% vol
	Mirabelle de Lorraine	45% vol
Italien	Brandy italiano Grappa di Barolo Südtiroler Grappa Südtiroler Williams Südtiroler Kirsch Südtiroler Marille Südtiroler Gravensteiner Slivowitz del Veneto Südtiroler Enzian	38% vol

1.2 Methanol

In der bereits erwähnten EWG-Verordnung Nr. 1576/89 sowie in ergänzenden Durchführungsbestimmungen sind folgende **Höchstwerte** für Methanol aufgeführt (**Mindest**werte f. Deutschland s. 2. Abschn.):

Branntwein, Brandy/Weinbrand	200 g/hl r. A.
Tresterbrand Obstbrand Brand aus Apfel- oder Birnenwein	1000 g/hl r. A.
Brand aus Obsttrester	1500 g/hl r. A.
Pflaumenbrand Mirabellenbrand Zwetschgenbrand Apfel- und Birnenbrand	1500 g/hl r. A. (vorläufiger Wert)

1.3 Weitere Inhaltsstoffe

In den unter 1.2 erwähnten EWG-Verordnungen sind zusätzlich Grenzwerte für den **Minimal**gehalt an **"flüchtigen Bestandteilen"**, d. h. die Gesamtheit flüchtiger Stoffe mit Ausnahme von Ethanol und Methanol angegeben:

Branntwein, Brandy/Weinbrand	125 g/hl r. A.
Tresterbrand	140
Obstbrand	200
Brand aus Obsttrester	200
Brand aus Apfel- oder Birnenwein	200

Für Obst- bzw. Obsttresterbrand aus **Steinobst** gilt zudem ein **maximaler Blausäuregehalt** von 10 g/hl r. A.

2 Deutschland

In der **Verordnung über den Gehalt an charakteristischen Begleitstoffen** (Bundesgesetzblatt I, S. 1678, 1971) sowie in einem Entwurf zu **Beschaffenheitsbedingungen von Obstbranntweinen** sind folgende **Mindest**gehalte für Methanol aufgeführt (N. B.: die Angabe in mg/100 ml r. A. entspricht der Angabe in g/hl r. A.):

Brände aus	Mindest-Methanolgehalt
Kirschen	400 mg/100 ml r. A.
anderem Steinobst	710
Kernobst außer Williams	320
Williamsbirnen	790
Weintrestern	480
Kernobsttrestern	630
Enzianwurzeln	1580
Weinhefe, Wein	Spuren

3 Schweiz

3.1 Alkohol

Bisher war der **Mindest**alkoholgehalt der für den Konsum bestimmten Branntweine gemäß **Lebensmittelverordnung** (LMV) **generell auf 40% vol** festgesetzt. Nach Inkrafttreten der revidierten LMV gelten die EG-Werte (s. 1.1). Der **Höchstgehalt** beträgt 55% vol.
Ergänzend wäre noch zu bemerken, daß auch Spirituosen mit einer Frucht (z. B. Williamsbirnen) trotz Frucht den Mindestalkoholgehalt aufweisen müssen. Die Anforderungen sind also nicht erfüllt, wenn die betreffende Spirituose den Mindestalkoholgehalt lediglich vor der Abfüllung aufwies.

3.2 Methanol

Seit einigen Jahren sind die Höchstwerte für Methanol in der **Fremd- und Inhaltsstoffverordnung** (FIV) geregelt. Für Spirituosen gilt generell ein Grenzwert von 16000 mg/l Alkohol (entspricht 1600 g/hl r.A.).

3.3 Weitere Inhaltsstoffe

Die FIV (s. 3.2) gibt für Spirituosen folgende **Höchstkonzentrationen** an (sog. Toleranzwerte, Angaben in mg/l r.A.):

Acetaldehyd	800
(Ausnahmen: Marc, Grappa	1600)
Alkohole, höhere (ohne Propanol)	5000
Cyanid (berechnet als HCN)	50
Propanol	35000
Säuren, flüchtige (als Essigsäure)	1500
Schweflige Säure (als SO_2)	50
Summe von Eisen, Kupfer und Zink	25

Die LMV (siehe 3.1) regelt außerdem den Extraktgehalt von Obstbränden. Dieser darf höchstens 10 g/l betragen. Ausnahmen: Brände aus Kirschen, Zwetschgen und Pflaumen dürfen höchstens 3 g/l Gesamtextrakt enthalten.

Das Kapitel 32 »Spirituosen« des Schweizerischen Lebensmittelbuches enthält **Erfahrungswerte** von handelsüblichen Branntweinen, die zwar keine Rechtsnormen darstellen, aber bei der Beurteilung entsprechender Produkte nützlich sein können. Die nachstehende Tabelle beruht zur Hauptsache auf gaschromatographischen Untersuchungen der Lebensmittelkontrolle. Zur Ermittlung der Tabellenwerte wurden 5% der Mindest- und Höchstwerte eliminiert und aus den verbleibenden Daten Mittelwert (m) und Standardabweichung (s) berechnet. Bei fehlender Angabe von s liegt keine Normalverteilung vor.

Tab. 17 : Erfahrungswerte handelsüblicher Branntweine (n = Anzahl Proben)

	Bestandteile in mg/l Ethanol	Kirsch n = 850		Williams n = 293		Pflaumen und Zwetschgen n = 129		Trauben-Trester n = 215		Hefe und Drusen n = 33		Grappa n = 50		Kernobst-Branntwein n = 135	
		m	s	m	s	m	s	m	s	m	s	m	s	m	s
1	Methanol	5200	920	11800	2600	9800	2400	11000		520	330	8600		3200	
2	1-Propanol	13000		3200		1400		700	400	650	90	600	250	1000	
3	2-Butanol	520		480		140		350		260		450		500	
4	2-Methyl-1-Propanol	380	120	630	270	550	250	750	190	850	340	800	260	800	300
5	1-Butanol	45		200	90	110		90		100		60	40		
6	2-Methyl- + 3-Methyl-1-Butanol	1000	270	1500	470	1250	500	2000	370	2400	970	1900	500	2700	650
7	Summe 3 + 4 + 5 + 6	1850	540	2600	800	2000	770	3050	550	3400	1270	3100	640	3900	850
8	Verhältnis 6 : 4	2,2	0,74	2,0	0,55	1,8	0,55	1,9	0,76	2,3	0,91	1,9	0,9	2,9	0,84

3.4 Anforderungen an den von der Eidgenössischen Alkoholverwaltung zu übernehmenden Kernobstbranntwein*

Merkmale		Aus Äpfeln, Birnen, Mischungen dieser Rohstoffe oder deren Teilen (Trub, Schönungstrub, Tropfsaft)		Aus Apfelwein, Birnenwein oder deren Gemischen	
		min.	max.	min.	max.
Gradstärke					
– Hafenbrand	% vol	55		55	
– Kolonnenbrand	% vol	70	76	70	76
Acetaldehyd	g/hl r. A.		80		60
Titrierbare Säure als Essigsäure	g/hl r. A.		120		80
Ester als Essigester	g/hl r. A.	40	300	40	200
Methanol	g/hl r. A.		1600		100
Höhere Alkohole ohne Propanol-1	g/hl r. A.		500		500
Propanol-1	g/hl r. A.		80		50
Eisen + Kupfer + Zink	g/hl r. A.		2,5		2,5
Trockenrückstand	g/hl r. A.		8		8
Schweflige Säure	g/hl r. A.		5		5
Acrolein	g/hl r. A.		0,5		0,5
Hexanol	g/hl r. A.		15		10
Verunreinigungen	g/hl r. A.		keine		keine

* Art. 3 Abs. 3 der Verordnung über die Übernahme gebrannter Wasser durch die Alkoholverwaltung vom 15. September 1993

4 Österreich

von Hofrat Univ. Prof. Dipl. Ing. Dr. J. Weiss, Klosterneuburg

Gemäß dem Kapitel B 23 (Spirituosen) des Codex Alimentarius Austriacus werden Spirituosen, d.h. »alle zum menschlichen Genuß bestimmten Getränke, in denen ... durch Brennverfahren gewonnener Alkohol als ein wertbestimmender Bestandteil enthalten ist und deren Mindestalkoholgehalt 15% vol ... beträgt«, verschiedenen Produktgruppen zugeordnet.

Für den bäuerlichen Abfindungsbrenner ist dabei die Produktgruppe »Edelbrände«, und innerhalb dieser der »österreichische Qualitätsbrand« von Bedeutung. Bei einem solcherweise bezeichneten Edelbrand müssen 100% des Alkohols von der angegebenen Obstart stammen und gewisse obstartspezifische chemisch-analytische Mindestanforderungen (Kennzahlen) erfüllt sein.

Beispiel Zwetschge:

Alkoholgehalt	> 38	% vol
Titrierbare Säuren (als Essigsäure)	max. 350	mg/100 ml r. A.
Flüchtige Ester (als Ethylacetat)	125– 700	mg/100 ml r. A.
Ethylacetat	max. 630	mg/100 ml r. A.
Gesamtester-Ethylacetat	mind. 30	mg/100 ml r. A.
Methanol	400–1500	mg/100 ml r. A.
Höhere Alkohole	mind. 100	mg/100 ml r. A.
Fuselalkohole	150–1500	mg/100 ml r. A.
Gesamtester/höhere Alkohole	max. 5,0	
Asche (auf Ware berechnet)	max. 0,2	g/l
Furfurolreaktion:	deutlich positiv	
Extrakt (grav., auf Ware berechnet)	5	g/l
davon höchstens 4 g Zucker pro Liter		
Zusätze von Abrundungsmitteln (z. B. Sorbit)	nicht nachweisbar	
Benzaldehyd	max. 6,5	mg/100 ml r. A.
Gesamt-Blausäure	max. 10	mg/100 ml r. A.

In einem Anhang des Codexkapitels wird auch für die Bestimmung jeder Kennzahl eine Analysenvorschrift angegeben.

5 Andere Staaten

In Kanada und in den USA ist maximal 0,35% vol **Methanol,** bezogen auf die trinkfertige Spirituose zulässig (entspricht bei einem Alkoholgehalt von 40% vol ca. 700 mg/100 ml r. A.).

Weitere Höchstgehalte für Methanol:

Italien	800 mg/100 ml r. A.
Finnland } Schweden	1200 mg/100 ml r. A.

6 Analysenbeispiele

Nachfolgende Tabelle enthält einige Analysenbeispiele. Naturgemäß ist der Gehalt der meisten Inhaltsstoffe gewissen Schwankungen unterworfen (s. Erfahrungswerte im Abschnitt 3.3 sowie Diskussion einer Analyse im Abschnitt 7).

Tab. 18: Analysenbeispiele (alle Angaben in mg/100 ml r.A.)

	Kirsch	Zwetschgen	Williams	Marc	Weinbrand	Apfel
Methanol	417	931	1546	1560	58	503
Ethylacetat (Ester)	350	280	200	393	61	99
1-Propanol	888	138	69	41	52	59
2-Butanol (sec.-Butanol)	28	0	28	3	1	0
2- Methyl-1-Propanol (Isobutanol)	42	50	43	98	108	106
1-Butanol	0	5	19	0	1	0
2-Methyl-1-Butanol	12	28	34	57	50	303
3-Methyl-1-Butanol	80	131	111	114	214	
Acetaldehyd	5	15	10	72	7	13
Titrierbare Säuren (b.a. Essigsäure)	100	33	90	45	40	55

7 Diskussion einer Kirschanalyse

			Bemerkungen
Alkohol	% vol	42	Mindestalkoholgehalte s. 1.1.
Methanol	mg/100 ml r.A.	460	Auch Methylalkohol genannt. Entsteht aus Pektin. Normaler Gehalt.
Ester (Ethylacetat, GC)	mg/100 ml r.A.	658	GC = gaschromatographisch bestimmt, d.h. spezifisch Ethylacetat. Gehalt zu hoch (aggressive Note). Ursache: stichige Maische (flüchtige Säure).
Gesamtester (berechnet als Ethylacetat)	mg/100 ml r.A.	750	Wird chemisch bestimmt. Erfaßt alle Ester. Gesamtester deshalb immer höher als GC-Ester. Gehalt zu hoch (ideal 250–450).
Aldehyd	mg/100 ml r.A.	90	Aldehyd wird als Acetaldehyd bestimmt. Gehalt zu hoch (s. 3.3). Wirkt dadurch aggressiv im Bukett.
1-Propanol	mg/100 ml r.A.	1252	Auch als n-Propanol bezeichnet. Gehalt kann von ca. 200–3000 variieren (bakteriell bedingt).
2-Butanol (sec. Butanol)	mg/100 ml r.A.	71	Höhere Alkohole (Fuselöl); gaschromatographisch bestimmt. Je nach Analysensystem werden die beiden Amylalkohole einzeln oder als Summe angegeben. 2-Methyl-1-Butanol ist immer nur ein Bruchteil von 3-Methyl-1-Butanol.
2-Methyl-1-Propanol (Isobutanol)	mg/100 ml r.A.	63	
1-Butanol	mg/100 ml r.A.	1	
2-Methyl-1-Butanol ⎫ Amylalkohole	mg/100 ml r.A.	12	
3-Methyl-1-Butanol ⎭	mg/100 ml r.A.	88	
Titrierbare Säuren (berechnet als Essigsäure)	mg/100 ml r.A.	220	Mit dieser Bestimmung werden auch nichtflüchtige Säuren erfaßt. Gehalt zu hoch (ideal ca. 100).
Flüchtige Säuren (berechnet als Essigsäure)	mg/100 ml r.A.	180	Summe aller flüchtigen Säuren. Differenz zu 220 Hinweis auf nichtflüchtige S. (z.B. Schwefelsäure).
Blausäure	mg/100 ml r.A.	12	Gehalt zu hoch (Limite 10). Ursache zu hoher Gehalt an beschädigten Steinen. Gehalte meist < 5.
Kupfer	mg/100 ml r.A.	1	Wird toleriert (s. 3.3). Bei Gehalten über 0,5 muß jedoch mit Trübungen gerechnet werden.
Furfural	mg/100 ml r.A.	2	Vom Anbrennen der Maische herrührend (s. F. 3.2.4).
Extrakt (Trockenrückstand)	mg/l	165	Angabe des Resultats bezieht sich meist auf die trinkfertige Spirituose. Angabe auch in g/l.
Ethylcarbamat	mg/l 40% vol	0,25	Normaler Gehalt, nicht zu beanstanden.

N FRAGEKASTEN

Im nachfolgenden Abschnitt sind Fragen und Probleme aus der Praxis aufgeführt, wie sie sich in dieser oder ähnlicher Form immer wieder stellen. Die Antworten sind im allgemeinen knapp gehalten, besonders dort, wo im Textteil nähere Angaben zu finden sind. Sie zeigen aber auch, daß gerade bei fehlerhaften Destillaten eine genauere Abklärung oft nur aufgrund einer Untersuchung im Fachlabor möglich ist.

Frage: In der Beilage erhalten Sie eine angebrochene Flasche Zwetschgenwasser. Wie Sie selber sehen können, ist eine leichte Verfärbung eingetreten. Ein Fehler bei der Lagerung ist ausgeschlossen, da die gesamte Lieferung am gleichen Ort aufbewahrt wird. Einige ungeöffnete Flaschen bleiben klar, während andere – ebenfalls ungeöffnete – wiederum eine Verfärbung aufweisen. Was mag der Grund sein?

Antwort: Die aufgetretene Färbung ist eindeutig auf die verwendeten Korken zurückzuführen, da diese bei ihrer Herstellung zwecks Verbesserung des Aussehens des öfteren leicht angefärbt werden. Werden nun Spirituosen fälschlicherweise liegend gelagert, so erfolgt durch die alkoholisch-wässerige Lösung eine Extraktion von Farbstoffen und löslichen Korkbestandteilen. Aus diesem Grunde sind viele Betriebe dazu übergegangen, Korkzapfen durch Drehverschlüsse zu ersetzen. Wir empfehlen Ihnen, die noch brauchbaren Flaschen für eine weitere Lagerung aufzustellen.

Frage: Wir bitten Sie, festzustellen, warum unser Kirsch in der Flasche trüb geworden ist. Mit den zur Filtration verwendeten Schichten haben wir bis heute nur gute Erfahrungen gemacht. Daß die Flaschen nicht ganz einwandfrei sauber sein könnten, ist ebenfalls nicht anzunehmen, da wir seit über drei Jahren nur noch Einwegflaschen einsetzen. Unmittelbar nach der Abfüllung sind uns keine Trübungen aufgefallen. Es ist selbstverständlich, daß das Filter vor und nach den Abfüllungen gründlich mit Quellwasser gewaschen und durchgespült wird.

Antwort: Die von Ihnen erwähnte Trübung konnten wir erst nach Kühlstellen des Musters reproduzieren. Wir haben das Destillat deshalb noch im kalten Zustand zentrifugiert. Im feinen weißen Bodensatz ließ sich eindeutig Calcium nachweisen. Falls Sie für das Herabsetzen, wie von uns wiederholt empfohlen, nur destilliertes oder enthärtetes Wasser verwendet haben, so dürfte die Calciumaufnahme im Filter erfolgt sein. Wir empfehlen Ihnen deshalb, dieses im Anschluß an das Waschen mit Quellwasser erschöpfend mit enthärtetem Wasser nachzuspülen. Übrigens sind in der Praxis vereinzelt auch Calciumphosphat-Trübungen beobachtet worden. Grund: Polyphosphate (zur Wasserenthärtung) im Kühlwasser; undichter Kühler!

Frage: Vierzehn Tage nach dem Abfüllen eines Weindrusenbranntweins habe ich eine Schwarzverfärbung des Korkstopfens und eine Ausscheidung von schwarzen Partikeln beobachtet (liegende Aufbewahrung der Flaschen). Das Destillat wurde vorerst in ein ausgekleidetes Anticorodalfaß verbracht und kurze Zeit später je zur Hälfte in rostfreie Stahltanks bzw. in Glasflaschen umgezogen. Die Abfüllung erfolgte nach dreijähriger Lagerung. Bisher hat nur der im Stahltank gelagerte Branntwein zu einer Verfärbung geführt. Wieso kommt es zu dieser unliebsamen Veränderung und was kann man dagegen tun?

Antwort: Beim liegend Aufbewahren von Spirituosen kann im Getränk anwesendes Eisen mit dem Gerbstoff des Korkstopfens unter Bildung einer tintenähnlichen Verbindung reagieren. Da die Verfärbung bei den in Glasballons gelagerten Destillaten nicht aufgetreten ist, muß angenommen werden, daß Spuren von Eisen aus dem rostfreien Stahlbehälter stammen. Eventuell im Drusenbranntwein enthaltene schweflige Säure hätte zu einer verstärkten Eisenabgabe aus dem Behälter führen können, da nicht alle Edelstahlbehälter SO_2-beständig sind.
Zur Wiederherstellung empfehlen wir Ihnen, eine Behandlung mit saurem Kationenaustauscher (z. B. Dowex 50 H$^+$, 20–50 mesh) vorzunehmen. Das Austauscherharz ist vor Gebrauch erschöpfend mit destilliertem Wasser zu spülen. Die benötigte Menge liegt bei ca. 0,5–1% des zu behandelndes Destillates. Man gibt den Austauscher in einen Trichterfilter und leitet das Destillat von einer erhöhten Lage aus langsam hindurch (evt. auch Kunststoffsäule mit Fritte verwenden).

Frage: Wir haben einem Kunden vor einiger Zeit eine Partie Kirsch (50% vol, unfiltriert) geliefert. Der Kunde hat diesen Kirsch nun filtriert und uns den beiliegenden Rückstand zur Untersuchung zugestellt. Das hochgrädige Kirschwasser wird in glasemaillierten Tanks mit dunkelblauer Auskleidung gelagert. Wir könnten uns nun vorstellen, daß es sich um losgelöste Teile dieser Auskleidung handelt. Der Tank war schon einige Jahre nicht mehr geöffnet, da er nie leer wurde. Wir bitten Sie um Ihre Stellungnahme.

Antwort: Die Untersuchung der uns eingesandten blaugrünen Ausscheidung hat ergeben, daß sie einerseits aus Kupfer und anderseits aus höheren Fettsäuren (Myristin- und Palmitinsäure) besteht. Entgegen Ihren Vermutungen können solche Ausscheidungen entstehen, wenn im Verlaufe der Destillation infolge Anwesenheit aggressiver Dämpfe (Essigsäure) Kupfer bzw. Zinn aus den absteigenden Apparaturteilen (Kühler usw.) herausgelöst wurden. Bei der anschließenden Lagerung bildeten sich dann mit den im Destillat enthaltenen höheren Fettsäuren die erwähnten unlöslichen Verbindungen. Als vorbeugende Maßnahme empfehlen wir Ihnen, die absteigenden Teile der Destillationsapparatur aus rostfreiem Stahl anfertigen zu lassen. Das beeinträchtigte Destillat kann mittels Kationenaustauscher-Behandlung wiederhergestellt werden (s. auch obige Antwort).

Frage: Beiliegend erhalten Sie ein Muster Kirsch (hergestellt für den Eigenbedarf), welches anfänglich von guter Qualität war. Im Laufe des Sommers nahm dieses jedoch einen mir unerklärbaren Säuregeruch an. Das Faß war einwandfrei. Ist eventuell das verwendete chemische Faßputzmittel schuld? Das Brenngut war gesund und ausgereift.

Antwort: Der eingesandte Kirsch erweist sich als überaus sauer (11,9 g flüchtige Säuren/l r. A.); degustativ ist zusätzlich ein Silogeschmack feststellbar. Wir empfehlen Ihnen, den Kirsch mit gleichen Anteilen Wasser zu versetzen und nach Zugabe von 500 g kohlensaurem Kalk pro hl einem Umbrand zu unterziehen. Vor- und Nachlauf sind abzutrennen.

Die Ursache der Verdorbenheit ist nicht beim Faßputzmittel zu suchen, sondern rührt eher davon her, daß sich im Verlaufe der Gärung eine bakterielle Zersetzung vollzogen hat. Ihre Feststellung, der Kirsch habe sich während des Sommers nachteilig verändert, dürfte sich weniger auf die Säure als auf Essigester beziehen, welcher im Verlaufe der Lagerung gebildet wird.

Frage: Mein Kirsch wurde von einem Kunden beanstandet, weil er, zum Kaffee crème zugesetzt, den Rahm zum Gerinnen brachte. Eigenartigerweise blieb die unerwünschte Erscheinung aus, wenn ich den Kaffee crème mit einem Konkurrenzprodukt vermischte. Was fehlt wohl meinem Kirsch?

Antwort: Kirschbrände enthalten in der Regel umso mehr flüchtige Säuren, je später die Maischen der Destillation unterzogen werden (eine Ausnahme bilden die angesäuerten Maischen, deren Gehalt an flüchtigen Säuren auch über längere Zeit konstant bleibt). Ein weiterer Grund für hohe Säuregehalte könnte in der Verwendung von offenen oder nur mit Senkdeckel versehenen Gärbottichen liegen. Wird nun ein solcher Kirsch mit Rahm zusammengebracht, so kann es zur Gerinnung dieses Produkts kommen, und zwar umso eher, wenn der Rahm seinerseits durch bakterielle Tätigkeit eine Erhöhung des Säuregehalts erfahren hat. Zur Herabsetzung der Säure empfiehlt sich ein Umbrand nach vorgängiger Teilneutralisation mit kohlensaurem Kalk (s. oben).

Frage: Mein Williamsdestillat weist einen ranzigen Fehlgeschmack auf. Was könnte der Grund dafür sein?

Antwort: Die Ursache solcher an ranzige Butter oder Silogeruch erinnernden Fehltöne sind auf die unerwünschte Tätigkeit von Bakterien des Clostridium-Typs zurückzuführen. Dabei wird Zucker in Butter- und Essigsäure umgewandelt, wobei besonders die Buttersäure und ihr Folgeprodukt Buttersäureethylester den erwähnten Fehler bewirken. Im Gegensatz zu den Essigbakterien sind die Buttersäurebakterien nicht auf Sauerstoff angewiesen, so daß auch Gärtrichter und hermetisches Verschließen der Gebinde keine tauglichen Schutzmaßnahmen darstellen. Dagegen kann mit einer Maischeansäuerung einem Buttersäurestich wirksam vorgebeugt werden. Bei dieser Gelegenheit möchten wir Sie noch darauf aufmerksam machen, daß neben den erwähnten Hauptprodukten bei der Buttersäuregärung außerdem Wasserstoffgas gebildet wird, so daß beim Abbrennen solcher Maischen infolge Knallgasbildung Explosionsgefahr besteht.

Frage: Irrtümlicherweise haben wir zum Abrunden von Apfelbrand statt Rohrzucker einen Gelierzucker zugesetzt. Nun kann das Destillat nicht mehr filtriert werden. Was soll ich tun?

Antwort: Gelierzucker ist ein Rohrzucker mit Zusatz von Pektin. Letzteres hat die Eigenschaft, in Lösung aufzuquellen und im Falle von Konfitüre eine beschleunigte Geleebildung zu bewirken. Bei Ihrem Destillat hat sich die Viskosität stark erhöht, so daß an eine Filtration nicht mehr zu denken ist. Wir empfehlen Ihnen, das Destillat mit 800–1000 g kohlensaurem Kalk pro hl zu rühren und anschließend zu filtrieren. Durch diese Behandlung wird das Pektin an Calcium gebunden (Bildung von unlöslichem Calciumpektat), so daß es in Salzform ausgeschieden werden kann.

Frage: Beim Abbrennen von Apfelmaischen ist mir aufgefallen, daß diese häufig zum Ankleben neigen; der nicht sehr dünnflüssige Blaseninhalt bildet einen Belag im Kessel. Auch dauert ein Abtrieb doppelt so lang, als dies normalerweise der Fall ist. Zudem habe ich ein starkes Schäumen festgestellt. Der Vergärungsgrad lag meist bei 2,5–3%. Zu welchen Maßnahmen können Sie mir raten?

Antwort: Die Vermutung liegt nahe, daß die Maischen noch nicht vollständig vergoren waren. Die noch relativ dickflüssige Maische bzw. der Vergärungsgrad von 2,5–3% ist ein Indiz dafür. Dadurch wird der Wärmetransport behindert, die Blasenwände werden zu heiß und es kommt zu einer ungleichmäßigen Ankochung in der Blase. Das starke Schäumen kann ebenfalls mit dem erhöhten Extraktgehalt erklärt werden; außerdem enthalten unvollständig vergorene Maischen viel gelöstes CO_2, was zusätzlich schaumbildend wirkt. Als Vorbeugungs- und Gegenmaßnahmen bieten sich einerseits eine vollständige Vergärung (Reinhefe- und Enzymzusatz), andererseits aber auch ein Vermischen von dick- und dünnflüssigem Brenngut an. Eventuell könnte einer dickflüssigen Maische auch etwas Wasser zugesetzt werden. In der Praxis hat sich auch gezeigt, daß angesäuerte Maischen viel weniger zum Schäumen neigen (Zusatz von ca. 60 ml konz. Schwefelsäure, verdünnt in der zehnfachen Menge Wasser, pro hl Maische).

Frage: Mein Birnenbrennsaft weist noch ein Mostgewicht von 9° auf. Ist die Gärung abgeschlossen? Wieviel Zucker ist noch vorhanden?

Antwort: Die Untersuchung ergab, daß weder Glucose noch Fructose vorhanden sind. Das gegenüber Apfelbrennsäften höhere Mostgewicht von 9° ist fast ausschließlich durch die Anwesenheit von Sorbit bedingt. Dieser unvergärbare Zuckeralkohol, der in einer Konzentration von 19,5 g/l aufgefunden wurde, täuscht in Ihrem Brennsaft 7–8 Mostgewichtsgrade vor. Der Brennsaft ist deshalb als vollständig vergoren zu betrachten.

Frage: Wann ist eine Kirschenmaische vollständig vergoren?

Antwort: Der Endvergärungsgrad kann nicht generell mit Saccharometer oder Mostwaage gemessen werden. Ausschlaggebend ist der Gehalt an Nichtzuckerstoffen, d. h. unvergärbaren Extraktbestandteilen wie Sorbit, Fruchtsäuren, Gerbstoffe, Mineralstoffe usw. Mit Ausnahme des Sorbits sind die Nichtzuckeranteile in allen Fruchtmaischen etwa gleich. Somit entscheidet, vereinfacht ausgedrückt, allein der Sorbitgehalt über den Endvergärungsgrad. Betrachten wir einmal die ungefähren Nichtzuckeranteile eines Kirschenmaische-Filtrates:

Fruchtsäuren	10 g/l
Sorbit	**40 g/l**
Mineralstoffe	2 g/l
Gerbstoffe	3 g/l
Eiweiß-Stoffe	3 g/l
Glycerin	4 g/l
Galakturonsäure	3 g/l
Extraktstoffe (unvergärbar)	65 g/l

Der **sorbitfreie Anteil** macht also etwa 25 g/l aus. Bei einem angenommenen Alkoholgehalt (im Maischefiltrat) von 8% vol und einem Extraktgehalt von 25 g/l wird mit der Spindel ein Mostgewicht von 0° gemessen; dies, weil der spezifisch leichtere Alkohol den Extrakt gerade etwa kompensiert. Nehmen wir nun aber unsere Kirschenmaische mit einem Sorbitgehalt von 40 g/l und setzen wir für den Sorbitgehalt (vereinfachend) den gleichen Zuckergehalt ein, so werden die 40 g Sorbit gemäß der Umrechnung »Zucker (in g/l) : 2 = Mostgewicht« etwa 20° entsprechen. Praktisch ist bei vergorenen Kirschenmaischen mit einem Mostgewicht von 12–24° zu rechnen. Übrigens liefern auch chemische Zuckerbestimmungen keine absolut verläßlichen Ergebnisse, da beispielsweise Galakturonsäure vergärbaren Zucker vortäuschen kann.

Frage: Zur Herstellung von destilliertem Wasser zum Herabsetzen der Destillate verwende ich einen Ionenaustauscher. Wie lange kann ich dieses Wasser in einem ausgekleideten Aluminiumfaß aufbewahren, damit es für obigen Zweck noch brauchbar ist?

Antwort: Zunächst möchten wir richtigstellen, daß destilliertes Wasser nur über eine Destillation gewonnen werden kann, während es sich bei dem von Ihnen verwendeten Verschnittwasser um enthärtetes bzw. vollentsalztes Wasser handelt. Grundsätzlich ist die Qualität des destillierten Wassers derjenigen von enthärtetem, also durch Ionenaustausch gewonnenem Wasser überlegen. Dest. Wasser kann, sofern es in saubere Gebinde gefüllt wird, bis zu einem Monat gelagert werden. Bei Ionenaustauscher-Wasser ist die Gefahr der bakteriellen Zersetzung bedeutend größer. Es empfiehlt sich deshalb, enthärtetes Wasser nicht aufzubewahren, sondern direkt nach Verlassen des Austauschers zu verwenden.

Frage: Seit einiger Zeit werden auf dem Markt Kunststoff-Flaschen für die Aufnahme bzw. Lagerung von Getränken angeboten. Können solche auch für Spirituosen empfohlen werden?

Antwort: Während bei Essig, Obstwein oder Maischen mit Kunststoffgebinden in der Praxis gute Erfahrungen gemacht werden konnten (ehemalige Chemikalienbehälter dürfen aber unter keinen Umständen verwendet werden!), sind bei Spirituosen Vorbehalte anzubringen. So mußten wir beispielsweise bei einem Lagerversuch von erstklassigem Zwetschgenwasser(45% vol) in grüngefärbten Niederdruck-Polyethylenflaschen feststellen, daß nach drei Monaten das ursprünglich fruchtige Sortenbukett, welches im Kontrollversuch (Glasflaschen) einwandfrei blieb, verschwunden bzw. durch einen dumpfen, getränkefremden Geruchston überdeckt war. Es erscheint uns jedenfalls zweckmäßig, vor jeder Verwendung von Kunststoff-Flaschen zum Zwecke der Lagerung von Spirituosen in mehrmonatigen Lagerversuchen die Eignung des einzusetzenden Materials zu erproben. Im Zweifelsfall würden wir Glas- oder Steinzeugbehältern den Vorzug geben.

Frage: Die Erfahrung zeigt, daß Eisentanks, in welchen Destillate, insbesondere aber auch Steinobstbrände gelagert werden, außen öfters überstrichen und innen periodisch mit Kunstharzen neu belegt werden müssen, woraus sich ziemlich hohe Unterhaltskosten ergeben. Nach meiner Ansicht kämen wohl rostfreie Stahltanks auf die Dauer billiger zu stehen. Ich möchte Sie nun fragen, ob V2A-Tanks gegenüber allen Spirituosen, selbst bei längerer Lagerung, absolut indifferent sind. Wäre es vielleicht besser, V4A-Stahl zu verwenden? Brauchen solche Tanks eine spezielle Außenbehandlung?

Antwort: Abgesehen von den hohen Anschaffungskosten können V2A-Tanks als ideale Behälter für die Spirituosenlagerung betrachtet werden. Sie bedürfen außer einer periodischen Reinigung mit Wasser, welchem etwas Schaummittel zugesetzt wird, keiner besonderen Außenbehandlung. Die Verwendung von V4A-Stahltanks erübrigt sich bei Spirituosen, sofern diese keine schweflige Säure enthalten.

Frage: Beim Abbrennen von Kernobsttrester habe ich eine viel zu tiefe Alkoholausbeute festgestellt. Was mag der Grund sein?

Antwort: Neben dem nächstliegenden Grund, nämlich einer steckengebliebenen Gärung (stichige Maische, Kälteeinbruch, Glanzgärer) sind noch weitere Erklärungen denkbar. Möglich wäre auch, daß ein Teil des Alkohols infolge ungeeigneter Lagerung verdunstet ist; anderseits könnte auch eine Mannitgärung stattgefunden haben (anstelle von Alkohol wird aus Fructose Mannit gebildet). Eine Abklärung des Sachverhalts wäre nur durch eine Laboruntersuchung möglich.

Frage: Mein Williams, den ich auf 42% vol eingestellt hatte, wurde vom Kunden mit der Begründung zurückgewiesen, der Alkoholgehalt entspräche nicht der Deklaration; er liege über 1% tiefer. Bitte untersuchen Sie das beiliegende Muster.
Antwort: Die Analyse ergab, daß der tatsächliche Alkoholgehalt dem deklarierten entspricht. Da wir gleichzeitig einen Extraktgehalt von 5,5 g/l feststellen konnten, ist anzunehmen, daß Ihr Kunde die Messung aräometrisch, d.h. mit Alkoholspindel, direkt im Produkt vorgenommen hat. Dies würde sein tieferes Ergebnis erklären. In extrakthaltigen Spirituosen dürfen aräometrische Alkoholbestimmungen nur nach vorgängiger Destillation durchgeführt werden. Zur Veranschaulichung nachstehend einige Beispiele:
Alkohol/Wasser-Lösung, auf 40,0% vol eingestellt. Zusätze von steigenden Mengen Saccharose. Aräometrische Messung direkt, d.h. ohne Destillation.

Saccharose-Zusatz (g/l)	abgelesener Alkoholgehalt (% vol)
–	40,0
2	39,4
4	38,8
6	38,3
8	37,8
10	37,2

Frage: Da wir jedes Jahr Weintrester brennen, möchten wir Sie höflichst um Rat fragen, wie wir das Destillat fachgerecht herabsetzen müssen und was vorzukehren ist, um etwas Farbe zu erhalten.
Antwort: Nach erfolgter Destillation, mit welcher übrigens nicht lange zugewartet werden sollte, wird das erhaltene Destillat mit destilliertem oder enthärtetem Wasser auf Trinkstärke 42–45% vol herabgesetzt. Die Menge des zu verwendenden Verschnittwassers ist dabei einer Kontraktionstabelle zu entnehmen. Die sich nach dem Wasserzusatz in der Regel einstellende Trübung ist auf etherische Oele und höhere Alkohole zurückzuführen. Zwecks Klärung wird das Destillat für einige Tage kühlgestellt und anschließend unter Anwendung eines Filterhilfsmittels solange filtriert, bis der abfließende Weintresterbrand völlig klar erscheint. Die Anfärbung wird in der Regel durch Zusatz von Zuckercouleur erreicht, welches im Fachhandel erhältlich ist. Auslagerung in Eichenholzfässern führt ebenfalls zu einer Farbaufnahme und zusätzlich zu einer erwünschten Alterung des Destillates. Dabei ist aber ein Ausfallen von kondensiertem Gerbstoff nicht ganz auszuschließen.

Frage: Kann eine Obstmaische, die mit ca. 50 ml konzentrierter Schwefelsäure versetzt wurde, nach dem Abbrennen noch als Viehfutter verwendet werden?
Antwort: Schlempen aus Obstmaischen dürfen nur verfüttert werden, wenn sie weder einen Säurezusatz erhalten haben noch einen zu hohen Gehalt an flüchtigen Säuren aufweisen. Ihr Futterwert ist, verglichen mit Kartoffel- und Getreideschlempen, ohnehin äußerst gering. Besser wäre ein großflächiges Ausbringen auf Felder, die zum Umpflügen anstehen; die Verfütterung an Rinder und Schweine ist eher eine Notlösung.

Frage: Kann ich ein Kernobstdestillat für das Einlegen von Himbeeren zwecks Herstellung von Himbeergeist verwenden? Das Destillat wurde hauptsächlich aus Äpfeln der Sorte Golden Delicious gewonnen.

Antwort: Erfahrungsgemäß werden die besten Himbeergeiste bei Verwendung von möglichst geruchs- und geschmacksneutralem Alkohol gewonnen. Zu diesem Zwecke müßten Sie den Apfelbrand mit einer beträchtlichen Menge Aktivkohle schönen (ca. 2 kg/hl). Vorteilhafter ist es allerdings, zum Überspriten einen hochrektifizierten Kernobstbranntwein oder 96prozentigen Trinksprit zu verwenden. Dabei sind pro 100 kg Himbeeren ca. 40 Liter erforderlich. Nach einer Standzeit von maximal 2 Tagen erfolgt die Destillation (vorgängig 50 Liter Wasser auf 100 Liter Maische zusetzen).

Frage: Beim Abfüllen von Spirituosen möchten wir darauf achten, daß die geforderte Füllmenge bei einer Temperatur von 15°C gewährleistet ist. Können Sie mir Angaben machen, welches Volumen die Spirituosen bei von 15°C abweichenden Temperaturen einnehmen. Wir füllen in der Regel in 7-dl-Flaschen ab.

Antwort: Die Volumenveränderung von Spirituosen ist nicht nur von der Temperatur, sondern auch vom Alkoholgehalt abhängig. Aus der folgenden, dem Fachbuch »Trinkbranntweine und Liköre« von *Wüstenfeld/Haeseler* entnommenen Tabelle lassen sich für zwei gebräuchliche Alkoholstärken (32–33, bzw. 40–42% vol) Faktoren entnehmen, mit denen man das bei einer bestimmten Temperatur gemessene Volumen multiplizieren muß, um das Volumen bei 15°C zu erhalten. In der zweiten Spalte ist das einzustellende Füllmaß bei den betreffenden Temperaturen für 0,7 Liter Spirituose (bezogen auf 15°C) wiedergegeben.

°C	32–33% vol Faktor	ml	40–42% vol Faktor	ml
0	1,0072	695,0	1,0094	693,4
2	1,0063	695,6	1,0082	694,3
4	1,0055	696,2	1,0070	695,1
6	1,0048	696,7	1,0061	695,7
8	1.0039	697,3	1,0049	696,6
10	1,0029	698,0	1,0036	697,5
12	1,0019	698,7	1,0023	698,4
14	1,0009	699,4	1,0010	699,3
16	0,9998	700,1	0,9997	700,2
18	0,9987	700,9	0,9983	701,2
20	0,9976	701,7	0,9970	702,1
22	0,9965	702,5	0,9957	703,0
24	0,9953	703,3	0,9942	704,0
26	0,9941	704,1	0,9928	705,1
28	0,9930	704,9	0,9913	706,1
30	0,9917	705,8	0,9899	707,1

Frage: Bedingt durch den diesjährigen großen Anfall an Williamsbirnen werden wir nicht in der Lage sein, die Maischen innert nützlicher Frist abzubrennen. Obgleich wir mit der Maischeansäuerung gute Erfahrungen gemacht haben, befürchten wir, daß bei mehrmonatiger Lagerung ein Bukettverlust eintreten könnte. Was wäre wohl in diesem Falle die beste Lösung?

Antwort: Um einerseits das typische Gärbukett zu erhalten und anderseits einer mikrobiellen Zersetzung vorzubeugen, empfehlen wir Ihnen, die ausgelagerten Birnen zwar einzumaischen, aber noch nicht zu vergären. Dies erreicht man durch Zugabe von konzentrierter Schwefelsäure. Der pH-Wert der Maische soll 2,2–2,4 betragen (mit Indikatorpapier kontrollieren!). Die erforderliche Säuremenge (80–120 ml pro hl) ist zunächst vorsichtig der zehnfachen Wassermenge zuzusetzen. Die Maische ist hierauf gut zu vermischen. Um zu gegebener Zeit die Gärung einzuleiten, ist der pH-Wert durch Zugabe von Lauge auf 3,2–3,3 anzuheben. Nachdem wiederum für eine gute Durchmischung gesorgt wurde, kann die Trockenreinzuchthefe beigefügt werden. Dieses Verfahren der verzögerten Gärung hat sich in der Praxis bestens bewährt.

Frage: Welche Werkstoffe kommen für Verstärker in Frage ?

Antwort: Früher bestanden Brennapparate ganz aus Kupfer. Gegenüber Edelstahl ist die Haltbarkeit aber beschränkt. Anderseits ist mit einem Edelstahlgerät die Qualität eines im Kupferkessel produzierten Destillates nicht zu erreichen (vermehrte Böckserbildung). Empfehlenswert ist eine Kombination von Kupfer und Edelstahl. Die inneren Verstärkerelemente sollten aus Kupfer angefertigt werden, die Ummantelung dagegen aus Edelstahl. Wie bereits mehrmals empfohlen, sollten die absteigenden Teile des Brennapparates, also Geistrohr, Kühler und Vorlage, aus Edelstahl hergestellt sein, um einer Kupferaufnahme durch das Destillat vorzubeugen (Isolation zwischen Kupfer und Stahl!). Kolonnenapparate können ohne weiteres aus Edelstahl bestehen, sofern die Böden aus Kupfer sind bzw. mit Kupferspiralen gefüllt werden.

Frage: Gibt es Unterschiede in der Qualität von Obstbränden, je nachdem, ob sie mit oder ohne Verstärker destilliert worden sind?

Antwort: Der Vorteil des einmaligen Abtriebs besteht vor allem darin, daß auch kleinere Maischemengen gebrannt werden können, weil das Destillieren des Rauhbrands entfällt, dessen Menge gewöhnlich nur etwa ein Viertel des ursprünglichen Maischevolumens beträgt. Dies ist in der Praxis vor allem für Stoffbesitzer (Brennauftraggeber) von Bedeutung. Im übrigen läßt sich die Frage nicht eindeutig beantworten, weil die Auffassungen über den Geschmack einer Spirituose sehr unterschiedlich sind. Nicht zuletzt hängt die Qualität auch von der Verstärkungseinrichtung, der Destillationstechnik und der Beschaffenheit der Maische ab. Fest steht nur, daß sich sowohl im einmaligen als auch im zweimaligen Abtrieb hochwertige Qualitätsbrände herstellen lassen, wobei aus wirtschaftlichen Überlegungen heraus in Zukunft wohl eher Brenngeräte mit Verstärker verwendet werden.

Frage: Kann ein Landwirt und Lieferant einer Zwetschgenmaische für einen Rohölschaden an einem 40 000 Liter fassenden Gärtank verantwortlich gemacht werden ?
Antwort: Anhand der Eingangskontrolle war es möglich, den Lieferanten des nach Rohöl riechenden Holzfasses ausfindig zu machen. Da der Inhalt dieses Fasses bereits mit dem Inhalt eines 40 000-Liter-Tanks vermischt worden war, hatte der ganze Tankinhalt den Rohölgeschmack angenommen. Eine Nachkontrolle im Landwirtschaftsbetrieb des Maischelieferanten ergab, daß das fragliche Holzfaß in einem für den Traktor bestimmten Abstellschuppen gelagert worden war. Ob das Faß selbst mit Rohöl in Berührung kam, z.b. durch Abfüllen bzw. Abstellen von Ölkannen oder Lappen auf der Faßdecke, konnte nicht mehr eruiert werden; jedenfalls läßt sich an diesem Beispiel klar ersehen, daß weder Maische- noch Weinfässer in die Nähe von Fahrzeugen und die sie meistens umgebenden Rohölbehälter gehören.
Es gehört aber auch zur Sorgfaltspflicht des Maischeankäufers, die gelieferten Gebinde und ihren Inhalt vor dem Entleeren einer strengen Geruchskontrolle zu unterziehen. Bereits sehr geringe Rohölanteile genügen nämlich, um größte Lagerbehälter zu deklassieren. Im vorliegenden Falle zeigte sich, daß der gesamte Rauhbrand nach Rohöl roch. Geruchliche und geschmackliche Einbußen sind auch nach massiven Schönungen (Paraffin- oder Kohle/Kieselgurfiltration) nicht zu umgehen. Nach unserer Ansicht müßte der Schaden im vorliegenden Fall durch Lieferanten und Ankäufer zu gleichen Teilen getragen werden.

Frage: Ich habe einen Zwetschgenbrand mit siloartigem Fehlton. Woher kommt dieser Fehler und was kann ich unternehmen ?
Antwort: Die Ursache kann von schlechtem Rohmaterial, aber auch von einer schlechten Gärung (Buttersäurebakterien) herrühren. Ein solcher Geruchs- und Geschmacksfehler läßt sich selten ohne Qualitätseinbuße beseitigen. Wir empfehlen aber dennoch, eine Schönung mit Zusatz von 300 g gelöschtem Kalk [$Ca(OH)_2$] und 300 g Magnesiumoxid (MgO)/hl vorzunehmen. Das Schönungsmittel wird mit wenig Destillat angerührt und der Hauptmenge unter gutem Vermischen zugegeben. Nach öfterem Umrühren muß spätestens nach 12 Stunden abfiltriert werden.

Frage: Ich frage mich manchmal, warum mir nach dem Genuß mancher »Schnäpse« unwohl ist. Am Alkohol kann der Unterschied doch nicht liegen, da die fraglichen Destillate immer Trinkstärke aufweisen.
Anwort: Nach Empfehlungen von Fachärzten liegt die (für Männer) schadlos verkraftbare Alkoholmenge pro Tag bei 60–80 ml reinem Alkohol (1,5–2 dl trinkfertige Spirituose). Neben Ethylalkohol sind aber in Destillaten in unterschiedlicher Menge Begleitstoffe wie Methanol, höhere Alkohole und ihre Ester vorhanden. Es ist bekannt, daß Alkohole und Ester mit steigender Molekülgröße immer weniger wasserlöslich sind. Damit steigen aber ihre Fettlöslichkeit und die Anreicherung im Gehirn. Da solche Stoffe auch langsamer abgebaut und ausgeschieden werden, wirken sie sich stärker und länger auf das zentrale Nervensystem aus als Ethanol. Damit wird verständlich, daß hochrektifizierte Destillate wie Wodka und Aquavit besser verträglich sind als Obstbrände mit bedeutend höherem Gehalt an obenerwähnten Begleitstoffen.

Frage: Wir sind uns nicht einig über den Kaloriengehalt von Spirituosen. Ein Bekannter behauptet, daß nur der Genuß von zuckerhaltigen Getränken, also z.B. Likören, mit einer Kalorienzufuhr verbunden sei. Stimmt das?

Antwort: Diese Ansicht entspricht nicht den Tatsachen. So beträgt der physiologische Brennwert von Ethylalkohol 7 kcal (30 kJ) pro Gramm, d.h. nahezu doppelt soviel wie der entsprechende Wert für Zucker (4 kcal bzw. 17 kJ). Für die Berechnung des Brennwerts müssen also sowohl Zucker- als auch Alkoholgehalt berücksichtigt werden. Nachstehend einige Beispiele (alle Angaben pro 100 g des betreffenden Getränkes):

Kaffee (ungezuckert)	5 kcal	21 kJ
Bier (hell)	47 kcal	197 kJ
Orangensaft	43 kcal	180 kJ
Branntwein (41–47% vol)	245–280 kcal	1026–1172 kJ
Likör (25% vol Alkohol, 12% Zucker)	186 kcal	778 kJ

Frage: Für den Eigenverbrauch möchte ich Likör herstellen. Können Sie mir entsprechende Rezepte angeben?

Antwort: Bei der häuslichen Likörbereitung kann der Liebhaber seiner Experimentierfreudigkeit freien Lauf lassen, vorausgesetzt, daß dabei einige Grundregeln beachtet werden. Falls Sie sich eingehender mit dieser Materie befassen wollen, empfehlen wir Ihnen das Büchlein »Likörbereitung« von *H. George* (erschienen im Ulmer-Verlag, Stuttgart). Nachstehend drei bewährte Rezepte für Fruchtliköre:

Kirschlikör
3 dl süßen oder vergorenen Kirschensaft,
3 dl Zuckerlösung (300 g Zucker durch Aufkochen in 1,3 dl Wasser lösen, abkühlen lassen),
2,5 dl Trinksprit (96%)
in dieser Reihenfolge vermischen und mit Wasser auf 1 Liter auffüllen. Einige Tage stehen lassen und anschließend filtrieren. Bei Aufbewahrung in einem dunklen und kühlen Keller ohne Qualitätseinbuße bis zu einem Jahr haltbar.

Likör aus schwarzen Johannisbeeren
500 g abgebeerte Früchte in einem verschließbaren Gefäß (Sterilisierglas oder Weithalsflasche) mit 5 dl Trinksprit (96%) versetzen, ohne die Beeren zu beschädigen. Nach kurzem Durchmischen Gefäß verschließen und 4–8 Wochen im Dunkeln stehen lassen. Nach dieser Zeit sind die Beeren vollständig extrahiert. Mischung mit Hilfe eines Preßtuches auspressen und Preß-Saft mit Zuckerlösung (300 g Zucker in 7 dl Wasser) versetzen. Nach gutem Durchmischen wird in Flaschen abgezogen.
Das gleiche Verfahren kann auch bei anderen Beerenarten wie Brombeeren und Preiselbeeren angewendet werden.

Birnenlikör
400–500 g Birnen (am besten Williamsbirnen) werden gewaschen und zerkleinert. Nun gibt man die Birnenstücke in den Mischbecher einer laufenden Küchenmaschine, in welchem bereits 500 ml Wodka (42 % vol) enthalten sind. Das Zusetzen der Birnenstücke soll rasch erfolgen, d.h. bevor sie sich durch Luftsauerstoff braun verfärben. Nun setzt man 1 g pektinspaltendes Enzym hinzu (z.B. Pectinol, Panzym Rapid, Pectinex usw.) und läßt den Ansatz in einem verschließbaren Glas während ca. 4 Wochen an einem dunklen, kühlen Ort stehen. Anschließend wird über ein Papierfilter oder Seihtuch in ein 1-Liter-Meßgefäß filtriert. Das Filtrat wird mit Wasser auf ca. 600 ml ergänzt. Hinzu kommen 50 ml Williamsbrand, 20 ml Weinbrand, 250 ml Zuckerlösung (siehe übernächste Frage) und Wasser bis zur 1-Liter-Marke. Fehlende Säure kann man durch Zusatz von etwas Zitronensaft ergänzen. Nach weiteren 3 Wochen wird nochmals filtriert. Der Likör enthält ca. 23 % vol Alkohol.

Frage: Ich möchte 3 Liter Kirschlikör von 30% vol herstellen. Können Sie mir angeben, wieviel Trinksprit von 96% vol ich verwenden muß?

Antwort: Nach unserem Rezept (s. oben) sollen die »Alkohollieferanten« aus Trinksprit (96% vol) und vergorenem Kirschensaft (0,3 l für 1 l Likör) bestehen. Berechnung:

Alkoholbedarf 3 x 0,3 l r.A. = 0,9 l r.A.

Alkohol aus Kirschensaft: 5 % vol oder 0,05 l r.A./l
3 x 0,3 = 0,9 l x 0,05 l r.A. = 0,045 l r.A.

Restmenge r.A.: 0,9 – 0,045 l r.A. = 0,855 l r.A.

Diese Alkoholmenge ist in 0,855/0,96 = **0,89 Liter** Trinksprit (96% vol) enthalten.

Falls nach dem gleichen Rezept unvergorener Kirschensaft verwendet würde, müßten 0,9/0,96 = **0,94 Liter** Trinksprit verwendet werden, um ebenfalls auf 30% vol zu kommen.

Frage: Bei der Likörherstellung wird öfters von Zuckerlösung gesprochen. Mich würde interessieren, wie man eine solche Zuckerlösung herstellen kann?

Antwort: Zuerst werden 450 ml Wasser aufgekocht. Hierauf setzt man ein Gramm Wein- oder Citronensäure zu, damit der Rohrzucker später in Invertzucker umgewandelt wird. Nun rührt man 1 kg Zucker in das kochende Wasser. Nach einer Viertelstunde sollte der Zucker umgewandelt sein. Ein während des Kochprozesses an der Oberfläche auftretender Schaum kann mit Schaumlöffel abgeschöpft werden. Die fertige Lösung wird nun noch heiß in einen Meßbecher filtriert und nach Bedarf mit heißem Wasser zu einem Liter aufgefüllt. Die so bereitete Zuckerlösung weist ungefähr 73% Zucker auf und kann für die Likörbereitung eingesetzt werden.

Frage: Können Sie mir erklären, was man unter Fruchtlikör versteht und wie man ihn zubereiten soll. Wieviel Fruchtsaft, Zucker und Alkohol werden ungefähr benötigt ? Wie steht es mit der Haltbarkeit ?

Antwort: Fruchtsaft-Liköre sollten mindestens 20 l Fruchtsaft pro 100 l Likör enthalten. Zu diesen Likören zählt man Ananas-, Brombeer-, Himbeer-, Erdbeer-, Kirschen-, Johannisbeer- und Heidelbeerlikör. Der Fruchtsaftanteil wird mit Trinksprit versetzt. Öfters werden auch ganze Früchte zerquetscht und in Alkohol eingelegt. Es empfiehlt sich, auch entsprechende Obstbrände anstelle von Trinksprit oder Teilen davon zu verwenden. Der Alkoholgehalt beträgt in der Regel 25–30 % vol, der Zuckeranteil schwankt zwischen 30 und 35%. Filtrierte Fruchtliköre sind ohne weiteres 1 Jahr haltbar. Eine Gärung ist nicht zu befürchten (s. auch Spezialrezepte).

Frage: Können Sie mir angeben, wieviel Wasser ich einem Grappa mit 64% vol zusetzen muß, um eine Trinkstärke von 42 % vol zu erhalten? Wie kann ich den Grappa filtrieren, sofern er sich beim Herabsetzen trüben sollte ?

Antwort: Als erstes empfehlen wir Ihnen, das Destillat durch Zusatz von 75 Liter enthärtetem Wasser/hl auf 37% vol herabzusetzen. Der Grappa wird hierauf während sieben Tagen bei −5°C gelagert und anschließend im gekühlten Zustand mit Hilfe eines Faltenfilters filtriert (s. E.3). Diese Maßnahme ist nötig, weil durch das Herabsetzen (auch Abkühlen) etherische Öle ausgeschieden werden. Nach erfolgter Filtration wird der Grappa mit 5% hochprozentigem Grappadestillat (oder Trinksprit) versetzt. Das Auftreten einer erneuten Trübung kann so verhindert werden.

Frage: Welche Kräutermischungen sind für die Herstellung von Kräuterbrand zu empfehlen ?

Antwort: Vom Fachhandel wird eine große Anzahl von Kräutern angeboten. Die richtige Wahl ist weitgehend Geschmackssache; zudem können die Qualitätsunterschiede beträchtlich sein. Als Beispiel sei die Zusammensetzung eines Gemisches angegeben, wie es vom Landesverband der Klein- und Obstbrenner in Nord-Württemberg für zartbitteren Kräuterbrand empfohlen wird (die angegebenen Mengen gelten jeweils für einen Liter Weingeist):

8 g Fenchelsamen	1 g ganze Nelken
3 g Anissamen	1 g Muskatblüte
20 g Kamille	1 g Wermutkraut
20 g Pfefferminz	1 g Kardamom
15 g Süßholzwurzel	1 g Angelikawurzel
10 g Wacholderbeeren	1 g Enzianwurzel
2 g Zimtrinde	1 g Beifuß
6 g Kümmelsamen	0,1 g Lavendelblüte
2 g Koreandersamen	2,5 g Thymian

Die benötigte Menge für einen Abtrieb muß möglichst genau zusammengestellt werden. Zum ganzen Abtrieb (25–30 Liter r. A.) sind außerdem die Schalen von 6–7 frischen Zitronen oder Orangen, 6–8 geriebene Möhren (mittelgroß), 2 mittlere Zwiebeln (geschnitten) sowie 1/2 mittlere Sellerieknolle (geschnitten) hinzuzufügen.

Frage: Welche Zusatzstoffe sind zur farblichen und geschmacklichen Abrundung von Weinbrand geeignet?

Antwort: Zur Herstellung sogenannter »Bonificateurs« kommen in erster Linie Zucker, Zuckercouleur und unschädliche Pflanzenextrakte in Frage. Verboten ist dagegen die Verwendung von Branntweinschärfen wie Pfeffer und Paprika, welche einen höheren Alkoholgehalt vortäuschen sollen. Bewährt hat sich die folgende Weinbrand-Typage:

    100 g Eichenholzspäne
    67 g Backpflaumen
    27 g geröstete Mandelschalen
    14 g getrocknete, grüne Walnuß-Schalen
    1 l Weindestillat 50% vol

in einem verschlossenen Gefäß während drei Tagen öfters schütteln. Nach gutem Auspressen nötigenfalls durch ein Faltenfilter filtrieren.
Filtrat mit Kandizuckerlösung (240 g Kandizucker und 3,3 dl Wasser) sowie 3,3 dl dunklem Malaga (15% vol) versetzen und gut mischen. Die optimale Dosierung läßt sich am besten durch Vorversuche ermitteln, wobei der maximal zulässige Extraktgehalt zu beachten ist.

O LITERATUR

Für den interessierten Leser folgt – neben einigen periodisch erscheinenden Schriften – eine Auswahl ergänzender oder weiterführender Literatur zum Thema Obstbrennerei und verwandten Gebieten.

1 Periodika

»Brennerei-Kalender«

Herausgeber: Dr. jur. Max Beck, Hagen-Hohenlimburg.
Handbuch für die Brennerei- und Alkoholwirtschaft mit Brennerei-Abece, Fachartikeln, Ausbeutetabellen, Branntweinstatistik, Kalendarium usw.
Erscheint jährlich.

»Die Branntweinwirtschaft«

Verlag der Versuchs- und Lehranstalt für Spiritusfabrikation und Fermentationstechnologie, Berlin.
Fachzeitschrift für Brennereien und die Spirituosen-, Essig- und Hefeindustrie.
Erscheint zweimal monatlich.

»Kleinbrennerei«

Verlag Eugen Ulmer, Stuttgart.
Biotechnologie der Obst- und Getreidebrennerei.
Erscheint monatlich.

»Schweizerische Weinzeitung«

Schweiz. Weinzeitung Verlag AG, Bülach.
Fachblatt des Weinhandels und der Spirituosenindustrie.
Erscheint 18 Mal jährlich.

»Spirituosen Jahrbuch«

Verlag der Versuchs- und Lehranstalt für Spiritusfabrikation und Fermentationstechnologie, Berlin.
Enthält u. a. Spirituosen-ABC, Fachartikel, Anschriften von Behörden, Fachverbänden und Lieferfirmen, Gesetzliches.
Erscheint jährlich.

2 Fachbücher und Tabellenwerke

Alkoholtafeln (CH)
Herausgegeben vom Eidg. Amt für Messwesen, Bern 1977.
62 Seiten mit 4 Tabellen.

Amtliche Alkoholtafeln (BRD)
Herausgegeben von der Physikalisch-Technischen Bundesanstalt und der Bundesmonopolverwaltung für Branntwein, Braunschweig/Berlin und Offenbach/M. 1980. 409 Seiten mit 7 Tabellen.

Brennen nach Vorschrift
Von R. Brose
Verlag Eugen Ulmer, Stuttgart, 2. Aufl. 1984. 232 Seiten.
Ratschläge und Informationen für Stoffbesitzer. Einführung in die branntweinmonopolrechtlichen Bestimmungen der BRD.

Brennereianalytik
Von L. Adam, W. Bartels, N. Christoph und W. Stempfl
B. Behr's Verlag, Hamburg 1994.
Band 1: Qualitätskontrolle in der Brennerei und beim Spirituosenhersteller
Band 2: Qualitätskontrolle und Analytik im Fachlabor.

Getränke-Analytik
Von H. Tanner und H. R. Brunner
Verlag Heller, Schwäbisch Hall, 2. Aufl. 1987. 236 Seiten, 42 Abbildungen, 30 Tabellen. Die wichtigsten Untersuchungsmethoden für Fruchtsäfte, Weine und Spirituosen unter besonderer Berücksichtigung vereinfachter Verfahren.

Getreide- und Kartoffelbrennerei
Von H. Kreipe
Verlag Eugen Ulmer, Stuttgart, 3. Aufl. 1981. 368 Seiten, 145 Abbildungen und 50 Tabellen.
Lehrbuch (Handbuch der Lebensmitteltechnologie). Biochemie, Technologie, Betriebsführung, Ausbildung, Recht.

Heilschnäpse, Magenbitter, feine Liköre
Von N. von Merhart
Verlag Steiger, Innsbruck, 5. Auflage 1993.
136 Seiten, 16 Bilder, 100 Rezepte für Anspruchsvolle.

Kontraktionstabellen Dr. Adam
Verlag Heller, Schwäbisch Hall 1995.
Auslieferung Schliessmann Kellerei-Chemie
GmbH & Co. KG, Schwäbisch Hall.

Likörbereitung
Von H. George
Verlag Eugen Ulmer, Stuttgart, 8. Aufl. 1989. 119 Seiten, 20 Farbfotos und 59 Zeichnungen.
Wissenswertes über Alkohol und alkoholische Getränke mit Rezeptbeispielen für die häusliche Zubereitung.

Schnapsbrennen
Von J. Pischl
Verlag Leopold Stocker, Graz, 6. Auflage 1994.
136 Seiten, 61 Zeichnungen / Bilder, 9 Tabellen
ein Ratgeber für Anfänger und Praktiker.

Technologie der Obstbrennerei
Von H. J. Pieper, E.-E. Bruchmann und E. Kolb
Verlag Eugen Ulmer, Stuttgart, 2. Aufl. 1993. 402 Seiten, 111 Abbildungen und 65 Tabellen.
Lehrbuch (Handbuch der Lebensmitteltechnologie). Chemische, biochemische, mikrobiologische und physikalische Grundlagen der Brennereitechnologie. Rohstoffe, Brennereieinrichtungen, Betriebsführung, Untersuchungsmethoden sowie Verarbeitung stärkehaltiger Rohstoffe.

Trinkbranntweine und Liköre
Von H. Wüstenfeld und G. Haeseler
Verlag Paul Parey, Berlin und Hamburg, 4. Aufl. 1964. 643 Seiten und 159 Abbildungen.
Umfassende Darstellung über Herstellung, Untersuchung und Beschaffenheit von Spirituosen aller Art.

Abbildungsverzeichnis

Abb. Nr.	Abschnitt		Seite
1	A.2.1	Strichformeln von Glucose, Fructose, Saccharose	15
2	A.2.1	Strichformel von Sorbit	16
3	A.2.2	Strichformeln von Äpfelsäure, Citronensäure und Weinsäure	17
4	B.1.3	Gäraufsatz	26
5	B.1.3	U-Röhre	27
6	B.1.3	Maischebehälter mit Tauchdeckel	27
7	B.2.1	Walzenmühle	29
8	B.2.1	Rätzmühle	29
9	B.2.1	Mixer	30
10	B.2.3	Strichformeln von Galakturonsäure und Pektin	32
11	B.2.6	Verarbeitungsschema zur Gewinnung methanolarmer Destillate	37
12	B.3.1	Apiculatus-Hefen	42
13	B.3.1	Hefe-Reinkultur	43
14	C.2.1	Einfache Hafenbrennerei mit direkter Beheizung	50
15	C.2.1	Blasenformen	50
16	C.2.2	Wasserbadbrennerei mit Helm	51
17	C.2.2	Dampfbrennerei mit Verstärker	52
18	C.2.2	Fahrbare Dreikessel-Dampfbrennerei	53
19	C.2.2	Kontinuierlicher Mostdestillierapparat	54
20	C.2.2	Wasserbadbrennerei, Verstärker aufgesetzt	55
21	C.2.2	Wasserbadbrennerei, Verstärker aufgesetzt	56
22	C.2.2	Wasserbadbrennerei, Verstärker seitlich	57
23	C.2.2	Wasserbadbrennerei, Verstärker aufgesetzt	58
24	C.2.2	Wasserbadbrennerei, Helm kugelförmig	59
25	C.2.2	Dampfbrennerei, Verstärker danebenstehend	60
26	C.2.2	Wasserbadbrennerei, Verstärker seitlich	61
27	C.2.2	Wasserbadbrennerei mit Helm	62
28	C.2.3	Gleichstrom-/Gegenstromdestillation	64
29	C.2.3	Cyanidabscheider	66
30	C.2.5	Kühlertypen	67
31	E.1.2	Funktion eines Kationenaustauschers	80
32	E.1.2	Schema eines Durchlaufenthärters	81
33	E.1.2	Wasserenthärtung im Kleinbetrieb	82
34	E.3	Trichterfilter	84
35	E.3	Zylinderfilter	84
36	E.3	Automatische Filtration	85
37	E.3	Schichtfilter mit Motorpumpe	86

Abbildungsverzeichnis

Abb. Nr.	Abschnitt		Seite
38	E.3	Kerzenfilter	86
39	E.4	Ablaßgarnitur für den Untenanstich	87
40	E.4	Druckheber für den Obenanstich	87
41	E.4	Flaschenverschließmaschine	87
42	E.4	Vakuumfüller	88
43	E.6	Entlüftung eingelegter Früchte	89
44	F.2.1	Calciumsulfat-Kristalle	91
45	G.3.1	Aräometer	108
46	G.3.1	Spindelzylinder	109
47	G.3.1	Ablesung des Aräometers	110
48	G.3.2	Hand-Refraktometer	111
49	G.3.4	Abhängigkeit der Alkoholausbeute vom Extraktgehalt	117
50	G.4.1	Temperaturabhängigkeit der Alkoholometrie	120
51	G.4.1	Destillationsvorrichtung	121
52	G.4.2	Ebullioskop nach Malligand	124
53	G.5	pH-Skala mit Beispielen	126
54	G.5	pH-Meßgerät	128
55	G.6	Flüchtigsäuremesser	129
56	G.8	Titrovin-Zylinder	132
57	G.10	Apparatur zur Esterbestimmung	133

Bildquellen

A. Adrian, Großheubach: Abb. 22
H. R. Brunner, Wädenswil: Abb. 10, 50
C. Carl, Göppingen: Abb. 14–17, 26, 28, 30
J. Carl, Göppingen: Abb. 25
Eidg. Alkoholverwaltung, Bern: Abb. 18
Gürtner, Endingen: Abb. 27
A. Holstein, Markdorf: Abb. 19, 21, 29
Hug, Bützberg: Abb. 9
U. Kothe, Eislingen: Abb. 20
H. Lüthi und U. Vetsch, Mikroskopische Beurteilung von Weinen und Fruchtsäften in der Praxis, Verlag Heller, Schwäbisch Hall 1981: Abb. 12, 13
Müller, Oberkirch-Tiergarten: Abb. 24
S. Nosko, Kleinbrennerei 26, 21 (1974): Abb. 49
C. Schliessmann, Schwäbisch Hall: Abb. 4–8, 31–43, 45–48, 51–57
Schweiz. Ferment AG, Basel: Abb. 11
H. Tanner und H. R. Brunner, Getränke-Analytik, Verlag Heller, Schwäbisch Hall 1987: Abb. 1–3, 44
R. Wengert, Grünkraut-Gullen: Abb. 23

Sachregister

Abbau
– von Fruchtsäuren 17, 48
– von Pektin 15, 31 ff.
Abbildungsverzeichnis 238
abbrennen s. Destillation
Abfindungsanmeldung 204
Abfindungsbrennerei 204 ff., 210 ff.
Abfüllung 87
Abfüllvorrichtungen 87 f.
Abschluß der Gärung 47
Abschnittsbrennerei 205
Absinth 196
absoluter Alkohol 196
Abtrieb s. Destillation
Acetaldehyd 17, 69, 76 f.
–, Grenzwerte 216 f.
s.a. Aldehyde
Acetaldehyd-diethylacetal 77
Acetale 19, 77
Acetalisierungen 77
Acrolein 95, 99, 103
–, Grenzwerte 217
Acroleinstich 99 f.
Aktivkohle 90, 94
Aldehyde 19, 49, 103
Aldehydgehalt 22, 41
Aldehydkühler 63
Alkohol 16, 118, 201 ff.
–, Eigenschaften 201 f.
–, Grenz- und Richtwerte 214 ff.
–, Herstellung 202 f.
–, Verwendung 202 f.
Alkoholausbeute s. Ausbeute
Alkoholbestimmung 118 ff.
Alkoholgesetz (CH) 207 ff.
Alkohole 19, 76, 217
s.a. Aromastoffe
s.a. höhere Alkohole
alkoholische Gärung s. Gärung
Alkoholometer 118 f.
Alkoholverluste 24, 26, 43, 47, 95
Alkoholverwaltung (CH) 207 f.
Alterung 75 ff.
Aluminium 101
Aluminiumbehälter 24
Ameisensäure 17
Aminosäuren 17 f., 35
Ammoniumsalze 35, 38, 40 f.
Amygdalin 39, 101

Amylalkohole 76, 220
Analysenbeispiele 219
Analysenzahlen 214 ff.
s.a. Betriebskontrolle
anbrennen 51, 102
Anforderungen
–, analytische s. Grenzwerte
– an das Rohmaterial 13 f., 20
– an Kernobstbranntwein
  (Übernahmebedingungen der
  Eidg. Alkoholverwaltung) 217
Ansäuerung der Maischen 30 ff., 38 ff.
Anschwemmfiltration 85
Anstellhefe 45
Anstelltemperatur 41, 44 ff.
Antischaum-Mittel 68, 97
Äpfel 13 f., 19, 38, 114 f., 125
s.a. Kernobst
Apfelbrand 75, 215, 219
Äpfelsäure 17, 48
–, zur Ansäuerung 30 f.
Apiculatus-Hefen 42, 95
Aprikosen 13 f., 21, 125
–, Verarbeitung 40
s.a. Steinobst
Aprikosenbrand 196
Aräometer 107 f., 118 f.
–, Ablesung 110
Aräometrie 107 ff., 118 ff.
Armagnac 23, 196, 215
Aromaschwäche 103
Aromastoffe 18 f.
Aromaverluste 43 f., 49, 94
Asbest 85
Ascorbinsäure 18, 89
ätherisch s. etherisch
Äthyl- s. Ethyl-
Ausbeute 14 (Tab.), 33 f., 36, 125
–, Berechnung 115 f.
–, voraussichtliche 16, 115 f.
Ausbeutefaktor 116, 122 f.
Ausbeutesätze 204, 212
Ausbeuteverminderung 16, 94
s.a. Alkoholverluste
Ausscheidungen s. Trübungen
Ausschuß 20
azeotropes Gemisch 196

bakterieller Abbau 17, 48
Bakterien 30, 48, 95
s.a. Mikroorganismen
Bakterienanfälligkeit 17
Barack s. Aprikosenbrand
Beerenbrände 99
Beerenobst 13 f., 21, 35, 114 f.
–, Verarbeitung 40
–, Zerkleinerung 29
Begriffe und Ausdrücke 196 ff.
Begriffsbestimmungen
  für Spirituosen (EG) 196, 214
Behälter 24 f.
–, Reinigung und Unterhalt 25
Behältermaterialien 24 f.
Beheizungsarten 49 ff.
Belüftung von Gärkellern 26
Bentonit 94
Benzaldehyd 39, 101, 218
Benzoesäure 46
Bernsteinsäure 42
Besteuerung 205, 209, 211
Betonbehälter 25
Betriebskontrolle 106 ff.
Birnen 13 f., 19, 38, 114 f., 125
  s.a. Kernobst
  s.a. Williamsbirnen
bitterkranke Weine 22
Bittermandelgeschmack 101
Blase 49 f., 64
–, Reinigung 73
Blasenform 50
Blasengeschmack 70
Blätter 20, 39, 102
Blättergeschmack 15
Blausäure 39, 65, 101, 220
–, Höchstgehalt 215 ff.
–, Bestimmung 136
Blauschönungstrub 22
Böckser s. Schwefelwasserstoffehler
Bonificateurs 88, 234
Bosnische Zwetschge 20
Bottiche s. Behälter
Brand 68 f., 214
  s.a. Branntwein
Branntwein(e) 197, 204, 207, 214 f.
  – aus Wein 22
Branntweinmonopolgesetz (A) 210
Branntweinmonopolgesetz (BRD) 204 f.
Branntweinstärke s. Alkoholgehalt
Bräunung 18, 88
  s.a. Oxidation

Brennapparaturen 49 ff., 211
–, mit direkter Beheizung 49 f.
–, mit indirekter Beheizung 51 ff.
Brennauftraggeber 208
Brenngeräte s. Brennapparaturen
Brennkarte 208
Brennkirschen 20
Brennobst 13, 19 ff., 210
Brennsäfte 38, 102, 132
Brennvorgang s. Destillation
brenzliger Geschmack 51, 102
Brombeeren 13 f., 125
  s.a. Beerenobst
Bukettstoffe s. Aromastoffe
Bukettveränderungen s. Alterung
Bukettverlust 38, 103
Bundesmonopolverwaltung (BRD) 205
Buttersäure 76, 94 f., 98
Buttersäurebakterien 95
Buttersäurestich 98 f.

Calcium 78 f.
Calciumbicarbonat 78
Calciumcarbonat 78, 96, 131
Calciumhydroxid 74, 97, 99, 131
Calciumsulfat 78, 91
Calvados 75, 197, 215
Cartiergrade 197
Cassis 125
Chinasäure 17
Citronensäure 17, 89
–, als Reinigungsmittel 74
Codex Alimentarius Austriacus 218
Cognac 23, 75, 197, 215
Cuprosulfit s. Kupfertrübungen
Cyanid s. Blausäure
Cyanidabscheider 65 f., 73

Dampfbrenngeräte 52 ff., 60, 63
Degustation 70, 198
Dehydroascorbinsäure 18
Dephlegmation 198
Dephlegmator 65, 63
Destillate, Zusammensetzung 76
  s.a. Analysenzahlen
Destillation 49 ff., 120 f.
– mit Verstärkungseinrichtung 71
– ohne Verstärkungseinrichtung 68 ff.
– spezieller Spirituosen 71 f.
Destillationstechnik 65, 68 ff.
Destillationsvorrichtung für die
  Alkoholbestimmung 121
Destillatlagerung 75, 84

241

Destillattemperatur 68
destilliertes Wasser 78
Deutschland
–, analytische Grenzwerte 214 ff.
–, monopolrechtliche Bestimmungen 204 ff.
Dichte von Alkohol/Wasser-Mischungen (Tab.) 192 f.
Disaccharide 16
Doppelaroma 103 f.
Dosierung
  – von Ansäuerungsmitteln 31
  – von Enzymen 34
  – von Gärhilfsmitteln 35
  – von Hefe 45 f.
  – von schwefliger Säure 38
Dreikesselbrennerei 53, 63
Drusen 23
Drusendestillate 100
Durchlaufenthärter 81

Ebullioskop 124
Ebullioskopie 123 f.
Edelbranntwein 198, 218
Edelstahl 24, 65, 67
–, Reinigung 25, 74
Edelstahlbehälter 24, 40, 75
EG-Staaten, analytische Grenzwerte 214 f.
Eichenholz 75
Eichenholzfässer 24, 75, 88
Eichenholzspäne 88
  s.a. Limousinspäne
Eigenbedarf 208
  s.a. Hausbedarf
Einbrand 25, 38, 44
einleiten der Gärung 44
einmaischen 24, 28 ff.
Eisen 46, 76, 91
–, Nachweis 135
Eisentrübungen 92
eiweißartige Substanzen 17 f.
Endvergärung 47, 115
Entfärbung 94
Entgeistung 63
Enthärtung von Leitungswasser 79 ff.
Enzian 198, 214 ff.
Enzianwurzeln 13 f., 23, 41, 46, 125
Enzymbehandlung der Maischen 31 ff., 38 ff.
Enzyme 18
–, pektolytische 31 f, 38 ff.
Erdbeeren 40, 125

Erfahrungswerte 106, 217
Erhitzung der Maische 36 f.
Erstickungsgefahr in Gärkellern 26
Erwärmung der Maische
  – zur Einleitung der Gärung 46
  – zur Enzymaktivierung 37
Essigbakterien 26, 30, 36, 95
Essigester 69, 76, 97
  s.a. Ester
Essigsäure 17, 42, 48, 67, 76, 94 ff., 127
  s.a. flüchtige Säure(n)
Essigsäureethylester s. Essigester
Essigstich 96 f.
Ester 19, 49, 103
Estergehalt 30, 39, 134
–, Bestimmung 133 f.
–, erhöhter 39, 97, 134
–, Grenzwerte 217 f.
Ethanol s. Alkohol
etherische Öle 49, 86
–, als Trübungsursache 93
Ethylacetat s. Essigester
Ethylalkohol 76 f.
  s.a. Alkohol
Ethylcarbamat 104, 220
Ethylmercaptan 100 f.
Extrakt 47, 107
–, Umrechnungstabelle 194
Extraktbestimmung 47, 107 ff.
Extraktgehalt 114 f. (Tab.), 88

Fachbücher s. Literatur
Fallobst 14
Färbung s. Zusatzstoffe
Fässer s. Behälter
Faßlagerung 75
Fehler s. Spirituosenfehler
Fehlgärungen 13, 20, 47, 94 ff.
Fehltöne 103
Feinbrand 64, 69 f.
Fellenbergzwetschge 20
Fertigstellung der Destillate 78 ff.
Fettsäuren 69, 76
–, höhere, als Trübungsursache 93
Feuerungsraum 51
Filterhilfsstoffe 85
Filtertypen 84 f.
Filtration 84 ff.
  s.a. Probenvorbereitung
Flaschen 87
Fließverhalten von Maischen 33
flüchtige Säure(n) 19, 30, 46, 95 f., 128, 216 ff.
–, Beseitigung 96 f.

–, Bestimmung 129 f.
Flüssighefe 45
s.a. Hefe(n)
Fragekasten 221 ff.
Fruchtbukett 19
Früchte, eingelegte 88 f.
Fruchtsäuren 17, 30, 74
s.a. Ansäuerung
Fruchtzucker s. Fructose
Fructose 15 f., 20, 72, 88
Furfural 102
Fuselöl(e) 42, 49, 65, 70
–, als Trübungsursache 93
Fuselölgehalt 45, 218
Futterwert von Schlempen 74
Galakturonsäure 32, 115
Gäraufsatz 26 f.
Gärbehälter 24 ff.
Gärbukett 19
Gärdauer 46
Gärgas s. Kohlendioxid
Gärhilfsmittel 35, 38 ff.
Gärstockungen 13, 18 f., 21, 35
–, Ursachen 46
Gärtemperatur 43
Gärtrichter 24
s.a. Gäraufsatz
Gärung 16, 42 ff.
s.a. Gärverlauf
Gärungsgleichung 16
Gärungsnebenprodukte 16, 42
Gärverlauf 46
Gärverzögerungen 35, 46
Gaschromatographie 106, 220
Gefrierpunkte von
 Alkohol/Wasser-Mischungen (Tab.) 202
Gegenstromdestillation 64
Gegenstromkühlung 68
Geiste 40, 65, 214
s.a. Obstgeiste
Geistrohr 49, 65 f.
–, Reinigung 73
Gelatineschönung 46
Gentianose 23
Gerbstoffe 18
–, als Trübungsursache 92
–, als Ursache von Gärstockungen 46
s.a. phenolische Stoffe
Gerbstoffgehalt 13, 19, 46
Geruchsfehler 94 ff.
Gesamtzuckergehalt 14 (Tab.), 16
Geschmacksfehler 94 ff.

Gesetzliches
 – lebensmittelrechtliche Bestimmungen
  214 ff.
 – monopolrechtliche Bestimmungen
  204 ff.
Gewerbebrenner 209
gewerbliche Brennereien 205
Gewichtsprozent s. Massenprozent
Gips s. Calciumsulfat
Glanzgärer 46
Glasbehälter 25, 40
Glasflaschen 45
s.a. Glasbehälter
Gleichstromdestillation 64
Glockenböden 65
Glucose 15 f., 39, 101
Glucose-Oxidase 36
Glycerin 42, 95
Golden Delicious 19
graphisches Verfahren zur
 Ermittlung der Ausbeute 117
Grappa 198, 214 ff.
Gravensteiner 19, 215
Grenzwerte 214 ff.

Hafenbrennerei 49 f., 63
Hagebutten 21
Hagelobst 19
Haltbarkeit
 – eingelegter Früchte 88
 – von Enzymen 34
 – von Preßhefe 46
 – von Trockenhefe 45
Haltbarmachung
 – eingelegter Früchte 88 f.
 – vergorener Maischen 48
Hand-Refraktometer s. Refraktometer
Härtebildner 78
–, als Trübungsursache 90 f.
Härtegrade 78 f., 130
Hausbedarf 206, 212
s.a. Eigenbedarf
Hausbrenner 208, 212
Hauszwetschge 20
Hefe(n) 42 ff.
Hefedestillate 100, 125, 217
Hefegeläger 13 f., 23, 68, 125
Hefenährstoffe 19, 31, 35
Hefevermehrung im Betrieb 45
Hefezersetzungsprodukte 100 f.
Heidelbeeren 14, 125
s.a. Beerenobst
Heizschlangen 63
Helm 49 f.

243

Herabsetzung von Destillaten 75, 78 ff., 91
Herabsetzungstabelle 190 f.
herber Beigeschmack 102
Hexanol 15, 29, 102
Himbeeren 13 f., 21, 40, 71, 125
　s.a. Beerenobst
Himbeergeist 40, 71 f.
　s.a. Obstgeist
Höchstwerte s. Grenzwerte
höhere Alkohole 42, 70, 76, 93, 216 f.
　s.a. Fuselöl(e)
Holunderbeeren 14, 125
　s.a. Beerenobst
Holzfässer 24 f., 36, 48, 75
Hydroxypropionaldehyd 99

Inaktivierung pektolytischer Enzyme 36 f.
Indikatoren 126 f.
Infektion 38
Inhaltsstoffe
　– des Obstes 15 ff.
　– von Spirituosen 76, 214 ff.
Inhaltsverzeichnis 7 ff.
Innenauskleidung 25
Interpretation von Meßergebnissen
　– der Alkoholbestimmung 124 f.
　– der Extraktbestimmung 113 ff.
　– der Flüchtigsäurebestimmung 128
　– der Wasserhärtebestimmung 130
Inulin 14, 23
Inversion 16
Ionen 80 f.
Ionenaustauscher 80 ff., 91 f.
Isocitronensäure 17
Johannisbeeren 13 f., 125
　s.a. Beerenobst, Cassis

Kahmhefen 26, 94 f.
Kaliumdisulfit 35, 38
Kalk
　–, gelöschter (Calciumhydroxid) 74, 97
　–, kohlensaurer (Calciumcarbonat) 78, 96
Kaltgärhefen 43, 45
Katalysator s. Cyanidabscheider
Kernobst 13 f., 19, 45
　–, Verarbeitung 38 f.
　–, Zerkleinerung 29
Kernobstbranntwein 198, 209, 214 ff., 217
Kernobstsaft 38, 45
Kernobsttrester 13 f., 22, 125
　s.a. Trester
Kernobstwein 22,125
Kerzenfilter 85 f.

Kesselstein 78
Ketone 19, 49
Kieselgur 94
Kirsch 39, 97, 198, 214, 217, 219
　s.a. Obstbrand
Kirschanalyse 220
Kirschdestillation 67, 70
Kirschen 13 f., 20, 114 f., 125
　–, Verarbeitung 39
　s.a. Steinobst
Knollen 13, 23
　–, Verarbeitung 41
Kochsalzlösung 82
Kohlendioxid 16, 26, 78, 96
Kohlenhydrate 15 f.
Kohlenwasserstoffe 19
Kohleschönung 94, 102 f.
Kolonnenbrennerei 54, 63, 102
kombinierte Säure/Enzym-Behandlung 35, 38
Konservierungsmittel 46
Kontaktkorrosion 67
Kontraktion 83, 201
Korken 92, 103
Korrektur
　– aräometrischer Messungen 111, 119 f.
　– refraktometrischer Messungen 112 f.
Korrekturtabellen 113, 138 ff.
Kräuter 72, 233
Kräuterspirituosen 72 f., 86
Kräuterextrakte 65
Kühler 49 ff., 67 f.
　–, Reinigung 73 f.
Kühllagerung 84
Kühlwasser 68, 79
　–, Regulierung 65, 71
künstliche Alterung 77
Kunststoffbehälter 24, 226
Kupfer 46, 76, 91, 101
　–, als Werkstoff 49
　–, Nachweis 135
　–, Reinigung 73 f.
Kupferacetat 67, 92
Kupferblech 75
Kupfersulfat 101
Kupfersulfid 101
Kupfertrübungen 92

Lagertemperaturen 48, 75, 84, 104
Lagerung
　– vergorener Maischen 48, 104
　– von Destillaten 75, 84
　– von Enzymen 34
　– von Früchten 19

– von Früchten in Flaschen 89
– von Rein- und Preßhefe 45 f.
– von Trestern 40 f.
Laugen 97 f., 131
Laugengeschmack 100
Lebensmittelbuch (CH) 217
Lebensmittelverordnung (CH) 197, 216
Leitungswasser 78 f.
Likör 199, 231 ff.
s.a. Spirituosen
Limousinspäne 75
Literatur 235 ff.
Lohnbrenner 208 f.
Luftkontakt 26, 75
Lutter 63, 68, 72
s.a. Rauhbrand
Lutterprober 69

Magnesium 78 f.
Magnesiumcarbonat 78
Magnesiumoxid (Magnesia) 94, 96
Maische(n) 28 ff., 107, 114
–, essigstichige 96
–, Tresteranteil 116
–, vergorene 48, 114
Maischebehälter 24 ff.
Maischebehandlung 28 ff.
Maischeerhitzung 36 f.
Maischeerwärmung 37
Maischeinfektion 26, 41
Maischekolonne 63
Maischelagerung 48, 104
Maischetemperatur 34, 45 f.
Maischeverflüssigung 33 f.
Maischezusätze 30 ff.
Mängel 90, 103 f.
Mannit 20, 95
Maraskakirsche 20
Marc 75, 92, 215 f., 219
Marillenbrand s. Aprikosenbrand
Massenprozent 118
Maximalwerte s. Grenzwerte
Mercaptane 100 f.
Meßergebnisse, Interpretation 113 ff., 124 ff.
Metallbehälter 24 f.
Metallgeschmack 101
Metalltrübungen 90 ff.
Methanol 32 f., 36, 76
–, Eigenschaften 36
–, Grenz- und Richtwerte 215 ff.
Methanolgehalt 33, 219 f.
Methylalkohol s. Methanol
mikrobiell bedingte Fehler 94 ff.

Mikroorganismen 94 f.
s.a. Hefe(n)
Milchsäure 17, 48, 95
–, zur Ansäuerung 30 f.
Milchsäurebakterien 95
Milchsäurestich 99
Mindestalkoholgehalte 214 ff.
Mindestwerte s. Grenzwerte
Mineralstoffe 19
Minimalwerte s. Grenzwerte
Mirabellen 125
Mischungstabelle 190 f.
Mittellauf 69 ff.
Mixer 29 f., 39
Monosaccharide 16
Most 63
Mostdestillierapparat, kontinuierlicher 54, 63
Mostgewicht 108, 114 (Tab.), 115, 194 (Tab.)
Mostobst 19
Mostwaage 108

Nachlauf 70 f., 102 f.
Nachweis von Schwermetallen 135
Näherungsformel zur Ermittlung der voraussichtlichen Ausbeute 115 f.
Natriumchlorid (Kochsalz) 80, 82
Natriumhydroxid 97 f.
Natriumpolyphosphate 79
Natronlauge 74, 97
Neutralisation 102, 126, 131
– essigstichiger Maischen 96 f.
– fehlerhafter Destillate 97 f., 102 f.
– von Schlempen 74
Nichtzuckerstoffe 115 f.
Normaltemperatur 108, 112, 118

Obstbrand 199, 214 ff.
Obstgeiste 75, 199
Obstwasser 199, 214
Obstwein 22, 125
Oel 72
s.a. etherische Oele
s.a. Fuselöle
Oesterreich
–, analytische Grenzwerte 218
–, monopolrechtliche Bestimmungen 210 ff.
Oxidation 76, 101
–, Verhinderung 26, 36

Pektin(e) 15, 31 ff.
Pektinesterase 32 f., 36
Pfirsiche 14, 125

245

–, Verarbeitung 40
s.a. Steinobst
Pflaumen 13 f., 21, 114, 125
–, Verarbeitung 40
s.a. Steinobst
Pflichtenhefte für Brenner (CH) 209
phenolische Stoffe 18, 75
Phlegma s. Dephlegmation
Phosphorsäure 30 f., 97 f.
Phosphorverbindungen 35
pH-Wert 17, 30, 34 f., 74 ff., 125 f.
–, Bestimmung 126 ff.
Polyesterharze 24
Polyethylen 24
Polygalakturonasen 32 f.
Preiselbeeren 21
s.a. Beerenobst
Preßhefe 39, 45 f.
Probenentnahme 107
Probenvorbereitung 107
Propanol 48, 76, 216 f., 219 f.
Propionsäure 76
Proteine 17 f.
Protopektin 15, 32

Qualitätsprüfungen von Spirituosen
(BRD) 199
Quitten 13 f., 38, 125
Quittengeist 38

Rätzmühlen 29
Rauhbrand 64, 68 f.
Refraktometer 111
Refraktometrie 111 f.
Reineclauden 125
Reinhefe 42 ff.
Reinigung
 – des Rohmaterials 28, 41
 – von Brennapparaturen 73 f.
 – von Maische- und Gärbehältern 25
Reinigungsmittel 25, 73
Reinzuchthefe s. Reinhefe
Rektifikation 199
Restzuckergehalt 16, 115
Richtwerte 214 ff.
Rohmaterial 13 ff.
Rohölgeschmack 13, 22
Röhrenkühler 67 f.
Rohrzucker s. Saccharose
Rohstoffe 19 ff.
Rostbildung 67, 76
Rübenzucker s. Saccharose
Rückfluß 64, 99, 103

Saccharometer 108
Saccharose 15 f.
Sauerkirschen 20
 s.a. Weichselkirschen
Sauerstoff 26, 36, 75 f., 101
Säureabbau, biologischer 17, 48
Säuregehalt 46, 126
 s.a. Grenzwerte
Säurekombinationen 30 f.
Säuren 30, 49
 –, Dosierung 30 f., 38 ff.
 –, Neutralisation 96 ff., 126, 131
 –, titrierbare 131 ff.
 –, Verdünnung 31
 s.a. flüchtige Säure(n)
 s.a. Fruchtsäuren
Säureschutz 38 ff.
Schaumbildung 68, 97
Schichtenfilter 85 f.
Schimmelbefall 25
Schimmelgeschmack 103
Schimmelpilze 95
Schlangenkühler 67 f.
Schlehen 125
Schlempe 63, 74
Schnellgärung 19, 39, 45
Schönungsmittel 93 f.
Schrumpfung 20 f.
Schwefeldioxid (SO_2) 25, 35, 69, 89, 102
 s.a. schweflige Säure
Schwefeldioxidfehler 102
Schwefelsäure 30 f.
Schwefelschnitten 25, 100
Schwefelung 35
 s.a. Einbrand
Schwefelverbindungen 49, 100 f.
Schwefelwasserstoffehler 100 f.
schweflige Säure 25, 35, 38, 67, 92, 216
 –, Geruch und Geschmack nach 102
 –, Bestimmung 132 f.
Schweiz
 –, analytische Grenzwerte 216 f.
 –, monopolrechtliche Bestimmungen
    207 ff.
Schweizerische Lebensmittelverordnung
    (LMV) 216
Schweizerisches Lebensmittelbuch
    (LMB) 217
Schwermetalle
 –, als Trübungsursache 91 f.
 –, Nachweis 135
Senkwaage s. Aräometer
Siebboden 51

Siedetemperatur
– von Acrolein 99
– von Alkohol 49
– von Methanol 36
– von Wasser 49
Silberchlorid 101
Silbercyanid 102
Silbernitrat 102
Sinnenprüfung s. Degustation
Slibowitz 20, 215
Soda 73
Sorbinsäure 21, 46
Sorbit 16, 20, 114
Spezialindikator 97
Spezialitätenbranntwein 209
Spindel s. Aräometer
Spindelzylinder 109
Spirituosen 200
–, Alterung 75 ff.
–, spezielle 71 ff.
Spirituosenfehler 90 ff.
–, in Geruch und Geschmack wahrnehmbare 94 ff.
–, sichtbare 90 ff.
–, Übersichtstabellen 105
Spontangärungen 42
Sporenbildung 43
Sprit 200, 203, 207
Sprossung 43
Stabilisierung vergorener Maischen 36, 48
Steinanteil 20, 101
Steine 39
Steingeschmack 39, 101 f.
Steinhäger 214
s.a. Wacholder
Steinobst 13 f., 20 f.
–, Verarbeitung 39 f.
–, Zerkleinerung 29 f.
Steuersatz für Branntwein 205, 209, 211
Stickstoffverbindungen 17, 35, 46
Stoffbesitzer 206
Süßkirschen 20
Synthesealkohol 200

Tabellen 138 ff.
Tafelobst 13, 19
Tauchdeckel 27
Teilentsalzung 79
Tellerkühler 67 f.
Temperaturabhängigkeit
– aräometrischer Messungen 111, 119 f.
– der Enzymaktivität 34
– der Hefevermehrung 43, 46

– der Löslichkeit 84
– refraktometrischer Messungen 112 f.
– von Alterungsvorgängen 75
Terpene, als Trübungsursache 93
Teststäbchen, zum Nachweis von Schwermetallen 135
Thiamin 18, 35
Titrovin-Zylinder 132
Topinambur 13 f., 23, 41, 46, 114
toxische Eigenschaften
– von Ethanol 202
– von Methanol 36
Trauben s. Weintrauben
Traubentrester 13 f.
s.a. Trester
Traubenwein 22
Traubenzucker s. Glucose
Trester 22, 65, 68, 125
–, Verarbeitung 40 f.
Tresteranteil 116
Tresterdestillate 22, 100, 125, 214 ff.
Tresterfaktor 116
Trichterfilter 84 f.
Trinksprit 203
s.a. Sprit
Trinkstärke 78
Trockenhefe 44 f.
s.a. Hefe(n)
Trockensubstanz s. Extrakt
Trübungen 84, 90 ff.

Überausbeute 206
Überhitzungen 102
Übernahme von Branntwein
– durch die Alkoholverwaltung (CH) 217
– durch die Bundesmonopolverwaltung (BRD) 205
überschwefeln 35, 102
umbrennen 51, 92, 94, 98, 102 f.
Umrechnungstabellen
– Alkoholgehalt 192 f.
– Extraktgehalt 194
umschalten auf Mittel- bzw. Nachlauf 68 ff., 104
Universalindikator 97
Unterhalt
– von Brennapparaturen 73 f.
– von Maische- und Gärbehältern 25
Untersuchungsmethoden (Übersicht) 106
unvergärbare Substanzen 16, 47
Urethan s. Ethylcarbamat

247

Vakuumentlüfter 37
Vakuumfüller 88
VA-Stahl 24
Verarbeitungshinweise 38 ff.
– für Beerenobst 40
– für Kernobst 38 f.
– für Steinobst 39
– für Trester 40
– für Wurzeln und Knollen 41
Verarbeitungsmöglichkeiten von Kernobst 19
Verdünnung s. Herabsetzung
Verdunstungsverluste 16, 48, 68
Veresterung 76
– von Pektinen 32
Verfärbungen 94
Verfütterung von Schlempen 74
Vergärung, vollständige 47, 114 f.
Vergärungsgrad 114
Verkostung s. Degustation
Vermehrung
– der Hefen 42 f.
– von Flüssighefen im Betrieb 45
verschließen
– der Flaschen 87
– der Gärbehälter 26 f.
Verschlußbrennereien 206, 210, 213
Verschnitt(e) 39, 200
Verschnittwasser 78, 83, 130
Verseifung 77
Verstärkung 69
Verstärkungseinrichtungen 64 f.
–, Reinigung 73
Verwertung von Schlempen 74
Vitamine 18
Vitamin B1 s. Thiamin
Vitamin C s. Ascorbinsäure
Vogelbeeren 21, 46
–, Verarbeitung 40
Vollentsalzung 79
Vollständigkeit der Gärung 47
Volumenkonzentration, Tabelle 138 ff.
Volumenprozent 118
–, Umwandlung in andere Gehaltsangaben 192 f.
Volumenveränderung von Alkohol/Wasser-Mischungen (Tab.) 195
Vorlage 50, 67 f.
Vorlauf 69 ff.
Vorlaufbehandlung 103
Vorlauftest 135
Vorproben s. Vorversuche
Vor- und Nachlauffehler 102 f.
Vorversuche 90, 99
Vorwort 5 f.

Wacholderbeeren 14, 21, 46
–, Verarbeitung 40
s.a. Beerenobst
Wacholder 72, 86, 125, 200
Walzenmühlen 29, 39
Waschvorrichtungen 28
Wasser
–, destilliertes 78
–, gebrannte 207
Wasseranteil von Früchten 15
Wasserbadbrenngeräte 51 f., 61 f.
Wasserenthärtung 79 f.
Wasserhärte 78 ff.
–, Bestimmung 130 f.
wässern von Holzbehältern 25
Wasserstrahlvakuum 89
Weichselkirschen 125
Weichwerden 15, 31
Wein 13 f., 22, 102, 125
Weinbrand 92, 200, 214, 219
Weindestillat 75
Weingeist 200
Weinhefe 125
Weinsäure 17
Weintrauben 14, 21, 125
Wermut 207
wilde Hefen 42, 95
Williams 86, 125, 214 ff., 219
Williamsbirnen 19, 30, 88 f., 114
–, Verarbeitung 38
Wurzeln 13, 23
s.a. Enzianwurzeln

Zerkleinerung 28 ff.
Zink 101
–, Nachweis 135
Zinn 65
Zitronensäure s. Citronensäure
Zucker 15 f., 45, 72, 88
Zuckeralkohole 20
Zuckercouleur 88
Zuckergehalt (Tab.) 14
–, Berechnung mittels Näherungsformel 115
–, Bestimmung s. Extraktbestimmung
Zuckerung 13
Zusatzstoffe 88
Zwetschgen 13 f., 20 f., 34, 114, 125
–, Verarbeitung 40
s.a. Steinobst
Zwetschgenrauhbrand 70
Zwetschgenwasser 214 f., 217 ff.
s.a. Obstbrand
Zylinderfilter 84 f.

248

Fachausdrücke

Deutsch	Französisch	Englisch
Rohmaterial	matières premières	raw material
Kernobst	fruits à pépins	pome fruits
Steinobst	fruits à noyaux	stone fruits
Beeren	baies	berries
Kirschen	cerises	cherries
Äpfel	pommes	apples
Birnen	poires	pears
Zwetschgen	pruneaux, quetsches	damsons
Pflaumen	prunes	plums
Aprikosen	abricots	apricots
Quitten	coings	quinces
Trester	marcs	residues, pomace
Wurzeln	racines	roots
Hefegeläger	lies	lees
Rätzmühle	cribleur	crusher
Walzenmühle	laminoir	grinder
Gärung	fermentation	fermentation
Gärbehälter	récipient de fermentation	fermenting vat
Reinigung	nettoyage	cleaning
Deckel	couvercle	cover
Gärtrichter	bonde de fermentation	fermentation valve
Maische	moût	mash
Ansäuerung	acidification	acidification
Hefen	levures	yeast
Ausbeute	rendement	yield
Destillation	distillation	distillation
Brennapparat	appareil de distillation	still
Heizung	chauffage	heating
Dampf	vapeur	steam
Kupfer	cuivre	copper
Blase	chaudière	boiler
Helm	chapeau	hat
Geistrohr	col de cygne	swan's neck
Kühler	refroidisseur	condenser
Vorlage	collecteur	receiver
Rauhbrand	flegme	first distillation
Feinbrand	bonne chauffe	second distillation
Vorlauf	tête	heads
Mittellauf	coeur	heart
Nachlauf	queue	tails
Spirituosen	spiritueux	spirits
Branntwein	eau-de-vie	brandy
Obstbrand	eau-de-vie de fruits	fruit brandy
Alterung	vieillissement	aging
Herabsetzung	réduction	dilution
Wasserhärte	dureté de l'eau	water hardness
Enthärtung	adoucissement	water softening
Verschnittwasser	eau de coupage	blending water
Lagerung	stockage	storage
Abfüllung	mise en bouteilles	bottling
höhere Alkohole	alcools supérieurs	higher alcohols
etherische Öle	huiles essentielles	essential oils
Extrakt	extrait	dry extract
Titrierbare Säuren	acidité totale	total acidity
Flüchtige Säuren	acidité volatile	volatile acids
schweflige Säure	acide sulfureux	sulfurous acid
Blausäure	acide cyanhydrique	hydrogen cyanide

Bessere Branntweine durch

PECTINEX
Ultra SP-L

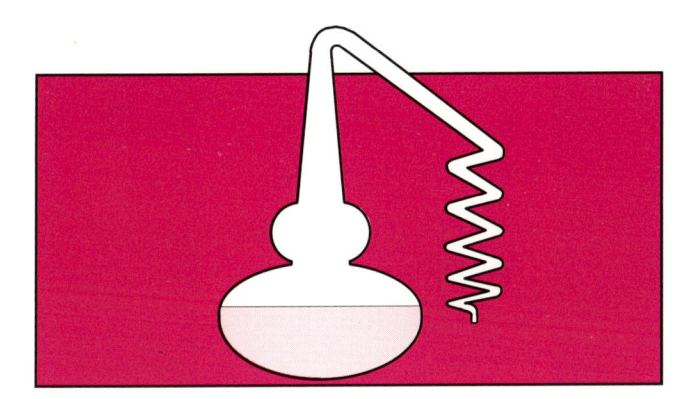

Zwischen dem Ergebnis des Brennens in qualitativer und quantitativer Hinsicht und dem Aufschluß der Brennmaische sowie deren Vergärung besteht ein enger Zusammenhang.

Pectinex Ultra SP-L ist der Schlüssel für perfekten biologischen Maischeaufschluss und optimale Vergärung mit Ausbildung eines ausgeprägt feinen Aromas.

Novo Nordisk Ferment AG   CH-4243 Dittingen

Unser Beitrag zur Erzeugung erstklassiger Branntweine:

Uvaferm CM Trockenhefe

für optimale Vergärung der Brennmaische

UVAFERM CEG™	Kaltgärhefe
SCHLIESSMANN Brennereihefe forte	Topinambur, mehlige Stoffe
DANSTILL C™ Sacc. diastaticus	Getreide- und Stärkemaischen
FERMAID™	Komplexer Hefenährstoff

Forschung, Produktion, Anwenderberatung:
DANSTAR FERMENT AG. Postfach 58, **CH – 6301 Zug / Schweiz**
Vertrieb durch den Fachhandel.

Handrefraktometer

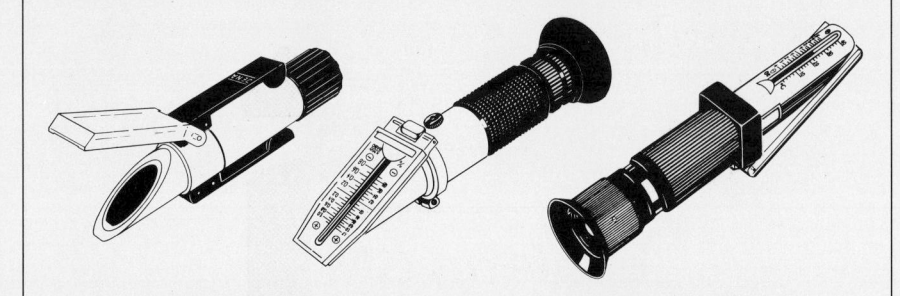

Alkoholbestimmungsgeräte

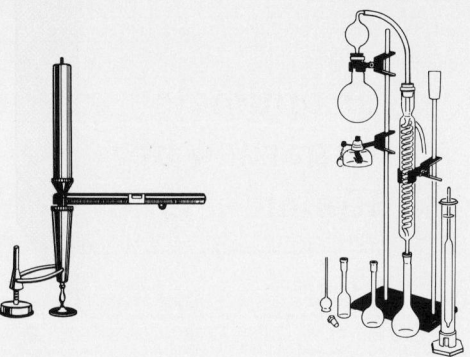

Aräometer, Gläser, Kolben, Zylinder

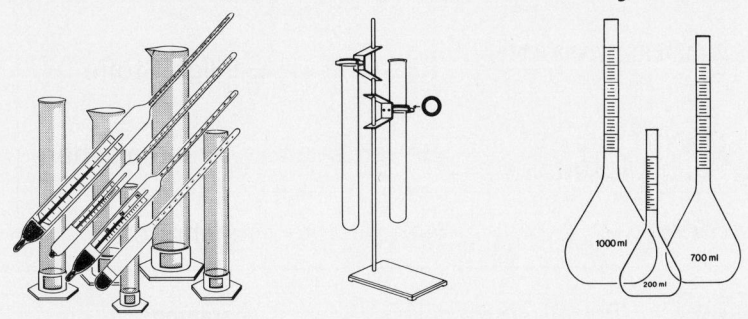

Schliessmann Kellerei-Chemie, Postf. 10 05 64, **74505 Schwäbisch Hall**
Telefon 07 91 - 7 20 25   Telefax 0791 - 8 44 25

PECTINEX

PECTINEX Ultra SP–L

für den gründlichen Aufschluss der Obst-Maischen

kühl lagern!

Uvaferm CM Trockenhefe

für die optimale Vergärung der Brennmaische

Zur problemlosen Maischeansäuerung

MS

MS-Säure-Kombination

Schaumfreies Brennen durch

Silicon Antischaum

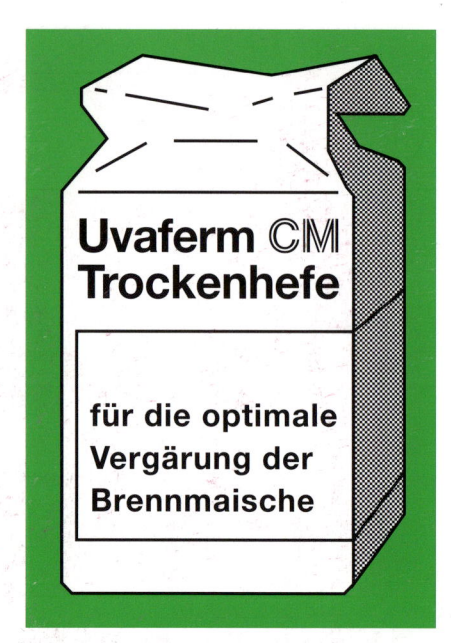

Schliessmann Kellerei-Chemie, Postf. 10 05 64, 74505 Schwäbisch Hall
Telefon 07 91 - 7 20 25   Telefax 07 91 - 8 44 25

PECTINEX Ultra SP-L

kühl lagern!

Angebrochene Flaschen
bitte im Kühlschrank
aufbewahren.